THE ART OF MODELING WITH SPREADSHEETS
Management Science, Spreadsheet Engineering, and Modeling Craft

THE ART OF MODELING WITH SPREADSHEETS

Management Science, Spreadsheet Engineering, and Modeling Craft

STEPHEN G. POWELL

Dartmouth College

KENNETH R. BAKER

Dartmouth College

Acquisitions Editor   *Beth Golub*
Assistant Editor   *Lorraina Raccuia*
Marketing Manager   *Gitti Lindner*
Editorial Assistant   *Ailsa Manny*
Media Editor   *Allie Keim*
Managing Editors   *Lari Bishop, Kevin Dodds*
Associate Production Manager   *Kelly Tavares*
Production Editor   *Sarah Wolfman-Robichaud*
Illustration Editor   *Benjamin Reece*
Cover Design   *Jaye Joseph*
Cover Image   *Isy Ochoa, The Palette, 1990. Private Collection/Isy Ochoa/SuperStock.*

This book was set in Times by Leyh Publishing LLP. It was printed by RR Donnelley & Sons Company. The cover was printed by Phoenix Color Corp.

This book is printed on acid-free paper. ∞

Library of Congress Cataloging-in-Publication Data
Powell, Stephen G.
   The art of modeling with spreadsheets / Stephen G. Powell, Kenneth R. Baker
      p. cm.
   Includes bibliographical references.
   ISBN 0-471-20937-6 (pbk. : alk. paper)
   1. Business—Computer simulation. 2. Electronic spreadsheets. I. Baker, Kenneth R.,
   1943- II. Title.
HF5548.2.P654 2004
650'.01'13--dc21   2003049717

USA ISBN: 0-471-20937-6
WIE ISBN: 0-471-45216-5

Printed in the United States of America

10   9   8   7   6   5   4   3   2   1

To Becky and Judy,
for all their encouragement and support

BRIEF CONTENTS

TABLE OF CONTENTS

PREFACE

This is a book about *modeling*, for business analysts. A *model* is a simplified representation of a situation or problem, and *modeling* is the process of building, refining, and analyzing that representation for greater insight or improved decision-making. There are many different types of models, including physical models (like a movie set or a toy airplane) and graphical models (like a roadmap or an organization chart), but in the business setting, the principal vehicle for modeling is the electronic spreadsheet. Among business analysts, we include MBA students, as well as practicing financial analysts, marketing specialists, operations planners, consultants, and business managers generally. These groups are concerned with business situations or business problems. They need to be able to build models, work with people who build models, and understand the results of analyzing models.

Models are everywhere in the business world, although they are often not recognized for what they are. Some models are so common that they are thought of as routine instruments rather than as models. The most mundane budget involves a simplified representation of the future and is, therefore, a model. Similarly, cash flow projections for existing firms involve models, as do the estimates contained in business plans for startups. In addition, many sophisticated models are not visible because they are embedded in software. Option pricing models are typically coded in dedicated software, as are credit scoring models for loans, or inventory models for stock control. Many business decisions, in fact, are influenced by model-based analysis. Managers and analysts who are skilled modelers can employ modeling effectively in a wide variety of situations where others might not recognize its power.

Millions of people routinely use spreadsheet software on the job to analyze business situations or problems. This group includes consultants who evaluate businesses for potential acquisitions or provide venture capitalists advice on the market value of startups. Marketing and financial analysts who build models to design advertising campaigns, estimate potential profits for a new product, or price new financial instruments also rely on spreadsheet models. So, too, do operations specialists who create efficient supply chains or schedule the flow of materials. Almost anyone who uses spreadsheets in business can benefit from training in modeling.

Models also play a central role in management education. A short list of models that nearly every MBA student encounters would include cash flow models, stock price models, option pricing models, product life cycle models, market diffusion models, order quantity models, and project scheduling models. For the management student, a basic ability to model in spreadsheets can be a powerful tool for acquiring a deeper understanding of the various functional areas of business. But to fully understand the implications of these models, a student needs to appreciate what a model is and how to learn from it.

Until quite recently, modeling was performed primarily by highly trained specialists using mainframe computers. Consequently, even a simple model was costly and could require many months of development time. The assumptions and results often seemed impenetrable to business managers because they were removed from the modeling process.

This situation has changed radically with the advent of personal computers and electronic spreadsheets. Now, managers and analysts can build their own models and produce their own analyses of business problems. We call this new kind of modeling, *end-user* modeling. With every analyst having access to a powerful computer, the out-of-pocket costs of modeling have become negligible. The major cost now is the analyst's *time*: time to formulate the problem, gather data, build and debug a model, and use the model to support the decision process. This book is designed to improve the *efficiency* with which business analysts approach modeling. Increased efficiency reduces the costs of modeling and opens up broader areas of application. This book is also designed to improve the *effectiveness* with which analysts use spreadsheet models. More effective modeling comes from the use of analytic tools and processes that provide deeper business insights.

One of our reasons for writing this book was the conviction that many analysts were not being appropriately educated as modelers. MBAs tend to receive strong training in statistics and management science but little training in practical modeling. (They often receive inadequate training, as well, in using spreadsheets for modeling.) In most educational programs, the emphasis is on *models*, rather than on *modeling*. That is, the curriculum covers a number of classical models that have proven useful in management education or in business. While studying the classics may be valuable for a number of reasons, studying models does not necessarily provide the skills needed to build models for new situations.

We also have met many analysts who view modeling as essentially a matter of having strong spreadsheet skills. But spreadsheet skills are not sufficient. The spreadsheet is only one tool in the creative, open-ended problem-solving process we call modeling. Modeling is both a technical discipline and a *craft*. The craft aspects of the process have largely been overlooked in the education of business analysts. The purpose of this book is to provide both the technical knowledge and the craft skills needed to develop real expertise in business modeling.

We believe that an effective business modeler needs an appropriate *balance* of skills in three areas: spreadsheets, management science/statistics, and modeling craft. It goes without saying that every business analyst must have at least elementary spreadsheet skills. But we find that even highly skilled Excel users sometimes lack critical skills for modeling, such as the ability to design and debug a spreadsheet model effectively. Thus we provide a careful treatment of what we call *spreadsheet engineering:* how to design, build, test and perform analysis with a spreadsheet model.

Management science and statistics comprise the second subject area we believe is essential to a business modeler. These sophisticated tools are not used in every modeling situation, but the effective analyst must be able to draw on them when appropriate. In some situations, the key insight from the modeling process comes from applying a technique drawn from statistics, optimization, or simulation.

In addition to technical skills in Excel and management science/statistics, an effective business modeler needs to acquire the craft skills of the trade. Modeling *craft* refers to the non-technical but essential skills that an expert modeler employs, such as abstracting the essential features of a situation in a model, debugging a model effectively, and translating model results into managerial insights. These skills may be more difficult to teach than narrow technical tools, but as in all professional fields, it is the craft skills that separate the expert from the novice. While experience is always necessary to acquire true expertise, we have found that novice modelers progress much faster if craft skills are identified and practiced. We therefore devote a chapter of the book to the essential craft skills, and we comment extensively throughout the text on the use of craft skills in the context of particular techniques or examples.

There are many fine books available on Excel, and many more on management science and statistics. Most of these books go into far more detail than the typical business analyst needs. Few of them devote attention to the craft aspects of modeling, and none presents all three skill areas in a manner accessible to the practical business analyst. Our book covers only those essential features of Excel that are heavily used in business modeling, and it develops spreadsheet skills in the context of spreadsheet modeling. We also cover basic topics in management science and statistics, again from the viewpoint of the practicing business analyst. Finally, we devote a considerable portion of the book to communicating the craft skills of modeling, because of our conviction that expertise lies more in acquiring these skills, and the judgment to use them wisely, than it does in piling on technical tools. Our goal throughout is to give the reader a solid foundation in modeling, without an overwhelming amount of technical detail.

For many years, we have passionately advocated modeling skills for business students and analysts. A decade ago, when spreadsheets were still somewhat new and far less powerful than they have since become, this was a difficult position to justify. But with each passing year we find more acceptance of this idea. More alumni call us for modeling advice. More consulting companies train their own analysts in modeling. All the trends we observe suggest that modeling will only become more vital in the future: computer hardware and software are becoming cheaper and more powerful; data sources are becoming more plentiful and accessible; the management community is becoming more aware of modeling skills; and modeling itself is becoming more appreciated as its successes are recognized. Finally, as the business environment becomes more competitive and chaotic, the value of timely and insightful analysis increases. In the future, the opportunities and rewards for modeling expertise will expand. We invite you to use this book in the journey toward becoming an expert modeler.

TO THE READER

Modeling, like painting or singing, cannot be learned entirely from a book. However, a book can establish useful principles, show how a variety of examples are addressed, and offer additional exercises for practice. We suggest that the reader take an *active learning* attitude toward this book. This means working to internalize the skills taught here by tackling as many new problems as possible. It also means applying these skills to everyday situations, in other classes in a business program, or on the job. Modeling expertise can only be acquired by *doing* modeling. We try here to teach basic principles, provide useful examples, and warn the reader about the pitfalls likely to be encountered. But there is no substitute for experience.

The book is organized into three parts. In the first part, comprising Chapters 1–4, we present modeling in the broader context of problem solving. Chapter 1 introduces our topic and establishes the groundwork. Chapter 2 discusses problem solving in general and the role modeling plays within it. Chapter 3 presents the essential craft skills of modeling that we call *modeling heuristics*. Finally, Chapter 4 presents a variety of visual tools that help to identify problem structure and that prepare for spreadsheet use.

The second part of the book comprises Chapters 5 and 6. Here we discuss the concrete details of how to construct and use an effective spreadsheet model, what we call *spreadsheet engineering*. Chapter 5 focuses on designing, building, and testing a spreadsheet so that the resulting analytic tool is efficient and effective. Chapter 6 discusses how to perform analysis using a spreadsheet model. As with the process of building a spreadsheet, the analytic process can, to some extent, be engineered.

The final part of the book covers advanced modeling skills from statistics and management science. Chapter 7 covers the essentials of data analysis and statistical modeling,

Chapter 8 is devoted to optimization, and Chapter 9 is devoted to simulation. While these topics do not arise in every modeling application, they can often be the key to obtaining effective results. The well-trained analyst must have an understanding of these tools and know when they should be employed.

TO THE TEACHER

It is far easier to teach technical skills in Excel or in management science/statistics than it is to teach modeling. Nonetheless, modeling skills *can* be taught successfully. Moreover, doing so can be great fun, both for the student and for the instructor. One reason students enjoy learning to model, beyond its obvious utility, is that it naturally offers room for their creativity. Some instructors enjoy teaching modeling because it brings them closer to their original reason for getting a business education, which was a love of solving practical business problems. Moreover, modeling is a rare skill among business educators, many of whom know the models of their discipline but do not know how to model. Start teaching your students how to model and you may well find yourself in demand among your colleagues for assistance with their own teaching.

We have used portions of this book to teach a variety of courses. In a short MBA course in Quantitative Analysis we would downplay the higher craft skills (Chapter 3) and focus on basic spreadsheet modeling skills (Chapter 5 and 6). Once we establish that foundation, we would teach the basics of data analysis, optimization, and simulation (Chapters 7, 8, and 9). If time were short, or if statistics were covered in a separate course, we would limit the coverage of Chapter 7 to basic exploration of databases (searching, sorting, filtering, pivot tables) and avoid the statistical analyses. We might also cover either optimization or simulation, but perhaps not both.

In an elective MBA course in modeling, for which students already had a background in some aspects of quantitative analysis, we would emphasize craft skills (Chapter 3) and downplay the advanced tools (Chapters 7, 8, and 9). In this course, we would assign several full-scale cases to illustrate the principles in Chapter 3, and we would give the students at least a week to work on each case. The final product each week would be a presentation to the client, so students could gain practice in translating model insights into managerial insights.

We have also taught elective MBA courses in Optimization and Simulation. These courses go beyond the coverage of Chapters 8 and 9, but they build on the spreadsheet material covered in Chapters 5 and 6 especially. While these courses focus on a particular set of tools and the associated applications, they still provide ample time for students to practice modeling skills.

SOFTWARE ACCOMPANYING THE TEXT

The CD-ROM that accompanies this text contains spreadsheet files for all the models presented in the text, as well as the three software applications *Premium Solver for Education*, *Crystal Ball 2000.2 Student Edition*, and the *Sensitivity Toolkit*.

The first time a spreadsheet is introduced in the text, we provide a CD symbol in the margin and the name of the file, indicating that the reader should go to the CD and open the file at this point. In most cases, each of the figures in the text corresponds to a single sheet in the related spreadsheet.

Premium Solver is used for linear and nonlinear optimization, which is the topic of Chapter 8. Detailed instructions for installing this application can be found in the README document in the Premium Solver folder.

Crystal Ball is used for Monte Carlo simulation, which is the topic of Chapter 9. Detailed instructions for installing this application can be found in the README document in the Crystal Ball folder.

The *Sensitivity Toolkit* is an Excel add-in that provides the capability to perform four types of sensitivity analysis:

- Data Sensitivity
- Tornado Chart
- Solver Sensitivity
- Crystal Ball Sensitivity

These tools are covered in Chapters 6, 8 and 9. Detailed instructions for installing this application can be found in the README document in the Sensitivity Toolkit folder. Note: Premium Solver and Crystal Ball must be properly installed *before* installing the Sensitivity Toolkit.

SUPPLEMENTARY MATERIALS

The following supplementary material is provided for adopting instructors and students on the text's companion Web site (www.wiley.com/college/powell):

For Instructors:

PowerPoint slides: A Microsoft PowerPoint presentation by Tava Olsen is available for each chapter of the text. Instructors may provide electronic copies of these presentations to their students.

Instructor's Manual: Sample syllabi and suggestions for course design, along with solutions to the exercises in the book.

Updates: Corrections and other information that becomes available after publication.

For Students:

PowerPoint slides: A Microsoft PowerPoint presentation by Tava Olsen is available for each chapter of the text. These may be printed off the website as a study tool.

Excel Spreadsheets: Copies of the spreadsheets that appear in figures. (These can also be found on the CD that accompanies the book.)

ACKNOWLEDGMENTS

A book such as this evolves over many years of teaching and research. Our ideas have been influenced by our students and by other teachers, not all of whom we can acknowledge here. Our students at Dartmouth's Tuck School have participated in our teaching experiments over the years and improved our courses through their inimitable feedback. Without the collaborative spirit our students bring to their education, we could not have developed our ideas as we have.

Among the many excellent teachers and writers whose ideas we have adapted, we would like to acknowledge Don Plane, Cliff Ragsdale, and Wayne Winston for their pioneering work in teaching management science with spreadsheets. We have also been influenced by Tom Grossman, Peter Bell, Zeger Degraeve, and Erhan Erkut. The book has benefited from careful reviews at many stages from the following reviewers: Jerry Allison

(University of Central Oklahoma), Jonathan Caulkins (Carnegie-Mellon University), Jean-Louis Goffin (McGill University), Roger Grinde (University of New Hampshire), Tom Grossman (University of Calgary), Raymond Hill (Air Force Institute of Technology), Alan Johnson (United States Military Academy), Prafulla Joglekar (LaSalle University), Tarja Joro (University of Alberta), Ron Klimberg (Saint Joseph's University), Larry Leblanc (Vanderbilt University), Jerry May (University of Pittsburgh), Jim Morris (University of Wisconsin), Jim Mote (RPI), Chuck Noon (University of Tennessee), Tava Olsen (Washington University), Fred Raafat (San Diego State University), Gary Reeves (University of South Carolina), Moshe Rosenwein (Columbia University), David Schilling (Ohio State University), Linus Schrage (University of Chicago), Donald Simmons (Ithaca College), George Steiner (McMaster University), and Stephen Thorpe (Drexel University). We have implemented some of their suggestions, many of which were given anonymously, and we only regret that we weren't able to adopt all of their creative ideas.

Beth Golub of John Wiley & Sons encouraged us to write this book for years and has been a supportive influence since we began. We appreciate the extensive network she tapped for feedback and her willingness to support us in writing what we hope will be a new kind of textbook. We owe her our thanks. We also want to acknowledge the organizational and copy editing help we received on early portions of the manuscript from Alison Baker.

ABOUT THE AUTHORS

Steve Powell is a Professor at the Tuck School of Business at Dartmouth College. His primary research interest lies in modeling production and service processes, but he has also been active in research in energy economics, marketing, and operations. At Tuck, he has developed a variety of courses in management science, including the core Decision Science course and electives in the Art of Modeling, Business Process Redesign, and Applications of Simulation. He originated the Teacher's Forum column in *Interfaces,* and has written a number of articles on teaching modeling to practitioners. He organized the Workshop on Teaching Management Science with Spreadsheets in the summer of 1998, and is the Academic Director of a new series of INFORMS workshops on teaching management science. In 2001, he was awarded the INFORMS Prize for the Teaching of Operations Research/Management Science Practice.

Ken Baker is a faculty member at Dartmouth College. He is currently Nathaniel Leverone Professor of Management at the Tuck School of Business and also Adjunct Professor at the Thayer School of Engineering. At Dartmouth, he has taught courses relating to Decision Science, Manufacturing Management, and Environmental Management. Over the years, much of his teaching and research has dealt with Production Planning and Control, and he is widely known for his textbook, *Elements of Sequencing and Scheduling,* in addition to a variety of technical articles. He has served as Tuck School's Associate Dean and directed the Tuck School's management development programs in the manufacturing area. In 2001, he was named a Fellow of INFORMS' Manufacturing and Service Operations Management (MSOM) Society.

CHAPTER 1

INTRODUCTION

MODELS AND MODELING

Modeling is the process of creating a simplified representation of reality and working with this representation in order to understand or control some aspect of the world. While this book is devoted to *mathematical* models, modeling itself is a ubiquitous human activity. In fact, it seems to be one of just a few fundamental ways in which humans understand the world.

As an example, a map is one of the most common models we encounter. Maps are models because they simplify reality by leaving out most geographic details in order to highlight the important features we need. A state road map, for example, shows major roads but not minor ones, gives rough locations of cities but not individual addresses, and so on. The map we choose must be appropriate for the need we have: a long trip home across several states requires a regional map, while a trip across town to find a new doctor's office requires a detailed street map. In the same way, a good model must be appropriate for the specific uses intended for it. A complex model of the economy is probably not appropriate for pricing an individual product. Likewise, a back-of-the-envelope calculation may be inappropriate for acquiring a multibillion-dollar company.

Models take many different forms: mental, visual, physical, mathematical, and spreadsheet, to name a few. We use mental models constantly to understand the world and to predict the outcomes of our actions. Mental models are informal, but they do allow us to make a quick judgment about the desirability of a particular proposal. For example, mental models come into play in a hiring decision. One person has a mental model that suggests that hiring older workers is not a good idea because they are slow to adopt new ways; someone else has a model that suggests hiring older workers is a good idea because they have valuable experience. We are often unaware of our own mental models, yet they can still have a strong influence on the actions we take, especially when they are the primary basis for decision making.

While everyone uses mental models, some people routinely use other kinds of models in their professional lives. Visual models include maps, as we mentioned above. Organization charts are also visual models. They may represent reporting relationships, reveal the locus of authority, suggest major channels of communication, and identify responsibility for personnel decisions. Visual models are used in various sports, where a coach will sketch the playing area and represent team members and opponents as X's and O's. Players seldom stop to think that they are adopting a model for the purposes of communication.

Physical models are used extensively in engineering to assist in the design of airplanes, ships, and buildings. They are also used in science, as, for example, in depicting the spatial arrangement of amino acids in the DNA helix or the makeup of a chemical compound. Architects use physical models to show how a proposed building fits within its surroundings.

Mathematical models take many forms and are used throughout science, engineering, and public policy. For instance, a groundwater model helps determine where flooding is most likely to occur, population models predict the spread of infectious disease, and exposure-assessment models translate the impact of toxic spills. In other settings, traffic-flow models predict the buildup of highway congestion, fault-tree models help reveal the causes of an accident, and reliability models suggest when equipment may need replacement. Mathematical models can be extremely powerful, especially when they give clear insights into the driving forces behind a particular result.

Why Study Modeling?

What are the benefits of building and using formal models, as opposed to relying on mental models or just "gut feel?" The primary purpose of modeling is to generate *insight,* by which we mean an improved understanding of the situation or problem at hand. While mathematical models consist of numbers and symbols, the real benefit of using them is to make better *decisions*. Better decisions are most often the result of improved understanding, not just the numbers themselves.

Thus, the most important reason to study modeling is that modeling improves our thinking skills. Modeling is a discipline that provides a structure for problem solving. The fundamental elements of modeling—such as parameters, decisions, and outcomes—are useful concepts in all problem solving. Modeling provides examples of clear and logical analysis and helps us set high standards for thinking.

Modeling also helps improve our quantitative reasoning skills. Building models demands care with units and orders of magnitude, and it teaches the importance of numeracy. Many people are cautious about quantitative analysis because they do not trust their own quantitative skills. In the best cases, a well-structured modeling experience can help such people overcome their fears, build solid quantitative skills, and improve their performance in a business world that demands (and rewards) these skills.

Any model is a laboratory in which we can experiment and learn. An effective modeler needs to develop an open, inquiring frame of mind to go along with the necessary technical skills. Just as a scientist uses the laboratory to test ideas, hypotheses, and theories, a business analyst can use a model to test the implications of alternative courses of action and develop not only a recommended decision but, equally important, the rationale for why that decision is preferred. The easy-to-understand rationale behind the recommendation often comes from insights the analyst has discovered while testing a model.

Models and Business

Given the widespread use of mathematical models in science and engineering, it is not surprising to find that they are also widely used in the business world. Quite a number of people routinely build and analyze formal models in their professional lives. When this work is done in the business setting, we call these people **business analysts,** and they are the intended audience for this book. In our years of training managers and management students, we have found that strong modeling skills are particularly important for consultants, as well as for financial analysts, marketing researchers, entrepreneurs, and others who face challenging business decisions of real economic consequence.

Just as there are many types of models in science, engineering, public policy, and other domains outside of business, many different types of models are used within business. We distinguish here one-time decision models, decision-support models, embedded models, and models used in business education. These categories exemplify different levels of interaction with and participation by the people in the business organization that uses the models.

Many of the models business analysts create are used in one-time decision problems. A corporate valuation model, for example, might be used during merger negotiations to make a go/no-go decision, but the model may never be used again. In other situations, a one-time model might be created to evaluate the profit impact of a promotion campaign, or to help select a health insurance provider, or to structure the terms of a supply contract. One-time models are usually built by decision makers themselves, often under time pressure. Managerial judgment is often used as a substitute for empirical data in such models, due to time constraints and data limitations. Most importantly, this type of model involves the user intensively, because the model is usually tailored to a particular decision-making need. One major benefit of studying modeling is to make the use of one-time models much more effective.

Decision-support systems are computer systems that tie together models, data, analysis tools, and presentation tools into a single integrated package. These systems are intended for repeated use, either by executives themselves or by their analytic staff. Decision-support systems are used in research and development planning at pharmaceutical firms, pricing decisions at oil companies, and product-line profitability analysis at manufacturing firms, to cite just a few examples. Decision-support systems are usually the province of computer personnel, but they represent the routine use of what were once one-time decision models. After a one-time model is established, it can be adapted for broader and more frequent use in the organization. Thus, the models within decision-support systems may initially be developed by managers and business analysts, but subsequently streamlined by information systems staff for a less intensive level of human interaction. An additional benefit of studying modeling is to recognize possible improvements in the design and operation of decision-support systems.

Embedded models are models that are contained within computer systems that perform routine, repeated tasks with little or no human involvement. Many inventory replenishment decisions are made by automated computer systems. Loan payments on auto leases or prices for stock options are also determined by automated systems. Routine real estate appraisals may also be largely automated. In these cases, the models themselves are somewhat hidden behind the software. Many users of embedded models are not aware of the underlying models, but simply assume that somehow the "system" knows how to make the right calculations. One ancillary benefit of studying modeling is to become more aware, and perhaps more questioning, of these embedded models.

Models are useful not only in the business world, but also in the academic world in which business analysts are educated. The modern business curriculum is heavily dependent on models for delivering basic concepts as well as for providing numerical results. An introductory course in Finance might include an option-pricing model, a cash-management model, and the classical portfolio model. A basic Marketing course might include demand curves for pricing analysis, a diffusion model for new-product penetration, and clustering models for market segmentation. In Operations Management, we might encounter inventory models for stock control, allocation models for scheduling production, and the newsvendor model for trading off shortage and surplus outcomes. Both micro- and macroeconomics are taught almost exclusively through models. Aggregate supply-and-demand curves are models, as are production functions. Most of the models used in education are highly simplified, or *stylized,* in order to preserve clarity. Stylized models are frequently used to provide insight into qualitative phenomena, not necessarily to calculate precise numerical results. In this book, we frequently use models from business education as examples, so that we can combine learning about business with learning about models.

Modeling can benefit business decision making in a variety of ways. For one thing, it can *provide more timely information* than alternative approaches. For example, while extensive surveys could be used to determine the potential demand for a product, effective modeling can often give useful bounds on the likely range of demand in far less time. Modeling can also *save costs:* surveys are expensive to create, distribute, and process. An effective modeler may be able to provide the same level of information at much lower cost. Another way in which modeling reduces cost is that it allows us to *make inexpensive errors.* Wind-tunnel tests are used in airplane design partly because if every potential wing design had to be built into a full-scale aircraft and flown by a pilot, we would lose far too many pilots. Similarly, using a model, we can propose ideas and test them in the model, without having to suffer the consequences of bad ideas in the real world. Yet another benefit of modeling is that it allows us to *explore the impossible.* Many companies have policies, procedures, or habits that prevent them from making certain choices. Sometimes, these habits prevent them from discovering better ways of doing business. Modeling can be used to explore these "impossible" alternatives, and if some of them prove attractive, modeling can be used to convince the skeptics to try them out.

A final benefit from studying modeling is that it can *improve business intuition.* As we have said, a model is a laboratory in which we perform experiments to learn. We can usually learn faster from laboratory experiments than from experience in the real world. With a model, we can try thousands of combinations that would take many years to test in the real world. We can also try extreme ideas that would be too risky to test in the real world. And we can learn about how the world works by simulating a hundred years of experience, all in an afternoon.

Even among those who do not build models, skill in working with models is very important. Most students eventually find themselves on a team charged with recommending a course of action. If these teams do not build models themselves, they often work with internal or external consultants who do. Experience in building and analyzing models is, in our minds, the best training for working effectively on problem-solving teams. People who have not actually built a few models themselves often accept model results blindly or become intimidated by the modeling process. A well-trained analyst not only appreciates the power of modeling but also remains skeptical of models as panaceas.

We believe that modeling skills are useful to a very broad range of businesspeople, from junior analysts without a business degree working in consulting to senior vice presidents of start-ups who do their own analysis. Many recent MBAs have only a superficial knowledge of these tools, because the typical MBA program still emphasizes passive consumption of other people's models rather than active model building. Thus, there is considerable potential even among those who hold MBAs to improve their modeling skills so they can become more capable of carrying out independent analyses of important decisions. The only absolute prerequisite for using this book and enhancing this skill is a desire to use logical, analytic methods to reach a better level of understanding in the decision-making world.

Organization of the Book

This book is organized around the three skills we believe business analysts most need in their modeling work:

- spreadsheet engineering
- modeling craft
- management science and statistics

Spreadsheet engineering deals with how to design, build, test, and perform analysis with a spreadsheet model. Modeling craft refers to the nontechnical but critical skills that an expert modeler employs, such as abstracting the essential features of a situation in a model, debugging a model effectively, and translating model results into managerial insights. Management science covers optimization and simulation. Along with statistics, a basic knowledge of these tools is important for the well-rounded analyst.

The heart of this book is the material on building spreadsheet models and using them to analyze decisions. However, before the analyst can build spreadsheet models successfully, certain broader skills are needed. Therefore, we begin in Chapter 2 with a discussion of the various contexts in which modeling is carried out and the role that modeling plays in a structured problem-solving process. Chapter 3 concentrates on the craft aspects of modeling—the tricks of the trade that experienced and successful modelers employ. These are not Excel tricks, but rather, approaches to dealing with the often ambiguous nature of analysis using models. In Chapter 4, we describe a set of visual modeling approaches, which often provide a powerful first step in building a detailed model. Chapter 5 provides guidelines for designing effective spreadsheets and workbooks, while Chapter 6 provides an overview of various tools available for analyzing spreadsheet models. Chapters 7 through 9 cover the advanced tools of the management scientist and their spreadsheet implementations, starting with an introduction to data analysis and statistics in Chapter 7. Chapter 8 deals with optimization, and Chapter 9 with simulation. Numerous examples throughout the text illustrate good modeling technique, and most chapters contain exercises for practice. Many of these exercises relate to a set of case problems, which are included at the end of the book. These problems provide an opportunity to gain experience with realistic modeling problems that build on concepts in different chapters.

THE ROLE OF SPREADSHEETS

Since spreadsheets are the principal vehicle for modeling in business, spreadsheet models are the major type we deal with in this book. Spreadsheet models are also mathematical models, but, for many people, spreadsheet mathematics is more accessible than algebra or calculus. Spreadsheet models do have limitations, of course, but they allow us to build more detailed and more complex models than traditional mathematics allows. They also have the advantage of being pervasive in business analysis. Finally, the spreadsheet format corresponds nicely to the form of accounting statements that are used for business communication; in fact, the word "spreadsheet" originates in accounting and only recently has come to mean the electronic spreadsheet.

It has been said that the spreadsheet is the *second best* way to do many kinds of analysis and is therefore the *best* way to do most modeling. In other words, for any one modeling task, there is almost certainly a more powerful, flexible, and sophisticated software tool available. In this sense, the spreadsheet is the Swiss Army knife of business analysis. Most business analysts lack the time, money, and knowledge to utilize a different software tool for each problem that arises, just as most of us cannot afford to carry around a complete toolbox to handle the occasional screw we need to tighten. The practical alternative is to use the spreadsheet (and occasionally one of its sophisticated add-ins) to perform most modeling tasks. An effective modeler will, of course, have a good sense of the limitations of the spreadsheet and will know when to use a more powerful tool, as well as when to call in experts for assistance.

Despite its limitations, the electronic spreadsheet is a breakthrough technology for practical modeling. Prior to the 1980s, modeling was performed only by specialists using demanding software on expensive hardware. This meant that only the most critical business problems could be analyzed using models, because only these problems justified the large budgets and long time commitments required to build, debug, and apply the models of the day. This situation has changed dramatically in the past fifteen years or so. First the personal computer, then the spreadsheet, and recently the arrival of add-ins for specialized analyses have put tremendous analytical power at the hands of anyone who can afford a laptop and some training. In fact, we believe the 1990s will come to be seen as the dawn of the "end-user modeling" era. End-user modelers are analysts who are not specialists in modeling, but who can create an effective spreadsheet and manipulate it for insight. The problems that end-user modelers can solve are typically not the multibillion-dollar, multi-year variety; these are still the preserve of functional-area specialists and sophisticated computer scientists. Rather, the end user can apply modeling effectively to hundreds of important but smaller-scale situations that in the past would not have benefited from this approach. We provide many illustrations throughout this book.

Spreadsheet skills themselves are now in high demand in many jobs, although experts in Excel may not be skilled modelers. Good training in spreadsheet modeling, in what we call **spreadsheet engineering,** is valuable because it can dramatically improve both the efficiency and effectiveness with which the analyst uses spreadsheets.

Lessons From the History of Spreadsheet Use

Spreadsheets represent the ubiquitous software platform of business. Millions of spreadsheet models are used each day to make decisions involving billions of dollars, and thousands of new spreadsheets come into being each day. Given this usage pattern, we might think that spreadsheet engineering is a well-developed discipline and that expertise in spreadsheet modeling can be found in just about any company. Amazingly, the opposite is true.

What is the current state of spreadsheet use by end-user modelers? The evidence available from audits that have been done on existing spreadsheets and from laboratory experiments on end users suggests that, despite the widespread use of spreadsheets, the quality with which they are engineered generally remains poor. There are four major problem areas:

- End-user spreadsheets frequently have major bugs.
- End users are overconfident about the quality of their own spreadsheets.
- The process that end users employ to create their spreadsheets is inefficient at best and chaotic at worst.
- End users fail to employ the most productive methods for generating insights from their spreadsheets.

A number of research studies have been conducted in the past decade to determine the error rate in existing spreadsheets. These studies range over many companies and many industries. The methods used in these studies to uncover errors differ as well. One major shortcoming of these studies is that only certain types of errors can be identified. In particular, careful audits can uncover errors in specific cells, but cannot reveal conceptual errors in the modeling behind the spreadsheet. We might wonder, for example, how many existing spreadsheets were designed to solve the wrong problem? Nevertheless, in a summary of this research, Ray Panko[1] cites the following disturbing statistic: in field audits of 367 spreadsheets in actual use, 24 percent were found to contain material errors. Even worse, recent studies that have used more accurate auditing methods show an error rate of 90 percent in fifty-four spreadsheets tested. It seems fair to conclude that most spreadsheets in actual use contain bugs. This fact alone should provide strong motivation for improving the spreadsheet-modeling process.

Laboratory experiments have uncovered another disturbing fact about spreadsheet modeling: end users appear to be overconfident about the likelihood of errors in their own spreadsheets. In these experiments, undergraduate volunteers were asked to build a

[1] See http://panko.cba.hawaii.edu/ssr/Mypapers/whatknow.htm.

spreadsheet for a well-defined problem. After they were done, the volunteers were given time to review and audit their models. Finally, they were asked to evaluate the likelihood that their model contained one or more bugs. While 18 percent of the subjects thought their models had one or more bugs, the actual proportion proved to be 80 percent. This finding of overconfidence is consistent with other studies: human beings tend to underestimate the possibility that they might make mistakes. Unfortunately, this overconfidence translates directly into a casual attitude toward spreadsheet design and ultimately into a disturbingly high error rate among spreadsheets in actual use.

Our observations of how end users actually construct spreadsheets suggest that the process is often inefficient and in many cases simply chaotic. End users typically do not plan their spreadsheets. Instead, they build them live at the keyboard and are drawn into endless rework. End users do not use a conscious prototyping approach, which involves building a series of models starting with the simplest and gradually adding complexity. End users rarely spend time debugging their models, unless the model performs in such a counterintuitive manner that it demands intervention. End users almost never subject their spreadsheets to review by another person. In general, end users appear to trust that the model they *thought* they had built is actually the model they see on their screens, despite the fact that spreadsheets show only numbers, not the relationships that make up the model behind the numbers.

Finally, many end users, even some who are experts in Excel, do not consistently use tools that can help generate the insights that make modeling worthwhile. Excel's Data Table and Goal Seek tools, to cite just two examples, are overlooked by the majority of end users. Without these tools, the end user either fails to ask questions of the model that can provide telling insights, or else wastes time generating results that could be found more easily.

The evidence is strong that the existing state of spreadsheet design and use is generally inadequate. This is one reason we devote a significant portion of this book to spreadsheet engineering. Only with a solid foundation in spreadsheet engineering can the business analyst effectively generate real insights from spreadsheet models.

How Much Knowledge of Mathematics and Computing Does Spreadsheet Modeling Require?

Many people new to modeling fear it because modeling reminds them of painful experiences with mathematics. We do not wish to downplay the essentially mathematical nature of modeling, even modeling using spreadsheets. However, an effective modeler does not need to know any really advanced math. Knowledge of basic algebra (including functions such as the quadratic, exponential, and logarithmic), simple logic (as expressed in an IF statement or the MAX function), and basic probability (distributions and sampling, for example) will usually suffice. When we find it necessary to use any higher math in this book, we provide explanations. But our focus here is less on the mathematical details of models than on the creative process of constructing and using models.

We assume throughout this book that the reader has a basic familiarity with Excel. This includes the ability to build a simple spreadsheet, enter and format text and data, use formulas and simple functions such as SUM, construct graphs, and so on. We do not assume the reader is an expert in Excel, nor do we assume knowledge of the advanced tools we cover, such as Solver and Crystal Ball. We have found that, in many situations, advanced Excel skills are not required for building effective models. And we believe that the main purpose of modeling is to improve the insight of the modeler. Thus, it is appropriate for a modeler with only basic Excel skills to build a model using only basic tools, and it is appropriate for a modeler with advanced skills to draw on advanced tools when needed. We have also found that too much skill in Excel can sometimes distract from the essential modeling tasks, which are almost always more about finding a simple and effective representation of the problem at hand than about finding some Excel trick.

For easy reference, we have provided an appendix that briefly outlines the basic Excel skills we assume as background. We have also provided reference guides where needed for the specialized tools and add-ins we present. We believe that, by working through the examples in the book, the reader's Excel skills will improve naturally and painlessly, just as ours have improved over years of building models and teaching modeling to students whose Excel skills often exceeded ours.

SUMMARY

The following statements summarize the principles on which this book is based.

- *Modeling is a necessary skill for every business analyst.*

  Models are encountered frequently in business education and in the business world. Furthermore, analysts are capable of formulating their own models.

- *Spreadsheets are the modeling platform of choice.*

  The wide acceptance and flexibility of the spreadsheet make it the modeling platform of choice for most business situations. Since familiarity with spreadsheets is required for almost everyone in business, the basis for learning spreadsheet-based modeling is already in place.

- *Basic spreadsheet modeling skills are an essential foundation.*

  While basic knowledge about spreadsheets is usually assumed in business, spreadsheet skills and spreadsheet modeling skills are not the same. Effective education in business modeling begins with training in how to use a spreadsheet to build and analyze models.

- *End-user modeling is cost-effective.*

  In an ever-growing range of situations, well-trained business analysts can build their own models without relying on consultants or experts.

- *Craft skills are essential to the effective modeler.*

  Craft skills are the mark of an expert in any field. The craft skills of modeling must be gradually refined through experience, but the process can be expedited by identifying and discussing them and by providing opportunities to practice their use.

- *Analysts can learn the required modeling skills.*

  Modeling skills do not involve complex mathematics or arcane concepts. Any motivated analyst can learn the basics of good modeling and apply this knowledge on the job.

- *Management science/statistics are important advanced tools.*

  Extensive knowledge of these tools is not required of most business analysts; however, a solid knowledge of the fundamentals can turn an average modeler into a power modeler.

REFERENCES

Many books are available on Excel, although most of these cover its vast array of features without isolating those of particular relevance for the business analyst. In the appendix on Excel we provide several references to books and other materials for learning basic Excel skills. A working business analyst should probably own at least one Excel guide as a reference book. Two such references are listed below.

Stinson, Craig, and Mark Dodge, 2001. *Microsoft Excel Version 2002 Inside Out.* Bellingham, WA: Microsoft Press.

Walkenbach, John, and Brian Underdahl. 2001. *Excel 2002 Bible.* New York: Wiley and Sons.

Several textbooks present the tools of management science using spreadsheets. We recommend these for a more detailed treatment of management science than we provide here.

Ragsdale, Cliff. 2001. *Spreadsheet Modeling and Decision Making.* 3d ed. Cincinnati: South-Western.

Winston, Wayne, and Chris Albright. 2000. *Practical Management Science.* 2d ed. Pacific Grove, CA: Duxbury.

The standard reference on the mathematics of management science is:

Hillier, Frederick, and Gerald Lieberman. 2002. *Introduction to Operations Research.* 7th ed. Oakland, CA: McGraw-Hill.

While this text does not rely on spreadsheets, it does provide in a relatively accessible form the methods behind much of the management science we present in this book.

For more narrowly focused books that apply spreadsheet modeling to specific business disciplines, consult:

Benniga, Simon. 2000. *Financial Modeling.* Cambridge, MA: MIT Press.

Lilien, Gary, and Arvind Rangaswamy. 1998. *Marketing Engineering.* Reading, MA: Addison-Wesley.

Finally, for a stimulating book on modeling and problem solving, we recommend:

Starfield, Anthony, Karl Smith, and Andrew Bleloch. 1990. *How to Model It.* New York: McGraw-Hill.

CHAPTER 2

MODELING IN A PROBLEM-SOLVING FRAMEWORK

INTRODUCTION

Modeling is an approach that helps us develop a better understanding of business situations. As a result, it helps us make better decisions. Thus, we don't view modeling as an end in itself, but rather, as part of a broader process. In this chapter, we discuss the roles modeling plays in that broader process. We refer to this broader process generically as a **problem-solving** process, although specific instances could involve making forecasts, evaluating business opportunities, or allocating resources.

Any successful problem-solving process begins with recognition of a problem and ends with implementation of a proposed solution. All the work that comes between these two points is the problem-solving process. In some cases, this process is highly structured and planned, perhaps involving a large team working over several months; in other cases, it is informal and unstructured, perhaps involving only one person for a couple of hours. Modeling is just one of many tools or strategies that can be used within problem solving. An effective problem solver knows when and how to use modeling effectively within the broader context of effective problem solving.

Modelers can play different roles in the problem-solving process. Primarily, these roles are:

- End user
- Team member
- Independent consultant

When the entire team consists of one person, then problem owner (or client) and modeler are one and the same. We refer to this role as the **end-user** modeler. The end user is often a small-business owner or an entrepreneur, who has no staff and no budget for consultants. In large firms, many managers are also end users at times, when there is no time to brief the staff or bring in consultants, or when the problem is too sensitive to share with anyone else. The end user carries out all of the activities in problem solving: identifying a problem worthy of attention, developing a model, using the model to develop insights and practical solutions, and implementing the results. There is an enormous untapped potential for end-user modeling, because there are so many relatively small problems for which modeling can provide insight, and because there are so many end users who have (or can acquire) the spreadsheet and modeling skills necessary to develop useful models.

In addition to the end-user role, modelers are often assigned to the role of **team member** on an internal committee or task force. In many cases, the problem-solving process may have begun before the committee was formed, and the modeler may or may not have been part of that process. Although chosen for expertise in modeling, the team-member modeler's role also requires good interpersonal and communication skills. A critical part of the work is communicating with nonmodelers on the team about the assumptions that go into the model and the intuition behind the model's results. Of course, the team-member modeler must also have the necessary technical skills to apply modeling successfully, but communication skills are more important than for the end-user modeler.

A third role for the modeler is that of **independent consultant.** This role differs from the role of team member because there is usually a client—someone who identifies the problem and ultimately manages the implementation of any solution. The role of consultant modeler also requires great communication and interpersonal skills. Despite being an organizational outsider, the consultant modeler must understand the client's problem deeply and translate the client's understanding of the problem into modeling terms. This role also requires the ability to translate model insights back into a language the client can understand, so that the client can proceed with implementing a solution.

This chapter describes a widely used problem-solving process and the role that modeling plays in this process. We then report on research into how expert modelers approach their work, and we draw some lessons for good modeling practice. Finally, we discuss the role that creativity plays in modeling and problem solving and various ways that teams and individuals can enhance their creativity.

THE PROBLEM-SOLVING PROCESS

While problem solving is an almost universal aspect of life, very few individuals follow a structured approach to it. This could indicate that effective problem solving is instinctive and intuitive and that the only way to improve in this area is through experience. We do not, however, subscribe to this point of view. In our experience, some degree of conscious attention to the process pays off in improved results and efficiency, even for experienced modelers and managers. This is especially true for problem-solving teams, where intuitive methods often fail because what is intuitive to one member makes no sense to another. While the end-user modeler can perhaps get by with short cuts, team members and independent consultants are more effective when they carefully manage the problem-solving process.

The problem-solving process is often described as a sequential, step-by-step procedure. While this makes for easy description, there is, in fact, no simple plan that represents the universal problem-solving process. Moreover, when people look back on their own problem-solving activities, they tend to recall more structure than was really there. Thus, a sequential description of problem solving should not be taken at face value. Even experts appear to jump around from one aspect of a problem to another as they attempt to formulate models. Any process must be flexible enough to accommodate different work styles, unexpected discoveries and disappointments, and inevitable fluctuations in effort and creativity. The process we discuss below helps focus attention on some of the critical aspects of effective problem solving, without providing a straitjacket that will cramp a problem solver's style. Our description comes from what experts tell us, from what we observe, and from what we have experienced in problem solving.

Defining Terms

We begin by making an important distinction between a **problem** and a **mess.** A mess is a morass of unsettling symptoms, causes, data, pressures, shortfalls, opportunities, and so on. A problem, on the other hand, is a well-defined situation that is capable of resolution. Why do we need the concept of a mess when we are problem solving? The idea is simple: problems do not come to us fully defined and labeled. Rather, we operate in a world full of confusion: causes and effects are muddled, data exist but there is little relevant information, problematic shortfalls or inadequacies appear alongside attractive opportunities, and so on. Where are the problems in this mess? Identifying a problem in the mess is itself a creative act that will do much to determine the quality of any solutions we propose. In most situations, a number of problems could be extracted from a given mess. Which one we choose depends on our understanding of the situation and on our insight into where analysis and action could be most effective. Our first piece of advice on problem solving, then, is to recognize that defining the problem to be solved is a critical step in the process—one that deserves considerable attention.

One way to focus attention on the problem definition is to use a problem statement of the form "In what ways might . . . ?" Imagine the situation facing a manufacturing company whose costs are rising sharply due to increasing wages. Here are some possible problem statements the company could use:

- In what ways might we increase the productivity of our workforce?
- In what ways might we reduce the labor content of our products?
- In what ways might we shift our manufacturing to lower-cost regions?
- In what ways might we increase revenues to keep pace with costs?
- In what ways might we change our product line to maintain profit margins?

This is just a sample of the problem statements that could apply to a given situation. It should be obvious that the approach taken to resolving the "problem" will be very different depending on which of these statements is adopted. Our advice is to pay close attention to the problem definition, take any problem definition as tentative, and prepare to alter it if evidence suggests that a different problem statement would be more effective.

At any stage in the problem-solving process, there are two quite different styles of thinking: **divergent** and **convergent.** Divergent thinking stresses generating ideas over evaluating ideas. It involves thinking in different directions or searching for a variety of answers to questions that may have many right answers. Brainstorming, in which the evaluation process is strictly prohibited, promotes divergent thinking and allows many ideas to flourish at the same time, even ideas that contradict each other. Convergent thinking, on the other hand, is directed toward achieving a goal, toward a single solution, answer, or result. It involves trying to find the one best answer. In convergent thinking, the emphasis shifts from idea generation to evaluation: Which of these ideas leads to the best outcomes? In many cases, this evaluation is carried out using a model.

Why is this distinction between divergent and convergent thinking useful? One reason is that some individuals naturally prefer, enjoy, or are skilled at one or the other type of thinking. When working as end users, these individuals should be conscious of their preference or skill and take steps to ensure that they devote sufficient time and energy to the other approach. Good evaluators need to encourage themselves to generate more ideas; good idea generators need to encourage themselves to test their ideas thoroughly. Since end users do it all, they must ensure that the balance between divergent and convergent thinking is appropriate throughout the problem-solving process.

An understanding of these concepts is just as important to members of a problem-solving team. In this situation, each member can afford to specialize in their preferred thought process: idea generators can take a lead role in that phase, while strong evaluators can take a lead role when that becomes the primary activity of the group. But each type of person needs to understand their own strengths and the strengths of others on the team and needs to appreciate that the other types make an important contribution. Finally, teams work best when they are aware of which type of thinking they are stressing at each point in the process. It is disruptive and inefficient to have one member of a team evaluating ideas during a brainstorming session; it is just as disruptive to have someone offering great new ideas during the preparation of a final presentation to the client.

A Six-Stage Process

We now describe a six-stage problem-solving process (Figure 2.1) that begins with a mess and ends with implementation of a solution. This process can be used to solve almost any problem, from the most immediate and well-defined (such as selecting a new supplier) to the most long-term and ill-defined (such as identifying a new corporate strategy). Since not all problem solving involves the use of formal models, we first describe the process in its most general form. Subsequently, we discuss how formal modeling fits within this overall framework. Throughout this section, we illustrate the stages of the process with the example of a pharmaceutical company whose blockbuster drug is due to come off patent in a year's time.

FIGURE 2.1
The Creative Problem-Solving Process

Exploring the mess
  Divergent phase
    Search mess for problems and opportunities.
  Convergent phase
    Accept a challenge and undertake systematic efforts to respond to it.

Searching for information
  Divergent phase
    Gather data, impressions, feelings, observations; examine the situation from many different viewpoints.
  Convergent phase
    Identify the most important information.

Identifying a problem
  Divergent phase
    Generate many different potential problem statements.
  Convergent phase
    Choose a working problem statement.

Searching for solutions
  Divergent phase
    Develop many different alternatives and possibilities for solutions.
  Convergent phase
    Select one or a few ideas that seem most promising.

Evaluating solutions
  Divergent phase
    Formulate criteria for reviewing and evaluating ideas.
  Convergent phase
    Select the most important criteria. Use the criteria to evaluate, strengthen, and refine ideas.

Implementing a solution
  Divergent phase
    Consider possible sources of assistance and resistance to proposed solution. Identify implementation steps and required resources.
  Convergent phase
    Prepare the most promising solution for implementation.

(After Couger, *Creative Problem Solving and Opportunity Finding*)

The six stages in this process are:

- Exploring the mess
- Searching for information
- Identifying a problem
- Searching for solutions
- Evaluating solutions
- Implementing a solution

Divergent thinking tends to predominate early in this process, while convergent thinking comes to dominate later on, but there is a role for each type of thinking in every stage of the process.

The first stage of problem solving explores the mess. As we have said, problems do not appear to us in the form of well-posed problem statements. Rather, we find ourselves in various messes, out of which problems occasionally emerge. It often takes a special effort to rise above the press of day-to-day activities and begin a problem-solving process. In this sense, the most important aspect of this phase may be more psychological than intellectual. The divergent thinking in this phase involves being open to the flow of problems and opportunities in the environment; the convergent phase distills a specific problem out of the mess. During this phase, we ask questions such as the following:

- What problems (or opportunities) do we face?
- Where is there a gap between the current situation and the desired one?
- What are the stated and unstated goals?

This stage will be complete when we have produced a satisfactory description of the situation and when we have identified (although not necessarily gathered) the key facts and data.

In our example, management in the pharmaceutical company is well aware that one drug has provided the bulk of profits over the past decade. Nevertheless, most of their day-to-day attention is devoted to tactical issues, such as resolving conflicts with suppliers or allocating R&D funds to the development of new drugs. As the date approaches on which their major drug loses its patent protection and alternative drugs can begin to compete, the managers gradually become more focused on the problem facing them. While the threat is obvious, the problem is not well defined. Each member of management probably explores this mess individually, in an informal way. They might make rough estimates of the magnitude of the threat (how much will profits fall when the patent expires?), and they might consider alternatives to improve outcomes (should I institute a cost-cutting program in manufacturing?). Eventually, management as a whole realizes the importance of the issue, and a task force is created to address it. All of this activity comes under the heading of exploring the mess.

The second stage searches for information. Here, we mean information in the broadest sense: opinions, data, impressions, published literature, and so on. This is a phase in which we cast about widely for any and all information that might shed light on what the problem really is. Examining the situation from many different points of view is an important aspect of this phase. We might survey similar companies to determine how they approach related problems. We might search the literature for related academic research. The search itself at this stage is divergent. Eventually, we begin to get a sense that some of the information is more relevant, or contains suggestions for solutions, or might otherwise be particularly useful. This is the convergent part of this phase. In this stage, we should expect to be using diagnostic skills, prioritizing, and constructing diagrams or charts. During this phase, we ask questions such as the following:

- ■ What are the symptoms and causes?
- ■ What measures of effectiveness seem appropriate?
- ■ What actions are available?

This stage will be complete when we have found and organized relevant data for the situation at hand and when we have made some initial hypotheses about the source of the problem and potential solutions.

The task force in our example holds several meetings to get to know each other and to get organized. They also hire a consultant to gather information and to bring an outside perspective to the discussion. The CEO charges the group to "find a strategy to deal with the patent situation," but the task force recognizes this is not a problem statement, only a vague indication of senior management's discomfort about the future of the company. The consultant, meanwhile, begins interviewing key managers inside the firm and gathering information externally. She collects information on general trends in the pharmaceutical industry, as well as case studies on the transition off patent for other drugs. A rough picture emerges as to the rate at which generics have invaded a market once patent protection has been lost. She also collects specific information on strategies that other market-dominating firms have used to limit their losses during similar transitions. The consultant interviews economists specializing in industry structure. Inside the firm, she interviews the scientists who develop new drugs, and she begins to formulate a picture of how the firm's portfolio of new drugs will contribute to future revenues. If the problem-solving process is to work well here, a broad search for information must precede any effort to narrow in on a specific problem that can be resolved. However, even while this search goes on, the members of the task force are beginning to form opinions as to the real problem they face and solutions they prefer.

The third stage defines the problem. In the divergent portion of this phase, we might pose four or five candidate problem statements and try them on for size. We will eventually choose one of these statements, perhaps somewhat refined, as our working problem statement. As mentioned before, there is a significant benefit for any problem-solving group to having an unambiguous statement of the problem they are solving. This is not to say that we can't modify or even replace one problem statement with another if the evidence suggests this is necessary. All problem statements should be viewed as tentative, although as time passes, the cost and risk of changing the problem statement increases. In this stage, we should be asking whether the situation fits a standard problem type, or whether we should be breaking the problem into subproblems. During this phase, we ask questions such as the following:

- ■ Which is the most important problem in this situation?
- ■ Is this problem like others we have dealt with?
- ■ What are the consequences of a broad versus narrow problem statement?

This stage will be complete when we have produced a working problem statement.

The consultant to the pharmaceutical firm in our example holds a series of meetings with the task force to present and discuss her preliminary research. The group now has a shared understanding of the financial state of their own firm, as well as a general idea of the state of the industry. They discuss how other firms fared when major drugs came off patent and what strategies were used to smooth the transition. At this point, the consultant leads an effort to define a problem statement around which the future efforts of the task force can be organized. In the discussion that ensues, two major points of view emerge. One group focuses on preserving the revenue-generating power of the patent drug as long as possible. They ask whether it would be possible to extend the patent, slow the introduction of generic competitors, or perhaps make an alliance with competitors that would share the profits from this category of drugs without significantly reducing its revenues. The other group is focused on a different issue: how to generate more revenue from other drugs now in the development pipeline. They ask whether the firm should increase its R&D spending, narrow its efforts to just the most promising drugs, or look for quicker ways to get regulatory approval. The consultant recognizes that no one is looking at reducing costs or shrinking the firm as possible strategies.

The task force has reached a critical stage in the problem-solving process. How they define the problem here will determine in large measure the solutions they eventually recommend. The consultant, recognizing this, makes an effort to have the group debate a wide range of problem statements. Here are some candidate problem statements they may consider:

- In what ways might we slow the decline in revenues from our patented drug?
- In what ways might we increase the chances of success of R&D on new products?
- In what ways might we increase market share for our existing products?
- In what ways might we resize the firm to match declining profits?
- In what ways might we develop more products with the same investment?
- In what ways might we partner with other firms?

Eventually, the task force comes to the conclusion that protecting the revenues from the existing drug is both difficult and risky. The most effective strategy probably involves developing a portfolio of new drugs as quickly and effectively as possible. Accordingly, they adopt the problem statement: "In what ways might we reduce the time to market for the six drugs currently under development?"

The fourth stage searches for solutions. Again, there is a divergent aspect to this phase, in which a deliberately open-ended search is conducted for good, even radical, solutions. Brainstorming or other creativity-enhancing techniques might be particularly useful, since the team has a well-considered problem statement to serve as a focal point for the creation of solutions. Prior to this point, it is premature to consider solutions. It can even be dangerous to do so, since superficially appealing solutions often gain support on their own, even if they solve the wrong problem. The convergent part of this phase involves a tentative selection of the most promising candidate solutions. The selection process must be tentative at this point, because criteria have not yet been established for a careful comparison of solutions. Nonetheless, there are costs to considering too many solutions, so some pruning is often necessary. During this phase, we ask questions such as the following:

- What decisions are open to us?
- What solutions have been tried in similar situations?
- How are the various candidate solutions linked to outcomes of interest?

This stage will be complete when we have produced a list of potential solutions and perhaps a list of advantages and disadvantages for each one.

Having decided to focus their efforts on improving the R&D process, our task force first forms a subcommittee composed mainly of scientists from the R&D division, along with a few business experts. The consultant conducts extensive interviews within the R&D group to uncover inefficiencies and possible ways to improve the process of bringing drugs to market. The subcommittee eventually develops a list of potential solutions, along with an evaluation of their advantages and disadvantages. Three areas for potential improvement stand out:

- Hire outside firms to conduct clinical trials and develop applications for Food and Drug Administration (FDA) approvals. This will speed up the approval process, although it will also increase costs.

- Invest a higher percentage of the R&D budget in drugs with the most promise of winning FDA approval. This should reduce the time required for the most promising drugs to reach the market, but it may also reduce the number of drugs that do so.

- Focus the drug portfolio on drugs in the same medical category. This should help develop an expertise in just one or two medical specialties, rather than spreading efforts over many technical areas and markets.

The fifth stage evaluates solutions. This stage can be considered the culmination of the process, as it is here that a preferred solution emerges. Any evaluation of the candidate solutions developed in the previous phase requires a set of criteria with which to compare solutions. Usually, there are many criteria that could be relevant to the outcome; some divergent thinking is useful in this phase to ensure that all relevant criteria, even those that are not obvious, are considered. Once the most important criteria are identified, the various solutions can be evaluated and compared on each criterion. This can lead directly to a preferred alternative. More often, this process leads to changes—and improvements—in the solutions themselves. Often, an aspect of one solution can be grafted onto another solution, or a particularly negative aspect of a generally attractive solution can be removed once the weakness has been recognized. So this phase, while generally stressing convergent thinking, still involves considerable creativity. During this phase, we ask questions such as the following:

- How does this solution impact each of the criteria?
- What factors within our control could improve the outcomes?
- What factors outside our control could alter the outcomes?

This stage will be complete when we have produced a recommended course of action, along with a justification that supports it.

During this phase, our task force first develops a set of criteria with which to evaluate each of the previously proposed solutions. The overall goal is to ensure that the firm remains profitable into the future, even as the main drug goes off patent and its revenues are lost. However, it is difficult to anticipate how any one solution will impact profits directly. For example, how much additional profit will the firm realize if it saves two months in the development process for a particular drug? For this reason, each solution is measured against many criteria, and the results are synthesized by the task force. Here are some of the criteria they develop:

- R&D cost reduction
- Increase in market share
- Months of development time saved
- Increase in probability of FDA approval

After extensive discussion, the task force finally decides that the one most critical area for improvement is how R&D funds are allocated over time. In the past, the firm has generally been very slow to cancel development of any particular drug. Each drug has the passionate support of the scientists working on it, and the commitment of this group to its own drug has superseded the business judgment needed to recognize that other drug-development teams can make better use of scarce R&D resources. With a more business-oriented allocation process, fewer drugs will get increased R&D funding, but, it is hoped, more drugs will come to market quickly.

The final stage implements the solution. This stage is included to remind us that a solution is useless if it cannot be implemented. Political resistance, departures from established tradition, and high personal cost or risk are some of the many reasons why apparently rational solutions cannot be implemented in real organizations. In the divergent portion of this phase, the problem-solving team will identify potential sources of resistance and support. As this phase proceeds and specific implementation plans for the proposed solution are developed, the thinking style turns from divergent toward convergent. In this stage, we should expect to be performing change management and focusing on communication. During this phase, we ask questions such as the following:

- What are the barriers to successful implementation?
- Where will there be support and motivation, or resistance and conflict?
- Are the resources available for successful implementation?

This stage will be complete when we have produced an implementation plan and executed enough of it to begin evaluating how well it is succeeding.

To implement its plan, the task force must first convince senior management to support the task force's recommended solution. The consultant has a major role to play here, in developing an effective presentation and in convincing both scientists and executives that this solution will work. The task force's role ends when it has won approval and has appointed a new committee to manage the implementation of the new R&D budget-allocation process. Of course, the problem-solving process does not really end here, as the new committee must carry the plan forward, monitor its impacts, modify it as needed, and solve a new set of problems as they arise. To this extent, no problem-solving process ever really ends; it just flows into a subsequent process.

Every successful problem-solving effort starts with a mess and concludes with an implemented solution. Sometimes, the cycle will be repeated more than once, so that the implementation itself creates a new situation and paves the way for follow-on problems to be identified. Nevertheless, the process passes through the stages we have outlined here. Knowledge of these stages is helpful in planning the overall tasks and resources, allocating effort, and setting expectations about progress. Within each stage, an awareness of the contributions from divergent and convergent thinking is helpful in balancing the need for creativity with the need for closure.

It is worth repeating that only rarely are these six stages followed in a strict sequence. Most problem-solving processes move back and forth from one stage to another, perhaps rethinking the problem statement while evaluating solutions, or returning to an information-gathering mode while searching for solutions. As in any creative endeavor, it is important for a problem-solving team (or individual) to remain flexible. That means remaining open to discoveries and to evidence that past work needs to be rethought.

Formal Modeling

The problem-solving process described above is generic in that it does not specifically address how formal modeling is used within the overall framework. Informal modeling, what is often called **mental modeling,** goes on constantly during problem solving. That is, problem solvers construct quick, informal mental models at many different points in the process. For example, when a potential solution is proposed, everyone on the team runs that idea through a mental model to get a quick first impression of its attractiveness. As an example, consider the following question: Would a tax on carbon emissions in developed countries significantly reduce global warming? What mental models do you use to evaluate this question? How do you think a tax would affect actual emissions of carbon? What would its impacts be on economic growth and quality of life? How would developing countries react to such a policy, and what would be the long-term impact on global temperature? Usually, when we consider questions like this, we use mental models to link causes (the tax) with their effects (changes in global temperature).

Mental models help us to relate cause and effect, but often in a highly simplified and incomplete way. Mental models also help us to determine what might be feasible in a given situation, but our idea of what is possible is often circumscribed by our personal experiences. Finally, mental models are always influenced by our preferences for certain outcomes over others, although those preferences may not be acknowledged or even understood. One of the sources of confusion and debate on topics such as global warming is that we all use different mental models, based on different assumptions and preferences for outcomes, and we have limited means of sharing those models because they are informal and hidden from view. So, while mental models may be useful, even necessary, they can also be extremely limiting. A common pitfall is to reject an unusual idea because it appears at first to be unworkable. Effective divergent thinking can help overcome this pitfall and allow unusual ideas to persist long enough to get a thorough hearing. But in some circumstances, mental models are simply not robust enough to provide sufficient insight, and formal models are called for.

Formal models provide the same kind of information as mental models. In essence, they link causes to effects and help us evaluate potential solutions. Once a set of potential solutions and a set of criteria have been identified, a formal model can be used to measure how well each solution performs according to the criteria. Formal models are undoubtedly costlier and more time-consuming to build than mental models, but they have the great advantage of making our assumptions, logic, and preferences explicit and open to debate.

Mental models were used extensively during the problem-solving process in our pharmaceutical company example. Every member of the task force was experienced in the industry, so each of them had developed mental models to think through the implications of the various proposals. For example, they each had some idea of the development and testing protocols for new drugs, the current process used to allocate R&D funds, and the profit streams new drugs typically generate. Using this experience, they were able to make rough, qualitative assessments of the impact the new R&D-allocation process would have on new-drug success, as well as the profit impact of introducing fewer drugs sooner. However, given the complexity of the drug-development process and the interaction of the various competing companies in the market, mental models would simply not support quantitative estimates of the overall profit impact of the proposed solution.

How could this company use formal modeling in the process? With a formal model, they could track the progress of each of the six drugs through the various stages of development. One of the key assumptions they need to agree on is how the new R&D process affects the completion time and probability of success at each stage. To this model, they probably want to add a module that projects the introduction of competing products in each medical category. This requires discussion and agreement on a set of assumptions about the plans of their competitors. Finally, they can complete the model by adding a financial component to determine their profits under any scenario. Taken as a whole, this model projects a stream of new-drug introductions by the firm itself and its competitors, then determines the price and market share for each drug, and ultimately calculates the resulting profits. Unlike mental models, a formal model built along these lines can be used to analyze whether the firm can generate enough revenues from new drugs to offset the loss in revenues from its blockbuster drug.

THE REAL WORLD AND THE MODEL WORLD

We stated at the outset of this chapter that modeling is a tool or a strategy that is used within the broader context of problem solving. Now that we have described that broader context, we can focus more narrowly on modeling itself.

A **model** is an abstraction, or simplification, of the real world. It is a laboratory—an artificial environment—in which we can experiment and test ideas without the costs and risks of experimenting with real systems and organizations. Figure 2.2 is a schematic showing how modeling creates an artificial world. We begin in the real world, with a problem statement that is already a selection of the most important features from the confusion and complexity of the mess. If we determine that modeling is an appropriate tool, we then move across an invisible boundary into the model world.

In order to move into the model world, we abstract the essential features of the real world, leaving behind all the inessential detail and complexity. We then construct our laboratory by combining our abstractions with specific assumptions and by building a model of the essential aspects of the real world. This is the process of **formulation.** It is an exercise in simplifying the actual situation and capturing its essence, with a specific purpose in mind. The formulation process typically forces us to confront four features of a model:

- Decisions
- Outcomes
- Structure
- Data

Decisions refers to possible choices, or courses of action, that we might take. These would be controllable variables, such as quantities to buy, manufacture, spend, or sell. (By contrast, uncontrollable variables such as tax rates or the cost of materials are not decision variables.) **Outcomes** refers to the consequences of the decisions—the performance measures we use to evaluate the results of taking action. Examples might include profit, cost, or efficiency. **Structure** refers to the logic and the mathematics that link the elements of our model together. A simple example might be the equation $P = R - C$, in which profit is calculated as the difference between revenue and cost. Another example might be the relationship $F = I + P - S$, in which final inventory is calculated from initial inventory, production, and shipments.

FIGURE 2.2
The Real World and
the Model World

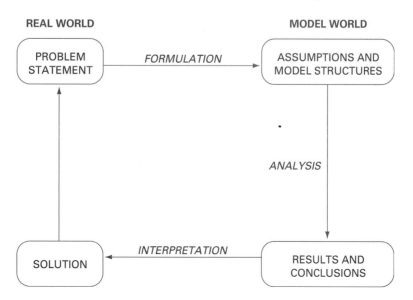

Finally, **data** refers to specific numerical assumptions. That may mean actual observations of the real world (often called "raw" or "empirical" data), or it may mean estimates of key uncontrollable variables in the problem's environment. Examples might include an interest rate on borrowed funds, the capacity of a manufacturing facility, or the first-quarter sales for a new product. (In Chapters 3 and 4, we examine the model-formulation process in more detail. In Chapter 5, we focus on how to build effective models using spreadsheets.)

Once it is built, we can use the model to test ideas and evaluate solutions. This is a process of **analysis,** in which we apply logic, often with the support of software, to take us from our assumptions and abstractions to a set of derived conclusions. Unlike formulation, which tends to be mostly an art, analysis is much more of a science. It relies on mathematics and reason in order to explore the implications of our assumptions. (In Chapter 6, we describe the major steps in this process. In Chapters 7 through 9, we elaborate on the major quantitative techniques for analyzing models.) This exploration process leads, hopefully, to insights about the problem confronting us. Sometimes, these insights involve an understanding of why one solution is beneficial and another is not; at other times, the insights involve understanding the sources of risk in a particular solution. In another situation, the insights involve identifying the decisions that are most critical to a good result, or identifying the inputs that have the strongest influence on a particular outcome. In each instance, it is crucial to understand that these insights are derived from the model world and not from the real world. Whether they apply to the real world is another matter entirely and requires managerial judgment.

To make the model insights useful, we must first *translate* them into the terms of the real world and then *communicate* them to the actual decision makers involved. Only then do model insights turn into useful managerial insights. And only then can we begin the process of evaluating solutions in terms of their impact on the real world. This is a process of **interpretation,** and here again, the process is an art. Good modelers can move smoothly back and forth between the model world and the real world, deriving crisp insights from the model, and translating the insights, modifying them as needed, to account for real-world complexities not captured in the model world.

This schematic description of the modeling process highlights some of the reasons why modeling can be a challenge to incorporate into problem solving. While powerful in competent hands, modeling is also somewhat esoteric. It involves deliberate abstraction and simplification of a situation, which appears to many people as a counterproductive exercise. Modeling requires a willingness to temporarily set aside much of the richness of the real world and to operate in the refined and artificial world of models and model insights. It also requires confidence that whatever insights arise in the model world can be translated into useful ideas in the real world. Additionally, it requires an ability to mix art with science in order to exploit the modeling process to its full potential. Until we have some experience with this process, we may be resistant and skeptical. And it is always easy to criticize a model as being too simple. In fact, good models are as simple as they can possibly be. But this very simplicity can appear to be a fatal flaw to skeptics. Despite all this, modeling is one of the most powerful tools in the problem solver's toolkit, simply because there is no more practical way to arrive at the insights modeling can provide.

LESSONS FROM EXPERT MODELERS

Perhaps the best way to become a good modeler is to serve an apprenticeship under an expert. Unfortunately, such opportunities are rare. Moreover, experts in all fields find it difficult to express their expertise or to teach it. While narrow, **technical** skills are relatively easy to teach (e.g., how to use the NPV function in Excel), expertise consists largely of **craft** skills that are more difficult to teach (e.g., what to include and exclude from the model). In the arts, there is a tradition of studio training, where a teacher poses artistic challenges to students and then coaches them as they work through the problems on their own. This is one way for students to acquire some of the difficult-to-articulate craft skills of the master. There is no comparable tradition in the mathematical fields; in fact, there is a long-standing belief that modeling cannot be taught, but must simply be acquired by experience.

An alternative to an apprenticeship under an expert is to study experts in a laboratory setting. Tom Willemain did this in a series of experiments with twelve expert modelers. He gave each expert a short problem description as it would come from a client and observed the subject working for one hour on the problem. The subjects were asked to think out loud so their thought processes could be recorded. Willemain's results concerning the "first hour in the life of a model" are highly suggestive of some of the ingredients of good modeling practice.[1]

Willemain was interested in determining the issues to which expert modelers devote attention as they formulate their models. He identified five topics important to modelers:

- problem context
- model structure
- model realization
- model assessment
- model implementation

Problem context refers to the situation from which the modeler's problem arises, including the client, the client's view of the problem, and any available facts about the problem. In this activity, the modeler tries to understand the problem statement as provided by the client and to see into the mess surrounding the problem statement.

Model structure refers to actually building the model itself, including issues such as what type of model to use, where to break the problem into subproblems, and how to choose parameters and relationships. In Figure 2.2, this is the process of moving into the model world, making abstractions and assumptions, and creating an actual model.

Model realization refers to the more detailed activities of fitting the model to available data and calculating results. Here, the focus is on whether the general model structure can actually be realized with the available data and whether the type of model under development will generate the hoped-for kinds of results.

Model assessment includes evaluating the model's correctness, feasibility, and acceptability to the client. Determining the correctness of a model involves finding whether the model assumptions correspond well enough to reality. Feasibility refers to whether the client has the resources to implement the developed model, whether sufficient data are available, and whether the model itself will perform as desired. Client acceptability refers to whether the client will understand the model and its results and whether the results will be useful to the client. In this phase, we can imagine the modeler looking from the model world back into the real world and trying to anticipate whether the model under construction will meet the needs of the client.

Finally, **model implementation** refers to working with the client to derive value from the model. This corresponds to the translation and communication activities in Figure 2.2.

One of the interesting observations Willemain made about his experts was that they frequently switched their attention among these five topics. That is, they did not follow a sequential problem-solving process, but rather, moved quickly among the various phases—

---

[1] Willemain, Thomas R., "Insights on Modeling from a Dozen Experts," *Operations Research* 42, no. 2 (1994): 213–222; "Model Formulation: What Experts Think About and When," *Operations Research* 43, no. 6 (1995): 916-932.

at one moment considering the problem statement, at another considering whether the necessary data would be available, and at another, thinking through whether the client could understand and use the model. A second significant finding was that model structure, presumably the heart of a modeler's work, received a relatively small amount of attention (about 60 percent of the effort) when compared to the other four topics. Finally, it turned out that experts often alternated their attention between model structure and model assessment. That is, they would propose some element of model structure and quickly turn to evaluating its impact on model correctness, feasibility, and acceptability. Willemain suggests that the experts treat model structuring as the central task, or backbone, of their work, but they often branch off to examine related issues (data availability, client acceptance, and so on), eventually returning to the central task. In effect, model structuring becomes an organizing principle, or mental focus, around which the related activities can be arrayed.

The experts in Willemain's study also offered their own perspectives on the important qualities of an effective *modeler,* an effective *model,* and an effective *modeling process.* As for an effective modeler, they listed first in order of importance the modeler's mind-set: creativity, sensitivity to client needs, persistence, and so on. Second in importance was nontechnical expertise, including communication and teamwork skills. Listed third was technical expertise and fourth, knowledge of the industry or problem type involved in the work. It is very revealing that even expert modelers, who might be expected to value technical expertise most highly, cite the modeler's mind-set and nontechnical skills as being most important. This reinforces the notion that craft skills are every bit as important to the successful modeler as technical skills.

When evaluating the qualities of an effective model, the experts listed validity, usability, value to client, feasibility, and aptness for client's problem—in that order. Validity refers to the technical correctness of the model: whether it is internally consistent, logical, and a faithful implementation of the modeler's intentions. It is not surprising that this is an absolute requirement. But notice the importance of model usability and value to client: a perfectly valid model may still be of little value to the client. Again, a good model and modeler must understand the problem context and the needs of the client.

Finally, when asked to compare the five modeling topics listed above and rate them on their importance to an effective modeling process, the experts listed problem context, model assessment, model structure, and model realization—in that order. Understanding the problem context, or discovering the real problem, again outranks the more technical aspects of the process in these experts' eyes.

The overall picture that emerges from this research is one in which craft skills are as essential to the effective modeler as technical skills. An effective modeler must understand the problem context, including the client, or modeling will fail. Likewise, a model that is technically correct but does not provide information the client can use, or does not gain the trust of the client, represents only wasted effort. Experts approach modeling with a general process in mind, but they move fairly quickly among the different activities, creating, testing, and revising constantly as they go. The experts appear to be comfortable with a high degree of ambiguity as they approach the task of structuring a model. They do not rush to a solution, but patiently build tentative models and test them, always being ready to revise and improve.

CREATIVITY IN MODELING

Creativity is a subject that makes many people uncomfortable, possibly because they underestimate how common it is. Nevertheless, creativity is a vital ingredient in successful problem solving, as it is in good modeling. Our purpose in this section is to dispel some of the myths surrounding creativity and to offer some practical tools for encouraging the creativity of problem-solving teams and individuals.

We begin with some common myths about creativity. The first is that creativity is instinctive and cannot be learned. This is similar to the belief that great teachers, or great chefs, or great architects, are simply born to their craft, and no amount of study will turn an ordinary professional into an extraordinary one. The truth seems to be somewhat different. Creativity, in fact, is an activity that results from the ordinary thought processes of ordinary people. Moreover, virtually everyone's creativity can be increased beyond its present level through training in the use of specific techniques.

Another common myth is that creative ideas arise in a flash of inspiration. Again, the truth is more mundane. All studies show that creative breakthroughs occur only after a considerable amount of time and effort has been expended. We need only read about the invention of the telephone, to which Alexander Graham Bell devoted decades of research before having a series of breakthroughs lead to success, to realize how critical it is to prepare the ground. While hard work is not a guarantee of creative breakthroughs, lack of hard work essentially rules them out. Louis Pasteur said this well: "Inspiration is the impact of a fact on a well-prepared mind."

A third myth is that creative individuals are geniuses—that is, different from the rest of us. This is the hardest myth to dispel, partly because we tend to focus on the few really awesome breakthroughs (the discovery of relativity or the DNA helix), while overlooking thousands of truly creative ideas that arise around us all the time. We have somehow elevated creativity to the status of a rare gem, when in fact it is an everyday matter. William James said, "Genius, in truth, means little more than a faculty of perceiving in an unhabitual way."

Creative individuals *are* different in some ways from average folk. They tend to display attributes we would expect—such as openness to new ideas, curiosity, independence, playfulness, impulsiveness, and risk taking. But they also display attributes that we do not traditionally attribute to them, such as discipline and perseverance. The widely-portrayed artist with great creativity but no discipline is truly a myth. Again, the biographies of the great inventors typically reveal years of toil and frustration punctuated by a few great insights. Truly creative breakthroughs are by their nature rare, but creativity is a characteristic everyone has and can improve.

Barriers to Creativity

What are some of the barriers to creativity? It is useful to distinguish **perceptual** barriers from **emotional** barriers. One perceptual barrier to creativity is stereotyping and labeling; that is, seeing the current situation as indistinguishable from some stereotypical situation, or labeling the current problem with a blanket label.

Another barrier is difficulty in isolating a problem. It is difficult to find creative solutions to a mess. Until we can isolate a problem from the confusion and distractions of the mess, it is almost impossible to focus our creativity.

A third barrier is adding artificial constraints to a problem. Many problem-solving teams have a hard time seeing beyond the current ways of doing business. Is the budget really fixed just because some higher manager has set budgets in the past, or can we make a case for expanded resources? Must we accept that each of our customers requires a personal sales call, or can our customers change their old habits and learn to order over the Internet? Every constraint limits the search for solutions. Every constraint diminishes the freedom of creative minds to explore.

A final perceptual barrier is an inability to see a problem from different points of view. Creative individuals seem to excel at holding many possible views of the problem, and even many possible solutions, in their head at the same time. This is one reason every step in the problem-solving process has a divergent phase, to encourage problem solvers to keep as many options open as long as possible. Some of these views or solutions may even contradict each other. Creativity is enhanced when multiple viewpoints and contradictions are encouraged and when premature focus on one viewpoint or solution is discouraged.

Creativity is also reduced by a number of emotional barriers. These include fear of making mistakes, intolerance of ambiguity, preference for judging ideas over generating them, inability to let ideas gestate, and a desire to succeed too quickly. To be creative, we need a certain degree of self-confidence. This involves a willingness to make mistakes, perhaps even to suggest silly solutions. It also involves a certain patience: a tolerance for ambiguity about what the real problem is and where a good solution might be found, the patience to let ideas percolate without knowing in advance which ones will pan out, and the confidence that success will come eventually. Finally, while an ability to evaluate ideas is critical to good problem solving, too strong a desire to judge ideas can hinder creativity. This last barrier is so important that we discuss it in detail in Chapter 3.

Techniques to Enhance Creativity

Many techniques have been developed to help individuals and groups to be more creative. While there is no guarantee of becoming highly creative by using these techniques, they are useful for freeing one's thinking. Groups are particularly given to behaviors that discourage creative thinking, so creativity techniques for groups may be particularly important. We discuss here a small sample of techniques for individuals and groups.

Boundary examination. In every problem-solving process, there are implicit assumptions that set the boundaries for the analysis. Boundary examination is used to uncover those assumptions, to challenge them, and to expand or replace them as needed. Boundaries are not intrinsically good or bad, but they are certainly necessary. In fact, the stages we have outlined in this chapter are designed to limit the scope of the problem-solving process so that it can reach an effective conclusion. One of the primary failings of many problem solvers is an inability to focus on one well-defined aspect of the mess that can be resolved.

Boundary examination begins with a description of the problem as it is currently understood. Then the assumptions behind this problem definition are isolated, and each one is challenged in turn. For example: Should we ignore the actions of competitors in our analysis of a new product? What are the consequences of doing so? How would we include the actions of competitors if we chose to do so? Once each assumption has been challenged, the problem can be restated based on a deeper understanding.

Force-field analysis. This technique is used to identify the forces that might move the situation under examination toward the best possible state and those that might move it toward the worst possible state. This technique first helps to identify the goals toward which we are working. Then it can stimulate creativity by identifying forces already at work in the situation—forces that will work with or against any proposed solution.

The first step in force-field analysis is to identify the goal to be reached. We next describe what the situation would be like in the worst possible case and the forces working to move the situation toward that outcome. Then we describe the best possible case and the forces moving the situation that way. For example, if the problem is to limit the impact of competing products on sales of our product, the worst possible state might involve a complete collapse of demand due to the introduction of a dominating product or due to product safety problems. The best possible case might arise if competitors fail to introduce any competing products or if the products they do introduce fail to gain customer loyalty.

These descriptions of extreme outcomes and the forces leading to them help to reveal the mental models behind our thinking. They also help to identify effective solutions, by revealing approaches that would strengthen the positive forces in play and weaken the negative ones.

Interrogatories. This method expands our view of a problem by asking five simple questions: Who, What, Where, When, and Why? These questions are helpful at almost any stage of the problem-solving process. They can help broaden our perspective and uncover hidden assumptions. In the example cited above, where the problem is to limit competitive inroads on our sales, we might ask:

- Who will buy our product if competitors offer a cheaper alternative?
- What qualities of the product we offer (for example, price, cost, or service) could we improve to reduce loss of business?
- Where can we most effectively place new advertising to expand our customer base?
- When can we expect competitors to introduce competing products?
- Why do existing customers purchase our product?

Brainstorming. Brainstorming is by far the best known of all creativity techniques. It is used when the goal is to generate a multitude of ideas, especially ideas outside the mainstream. The method works by separating idea generation from evaluation. In fact, evaluation is explicitly forbidden during brainstorming.

Usually, a group engages in a brainstorming session for an hour or so, under the guidance of a facilitator. The facilitator's role is to encourage all members to participate, to help the group build on the ideas already generated, to record the ideas as they arise, and to remind the group of the rules in brainstorming. The essential rule is to *accept all ideas*—no matter how wild, dangerous, or outrageous—*without evaluation.* Any attempt to evaluate an idea, even to provide a positive comment, should be avoided. It is permissible—indeed, members are encouraged—to build on an idea by refining or extending it.

Nominal group technique. One of the drawbacks of brainstorming is that ideas are generated in public, so the group knows the author of each idea. This may inhibit creativity, since it is likely that some members of the group have higher positions of authority or higher status, so their ideas may be better received than others. Even without any overt evaluation of ideas, members can perceive (or even simply imagine) that sharing certain ideas may be dangerous to their reputations or careers.

The nominal group technique is used for the same purposes as brainstorming, but the ideas are initially generated in written form. Once each member has listed as many ideas as possible, the ideas are shared anonymously. For example, the facilitator might randomize the cards on which each member has recorded ideas and write down one from each card in turn. Members are then encouraged to discuss the ideas, clarifying them and using them to stimulate new ideas, but not to evaluate them or make their authorship public. This public discussion is often followed by another round of writing and sharing.

Wildest idea. Groups are generally quite conservative in their approach to problem solving, preferring tried-and-true ideas to the truly creative. When it is necessary to break out of this bind, the wildest-idea technique can help.

The process begins with the first wild idea anyone can offer. The facilitator guides the group through an exploration of the idea, trying to vary it or extend it to better solve the problem at hand. While this process involves evaluation to some extent, the general tone should be kept positive, looking for the useful parts of a given idea and not rejecting it out of hand because it is impractical in some ways. Once the first idea has been fully explored, the group moves on to another wild idea—until an idea is found that offers a potential solution. Often, the solution adopted will share some features of several of the wild ideas generated in this session.

SUMMARY

Effective modeling takes place within a larger problem-solving process. Modeling can be useful both in finding a good solution and in facilitating communication as the solution is developed, refined, and implemented. Therefore, it is important to recognize the larger context in which modeling occurs. We organize the problem-solving process into six stages. At the outset, the "problem" is no more than an unstructured situation where there is some unsatisfied need, some goal (possibly unarticulated) waiting to be met, or some opportunity remaining unrealized. During the process, this initial unstructured mess is gradually transformed—first by gathering information, then by articulating a problem, and finally, by creating, evaluating, and implementing a solution. Although it's convenient to describe these stages as if they were separate and occurred in a strict sequence, that is seldom the case. In fact, we can't always identify the specific activities at each stage until after the fact. Nevertheless, every implemented solution comes about through some version of the problem-solving process. Generally speaking, the bigger the problem at hand or the larger the team working on it, the more important it is to use a structured problem-solving process.

Mental modeling is an essential tool in problem solving. A mental model allows us to trace the consequences of a course of action without actually implementing it. In that way, mental models save us the time and cost, not to mention the occasionally disastrous consequences, of actually trying out alternative solutions to a problem.

Formal models provide the same kind of benefits as mental models. A formal model is a laboratory within which we can search for the best solution, without incurring the time and cost of trial-and-error approaches. Formal models are costlier and more time-consuming to build than mental models, but they have the great advantage that they make our assumptions, logic, and preferences explicit. They also allow us to search among many more solutions than would otherwise be possible. Finally, an effective formal model can help communicate the reasoning behind a solution and in that way help to motivate an individual or organization to act.

Modeling involves abstracting the essential features of a situation and building a logical structure that mimics some aspects of the real world. We use the metaphor of the "model world" to emphasize the artificial nature of modeling and the need to be aware of whether we are reasoning about the real world or a simplified representation of it. An effective modeler can comfortably move back and forth between the real world and the model world. Moving into the model world requires abstracting the essential features of the real world; moving back to the real world requires translating model insights into managerial insights.

Research on expert modelers has shown that they develop their models in a cyclic fashion, not in a predictable sequence of steps. Structuring the model provides a central focus, but experts frequently shift their focus to consider related issues, such as data availability or the needs of a client. Experts themselves consider it essential that a modeler possess nontechnical skills such as creativity, persistence, and sensitivity to the client's needs. Thus, the craft skills of modeling, which are a major theme of this book, are vital for effective modelers.

Creativity is an essential ingredient in successful problem solving, just as it is in modeling. Creativity involves an element of play; likewise, effective modelers often seem to play with their models. Myths are common about creativity, and it is generally an uncomfortable subject. Creativity is, in fact, common among ordinary people, especially those who have immersed themselves in a problem. Moreover, creativity can be enhanced through self-awareness and the use of specific techniques, such as force-field analysis or brainstorming.

REFERENCES

For more information on problem solving, creativity in general, and specific creativity techniques, consult the following books:

Adams, James L. *Conceptual Blockbusting.* 2001. Reading, MA: Addison-Wesley.

Couger, J. Daniel. *Creative Problem Solving and Opportunity Finding.* 1995. Danvers, MA: Boyd & Fraser.

Evans, James R. *Creative Thinking.* 1991. Cincinnati: South-Western.

EXERCISES

1. Refer to the Retirement Planning case.
   a. Explore the mess by answering the following questions:
      What do we know?
      What can we assume?
      What could the results look like?
      What information can be brought to bear?
      What can we ask the client?
      Are there any similar situations or problems?
   b. Formulate one or more problem statements.

2. Refer to the Draft TV Commercials case.
   a. Explore the mess by answering the following questions:
      What do we know?
      What can we assume?
      What could the results look like?
      What information can be brought to bear?
      What can we ask the client?
      Are there any similar situations or problems?
   b. Formulate one or more problem statements.

3. Refer to the Icebergs for Kuwait case.
   a. Explore the mess by answering the following questions:
      What do we know?
      What can we assume?
      What could the results look like?
      What information can be brought to bear?
      What can we ask the client?
      Are there any similar situations or problems?

    b. Formulate one or more problem statements.

4. Refer to the Racquetball Racket case.

    a. Explore the mess by answering the following questions:

        What do we know?

        What can we assume?

        What could the results look like?

        What information can be brought to bear?

        What can we ask the client?

        Are there any similar situations or problems?

    b. Formulate one or more problem statements.

CHAPTER 3

THE CRAFT OF MODELING

INTRODUCTION

Successful modelers can draw on both technical and craft skills in their work. **Technical skill** refers to the ability to carry out specific, narrow, well-defined tasks in the modeling process. This includes, for example, calculating present values, linking balance sheets and income statements correctly, or identifying a tail probability in the results of a simulation model. Proper use of technical skill leads to a correct result, and there is little room for creativity. **Craft skill,** on the other hand, does not lead to a single correct result and does require creativity. Some examples of craft skill are making useful simplifications in a complex problem, designing a prototype, or brainstorming ways to increase demand for a new product. Craft skills develop slowly, over time and with experience, whereas technical skills can be learned at one pass. In playing the piano, technical skill is developed by practicing scales, while real craft is needed to interpret the music while playing it. Craft skills are harder to describe and teach than technical skills, but they are just as important to successful modeling. In fact, it is the high level of craft skill that distinguishes the expert modeler from the journeyman. In this chapter, we describe some of the most important craft skills and discuss the role that these skills play in modeling. The collection of modeling cases, which appears later in the book, provides opportunities to practice these skills in unstructured problem situations.

Craft skills are rarely discussed in books on spreadsheets or management science. One reason may be the common perception that problem solving is an art that cannot be taught, only learned through long experience. Another reason may be that expert modelers, like experts in all fields, are largely unconscious of their own craft skills. There is also no well-accepted theory or classification for the craft skills in modeling. Nevertheless, we have found that awareness of these skills is essential to the successful development of truly skilled modelers. We commonly encounter highly skilled spreadsheet users whose craft skills are weak. As a consequence, they cannot successfully employ modeling in new and unstructured situations. On the other hand, we rarely encounter analysts with good craft skills who cannot learn enough Excel to become good modelers. Furthermore, craft skills *can* be learned, despite the impediments cited above. The first step in this process is to identify the skills themselves so the modeler in training can begin to develop an awareness of modeling on a higher level than the merely technical.

It is helpful to classify craft skills into useful rules of thumb, or **modeling heuristics.** In general, a heuristic is an approach, a strategy, or a trick that has often proved effective in a given situation. A widely cited example from general problem solving is to write down everything we know about a problem. Heuristics are thought to be one of the most common ways humans deal with the complexities of the world around them, so it should not be surprising to find that modelers have their own. A modeling heuristic is a rule of thumb that experienced modelers use to help them over the inevitable difficulties that arise in modeling. We believe that novices can improve their modeling abilities by observing how these heuristics are used in a number of different situations. However, the only way to acquire and perfect these skills is to practice them on new problems.

In this chapter, we describe eight fundamental heuristics and illustrate how they can be used in practice. Some of these heuristics may be familiar. For the novice modeler, our purpose here is to raise awareness of the role these skills play so that they can be called on routinely in modeling work. Some of these heuristics may be new. They require practice and refinement until they become as familiar as the ones already known. Implementing these ideas will lead to a stronger personal tool kit of modeling skills. The collection of modeling cases provides an opportunity to begin practicing these skills. In fact, we initiate that process in this chapter.

Throughout this chapter, we will refer to four modeling cases that describe unstructured problems. One involves assisting a friend in planning for retirement, another deals with determining how many draft TV commercials to commission, the third requires evaluating the feasibility of towing icebergs to Kuwait for drinking water, and the fourth involves determining the profitability for a new process. Short synopses of these cases are given here, while the complete versions can be found in the collection of modeling cases at the end of the book. Before proceeding any further, it would be helpful to read these synopses and give some thought to how to model them.

RETIREMENT PLANNING

The client currently is forty-six years old, with an income of about $126,000 per year. His goal is to retire between ages sixty-two and sixty-seven and to have enough savings to live comfortably in about the same fashion he does now (with some money available for expanded travel). The client's accumulated savings for retirement total $137,000. His employer contributes around $10,000 per year into the retirement fund, while he has been contributing $7,500. How much should he be saving?

DRAFT TV COMMERCIALS

The client directs TV advertising for a large corporation. His budget for a single ad campaign is typically around $10 million. Under current procedures, a single TV advertisement is commissioned for about $500,000, and the remainder of the budget is spent on airing the ad. The client is considering a new approach, in which two or more draft commercials (at about the same cost) would be commissioned from different agencies. The best of these drafts would then be aired using the remainder of the budget. Is this new plan more effective than the old procedure?

ICEBERGS FOR KUWAIT

Freshwater is in short supply in Kuwait and is therefore very expensive. One suggested remedy is to tow icebergs from Antarctica to Kuwait (a distance of about 9,600 kilometers) and melt them for freshwater. The volume of an iceberg ranges from about 500,000 cubic meters to more than 10 million cubic meters. Theoretical analysis suggests that an idealized spherical iceberg would lose about 0.2 meter of radius per day during transport, although this amount increases with the speed of towing and the distance from the pole. Fuel costs for towboats depend on the size of the boat, the speed, and the volume of the iceberg being towed. Would it be cost-effective to tow icebergs to Kuwait for freshwater, and, if so, how should this be done?

THE RACQUETBALL RACKET

A new and cheaper process has been invented for manufacturing racquetballs. The new ball is bouncier but less durable than the major brand. Unit variable costs of production for the new process will run about $0.52, while the current process costs $0.95. A new plant would cost between $4 million and $6 million. We have fourteen years of data on the number of racquetball players in the United States, the average retail price of balls, and the number of balls sold. The number of players is expected to increase about 10 percent per year for ten years and then level off. In a recent survey, 200 users were asked to use both balls over several months, and their preferences were assessed at several different prices for the new ball. What is the net present value of an investment in a new plant to manufacture balls using this new process? What is the best price for the new ball, and how might the competitor react to introduction of a new ball?

SIMPLIFY THE PROBLEM

Without a doubt, the most fundamental heuristic in all modeling is to *simplify*. Simplification is the very essence of modeling. We should never criticize a model for being simple, only for being too simple for the purposes at hand. Remember: a model that is too simple can often be modified to better suit the desired purposes.

On the other hand, a model that is more complex than necessary already represents a waste of some modeling effort. Worse yet, a model may be so complex that it cannot be simplified effectively. It is, in fact, much harder to detect when a model is more complex than needed than it is to detect when a model is too simple. Overly simple models make us uncomfortable and motivate us to improve them; overly complex models may simply confuse and overwhelm us.

In discussing the importance of simplicity in models, Michael Pidd, in his book *Tools for Thinking,* offers the following aphorism: "Model simple, think complicated." By this, he reminds us that models are not independent of their users. So the right question to ask about a model is not whether the model by itself is adequate, but whether the user can discover helpful insights with the model. Simple models can support rigorous, critical thinking on the part of the user. Simple models are also more transparent and therefore easier to understand and apply. Users (and their managers) are more likely to trust simple models and implement the recommendations that are developed from their analysis. A modeling team will find that a simple model facilitates communication within the team, while only the modeling experts may understand a complex model.

There is no more useful tool in the modeler's kit than "keeping it simple." Thus, we try to cut away all complexity that is not essential. Never stop asking whether any particular aspect of a model is necessary to achieving the goals at hand. Novice modelers are often amazed at the simplicity of experts' models, particularly the simplicity of an expert's *first* model. Two other heuristics we will discuss later, decomposition and prototyping, are themselves powerful tools for keeping models simple.

How does one go about simplifying situations for modeling? One approach is to focus on the connections between the key decisions to be made and the outcomes that result from those decisions. Then, ask what central trade-offs make these decisions difficult and build a model to explore those trade-offs. In the Retirement Planning case, for example, increasing one's savings rate reduces current disposable income but increases one's assets at retirement. If that trade-off makes the problem difficult, focus the modeling effort on that issue and leave out anything that seems peripheral.

In the Draft TV Commercials case, money spent on creative work will increase the quality of the advertisement, while money spent on buying airtime will increase the number of consumers who see the advertisement. If the budget is limited, there is an inevitable trade-off between spending money on creative work and spending money on airtime. Focus the modeling efforts on illuminating this trade-off.

In the Icebergs for Kuwait case, we know that large icebergs will provide more water, but they may take longer and cost more to transport. Small icebergs provide less water but may be more efficient to move. Here is an essential trade-off to capture in the model.

The goal in the Racquetball Racket case is not to make a highly accurate forecast of profits from the venture, but rather, to understand the risks introduced by various factors such as the competitor's response to our entry. This argues for a simple but highly flexible model. Obviously, the pricing decision will be a key one. A high price may provide attractive margins but also limit our market share. On the other hand, a low price may provide a large market share but leave us with very tight margins. The relationship between price and profitability is one important aspect of the problem, but it will help to keep this relationship simple because we are interested in understanding how it will be affected by the competitive response.

Simplification by its nature involves making assumptions. Boldness and self-confidence in making assumptions is a mark of an experienced modeler. Many modelers, however, make assumptions but do not recognize that they are doing so. For example, in the Racquetball Racket case, many student modelers assume that sales will immediately reach a steady state. But if they don't realize this is an assumption, they miss the opportunity to test the sensitivity of their results to it. Thus, it is important both to make assumptions and to recognize them as they are being made. Every assumption should be revisited at some point in the analysis, to see if an alternative assumption would substantially change the results or provide new insights.

BREAK THE PROBLEM INTO MODULES

One of the most fundamental ways to approach any type of problem solving is to decompose the problem into simpler components. This decomposition heuristic is basic to Western science and, some would say, to Western thought itself. The rub, of course, is to know where to draw the lines; that is, which are the most productive components to create. One approach is to divide the problem into components that are as *independent* of each other as possible.

In the Retirement Planning case, it is natural to decompose the problem into a working-life module and a retirement module. Within the working-life module, we will want to keep track of salary and other income as well as accumulating retirement assets. In the retirement module, we will follow the accumulated assets as they are drawn down for consumption. We may also track certain aspects of consumption, such as travel expenses. These modules are nearly independent: the only necessary connection is that the final assets from the working-life module become the initial assets in the retirement module.

In the Draft TV Commercials case, one module can be devoted to determining the quality of the advertisement that is ultimately aired, while another can be devoted to determining the impact of a budget for airing an advertisement of a given quality. These modules are largely independent: the quality of the advertisement chosen depends on the distribution of quality in the population from which advertisements are drawn, as well as on the number of drafts purchased. Meanwhile, the impact of a given budget in creating audience impressions depends on the size of the budget and the quality of the ad being aired. This latter module requires some assumption about the influence of incremental advertising dollars on incremental impact. The simplest assumption would be that impact is proportional to advertising spending, although we might expect diminishing returns to set in eventually.

In the Icebergs for Kuwait case, a common approach would be to create three modules: the first determines the supply of icebergs at the edge of the ice cap in Antarctica (by size, shape, etc.); the second determines how large the iceberg is when it arrives in Kuwait, given its size and shape at the start of the trip, the speed at which it is towed, melting rates, and other factors; and the third converts the iceberg into a certain quantity of drinking water and a corresponding economic value.

In the Racquetball Racket case, a typical decomposition is to determine annual dollar sales of our ball by multiplying the number of users by the average number of balls purchased per year. The number purchasing our ball is the total number of users multiplied by our share of the market. Our share, in turn, is a function of our price and quality relative to the competitor's price and quality. There are, of course, other ways to decompose sales: by geographic region, by age of buyer, by product type, and so on. Which of these to choose in a given situation depends on two things: how effective it is to build a model of one component and how easy it is to extend the model for one component to cover all the other components.

Why does the decomposition heuristic work? The great advantage of decomposing a problem is that the components are simpler to deal with than the whole. In addition, the process provides a natural structure to the analysis, thereby allowing the analyst to focus effort on one area at a time. Finally, this heuristic naturally leads us to think in terms of modules, and from there, it is a short step to discover the *interchangeability* of modules. For example, we can change our approach to modeling market share in the Racquetball Racket case without changing any other module. This leads us naturally to another powerful heuristic: *prototyping*.

BUILD A PROTOTYPE AND REFINE IT

A **prototype** is just a working model. A prototype of a new car, for example, is a working model of the car, built to test design concepts prior to high-volume manufacturing. A prototype of a computer program is a working model that can be used to test whether the program works as intended. It can also be used to test the reactions of the users, who may not be able to specify their needs in the abstract, but can discover their needs through experimenting with the prototype. A prototype of a model (in our sense) is nothing more than a working model of a model. As a working model, it should take data and inputs from the user and produce key outputs in response. However, the model is very likely to need further refinements, since there will probably be gaps between its current performance and the desired results. These gaps describe the tasks that remain, either in terms of interaction with the user or in terms of analysis yet to be done, if the prototype is to be elevated to a finished version. Prototyping is an essential part of an effective modeling approach, especially so when modeling is performed under tight limits on the available time and cost.

What would a prototype for the Retirement Planning case look like? In this case, the essential concern is to explore the relationship between the working life savings rate and retirement assets. We might take as our objective the number of years that we can live off our retirement assets before they are exhausted. In order to estimate this result, it will be useful to simplify some of the many complexities of the problem. For a first prototype, we could make the following assumptions:

- Income grows at a constant rate during the working years.
- The savings rate is a constant percentage of annual income in the working years.
- Retirement assets provide a fixed rate of return.
- The retirement date is fixed.
- Postretirement consumption is a fixed percentage of income in the final work year.

Using these assumptions, it is a fairly simple matter to build a model that projects our income (at some assumed growth rate) from the present to retirement, calculates our retirement contributions (given a constant savings rate), accumulates our retirement assets (at some assumed rate of return), projects our assets as they are drawn down during retirement (at the assumed consumption rate), and finally determines the year in which they are exhausted. This simple model allows us to create a plot that shows how long our assets last as a function of our savings rate (Figure 3.1). If that relationship is the essential summary of our analysis, we have completed our first prototype. We can now test the model, varying decisions and parameters in an attempt to gain insight into the problem. Eventually, we may want to build a refined model, if the first prototype proves inadequate in some way.

In an initial approach to the Draft TV Commercials problem, we might avoid the complexities of sampling from a population of potential drafts and simply assume that advertisement quality increases with the number of draft ads, but with diminishing returns. We might implement this relationship using a power function:

$$Quality = (Number\ of\ drafts)^a$$

We might also assume that the total budget is fixed and that each draft advertisement costs a fixed percentage of the budget. It follows that each additional draft advertisement reduces the budget available for airing by the same amount. If we assume that the total impact created by an advertisement is the product of the quality of the advertisement (in impressions per dollar spent on airing) and the airing budget, we have the basis for a prototype. From this simple model, we can plot a graph that relates the total number of impressions created to the number of draft advertisements (Figure 3.2).

Are we content with this first prototype? Probably not. Assuming that we have or can acquire some data on the variability of ad quality, we might later refine the portion of the model in which the quality of the best draft is determined. Sampling from a distribution

FIGURE 3.1
Sketch of Results for the Retirement Planning Case

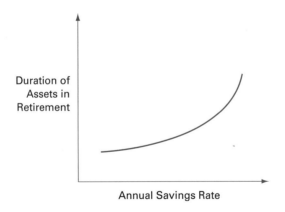

FIGURE 3.2
Sketch of Results for the Draft TV Commercials Case

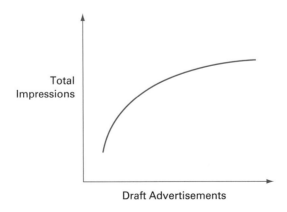

of ad quality will give us the average quality of the best advertisement as a function of the number of drafts. We expect this function to have the same concave shape as the power function in our first prototype. But it will be a better component in at least two ways: first, it more closely resembles the actual process by which the best advertisement is created; second, it allows us to test the sensitivity of the results (total impressions created) to the variability in the distribution of quality.

A prototype for the Icebergs for Kuwait problem could be a model for the radial shrinking of a spherical iceberg of fixed initial size being towed at constant speed from the ice pack to Kuwait. If we calculate the final volume of the iceberg and multiply by the price of water, then we can compute an initial estimate of the value of the project.

This is the information the client wants, so our simple model is a legitimate prototype. Is this a simplified approach? Of course it is. But the model's simplicity is its strength, not its weakness. If we have built our prototype quickly, we have time left over to refine it. Rather than having a number of separate pieces to try to integrate, we have one unified model to work with.

Before refining this model, we would want to use it to explore the problem. For example, we would want to test the sensitivity of the final cost to the initial size of the iceberg, the towing speed, and the size of the boat. These tests will give us ideas not only about the ultimate results the model will generate, but also about where improvements might be warranted. We might, for example, want to test towing strategies that involve changes in speed over the trip. On the other hand, perhaps the weakest part of the model is the assumption that the iceberg is spherical and melts with a constant radius. Does the submerged portion of an iceberg melt faster or slower than the visible part? Does the ratio of these parts change with size? Every assumption is an opportunity to improve the analysis. The trick to effective prototyping is to find in the model those improvements that lead to significant improvements in the results, not merely to a more elegant, more complex, or more "realistic" model.

In the Racquetball Racket case, the objective is to help the client make a go/no-go decision. A highly accurate forecast of the NPV is not necessarily required, especially if the estimated NPV is clearly positive or negative. Thus, a prototype should give us a first, rough estimate of project NPV. It will move us closer to that goal if we assume that:

- Our competitor will price at its current level,
- Our price and our competitor's price both remain constant over the life of the analysis,
- No third competitor will enter, and
- Total demand for balls will grow at a constant percentage rate, independent of prices.

The only remaining component involves our market share, which we could model as an S-shaped function of our price. The following function is useful in this context:

$$Share = b + (a - b)[Price^c / (d + Price^c)]$$

We can use the market-research data to help us determine plausible values for the parameters $a, b, c,$ and d. With this module in place, we have a full prototype, because the model can generate an NPV for any price we choose. With the model, we can develop a chart showing how project NPV varies with our price and whether there is a price we can charge at which the project looks attractive (Figure 3.3). Once again, we are not done with the analysis. These results are only the first in what will most likely be a long sequence of estimates for project NPV, but this prototype supports the next stage in the analysis, which involves testing the sensitivity of our results to our assumptions.

FIGURE 3.3
Sketch of Results for the
Raquetball Racket Case

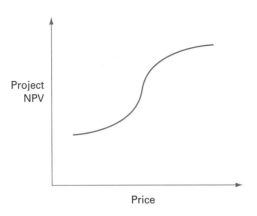

In general, how do we know when we have a completed prototype? If we have

■ decomposed the problem into modules,

■ built at least a simple model for every module, and

■ coordinated the modules so that they work together to generate results in the form we think the client wants,

then we have a prototype. If we cannot provide at least a tentative answer to the client's major questions, we don't yet have a prototype. If one or more modules are missing, we do not have a prototype. But once our ideas come together in a working model, the event marks a key milestone, for then the emphasis will shift from creation to refinement, in collaboration with the client.

The cyclic nature of prototyping is worth some elaboration. Many people think that prototyping involves building one model after another until we are satisfied that we have the final model, and *then* carrying out the analysis. This is a fundamental misunderstanding of the process. It is essential to use each successive prototype to answer the managerial questions in the problem before refining the model further. This discipline helps keep the modeler's attention on the *problem,* and not exclusively on the model or the modeling process. One reason modelers sometimes hesitate to use prototypes in this way is that they are embarrassed by the shortcomings of their early models and don't want to see them being used "for real." But it is only in this way that a modeler can see the value of each successive refinement.

Why is prototyping such a powerful idea? One reason is that a prototype keeps the entire problem in the mind of the modeler. It is impossible to perfect a module in isolation because it has value only as part of the entire model. In most situations, we cannot know how well a module works until it is integrated with the others, so it is vital to build prototypes in which every major component is represented. Prototyping also helps avoid the seduction of modeling for its own sake. Remember that the task is to provide management with *insight.* Modeling is merely a means to that end. One way to maintain focus on the managerial question at hand is to use a series of prototypes to generate tentative answers to the client's questions. By using each model to provide an answer, and by performing sensitivity analysis on each model, the focus will remain, appropriately, on the problem rather than on the model.

Prototyping is a particularly critical tool for novice modelers, who frequently struggle with psychological reactions to the vagaries of the creative process. Many of our students have never struggled as hard as they do in a modeling assignment. Some of them suffer from all the symptoms of depression when they have worked for a week and feel they have nothing to show for it. For these students, as for most modelers, having a working prototype, *no matter how primitive,* is a great psychological boost. Once we have a prototype, we have not only a tentative answer for the client, but also a road map for future work.

Finally, prototyping is an essential tool for the practicing analyst who operates under severe time constraints. Once a prototype is up and running, the analyst should ask this question: Where would my model benefit most from additional work? Or, to put it more precisely: Where should I focus my efforts to most improve the quality of my advice to the client? This is an impossible question to answer in the abstract. But with a prototype and some skill in sensitivity analysis, we can get a fair idea of which modules or which components within a given module have the biggest impact on the results. Thus, the prototype is itself a necessary tool in the analyst's efforts to use time effectively.

SKETCH GRAPHS OF KEY RELATIONSHIPS

One of the reasons modeling is so difficult for many people is that it appears to be highly abstract or mathematical, and they cannot find a way to express their thoughts in these terms. Most people have good intuitions about the modeling challenges they face, but they lack the skills to represent those intuitions in a useful way. The ability to change representation systems is one of the powerful heuristics that experts suggest for general problem solving. Good problem solvers can look at a problem from many angles—inventing analogies, drawing pictures, hypothesizing relationships, or perhaps carrying out suggestive physical experiments.

Novice modelers rarely use drawings or sketches to represent their understanding of a problem. They haven't discovered that visual depictions of models are often much easier to work with than verbal or mathematical ones. When it comes to creating a relationship between two variables, sketching a graph is a very useful first step.

The inability to visualize the relation between variables is a common stumbling block in modeling. If we ask whether the relation between advertising and sales is linear or concave, we typically get little response. Yet if we draw coordinate axes and label the horizontal axis "Advertising," and the vertical "Sales," most anyone will say the graph slopes up and probably "bends over" at some point. So the *intuition* for a concave relation in this case is widely shared; what many people lack is a representation system within which they can express their intuition. Such people are without the mathematical sophistication to select a plausible family of functions to represent a given graphical relation.

Here is another example of the power of visualization. When a novice modeler is completely stuck about how to start a modeling problem, we might draw a simple diagram (Figure 3.4) consisting of a box with one arrow coming in from the top and another going out to the right. Along with the drawing, we'll say that the way we see the problem, we have some decisions to make (arrow going into box), then the future will evolve in some way (inside the box), and in the end, we'll have some outcomes (arrow going out of box). The model we need to build is going to transform alternative decisions into outcomes we can evaluate. This simple picture does wonders—it focuses the novice on three key issues: What *decisions* do we have? How will we evaluate *outcomes?* and What system of *relationships* connects the decisions to the outcomes? To an experienced modeler, this picture may seem trivial. To a struggling novice, however, it can be a revelation. Somehow, the picture itself is far more powerful than an equivalent verbal or algebraic description.

Why does this visualization heuristic work? We suspect one reason has to do with the power of looking at a problem from different viewpoints. Somehow changing how we look at a problem often helps us overcome a sense of being stuck, of having no useful knowledge about a particular issue. (Novice modelers never seem unable to sketch a graph for a relation, even when they said they knew nothing about the mathematical function involved.)

Visualization probably works by *externalizing* the analysis—that is, by moving the focal point of analysis from inside the mind to an external artifact (such as a graph or equation). This is clearly essential for modeling in groups, where thoughts in the mind cannot be debated

FIGURE 3.4
Visualization of the
Modeling Process

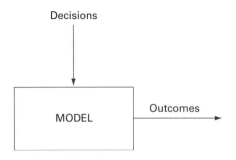

unless they are represented outside the mind. But it is also crucial for the solo modeler, because it is far easier to test and refine an external artifact than an inchoate idea in the mind.

Sketching graphs is also a powerful heuristic because there is only a small set of possible relations between two variables that are useful in a typical modeling problem, and common sense can be used to rule out most of them. The most often used is the simple straight line (with either positive or negative slope). In the spirit of prototyping, we often suggest that the *first* relation we would propose between *any* variables is a linear one. Build a working prototype first and gain some experience with it. Come back later and refine the linear relation if theory or intuition suggests a more complex relation and if model testing suggests that the results will be sensitive to this relation.

In order to make full use of this heuristic, the modeler also needs to know a few useful families of functions. Here is a basic list. These families are also depicted in Figure 3.5.

■ Linear function, showing constant returns (positive or negative), $y = a + bx$.

■ Power function with increasing returns, $y = ax^b$ with ($b > 1$).

■ Exponential function, representing decline and decay, $y = ae^{-bx}$.

■ Exponential function, representing leveling off at an asymptote, $y = a(1 - e^{-bx})$.

■ Power function, with diminishing returns, $y = ax^b$ with ($b < 1$).

■ The S-shaped curve, for rapid, then slowing growth, $y = b + (a - b)[x^c / (d + x^c)]$.

This use of graphs to select a family of curves to represent a relation ties in closely to another important heuristic, *parameterization*.

FIGURE 3.5
Useful Functions
for Modeling

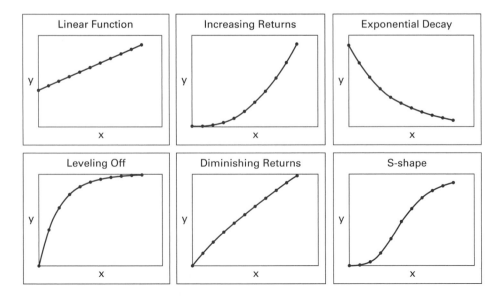

IDENTIFY PARAMETERS AND PERFORM SENSITIVITY ANALYSIS

We have seen that sketching a graph is a powerful way to express one's intuitions about the relationship between two variables. (The idea could be extended to three variables, although it gets more complicated.) But there is no direct way as yet to enter a sketch into a spreadsheet. Some explicit formula must be created to stand for the sketch in the model itself. This could take the form of a traditional mathematical function, for example:

D5 = $A$1+$A$2*D4

or it could be a complex combination of spreadsheet functions, for example:

D5 = IF(D2–D1>$E$4,VLOOKUP(E7,Data,3),VLOOKUP(E7,Data,2))

In either case, the relations involve input numbers, and these parameters play an essential role in spreadsheet modeling and analysis.

For example, we might hypothesize that there is a downward-sloping relation between the quantity we sell and the price we can charge. This assumption is consistent with the linear demand curve

$$Price = a - b \times (Quantity)$$

and also with the constant-elasticity demand curve

$$Price = a \times (Quantity)^b \qquad (b < 1)$$

In each of these functions, the symbols a and b are parameters that stand for as-yet-undetermined numbers. Each of these functions represents a *family* of relations having the common property of sloping downward; the linear family declines at a constant rate, while the other declines at a decreasing rate. When we implement one of these families in a spreadsheet model, we choose particular values of the parameters; that is, we select one from among the family of curves. Rarely will we know the values of these parameters exactly. This is where sensitivity analysis comes in. With sensitivity analysis, we can determine plausible ranges for the parameters and test the impact of changing parameter values on model outputs. In fact, we will recommend in Chapter 6 that testing the sensitivity of the critical outputs to model parameters is an essential step in any modeling activity. One reason we can be creative in the functional relationships we put in our models is that we have confidence that we can eventually test our results with respect both to the functions we have used and to the parameters that drive those functions.

Parameterization plays a key role in one of our favorite short modeling problems, called Hot and Thirsty.[1] The goal is to model the temperature of a warm beer as it cools over time in a refrigerator. Common sense leads to a difference equation of the form

$$T_{t+1} = T_t - Heat\ loss\ over\ the\ interval\ (t,\ t + 1)$$

where T_t represents the temperature of the beer at time t. What factors influence the heat loss? Clearly the type of beer may be relevant, as is the material used in its container, the shape of the container, the humidity of the refrigerator, how frequently it is opened, and so on. There are, in fact, so many factors that influence heat loss that one might think the only feasible approach is to gather data on all of them, a daunting task. However, there is an easier way.

A little understanding of thermodynamics (or some experience with refrigerators) will suggest that heat loss is proportional to the temperature difference between the beer and the air in the refrigerator, with the constant of proportionality depending on all the factors cited above; that is:

$$T_{t+1} = T_t - k \times (T_t - T_{fridge})$$

[1] Starfield, A., K. Smith, and A. Bleloch. *How to Model It* (New York: McGraw-Hill, 1990), 54–69.

If, for the moment, we assume some arbitrary value for the constant of proportionality k, it is straightforward to build a spreadsheet model for this relation. Then, as we choose different values of the parameter k, we can graph different decline curves for the temperature (see Figure 3.6). It is surprising but true that we can use common sense and a little experience with beer to determine plausible values for k within a rather narrow range, just based on the time it takes to cool to refrigerator temperature. We could also determine k rather accurately by cooling a beer for, say, fifteen minutes and then determining its temperature. We can then use the family of curves in Figure 3.6 to read off the value of k that gives us this temperature. This looks like sleight of hand, as if we were manufacturing knowledge out of ignorance. After all, we know that k depends on a long list of factors, none of which is known in this problem. Yet here we lump all these influences into a single number. What really has happened is that we have used intuition and common sense to build a structure (or model) that is more general than needed for the immediate purpose, and then we have specialized it to the case at hand by varying the single number k. We have also saved a lot of effort by building a model structure before we tried to collect data, because, using this approach, we never have to know the type of beer, its container, or anything about the refrigerator.

Why is parameterization such a powerful heuristic? We believe its power comes, as the previous example suggests, from our ability to select one from a family of curves by using sensitivity analysis. Parameterization also reduces the vagueness in a relation to a single dimension, which itself is a great simplification. Then, if we can find ways (such as the graphical approach described above) to display the implications of a particular choice for the parameter, we can bring to bear our usually considerable intuition about the problem. So the power of parameterization, in part, lies in building links between our rational knowledge and our intuition.

SEPARATE THE CREATION OF IDEAS FROM THEIR EVALUATION

Jim Evans, who has written extensively on the role of creativity in management science, points out in his book *Creative Thinking* that one of the important emotional blocks to creativity is the tendency to judge ideas before they receive an adequate hearing. Many modelers we have worked with show a marked *preference* for judging ideas over generating them, especially if generating ideas means coming up with wild notions that will probably not work. But some wild notions actually do work, and others spark the mind to generate additional creative solutions. It is, therefore, essential to have methods available that help *quiet the critical voice* during the most creative phases of the problem-solving process.

FIGURE 3.6
Temperature of Beer Over Time

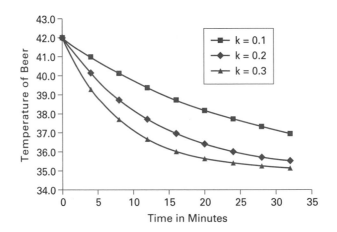

The "quiet the critic" heuristic is based on the distinction, discussed in Chapter 2, between **divergent** and **convergent** thinking. Divergent thinking involves generating alternative problem statements, approaches, and possible solutions, with a minimum of evaluation. Convergent thinking, on the other hand, involves the rational analysis of these alternatives, with the goal of choosing the best (and rejecting the rest). Each stage of the problem-solving process involves both divergent and convergent thinking. However, it is generally most effective to stress divergent types of thinking early in the modeling process and to gradually shift to more convergent thinking as the model and analysis take shape.

The quintessential divergent-thinking process is **brainstorming,** in which a group or individual generates as many ideas on an issue as possible, without any critical evaluation. The most effective brainstorming sessions involve a facilitator, who can set the ground rules and remind participants not to criticize the ideas of others. The purpose, of course, is to prevent premature selection of obvious or mundane approaches to a problem by generating large numbers of alternatives. Some participants always seem to have difficulty refraining from evaluating their own ideas or those of others during such a session. It is often equally difficult for them to show overt enthusiasm for ideas, from whatever source. Fostering a climate in which ideas are celebrated, regardless of their source or their apparent usefulness, should be a goal of modeling teams and individuals.

It's difficult to appreciate the power of brainstorming without seeing it in action. We recall a class session in which we were analyzing the problem of how to configure a highway tunnel to accommodate the maximum traffic volume. We had determined the optimal speed and heading for cars to follow, but were stuck on how to ensure that drivers would actually follow our solution. We then had a short brainstorming session focused on how to accomplish this. Among many other creative ideas, one student suggested installing rows of lights in the tunnel that would blink on and off at a speed set by the traffic engineers to guide drivers to the correct speed. This student was from another country, and the other students' first reaction was that this solution must be something she had seen in use in her home country. Once they began to realize it was not a known solution but something she had invented on the spot, they were more willing to think of alternatives beyond their own experience.

Why does this heuristic work? Apparently, our educational systems encourage students to criticize their own ideas and those of others, but not to create ideas or to appreciate their own and others' creative ideas. This imbalance can be so extreme that an open-ended project such as modeling becomes overwhelming because the pitfalls of every approach seem so clear to the modeler. When the critical faculty is so strong, the modeler needs reassurance that mistakes and blind alleys are a necessary part of the creative process. By finding ways to "quiet the critic," the novice modeler gains time to find a solution that will stand up to their own scrutiny and to the scrutiny of others.

WORK BACKWARD FROM THE DESIRED ANSWER

Most modeling projects proceed from the ground up: make assumptions, gather data, build a prototype, and so on. This is a reasonable approach in many ways, and to some extent, there is no alternative. But the bottom-up approach can lead to difficulties, especially in the hands of creative individuals. Creative exploration of a problem with a succession of models sometimes leaves the modeling team in a quandary about which approach among many to take and which results to show the client.

One way to break through this dilemma is to work backward from the desired answer. That is, imagine the *form* the answer will take, and then work backward from that point to select the model and analysis necessary to generate the chosen form of answer. An example will clarify this point.

It is clear in the Retirement Planning case that the client wants to know how his savings during his working life will influence his retirement years. But there are many ways to measure the quality of retirement living; which ones are best suited to this client? Would he like to know his asset level at retirement, or the number of years his assets will hold out, or the maximum amount he can afford to spend if he lives to seventy-five, or the probability of running out of money before he is ninety? Before we can focus our modeling, we must have an answer (even a tentative one) to this question. Likewise, we need to know how the client thinks about his savings decision—in terms of a constant percentage of his income or a constant dollar amount, or perhaps a percentage rising at a certain rate. Until we settle this question, we are also not ready to think about how we are going to present our results. If, after sufficient thought, we decide we want to show the client how his final assets depend on his (constant percentage) savings rate and how this relationship itself depends on the returns he can earn on his assets, we can sketch the chart shown in Figure 3.7. Notice that we do not need a model, nor do we need any data, to sketch this chart because it is only an illustration. But the chart has considerable value because it focuses our modeling effort on a clear end product.

We sometimes facetiously call this the **PowerPoint heuristic.** Here's the idea: most decision makers are very busy, so they cannot sit through a long-winded presentation. In fact, we like to imagine that our client is so busy that we have to condense our entire presentation to *one PowerPoint slide.* If that's all we have, that one slide must contain the essential message we have to deliver. What is that message? Is it a number, a table, a chart, a procedure, a recommendation? Sketching out what that one slide might look like involves making decisions about the critical outputs, thus focusing the modeling effort on the essential message.

The power of this heuristic lies not just in being able to organize one's thoughts at the end of a modeling effort, but also in organizing the work itself by asking periodically: What will our final results look like?

FOCUS ON MODEL STRUCTURE, NOT ON DATA COLLECTION

Novice modelers often spend a high proportion of their time searching for and analyzing *data.* Expert modelers, on the other hand, spend most of their time working on the *structure* of their models. This contrast has significant implications for the appropriate conduct of a modeling project.

Why do novices emphasize data analysis over model structure? This attitude appears to be based on three beliefs. First, novices assume that the available empirical data are an accurate indicator of the information needed in the modeling process. Second, they believe that obtaining empirical data moves the process forward in a productive direction.

FIGURE 3.7
Sketch of Results for
Retirement Analysis

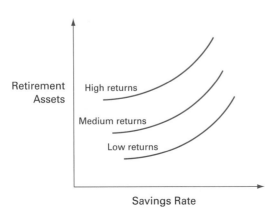

Third, they believe that the available empirical data will ultimately improve the quality of the recommendations developed as a result of modeling. From these beliefs, it seems to follow logically that data collection and analysis should be an important and early activity in any modeling project. But these beliefs are not supported by experience.

Novice modelers tend to accept, without critical screening, any data provided to them. By contrast, expert modelers know that most data contain hidden biases and errors. Perhaps the biggest single problem with empirical information is that it reports on the past, while modeling looks to the future. Even if we have accurate data on the growth in sales over the past ten years, can we be sure next year's growth will follow the same pattern? Other common sources of biases and errors in empirical data include:

- *Sampling error* (e.g., a phone survey does not contact the homeless)
- *Differences in purpose* (e.g., accounting profits do not correspond to economic profits)
- *Masking* (e.g., actual sales may not reflect underlying customer demand)
- *Inappropriateness* (e.g., growth rates on one product may not predict those on another)
- *Definitional differences* (e.g., demand histories do not reveal price elasticity)

Experts look at all data skeptically, asking where the information came from and who gathered it (with what motivations). They try to determine all the ways in which it may be flawed for the purpose they have in mind. Even when high-quality data are available, the modeler must use judgment before incorporating the data into a model. Sometimes, good judgment involves discarding parts of the data as irrelevant or misleading; sometimes it involves choosing how to summarize the data (whether to use the average or the worst case, for example). Experts, then, are much more skeptical than novices about the accuracy and appropriateness of empirical data, and therefore more skeptical about the usefulness of empirical data in a modeling effort.

While novices believe that collecting empirical data will move the modeling process forward beneficially, they seldom recognize that data collection can also be distracting and limiting. For example, if the familiar corporate database documents sales by industry and by company size, most likely a model for sales will relate it to these two driving variables, rather than to less readily available, but perhaps more important, factors. A better model will result in most cases if it is built up from first principles, without being channeled by the available data.

The Racquetball Racket case provides another example of how the availability of data can limit modeling creativity. The market-research firm has given us information on the percentage of people who would buy our ball at various prices. They present the data in the form of a ratio of our competitor's price to our price. Does this imply that we should use the price *ratio* as the driving variable in our model of market share? The implication of such an approach would be that consumers do not react to the actual level of prices but only to relative prices. In other words, our share would be the same if we charged $5 and the competition $10, or if we charged $1 to their $2. Is this a plausible model, or might consumers react instead to the *difference* in prices? If we focus first on the data as presented, we may not even recognize the relevance of this question.

Thus, experts first build an appropriate model structure and use data to refine that model. The principle, in essence, is to let the model tell us what data we need rather than letting the data dictate our model.

Novice modelers often think they cannot build a useful model without acquiring good data first. Worse, they often feel that collecting good data, or at least better data than they currently have, is necessary before they even begin to *think* about a model. In either case, their premise is that data hold the key to a successful analysis. Some companies foster this attitude by emphasizing "data-driven decision making." A popular textbook even offers the advice that, ". . . one of the *first jobs* of an analyst is to gather exactly the *right data* and summarize the data appropriately." [Emphases added.] But how can a modeler identify the right data before building an initial model within which these questions can be answered? Most important, how can the modeler know what data will have the biggest impact on the ultimate recommendations that flow out of the modeling process?

Inexperienced modelers appear to believe that the quality of a model's recommendations depends critically on the quality of the model's data. But the managerial recommendations that evolve from modeling and analysis are often driven far more by the structure of the model than by the specific parameters in it. Therefore, it is imperative to get the model structure right, but it may be quite acceptable to work with rough parameter estimates. Once the modeling process has begun and a prototype provides us a basis for determining which data would be desirable, we can address the question of whether rough parameter estimates will work. The precision needed for the numerical inputs can be determined only through testing the model itself. This is an additional benefit from sensitivity analysis, beyond the plausibility tests that we mentioned earlier. Sensitivity tools can help identify which parameters require precise values—that is, the ones for which data analysis would be most beneficial. Experts, then, focus on getting model structure right and on acquiring only data that will materially affect their conclusions.

Based on our observations of expert modelers, we believe that data collection should rarely be the main concern in modeling. It is quite possible to build models, analyze models, and draw insights from models without relying on data analysis or statistical methods at all. In fact, we endorse that approach as a first cut. Data collection should ideally be undertaken only after a model-based determination has been made as to precisely which data are needed and with what level of precision. We have come to this point of view after repeatedly observing problem-solving teams waste large amounts of precious time and effort on poorly conceived data-collection expeditions. This is not to say that data collection is irrelevant; there are circumstances in which empirical data have a major impact on the quality of model-based recommendations. However, most business analysis takes place under a fairly severe time constraint. In such circumstances, modelers seldom have the luxury to search for the best possible data. Sometimes, we can find only data that were collected for other purposes and may not be tailored to our needs. At other times, very little data are available at all. Nevertheless, we must remember that *modeling* is central, not data.

SUMMARY

Modeling heuristics are rules of thumb that help in the design and use of models. They enhance pure technical skill by enabling us to invent models for new and unfamiliar situations. They also play a major role in the craft of modeling. Our list of modeling heuristics includes:

1. Simplify the problem.
2. Break the problem into modules.
3. Build a prototype and refine it.
4. Sketch graphs of key relationships.
5. Identify parameters and perform sensitivity analysis.
6. Separate the creation of ideas from their evaluation.
7. Work backward from the desired answer.
8. Focus on model structure, not on data collection.

Some of the items on the list are useful to help a modeling effort get off to a good start. If we think in terms of the chronological steps in a typical modeling project, the last heuristic may be the first one to apply: focus first on structuring a model rather than on obtaining data. The first model ought to be simple. It should be guided mainly by the desire to capture an essential trade-off in the problem. Simplification, by its nature, involves making assumptions about the problem, and these should be explicit. In any stage of model development, there should be a companion phase in which those assumptions are subjected to sensitivity analysis so that we can determine which ones need refinement. Devising a model structure made up of modules enables us to focus on the components of the model as a means of overcoming complexity in the overall problem. An ideal structure contains independent modules and allows interchangeable substitutes for the original module.

In building an initial model structure, we might start with visual representations, such as diagrams or graphs, for the inputs and also for the outputs. Visualizing the outputs, in the sense of working backward, keeps us focused on the precise requirements of the problem. Then, in order to convert graphical representations to mathematical representations, we might want to draw on a small family of familiar functions, specifying parameters as needed. Parameters used in this way are numerical assumptions, and, as with structural assumptions, they deserve sensitivity analysis. Sensitivity testing will tell us which parameters or which functional relationships are most critical to the ultimate outcomes.

Some of the heuristics on our list may be applied repeatedly during a modeling project. Developing a good model is a multistep process involving successive refinement. We start with a first prototype, and we test it to determine how well it addresses the problem. This testing may suggest we do some data collection, and it might stimulate our thinking about enrichments to the model. At various stages in the process, especially when the project is team-based, we may need some creative input from brainstorming activity. However, with the repeated cycles of model enhancement and model testing, we will have compiled some analysis, perhaps overly simple, that we can bring to bear on the problem. As we improve the model, we continually add to our store of knowledge and insight about the problem, so that at every stage in the process, we have an answer for the client and a sense of whether our analysis is adequate. Prototyping thus creates an important dialogue with the client and helps assure that the focus remains on the problem rather than the model.

REFERENCES

Very little has been written on the craft aspects of modeling, whether in business or science. The original work on heuristics in problem solving is the following:

Polya, George. 1971. *How to Solve It.* Princeton, NJ: Princeton University Press.

This little classic, which is still in print sixty years after it was written, is focused on problem solving in mathematics, but it still provides worthwhile reading.

A more recent book that discusses some of the ideas in this chapter is:

Pidd, Michael. 1996. *Tools for Thinking: Modelling in Management Science.* Chichester: John Wiley.

The following articles, which are classics of a sort, are still relevant after many years and remain worth reading:

Geoffrion, Arthur M. 1976. "The Purpose of Mathematical Programming Is Insight, Not Numbers," *Interfaces* 7, 81–92.

Little, John D. C. 1970. "Models and Managers: The Concept of a Decision Calculus," *Management Science* 16, B466–B485.

Morris, William T. 1967. "On the Art of Modeling," *Management Science* 13, B707–717.

Urban, Glen L. 1974. "Building Models for Decision Makers," *Interfaces* 4, 1–11.

EXERCISES

1. Refer to the Retirement Planning case. Review the problem statement developed in the corresponding exercise in chapter 2.

   Questions

   a. What are the decisions, objectives, and constraints in the problem?

   b. In what ways could we simplify the problem?

   c. What modules will we need to build?

   d. What are the parameters of the problem?

   e. What are the key relationships in the problem? Draw their graphs.

2. Refer to the Draft TV Commercials case. Review the problem statement developed in the corresponding exercise in chapter 2.

   Questions

   a. What are the decisions, objectives, and constraints in the problem?

   b. In what ways could we simplify the problem?

   c. What modules will we need to build?

   d. What are the parameters of the problem?

   e. What are the key relationships in the problem? Draw their graphs.

3. Refer to the Icebergs for Kuwait case. Review the problem statement developed in the corresponding exercise in chapter 2.

   Questions

   a. What are the decisions, objectives, and constraints in the problem?

   b. In what ways could we simplify the problem?

   c. What modules will we need to build?

   d. What are the parameters of the problem?

   e. What are the key relationships in the problem? Draw their graphs.

4. Refer to the Racquetball Racket case. Review the problem statement developed in the corresponding exercise in chapter 2.

   Questions

   a. What are the decisions, objectives, and constraints in the problem?

   b. In what ways could we simplify the problem?

   c. What modules will we need to build?

   d. What are the parameters of the problem?

   e. What are the key relationships in the problem? Draw their graphs.

CHAPTER 4

VISUAL MODELING TOOLS FOR PROBLEM FORMULATION

INTRODUCTION

Spreadsheets provide a powerful and flexible modeling platform, but they have a number of limitations. Perhaps the most serious limitation is that the row-and-column format does not allow for the development of model *boundaries* and *structure* independent of the numerical details. The boundaries of a model determine which factors are included and which are excluded. Model structure includes the key inputs and outputs, as well as the relationships that link outputs to inputs. In every spreadsheet, the numerical details are commingled with model boundaries and structure.

This commingling of boundaries, structure, and numbers is not a problem for experienced modelers, because they have learned to develop a model structure before approaching the spreadsheet. In contrast, we often observe novice modelers taking whatever information is at hand and entering it into a spreadsheet before they have sufficiently developed the model itself. In other words, novices generally approach a spreadsheet-modeling task from the **bottom up,** without deciding such essential modeling issues as what the key outputs are, how those outputs will be obtained from the inputs, and how essential relationships will be modeled. Experts, on the other hand, usually develop a **top-down,** or high-level, view of their model, often using a table, chart, or sketch. That is to say, experts concentrate on defining the boundaries and the essential structure of their models first. Experts may choose a bottom-up approach (starting with the details) when they are working on a familiar problem, but it is an ineffective approach for novices. It is also ineffective for anyone, novice or expert, who is confronting an unfamiliar type of modeling problem. Bottom-up modeling is also an ineffective approach for teams. An early task for a modeling team is to bring to light each other's mental models of the situation at hand. Only then can they develop a shared understanding of model boundaries and structure.

Expert modelers use a variety of visual modeling tools in the early stages of model formulation and design. These tools are useful in providing a high-level structure to a model before implementing it in a spreadsheet. Individuals can use these tools to develop their understanding of the fundamental interconnections that drive the problem. Teams can use these tools to develop a shared understanding of the essential elements in the model. A number of these tools can also be used to present the essential features of a model to clients. In this chapter, we describe four visual modeling tools:

- Influence charts
- Outlines
- Decision trees
- Network diagrams

Influence charts are the most general and powerful of these tools. They identify the main elements and delineate the boundaries of a model. We recommend using them in the early stages of any unstructured problem-formulation task. Outlines can be useful in organizing the components of a model and ultimately in laying out the rows of a spreadsheet. Many standard spreadsheets, such as financial statements, can be structured in outline form. Decision trees are particularly useful in situations where there are random variables and a sequential logic to events. Finally, network diagrams are handy for creating a specialized structure where material flows across space or time.

INFLUENCE CHARTS

We pointed out in Chapter 2 that model building and analysis are used within the broader context of problem solving. To be successful, this process must begin with the recognition of a problem and end with implementation of a solution. At a minimum, modeling should help in evaluating alternative solutions, but it can also provide the analyst with an enhanced intuitive understanding of the problem and the forces within it.

One of the key challenges modelers face in the problem-solving process is how to translate an initial, vague understanding of a problem into a concrete model. A mathematical model, of course, requires specific numerical inputs and outputs and also the precise relationships that connect them. As we have mentioned, many modelers make the mistake of plunging into the details of a model before they think through the role the model will play in the overall process. We recommend a different approach, using the power of visualization to develop a broad understanding of the critical inputs, outputs, and relationships in a model before building a prototype. An **influence chart** is a simple diagram that shows what outcome variables the model will generate and how these outputs are calculated from the necessary inputs. The process of building an influence chart is an instance of the decomposition heuristic that we described in Chapter 3. As with any form of decomposition, the benefit of using the heuristic is the clarity it brings to the task. Note, however, that influence charts are not designed to provide numerical results or even insights into which particular solutions are desirable.

Influence charts are particularly powerful in the early, conceptual stages of a modeling effort. They encourage the modeler or modeling team to focus on major choices, such as what is included and what is excluded, rather than on details that may ultimately turn out to be unimportant. Influence charts thus provide a high-level view of the entire model that can be comprehended at one glance. This high-level perspective, in turn, supports modeling in teams by facilitating communication among team members. As a result, areas of agreement and disagreement among team members surface early. Influence charts can also be highly effective in communicating the essence of the modeling approach to clients.

Influence charts are flexible, so they support the kind of frequent revision that effective modeling requires. We often encourage our student teams to devote the first hour in the life of a model to working out an influence chart. In addition, we ask them not to turn on the computer until all members of the team agree that their chart represents a suitable initial description of their model.

EXAMPLE

A Pricing Decision

The task at hand is to determine the price we should set for our product so as to generate the highest possible profit this coming year. Since our plan will ultimately be measured by its profitability, we define Profit as the outcome measure and enclose it in a hexagon (Figure 4.1A). Next we ask what we need to know to determine Profit. The necessary components, Total Revenue and Total Cost, are drawn as variables enclosed in circles to the left of Profit and connected to it by arrows (Figure 4.1B). These arrows

FIGURE 4.1A
Start the Influence Chart with the Objective (Profit)

FIGURE 4.1B
Decompose Profit into Total Revenue and Total Cost

identify which variables are required to calculate the outcome. Next, Total Cost is determined by Fixed Cost and Variable Cost, which are drawn to the left of Total Cost (Figure 4.1C). Variable Cost in turn is the product of Quantity Sold and Unit Cost (Figure 4.1D). Now we turn to Total Revenue, which is the product of Quantity Sold and Price. We add Price and enclose it in a box to show it is our decision variable (Figure 4.1E). Finally, Price Elasticity, along with the price we set, determines Quantity Sold. So, in Figure 4.1F, we add the Price Elasticity variable and an arrow from Price to Quantity Sold.

Traditionally, influence charts are built from right to left, using diagrammatic conventions that distinguish the roles of different types of variables. For example, we use hexagons to represent outputs and boxes to represent decisions, as indicated in our example. We also use circles to represent other variables. As we complete the layout, we can identify certain of the variables as inputs. These are shown in the diagram as triangles. Later, we will also use double circles to represent variables that are random.

While this is a highly simplified example, its development does involve a number of modeling choices. For example, we can see in the influence chart that Fixed Cost is assumed to be a known quantity, since there are no variables that are needed to determine

FIGURE 4.1C
Decompose Total Cost into Variable Cost and Fixed Cost

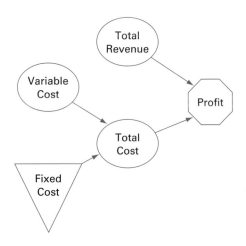

FIGURE 4.1D
Decompose Variable Cost
into Quantity Sold and
Unit Cost

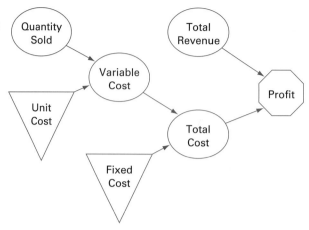

FIGURE 4.1E
Decompose Total
Revenue into Quantity
Sold and Price

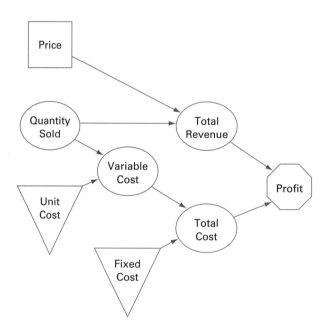

Fixed Cost. In another situation, we might face a set of choices as to which production technology to choose for the coming year. In this case, Fixed Cost would not be known but would be influenced by our technology choices, and the chart would have to reflect those complexities. Another modeling choice is evident in how Quantity Sold is determined. In our chart, both Price and Price Elasticity influence Quantity Sold. This reflects our modeling judgment that we face a price-dependent market. In many situations, we might assume instead that Sales are independent of Price, at least within a reasonable range of prices. One final modeling decision is evident in our chart: since Quantity Sold determines Variable Costs, we are assuming that production and sales are simultaneous. If, on the other hand, it were our practice to produce to stock and to sell from inventory, we would need to modify the chart to reflect this process.

This example illustrates that influence charts help the modeler make explicit decisions about what is included in the model and how the variables interact to determine the output.

FIGURE 4.1F
Decompose Quantity
Sold into Price and Price
Elasticity

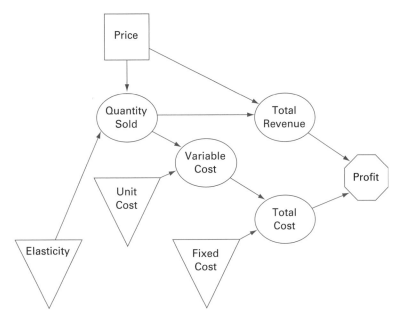

EXAMPLE

A Pro Forma Income Statement

An income statement is a standard accounting framework that is widely used for projecting the financial future of a company. The bottom line in an income statement is Retained Earnings, which is roughly the difference between revenue and costs, adjusted for taxes and dividends. A simple income statement is shown in the form of an influence chart in Figure 4.2.

If our purpose were simply to record the historical performance of a company, then the relationships depicted in Figure 4.2 would be sufficient. Moreover, the related spreadsheet would consist entirely of numbers; no formulas would be needed because all variables are already determined. However, Figure 4.2 would be inadequate if our purpose were to make projections into the future because it reveals nothing about how critical variables such as Sales Revenue and Cost of Goods Sold will be determined. In other words, Figure 4.2 represents only a static accounting framework and not a *model* of the future. To convert a static income statement into a model, we will need to determine how underlying variables such as Quantity Sold will evolve over time. In a simple model, we could assume that Unit Cost and Price will be constant and that Quantity Sold will be determined by Initial Sales and Sales Growth Rate. Figure 4.3 shows an influence chart for this model.

It is noteworthy that even in this case, where accounting rules determine much of the model structure, an influence chart is useful for depicting the underlying forces that drive the results.

PRINCIPLES FOR BUILDING INFLUENCE CHARTS

An influence chart is not a technical flowchart that must conform perfectly to a rigid set of rules. Rather, it is a somewhat free-form visual aid for thinking conceptually about a model. We offer the following guidelines for constructing such charts:

FIGURE 4.2
Influence Chart for a
Static Income Statement

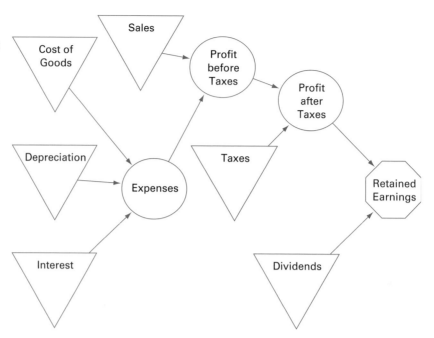

FIGURE 4.3
Influence Chart for an
Income-Statement Model

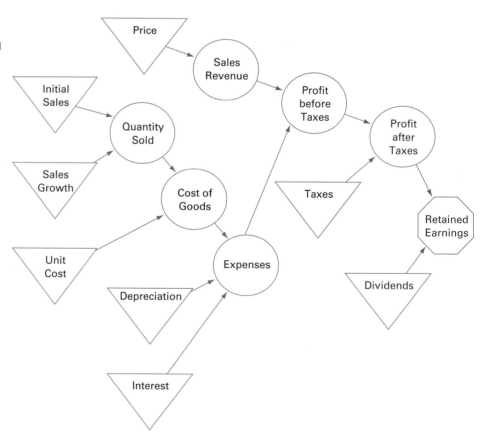

- Start with the outcome measure. To decide which variable this is, ask what single variable the decision maker will use to determine success or failure.

- Decompose the outcome measure into a small set of variables that determine it *directly*. Each of these influencing variables should be independent of the others, and together they should be sufficient to determine the result.

- Take each variable in turn and repeat this process of decomposition. For each variable, ask, "What do I need to know to determine. . . ?"

- Identify input data and decisions as they arise.

- A variable should appear only once in the diagram.

- Highlight special types of elements with special symbols. For example, we use squares for decision variables and double circles for random variables, but any consistent code will work.

The most common error in drawing influence charts is to draw an arrow from the output back to the decisions. The motivation for this seems to be that the outcome will be used to determine the best decisions. Remember, however, that an influence chart is simply a *description* of how we will calculate outcomes for any set of decisions and other parameters. It is not intended to be used to find the best decisions. That is a separate process, requiring an actual model, not simply a diagram.

In what follows, we present two detailed exercises in building influence charts for unstructured problems. Read each case and draw an influence chart before proceeding. We will then describe the process of building an influence chart and discuss some of our modeling choices. Keep in mind, however, that there is no one correct diagram, just as there is no one correct model.

EXAMPLE

The SS *Kuniang**

In the early 1980s, New England Electric System (NEES) was deciding how much to bid for the salvage rights to a grounded ship, the SS *Kuniang*. If the bid were successful, the ship could be repaired and fitted out to haul coal for the company's power-generation stations. But the value of doing so depended on the outcome of a U.S. Coast Guard judgment about the salvage value of the ship. The Coast Guard's judgment involved an obscure law regarding domestic shipping in coastal waters. If the judgment were to indicate a low salvage value, then NEES would be able to use the ship for its shipping needs. If the judgment were high, the ship would be considered ineligible for use in domestic shipping unless a considerable amount of money was spent in fitting her with fancy equipment. In effect, this would mean additional expenses for NEES. The Coast Guard's judgment would not be known until after the winning bid was chosen, so there was considerable risk associated with submitting the winning bid. If the bid were to fail, the alternatives would include purchasing either a new ship or a tug/barge combination, both of which were relatively expensive alternatives. One of the major issues was that the higher the bid, the more likely that NEES would win. NEES judged that a bid of $2 million would definitely not win, whereas a bid of $12 million definitely would win. Any bid in between was possible.

The goal here is to select an amount to bid for the SS *Kuniang* that will allow NEES to supply coal to its plants in the most economical way. We assume that the amount of coal

* D. E. Bell, "Bidding for the S.S. Kuniang," *Interfaces* 14 (1984): 17–23.

to be shipped is fixed and that NEES will either use the *Kuniang* or buy a new ship or a tug/barge combination. That is, we explicitly rule out the possibility that NEES can avoid meeting the demand for shipped coal. We further assume that the outcome measure is the NPV of profits from this shipping operation over an appropriate time period (in the case of a ship, perhaps twenty years).

Our influence chart starts with an outcome measure for NPV and two influences: Costs and Revenues (Figure 4.4). Since the revenues are most likely independent of the ship chosen, that part of the diagram does not need to be developed further. The costs incurred in coal shipping depend on which option is chosen. Apparently, NEES can always buy a new ship or a tug/barge combination, and it may have the option to buy the *Kuniang* if its bid wins. So Costs will be calculated as the minimum of these three costs. The costs of the *Kuniang* are the essential part of the model. These costs are dependent on the salvage value set by the Coast Guard, which is unpredictable and is therefore shown as a random variable (a double circle). The cost is also influenced by our bid and by whether we win the auction. In Figure 4.4, we have shown the outcome of the auction as the random variable "Win?" We have in mind a simple model in which the probability of winning increases as our bid increases. But this is an area of the diagram where further elaboration could be productive. We could, for example, add modules for the bids of our competitors. We could also add a module for the auction process itself. Whether to add further detail is always the modeler's judgment. But this simple influence chart is sufficiently detailed to support the building of a prototype model.

One additional point to notice here is that the numerical information in the problem statement, which places some limits on reasonable bids, plays no role at all in constructing the influence chart. In fact, we routinely ignore all available numerical data when we build influence charts because the goal is to develop a problem structure, not to solve the problem. Problem structure is not influenced by the values of parameters. This principle conflicts with another that many of us learned in early math classes, which was to use all the given data to solve the problem. This may be an appropriate problem-solving heuristic for simple math problems in school, but it is not necessarily helpful in structuring real business decisions.

FIGURE 4.4
S.S. *Kuniang*
Influence Chart

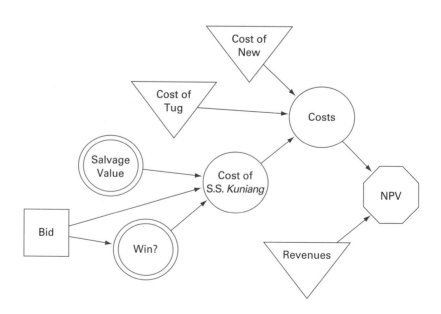

EXAMPLE

National Leasing, Inc.

During the 1990s, leasing grew to 40 percent of new-car sales. Nowadays, the most popular leases are for expensive or mid-range vehicles and carry terms of twenty-four or thirty-six months. The most common form of leasing is the **closed-end** lease, where the monthly payment is computed based on three factors:

- Capitalized Cost: the purchase price for the car, net of trade-ins, fees, discounts, and dealer-installed options.

- Residual Value: the value of the vehicle at the end of the lease, specified by the leasing company (the "lessor") in the contract. The customer has the right to purchase the vehicle at this price at the end of the lease.

- Money Factor, or Rate: the interest rate charged by the leasing company.

A lower residual value results in higher monthly payments. Therefore, a leasing company with the highest residual value usually has the lowest, and most competitive, monthly payment. However, if the actual end-of-lease market value is lower than the contract residual value, the customer is likely to return the car to the lessor. The lessor then typically sells the vehicle, usually at auction, and realizes a "residual loss."

A low residual value results in a high monthly payment (which is relatively less attractive), but, at the end of the lease, if the actual market value is greater than the contract residual, the customer is more likely to purchase the vehicle. By then selling the vehicle for the prevailing market value, the customer in essence receives a rebate for the higher monthly payments. (Of course, the customer may also decide to keep the car.) When customers exercise their purchase option, the lessor loses the opportunity to realize "residual gains."

The primary challenge for companies offering a closed-end lease is to select the residual value of the vehicle. Intelligent selection means offering competitive monthly payments on the front end without ignoring the risk of residual losses on the back end. In approaching this problem from a modeling perspective, the first task is to find ways to cut it down to size. After all, any leasing company offers leases on dozens of vehicles at any one time. Furthermore, unless it is just starting to do business, the company has an existing portfolio of hundreds of leases on its books, and the risk characteristics of this portfolio may influence the terms offered on new leases. We can become overwhelmed by complexity if we start by trying to model the entire problem. A modular, prototyping approach is vital here.

One reasonable approach is to develop a prototype for a specific lease on a single type of vehicle. Once a prototype model based on this diagram is tested and proved, we can expand on it by bringing in excluded aspects of the problem.

An example will make the problem more concrete. Consider new Honda Accord models, which sell for $25,000. Also consider only three-year leases, and assume the money rate is fixed at 5 percent. Given these assumptions, our goal is to determine the best contract residual value (CRV) for a single lease on a single class of vehicles.

The CRV is clearly our decision variable. How will we determine whether we have made a good choice? Once we have chosen the CRV (and the other terms of the lease), we will offer it to the leasing market. Some number of customers will purchase our lease and pay us the monthly lease payments for three years. (A few will default during this period, but we ignore that factor in our initial prototype.) Our monthly lease revenues will be the product of the monthly payment and the number of leases sold. The monthly payment, in turn, will depend on the term, the money factor, and the CRV.

At the end of three years, all our leases will expire. Some customers will buy their vehicles at the CRV; others will return their vehicles and take a new lease with us; still others will return their vehicles and not purchase another lease with us. (We ignore the value of follow-on leases in our initial prototype.) When all is said and done, we will have made some level of profit. Profit, then, is our outcome measure, and it is influenced by three factors: lease revenues, our cost of borrowing (to pay for new vehicles), and the residual value of vehicles at the end of the lease (Figure 4.5).

So far, this is a rather straightforward influence chart. But two parts of it deserve additional attention. First, what determines how many leases are sold? Presumably, customers are sensitive to the monthly payment, and that influence is shown in the diagram, but what else influences volume? One simple approach is to assume a value for demand elasticity: volume increases (or decreases) by x percent when our monthly payments decrease (or increase) by 1 percent. This relationship is sufficient to generate some realistic aspects of the lease market—namely, a decline in volume with increasing payments—and it may be sufficient for a prototype model. But it does not explicitly include any information about our competitor's monthly payments. In particular, the elasticity is probably different when our payments are above the competition than when they are below. This may be a fertile area for refinement in later prototypes.

We should also consider what factors determine the residual value of the vehicle to the leasing company. When a lease expires, the contract allows the customer to purchase the vehicle for the CRV or to return it to the leasing company. The customer's decision at this point is crucial to determining the profitability of the lease. If used-car prices are high relative to the CRV, it is in the customer's interest to buy the car at the CRV and then sell it for the higher market price. On the other hand, if used-car prices are low, customers will tend to return their leased vehicles and buy a cheaper equivalent used car. In this case, the leasing company will have to sell the vehicle at the low market price. And, of course, some customers will lease a new vehicle regardless of used-car prices, and some may not behave in an economically rational manner at all. Should we include all of these factors in our influence chart?

FIGURE 4.5
National Leasing
Influence Chart

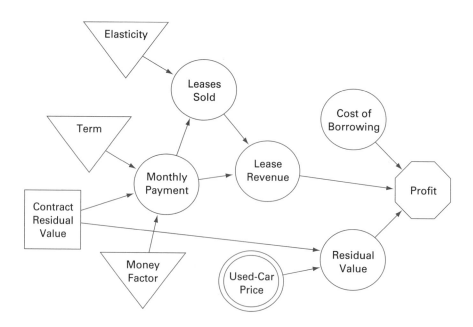

One approach would be to assume that all vehicles will be purchased if used-car prices exceed the CRV, and none will be purchased if the reverse holds. But how do we know how much used cars will be worth three years from now? In our chart, we model used-car prices as a random variable—for example, a normal distribution with a mean of $15,000 and a standard deviation of $2,000. Alternatively, we might assume that this class of vehicles loses a random amount of its value each year, where the annual loss is uniformly distributed between 8 and 12 percent. This slightly more detailed model will also generate a distribution of values three years from now. In further refinements of the chart, we might expand on these ideas and model the fundamental determinants of used-car values: new-vehicle quality, the macro economy, and so on. In any case, a random value for used-car prices captures one of the essential features of this problem—namely, the risk of residual losses and residual gains. This influence chart is probably sufficiently detailed to support construction of a prototype model. Working with this model will help us discover whether we have captured the essential trade-offs in the problem.

As we have stressed before, the influence chart documents the simplifying assumptions made during the modeling process. Here are some of the critical assumptions embodied in Figure 4.5:

- one vehicle/one lease term
- no lease defaults
- no follow-on leases
- rational behavior of customers at lease end
- random used-car prices

We recommend that the modeler or one member of the modeling team record each assumption as it is made during the process of developing an influence chart. This is useful for two reasons. First, it focuses attention and discussion on assumptions as they are being made. Second, each assumption should be viewed as a potential area for later refinement of the model.

OUTLINES

Influence charts and other visual modeling tools are powerful because they assist the modeler in separating the design of a *model* from the design of the *spreadsheet* that implements the model. As we have noted elsewhere, modelers too often begin the modeling process by entering information in a spreadsheet without first establishing the model's essential relationships. This approach is generally ineffective for novice modelers and for unstructured problems. Learning to use visual modeling tools such as influence charts is an important step in the development of modeling expertise.

The influence chart is the tool of choice for complex, unstructured problems. These are problems in which the highly structured row-and-column format of the spreadsheet would limit the creativity of the modeler during the initial phases of problem structuring. However, there are circumstances in which the row-and-column layout of the spreadsheet corresponds so closely to the desired model logic that it can provide a useful visual modeling paradigm. Usually, the model involves projecting a set of variables over time, so that the column headings naturally represent the time dimension (months, quarters, years, etc.). The rows represent variables in the model. Since we know that the columns will correspond to time periods, it is effective to concentrate initially on determining the appropriate row headings. Two things must be determined at this stage: what are the appropriate variables, and what is the most logical sequence in which to calculate them? Developing an *outline* of a model by concentrating on the headings of rows in a spreadsheet can be an effective way to conceptualize a model without becoming buried in details.

Outline for the Pricing Decision

To illustrate the use of outlines as a modeling tool, we return to the pricing example discussed in the previous section. Since we are interested in setting a price that maximizes our profits over the coming year, the time dimension across the columns of the spreadsheet will most likely consist of either twelve months or four quarters. The different variables will appear down the rows. Initially, we might simply describe Profit as determined by Total Revenue and Total Cost, as follows:

Initial Pricing Model in Outline Form

> Profit
>> Total Revenue
>> Total Cost

At a more detailed level, we can decompose Total Revenue into Quantity Sold and Unit Price, and Total Cost into Fixed Cost and Variable Cost:

Second Pricing Model in Outline Form

> Profit
>> Total Revenue
>>> Quantity Sold
>>> Unit Price
>> Total Cost
>>> Fixed Cost
>>> Variable Cost

At an even more detailed level, we can add the determinants of these components:

Third Pricing Model in Outline Form

> Profit
>> Total Revenue
>>> Quantity Sold
>>>> Unit Price
>>>> Price Elasticity
>>> Unit Price
>> Total Cost
>>> Fixed Cost
>>> Variable Cost
>>>> Quantity Sold
>>>> Unit Cost

As we develop these outlines in more and more detail, we often find that some variables begin to repeat. For example, Unit Price repeats under Total Revenue, because it directly influences both the Quantity Sold and Total Revenue. Similarly, Quantity Sold repeats because it influences both Total Revenue and Total Cost. This is not necessarily bad practice when outlining a model, but, as we might expect, repeating calculations in a spreadsheet model is to be avoided. Here, we can avoid the repetition by adding formulas for calculating variables that use information from previous rows, as shown below. We also add headings to group related variables. Finally, we have reordered the rows to ensure that inputs appear before the variables that depend on them. As discussed in Chapter 5, when we cover the principles of good spreadsheet design, it is advantageous to have all rows calculated from inputs that appear above them.

Final Pricing Model in Outline Form

Revenue
    Unit Price
    Price Elasticity
        Quantity Sold   = *function of Unit Price and Elasticity*
        Total Revenue   = *Quantity Sold × Unit Price*
Cost
    Fixed Cost
    Unit Cost
        Variable Cost   = *Quantity Sold × Unit Cost*
        Total Cost   = *Fixed Cost + Variable Cost*
Profit   = *Total Revenue – Total Cost*

Outline for the Pro Forma Income Statement

A pro forma income statement is another common example of a model structure that takes the form of an outline. In the previous section, we described the process of creating an influence chart for an income statement. In its simplest form, an income statement is a list of financial variables:

Income Statement in List Form

Sales
Cost of Goods Sold
Depreciation
Interest
Profit before Taxes
Taxes
Profit after Taxes
Dividends
Retained Earnings

While all the necessary variables are included here, the list form disguises some of the structure behind the income statement. A more useful format is an outline, in which we indent items that are components of other calculations. We also add the heading Expenses to show that three items (Cost of Goods Sold, Depreciation, and Interest) all belong to the same category.

Income Statement in Outline Form

Sales

Expenses

    Cost of Goods Sold

    Depreciation

    Interest

Profit before Taxes

    Taxes

Profit after Taxes

    Dividends

Retained Earnings

One advantage of standard formats such as the income statement is that many of the variables are determined by standard definitions and therefore require no explicit modeling. For example, Profit before Taxes *always* equals the difference between Sales and Expenses. On the other hand, a variable such as Cost of Goods Sold could be represented as a percentage of Sales (where the percentage is an input parameter that could be modeled as constant or as varying with time), or as the sum of Fixed Costs and Variable Costs. Likewise, Variable Costs could be modeled in turn as a percentage of Sales. If an element in the outline is not determined by a definition, then it must be modeled in some way. Such choices should be made taking into account the specifics of the situation at hand. The definitional relationships, by contrast, require no explicit modeling; in effect, they come for free. We have added these definitional relationships to the outline below:

Income Statement with Definitional Relationships

Sales

Expenses   *= Cost of Goods Sold + Depreciation + Interest*

    Cost of Goods Sold

    Depreciation

    Interest

Profit before Taxes   *= Sales – Expenses*

    Taxes

Profit after Taxes   *= Profit before Taxes – Taxes*

    Dividends

Retained Earnings   *= Profit after Taxes – Dividends*

In our final version, we have formulated equations for each of the variables not given by a definition. For example, we have projected Sales each year by multiplying the previous year's sales by a constant growth rate.

Fully Specified Income Statement

Sales   *= Previous sales × (1 + Sales growth rate)*

Expenses   *= Cost of Goods Sold + Depreciation + Interest*

    Cost of Goods Sold   *= Sales × Cost of Goods Sold percentage*

    Depreciation   *= Current assets × Depreciation rate*

    Interest   *= Current year's debt × Interest rate*

Profit before Taxes   *= Sales – Expenses*

    Taxes   *= Profit before Taxes × Tax rate*

Profit after Taxes	= *Profit before Taxes – Taxes*
Dividends	= *Profit after Taxes × Dividend rate*
Retained Earnings	= *Profit after Taxes – Dividends*

It might seem that outlines are useful only for accounting models, in which much of the model structure is predefined. However, we have found that outlines can be used more broadly to structure the thinking of an individual or a group in open-ended situations.

EXAMPLE

Buying a Cottage

Bruce and Amy, both fifty-eight, are considering buying a cottage at a nearby lake. Amy expects to inherit a substantial sum of money within the next ten to fifteen years, which she can use to help pay the costs of the cottage. However, she is concerned that their income will be insufficient to meet their other needs after Bruce retires. Bruce's main concern is that his retirement may have to be postponed if their income does not grow as expected.

The couple has tried to discuss this situation several times but found it difficult. One problem is that each of them focuses on different aspects of the problem, such as whether the inheritance will become available, how quickly other assets will appreciate, when Bruce will decide to retire, and so on. Another complication is that each person evaluates the risks differently. For example, Amy fears becoming strapped for cash ten years from now and having difficulty paying for the cottage. Bruce, on the other hand, feels they can always sell the cottage if necessary, so the financial risks seem much smaller to him. The two need some way to agree on a set of assumptions and to trace through their implications. A simple but flexible financial model would be of considerable help.

Any model for this situation will probably involve projections of the couple's cash flows and assets from the present into the future. Since the time dimension is obvious, attention should focus on the variables to project. An initial outline could simply track income, expenses, and assets:

Initial outline

Income	
Expenses	
Excess cash	= Income – Expenses
Assets	

At the next level of detail, the couple might want to expand these general categories with an eye toward representing the major issues, such as the inheritance and cottage expenses.

First refinement

Income	= *Bruce's salary + Social Security + Retirement-plan income + Inheritance*
Bruce's salary	
Social Security	
Retirement-plan income	
Inheritance	
Expenses	= *Normal living expenses + Cottage expenses*
Normal living expenses	
Cottage expenses	= *Mortgage + Taxes + Upkeep*
Mortgage	

Taxes

Upkeep

Excess cash   = *Income – Expenses*

Assets   = *Retirement savings + Inheritance assets*

Retirement savings

Inheritance assets

Obviously, this outline can be further elaborated if that is needed. In the end, the model may look like a standard spreadsheet, but the end product will not necessarily reveal the value the process brings to the couple making the decision. Elaborating this outline should help the two understand each other's assumptions and values. For example, when is Bruce planning to retire, and how does he feel about retiring a year or two later, if that proves necessary? When does Amy think her inheritance is likely to be available, and how does she feel about using it to cover their expenses? Which categories of living expenses do they feel will change during retirement? Many of these questions can be answered fully only by building a more complete model and using it to analyze the situation. But the process of constructing the outline itself begins to raise questions about what is known, what can be assumed, what is random, and what is a decision. Answering such questions is the essence of modeling. Outlines can be a useful tool in the process.

DECISION TREES

Decision-tree models offer another visual tool that can complement influence charts and provide a more detailed picture of the uncertain elements in decision making. Decision trees are especially useful in situations where there are multiple sources of uncertainty and a sequence of decisions to make. They help organize the elements in a problem by distinguishing between decisions (controllable variables) and random events (uncontrollable variables). As a first step in describing decision trees, we introduce a simpler structure that is useful in its own right.

A **probability tree** depicts one or more random factors. For example, if we believe that demand for our product is uncertain, we might model that uncertainty using the probability tree in Figure 4.6. In this simple tree, we assume that demand may take on one of the three alternative values: High, Medium, or Low. The node from which the branches emanate is called a **chance node,** and each branch represents one of the possible **states** that could occur. Each state, therefore, is a possible resolution of the uncertainty represented by the chance node. Later, when we make calculations to analyze the model, we specify probabilities for each of the states, thus creating a probability distribution to describe the uncertainty at the chance node.

FIGURE 4.6
Simple Probability Tree

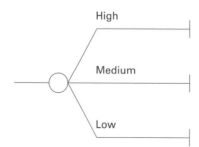

In other circumstances, we might want to show greater detail than just three qualitative states for demand, so we might use a tree with more branches, perhaps quantifying the states as $10 million, $20 million, $30 million, $40 million, and $50 million, as shown in Figure 4.7. Again, the tree is meant to show that demand is uncertain and that one of the alternative states will actually occur. When we specify the probabilities for each of these five states, we create a probability distribution for the dollar value of demand.

Probability trees can accommodate more than one source of uncertainty. In addition to the demand uncertainty in Figure 4.6, suppose we face uncertainty in both the number of competing products and the competitive effectiveness of our advertising. Now we can draw a tree with three chance nodes. The first chance node represents demand states, characterized as High, Medium, or Low. For each demand state, one of several possible numbers of competitors will occur. Likewise, for each combination of demand and number of competitors, one of several levels of advertising effectiveness will occur. We can depict this situation either in a telegraphic form (Figure 4.8), in which only one chance node of each type is displayed, or in exhaustive form (Figure 4.9), where all possible combinations are displayed. In either case, the tree conveys the idea that there are forty-five possible

FIGURE 4.7
Probability Tree with
Five States

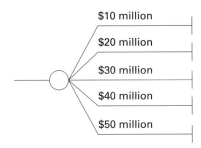

FIGURE 4.8
Three Chance Nodes in
Telegraphic Form

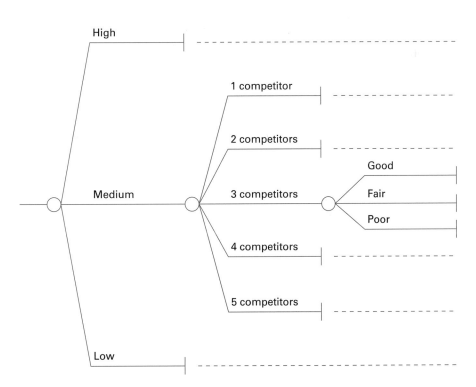

FIGURE 4.9
Three Chance Nodes
in Exhaustive Form

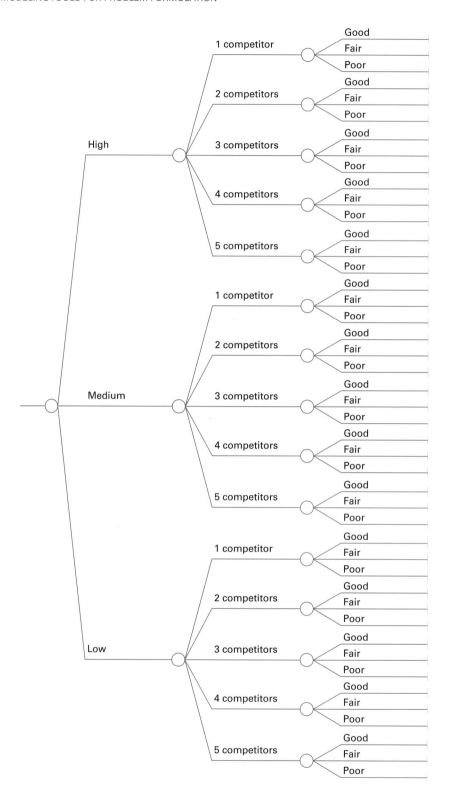

states, corresponding to (three demand levels) × (five competitors) × (three levels of advertising effectiveness). Once we realize this fact, we could equivalently represent the outcomes with one chance node and forty-five states. To perform the steps in analyzing the tree, we would need to examine all of the details. For that purpose, the telegraphic form is not sufficiently detailed, and we would instead need to represent the entire set of forty-five alternatives, as in Figure 4.9.

While probability trees are helpful for displaying chance events and their outcomes, they can quickly become complex when there are several sources of uncertainty, as our forty-five-state example suggests. At an early stage in building a tree, it is not necessary to be precise in specifying the number of alternatives at a chance node. It is more important to recognize which outcomes are uncertain and how to structure the tree to represent them.

In a **decision tree,** we represent decisions as well as chance nodes. For example, suppose that we are introducing a new product and that the first decision determines which channel to use during test-marketing. When this decision is implemented, and we make an initial commitment to a marketing channel, we can begin to develop estimates of demand based on our test. At the end of the test period, we might reconsider our channel choice, especially if the demand has been low, and we may decide to switch to another channel. Then, in the full-scale introduction, we attain a level of profit that depends, at least in part, on the channel we chose initially. In Figure 4.10, we have depicted (in telegraphic form) a situation in which we choose our channel initially, observe the test market, reconsider our choice of a channel, and finally observe the demand during full-scale introduction.

Decision trees are used to describe the choices and uncertainties facing a single decision-making agent. This usually means a single decision maker, but it could also mean a decision-making group or a company. Decisions are represented as boxes, and we can think

FIGURE 4.10
A Decision Tree

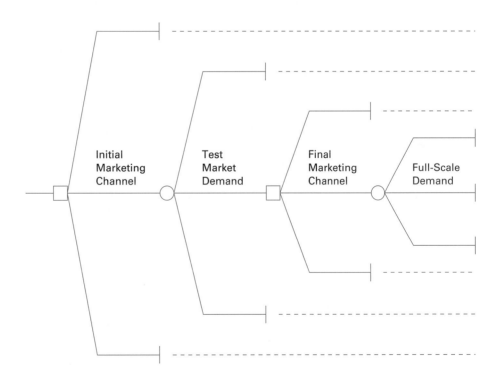

Initial Marketing Channel

Test Market Demand

Final Marketing Channel

Full-Scale Demand

of them as controllable variables. For each decision, the alternative choices are represented as branches emanating from the decision node. These are potential actions that are available to the decision maker. Uncertainties are represented as circles, and we can think of them as uncontrollable variables. For each source of uncertainty, the possible alternative states are represented as branches emanating from a chance node. If there are other players or agents in the scenario, their actions can be depicted as chance nodes, although this may be an oversimplification. For example, if we were to sue a competitor for patent infringement, it is unlikely that they would toss a coin to decide whether to settle or go to court against us. More likely, they would act as we would in that situation—that is, they would study the situation and make a decision aimed at reaching the best outcome for *them*. The analysis of the interrelated decisions of two (or more) actors is quite difficult, and we will not discuss it at length except to mention that representing a competitor's actions as random probably overstates the value we can extract from the situation.

Decision Tree for the S.S. *Kuniang*

To illustrate the use of a decision tree, we return to the problem of the SS *Kuniang,* which was introduced earlier. Two decisions must be made: how much to bid for the salvage rights and which ship to use for hauling coal (a new ship, a tug/barge combination, or the salvaged *Kuniang*). Two of the uncertainties are whether NEES will win the auction and whether the Coast Guard will award a low or high salvage value.

In order to draw a decision tree, it is essential to understand the sequence in which these decisions and uncertainties occur. NEES must first decide on an amount to bid, before it can know the results of the auction or the Coast Guard judgment. Furthermore, the decision as to which ship to use can be delayed until after these uncertainties are resolved. It is immaterial whether the results of the auction are resolved before or after the outcome of the Coast Guard judgment, so we assume that the auction result is known first.

We begin the *Kuniang* tree (Figure 4.11) with a decision node representing the amount NEES will bid for the salvage rights. For simplicity, we distinguish three choices of bid level: $2 million, $8 million, and $12 million. These three choices encompass the high and low extremes, along with an intermediate option. Later, we can return to this part of the model and add more detail.

After making its bid, NEES finds out whether it won the auction. We represent this result with a chance node at the end of each of the branches coming from the decision node. Each of these chance nodes generates two states: win the auction or lose it. Sometime after the auction, the result of the Coast Guard judgment also becomes known. This uncertain event can be represented by another chance node, appearing on each path through the auction nodes, except where there is no chance of winning the auction. Chance nodes for the Coast Guard judgment also have two states: low salvage value and high salvage value. Finally, NEES must decide which of three alternatives to adopt for transporting coal: buying a new ship, buying a tug/barge combination, or salvaging the *Kuniang*. As shown in the tree, this decision is represented by a decision node on each path, although the *Kuniang* is not an option on some of the paths. Note that the decision about how to transport coal occurs *after* NEES has determined whether the company has won the bid and after NEES has learned whether the salvage rights are low or high.

This completes the building phase for this tree. In principle, we have thirty-six ($= 3 \times 2 \times 2 \times 3$) paths through the tree, although some combinations cannot occur. For example,

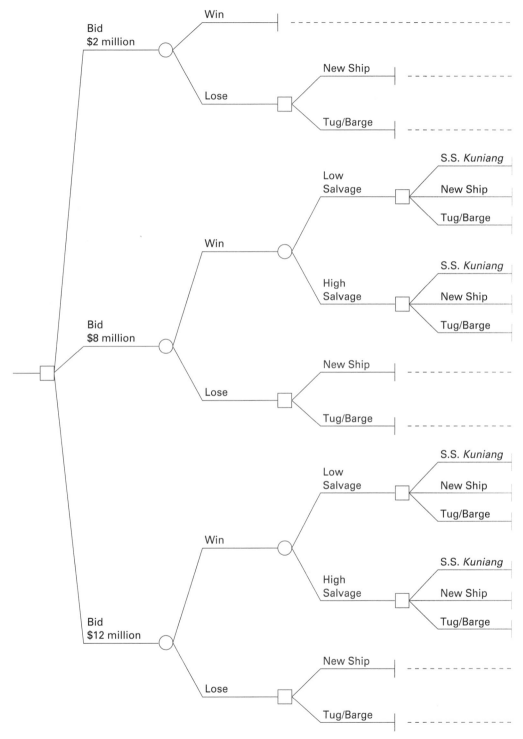

FIGURE 4.11 Decision Tree for the S.S. *Kuniang* Example

we cannot lose the bid and salvage the *Kuniang.* The tree diagram shows only nineteen distinct paths through the tree. Each of these paths represents one distinct combination of choices and states; each path thus represents one way the story can turn out. The question now is which of these stories does NEES wish will occur? To put it another way, which bid level should NEES choose, and when the time comes, which ship should it use?

To answer these questions requires some quantitative analysis and two kinds of detailed information. First, we must specify the probabilities corresponding to the states at each chance node. Second, we must determine an overall value to NEES of arriving at the end of the tree along any of the possible paths. Once we have this information, we can analyze the decisions represented in the tree.

The probability of winning the bid was thought to increase from 0 at a bid of $2 million to 1.0 with a bid of $12 million. In our tree diagram, we have simplified the situation by including only three possible bids that NEES might make for the salvage rights to the *Kuniang*: $2 million, $8 million, or $12 million. As the company's bid increases, so, too, does the probability that NEES will win the auction. For example, if they bid $2 million, they will not win; if they bid $8 million, the estimated chance of winning is 60 percent; and if they bid $12 million, they are sure to win. The other uncertainty is the legal decision regarding the salvage value. As this is independent of who wins the auction, the relevant probabilities do not change within the tree. Experts within the company have estimated that the Coast Guard would assign a low salvage value with probability 0.3, and a high value with probability 0.7, regardless of which firm wins the auction. At the end of each path through the tree, we place the dollar value of the profits to NEES (in millions). These values, developed from economic details available to the company's analysts, include the cost of the bid as well as the estimated future net revenues. The numerical values are shown in Figure 4.12.

To evaluate this situation and determine which bid level is best, we analyze the tree using a procedure called **rollback.** Rolling back the tree involves two operations: choosing the best alternative at decision nodes and evaluating the expected value at chance nodes. We proceed from right to left, or backward in time, since we will need the results of later stages to evaluate the implications at earlier stages.

Starting with the decision node labeled A in Figure 4.12, we compare the profits from the three alternatives, and we choose the *Kuniang* over the other alternatives because it offers the highest profit. In effect, we are saying that *if* we bid $8 million, and *if* we win the auction, and *if* the salvage value is low, *then* we will use the *Kuniang* rather than build a new ship or employ a tug/barge combination. We can now erase node A and its branches and simply replace it with the value $7.5 million. Moving to node B, also a decision node, we see that the *Kuniang* is again the best choice. So if we bid $8 million, and if we win, and if the salvage value is high, then we also choose the *Kuniang,* making a profit of $4.5 million.

Node C is a chance node. From this node, we have a 30 percent chance of going to node A, where the value is $7.5 million, and a 70 percent chance of going to node B, where the value is $4.5 million. We evaluate the chance node at the expected value of its outcomes, which is $5.4 million ($= 0.3 \times 7.5 + 0.7 \times 4.5$).

Moving back to node E, we see we have a 60 percent chance of going to node C, worth $5.4 million, and a 40 percent chance of going to node D, where the best choice (New Ship) is worth $3.2 million. The expected value of these outcomes is $4.52 ($= 0.60 \times 5.4 + 0.40 \times 3.2$). Thus, if we bid $8 million, our expected outcome, given all the uncertainties and decisions yet to come, is $4.52 million.

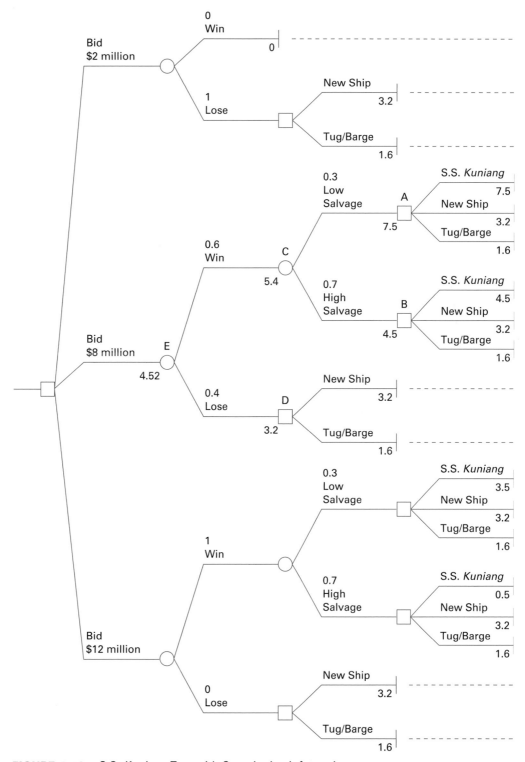

FIGURE 4.12 S.S. *Kuniang* Tree with Quantitative Information

Similar analyses lead to an expected value of $3.2 million for a bid of $2 million and an expected value of $3.29 million for a bid of $12 million. Thus, the best decision (among these three bid levels) is to bid $8 million. The completed tree is shown in Figure 4.13, where the expected values are shown next to each node. We have also used arrows to show which decisions should be taken.

We should point out that the expected profit of $4.52 million is *not* the payoff that NEES should expect to receive. Rather, like all expected values, it is the probability-weighted average of all the outcomes that can occur. Expected values represent a way of summarizing the results of an uncertain process in just one figure. They are the most frequent means of summarizing the value of a chance node, given the values and probabilities corresponding to each of its states. But this is not done simply for convenience. Faced with a series of decisions to make where uncertainty plays a role, the decision maker's best choices are the ones that maximize the expected value of uncertain outcomes, provided that none of the states represents a threat to the viability of the company.

Should we wish to look beyond the expected value as a measure of value, the tree also lets us determine the full range of outcomes and their associated probabilities. Examining the tree in Figure 4.13, we can see that if we lose the auction, we make $3.2 million, and the probability that this will occur is 0.4. If we win and the salvage value is low, we make $7.5 million. The probability of this occurring is the probability of winning (0.6) times the probability of a low salvage value (0.3), or 0.18. On the other hand, if we win and the salvage value is high, we make $4.5 million with probability 0.42 (= 0.6 × 0.7). These three possible outcomes are shown as a probability distribution in Figure 4.14, along with the expected value, which lies at the center of gravity of the three possible outcomes. Note that the probabilities of the three outcomes sum to 1.0, which is a check to confirm that we have constructed a valid probability distribution.

The detailed analysis of the SS *Kuniang* decision in Figure 4.13 illustrates all the important features of a decision-tree analysis. First, the expected value of the optimal decision is the probability-weighted average of the outcomes, taking into account future optimal decisions. Second, even under the set of optimal decisions, there is a range of potential economic outcomes with corresponding probabilities. This probability distribution can be used to understand the risks associated with the optimal decision. For example, there is a 40 percent chance in this case that we will make only $3.2 million; on the other hand, there is a 18 percent chance that we will make $7.5 million. We refer to the probabilities of extreme outcomes as **tail probabilities.**

Decision trees can be evaluated by hand, as we have done in this example, or within a spreadsheet. Specialized add-ins, which preserve the tree structure of the problem, are available for this purpose but are beyond the scope of this book.[1] Alternatively, we can build a simple spreadsheet model for the *Kuniang* example. Only two specialized mathematical operations are needed for the tree: calculating the maximum value at decision nodes and calculating the expected value at chance nodes. One advantage of the spreadsheet approach in this case is that we can introduce the bid level as a parameter and optimize its value directly, without considering each discrete value separately. Our spreadsheet is shown in Figure 4.15.

---

[1] See, for example, Treeplan at the Web site www.treeplan.com.

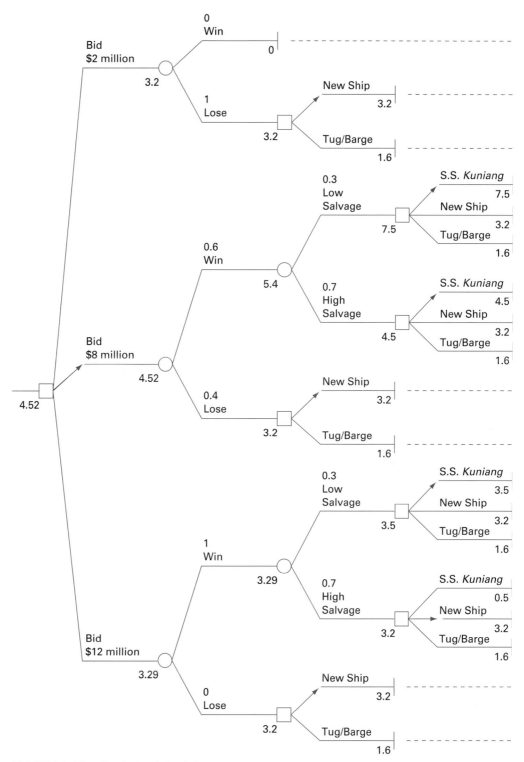

FIGURE 4.13 Analysis of the S.S. *Kuniang* Tree

FIGURE 4.14
Probability Distribution for Profits

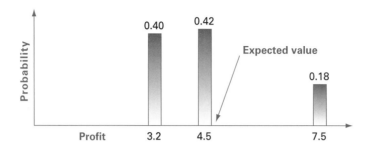

FIGURE 4.15
Spreadsheet Analysis of the S.S. *Kuniang* Tree

SSKuniang.xls

Bid	Exp.Profit
	3.410
2.0	3.200
2.5	3.645
3.0	4.040
3.5	4.385
4.0	4.680
4.5	4.925
5.0	5.120
5.5	5.265
6.0	5.360
6.5	5.405
7.0	5.400
7.5	5.345
8.0	5.240
8.5	5.085
9.0	4.880
9.5	4.670
10.0	4.488
10.5	4.271
11.0	4.019
11.5	3.732
12.0	3.410

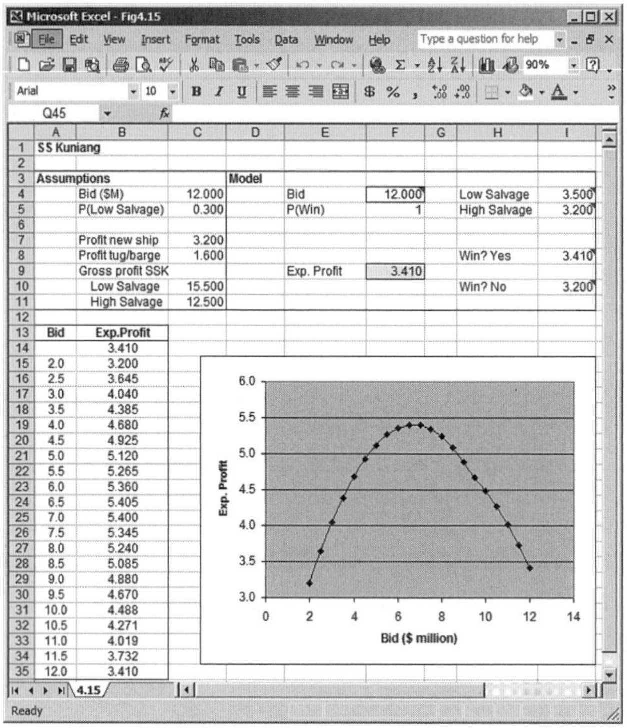

Given a bid level and the other parameters, the model first calculates the probability of winning the auction (cell F5). We use a simple formula for the probability of winning for any particular bid:

$$P(\text{Win}) = (Bid - 2)/10, \quad \text{for } 2 <= Bid <= 12$$

where the variable *Bid* represents the size of the bid in millions of dollars. This formula is consistent with the assumption that we lose for sure with a bid of \$2 million and that we win for sure with a bid of \$12 million. In cells I4 and I5, we calculate the gross profit for the *Kuniang,* given that we win, for the two salvage levels. In cell I8, we calculate the expected value of these two outcomes, while in I10 we calculate the expected profit if we lose the auction. Finally, in cell F9, we calculate the expected profit based on the winning and losing states and their probabilities. By comparing different values of the bid, as shown in the accompanying table and graph, we can estimate that the best bid level is about \$6 million.

Principles for Building and Analyzing Decision Trees

Decision trees can be built using a fairly standard procedure. Judgment is required, however, in determining which decisions and uncertainties are critical to the situation and therefore must be captured in the tree, as well as in selecting the specific choices and states to recognize. Beginners tend to draw overly complex trees. The more experienced analyst starts with a small number of nodes and a small number of outcomes and expands only when the results suggest that more detail is required. Here is a general procedure for constructing trees:

- Determine the essential decisions and uncertainties.
- Place the decisions and uncertainties in temporal sequence.
- Start the tree with a decision node representing the first decision.
- Select a representative but not exhaustive number of possible choices for the decision node.
- For each choice, draw a chance node representing the first uncertain event that follows the initial decision.
- Select a representative but not exhaustive number of possible states for the chance node.
- Continue to expand the tree with decision and chance nodes until the overall outcome can be evaluated.

While decision trees can be used to develop a purely qualitative understanding of a situation, they usually lead to a quantitative analysis. This analysis can identify which decisions are best and can construct the probability distribution of results. To carry out this analysis, we need two types of information: the probability for each possible state and the overall value of arriving at the end of the tree along a particular path. Here is the rollback procedure for analyzing trees:

- Start from the last set of nodes—those leading to the ends of the paths.
- For each chance node, calculate the expected value as a probability-weighted average of the values corresponding to the branches.
- Replace each chance node by its expected value.
- For each decision node, find the best value (maximum benefit or minimum cost) among the choices corresponding to the branches.
- Replace each decision node by the best value and note which choice is best.
- Continue evaluating chance nodes and decision nodes, backward in sequence, until the first node is resolved.

In the rollback procedure, any chance node, or any decision node, can be evaluated once the nodes connected to its emanating branches have been evaluated. In that way, the calculations move from the end of the tree toward the beginning, ultimately identifying the optimal choice at the initial decision node.

EXAMPLE

A Patent-Infringement Suit

One of our corporate competitors is threatening us with a lawsuit for patent infringement. The competitor is already in court in a similar lawsuit against another firm. One option open to us is to settle out of court now; the alternative is to wait until the other suit is settled before taking action. If the competitor loses the other suit, it will not pursue its action against us. If, on the other hand, the competitor wins, it is likely (but not certain) to sue us. If the competitor sues at that point, we can settle, go to trial and contest the patent-infringement claim, or go to trial and concede the patent infringement but fight the settlement amount. In either case, of course, we will either win or lose in court.

Figure 4.16 shows a decision tree for this case. The first decision is whether to settle now or wait for the outcome of the competitor's current suit. If that suit fails, we will not be sued, and the tree ends at that point. However, if the competitor wins that suit, it may sue us. This outcome is shown as a chance node. Again, if there is no suit, the tree ends. If the opponent does sue, we have the three choices shown on the tree. Finally, the outcome of each of the trial branches is shown as random.

One essential feature of legal proceedings is that both parties have a series of options. This example illustrates how decisions typically alternate with random events. In the specific scenario of the example, the random events are either the decisions of opponents or the results of trials. The objective of a quantitative analysis in this case is not simply to determine the optimal decision, but also to choose an appropriate value for settling the suit now. The first step is to evaluate the expected outcome if we wait. In Figure 4.16, we have

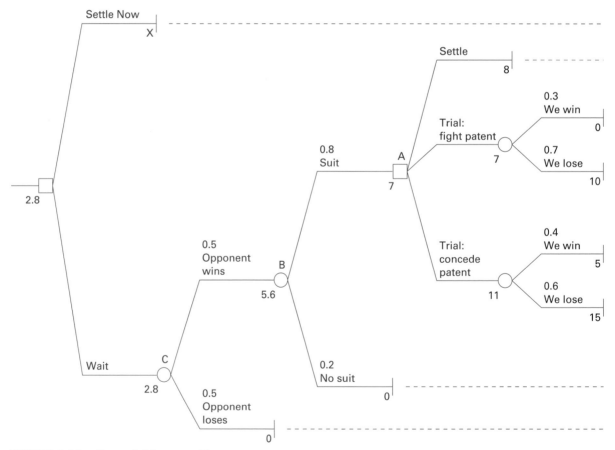

FIGURE 4.16   Patent-Infringement Tree

included the necessary probabilities and outcome values. Here, the outcomes are all costs, so the objective is to minimize expected cost.

We roll back the tree from right to left, calculating expected values at chance nodes and minimizing costs at decision nodes. If the opponent wins the current suit and sues us, we have three choices (node A): Settle, Go to Trial / Fight the Patent, or Go to Trial / Concede the Patent. The expected values for the last two options are $7 million and $11 million, respectively. Since settling at this stage costs us $8 million, the lowest-cost choice is to Go to Trial / Fight the Patent.

At node B, we will either be sued and lose $7 million in expected value, or not be sued and lose nothing. Given that the probability of a suit is 0.8, the expected value at node B is $5.6 million ($= 0.8 \times 7 + 0.2 \times 0$). At node C, we have a 50 percent chance of losing $5.6 million and a 50 percent chance of losing nothing. The expected value here is $2.8 million ($= 0.5 \times 5.6 + 0.5 \times 0$).

Now we can see that if we could settle the suit today for $2.8 million, we would be no better or worse off than if we were to wait, at least in terms of expected costs. But the risks of these two choices are quite different. No risks attach to settling now. On the other hand, if we wait, then we have a 72 percent chance of losing nothing and a 28 percent chance of losing $10 million. [We lose nothing in three cases: if the opponent loses the current suit (probability 0.5), if the opponent wins and does not sue (probability $0.1 = 0.5 \times 0.2$), and if the opponent wins and sues and we win (probability $0.12 = 0.5 \times 0.8 \times 0.3$). The probabilities of these outcomes sum to 0.72.] Given the 28 percent chance of an outcome we'd like to avoid, it might even be preferable to offer somewhat more than $2.8 million to settle immediately.

Decision trees are particularly appropriate for situations like those we have illustrated, where there are just a few uncertainties and a few decisions. By contrast, trees with many decisions and events can become unwieldy. When there are many uncertainties, the calculations become tedious if done by hand, and they become error-prone if done on a spreadsheet. In principle, we can imagine the limiting case in which a large number of discrete branches at a chance node are instead represented by a continuous distribution. Unfortunately, the process of calculating expected values, while straightforward for simple discrete distributions, can become impractical with continuous distributions. Simulation is the tool of choice when we have a large number of uncertainties, especially when these are represented by continuous distributions. Simulation is also a practical method for analyzing decisions with uncertainty when the underlying model is highly complex, as we illustrate in Chapter 9.

NETWORK DIAGRAMS

Network diagrams (or **flow diagrams**) provide a visual modeling tool for situations in which material flows through a system. One example would be consumer products flowing through a physical distribution system; another would be cash in an investment account accumulating over time periods. Thus, the material that "flows" could be physical or nonphysical, and the system could be dispersed geographically or in time. As with influence charts, network diagrams show the relationships among elements of a problem, and they delineate the boundaries of the system under study. For the analyst, network diagrams can also be useful in organizing the analysis by making sure that no important elements are overlooked. A diagram may not provide all of the analysis, but it can often help identify the elements that have to be considered.

In general terms, a **network** is a collection of connected elements. The elements could be factories, bank accounts, people, and so on. The connections among factories could be delivery routes, the connections among bank accounts could be electronic funds-transfer routes, and the connections among people could be organizational reporting relationships. In a network diagram, the elements are shown as circles and boxes (or **nodes**) and the connections as arrows (or **arcs**). Many different kinds of systems lend themselves to network modeling, where the analysis of the model provides insight into the nature of the activities or flows that occur in the network. In what follows, we present three examples where a network diagram can organize the modeling effort as well as provide a convenient place to perform some of the analysis. For each example, we give a systematic procedure for developing the network diagram.

EXAMPLE

Distribution at Western Paper

The Western Paper Company manufactures paper at two factories (F1 and F2) on the West Coast. Their products are shipped by rail to a pair of depots (D1 and D2), one in the Midwest and one in the South. At the depots, the products are repackaged and sent by truck to three regional warehouses (W1, W2, and W3) around the country, in response to replenishment orders.

Each of the factories has a known monthly production capacity, and the three regional warehouses have placed their demands for next month. Knowing the costs of transporting goods from factories to depots and from depots to warehouses, Western Paper is interested in planning its logistics operations and costs for the month.

The distribution network for Western Paper contains three kinds of elements—factories, depots, and warehouses. The routes of flow for paper include rail routes from factories to depots and truck routes from depots to warehouses. In what follows, we specify the steps in building a flow diagram for the distribution network (Figure 4.17).

Inputs and outputs. At Western Paper, input flows originate at the factories, and we can view the capacities as inputs. The outputs are deliveries to meet demand at the warehouses. Thus, we will have two input nodes and three output nodes in our diagram, each indicated by a triangle. In addition, the depots represent intermediate nodes. Material flows into the depots from the factories and out of the depots to the three warehouses.

FIGURE 4.17
Network Diagram for
Western Paper

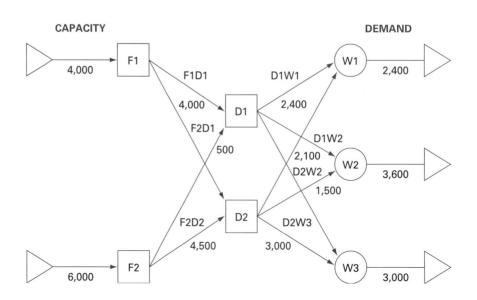

Capacities and demands. The capacities at the factories limit the flow. We might list the capacities in a simple table such as the following:

Factory	F1	F2
Capacity	4,000	6,000

With a similar table, we can record the demands at each of the warehouses:

Warehouse	W1	W2	W3
Demand	2,400	3,600	3,000

Certain elements may not have capacities. That would be the case for the nodes representing depots in this problem. At these intermediate nodes, there is apparently unlimited space available, the assumption being that Western Paper is able to obtain whatever space it needs in a public warehouse.

Decisions. Once the nodes of the diagram are determined, the next step is to identify the arcs, or the routes on which flows occur. While some flows in a network may be dictated by inputs and outputs, or by technology, other flows are redirected at the discretion of the decision maker. Thus, at some points in the system, flows are determined by conscious decisions. We refer to these as decision nodes, or simply **decisions,** and we show them as boxes in the diagram. Decisions determine the flow along some or all of the arcs.

In the case of Western Paper, all possible factory-depot pairs represent possible routes of flow by rail. Similarly, all possible depot-warehouse pairs represent possible routes of flow by truck. Each of these arcs should be labeled with a distinct name. For example, the flow from factory F1 to depot D2 can be labeled F1D2.

At this stage, we have produced a network diagram that reflects the nodes and arcs we have identified, along with the relevant capacities and demands. Showing nodes as boxes underscores the fact that there are decisions affecting the flows at those locations. On the arcs is a set of shipment quantities that make up a proposal for next month's distribution plan at Western Paper. At this point, the diagram makes it possible to perform some basic analyses related to this proposed plan.

Feasibility check. The first step is to confirm the feasibility of this plan. This means making sure that the flow pattern can be implemented. At factory F2, for instance, we compare the total flow out of the factory node (5,000) with the capacity (6,000), to confirm that the plan is workable. A similar comparison can be done, on the network diagram itself, for F1.

A similar check must be made for the outputs. At warehouse W2, for instance, we compare the total flow into the warehouse (3,600) with the demand (3,600), to confirm that the planned deliveries meet the demand. A similar comparison can be done for the other two warehouses.

Finally, we must check that the flows at the depots are feasible. At depot D1, we compare the total flow into the depot (4,500) with the total flow out of the depot (4,500). A requirement that the total flow into a node must equal the total flow out of the node is sometimes called a **material-balance** constraint. Another material-balance constraint applies at depot D2.

Costs and revenues. Another part of the analysis traces the financial implications of the proposed flow pattern. In general, this type of analysis requires an accounting of the various costs and revenues in order to determine profit. In a distribution problem, such as Western Paper's, we find ourselves dealing with a database that includes the unit cost for each route in the system, so the focus tends to be on costs, not on revenues. The unit costs can be displayed in a pair of tables, as shown below. The first table shows the unit cost of rail shipment from factory to depot, while the second table shows the unit cost of truck shipment from depot to warehouse.

Depot

Factory	D1	D2
F1	$0.56	$0.58
F2	0.60	0.66

Warehouse

Depot	W1	W2	W3
D1	$1.25	$1.50	$1.60
D2	1.45	1.30	1.28

In Figure 4.18, we have relabeled the same diagram with the costs and quantities in order to make the cost calculations. The figure ignores the zero shipments on some of the arcs. By multiplying the volume on each route by its unit cost, we can compute the total rail cost at $5,510 and the total truck cost at $11,940—for a total distribution cost of $17,450.

Western Paper's distribution system lends itself to a particular type of network diagram that is often called a **transshipment** network. To demonstrate some other features of network diagrams, we next look at a somewhat different example.

EXAMPLE

Planning for Tuition Expenses

Two parents want to provide for their daughter's college expenses with some of the $80,000 they have recently inherited. They hope to set aside part of the money and establish an account that would cover the needs of their daughter's college education, which begins four years from now, with a one-time investment. Their estimate is that first-year college expenses will come to $24,000 and will increase $2,000 per year during each of the remaining three years of college. The following investment instruments are available:

Investment	Available	Matures	Return at Maturity
A	Every year	in 1 year	5%
B	In years 1, 3, 5, 7	in 2 years	11%
C	In years 1, 4	in 3 years	16%
D	In year 1	in 7 years	44%

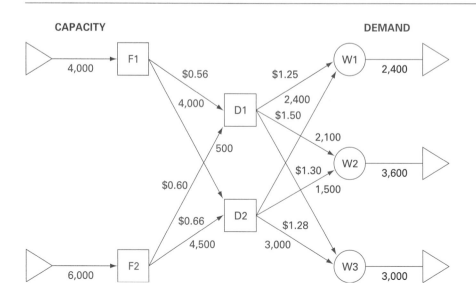

FIGURE 4.18
Cost Calculation for
Western Paper

In this case, a key concern is the timing of various financial flows. The nodes in the diagram of Figure 4.19 correspond to points in time, and we can think of them as representing the start of this year, the start of next year, and so on. (For convenience, we treat the first year as year 1 and its starting point as time 0.)

Inputs and outputs. The one input flow is the initial fund (shown as IF), which will be established at time 0, corresponding to the start of this year. The four outputs are the tuition expenses anticipated at the start of years 5–8.

Capacities and demands. The initial fund is actually a decision as well as an input, and it does constrain the initial investments. Therefore, we show it as a box in the diagram to emphasize that it is a decision. However, once the initial fund is determined, its size will limit the choice of the four initial investments. The four outputs are the tuition expenses anticipated at the start of years 5–8. These are known quantities, analogous to the demands at Western Paper's warehouses, and they are indicated by output triangles.

Decisions. The flows in this network correspond to the amounts invested. Investment A can be selected in each year, so we use A1 to represent the amount invested in year 1, A2 for the amount invested in year 2, and so on, up to A7. Investment B can be selected only every other year, so we use B1 to represent the amount invested in year 1, B3 for the amount invested in year 3, and B5 for the amount invested in year 5. Similarly, we use C1, C4, and D1 to complete the investment alternatives. In the network diagram, a one-year investment instrument connects two successive nodes, while a two-year instrument skips a node, and so on.

All nodes in this model correspond to decisions about the allocation of financial assets. Not only is there an allocation decision needed initially, to distribute funds among the instruments available at the start, but there are also subsequent decisions needed as investments mature. On occasion, as at the start of year 2, there is only one investment alternative given, so the allocation decision is trivial. However, in most years, an allocation is needed.

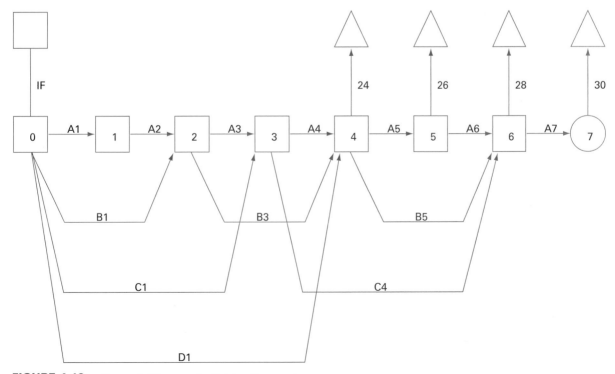

FIGURE 4.19   Network Diagram for Tuition Payments

Each arc represents the investment in a particular financial asset over a specified period of time. As a result, each such asset grows in value by accumulating interest at a rate given in the problem scenario. Thus, on the diagram, we can think of the head of the arc as being worth more than the tail, reflecting the appreciation of the corresponding asset. While we write A1 to represent the investment in A at time 0, we know that when the arc arrives at the start of year 2, it is worth $1.05 \times A1$, due to the 5 percent annual return. In order to make the tracking of funds on the diagram more convenient, we can split each arc into two parts, as shown in Figure 4.20. Here, a circle depicts the transformation of its input flow to a corresponding output flow. When such a node represents investment A, the output flow is 5 percent larger than the input flow; when the node represents investment B, the output flow is 11 percent larger, and so on. In order to label the outflows from such nodes, we may need to make some brief side calculations.

As an example, suppose the initial investment is $80,000, split equally among the four instruments available at the outset. Furthermore, suppose that we follow a rule that calls for an investment of $20,000 in A whenever there is an allocation to make. We can now determine whether this plan is feasible.

Feasibility check. Given the equal split dictated by our rule, the output flows from the initial node are $20,000 each in A1, B1, C1, and D1. A1 is transformed into $21,000 by its 5 percent return, and the only alternative at the start of year 2 is to reinvest this amount as A2. Then, A2 is transformed into $22,050, and B1 into $22,200, so that the total input into year 3 comes to $44,250. Following our rule, $20,000 is allocated to A3, and the rest ($24,250) to B3. At the start of year 4, the input flows are $21,000 from A3 and $23,200 from C1—for a total of $44,200. Following our rule, $20,000 is allocated to A4, and the rest ($24,200) to C4.

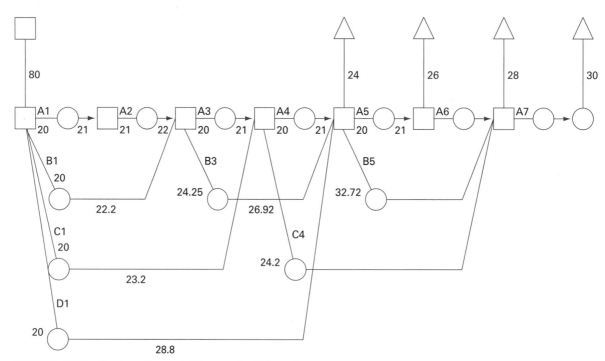

FIGURE 4.20 Revised Network Diagram for Tuition Payments

At the start of year 5, there are three input flows, totaling about $76,720. The output flows are $24,000 to cover the first tuition payment, $20,000 for A5 under our rule, and the remainder ($32,720) for B5.

At the start of year 6, there is only one input flow, $21,000 from A5. However, there is a need to cover a tuition payment of $26,000. Thus, the calculations on the diagram allow us to see that our investment rule will not be feasible. On the other hand, if we simply raise A5 to $25,000, all tuition payments will be covered, and we will wind up with a surplus of more than $3,500 (Figure 4.21).

The flow diagrams in Figures 4.20 and 4.21 contain inputs, outputs, capacities, and demands—just like the Western Paper diagram—as well as allocation decisions. The new element is a **transformation node,** for which the output flow is larger than the input flow due to financial returns. In principle, transformation nodes can work to reduce flows as well as to increase them. The next example provides a case in point.

EXAMPLE

Production at Delta Oil

The refining process at Delta Oil Company separates crude oil into components that eventually yield gasoline, heating oil, jet fuel, lubricating oil, and other petroleum products. In particular, gasoline is produced from crude oil by either a distillation process alone or by a distillation process followed by a catalytic-cracking process. The outputs of these processes are subsequently blended to obtain different grades of gasoline.

The distillation tower at Delta's refinery uses five barrels of crude oil to produce three barrels of distillate and two barrels of other "low-end" by-products. Some distillate is blended into gasoline products; the rest becomes feedstock for the catalytic cracker.

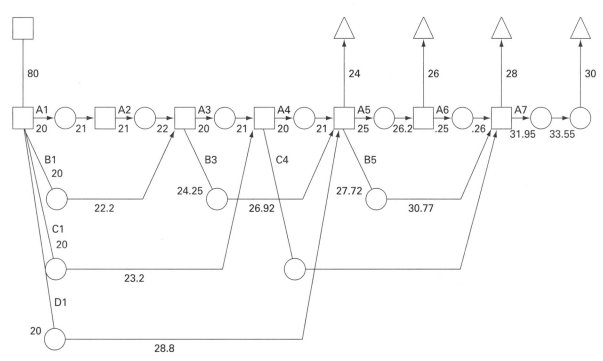

FIGURE 4.21   Feasible Plan for Tuition Payments

The catalytic-cracking process produces high-quality catalytic gasoline (or catalytic, for short) from the feedstock. Delta's catalytic cracker requires 2.5 barrels of distillate to produce 1.6 barrels of catalytic and 1 barrel of "high-end" by-products. (The cracking process creates output volume that exceeds input volume.)

Finally, distillate from the distillation tower is blended with catalytic to make regular gasoline and premium gasoline. The blend of distillate and catalytic must be at least 50 percent catalytic to meet the quality requirements of regular and at least 65 percent catalytic to meet the quality requirements of premium.

Planning and scheduling operations at Delta's refinery must take into account the capacity requirements of the equipment while matching product flows with demands in the various product markets. A diagram for Delta Oil is shown in Figure 4.22. In this diagram, the nodes represent stages of the manufacturing process (purchase, production, and distribution).

Inputs and outputs. At Delta Oil, there is only one input, described as crude oil, but there are several outputs. These include by-products (broken down into low-end and high-end categories) and gasoline products (consisting of regular and premium). Thus, we can distinguish four outputs. The one input and four outputs are represented by triangles in the diagram.

Transformation processes. In our previous example, flows were transformed by the process of financial appreciation. In a production environment, transformation nodes are associated with changing one kind of flow into another. At Delta Oil, there are two processes—the distillation tower and the catalytic cracker—which are represented as nodes in the network. Distillation takes crude oil as input, and it produces distillate and low-end by-products. Cracking takes feedstock (which in this case happens to be distillate) as input, and it produces catalytic and high-end by-products.

Capacity levels. In some cases, capacities may be unlimited, as we saw in the depots of the Western Paper network, but for production processes, capacities are usually limited. When we come to the analysis, we will want to know the restrictions these processes

FIGURE 4.22
Network Diagram for Delta Oil

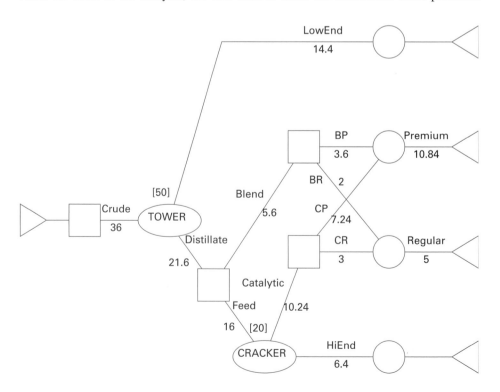

impose on the rates of flow through the network. In the case of Delta Oil, the distillation tower has a capacity of 50,000 barrels per day, while the catalytic cracker has a capacity of 20,000 barrels per day. These capacities are noted in brackets on the diagram.

Decisions. Delta Oil's production system allows for a decision regarding how much of the distillate generated by the distillation tower should be sent as feedstock to the catalytic cracker and how much should be sent directly to gasoline blending. There are also two decisions regarding the blending of distillate and catalytic. Since the outputs are "regular" and "premium," we must decide how much distillate and how much catalytic should be allocated to each. Decisions are again represented in the diagram by boxes.

Note the distinction between transformation nodes and decision nodes. For a transformation node, outputs may take a different form than the inputs, and the total output quantity may not equal the total input quantity. For example, crude oil is an input to the distillation tower, but the outputs are distillate and by-products. On the other hand, for a decision node, the outputs are the same material as the inputs. For example, the distillate that comes out of the tower is still distillate when routed to the cracker as feedstock or when blended with gasoline. In addition, a material-balance requirement holds at each decision node: the sum of the quantities flowing in must equal the sum flowing out.

Once the nodes have been determined, we can place arcs in the diagram to represent every possible flow route. Each of these arcs should be labeled with a distinct name. For example, the distillate that we allocate to the cracker is labeled Feed, while the distillate that we allocate for blending is labeled Blend. Premium gasoline is made from a combination of BP (from Blend) and CP (from Catalytic), while regular gasoline involves a combination of BR and CR. Labeling each arc makes it possible to trace the entire pattern of flows in the network.

The network diagram allows us to analyze various production plans for Delta Oil. For example, we might simply check a proposed plan for consistency. We would need to know, of course, how much crude and how much of the four outputs were to be produced. But, having created the diagram and having identified the embedded decisions, we also know that we must obtain information on the feedstock quantity and how the gasoline is split between regular and premium.

Feasibility check. Suppose we were asked to evaluate a plan to buy 36,000 barrels of crude oil and produce approximately 16,000 barrels of gasoline and 21,000 barrels of by-products. These figures would not be sufficient to label all the flows in the diagram. However, if further inquiry revealed that 16,000 barrels would be fed to the catalytic cracker and that regular gasoline would be made up of 2,000 barrels of distillate blend along with 3,000 barrels of catalytic, then we could label the entire diagram. First, we calculate the outflow from the tower, using the input volume of 36,000 and the fact that distillate represents 60 percent of the output. This places the distillate volume at 21,600. Since 16,000 is fed into the cracker, the remaining 5,600 must be allocated as Blend. Furthermore, we can calculate the outflow from the cracker, using the input volume of 16,000 and the fact that Catalytic represents 64 percent of the output. This places the catalytic volume at 10,240. With Blend and Catalytic known, and with BR and CR specified at 2,000 and 3,000, respectively, we can use material-balance arithmetic to calculate BP as 3,600 and CP as 7,240. Figure 4.22 contains the numerical summary.

With some side calculations, we can also confirm that this plan calls for regular gasoline consisting of 60 percent catalytic and premium gasoline consisting of 66.8 percent catalytic, both above the minimum levels that are required. In addition, the crude-oil volume and the feedstock quantity are well within the capacity limits of the distillation tower and the catalytic cracker, so the proposed plan is a feasible one.

Costs and revenues. In the case of Delta Oil, there are purchase costs for crude oil and operating costs for the two processes. There are also revenues for each of the four products sent to market. These unit costs and revenues are shown in the following table:

Activity	Item	Cost per bbl.	Price per bbl.
Purchase	Crude	$28	
Distillation	Crude	5	
Cracking	Feed	6	
Sales	Low-end		$25
Sales	High-end		38
Sales	Regular		40
Sales	Premium		42

In Figure 4.23, we label the diagram with these values, in order to evaluate the profitability of the proposed plan. We multiply purchase quantity by unit purchase cost, and we multiply operating levels by unit operating costs; these calculations give us a figure for total cost. When we multiply sales quantities by unit prices, we obtain total revenue. Finally, we can calculate profit as the difference between total revenue and total cost. As shown in the figure, the proposed plan leads to a loss of nearly $64,000 for the month. Evidently, Delta Oil will want to use the diagram to search for a more profitable plan.

SUMMARY

Although we emphasize the use of spreadsheets in modeling, there are often many useful steps that can be taken before opening up a workbook. In this chapter, we have discussed a number of tools that reinforce the visual aspects of modeling activity. The ability to visualize model structure (and to communicate that visualization) can be a powerful and effective factor in an expert's set of modeling skills.

FIGURE 4.23
Profit Calculation for
Delta Oil

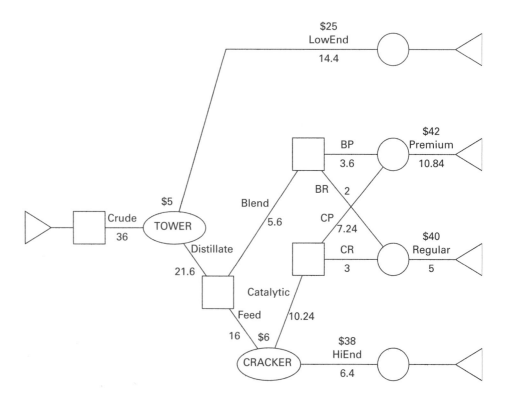

Influence charts provide a way to begin organizing a model. They start with the model outputs and break them down into constituent parts. By following the logical trail from what we want to learn back to what we already know, or what we can readily find out, an influence chart allows us to map out the main structure of our model. At the same time, the chart helps us distinguish among inputs, outputs, and decisions. Moreover, an influence chart reinforces a top-down approach, which helps us avoid the traps associated with bottom-up analysis.

Outlines serve to organize our models into categories, subcategories, and individual elements. They are particularly helpful when our models resemble accounting statements, because we can draw on accounting definitions and relationships in structuring our outline. Thus, the elements of income statements, balance sheets, and cash-flow statements can often serve as a framework for our modeling logic. In addition, these model forms communicate effectively with clients who are more familiar with accounting information than they are with model output.

A decision tree is a somewhat specialized tool for recognizing the role of random factors in a model. Trees help us distinguish between decisions and random events, and, more importantly, they help us sort out the sequence in which they occur. Probability trees provide us with an opportunity to consider the possible states in a random environment when there are several sources of uncertainty, and they can become components of decision trees. Using the rollback procedure, we can identify those decisions that optimize the expected value of our criterion. Furthermore, we can produce information in the form of a probability distribution to help assess the risk associated with any decision in the tree.

Network diagrams represent another tool that helps us specify the boundary of a model and sort out its major elements. In networks, we trace the progress of a certain material as it moves through a complicated system. We begin by identifying inputs and outputs and by noting whatever capacities and demands occur at those points. We then look within the network for decisions that reallocate flows at the various stages of progress. Network diagrams allow us to represent transformations that commonly occur in production or financial systems, as well as material-balance relationships that apply to particular allocation decisions. The diagrams themselves serve as tools to help test the feasibility of any proposed plan, and they provide a laboratory for basic cost and profitability analysis.

These four kinds of visual tools can be useful at the outset of a modeling project, to help build an initial structure and to identify key elements of that structure. In addition, in the case of network diagrams, optimization techniques can build on basic diagramming tools. We highlight this approach in Chapter 8.

REFERENCES

Some related material can be found in the following books:

Clemen, Robert T. 1996. *Making Hard Decisions*, 2d ed. Pacific Grove, CA: Duxbury.

Golub, Andrew Lang. 1997. *Decision Analysis: An Integrated Approach*. New York: John Wiley.

Kammen, Daniel M., and David M. Hassenzahl. 1999. *Should We Risk It?* Princeton, NJ: Princeton University Press.

EXERCISES

Influence Charts

1. The Boeing Company faces a critical strategic choice in its competition with Airbus S.A.S. for the long-haul flight segment: Should it design and build a super-747 model that can carry 550 passengers at speeds around 350 mph, or a plane that can fly at 95 percent of the speed of sound but carry only about 350 passengers? Draw an influence diagram for this decision.

2. Many forms of cancer can be cured or controlled if identified early. Blood tests exist for many cancers, but they are costly and do not provide 100 percent reliable results. Each test would involve drawing one blood sample and testing it for between five and ten forms of cancer. Each test has its own accuracy, both for false positives and for false negatives. Some cancers can be cured with high probability when detected by blood test, while others either cannot be cured or can only be slowed. Would it be cost-effective for HMOs to offer cancer screening every year to patients more than, say, fifty years old? Draw an influence diagram.

3. The Red Cross provides about 40 percent of the replacement blood supply for the United States. The available donor base has been shrinking for years, and although increased advertising has kept Red Cross supplies adequate, the time is approaching when demand will outstrip supply. For many years, the Red Cross has refused to pay donors for blood, on the grounds that to do so would "put the blood supply of the country at risk." Evaluate a policy under which the Red Cross would pay each donor a set fee. Draw an influence diagram

4. Refer to the Retirement Planning case. Review the problem statement that was generated for this case in conjunction with the corresponding exercises in Chapters 2 and 3. (If this has not yet been done, develop the problem statement as a first step.) Draw an influence diagram for the case based on the problem statement already developed, modifying it if necessary.

5. Refer to the Draft TV Commercials case. Review the problem statement that was generated for this case in conjunction with the corresponding exercises in Chapters 2 and 3. (If this has not yet been done, develop the problem statement as a first step.) Draw an influence diagram for the case based on the problem statement already developed, modifying it if necessary.

6. Refer to the Icebergs for Kuwait case. Review the problem statement that was generated for this case in conjunction with the corresponding exercises in Chapters 2 and 3. (If this has not yet been done, develop the problem statement as a first step.) Draw an influence diagram for the case based on the problem statement already developed, modifying it if necessary.

7. Refer to the Racquetball Racket case. Review the problem statement that was generated for this case in conjunction with the corresponding exercises in Chapters 2 and 3. (If this has not yet been done, develop the problem statement as a first step.) Draw an influence diagram for the case based on the problem statement already developed, modifying it if necessary.

Outlines

8. You have been asked to serve as chair of a professional conference that will take place six months from now. You must arrange for the physical requirements of the event, which include hotel and room space, meals, vendor space, and breakout space. You must also arrange for advertising in professional and public media. You must hire and train staff to accept reservations and communicate with attendees, both before and during the event. Finally, you must anticipate and budget for unforeseen events. Develop the outline of a budget for this project.

9. Refer to the XYZ Company case. Compose a list of categories that will allow an analyst to predict monthly cash needs and profitability for the first six months of the year, for the case where there are payment lags and the firm is using accrual accounting.

10. Refer to the Damon Appliances case. Compose a list of categories for the pro forma income statement and the pro forma balance sheet, as desired by the CFO.

Decision Trees

11. Copy Makers Inc. (CMI) has just received a credit request from a new customer who wants to purchase a copying machine. As input to its decision of whether to grant credit, CMI has made the following estimates and assumptions:

   ■ If CMI denies the customer credit, there is a 20 percent chance that the customer will buy the copying machine with cash anyway.

- If CMI grants credit, there is a 70 percent chance the customer will be a good credit risk.
- If CMI grants credit and the customer is a good credit risk, CMI will collect 100 percent of the purchase price.
- If CMI grants credit and the customer is a bad credit risk, CMI has two options. Under the first option, CMI would continue to send the customer a bill and hope it is eventually paid. Under this option, CMI will collect 100 percent, 50 percent, or 0 percent of the amount owed, with probabilities 0.3, 0.5, and 0.2, respectively. Under the second option, CMI would vigorously pursue the collection of the amount owed. To do so would cost CMI 25 percent of the amount owed, regardless of the amount eventually collected. Under this second option, CMI will again collect 100 percent, 50 percent, or 0 percent of the amount owed, with probabilities 0.1, 0.2, and 0.7, respectively.
- The copy machine sells for $8,000 and costs CMI $5,000. Nonvigorous enforcement has no cost, while vigorous enforcement costs $2,000.

Draw a decision tree for CMI's problem. Using the rollback procedure, determine the optimal decision and its expected value.

12. TCS Corporation has recently decided to manufacture a product in its own facilities rather than outsource to Asian manufacturers. Its new plant will last about ten years. TCS is considering two options: build a large plant now that will have sufficient capacity to handle demand into the foreseeable future, or build a small plant that can be expanded two years later, after demand is better known. TCS will not expand the small plant unless demand in the first two years exceeds a threshold level.

    TCS assumes that the level of demand in subsequent years will be the same as in the first two years (e.g., if demand is high in the first two years, it will continue to be high in the next eight years).

    Draw a decision tree for TCS's problem. What additional data are needed to determine the optimal decision?

13. A small manufacturer uses an industrial boiler in its production process. A new boiler can be purchased for $10,000. As the boiler gets older, its maintenance expenses increase while its resale value declines. Since the boiler will be exposed to heavy use, the probability of a breakdown increases every year.

    Assume that when a boiler breaks down, it can be used through the end of the year, after which it must be replaced with a new one. Also, assume that a broken-down boiler has no resale value.

    Some basic data are given in the table below:

Year of Operation	Expenses	Resale Value	Breakdown Probability
1	1,500	7,000	0.1
2	2,000	5,000	0.2
3	3,000	4,000	0.4
4	4,500	2,000	0.5
5	6,000	500	0.8

    Draw a decision tree for this problem. Using the rollback procedure, determine the optimal decision and its expected value.

14. Delta Electric Service is an electrical-utility company serving parts of several states. It is considering replacing some of its equipment at generating substations and is trying to decide whether it should replace an older, existing PCB transformer. (PCB is a toxic chemical known formally as polychlorinated biphenyl.) Although the PCB generator meets all current regulations, if an incident such as a fire were to occur, and PCB contamination caused harm either to neighboring businesses or farms, or to the environment, the company would be liable for damages. Recent court cases have shown that simply meeting regulations does not relieve a utility

of liability if an incident causes harm to others. In addition, courts have been awarding very large damages to individuals and businesses harmed by incidents involving hazardous material.

If Delta replaces the PCB transformer, no PCB incidents will occur, and the only cost will be the cost of the new transformer, estimated to be $85,000. Alternatively, if the company elects to keep the existing PCB transformer in operation, then, according to their consultants, there is a 50/50 chance that there will be a high likelihood of an incident or a low likelihood of an incident. For the case of a high likelihood of an incident, there is also a 0.004 probability that a fire will occur sometime during the remaining life of the transformer, and a 0.996 probability that no fire will occur. If a fire occurs, there is a 20 percent chance that it will be severe and the utility will incur a very high cost, whereas there is an 80 percent chance that it will be minor and the utility will incur a low cost. The high- and low-cost amounts, including both cleanup and damages, are estimated to be $100 million and $10 million, respectively, based on results from other incidents in the industry. For the case of a low likelihood of an incident, there is a 0.001 probability of a fire during the remaining life of the transformer, and a 0.999 probability of no fire. If a fire does occur, then the same probabilities exist for the severe and minor outcomes as in the previous case. In both cases, there will be no cost if no fire occurs.

Draw a decision tree for this problem. Using the rollback procedure, determine the optimal decision and its expected value.

Network Flow Diagrams

15. Refer to the Gulfport Oil case. Draw a network diagram showing the inputs, outputs, and flows in this problem.

Questions

a. Find a feasible set of flows consistent with the given information on input capacities, quality constraints, production capacities, and output requirements.

b. For the set of flows in (a), find the total profit.

16. Refer to the Coastal Refining Company case. Draw a network diagram showing the inputs, outputs, and flows in this problem.

Questions

a. Find a feasible set of flows consistent with the given information on input capacities, quality constraints, production capacities, and output requirements.

b. For the set of flows in (a), find the total profit.

17. Refer to the Quincy Chocolate case. Draw a network diagram showing the inputs, outputs, and flows in this problem.

Questions

a. Find a feasible set of flows consistent with an output of 2 million pounds of milk chocolate.

b. For the set of flows in (a), find the total profit.

18. Refer to the Workforce Management case. Draw a network diagram showing the inputs, outputs, and flows in this problem.

Questions

a. Find a feasible set of flows consistent with the given information on initial workforce size, monthly requirements, and other features of the problem.

b. For the set of flows in (a), find the total profit.

CHAPTER 5

SPREADSHEET ENGINEERING

INTRODUCTION

Builders of ships, bridges, and skyscrapers all spend considerable time and money planning the structure before they order concrete and steel. Even the builder of a modest house starts with blueprints and a plan of activities. Without detailed planning, complex structures cannot be built efficiently, and they sometimes fail in use. The same is true of spreadsheet models. Spreadsheets can be as important to a business as a bridge is to the users of a road network. If a business relies on a spreadsheet, the business should devote sufficient resources to ensuring that the spreadsheet is suitably *engineered*.

Advance planning can speed up the process of implementing a complex design. Some years ago, the auto industry learned that more resources invested in preproduction activities saved a great deal of money when a new car was being prepared for manufacturing. One of the major sources of efficiency in this case was avoiding cycles of rework and redesign. Without good planning, the need for design improvements is detected only after implementation has begun, and much of the implementation effort is wasted. The same is true of spreadsheet models: extra time spent in planning can actually *reduce* the overall time required to perform a spreadsheet analysis.

Sometimes, at the outset, it seems as if a spreadsheet project will be fairly straightforward. The flexibility of the spreadsheet environment seduces us into believing that we can jump right in and start entering formulas. Then, as we move further into the process of building the spreadsheet, it turns out that the project is a bit more complicated than it seemed at first. We encounter new user requirements, or we discover obscure logical cases. We redesign the spreadsheet on the fly, preserving some parts of the original design and reworking others. The smooth logical flow of the original spreadsheet gets disrupted. Rather quickly, a simple task becomes complicated, driven by a cycle of unanticipated needs followed by rework and additional testing. Before long, we face the prospect of a spreadsheet containing "spaghetti logic," and, as a result, we have reason to worry that the spreadsheet contains errors.

Advance planning can also help the designer avoid critical errors in a design. A mistake in the design of a building or bridge can cause it to collapse; a bug in a spreadsheet can lead to poor decisions and substantial losses. The available research suggests that many spreadsheets actually in use contain hidden errors. Learning how to avoid bugs is an essential aspect of spreadsheet modeling. Many analysts spend 80 percent of their time building (and fixing) models, and only 20 percent using them for analysis. With good design skills, that ratio can be reversed, so that analysts can spend the majority of their effort improving actual decisions.

In this chapter, we offer guidelines for engineering spreadsheets. Our motivation is to improve both the efficiency and the effectiveness with which spreadsheets are created. An *efficient* design process uses the minimum time and effort to achieve results. An *effective* process achieves results that meet the users' requirements. Although spreadsheet modeling is a creative process, and thus cannot be reduced to a simple recipe, every spreadsheet passes through a predictable series of stages. Accordingly, we organize our guidelines around these phases:

- designing
- building
- testing

We also use a simple example in this and several subsequent chapters to illustrate our precepts and methods.

ARE SPREADSHEETS ERROR-FREE?

Countless companies and individuals rely on spreadsheets every day. Most users assume their models are error-free. However, the available evidence suggests just the opposite: many, perhaps most, spreadsheets contain internal errors, and more errors are introduced as these spreadsheets are used and modified. Given this evidence, and the tremendous risks of relying on flawed spreadsheet models, it is absolutely essential to learn how to create spreadsheets that are as close to error-free as possible.

It is rare to read press reports on problems arising from erroneous spreadsheets. Most companies do not readily admit to these kinds of mistakes. However, the few reports that have surfaced are instructive. Dhebar, for example, reports on the case of a *Fortune* 500 company that relied on a spreadsheet model to evaluate investment proposals. The formulas and the discount rate in the model were established in the distant past, were never documented, and were made by someone who had left the company. Although the prime rate rose from 8 percent to more than 20 percent between 1973 and 1981, the spreadsheet was never updated to reflect the change, with presumably serious consequences to the quality of the investment decisions it supported.[1]

Savitz reports another case, at Fidelity Investments, where a spreadsheet was used to report distributions for various funds. For the huge Magellan Fund, a $4.32-per-share capital-gains distribution was forecast in November, and investors were notified. However, in December, the company announced that there would, in fact, be no distribution at all. A clerical worker had put the wrong sign in front of a $1.2 billion ledger entry. This created an apparent $2.3 billion gain in place of the real $0.1 billion loss. The error may have affected buyers, some of whom might have sold to avoid the distribution, thus missing a price rise. Others might have postponed their purchases to avoid the distribution, thus also missing the price rise.[2]

These two cases involve improper *use* of spreadsheets. But are spreadsheets themselves properly *built* in the first place? Apparently not, at least according to the evidence cited by Panko. He summarizes the results of seven field audits involving 367 real-world spreadsheets. Overall, 24 percent were found to contain material errors. Since 1997, 91 percent of the fifty-four spreadsheets tested contained errors, presumably because auditing methods have improved.[3] This evidence should be sufficient to put us all on notice that errors in spreadsheets are rampant and insidious.

Why are errors in spreadsheets so common? Traditional computer programming, which is much older than spreadsheet programming and is carried out largely by trained professionals, typically relies on elaborate and formalized development methods. One aspect of these methods is code inspection, which involves a line-by-line audit of finished computer

---

[1] Dhebar, A. "Managing the Quality of Quantitative Analysis," *Sloan Management Review* 34, (Winter 1993): 69–75.

[2] Savitz, E "Magellan Loses Its Compass," *Barron's* 74, (12 December 1994).

[3] Panko, R. "What We Know about Spreadsheet Errors," *Journal of End User Computing* 10, (Spring 1998): 15–21.

code by a team not involved in the original development. A typical code inspection finds errors in 5 percent of the lines of code written (and tested) by professional programmers. If this level of error rates characterizes professional programmers, how much more prevalent are errors among end-user programmers of spreadsheets?

Despite this evidence, very few corporations (and even fewer individuals) employ even the most basic design and inspection procedures. These procedures take time and effort, whereas one of the great appeals of spreadsheet modeling is that it is quick and easy for business analysts who are not professional programmers. But this ease of use is a delusion if the spreadsheets that result contain significant errors. One reason for the lack of careful design and testing procedures seems to be overconfidence. In one experiment, for example, subjects were asked whether they thought their spreadsheets contained errors. Only 18 percent said they suspected errors in their spreadsheets, while 86 percent of the spreadsheets actually contained errors.

Panko summarizes this evidence well:

> Overall, these studies show that many spreadsheets are large, complex, important, and affect many people. Yet [spreadsheet] development tends to be quite informal, and even trivial controls such as cell protection are not used in most cases. In [traditional] programming, code inspection and data testing are needed to reduce error rates after a module is developed. Yet code inspection is very infrequent [in spreadsheet programming], and while data testing is done, it lacks such rigors as the use of out-of-bounds data. *In general, end-user development in spreadsheeting seems to resemble programming practice in the 1950s and 1960s.*[4] [emphasis added]

Our purpose in this chapter is to provide practical but effective tools to help end users build error-free spreadsheets.

DESIGNING A SPREADSHEET

The essential first step in developing any spreadsheet model is to *design* it. We first offer some tips on good design practices for single-worksheet models, and we then discuss how to design an effective workbook composed of interconnected worksheets. To make our suggestions more tangible, we introduce the following example:

EXAMPLE

The Advertising Budget Decision

As product-marketing manager, one of our jobs is to prepare recommendations to the Executive Committee as to how advertising expenditures should be allocated. Last year's advertising budget of $40,000 was spent in equal increments over the four quarters. Initial expectations are that we will repeat this plan in the coming year. However, the committee would like to know whether some other allocation would be advantageous and whether the total budget should be changed.

Our product sells for $40 and costs us $25 to produce. Sales in the past have been seasonal, and our consultants have estimated seasonal adjustment factors for unit sales as follows:

Q1   90%

Q2 110%

Q3   80%

Q4 120%

[4] Ibid.

(A seasonal adjustment factor measures the percentage of average quarterly demand experienced in a given quarter.)

In addition to production costs, we must take into account the cost of the sales force (projected to be $34,000 over the year, allocated as follows: Q1 and Q2, $8,000 each; Q3 and Q4, $9,000 each), the cost of advertising itself, and overhead (typically around 15 percent of revenues).

Quarterly unit sales seem to run around 4,000 units when advertising is around $10,000. Clearly, advertising will increase sales, but there are limits to its impact. Our consultants several years ago estimated the relationship between advertising and sales. Converting that relationship to current conditions gives the following formula:

$$Unit\ sales = 35 \times Seasonal\ Factor \times \sqrt{3,000 + Advertising}$$

Rule 1: Sketch the Spreadsheet

Carpenters have the saying, "Measure twice, cut once." That is, since planning is inexpensive and miscut wood is useless, plan carefully to avoid waste and rework. A similar rule applies to spreadsheets: planning the work carefully will result in far less time spent correcting mistakes.

Turn the computer *off* and *think* for a while, before hitting any keys. This may seem like harsh advice at the start, but we have seen many modelers create a spreadsheet in a flurry of keystrokes, only to discover at some later point that their design is flawed and in need of wholesale revision. To those who are relatively new to spreadsheet modeling, we recommend beginning with a sketch of their spreadsheet before entering anything into the computer. We also believe this is a good first step for experienced modelers. A sketch should show the physical layout of major elements and should contain at least a rough indication of the flow of calculations. Instead of laboriously writing out formulas with cell addresses, we use variable names to indicate how calculations will be performed. For example, we might write: *Profit = Total Revenue – Total Cost*. In order to show the logic for calculating unsold goods, we might write: IF(*Stock > Demand, Stock – Demand, 0*). The acid test for whether a sketch is sufficiently detailed is whether a spreadsheet can be built from it in a straightforward manner without any significant redesign. (Both influence charts and outlines, as described in Chapter 4, can be used as inputs in the design process.)

For the Advertising Budget example, a sketch of the spreadsheet might include boxes to depict four major sections (Parameters, Decisions, Outputs, and Calculations), row headings for the entries in the Calculations section, and a brief indication of how each row in the model will be calculated. For example, *Gross Margin = Revenue – Cost of Goods*. Figure 5.1 shows an initial sketch along these lines.

The normal logical flow would require calculations to precede outputs. Why have we placed calculations at the bottom of the spreadsheet? The reason has to do with the use we envision for the model. We expect to vary some of the decision variables, and we'll want to know the consequences for the output measure. Since we want to see the effects of varying decisions on the output, it makes sense to place these items close together in the spreadsheet. In addition, we may also want to alter one or more of the input parameters and revisit the relationship between decisions and output. Therefore, it also makes sense to have inputs in close proximity to output and decisions. The one part of the spreadsheet we won't be examining or altering, once we've tested it, is the set of calculations. Therefore, we place the calculations in a secondary location.

Part of the thinking process, then, is anticipating what use will be made of the model. We will return to this point later, but for now, the planning process should take this into consideration when the model structure is sketched.

FIGURE 5.1
Sketch of the Advertising
Budget Spreadsheet

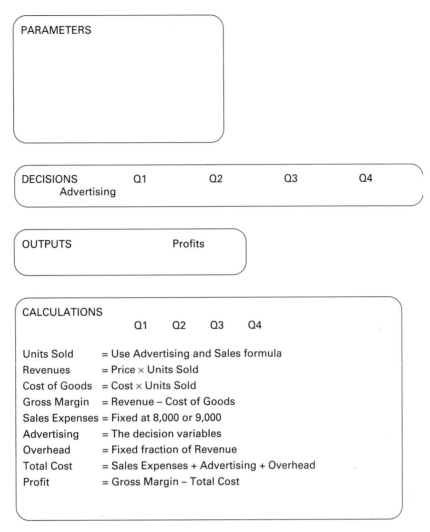

PARAMETERS

DECISIONS	Q1	Q2	Q3	Q4
Advertising				

OUTPUTS   Profits

CALCULATIONS

	Q1	Q2	Q3	Q4

Units Sold   = Use Advertising and Sales formula
Revenues   = Price × Units Sold
Cost of Goods   = Cost × Units Sold
Gross Margin   = Revenue – Cost of Goods
Sales Expenses = Fixed at 8,000 or 9,000
Advertising   = The decision variables
Overhead   = Fixed fraction of Revenue
Total Cost   = Sales Expenses + Advertising + Overhead
Profit   = Gross Margin – Total Cost

Rule 2: Organize the Spreadsheet into Modules

Modules create groups of similar items and separate unlike items. Modularization is a
basic principle of good design and a useful first step in organizing information. In spreadsheets, this means separating data, decision variables, outcome measures, and detailed calculations. If an influence chart has been constructed, as discussed in Chapter 4, then a lot
of this work will already have been done. An influence chart will have identified the outcome measure (or measures) of major interest, as well as the data and decisions that make
up the inputs. Most importantly, the influence chart will also have organized the major
steps in the calculations required to produce the outputs.

  Along with grouping and separating, the next step is to consider the flow of information in the model—that is, to specify which information will need to pass from one group
to another. Data and decisions will serve as inputs to some of the calculations, and a small
number of the calculations will eventually be highlighted as outputs. After these key link-
ages are identified, the additional development of one module can go on somewhat independently of modifications in other modules. Keep in mind that formulas should generally
reference cells located above and to the left. (The principle of modularization also applies
to using multiple worksheets to organize a workbook.)

Figure 5.2 displays our spreadsheet for the Advertising Budget example. Following the layout in our initial sketch, we use four modules and surround each one with a border for clarity. The output module contains an additional block that houses the base-case value, for later reference. The detailed calculations are simple enough to include in a single block, but even here, we use blank lines to separate net income, expenses, and profits. We highlight values of decision variables (the quarterly advertising expenditures) and the output measure (annual profit) with color shading. Models that are more complex may, of course, contain many more modules and require layouts that are more elaborate.

As planned, the modules for parameters, decisions, and outputs are in close proximity. Therefore, we can change the value of an input and immediately see the impact on the output in the same Excel window. Although we reduced the size of the spreadsheet image to 80 percent in Figure 5.2, in order to show the entire spreadsheet, the one-window summary of inputs and outputs will remain intact when the spreadsheet is viewed at its original size.

Rule 3: Start Small

Do not attempt to build a complex spreadsheet all at once. Isolate one part of the problem or one module of the spreadsheet; then design, build, and test that one part. Once that part of the model is in good shape, go on to the next one. By making (and correcting) many little mistakes in each module, and thus keeping the mistakes local if they occur, it is possible to avoid making really large and complex mistakes that require much more effort to detect and correct.

If we were building a model to cover 100 customers, it would make sense to build a model for one customer, or perhaps a few customers. If the model structure is the same or similar for each of the customers, it will be easy to replicate this initial building block. Then, when the replication is working, the model can be expanded to include the

FIGURE 5.2
The Advertising Budget Spreadsheet

Adbudget.xls

remaining customers. Similarly, if we were building a model to cover twelve months, we would start by building a model for the first month; then we would expand it to two months and ultimately to all twelve.

In the Advertising Budget example, we start by creating the Parameters and Decisions modules, since those simply organize and display the information we have gathered. Since we do not know at the outset what values we will ultimately choose for the decision variables, we enter convenient values (last year's expenditures of $10,000 each quarter seem appropriate), simply to hold a place and to assist us in debugging the logic of the spreadsheet. When we begin work on the financial logic, we focus on the first quarter. Only when the profit in the first quarter has been calculated successfully should we move on to the rest of the year. (Recursive formulas, which use a previous value to calculate the current value, will facilitate this process.)

Rule 4: Isolate Input Parameters

Place the numerical values of key parameters in a single location and separate them from calculations. This means that formulas will contain only cell references, not numerical values. It also means that a parameter contained in several formulas appears only once as a numerical value in the spreadsheet, although it may appear several times as a cell reference in a formula.

Parameterization offers several advantages. First, placing parameters in a separate location makes it easy to identify them and change them. It also makes a particular scenario immediately visible. Parameterization ensures that changing a numerical value in one cell is sufficient to induce a change throughout the entire model. In addition, parameterization is required for sensitivity-analysis tools, as we discuss in Chapter 6. Finally, it is relatively easy to document the assumptions behind parameters, or the sources from which they were derived, if those parameters appear in a single location.

A common source of error in spreadsheets is the tendency to bury parameters in cell formulas and to replicate the same parameter in multiple cells. This makes identifying parameters difficult, because they are not immediately visible. It's also difficult to know whether all numerical values of a parameter have been changed each time an update is required. By contrast, the habit of using a single and separate location considerably streamlines the building and debugging of a spreadsheet.

In our sample spreadsheet, all the essential parameters are located in a single module (cells B6:G15). Notice, for example, that price is referenced in cells D28:G28. When price is changed in C7, it is automatically changed in these other cells as well.

Rule 5: Design for Use

While designing a spreadsheet, try to anticipate who will use it and what kinds of questions they will want to address. Make it easy to change parameters that can be expected to change often. Make it easy to find key outputs by collecting them in one place. Include graphs of the outputs to make it easier to learn from the spreadsheet. Record the numerical values of base-case outputs as a prelude to sensitivity analysis. (We call this idea **benchmarking,** and we develop it further in Chapter 6.)

In our example spreadsheet, we have anticipated that when we move into the analysis phase, we will primarily be changing one or more values in the Parameters module (or the Decisions module) and observing the effect on the key output, annual profits. That is why we have copied the value of profits from cell H37 to cell C21, where it can be read more conveniently. We have also benchmarked (or "hard-coded") the base-case value in cell F21, so that it remains the same while changes are made in the parameters and other calculations. In a larger model, the outputs may be scattered over many locations in different worksheets. It is very helpful to gather them together and place them near the inputs so that the details of the model itself do not interfere with the process of analysis.

Rule 6: Keep it Simple

Just as good models should be simple, good spreadsheets should be as simple as possible while still getting the job done. Complex spreadsheets require more time and effort to build, and they are much more difficult to debug than simple ones. Some of our earlier rules, such as modularization and parameterization, help keep models simple.

Long formulas are a common symptom of overly complex spreadsheets. The most serious constraint on effective spreadsheet modeling is not computing power, but human brainpower. Therefore, there is little to be gained from minimizing the number of cells in a spreadsheet by writing a long formula in one cell. It is better to decompose a complex calculation into its intermediate steps and to display each step in a separate cell. This makes it easier to spot errors in the logic and to explain the spreadsheet calculations to others. Overall, it is a more efficient use of the combined human-computer team.

In the Advertising Budget example, we could calculate *Gross Margin* (cell D30) in a single row rather than use three rows to calculate its components (*Units Sold, Revenue,* and *Cost of Goods*). However, the detail helps in checking the logic, and it may eventually prove helpful during analysis. Later on, for example, we may decide that it would be more realistic to model sales as a function of price. Instead of modifying a complicated *Gross Margin* formula, we will find it easier to work with the formula for *Units Sold*.

Rule 7: Design for Communication

Spreadsheets are almost always used long after the builder ever thought they would be, and often by people who are not familiar with them. Logical design will help users understand what the spreadsheet is intended to accomplish and how to work with it effectively. The look and the layout of a spreadsheet will often determine whether its developer or another user will understand it several months or years after it was built. Visual cues that reinforce the model's logic will also pay dividends when the spreadsheet gets routine use as a decision-support device.

The use of informative labels and the incorporation of blank spaces can go a long way toward conveying the organization of a spreadsheet. The specialized formatting options in Excel (outlines, color, bold font, and so on) can also be used to highlight certain cell entries or ranges for quick visual recognition. This facilitates navigating around the spreadsheet, both when building the spreadsheet and when using it. However, formatting tools should be applied with care. If used to excess, formatting can confuse, obscure, and annoy rather than help. In our example spreadsheet, we use various formatting tools to improve readability, including bold font, borders, color shading, and capitalization. Within a team or an organization, or when creating a series of spreadsheets, it also helps to use these formatting tools consistently. For example, we use yellow shading and a border to designate cells that represent decision variables in virtually all of our spreadsheet models.

Sometimes, large spreadsheets can be reorganized with the help of split windows. For example, if we were to display the Advertising Budget spreadsheet at normal size, it would not fit within one (laptop) window. As a result, the lower part of the Calculations module would drop out of view. If we wanted to preserve the top portion of the spreadsheet, but also view the quarterly profit levels and the profit-margin percentages, we could split the window vertically, as shown in Figure 5.3.

Rule 8: Document Important Data and Formulas

Spreadsheets have become widespread in the business world because they are easy to build and use. Originally, many analysts learned to build spreadsheets because their corporate information-technology departments could not serve their needs in a timely fashion. One reason for the lack of a timely response is that information-technology professionals use a careful and time-consuming design process for creating computing applications, including extensive documentation. Spreadsheet users rarely apply the same level of effort to their applications. The question, then, is: How can we preserve the benefits of using spreadsheets, while also gaining the benefits of a careful design process?

One answer to this question is to find *practical* ways to document a spreadsheet. Creating separate documentation or user manuals is usually impractical. But it can be very practical to record the source of each important parameter and explain each important calculation in the spreadsheet itself. A design sketch of the spreadsheet provides documentation, in a fashion, for every important relationship in the model. Transferring this information to the actual spreadsheet helps preserve the underlying logic of the model and ultimately helps convey that logic to users of the spreadsheet.

In our example spreadsheet, we have documented both input parameters and the model logic in column J (refer to Figure 5.2). We have noted the source of each of the parameters: the accounting department, consultants, and so on. For each formula, we have provided a short explanation of the arithmetic, such as *Revenue = Price × Units*.

At the detailed level, we can provide documentation within individual cells by inserting cell comments. The command Insert→Comment brings up a small window in which we can describe the contents of the cell where the cursor is located. Figure 5.4 shows an example in which the Comment window explains that last year the budget was distributed equally among the quarters. The format of the comment is controlled by a selection from the Tools→Options menu. On the View tab within this menu are three buttons controlling the display of cell comments. A comment can be displayed permanently by clicking on Comment & indicator. Or we can click on Comment indicator only, in which case there will be a red triangle in the upper-right-hand corner of the cell, but the comment will be

FIGURE 5.3
Split-Window Display in the Advertising Budget Spreadsheet

Adbudget.xls

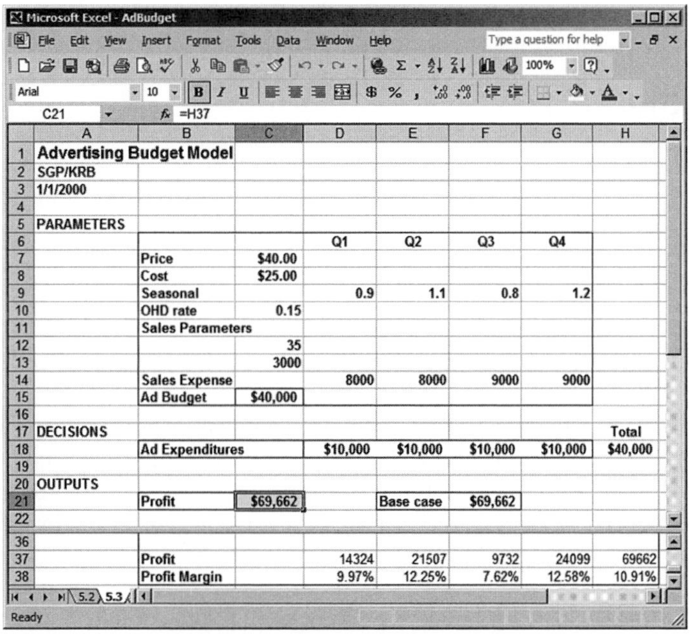

	A	B	C	D	E	F	G	H
1	Advertising Budget Model							
2	SGP/KRB							
3	1/1/2000							
4								
5	PARAMETERS							
6				Q1	Q2	Q3	Q4	
7		Price	$40.00					
8		Cost	$25.00					
9		Seasonal		0.9	1.1	0.8	1.2	
10		OHD rate	0.15					
11		Sales Parameters						
12			35					
13			3000					
14		Sales Expense		8000	8000	9000	9000	
15		Ad Budget	$40,000					
16								
17	DECISIONS							Total
18		Ad Expenditures		$10,000	$10,000	$10,000	$10,000	$40,000
19								
20	OUTPUTS							
21		Profit	$69,662		Base case	$69,662		
22								
36								
37		Profit		14324	21507	9732	24099	69662
38		Profit Margin		9.97%	12.25%	7.62%	12.58%	10.91%

Microsoft Excel - AdBudget

File Edit View Insert Format Tools Data Window Help — Type a question for help

Arial 10 B I U $ %

C21 = =H37

5.2 5.3

Ready

FIGURE 5.4
Comment Window for
the Budget Parameter

Adbudget.xls

	A	B	C	D	E	F	G	H	I	J
1	Advertising Budget Model									
2	SGP/KRB									
3	1/1/2000									
4										
5	PARAMETERS									
6				Q1	Q2	Q3	Q4			Notes
7		Price	$40.00							Current price
8		Cost	$25.00							Accounting
9		Seasonal		0.9	1.1	0.8	1.2			Data analysis
10		OHD rate	0.15							Accounting
11		Sales Parameters								
12			35							Consultants
13			3000							
14		Sales Expense				9000	9000			Consultants
15		Ad Budget	$40,000							Current budget
16										
17	DECISIONS							Total		
18		Ad Expenditures				$10,000	$10,000	$40,000		sum
19										
20	OUTPUTS									
21		Profit	$69,662		Base case	$69,662				
22										
23	CALCULATIONS									
24		Quarter		Q1	Q2	Q3	Q4	Total		
25		Seasonal		0.9	1.1	0.8	1.2			
26										
27		Units Sold		3592	4390	3192	4789	15962		given formula
28		Revenue		143662	175587	127700	191549	638498		price*units
29		Cost of Goods		89789	109742	79812	119718	399061		cost*units
30		Gross Margin		53873	65845	47887	71831	239437		subtraction
31										
32		Sales Expense		8000	8000	9000	9000	34000		given

The comment window note near C15 reads: "The budget was split equally among the quarters last year."

displayed only when the cursor is placed within that cell. If we click on None, then neither the comment nor the indicator will be visible at all.

Finally, it may be worth creating a separate module to list the assumptions in the model, particularly the structural simplifications adopted at the outset of the model-building process. In the Advertising Budget example, we assumed that production quantities would be equal to demand quantities each quarter and that there would be no inventory. That is, we assumed that we could ignore the detailed timing problems that might arise in the supply chain when we attempt to meet demand directly from production.

DESIGNING A WORKBOOK[5]

Although many effective spreadsheet models use only a single worksheet, it is often desirable to use multiple sheets in a workbook. In fact, the multisheet format can be exploited to better accomplish many of the goals cited above, such as modularization and ease of use. Most of the design principles described above apply equally well to the design of workbooks. However, some additional issues arise, as we discuss below.

Rule 1: Use Separate Sheets to Group Similar Kinds of Information

Workbooks are often used to make a model easier for an outsider to understand and use. To facilitate this understanding, isolate the technical details of the model and bring to the fore the assumptions behind the model and the results it produces. This allows an outsider to view assumptions and results without being distracted by the details of the calculations.

[5] Thanks to Peter Regan for his contributions to this section.

As an example, we have created a workbook for the Delta Oil example introduced in Chapter 4. The Contents sheet, shown in Figure 5.5, describes the purpose of the model, gives an overview of the other four worksheets, and provides some simple notes to explain the process of carrying out the analysis. The Database sheet (Figure 5.6) is mainly information compiled from the corporate database. Although the downloaded information takes this form, it is not an intuitive display. The Parameters sheet (Figure 5.7) restates this same information in tables. Users who are familiar with the production process at Delta Oil can view this sheet and quickly appreciate the parametric case under consideration. The fourth sheet contains an optimization model, but the details would not be of interest to the typical user. The results of the model, however, are tabulated in the Summary sheet (Figure 5.8), which includes a chart that summarizes the distribution of revenues across Delta Oil's various products.

Note that the Database sheet contains data for each of several years, starting in 2001. To analyze a particular year's data, the user copies a column of data into the range C2:C19. This information then appears in a more practical form in the Parameters sheet. In other words, the Parameters sheet contains formulas that reference cells on the Database sheet, deriving all of its information from the given database. Once this information is confirmed, the user can proceed to the Model sheet and implement the optimization. Immediately, the results appear in the Summary sheet. Thus, the Summary sheet contains no new parameters; its information is derived from the Model sheet. Finally, several key pieces of information—the annual profit, the utilizations, and the sales distribution—are reproduced in the Database sheet. In other words, the values in cells C21:C27 of the Database sheet are simply cell references to the corresponding data on the Summary sheet. Having analyzed a given year (2001, in our example), the user can preserve the results by copying the values in cells C21:C27 to cells E21:E27, and can then proceed to analyze some other year.

Workbooks should be designed so that users need to interact with only a few, easily recognized sheets. In our example, a user can view the input data in the Parameters sheet, and subsequently the output data in the Summary sheet, but there is no need to alter anything on those worksheets.

FIGURE 5.5
The Contents Sheet in
the Delta Oil Workbook

Delta.xls

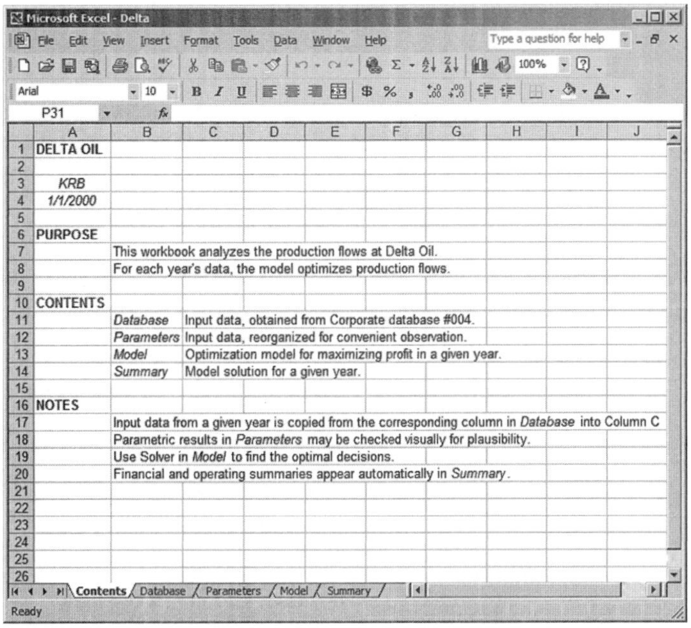

FIGURE 5.6
The Database Sheet in
the Delta Oil Workbook

Delta.xls

	A	B	C	D	E	F	G	H	I
1	Type	Detail	Value		2001	2002	2003	2004	2005
2	Capacity	Tower	50,000	bbl.	50,000	50,000	50,000	60,000	60,000
3	Capacity	Cracker	20,000	bbl.	20,000	20,000	20,000	20,000	24,000
4	Yield	Distillate fr. Crude	0.40		0.40	0.40	0.40	0.40	0.40
5	Yield	Low-End fr. Crude	0.60		0.60	0.60	0.60	0.60	0.60
6	Yield	Catalytic fr. Feed	0.64		0.64	0.64	0.64	0.64	0.64
7	Yield	Hi-End fr. Feed	0.40		0.40	0.40	0.40	0.40	0.40
8	Contract	Crude	36,000	bbl.	36,000	36,000	36,000	36,000	36,000
9	Demand	Regular gas	5,000	bbl.	5,000	5,000	5,000	5,000	5,000
10	Demand	Premium gas	10,000	bbl.	10,000	10,000	10,000	10,000	10,000
11	Quality	Min Cat in Reg	0.50		0.50	0.50	0.50	0.50	0.50
12	Quality	Min Cat in Prem	0.65		0.65	0.65	0.65	0.65	0.65
13	Cost	Tower	$6.00	per bbl.	$6.00	$6.18	$6.37	$6.56	$6.75
14	Cost	Cracker	$5.00	per bbl.	$5.00	$5.15	$5.30	$5.46	$5.63
15	Cost	Crude	$25.00	per bbl.	$28.00	$29.40	$30.87	$32.41	$34.03
16	Price	Low-End	$28.00	per bbl.	$25.00	$26.75	$28.62	$30.63	$32.77
17	Price	Regular gas	$40.00	per bbl.	$40.00	$43.20	$46.66	$50.39	$54.42
18	Price	Premium gas	$42.00	per bbl.	$42.00	$45.36	$48.99	$52.91	$57.14
19	Price	Hi-End	$36.00	per bbl.	$32.00	$33.92	$35.96	$38.11	$40.40
20									
21	Profit	Annual net income	$31,751		$31,751				
22	Efficiency	Tower utilization	100%		100%				
23	Efficiency	Cracker utilization	53%		53%				
24	Sales	Low-End	21,600		21,600				
25	Sales	Regular	580		580				
26	Sales	Premium	10,000		10,000				

FIGURE 5.7
The Parameters Sheet in
the Delta Oil Workbook

Delta.xls

	A	B	C	D	E	F	G	H	I	J
1	Parameters									
2										
3	Production							Unit cost	Capacity	
4		Distillation Tower		Crude	Distillate	Low-End				
5			per lb. of input	1	0.40	0.60		6.00	50,000	
6			per lb. of output	2.5	1	1.5				
7										
8		Catalytic Cracker		Feedstock	Catalytic	Hi-End				
9			per lb. of input	1	0.64	0.40		5.00	20,000	
10			per lb. of output	1.56	1	0.63				
11										
12	Quality									
13		Regular gas								
14			min Catalytic	0.50						
15		Premium gas								
16			min Catalytic	0.65						
17										
18	Sales	Prices per bbl.								
19			Low-End	28.00						
20			Regular	40.00					5,000	
21			Premium	42.00					10,000	
22			Hi-End	36.00						
23										
24	Purchases									
25			Crude	25.00						

Note that a reference to a cell on another sheet begins with the name of that sheet followed by an exclamation mark. For example, Database!C13 refers to cell C13 on the Database sheet. When using formulas that contain references to other sheets, the references themselves begin to look complicated, and most users find it convenient to create these references by pointing and clicking. The complexity of multisheet references reinforces the importance of keeping formulas simple (as well as sheet names) so that someone examining the logic for the first time can follow the calculations. Another way to make formulas look simple is to use range names, which we discuss later.

FIGURE 5.8
The Summary Sheet in
the Delta Oil Workbook

Delta.xls

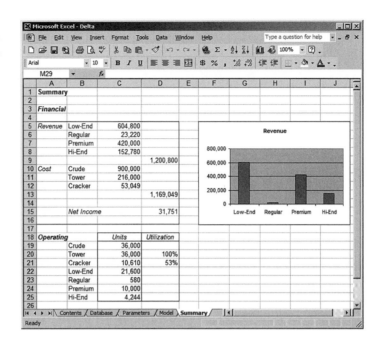

Rule 2: Design Workbooks for Ease of Navigation

Since the purpose of a structured workbook is to facilitate understanding by other users, any form of structural help for finding their way around the workbook is beneficial. Using revealing names for individual sheets is one helpful approach. (To change a sheet name, double-click on the name tab at the bottom of the spreadsheet and edit the name.)

Rule 3: Protect Workbooks from Unwanted Changes During Use

Several tools protect the contents of a workbook from unwanted changes and make it more user-friendly. In the Advertising Budget example, if we wanted to protect all the cells other than the decision variables, we would first lock all cells, then unlock the cells for the advertising allocation, and finally protect the entire sheet. The details are as follows. First, we select the entire worksheet. Then, we select Format→Cells, choose the Protection tab, and check the box for locked. Next, we repeat the process for the decision variables, first selecting the range C18:F18. Again, we select Format→Cells, choose the Protection tab, but this time we uncheck the box for locked. Finally, we protect the entire worksheet, using Tools→Protection→Protect Sheet. At the top of the Protect Sheet window, we check the box for Protect worksheet. In the lower window, there is a long list of options to allow users. If we check only the box for Select locked cells, then a user will be able to select and modify only the decision-variable cells. It will not be possible to select other cells. On the other hand, if we check the boxes for Select locked cells and Select unlocked cells, then the user will be able to select any of the locked cells (e.g., to verify a formula), but will not be permitted to alter the contents of those cells.

In addition, we can ensure that only legitimate values are used as inputs. This process is called **data validation,** a technique that is highly recommended for workbooks available to multiple users over an extended period. To invoke data validation, highlight the cells involved and click on Data→Validation. The Data Validation window contains three tabs, as shown in Figure 5.9. On the first tab, we can restrict the allowable inputs to a cell—for example, to require a number (as opposed to text) and one that lies between

FIGURE 5.9
The Data Validation
Window

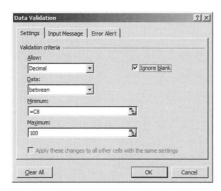

certain minimum and maximum values. In the Advertising Budget example, we require a user to enter a price that lies between unit cost (cell C8) and $100. On the second tab, we have an option of creating an input message that will appear whenever the cursor is placed on this cell. This message functions like a cell comment. On the third tab, we can design an error alert for the case of an invalid entry. An example for the Advertising Budget spreadsheet is shown in Figure 5.10, which shows the error alert when we attempt to enter a price greater than $100 or less than the unit cost.

BUILDING A SPREADSHEET

The second stage in creating a useful spreadsheet model is actually building it. Since most spreadsheet users do not consciously design their spreadsheets, they merge the designing and building processes. The usual result is that a great deal of time and energy are wasted fixing mistakes and redesigning a model that should have been designed once at the start.

A well-*designed* spreadsheet should be easy and quick to *build.* However, speed is not the only criterion here. Most bugs in spreadsheets are introduced during the building process. Therefore, learning to build spreadsheets without introducing errors is also vital. Here are some tips for building spreadsheets efficiently and effectively:

Rule 1: Follow a Plan

Having gone to the trouble of sketching the spreadsheet, it only makes sense to follow the sketch when building. With a sufficiently detailed sketch, the building process itself becomes more mechanical and therefore less prone to mistakes. All of the rules in this section are designed to make the building process routine, repeatable, and error-free.

Rule 2: Build One Module at a Time

Rather than trying to build an entire spreadsheet at one pass, it is usually more efficient to build a module and test it out before proceeding. For one thing, as we build the first module, we may discover that the design itself can be improved, so it is best to have made a limited investment in the original design before revising it. Another reason for this advice is to localize the potential effects of an error. If we make an error, its effects are likely to be limited mainly to the module we're building. By staying focused on that module, we can fix errors early, before they infect other modules that we build later.

FIGURE 5.10
Error Alert Produced by
Data Validation

Rule 3: Predict the Outcome of Each Formula

For each formula entered, predict the numerical value expected from it before pressing the Enter key. Ask what order of magnitude to expect in the result, and give some thought to any outcomes that don't correspond to predictions. This discipline helps to uncover bugs: without a prediction, every numerical outcome tends to look plausible. On the other hand, a prediction that is orders of magnitude different from the calculated number provides an opportunity. For example, if we predict $100,000 for annual revenue, and the calculated value comes to $100,000,000, then there is a flaw either in our intuition or in our formula. Either way, we can benefit: our intuition may be sharpened, or we may detect an error in need of fixing.

Rule 4: Copy and Paste Formulas Carefully

The Copy and Paste commands in Excel are not simply time-savers; they are also helpful in avoiding bugs. Instead of entering structurally similar formulas several times, we copy and paste a formula instead. Repetition can be a source of errors, and copying formulas can diminish the potential for this type of error. On the other hand, careless copying is also a source of bugs. One of the most common errors is to select the wrong range for copying—for example, selecting one cell too few in copying a formula across a row. Recognizing this problem helps keep us alert to the possibility of a copying error, and we are therefore more likely to avoid it.

Rule 5: Use Relative and Absolute Addressing to Simplify Copying

Efficient copying depends on skillful use of relative and absolute addressing. Remember that an address such as B7 is interpreted in a *relative* fashion in Excel: if the highlighted cell is A6, B7 is read as the cell one row down and one column to the right. When we include a cell with a relative address in a formula and then copy the formula, the cell address will change to preserve the relative position between the highlighted cell and the input cell. On the other hand, an *absolute* address such as $B$6 refers to the cell B6 regardless of the location of the highlighted cell. When a formula with an absolute address is copied, the address will remain $B$6. Absolute addresses are usually used when referring to a parameter, since the location of the parameter is fixed.

Rule 6: Use the Function Wizard to Ensure Correct Syntax

The button f_x on the standard toolbar brings up the Function Wizard, which is a complete listing of all the functions built into Excel. It is not necessary to memorize the exact syntax of an occasionally used function, or to guess at the correct syntax, because the Function Wizard is there to help. For example, we might want to calculate the payment on a car loan once in a while, but it may be difficult to memorize the exact form of the PMT function. Whenever this function is needed, click on the Function Wizard and select PMT. A window then appears that shows what inputs the function needs and in what order. This window even calculates the value of the function when its inputs are specified, thus providing quick feedback on whether the results are as expected.

Rule 7: Use Range Names to Make Formulas Easy to Read

Any cell or range of cells in a spreadsheet can be given a name. This name can then be used in formulas to refer to the contents of the cell. If cell B6 is named VblCost, we can use either B6 or VblCost interchangeably in any formula. Obviously, it is easier to understand a formula that uses range names than one that uses cell addresses. Formulas that are easier to understand are easier for the developer to debug and easier for new users to understand.

Range names require extra work to enter and maintain, so they may not be worth the effort in simple spreadsheets destined for one-time use. But in a spreadsheet that will become a permanent tool, and that will be used by other analysts long after the designer has moved on, it is a good idea to use range names to help subsequent users understand the details. Some firms have a policy requiring that all major spreadsheets use range names throughout.

We can assign a name to a cell or a range of cells by selecting Insert→Name→Define and specifying the relevant cell range. For example, in the spreadsheet of Figure 5.3, we have assigned the name TotProfit to cell H37. This allows us to use the formula =TotProfit in C21, our main output cell. (To view all the range names in use, look in the pull-down window at the top of the spreadsheet, to the left of the formula window.) As a more ambitious example, we can assign the name Price to cell C7 and the name Sales to the range D27:G27 (by highlighting the four-cell range before defining the name). Then, the revenue formulas in cells D28:G28 can be entered as =Price*Sales. This makes the formulas easier to interpret and reduces the possibility for errors.

Rule 8: Use Dummy Input Data to Make Errors Stand Out

Most modelers naturally use realistic values for input parameters as they build their spreadsheets. This has the advantage that the results look plausible, but it has the disadvantage that the results are difficult to check. For example, if the expected price is $25.99 and unit sales are 126,475, revenues will be calculated as $3,287,085.25. We could check this with a calculator, but it is not easy to check by eye. However, if we input arbitrary values of $10 for price and 100 for unit sales, we can easily check that our formula for revenue is correct if it shows a result of $1,000. Generally speaking, it saves time in the long run to input arbitrary but simple values for the input parameters (for example, 1, 10, and 100) during the initial building sequence. Once the spreadsheet has been debugged with these arbitrary values, it is then a simple matter to replace them with the actual input values.

TESTING A SPREADSHEET

Even a carefully designed and built spreadsheet may contain errors. Errors can arise from incorrect references in formulas, from inaccurate copying and pasting, from lack of parameterization, and from a host of other sources. There is no recipe to follow for finding all bugs. Many bugs are found late in the analysis phase, forcing the user to backtrack and not only fix the bug, but repeat a lot of the previous work. This can be avoided by carefully testing the spreadsheet before using it for analysis.

The tips we offer here can help an end user test whether a model is correct. However, common sense and the experience of thousands of professional programmers suggest that one of the most effective ways to find errors in a model is to *give it to an outsider* to test. Another pair of eyes can often find errors that have eluded the builder, who is so immersed in the details that errors are no longer detectable. Finding another pair of eyes may be impractical for many end users who work on their own, but it should be feasible in almost any company, especially when the spreadsheet is large, complex, and important. Formal code inspection, as practiced by professionals, is rarely carried out for spreadsheet models. However, a few consulting companies practice something similar, and we suspect that it will become more common as the risks of spreadsheet errors become more widely appreciated.

Rule 1: Check that Numerical Results Look Plausible

The most important tool for keeping a spreadsheet error-free is a *skeptical attitude*. As we build the spreadsheet, we transform input parameters into a set of intermediate results that will eventually lead to final outcomes. As these numbers gradually appear, it is important to check that they look reasonable. We suggest three distinct ways to accomplish this:

- Make rough estimates.
- Check with a calculator.
- Test extreme cases.

Make Rough Estimates

In an earlier section, we recommended predicting the rough magnitude of the result of each formula before pressing Enter. This trick helps catch errors as they are made. Similarly, it is a good idea to scan the completed spreadsheet and to check that critical results are the correct order of magnitude. For example, in the Advertising Budget example, if we sell about 3,000 units in Q3 at $40 each, we should make about $120,000. This calculation can be made in our heads, and it helps to confirm that the value in cell F28 ($127,700) is probably accurate.

Use a Calculator

A more formal approach to error detection is to check some portion of the spreadsheet on a calculator. Pick a typical column or row and check the entire sequence of calculations. Errors often occur in the last row or column due to problems in Copy and Paste operations, so check these areas, too.

Test Extreme Cases

If the logic behind a spreadsheet is correct, it should give logical results even with unrealistic assumptions. For example, if we set Price to $0, we should have zero revenues. Extreme cases such as this are useful for debugging because the correct results are easy to predict. Note, however, that just because a spreadsheet gives zero revenues when we set Price to $0 does not guarantee that the logic will be correct for all cases.

In the Advertising Budget example, if we price at cost, we should get a Gross Margin of zero. We can make this test by entering $25 for Price in C7 and then observing that Gross Margin in D30:G30 becomes zero. Testing extreme cases is one of the tools of professional programmers that end users should adopt as their own.

Rule 2: Check that Formulas are Correct

Most spreadsheet errors occur in formulas. We can reduce the possibility of errors by making formulas short and using multiple cells to calculate a complex result. We can also reduce errors by using recursive formulas wherever possible, so that successive formulas in a row or column have essentially the same form. Yet another good idea is to design the spreadsheet so that formulas use as inputs only cells that are above and to the left and are as close as possible. But having taken all these precautions, it is still necessary to test that formulas are correct before beginning the analysis. We offer five ways to accomplish this:

- Check manually.
- Display individual cell references.
- Display all formulas.
- Use the Auditing Tools.
- Use Error Checking.

Check Manually

Most end users check formulas one at a time, by highlighting each cell in a row or column in sequence and visually auditing the formula. This procedure works fairly well, especially if the formulas are recursive so that many cell references change in a predictable way or do not change at all from cell to cell. It also works best if range names are used. This method is, however, extremely tedious, and tedious methods encourage carelessness. Several better methods are described below.

Display Individual Cell References

Another way to check formulas is to use the cell-edit capability, invoked either by pressing the F2 key or by double-clicking on the cell of interest. This step reveals the formula in the cell, displayed with color-coded cell references. Each cell that appears in the formula is highlighted by a selection border, which is color-coded to the cell reference in the formula. Often, the locations of the cell references in a formula give visual clues to whether a formula is correctly structured. When an error occurs, it is often possible to drag a highlighted border to a different cell as a means of correcting the address in the formula. This method is preferred to manual checking because it provides stronger visual clues for locating errors.

Display All Formulas

Another excellent device is to display all the formulas in the spreadsheet by holding down the Control key and pressing the Apostrophe key on the upper-left corner of the main keyboard. This will display the spreadsheet formulas, as shown in Figure 5.11, making them easier to scan. Usually, successive formulas in a row or column have some consistent pattern. For example, one cell reference is absolute and does not change, while another is relative and changes from D28 to E28 to F28, and so on. If there is an error, it can often be detected as a break in a pattern. (Return the spreadsheet to its normal form by pressing Control-Apostrophe again.)

FIGURE 5.11
Displaying Formulas in
the Advertising Budget
Spreadsheet

Adbudget.xls

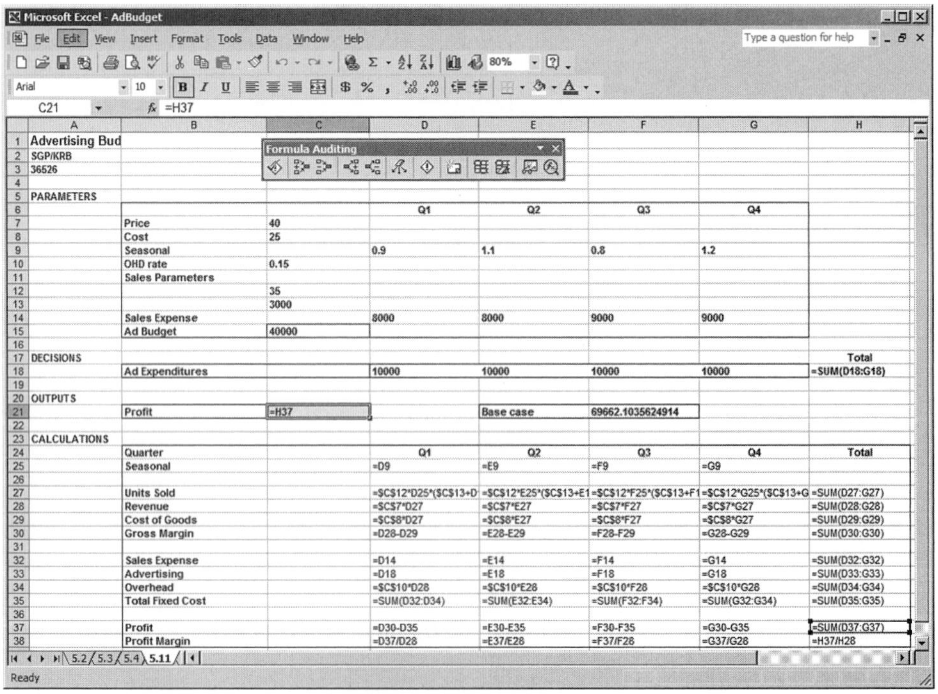

In the spreadsheet for the Advertising Budget example, note the similar structure in the four formulas for Gross Margin in the range D30:G30. A copying error would show up as a break in the pattern here.

Use the Auditing Tools

Another useful and underutilized set of debugging tools in Excel is available on the Auditing toolbar. (To display the Auditing toolbar, select Tools→Formula Auditing→Show Formula Auditing Toolbar.) These options can be used to identify the cells used to calculate a given cell (its **predecessors**) or the cells it is used to calculate (its **successors**). The Trace Precedents option draws colored arrows to the predecessors of a given cell. Invoking the Trace Precedents option again from this point will identify the predecessors of the predecessors, and so on, reaching backward into the logic of the calculations. The Trace Dependents option works similarly, but in the forward direction. The arrows convey a pattern of information flow, which should conform to the underlying logic of the model. For debugging purposes, the Auditing tools can be used to display the information flows related to a group of cells. If these cells have a parallel or iterative structure, there should be a distinctive pattern in the arrows produced by the Auditing tools. As with displaying formulas, bugs often show up as unexpected breaks in the pattern of these arrows.

In the spreadsheet for the Advertising Budget example, suppose we select cell H37. Next, we display the Formula Auditing toolbar and choose the option for Trace Precedents several times in succession. The cells that are used to calculate profit are highlighted, then their predecessors are highlighted, and so on, as shown in Figure 5.12. Again, an error in the formulas would show up as a break in these visual patterns. (Use the Remove All Arrows option to erase the auditing arrows.)

FIGURE 5.12
Using the Auditing Toolbar in the Advertising Budget Spreadsheet

Adbudget.xls

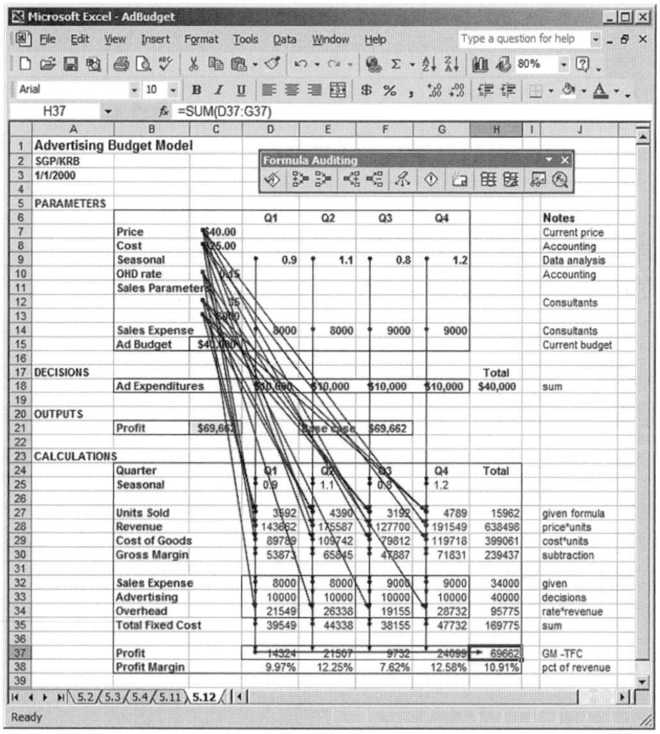

Use Error Checking

Microsoft has introduced automatic Error Checking in Excel 2002, with a new tab located under Tools→Options (see Figure 5.13). This is the spreadsheet equivalent of grammar checking in word processing. Error Checking as a whole can be turned on or off, as can each of the options. If Error Checking is turned on, all cells that are identified as possibly containing errors are noted with a colored triangle. The following seven errors are flagged:

- Evaluates to error value
- Text date with two-digit years
- Number stored as text
- Inconsistent formula in region
- Formula omits cells in region
- Unlocked cells containing formulas
- Formulas referring to empty cells

Three of these categories of possible errors seem to be most prevalent: Inconsistent formula in region, Formula omits cells in region, and Formulas referring to empty cells. Inconsistent formulas are those that violate a pattern. For example, a recursive formula that is copied across a row but that changes its pattern of references to absolute addresses would be flagged under this category. Often, these potential errors are consciously designed into the spreadsheet, and although they are not errors, they are nonetheless indicative of poor programming practice. Formulas that omit cells in a region also violate an expected pattern. Finally, formulas that refer to empty cells are either wrong outright or at least indicate dangerous programming practice. While this new Error Checking capability can highlight only certain well-defined categories of potential errors (and the user can determine which categories by using the check boxes), it is a useful tool—one that should be employed during the design and testing phases of spreadsheet construction.

Rule 3: Test that Model Performance is Plausible

For many end users, the analysis phase begins while testing is still in progress. This is natural and perhaps unavoidable, although we have stressed the importance of taking a careful and structured approach to designing, building, and testing spreadsheets before using them for analysis. However, if analysis begins before testing is complete, it is at least desirable to retain a skeptical attitude toward the early results from using the model. Many minor bugs come to light during analysis. More importantly, actually using the model can reveal

FIGURE 5.13
The Error Checking
Window

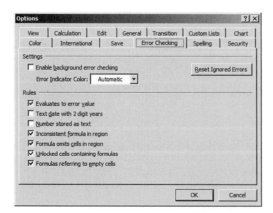

major logical flaws. These types of errors, which usually cannot be uncovered by the most meticulous checking of formulas, can destroy the credibility of the entire modeling process.

If a spreadsheet model is logically sound and built without errors, it should react in a plausible manner to a range of input values. Thus, sensitivity testing, which we discuss in Chapter 6, can be a powerful way to uncover logical and mechanical errors. In our Advertising Budget example, if profit were to go *down* as we increased the price, we could be fairly sure we had a bug in the model. But even if we have confirmed that profits rise with price, would we expect that relationship to be linear or nonlinear? We can test our intuition and the model by calculating profit for a range of prices and graphing the results. Figure 5.14 shows that the relationship in the model is linear. We might conclude that this is as we expected and intended. On the other hand, we might decide that demand should instead depend on price (which, in our model, it does not) and that the model needs further refinement.

SUMMARY

Spreadsheets are important throughout business, and important tools deserve careful engineering. While spreadsheet modeling is not a science, we can enumerate a set of guidelines for designing, building, and testing our spreadsheets. Our guidelines have evolved from our observations working with both experienced and inexperienced model builders. These guidelines are designed to make the process of spreadsheet development both more efficient and more effective.

The available evidence suggests strongly that most spreadsheets in use contain errors and that their developers are overconfident about the reliability of their models. This suggests that we should be humble about our ability to develop spreadsheets that correctly implement the models we have conceived. Care and effort are required to build models successfully. Some useful lessons can be learned from professional programmers—most importantly, to be skeptical and to test thoroughly.

Here is a summary of the rules given in this chapter.

Designing a Spreadsheet
Sketch the spreadsheet.
Organize the spreadsheet into modules.
Start small.
Isolate input parameters.
Design for use.

FIGURE 5.14
The Price-Profit
Relationship in the
Advertising Budget
Spreadsheet

Adbudget.xls

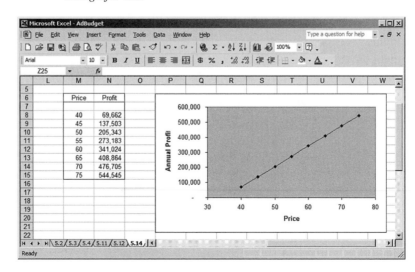

Keep it simple.
Design for communication.
Document important data and formulas.

Designing a Workbook

Use separate spreadsheets to group like information.
Design workbooks for ease of navigation.
Protect workbooks from unwanted changes during use.

Building a Spreadsheet

Follow a plan.
Build one module at a time.
Predict the outcome of each formula.
Copy and Paste formulas carefully.
Use relative and absolute addressing to simplify copying.
Use the Function Wizard to ensure correct syntax.
Use range names to make formulas easy to read.

Testing a Spreadsheet

Check that numerical results look plausible.
Check that formulas are correct.
Test that model performance is plausible.

SUPPLEMENTARY READING

The most thoughtful writing on spreadsheet design has appeared not in books but in journal articles. We list some useful articles below. More information can be found in references compiled in the Edwards and Panko articles.

Caine, D. J. and A. J. Robinson. 1993. "Spreadsheet Modeling: Guidelines for Model Development." *Management Decision* 31: 38–44.

Conway, D. G. and C. T. Ragsdale. 1997. "Modeling Optimization Problems in the Unstructured World of Spreadsheets." *Omega* 25: 313–322.

Edwards, J. S., P. N. Finlay, and J. M. Wilson. 2000 "The Role of OR Specialists in 'Do It Yourself' Spreadsheet Development." *European Journal of Operational Research* 127: 14–27.

Panko, R. R. 1999. "Applying Code Inspection to Spreadsheet Testing." *Journal of Management Information Systems* 16: 159–176.

The following short monograph and the accompanying Web site may also be helpful:

Raffensperger, John F. 2002. "The Art of the Spreadsheet." www. SpreadsheetStyle.com.

EXERCISES

1. Refer to the Flexible Insurance Coverage case. Design a spreadsheet that will allow an individual employee to compare the annual expenses for each plan.

   Questions

   a. Sketch the spreadsheet on paper.

   b. Build and test a prototype model.

2. Refer to the Two-Part Tariff case. Design a spreadsheet that will allow management to select an access fee and usage rate for each segment and determine the overall profitability of the pricing scheme.

   Questions

   a. Sketch the spreadsheet on paper.

   b. Build and test a prototype model.

3. Refer to the Producer Responsibility case. Design a spreadsheet that will allow BMW management to estimate the cost of disposal a decade into the future (i.e., in 1999), as a percentage of net income.

   Questions

   a. Sketch the spreadsheet on paper.

   b. Build and test a prototype model.

4. Refer to the XYZ Company case. Review the list structure developed for this case in conjunction with the corresponding exercise in Chapter 4. (If this has not yet been done, develop the list as a first step.) Design a spreadsheet that will allow an analyst to predict monthly cash needs and profitability for the first five months of the year.

   Questions

   a. Sketch the spreadsheet on paper.

   b. Build and test a prototype model.

5. Refer to the Damon Appliances case. Review the list structure developed for this case in conjunction with the corresponding exercise in Chapter 4. (If this has not yet been done, develop the list as a first step.) Design a spreadsheet for the monthly pro forma income statements and balance sheets for the coming year.

   Questions

   a. Sketch the spreadsheet on paper.

   b. Build and test a prototype model.

6. Refer to the Retirement Planning case. Review the problem statement and influence diagram that were generated for this case in conjunction with the corresponding exercises in Chapters 3 and 4. (If this has not yet been done, develop the problem statement and influence diagram as preliminary steps.) Design a spreadsheet to help analyze the problem.

   Questions

   a. Sketch the spreadsheet on paper.

   b. Build and test a prototype model.

7. Refer to the Draft TV Commercials case. Review the problem statement and influence diagram that were generated for this case in conjunction with the corresponding exercises in Chapters 3 and 4. (If this has not yet been done, develop the problem statement an influence diagram as preliminary steps.) Design a spreadsheet to help analyze the problem.

   Questions

   a. Sketch the spreadsheet on paper.

   b. Build and test a prototype model.

8. Refer to the Icebergs for Kuwait case. Review the problem statement and influence diagram that were generated for this case in conjunction with the corresponding exercises in Chapters 3 and 4. (If this has not yet been done, develop the problem statement and influence diagram as preliminary steps.) Design a spreadsheet to help analyze the problem.

   Questions

   a. Sketch the spreadsheet on paper.

   b. Build and test a prototype model.

9. Refer to the Racquetball Racket case. Review the problem statement and influence diagram that were generated for this case in conjunction with the corresponding exercises in Chapters 3 and 4. (If this has not yet been done, develop the problem statement and influence diagram as preliminary steps.) Design a spreadsheet to help analyze the problem.

   Questions

   a. Sketch the spreadsheet on paper.

   b. Build and test a prototype model.

CHAPTER 6

ANALYSIS USING SPREADSHEETS

INTRODUCTION

In the previous chapter, we pointed out that spreadsheet models often play a critical role in business planning and analysis. Because of their importance, spreadsheets should not be created haphazardly. Instead, they should be carefully engineered. We recommended a process for designing, building, and testing a spreadsheet that is both efficient and effective. Not only does this process minimize the likelihood that the spreadsheet contains errors, but it also prepares the user to investigate the business questions at hand. That is the analytic phase of the modeling process. Our purpose in this chapter is to provide a structure for this investigation and to present the essential Excel tools that support analysis. Advanced methods, and the Excel tools that go with them, are elaborated in subsequent chapters.

We have found that, over time, most analysts develop their own informal approaches to the analytic phase of modeling. Many of us have favorite tools that we tend to use over and over, even when they are not really adequate to the task. But it is difficult to develop a *complete* set of analytic tools simply through experience. An analyst who does not know a particular tool generally does not think to ask the business question that the tool helps answer. By the same token, an analyst with a complete analytic toolkit would be more likely to ask the right questions.

Although Excel itself has thousands of features, most of the analysis done with spreadsheets falls into one of the following five categories:

- base-case analysis
- what-if analysis
- breakeven analysis
- optimization analysis
- risk analysis

Within each of these categories, there are specific Excel tools, such as the Goal Seek tool, and add-ins, such as Crystal Ball, which can be used either to automate tedious calculations or to find powerful business insights that cannot be found any other way. Some of these tools, such as Solver, are quite complex and will be given more complete treatment in later chapters. Here, we provide only a brief introduction to these tools so as to give the reader a complete overview of the process of spreadsheet analysis. By contrast, some of the other tools we describe in this chapter are extremely simple, yet they seem to be underutilized by the majority of analysts.

Once again, we draw on the Advertising Budget example, which was introduced in Chapter 5, to illustrate the different kinds of analysis. Here is a sample of the kinds of questions we answer in this chapter:

- If we follow last year's plan to spend the same amount on advertising in each quarter, how much profit can we expect to make?

- How much will profit change if our product costs turn out to be 10 percent higher or lower than we have assumed?

- If our product costs rise, at what point will profit reach zero?

- What is the maximum profit we can make with an advertising budget of $40,000?

- How likely is it that we will lose money if price and cost are uncertain?

Base-Case Analysis

Almost every spreadsheet analysis involves measuring outcomes relative to some common point of comparison, or **base case.** Therefore, it's worth giving some thought to how the base case is chosen. A base case is often drawn from current policy or common practice, but there are many other alternatives. Where there is considerable uncertainty in the decision problem, it may be appropriate for the base case to depict the most likely scenario; in other circumstances, the worst case or the best case might be a good choice.

Sometimes, several base cases are used. For example, we might start the analysis with a version of the model that takes last year's results as the base case. Later in the analysis, we might develop another base case using a proposed plan for the coming year. At either stage, the base case is the starting point from which an analyst can explore the model using the tools described in this chapter, and thereby gain insights into the corresponding business situation.

In the Advertising Budget example, most of the input parameters such as price and cost are forecasts for the coming year. These inputs would typically be based on previous experience, modified by our hunches as to what will be different in the coming year. But what values should we assume for the decision variables in the base case? Our ultimate goal is to find the best values for these decisions, but that is premature at this point. A natural alternative is to take last year's advertising expenditures ($10,000 in each quarter) as the base-case decisions, both because this is a simple plan and because initial indications point to a repeat for this year's decisions.

What-If Analysis

Once a base case has been specified, the next step in analysis often involves nothing more sophisticated than varying one of the inputs to determine how the key outputs change. Assessing the change in outputs associated with a given change in inputs is called **what-if analysis.** The inputs may be *parameters,* in which case we are asking how sensitive our base-case results are to forecasting errors or other changes in those values. Alternatively, the inputs we vary may be *decision variables,* in which case we are exploring whether changes in our decisions might improve our results, for a given set of input parameters. Finally, there is another type of what-if analysis, in which we test the effect on the results of changing some aspect of our model's *structure.* For example, we might replace a linear relationship between price and sales with a nonlinear one. In these three forms of analysis, the general idea is to alter an assumption and then trace the effect on the model's outputs.

We use the term **sensitivity analysis** interchangeably with the term what-if analysis. However, we are aware that sensitivity analysis sometimes conveys a distinct meaning. In the optimization models of Chapter 8, where optimal decision variables themselves depend on parameters, we use the term sensitivity analysis specifically to mean the effect of changing a parameter on the *optimal* outcome. (In optimization models, the term what-if analysis is seldom used.)

When we vary a *parameter,* we are implicitly asking what would happen if the given information were different. That is, what if we had made a different numerical assumption at the outset, but everything else remained unchanged? This kind of questioning is important because the parameters of our model represent assumptions or forecasts about the environment for decision making. If the environment turns out to be different than we had assumed, then it stands to reason that the results will also be different. What-if analysis measures that difference and helps us appreciate the potential importance of each numerical assumption.

In the Advertising Budget example, if unit cost rises to $26 from $25, then annual profit drops to $53,700. In other words, an increase of 4 percent in the unit cost will reduce profit by nearly 23 percent. Thus, it would appear that profits are quite sensitive to unit cost, and, in light of this insight, we may decide we should monitor the market conditions that influence the material and labor components of cost.

When we vary a *decision variable,* we are exploring outcomes that we can influence. First, we'd like to know whether changing the value of a decision variable would lead to an improvement in the results. If we locate an improvement, we can then try to determine what value of the decision variable would result in the best improvement. This kind of questioning is a little different from asking about a parameter, because we can act directly on what we learn. What-if analysis can thus lead us to better decisions.

In the Advertising Budget example, if we spend an additional $1,000 on advertising in the first quarter, then annual profit rises to $69,882. In other words, an increase of 10 percent in the advertising expenditure during Q1 will translate into an increase of roughly 0.3 percent in annual profit. Thus, profits do not seem very sensitive to small changes in advertising expenditures in Q1, all else being equal. Nevertheless, we have identified a way to increase profits. We might guess that the small percentage change in profit reflects the fact that expenditures in the neighborhood of $10,000 are close to optimal, but we will have to gather more information before we are ready to draw conclusions about optimality.

In addition to testing the sensitivity of results to parameters and decision variables, there are situations in which we want to test the impact of some element of model structure. For example, we may have assumed that there is a linear relationship between price and sales. As part of what-if analysis, we might then ask whether a nonlinear demand-price relationship would materially alter our conclusions. As another example, we may have assumed that our competitors will not change their prices in the coming year. If we then determine that our own prices should increase substantially over that time, we might ask how our results would change if our competitors were to react to our pricing decisions by matching our price increases. These what-if questions are more complex than simple changes to a parameter or a decision variable because they involve alterations in the underlying structure of the model. Nonetheless, an important aspect of successful modeling is testing the sensitivity of results to key assumptions in the structure of the model.

In the Advertising Budget example, the nonlinear relationship between advertising and sales plays a fundamental role. In the spirit of structural sensitivity analysis, we can ask how different our results would be if we were to replace this relationship with a linear one. For example, the linear relationship

$$Sales = 3{,}000 + 0.1(Advertising \times Seasonal\ Factor)$$

lies close to the nonlinear curve for advertising levels around $10,000. When we substitute this relationship into the base-case model, holding advertising constant at $10,000 each quarter, we find that profit changes only slightly, to $70,000. But in this model, if we then increase Q1 advertising by $1,000, we find that profit *decreases*, while in the base-case model it increases. Evidently, this structural assumption does have a significant impact on the desired levels of advertising.

We have illustrated what we might call a "one-at-a-time" form of what-if analysis, where we vary one input at a time, keeping other inputs unchanged. We could, of course, vary two or more inputs simultaneously, but these more complex experiments become increasingly difficult to interpret. In many cases, we can gain the necessary insights by varying the inputs one at a time.

It is important not to underestimate the power of this first step in analysis. Simple what-if exploration is one of the most effective ways to develop a deeper understanding of the model and the system it represents. It is also part of the debugging process, as we pointed out in the previous chapter. When what-if analysis reveals something unexpected, we have either found a useful insight or perhaps discovered a bug.

Predicting the outcome of a what-if test is an important part of the learning process. For example, in the Advertising Budget example, what would be the result of doubling the selling price? Would profits double as well? In the base case, with a price of $40, profits total $69,662. If we double the price, we find that profits increase to $612,386. Profits increase by much more than a factor of two when prices double. After a little thought, we should see the reasons. For one, costs do not increase in proportion to volume; for another, demand is not influenced by price in this model. Thus, the sensitivity test helps us to understand the nature of the cost structure—that it's not proportional—as well as one limitation of the model—that no link exists between demand and price.

Benchmarking

During what-if analysis, we repeatedly change inputs and observe the resulting change in outputs. This can get confusing unless we keep a record of the results in some organized fashion. One simple solution to this problem is to **benchmark** sensitivity results against the base case by keeping a record of the base-case outcome on the spreadsheet.

In the Advertising Budget spreadsheet, we recorded the base-case profit of $69,662 on the spreadsheet in cell F21, as shown Figure 6.1. Note that this cell contains the *number* $69,662, not a cell reference to profit in C21. We construct this entry by selecting C21 and choosing Edit→Copy, then selecting F21 and choosing Edit→Paste Special with the option Paste Values, as shown in Figure 6.2. With this structure, the result of any new sensitivity test will appear in C21, while the base-case value will be maintained in F21. If we wish, we can add a cell to measure the difference in profit between the base case and the sensitivity test, or the percentage difference, if that seems more useful.

Scenarios

Up to this point, we have viewed each parameter in our model as independent of all the others. But it is often the case that certain *sets* of parameters go together in some natural way. For example, in the airline industry during a recession, we might expect passenger miles to be low and the interest rate also to be low. Thus, in using a model to forecast future airline profitability, we might want to analyze a scenario involving a recession, and to do so, we would choose low values for these two inputs. Furthermore, when we perform what-if analysis on this scenario, we would vary both parameters up and down together, not independently.

In general, we can think of a **scenario** as a story about the future decision-making environment translated into its effects on several of the model's parameters. Specifically, in modeling terms, a scenario is a set of parameters that describes an internally consistent view of the future. In our airline example, the story involves a recession and the impact the recession has on specific parameters affecting demand and investment. In the oil industry, a scenario might depict the breakup of the OPEC cartel and its impacts on

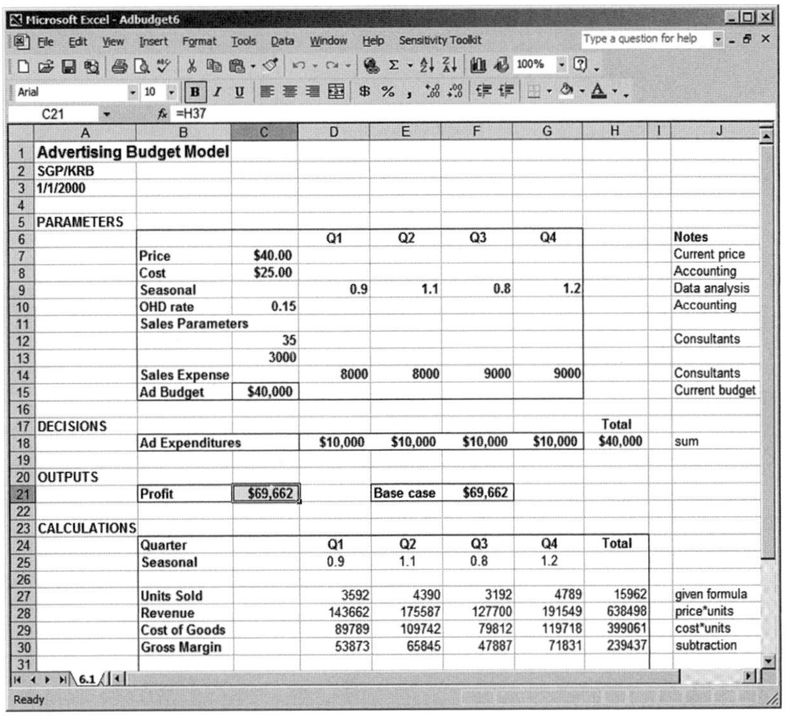

FIGURE 6.1
The Advertising Budget
Spreadsheet

AdBudget6.xls

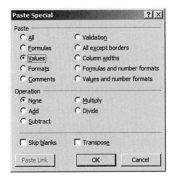

	A	B	C	D	E	F	G	H	I	J
1	Advertising Budget Model									
2	SGP/KRB									
3	1/1/2000									
4										
5	PARAMETERS									
6				Q1	Q2	Q3	Q4			Notes
7		Price	$40.00							Current price
8		Cost	$25.00							Accounting
9		Seasonal		0.9	1.1	0.8	1.2			Data analysis
10		OHD rate	0.15							Accounting
11		Sales Parameters								
12			35							Consultants
13			3000							
14		Sales Expense		8000	8000	9000	9000			Consultants
15		Ad Budget	$40,000							Current budget
16										
17	DECISIONS							Total		
18		Ad Expenditures		$10,000	$10,000	$10,000	$10,000	$40,000		sum
19										
20	OUTPUTS									
21		Profit	$69,662		Base case	$69,662				
22										
23	CALCULATIONS									
24		Quarter		Q1	Q2	Q3	Q4	Total		
25		Seasonal		0.9	1.1	0.8	1.2			
26										
27		Units Sold		3592	4390	3192	4789	15962		given formula
28		Revenue		143662	175587	127700	191549	638498		price*units
29		Cost of Goods		89789	109742	79812	119718	399061		cost*units
30		Gross Margin		53873	65845	47887	71831	239437		subtraction
31										

FIGURE 6.2
The Paste Special
Window

production and exploration worldwide. In the semiconductor business, a scenario might involve a breakthrough in optical technology that leads to the first chip powered by light. To translate these stories into useful terms, we would have to determine how such events influence specific parameters in a co-ordinated fashion.

In the Advertising Budget example, we can construct an optimistic scenario in which prices are high ($50) and costs are low ($20), yielding a profit of $285,000. Similarly, we could construct a pessimistic scenario, in which prices are low ($35) and costs are high ($30), leading to a loss of $78,000. Each scenario tells a coherent story that has meaning to the decision makers and is implemented in the model through a set of two or more parameters. Excel offers a way to record the inputs and outputs of multiple scenarios in the Scenario Manager. We select Tools→Scenarios and enter the first scenario by clicking on the Add button and entering the information required in the Add Scenario window and (after clicking OK) the Scenario Values window. Thereafter, we can use the Edit button to change the details, or the Add button to enter another scenario. Figure 6.3 shows the window for the Scenario Manager after the optimistic and pessimistic scenarios have been

FIGURE 6.3
The Scenario Manager
Window

added. If we click on the Show button, the values corresponding to the selected scenario are placed in the spreadsheet. If we click on the Summary button, we obtain the summary table shown in Figure 6.4.

As an application of scenario analysis, consider the case of Heineken Brewery. The modeling task in this case was to develop a forecast for Heineken profits over the five years 1999–2003. Because of uncertainty over the strategies that major players in the beer industry would pursue over this time period, no single base case was considered appropriate. Three scenarios were developed, as described below.

Business As Usual: The industry avoids major price wars, and financial returns improve slightly. Heineken's performance is the same as in the late 1990s, and, in the near future, the company makes two major acquisitions and some small ones. Heineken continues to globalize and augments its market share by 8% over the five years.

Price War: The industry price wars started by Miller and Busch continue worldwide, dropping returns toward the cost of capital. Heineken's performance is stable, but with weaker margins and no new acquisitions.

Market Discipline: The industry consolidates and avoids price wars. Heineken improves gross margins through an aggressive mergers-and-acquisitions program. It becomes a leader in the drive for industry consolidation.[1]

FIGURE 6.4
The Summary Produced
by the Scenario Manager

AdBudget6.xls

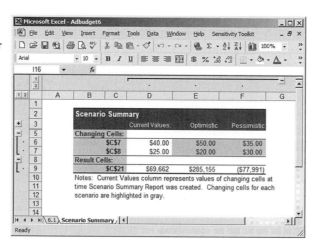

---

[1] Copeland, T., T. Koller, and J. Murrin, *Valuation* (New York: John Wiley, 2002), 252.

These alternative futures were then translated into alternative sets of input parameters. For the Price War scenario, two adjustments were made to the Business As Usual assumptions: revenue growth would be 0 percent rather than 2 percent, and 1 percent (rather than 3 percent) of revenue growth would come from acquisitions. In the Market Discipline scenario, growth by acquisitions was increased so that Heineken augments its market share by 15 percent.

The results of the Heineken scenario analysis are summarized below. To focus on just one result, we can see that equity per share is 19.3 guilders lower in the Price War scenario, and 40.5 guilders higher in the Market Discipline scenario, relative to the Business As Usual scenario.

Result	Units	Price War	Business As Usual	Market Discipline
Average annual growth	Percentage	2.4	5.6	7.0
Average ROIC	Percentage	13.0	13.1	14.2
Company value	NLG Billion*	29.8	35.8	48.5
Equity value	NLG Billion	27.5	33.5	46.2
Equity value per share	NLG	87.6	106.9	147.4
Probability	Percentage	15.0	60.0	25.0

*Netherlands guilders

Data Sensitivity

The **Data Sensitivity** tool automates certain kinds of what-if analysis. It simply recalculates the spreadsheet for a series of values of an input cell and tabulates the resulting values of an output cell. This allows the analyst to perform several related what-if tests in one pass rather than entering each input value and recording each corresponding output.

The Data Sensitivity tool is one module in the **Sensitivity Toolkit,** which is an add-in that accompanies this book. Once the Toolkit is installed, the Sensitivity Toolkit option will appear on the far right of the menu bar (see Figure 6.1). Data Sensitivity and the other modules can be accessed from this menu.

We illustrate the use of the Data Sensitivity tool in the Advertising Budget model by showing how variations in unit cost from a low of $20 to a high of $30 affect profit. We first select Sensitivity Toolkit→Data Sensitivity. The first window provides a choice for Table Type, which we leave at the default of One-Way Table. For the result cell, we enter C21, which is the output cell in our model.

After pressing the Next button, we proceed to a window that asks for the information needed to produce a one-way table. The Cell to Vary is C8, which contains the unit-cost parameter. The Input Type has two options: Begin, End, Increment and Begin, End, Num Obs (Number of Observations). We most often use the default choice of Begin, End, Increment. In the three blank windows, we enter the values describing the series of unit costs we wish to investigate: 20, 30, 1, as shown in Figure 6.5. This designs a table in which the unit cost varies from $20 to $30 in steps of $1.

Figure 6.6 shows the output generated by the Data Sensitivity tool. A worksheet has been added to the workbook, and the first two columns on the sheet contain the table of what-if values. In effect, the what-if test has been repeated for each unit-cost value from $20 to $30 in steps of $1, and the results have been recorded in the table. In addition, the table is automatically converted to a graph, which can be edited at the user's discretion for cosmetic purposes. As the table and graph both show, annual profits drop as the unit cost increases, and the cost-profit relationship is linear. We can also see that the breakeven value of the unit cost falls between $29 and $30, since profits cross from positive values to negative values somewhere in this interval.

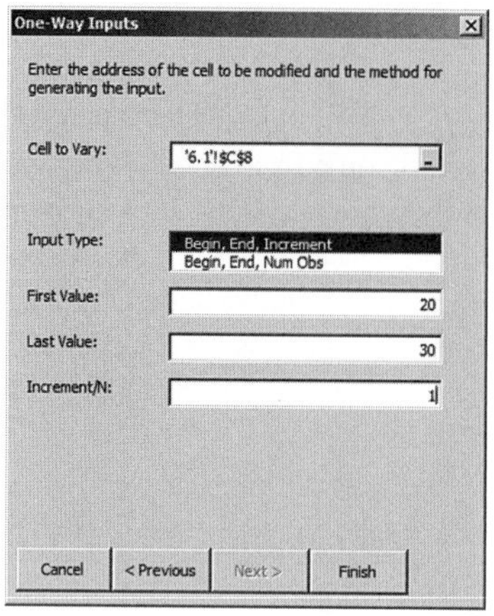

FIGURE 6.5
The One-Way Inputs for Data Sensitivity

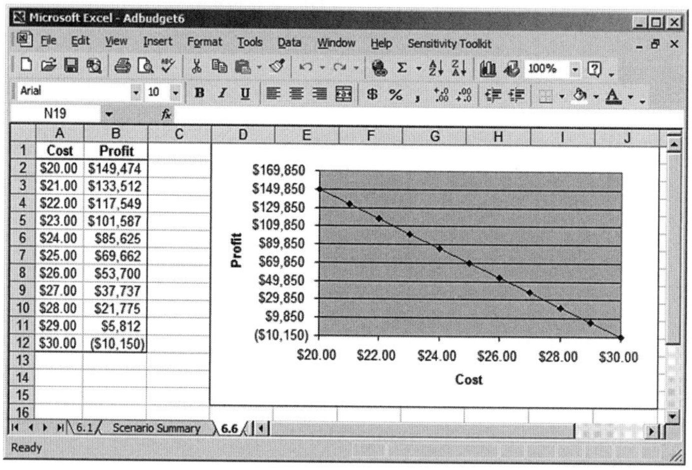

FIGURE 6.6
A Graph Based on Data Sensitivity

AdBudget6.xls

Note that the Data Sensitivity tool requires that we provide a single cell address to reference the input being varied in a one-way table. The tool will work correctly only if the input has been placed in a single location. By contrast, if an input parameter had been embedded in several cells, the tool would have given incorrect answers when we tried to vary the input. Thus, the use of single and separate locations for parameters (or for decisions), which we advocated in Chapter 5, makes it possible to take advantage of the tool's capability.

We can also use the Data Sensitivity tool to analyze the sensitivity of an output to *two* inputs. This option gives rise to a two-way table, in contrast to the one-way sensitivity table illustrated above. To demonstrate this feature, we can build a table showing how profits are affected by both Q1 advertising and Q2 advertising. When we invoke the Data Sensitivity tool after using it for the one-way analysis, some of the values we specified remain visible. Thus, for example, the Result Cell remains C21 and does not need editing. In the Two-Way Inputs window, we ask for both cells to vary from $5,000 to $15,000 in steps of $1000, giving rise to the table shown in Figure 6.7 (after some modest reformatting), which appears on another newly added sheet. A quick check that helps us confirm our work is to look up the profit value in the table corresponding to advertising expenditures of $10,000 in both Q1 and Q2. In the center of the table, we see that this value is $69,662, as expected.

FIGURE 6.7
Data Sensitivity: Profit
as a Function of Q1
and Q2 Advertising

AdBudget6.xls

Microsoft Excel - Adbudget6											

	A	B	C	D	E	F	G	H	I	J	K	L
1	Profit: $D$18 by $E$18											
2												
3	Q1						Q2					
4		$5,000	$6,000	$7,000	$8,000	$9,000	$10,000	$11,000	$12,000	$13,000	$14,000	$15,000
5	$5,000	$64,180	$65,060	$65,838	$66,529	$67,145	$67,695	$68,187	$68,625	$69,017	$69,366	$69,676
6	$6,000	$64,718	$65,598	$66,376	$67,067	$67,683	$68,233	$68,725	$69,164	$69,555	$69,904	$70,214
7	$7,000	$65,173	$66,053	$66,831	$67,522	$68,138	$68,688	$69,179	$69,618	$70,010	$70,359	$70,669
8	$8,000	$65,557	$66,437	$67,215	$67,906	$68,522	$69,072	$69,563	$70,002	$70,394	$70,743	$71,053
9	$9,000	$65,879	$66,759	$67,537	$68,228	$68,844	$69,394	$69,885	$70,324	$70,716	$71,065	$71,375
10	$10,000	$66,147	$67,027	$67,805	$68,496	$69,112	$69,662	$70,153	$70,592	$70,984	$71,333	$71,643
11	$11,000	$66,367	$67,247	$68,025	$68,716	$69,332	$69,882	$70,374	$70,813	$71,204	$71,553	$71,863
12	$12,000	$66,544	$67,424	$68,203	$68,894	$69,510	$70,060	$70,551	$70,990	$71,382	$71,731	$72,040
13	$13,000	$66,683	$67,563	$68,341	$69,033	$69,648	$70,198	$70,690	$71,129	$71,520	$71,869	$72,179
14	$14,000	$66,787	$67,667	$68,445	$69,136	$69,752	$70,302	$70,793	$71,232	$71,624	$71,973	$72,283
15	$15,000	$66,858	$67,738	$68,517	$69,208	$69,824	$70,374	$70,865	$71,304	$71,696	$72,045	$72,354
16												

By studying Figure 6.7, we can make a quick comparison between the effect of additional spending in Q1 and the effect of the same spending in Q2. As we can observe in the table, moving across a row generates more profit than moving the same distance down a column. This pattern tells us that we can gain more from spending additional dollars in Q2 than from the same additional dollars in Q1. Thus, starting with the base case, we could improve profits by shifting dollars from Q1 to Q2. We can also note from the table, or from the three-dimensional chart that automatically accompanies it, that the relationship between profits and advertising expenditures is not linear. Instead, profits show diminishing returns.

Tornado Charts

Another useful tool for sensitivity analysis is the **tornado chart.** In contrast to the information produced by the Data Sensitivity tool, which shows how sensitive an output is to one or perhaps two inputs, a tornado chart shows how sensitive the output is to several different inputs. Consequently, it shows us which parameters have a major impact on the results and which have little impact.

Tornado charts are created by changing input values one at a time and recording the variations in the output. The simplest approach is to vary each input by a fixed percentage, such as ±10 percent, of its base-case value. For each parameter in turn, we increase the base-case value by 10 percent and record the output, then decrease the base-case value by 10 percent and record the output. Next, we calculate the absolute difference between these two outcomes and depict the results in the order of these differences.

The Sensitivity Toolkit contains a tool for generating tornado charts. For the Advertising Budget example, we select Sensitivity Toolkit→Tornado Chart and specify cell C21 as the result cell, just as we did when using the Data Sensitivity tool. Next, we designate the Input Parameters for the chart. Given the structure of our model (refer to Figure 6.1), we can simply enter the range C7:G15, since the tool will ignore blank cells and titles. However, it is also possible to enter a list of cells in the usual fashion, by holding down the Control key and pointing to each cell or cell range desired.

The Tornado Chart tool provides a choice of three options:

- Constant Percentage
- Variable Percentage
- Percentiles

Suppose we select Constant Percentage and click the Next button. In the Constant Inputs window, we enter 10. In this instance, we are varying the following parameters by ±10 percent of their base-case values: price, unit cost, overhead percentage, two sales parameters, four seasonal factors, four quarterly sales expenses, and the advertising budget. The final step is to click Finish.

The tornado chart appears on a newly inserted worksheet, as shown in Figure 6.8. The horizontal axis at the top of the chart shows profits; the bars in the chart show the changes in profit resulting from ±10 percent changes in each input. After calculating the values, the bars are sorted from largest to smallest for display in the diagram. Thus, the most sensitive inputs appear at the top, with the largest horizontal spans. The least sensitive inputs appear toward the bottom, with the smallest horizontal spans. Drawing the chart using horizontal bars, with the largest span at the top and the smallest at the bottom, suggests the shape of a tornado, hence the name. If some of the information in the chart seems unclear, details can usually be found in the accompanying table, which is constructed on the same worksheet by the Tornado Chart tool. In our example, we can see in the table that price has the biggest impact (a range of more than $108,000), with unit cost next (a range of nearly $80,000), and the other inputs far behind in impact on profit.

The standardization achieved by using a common percentage for the change in inputs (10 percent in our example) makes it easy to compare the results from one input to another, but it may also be misleading. A 10 percent range may be realistic for one parameter, while 20 percent is realistic for another, and 5 percent for a third. The critical factor is the size of the forecast error for each parameter. If these ranges are significantly

FIGURE 6.8
Tornado Chart using the
Constant Percentage
Option

AdBudget6.xls

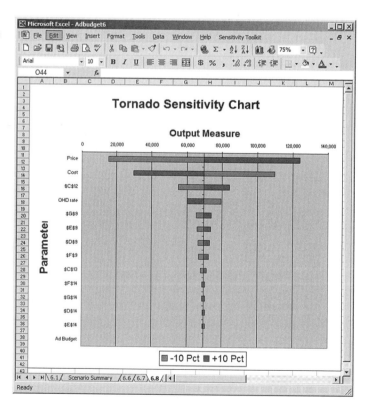

different, we should assign different percentages to different inputs. This can be accomplished using the Variable Percentage option in the Tornado Chart tool.

To illustrate the Variable Percentage option in the Advertising Budget example, we will limit ourselves to including price, cost, seasonal factors, and overhead rate. Suppose that, based on a detailed assessment of the uncertainty in these parameters, we want to vary price by 5 percent, cost by 12 percent, seasonal factors by 8 percent, and overhead rate by 3 percent. Before invoking the tool, we must enter this information into our spreadsheet. A reliable way to do so is to duplicate the range containing the input parameters in an unused region of the spreadsheet and then replace each parameter with the corresponding percentage. In this example, we can copy cells B6:G10 and paste into the range K6:P10. Then, we can replace the parameters we wish to vary with the corresponding percentages.

When we invoke the Tornado Chart tool, the Result Cell remains unchanged. For Input Parameters, we enter the range C7:G10 and select the Variable Percentage type of analysis. When we click on the Next button, we come to the Variable Inputs window, where we can enter the range L6:P10 and click Finish.

The resulting tornado chart is shown in Figure 6.9. As the results show, cost now has the biggest impact on profits, partly because it has a larger range of uncertainty than price.

In Chapter 7, we discuss how to use confidence-interval information to guide the Variable Percentage analysis when some of our parameters are based on sample data. Later, in Chapter 9, we show how to use Monte Carlo simulation to fully account for uncertainty in spreadsheet models. There, we also explain how to use the Percentiles option in the Tornado Chart tool, and we show how a tornado chart can serve as a useful first step in simulation analysis.

FIGURE 6.9
Tornado Chart Using the Variable Percentage Option

AdBudget6.xls

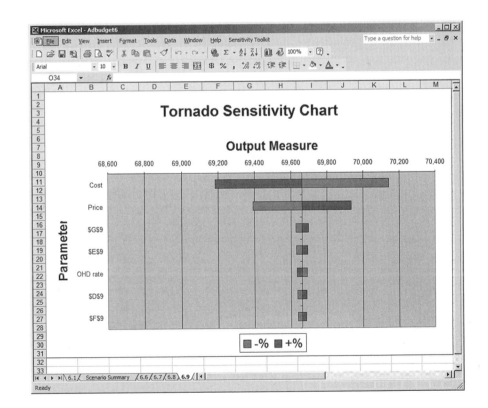

Breakeven Analysis

Many managers and analysts throw up their hands in the face of uncertainty about critical parameters. If we ask a manager to directly estimate market share for a new product, the reply may be: "I have *no idea* what market share we'll capture." A powerful strategy in this situation is to reverse the sense of the question and ask not, "What will our market share be?" but rather, "How high does our market share have to get before we turn a profit?" The trick here is to look for a **breakeven,** or cutoff, level for a parameter—that is, a target value of the parameter at which some particularly interesting event occurs, such as reaching zero profits or making a 15 percent return on invested assets. Managers who cannot predict market share can often determine whether a particular breakeven share is likely to occur. This is why breakeven analysis is so powerful.

Even if we have no idea of the market share for the new product, we should be able to build a model that calculates profit given some *assumption* about market share. Once market share takes the role of a parameter in our model, we can use the Data Sensitivity tool to construct a graph of profit as a function of market share. Then, from the graph, we can find the breakeven market share quite accurately.

New capital investments are usually evaluated in terms of their net present value, but the appropriate discount rate to use is not always obvious. Rather than attempting to determine the appropriate discount rate precisely, we can take the breakeven approach and ask how high would the discount rate have to be in order for this project to have an NPV of zero? (The answer to this question is generally known as the *internal rate of return.*) If the answer is 28 percent, we can be confident that the project is a good investment. On the other hand, if breakeven occurs at 9 percent, we may want to do further research to establish whether the discount rate is clearly below this level.

Breakeven values for parameters can be determined manually, by repeatedly changing input values until the output reaches the desired target. This can often be done fairly quickly by an intelligent trial-and-error search in Excel. In the Advertising Budget example, suppose we want to find the breakeven cost to the nearest penny. Recall our example earlier, where we noted that profit goes to zero between a unit cost of $29 and a unit cost of $30. By repeating the search between these two costs in steps of $0.10, we can find the breakeven cost to the nearest dime. If we repeat the search once more, in steps of $0.01, we will obtain the value at the precision we seek.

However, Excel also provides a specialized tool called **Goal Seek** for performing this type of search. Three pieces of information are required: the output-cell address, the target level sought, and the input for which the search is conducted. To determine the breakeven cost in the Advertising Budget example, we select Tools→Goal Seek. The Set Cell is Profit in C21; the To Value is the profit target of zero; and the Changing Cell is unit cost, in C7. With these three specifications, the Goal Seek window takes the form shown in Figure 6.10. The tool locates the desired unit cost as $29.36, and the corresponding calculations will be displayed on the spreadsheet (see Figure 6.11). Choosing the OK button in the Goal Seek Status window preserves these values in the spreadsheet; choosing the Cancel button returns the spreadsheet to its base case.

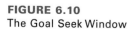

FIGURE 6.10
The Goal Seek Window

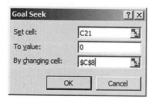

FIGURE 6.11

Using the Goal Seek Tool in the Advertising Budget Example

AdBudget6.xls

	A	B	C	D	E	F	G	H	I	J
1	Advertising Budget Model									
2	SGP/KRB									
3	1/1/2000									
4										
5	PARAMETERS									
6				Q1	Q2	Q3	Q4			Notes
7		Price	$40.00							Current price
8		Cost	$29.36							Accounting
9		Seasonal		0.9	1.1	0.8	1.2			Data analysis
10		OHD rate	0.15							Accounting
11		Sales Parameters								
12			35							Consultants
13			3000							
14		Sales Expense		8000	8000	9000	9000			Consultants
15		Ad Budget	$40,000							Current budget
16										
17	DECISIONS							Total		
18		Ad Expenditures		$10,000	$10,000	$10,000	$10,000	$40,000		sum
19										
20	OUTPUTS									
21		Profit	$0		Base case	$69,662				
22										
23	CALCULATIONS									
24		Quarter		Q1	Q2	Q3	Q4	Total		
25		Seasonal		0.9	1.1	0.8	1.2			
26										
27		Units Sold		3592	4390	3192	4789	15962		given formula
28		Revenue		143662	175587	127700	191549	638498		price*units
29		Cost of Goods		105463	128899	93745	140617	468724		cost*units
30		Gross Margin		38199	46688	33955	50932	169775		subtraction
31										

Note that the Goal Seek tool searches for a prescribed level in the relation between a single output and a single input. Thus, it requires the parameter or decision being varied to reside in a single location, reinforcing one of the design principles we introduced in Chapter 5.

Optimization Analysis

Another fundamental type of managerial question takes the form of finding a set of decision variables that achieves the best possible value of an output. In fact, we might claim that the fundamental management task is to make choices that result in optimal outputs. **Solver** is an important tool for this purpose. Solver is an add-in for Excel that makes it possible to optimize models in which there may be constraints on the choice of decision variables. Optimization is a complex subject, and we devote Chapter 8 to it and to the use of Solver. However, we can provide a glimpse of its power by demonstrating a simple application in the Advertising Budget example.

Suppose we wish to maximize total profits with an advertising budget of $40,000. We already know that, with equal expenditures in every quarter, annual profits come to $69,662. The question now is whether we can achieve a higher level of annual profits. The answer is that a higher level is, in fact, attainable. An optimal reallocation of the budget produces annual profits of $71,447. The chart in Figure 6.12 compares the allocation of the budget in the base case with the optimal allocation. As we can see, the optimal allocation calls for greater expenditures in quarters Q2 and Q4 and for smaller expenditures in Q1 and Q3. We defer the details of using the Solver until Chapter 8.

This is just one illustration of Solver's power. Among the many questions we could answer with Solver in the Advertising Budget example are these:

■ What would be the impact of a requirement to spend at least $8,000 each quarter?

FIGURE 6.12
Comparison of Base-
Case and Optimal
Allocations

AdBudget6.xls

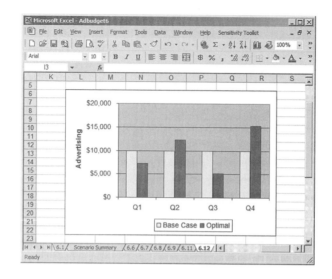

- What would be the marginal impact of increasing the budget?
- What is the optimal budget size?

Chapter 8 develops the tools and techniques to answer these and a host of related questions for a variety of spreadsheet models.

Simulation and Risk Analysis

Uncertainty often plays an important role in analyzing a decision, because with uncertainty comes risk. Until now, we have been exploring the relationship between the inputs and outputs of a spreadsheet model as if uncertainty were not at issue. However, risk is an inherent feature of all managerial decisions, so it is frequently an important aspect of spreadsheet models. In particular, we might want to recognize that some of the inputs are subject to uncertainty. In other words, we might want to associate probability models with some of the parameters. When we take that step, it makes sense to look at outputs the same way—with probability models. The use of probability models in this context is known as **risk analysis.**

The tool we use for risk analysis in spreadsheets is **Crystal Ball,** an add-in for Monte Carlo simulation that is supplied with this book. This tool allows us to generate a probability distribution for any output cell in a spreadsheet, given probability assumptions about some of the input cells. Simulation and risk analysis are the subjects of Chapter 9. Here, we simply illustrate how Crystal Ball can help us answer an important question about risk.

In the Advertising Budget example, we return to the base case, with equal expenditures of $10,000 on advertising each quarter. Our base-case analysis, which assumed that all parameters are known exactly, showed an annual profit of $69,662. However, we might wonder about the distribution of profits if there's uncertainty about the unit price and the unit cost. Future prices depend on the number of competitors in our market, and future costs depend on the availability of raw materials. Since both level of competition and raw-material supply are uncertain, so, too, are the parameters for our price and cost. Suppose we assume that price is normally distributed with a mean of $40 and a standard deviation of $10, and that unit cost is equally likely to fall anywhere between $20 and

$30. Given these assumptions, what is the probability distribution of annual profits? And how likely is it that profits will be *negative?*

Figure 6.13 shows the probability distribution for profits in the form of a histogram, derived from the assumptions we made about price and cost. The graph shows us that the estimated average profit is $69,756 under our assumptions. It also shows that the probability is about 33 percent that we will lose money. This exposure may cause us to reevaluate the desirability of the base-case plan.

We defer the details of using Crystal Ball until Chapter 9. There, we show how to:

- Determine which inputs require probability models.
- Select appropriate probability models for those inputs.
- Configure Crystal Ball to generate a histogram for any output cell.

Chapter 9 develops the tools and techniques to address uncertain elements in the analysis, for a variety of spreadsheet models.

SUMMARY

The process of analyzing a spreadsheet model has several identifiable steps. The first step is to construct a base case, which becomes a key point of comparison for all of the subsequent analyses. The next step is what-if analysis: changing inputs and tracing the effects on one or more of the outputs. Early in the development of a spreadsheet, this step is an aid in debugging the model, as we mentioned in Chapter 5. Once the spreadsheet has been debugged and tested, what-if analysis helps us discover how sensitive an output is to one or more of the inputs. Furthermore, the Data Sensitivity tool helps us automate one-at-a-time sensitivity analysis. The information produced by this tool is also translated into a chart so that relationships can be portrayed visually.

A tornado chart provides another form of what-if analysis, treating several of the inputs at once. Scenario analysis can be used to analyze the outputs for a set of inputs that together tell a story. Whatever tool we use, probing for sensitivities helps provide useful insight in support of management decisions. In the Advertising Budget example, our early probing revealed that profits respond in straight-line fashion to changes in the unit cost and that profits show diminishing returns to additional advertising expenditures.

A related step involves inverting the analysis, where we start with a target for a particular output and "back into" the input value that achieves that target level of performance. The most prominent form is breakeven analysis, which aims at a target of zero, but the concept can be applied to any target level. Excel provides the Goal Seek tool to automate the search for a single input value that achieves a desired output value. Breakeven analysis provides us with an early indication of risk: we can determine how much of a "cushion" there is in any one of our parameter forecasts. Should the actual value turn out to be worse than

FIGURE 6.13
Distribution of Profits from the Advertising Budget Example

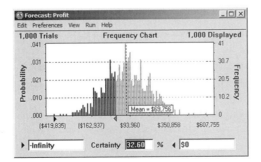

our base-case assumption, breakeven analysis tells us how much of a difference we can tolerate before our output measure drops to zero. In the Advertising Budget example, the $25 unit cost could grow to more than $29 before we would face negative profits.

The most ambitious forms of analysis are optimization and simulation. Optimization methods look for the best value of an output by searching through various combinations of the decisions. Simulation methods allow some of the inputs to be treated as probabilistic, tracing the implications for outputs. These two methods represent advanced techniques of modeling, and we devote full chapters to them. In our analysis framework, they play the role of powerful tools capable of delivering further insights. In the Advertising Budget example, the insight obtained from optimization was that the allocation of advertising expenditures across the four quarters should not be equal, but should, in some way, reflect the size of the seasonal factors. In fact, further optimization analysis reveals that the $40,000 budget itself is probably too small. A larger budget could increase profitability.

The progression from a base case to what-if and breakeven analysis, then to optimization and simulation analyses, represents a logical and increasingly sophisticated set of methods for *experimenting* with a spreadsheet model. This kind of experimentation provides the opportunity for the same kind of learning that a scientist derives from laboratory experiments. Indeed, the spreadsheet is the electronic laboratory for an analyst, and in supporting management decisions with laboratory work, the analyst is serving as a *management scientist*. In the next chapters, we develop the management scientist's advanced modeling tools.

EXERCISES

1. Refer to the Flexible Insurance Coverage case. From the corresponding exercise in Chapter 5, review the design of a spreadsheet that will allow an individual employee to compare the annual expenses for each plan and thereby choose the cheapest alternative.

   Questions

   a. Consider the case of a single employee with estimated annual expenses of $400. What plan is the cheapest? What is the total annual cost associated with this plan?

   b. For the analysis in (a), construct a table to show the best plan and the associated cost for annual expenses ranging from $100 to $1,200 in steps of $100.

   c. Consider the case of a married employee with estimated annual expenses of $800 and $250 for the spouse. What plan is the cheapest? What is the total annual cost associated with this plan?

   d. For the analysis in (c), construct a table to show the best plan and the associated cost for annual expenses ranging from $400 to $1,400 in steps of $100 for the employee and from $200 to $1,200 in steps of $100 for the spouse.

2. Refer to the Two-Part Tariff case. From the corresponding exercise in Chapter 5, review the design of a spreadsheet that will allow management to compare choices of access fee and usage rate and thereby choose the most profitable alternative.

   Questions

   a. Find a pricing scheme (access fee and usage rate for each segment) that satisfies the required conditions.

   b. Construct a table to determine the range of values for the unit cost ($1.00 in the base case) for which the solution in (a) will hold.

3. Refer to the Producer Responsibility case. From the corresponding exercise in Chapter 5, review the design of a spreadsheet that will allow BMW management to estimate the cost of disposal a decade into the future (i.e., in 1999) as a percentage of net income.

Questions

a. What percentage is predicted for 1999, assuming there are no changes in trends and policies?

b. Construct a tornado chart for the analysis in (a). List the relevant parameters in descending order of their impact on the disposal cost.

4. Refer to the XYZ Company case. From the corresponding exercise in Chapter 5, review the design of a spreadsheet that will allow an analyst to predict monthly cash needs and profitability for the first five months of the year.

Questions

a. In what month does the cash balance fall below zero, signaling a need to borrow money?

b. What is the net income, as a percentage of sales, in April?

c. Suppose the monthly increment in sales is 600—instead of 500, as in the base case. How does this change affect the answers in (a) and (b)? Construct a table to examine the month in which cash balance disappears as a function of the monthly increment in sales.

d. Suppose the monthly increment in sales is 300—instead of 500, as in the base case. How does this change affect the answers in (a) and (b)? Construct a graph showing the profitability percentage in (b) as a function of the monthly increment in sales.

5. Refer to the Damon Appliances case. From the corresponding exercise in Chapter 5, review the design of a spreadsheet that will generate the monthly pro forma income statements and balance sheets for the coming year.

Questions

a. For the given production plan, what is the profit for the year and the maximum amount of money that will need to be borrowed (i.e., the credit limit)?

b. What if the production plan corresponds to the figures in the following table: how does this change the answers in (a)? (The first row of this table gives the workforce size, and the second row gives the production quantity each month.)

Jan	Feb	Mar	Apr	May	Jun	Jul	Aug	Sep	Oct	Nov	Dec
40	40	40	40	40	40	56	56	56	56	56	40
320	320	320	320	320	420	558	548	548	548	448	320

6. Refer to the Retirement Planning case. From the corresponding exercise in Chapter 5, review the design of a spreadsheet for this problem.

Questions

a. Develop a base case. You may create any data you need for this purpose. Why is this base case appropriate for this situation?

b. Perform an appropriate sensitivity analysis. Which parameters have the most significant impact on the results? Can you find applications for the Data Sensitivity, Tornado Chart, and Scenario Manager tools?

c. Identify applications of the Goal Seek tool in this situation. (For example, find the savings rate needed to ensure that assets do not run out before age ninety.)

d. Identify a potential application of *optimization* in this case.

e. Identify potential applications of *simulation* in this case.

7. Refer to the Draft TV Commercials case. From the corresponding exercise in Chapter 5, review the design of a spreadsheet for this problem.

Questions

a. Develop a base case. You may create any data you need for this purpose. Why is this base case appropriate for this situation?

b. Perform an appropriate sensitivity analysis. Which parameters have the most significant impact on the results? Can you find applications for the Data Sensitivity, Tornado Chart, and Scenario Manager tools?

c. Identify applications of Goal Seek in this situation. (For example, what percentage of the overall budget should be devoted to draft commercials in order to achieve a preset target number of impressions?)

d. Identify a potential application of *optimization* in this case.

e. Identify potential applications of *simulation* in this case.

8. Refer to the Icebergs for Kuwait case. From the corresponding exercise in Chapter 5, review the design of a spreadsheet for this problem.

Questions

a. Develop a base case. You may create any data you need for this purpose. Why is this base case appropriate for this situation?

b. Perform an appropriate sensitivity analysis. Which parameters have the most significant impact on the results? Can you find applications for the Data Sensitivity, Tornado Chart, and Scenario Manager tools?

c. Identify applications of Goal Seek in this situation. (For example, how large an iceberg should they tow in order to break even at the current price for drinking water?)

d. Identify a potential application of *optimization* in this case.

e. Identify potential applications of *simulation* in this case.

9. Refer to the Racquetball Racket case. From the corresponding exercise in Chapter 5, review the design of a spreadsheet for this problem.

Questions

a. Develop a base case. You may create any data you need for this purpose. Why is this base case appropriate for this situation?

b. Perform an appropriate sensitivity analysis. Which parameters have the most significant impact on the results? Can you find applications for the Data Sensitivity, Tornado Chart, and Scenario Manager tools?

c. Identify applications of Goal Seek in this situation. (For example, what percentage of the market must they achieve to break even on their investment?)

d. Identify a potential application of *optimization* in this case.

e. Identify potential applications of *simulation* in this case.

CHAPTER 7

DATA ANALYSIS IN THE SERVICE OF MODELING

INTRODUCTION

In this chapter, we discuss the roles that data, data analysis, and statistics play in modeling, and we present a variety of relevant Excel tools. Data analysis and statistical techniques are used in many situations, not all of which are pertinent to the building of spreadsheet models for decision making. Since that has been our focus throughout the book, we organize this chapter around tools that are most useful in that context.

We emphasize that modeling is motivated by the existence of a problem to be resolved or a decision to be made. In the course of developing and testing a model for the purpose of shedding light on the problem, we may decide to collect empirical data. However, the collection and analysis of that data is a means to an end, not a primary goal. Data analysis should be undertaken only to improve the accuracy and usefulness of the conclusions drawn from the model, not to enhance the model for its own sake. In that sense, data analysis *supports* the modeling process, but modeling remains the primary focus.

As we have mentioned, data analysis and statistical techniques are often used in contexts other than in modeling. Data analysis, for example, is often used to provide general background for managers. A marketing manager might ask for a report on company sales by geographic region and by product line—not to help make a specific decision, but simply to better understand the business environment. A credit card company might request a study to identify the predictors of overdue accounts, even though no specific decision is at hand. These uses of data analysis and statistical methods, while valuable in their own right, are not the focus of this chapter.

In Chapter 3, we recommended an emphasis on *structuring the model,* not on collecting data. Novice modelers generally place too much reliance on empirical data and fail to recognize biases, distractions, and irrelevancies in the data collection process. That is why, in Chapter 5, we stressed the importance of prototyping using readily available data, even roughly estimated data. Moreover, in Chapter 6, we noted the importance of using sensitivity analysis to determine which parameters have a significant impact on the results and may therefore be worthy of further refinement through data analysis.

We emphasize model structure over data analysis because we find that model structure almost always has a strong impact on the ultimate recommendations. Analysis of empirical data, on the other hand, may or may not have such an impact. The modeling process itself, as described in earlier chapters, suggests what data to collect and how accurate that data must be for the purposes at hand.

As with optimization and simulation, which are the advanced techniques covered in later chapters, we have found that working analysts can themselves do much of the data analysis they need. To do so, they need an understanding of the fundamentals of data analysis and statistics. Most analysts will call on experts when their needs go beyond the fundamentals. With that in mind, our coverage in this chapter includes four major topics:

- finding facts in databases (searching, editing, sorting, and filtering)
- estimating parameters (point estimates and interval estimates)
- estimating relationships among two or more variables (simple, multiple, and nonlinear regression)
- forecasting a single variable (time-series methods)

Throughout this chapter, we use an extended example to illustrate some of the practical issues surrounding the use of data in spreadsheet modeling. Our example involves a typical spreadsheet model, built to help determine the capacity of a new manufacturing plant. In the next section, we describe the problem and present a base-case analysis. In subsequent sections, we illustrate how to apply data-analysis tools in this model. By focusing on the business decision to be made, rather than on the model itself, we illustrate how data can sometimes, but not always, materially influence a decision.

A Decision-Making Example

Forecasts of future sales are an essential ingredient in selecting the capacity of a new manufacturing facility. While capacity can be adjusted up or down during the life of a plant, it is usually less expensive to build the appropriate size at the start. In this example, we illustrate how to build a model to help determine the size for a new plant.

EXAMPLE

A Capacity Decision

Bundy Pharmaceuticals, Inc. (BPI) is planning to shift production of its popular arthritis drug from overseas contract suppliers to domestic manufacturing. The question BPI faces is how big a plant to build. Sales of the drug have been growing over the past decade, but future sales cannot be known for certain. Too small a plant will leave some demand unsatisfied, while too large a plant will lead to inefficiencies.

The current price of the drug is $10 per unit. Since sales have increased from around 500,000 units to more than one million units over the past ten years, BPI is currently considering plant capacities in the range from 1.2 million to 2.5 million units annually. Within this range, it costs a minimum of $5 million to build a plant, with an incremental cost of approximately $10 per unit of annual capacity. For example, a 1.5 million-unit plant costs $20 million.

Once a plant has been built, its capacity determines both its variable and fixed costs of operation. The fixed costs are estimated to be $1.50 for each unit of capacity. Assuming a capacity of at least one million units, the maximum variable costs are $6 per unit. Each incremental 100,000 units of capacity above one million reduce variable costs by $0.10. For example, variable costs are $5.50 for a 1.5 million-unit plant. Corporate policy specifies that new plant decisions be made on the basis of a ten-year NPV using a discount rate of 10 percent.

Base-Case Analysis

Our first cut at creating a model for this situation should be based on simple, but reasonable, assumptions. The purpose of this prototype is primarily to translate the given information into a usable model structure with limited effort and rework. As shown in Figure 7.1, the model includes seven parameters that are given in the problem description. The

FIGURE 7.1
Base-Case Spreadsheet

Bundy.xls

	Microsoft Excel - Bundy										

E20   fx =H36

	A	B	C	D	E	F	G	H	I	J	K
1	Bundy Pharmaceuticals Inc.										
2	SGP/KRB										
3	1-Jan-00										
4											
5		Parameters	Interest rate		10%						
6			Unit revenue		$10.00						
7			Plant construction cost								
8				fixed	$5,000,000						
9				variable	$10.00						
10			Fixed operating cost		$1.50						
11			Variable operating cost								
12				maximum	$6.00						
13				decline rate	$0.10						
14			Demand								
15				Initial level	1,010,000						
16				Annual growth	50,000						
17											
18		Decisions		Capacity	1,500,000						
19											
20		Results		NPV	$561,374						
21											
22		Model	Plant Cost	$20,000,000							
23											
24				Year	Demand	Sales	Vcost	Fcost	Cash Flow		
25				0	1010000				($20,000,000)		
26				1	1060000	1060000	5.50	2250000	$2,520,000		
27				2	1110000	1110000	5.50	2250000	$2,745,000		
28				3	1160000	1160000	5.50	2250000	$2,970,000		
29				4	1210000	1210000	5.50	2250000	$3,195,000		
30				5	1260000	1260000	5.50	2250000	$3,420,000		
31				6	1310000	1310000	5.50	2250000	$3,645,000		
32				7	1360000	1360000	5.50	2250000	$3,870,000		
33				8	1410000	1410000	5.50	2250000	$4,095,000		
34				9	1460000	1460000	5.50	2250000	$4,320,000		
35				10	1510000	1500000	5.50	2250000	$4,500,000		
36								NPV	$561,374		
37											

Construction costs occur throughout year 0. They are recognized at the end of the year and discounted back to the start of the year.

Ongoing revenues and costs are recognized at the end of each year.

All costs are discounted back to the start of year 0.

Ready

model also has one decision variable (plant capacity), which is arbitrarily set to 1.5 million at this stage. One area that needs special consideration is the forecast of demand over the next ten years. Historical data on sales over the past ten years are given in the table below. (Note: since offshore production capacity has been used, there has not been a year in which demand exceeded sales.)

Year	Unit Sales
1	487,000
2	560,000
3	601,000
4	689,000
5	788,000
6	854,000
7	902,000
8	957,000
9	991,000
10	1,010,000

This is not the time, however, to undertake an elaborate and time-consuming statistical analysis of these data. At this early stage in the modeling process, we have no idea how critical the demand forecast is to the decision at hand. For this first prototype, we will look for a way to incorporate the essential features of the given data with minimal effort.

A quick glance at the demand history shows that sales have grown from about 500,000 ten years ago to about one million last year. A simple but plausible forecast of future demand would be to assume that this rate of increase (about 50,000 units per year) will continue for the next ten years. We need two parameters to represent demand according to these assumptions: an initial value (1.01 million) and the annual growth rate (50,000). Accordingly, demand next year is 1.06 million, growing to 1.51 million ten years out. We will continue to assume a capacity of 1.5 million, since the task of finding the *best* capacity level is yet to come. Under these assumptions, demand first exceeds 1.5 million (causing unsatisfied demand) only in the tenth year. The NPV for this case is $0.561 million, as calculated by the model in Figure 7.1.

Sensitivity Analysis

Given that the base-case model accurately represents our understanding of the problem, we next wish to explore the implications for the capacity decision. Since we have only a single decision variable, we can use the Data Sensitivity tool to find the optimal capacity. The results are shown in Figure 7.2. It appears that the best we can do here is an NPV of $1.811 million with a 1.25 million-unit plant. Notice that with a capacity of 1.25 million, demand begins to exceed capacity in year 5. The optimal capacity level balances the costs of building additional capacity with the benefits of increased sales and lower variable costs. This result is, of course, only a first estimate—an initial, rough idea of where the best capacity level may lie, given a simple model and a number of assumptions, each of which should be tested. (A refinement of the table in Figure 7.2 shows that a slight improvement can be made by choosing capacity of 1.26 million, but we don't imagine that capacity plans would distinguish alternatives at this level of precision.)

One way to test our model is to determine the sensitivity of the NPV to each of the input parameters. This can be accomplished using a tornado chart, as shown in Figure 7.3. In this chart, each of the parameters was varied by 10 percent from its base-case value. Keeping in mind the caveats we mentioned in Chapter 6 about tornado charts, this chart shows that two parameters, unit revenue and minimum variable operating cost, have the largest impacts on NPV. The initial demand level has some impact on the NPV, but the growth rate in demand has a relatively small impact, assuming that a 10 percent deviation is an accurate representation of the true uncertainty. This is at least partly because at a

FIGURE 7.2
Optimal Capacity
Determination for
the Base Case

Bundy.xls

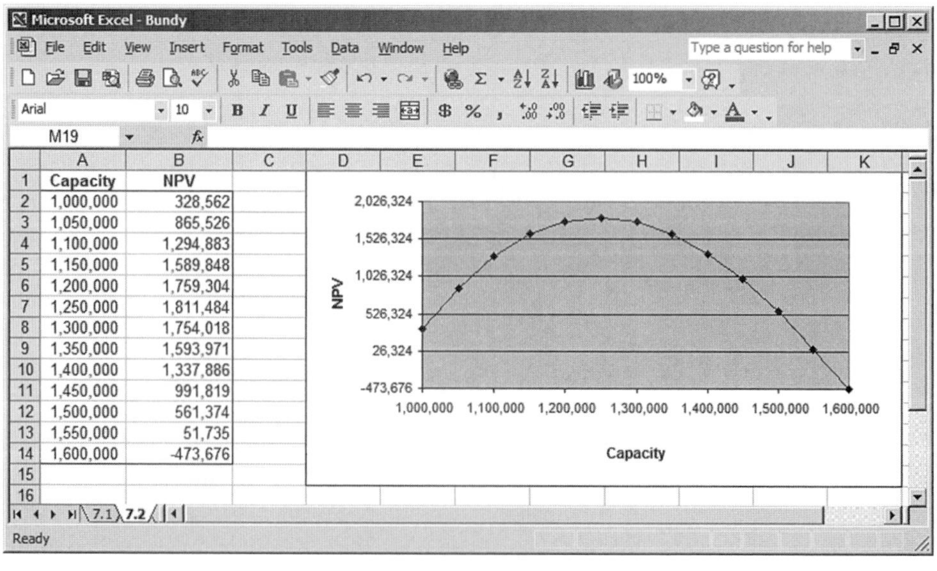

	A	B
1	Capacity	NPV
2	1,000,000	328,562
3	1,050,000	865,526
4	1,100,000	1,294,883
5	1,150,000	1,589,848
6	1,200,000	1,759,304
7	1,250,000	1,811,484
8	1,300,000	1,754,018
9	1,350,000	1,593,971
10	1,400,000	1,337,886
11	1,450,000	991,819
12	1,500,000	561,374
13	1,550,000	51,735
14	1,600,000	-473,676

FIGURE 7.3
Tornado Chart for the
Base Case

Bundy.xls

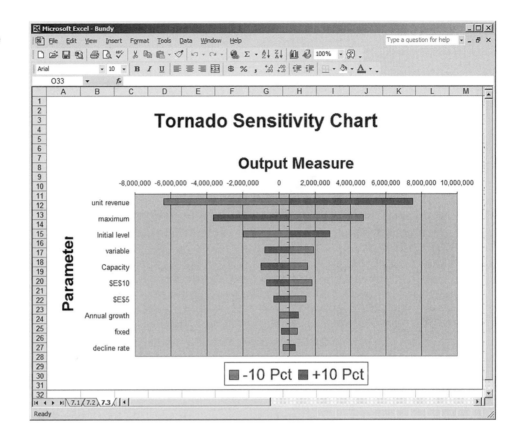

capacity of 1.25 million, sales reach capacity in year 4, so later growth in sales has no impact on the NPV.

Another useful insight can be derived from sensitivity analysis. For example, let's examine the annual growth rate of 50,000 units. How sensitive is the optimal capacity to this assumption? We can repeat the sensitivity test of capacity for a variety of growth parameters. This gives rise to a two-way sensitivity table (see Figure 7.4)—resembling the first sensitivity table, but with a different column for each different growth rate. We've used a bold font in the table to highlight the maximum NPV in each column, showing the location of the optimal capacity for each growth rate. The results show that optimal capacity is relatively insensitive to the growth parameter. When we vary the growth parameter from 10,000 to 90,000 units per year, a factor of nine, the optimal capacity increases from 1.05 million to 1.5 million, or only about 50 percent. Now, it is unlikely that future growth is as uncertain as we have depicted it here. If, in fact, future growth lies somewhere between 40,000 and 60,000 units per year, and we build a plant based on an assumed rate of 50,000 units, our resulting NPV will fall short of the optimum by less than 5 percent.

Base-Case Summary

Our base-case results suggest that if demand growth is around 50,000 units per year over the next ten years, we should build about 1.25 million units of capacity. Sensitivity analysis shows that if we are confident that actual demand growth will be between, say, 40,000 and 60,000 units annually, then 1.25 million units is close to the optimal level. This may well be enough precision for making a good decision. After all, many things about the future are uncertain, in addition to demand. Recommending an optimal plant capacity of

FIGURE 7.4
Sensitivity of Optimal
Capacity to Demand
Growth

Bundy.xls

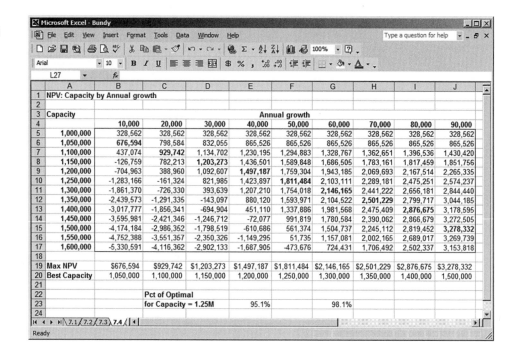

1.234567 million units would suggest an implausible level of precision in the analysis. Later, we return to this example and apply statistical methods to explore their impact.

FINDING FACTS FROM DATABASES

One of the ways we encounter data is in the form of a database. For our purposes, a **database** is a table of information, with each row corresponding to a **record** in the database and each column corresponding to a **field** for the various records. For example, one record might correspond to a single customer order, and the fields might include the customer's name, items ordered, and total value of order. Excel refers to a table of this type as a **list.** The first row of a list contains names for each of the fields. Each successive row contains one record. In this section, we cover some basic Excel commands that help us manipulate lists and thus seek out information in a given database. We consider commands that edit, search, sort, or filter information in a database, along with the Pivot Table command.

As examples, we'll work with three databases:

- Analgesics.xls, with data on retail sales of painkillers
- Applicants.xls, with data on MBA applicants from one year's pool
- Executives.xls, with data on executive compensation for a sample of companies

Figure 7.5 shows a portion of the Analgesics.xls database. A second worksheet in the database provides definitions of the fields, in case the column titles are not self-explanatory. The information in the database describes more than 7,500 sales transactions for a variety of painkillers over a ten-week period at six different stores that form part of a retail chain. We might use this database to answer such questions as the following:

- What were the market shares of the various brands?
- What were weekly sales volumes at the different stores?

FIGURE 7.5
First Portion of the
Analgesics Database

Analgesics.xls

	A	B	C	D	E	F	G	H	I	J	K
1	ID	ITEM	UPC	DESCRIPTION	SIZE	STORE	WEEK	SALES			
2	1	6122741	2586610502	ALEVE CAPLETS	24 CT	101	383	0			
3	2	6122741	2586610502	ALEVE CAPLETS	24 CT	101	384	0			
4	3	6122741	2586610502	ALEVE CAPLETS	24 CT	101	385	0			
5	4	6122741	2586610502	ALEVE CAPLETS	24 CT	101	386	0			
6	5	6122741	2586610502	ALEVE CAPLETS	24 CT	101	387	0			
7	6	6122741	2586610502	ALEVE CAPLETS	24 CT	101	388	0			
8	7	6122741	2586610502	ALEVE CAPLETS	24 CT	101	389	0			
9	8	6122741	2586610502	ALEVE CAPLETS	24 CT	101	390	0			
10	9	6122741	2586610502	ALEVE CAPLETS	24 CT	101	391	0			
11	10	6122741	2586610502	ALEVE CAPLETS	24 CT	101	392	0			
12	11	6122741	2586610502	ALEVE CAPLETS	24 CT	103	383	0			
13	12	6122741	2586610502	ALEVE CAPLETS	24 CT	103	384	0			
14	13	6122741	2586610502	ALEVE CAPLETS	24 CT	103	385	0			
15	14	6122741	2586610502	ALEVE CAPLETS	24 CT	103	386	0			
16	15	6122741	2586610502	ALEVE CAPLETS	24 CT	103	387	0			
17	16	6122741	2586610502	ALEVE CAPLETS	24 CT	103	388	0			
18	17	6122741	2586610502	ALEVE CAPLETS	24 CT	103	389	0			
19	18	6122741	2586610502	ALEVE CAPLETS	24 CT	103	390	0			
20	19	6122741	2586610502	ALEVE CAPLETS	24 CT	103	391	0			
21	20	6122741	2586610502	ALEVE CAPLETS	24 CT	103	392	0			
22	21	6122751	2586610504	ALEVE CAPLETS	50 CT	102	383	0			
23	22	6122751	2586610504	ALEVE CAPLETS	50 CT	102	384	0			
24	23	6122751	2586610504	ALEVE CAPLETS	50 CT	102	385	0			
25	24	6122751	2586610504	ALEVE CAPLETS	50 CT	102	386	0			

(We use past tense here to emphasize that, although we are interested in projecting into the future, the data actually tell us something about the past.)

Figure 7.6 shows a portion of the Applicants.xls database. Again, a second worksheet provides a glossary for the field names. The information was collected on nearly 3,000 applicants to a well known MBA program, showing the status of the applicant pool on a date early in the summer. We might use this database to answer such questions as the following:

FIGURE 7.6
First Portion of the
Applicants Database

Applicants.xls

	A	B	C	D	E	F	G	H	I
1	ID	ROUND	AGE	SEX	CITZ CODE	1ST CONTACT	JOB MONTHS	INDUSTRY	INDUSTRY DESC.
2	1	1	30	M	U	Email	84	260	Finan Serv-Diversified
3	2	1	29	M	U	Phone call	86	370	Government
4	3	1	27	M	U	Phone call	40	260	Finan Serv-Diversified
5	4	1	30	M	U	Email	48		
6	5	1	32	M	U	Home Page	85	290	Finan Serv-Invest Mgt/Research
7	6	1	26	M	U	Home Page	32	280	Finan Serv-Invest Bk/Brokerage
8	7	1	29	M	U	Phone call	60	10	Accounting
9	8	1	27	F	U		44	220	Entertainment/Leisure/Media
10	9	1	29	M	U	Phone call	66	40	Agribusiness
11	10	1	31	M	U	Letter	78	420	Nonprofit
12	11	1	27	M	U	Phone call	24	460	Retail
13	12	1	27	M	U	Phone call	51	370	Government
14	13	1	28	M	U		26	230	Environmental Services
15	14	1	30	M	U	Phone call	72	20	Advertising/Marketing Services
16	15	1	27	F	U	Phone call	48	420	Nonprofit
17	16	1	25	M	U	Home Page	31	260	Finan Serv-Diversified
18	17	1	24	F	U	Phone call	24	210	Energy/Utilities
19	18	1	28	M	U	Phone call	31	400	Law
20	19	1	27	M	N	Home Page	54	80	Construction
21	20	1	26	M	U	Letter	32	230	Environmental Services
22	21	1	24	M	U	World Wide Web	24	580	Other Services
23	22	1	27	M	U	Phone call	46	260	Finan Serv-Diversified
24	23	1	28	M	U	Home Page	50	160	Consumer Gds-Food/Beverage
25	24	1	28	M	U	Home Page	60	10	Accounting

- How many applicants had nonprofit work experience?
- How did GMAT score vary with the timing of the application?

Figure 7.7 shows a portion of the Executives.xls database. The information constitutes sample of 100 records from a publicly available survey of executive compensation. We might use this database to answer such questions as the following:

- What proportion of compensation was due to annual bonuses?
- What factors seemed to explain the value of an executive's salary?

These three databases contain what we might think of as "raw" data. That is, the databases were not necessarily compiled for the purpose of answering the questions we posed. They were likely built for other purposes, or on the hope that they might be generally helpful to unspecified users.

Searching and Editing

It is usually helpful to assign a range name to a list. For example, we assign the range name *Data* to our lists, so that we can easily select the entire database, including column titles. With the database selected, we choose Data→Form. A form appears that is tailored to the structure of the database, as shown in Figure 7.8 for the Analgesics list. This form allows us to examine the records one at a time, using the Find Prev and Find Next buttons. We can also enter a record, using the New button, or delete a record, using the Delete button.

A simple way to search for a record in the database is to click on the form's Criteria button, type an identifying entry into one of the field windows, and then click on Find Next. A broader search of the entire database, which does not rely on the form, uses the Edit→Find command, after the database has been selected. With this command, entries in the database can be edited by using the Find and Replace commands in tandem. One of

FIGURE 7.7
First Portion of the
Executives Database

Executives.xls

ID	EXECID	GENDER	SALARY	BONUS	OTHER	SHARES	CONAME	TICKER
2611	6	MALE	683.462	412.768	0.000	207.828	ADC TELECOMMUNICATIONS INC	ADCT
4666	29	MALE	750.000	1012.500	0.000	641.691	ALLTEL CORP	AT
2702	74	MALE	875.000	1000.000	22.100	2234.402	ARROW ELECTRONICS INC	ARW
5562	85	MALE	324.389	80.563	0.000	16632.050	ATMEL CORP	ATML
314	111	MALE	750.000	825.000	294.770	183.031	BAXTER INTERNATIONAL INC	BAX
2766	140	MALE	509.734	77.257	0.000	354.541	BOB EVANS FARMS	BOBE
2777	152	MALE	700.000	317.665	0.000	39.928	KEYSPAN CORP	KSE
5588	167	MALE	820.677	500.000	45.687	1208.415	CALLAWAY GOLF CO	ELY
516	197	MALE	1350.000	1965.000	0.000		CHEVRON CORP	CHV
2962	223	MALE	1000.000	0.000	0.000	255.198	CMS ENERGY CORP	CMS
2654	246	MALE	1357.026	2162.508	91.721	1517.168	AFLAC INC	AFL
5865	313	MALE	933.333	5554.350	300.034	6033.567	TRIARC COS INC -CL A	TRY
822	315	MALE	771.018	463.200	0.000	224.861	EASTERN ENTERPRISES	EFU
9283	393	MALE	1000.000	2750.000	143.698	643.966	FREEPRT MCMOR COP&GLD -CL B	FCX
5067	398	MALE	205.000	0.000	56.891	9040.113	HUMANA INC	HUM
16384	415	MALE	550.000	275.000	60.703	48.542	BARNES GROUP INC	B
1016	418	MALE	620.000	952.468	0.000	334.430	GENUINE PARTS CO	GPC
10891	474	MALE	410.004	400.000	0.000	1469.256	HORACE MANN EDUCATORS CORP	HMN
3296	482	MALE	450.000	0.000	0.000	151.477	HUNT (JB) TRANSPRT SVCS INC	JBHT
3367	522	MALE	750.000	0.000	46.067	740.528	KANSAS CITY SOUTHERN INDS	KSU
1329	555	MALE	1185.577	3331.968	0.000	46497.711	LIMITED INC	LTD
4837	563	MALE	1051.946	0.000	712.393	17308.998	LOEWS CORP	LTR
1459	608	MALE	369.231	0.000	77.757	141.572	MCKESSON HBOC INC	MCK
1679	705	MALE	730.769	0.000	159.776		OGDEN CORP	OG

FIGURE 7.8
Form for the
Analgesics Database

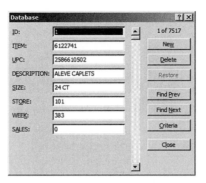

the flexible aspects of the Find/Replace command is the use of the symbols "?" and "*" to assist in these operations. The question mark stands for a single symbol, and the asterisk stands for any sequence of symbols.

Question: In the Analgesics database, which transactions involve the brand Aleve?

In the database, there are entries for individual brands with tablets, caplets, gelcaps, and the like, each indicated in the Description field. For the purposes of investigating sales by brand name, we would like to combine all of these variations into a single descriptor for each brand. To accomplish this conversion, we use the Find command to locate Aleve* (where the asterisk stands for anything that may follow the brand name in the description of the item). Then, we use the Replace window to designate the replacement as Aleve. By clicking on the Replace All option, we convert the description of all Aleve brand items to the same description (see Figure 7.9).

Sorting

The Sort command can be used not only for database sorting but also for sorting any contiguous set of rows and columns on a spreadsheet. It is found on the Data menu. We give an example using the Executives database and another using the Applicants database.

Question: In the Executives database, are there any duplicate records?

Suppose we wish to determine whether any executive (identified by the identification number in column B) is represented more than once in the sample. We begin by selecting the database. (Exploiting the range name, we do this by clicking the pull-down menu of range names, located directly above column A, and selecting the name Data.) Then, we choose Data→Sort. By default, the Sort command is set up to sort by rows and to preserve column titles while doing so. We next go to the pull-down menu associated with the Sort by window, where we select the title EXECID and click on Ascending (see Figure 7.10). When we click on OK, the sorting procedure is carried out. Then, when we scan the ID numbers in the sorted list, we can see that no two adjacent entries match. Therefore, no executive appears twice in the list.

EXCEL TIP: THE SORT COMMAND

When we want to use the Sort command, but a row of titles is not present, the corresponding button in the command window should be selected. Meanwhile, the Options button offers the possibility of sorting by columns instead of by rows. Note also that although the Sort operation can be reversed by the Undo command, it is often a good idea to save the data to a new worksheet before sorting, so that the sorted data can be saved separately.

FIGURE 7.9
Replacing Compound
Descriptions with a
Simple Brand Name

Analgesics.xls

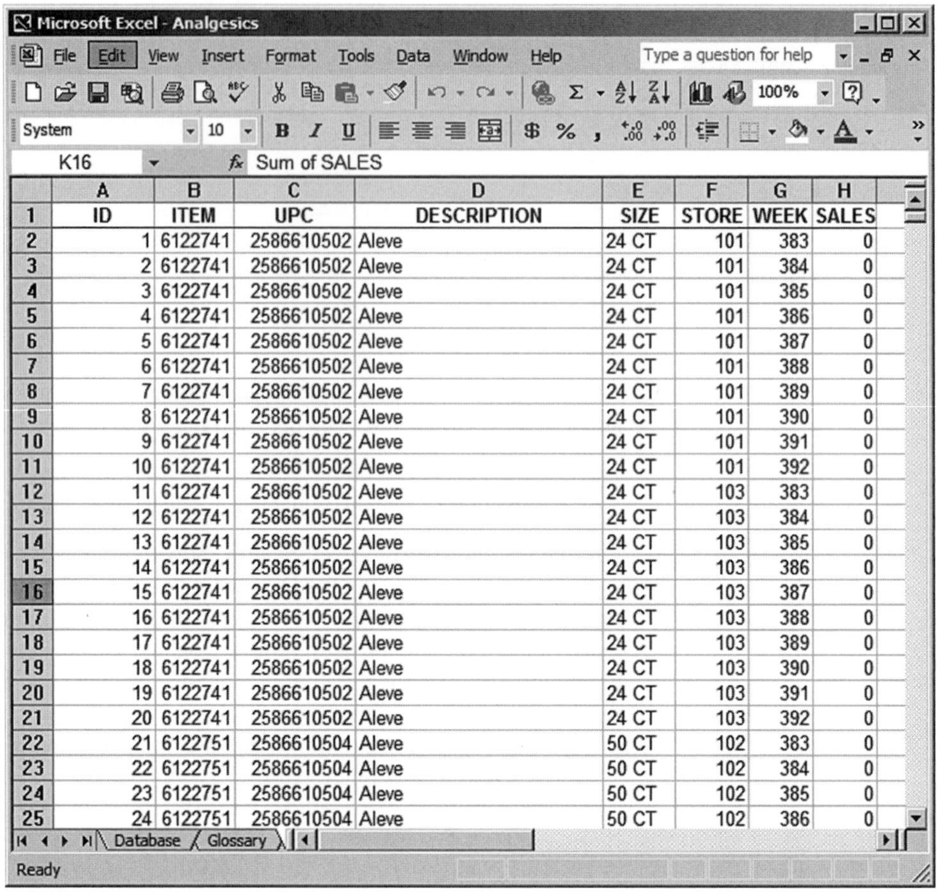

	A	B	C	D	E	F	G	H
1	ID	ITEM	UPC	DESCRIPTION	SIZE	STORE	WEEK	SALES
2	1	6122741	2586610502	Aleve	24 CT	101	383	0
3	2	6122741	2586610502	Aleve	24 CT	101	384	0
4	3	6122741	2586610502	Aleve	24 CT	101	385	0
5	4	6122741	2586610502	Aleve	24 CT	101	386	0
6	5	6122741	2586610502	Aleve	24 CT	101	387	0
7	6	6122741	2586610502	Aleve	24 CT	101	388	0
8	7	6122741	2586610502	Aleve	24 CT	101	389	0
9	8	6122741	2586610502	Aleve	24 CT	101	390	0
10	9	6122741	2586610502	Aleve	24 CT	101	391	0
11	10	6122741	2586610502	Aleve	24 CT	101	392	0
12	11	6122741	2586610502	Aleve	24 CT	103	383	0
13	12	6122741	2586610502	Aleve	24 CT	103	384	0
14	13	6122741	2586610502	Aleve	24 CT	103	385	0
15	14	6122741	2586610502	Aleve	24 CT	103	386	0
16	15	6122741	2586610502	Aleve	24 CT	103	387	0
17	16	6122741	2586610502	Aleve	24 CT	103	388	0
18	17	6122741	2586610502	Aleve	24 CT	103	389	0
19	18	6122741	2586610502	Aleve	24 CT	103	390	0
20	19	6122741	2586610502	Aleve	24 CT	103	391	0
21	20	6122741	2586610502	Aleve	24 CT	103	392	0
22	21	6122751	2586610504	Aleve	50 CT	102	383	0
23	22	6122751	2586610504	Aleve	50 CT	102	384	0
24	23	6122751	2586610504	Aleve	50 CT	102	385	0
25	24	6122751	2586610504	Aleve	50 CT	102	386	0

K16   *fx* Sum of SALES

Microsoft Excel - Analgesics

File Edit View Insert Format Tools Data Window Help   Type a question for help

System   10   B I U $ % ,   100%

Database / Glossary

Ready

FIGURE 7.10
Sorting the Executives
Database by the
EXECID Field

Question: In the Applicants database, how does work experience vary among the applicants in successive rounds?

In the previous example, we chose one basis for sorting—the executive identification. Note that we left two windows blank in the Sort by window. Excel allows up to three sort criteria. When two are specified, ties on the first criterion are broken by the second; and when three are specified, ties on the second criterion are broken by the third. In the Applicants database, for example, we can sort first by Round, then by Industry, and then by Job Months (see Figure 7.11) to get a sense of how applications arrive over time from people in different industries and with different lengths of service in their current job. We might observe, for example, that the applicants with relatively fewer months in advertising tend to apply in the first two rounds.

Filtering

The Filtering capabilities in Excel allow us to probe a large database and extract a portion of it that deals with the specific records in which we are interested. We may simply want to view the extracted portion temporarily, or we may want to store it separately, for further analysis. As an illustration, we use the Applicants database.

Question: In the Applicants database, what are the characteristics of the applicants from nonprofit organizations?

Suppose we want to view only the applicants who worked in nonprofit organizations. We first select the database and then the Data→Filter menu item, finally choosing AutoFilter from the submenu. This step adds a list arrow to the title of each column. If we click on the Industry Description list arrow and choose Nonprofit, we see the subset of the database that contains Nonprofit entries (Figure 7.12). Notice that Filtering does not actually extract any records, but merely hides rows that do not match the filter criteria. Thus, in Figure 7.12, we see that applicants from the Nonprofit sector appear in rows 11, 16, 87, 103, and so on. We can copy and paste this subset to a different sheet, if we wish. Alternatively, to restore the view of the entire database, we can either select (All) using the list arrow again, or we can return to the submenu from which we selected AutoFilter and select Show All. Note that while we are viewing a filtered subset of the database, the triangle marking the list arrow we had used shows up in a blue color. This is a reminder that the information on the screen is filtered.

Notice that one of the options on the arrow list is the Top 10 option. We can use this option with numerical data to isolate the records with the smallest or largest values of a numerical record.

Question: In the Applicants database, what are the ages of the oldest applicants?

For example, to find the ten oldest applicants, we select the Top 10 option for the Age field (see Figure 7.13 for the result). We could similarly create a list of the Top 10 percent, by editing the "items" window. By editing the "10" window, we can restrict ourselves to the Top 5 or the Top 12, and so on; and by editing the "Top" window, we can obtain the Bottom 5, or the Bottom 15 percent, and so on. Figure 7.14 shows the windows for the Top 10 option.

FIGURE 7.11
Sorting the Applicants
Database Using
Three Fields

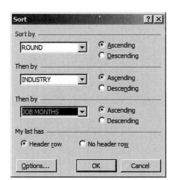

FIGURE 7.12
Filtering the Applicants Database to Highlight Nonprofit Backgrounds

Applicants.xls

Microsoft Excel - Applicants

	A II	B ROUN	C AG	D SE	E CITZ COD	F 1ST CONTACT	G JOB MONTH	H INDUSTR	I INDUSTRY DES
11	10	1	31	M	U	Letter	78	420	Nonprofit
16	15	1	27	F	U	Phone call	48	420	Nonprofit
87	86	1	29	M	U	Test Score Tape (DNU)	4	420	Nonprofit
103	102	1	27	M	U	World Wide Web	30	420	Nonprofit
174	173	1	26	M	U	Home Page	37	420	Nonprofit
176	175	1	28	M	U	Phone call	60	420	Nonprofit
209	208	1	32	F	U	Home Page	108	420	Nonprofit
328	327	1	30	M	U	Phone call	62	420	Nonprofit
336	335	1	35	M	U	Phone call		420	Nonprofit
344	343	1	27	M	U	Phone call	44	420	Nonprofit
375	374	1	32	M	U	Home Page	88	420	Nonprofit
412	411	1	27	F	U	Phone call	48	420	Nonprofit
428	427	1	29	F	U	Phone call	62	420	Nonprofit
454	453	1	29	F	N	Test Score Tape (DNU)	56	420	Nonprofit
470	469	1	32	M	N	World Wide Web	61	420	Nonprofit
521	520	1	29	M	U	Home Page	72	420	Nonprofit
578	577	2	26	M	U	Test Score Tape (DNU)	26	420	Nonprofit
614	613	2	30	M	U	Home Page	6	420	Nonprofit
686	685	2	37	M	U	Letter	144	420	Nonprofit
748	747	2	28	F	U	Phone call	60	420	Nonprofit
825	824	2	29	M	N	Letter	58	420	Nonprofit
990	989	2	29	F	U	Phone call	67	420	Nonprofit
998	997	2	32	M	U	Reapplicant	98	420	Nonprofit
1120	1119	3	28	F	U	Phone call	35	420	Nonprofit
1172	1171	3	26	M	U	Home Page	36	420	Nonprofit

Database / Glossary \ Nonprofit /

Filter Mode

FIGURE 7.13
Filtering the Applicants Database to Find the Ten Oldest Applicants

Applicants.xls

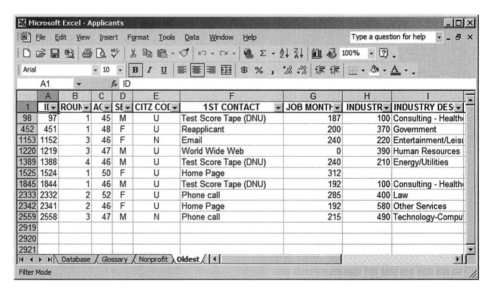

FIGURE 7.14
The Windows for the Top 10 Option

Question: Isolate the applicants who worked in either the Nonprofit or Government sectors.

Another option on the arrow list is the Custom option, which allows us to filter data using compound criteria. For example, to isolate the applicants who worked in *either* the Nonprofit or Government sectors, we select the Custom option and click the Or button in the AutoFilter Custom window to set up the appropriate logical structure (see Figure 7.15).

Question: Isolate the applicants who worked in either the Nonprofit or Government sectors and had GMAT scores above 700.

For more complicated descriptions of compound criteria, we use the Advanced Filter option on the Data→Filter submenu. Suppose, for example, that we wish to isolate the applicants who worked in either the Nonprofit or Government sectors and had GMAT scores above 700. First, we must add our selection criteria to the list. We begin by adding four rows to the sheet containing the original database (one of which will remain blank, just for spacing). In row 1, we duplicate the field names by copying row 5. Then, in column I, we enter Nonprofit and Government in rows 2 and 3, and we enter ">700" under GMAT in these same rows. Row 2 will select for Nonprofit and GMAT > 700. Row 3 will select for Government and GMAT > 700. Thus, multiple criteria in a single row are connected by AND; criteria in separate rows are connected by OR. Now we select the original database and the Advanced Filter item on the submenu, which brings up the display shown in Figure 7.16. The windows that this command provides allow us to specify the location of the database (which has already be selected) and the location of the criteria (A1:K3). Before filling in these two windows, we can click on a button to indicate whether we want to view the results or copy the results to a separate location in the workbook.

FIGURE 7.15
Setting Up a
Compound Filter

FIGURE 7.16
Setting Up an
Advanced Filter

Tabulating

The Pivot Table option on the Data menu allows us to view summaries of the data in convenient tables, most often in formats known as **cross-tabulation tables,** or **cross-tabs.** To appreciate how pivot tables work, we return to the Analgesics database and specifically to the edited version where we combined all of the item descriptions into single-word brand names. (The modified data are saved as a separate worksheet, with the database named Data2.) In what follows, we describe the construction of three pivot tables, each an elaboration on the one before.

Question: What are total sales of painkillers, and how do they break down by brand name and by store?

We begin by selecting the database and then choosing the Pivot Table option (actually, the Pivot Table Wizard) from the Data menu. The first two steps automatically apply, and we can proceed by clicking the Next button. At step 3, we can choose to put results on the existing worksheet, in cell K1.

Now we click on the Layout button. A map of a pivot table appears, as shown in Figure 7.17, and we drag the SALES icon into the DATA box. The icon in the DATA box gets renamed Sum of SALES. (If it is renamed something else, such as Count of SALES, double-click on that name, and a small window appears, similar to the one in Figure 7.18. Select Sum in the main window of this option and click OK.) Then, we click OK in the Layout window and click Finish in the wizard. These steps place the first pivot table in the spreadsheet (in cells K1:L2), revealing a total sales quantity of 9,432 units.

FIGURE 7.17
Layout Options for
a Pivot Table

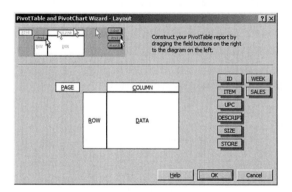

FIGURE 7.18
Display Options for the
Data in the Pivot Table

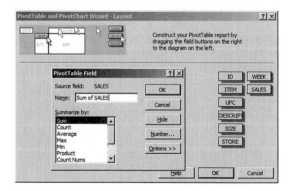

To build our second table, we close the small windows on the screen, return to the Pivot Table Wizard, and repeat the process. At step 3, we revise the layout. This time, we designate cell K4 as the home for the table, and we drag the DESCRIPTION icon to the ROWS box, as well as dragging the SALES icon to the DATA box, as we did before. When we click on Finish, we see a table in cells K4:L14 that breaks down the 9,432 sales transactions by brand name. For example, we see that Tylenol has the highest sales, at 2,770 units.

To build our third table, we repeat the steps once more, choosing cell K16 as the home cell. This time, we drag the STORE icon to the COLUMNS box, the DESCRIPTION icon to the ROWS box, and the SALES icon to the DATA box. When we click on Finish, we see a table that breaks down the sales transactions by brand and by store, with row and column totals provided. The table resides in the range of cells K16:R26. Figure 7.19 shows all three tables as they appear in the spreadsheet. In the third table, we can see that whereas store 102 has the highest number of transactions, store 100 sells the most Tylenol.

Having constructed our pivot table, we can modify it after the fact. For example, we can use the arrows in the row or column headings to limit our table to just certain row and column entries. The Pivot Table window that remains on the screen also allows us to edit the table we created. We can, for example, substitute WEEK for STORE in the column location, to obtain a breakdown of sales by week and by brand.

Question: In the Applicants database, how does GMAT score vary according to the round in which the application is filed?

FIGURE 7.19
Three Pivot Tables Showing Sales Data at Various Levels of Detail

Analgesics.xls

	J	K	L	M	N	O	P	Q	R
1		Sum of SALES	Total						
2		Total	9432						
3									
4		Sum of SALES							
5		DESCRIPTION ▾	Total						
6		Advil	2136						
7		Aleve	996						
8		Anacin	365						
9		Bayer	1019						
10		Bufferin	156						
11		Excedrin	1325						
12		Motrin	665						
13		Tylenol	2770						
14		Grand Total	9432						
15									
16		Sum of SALES	STORE ▾						
17		DESCRIPTION ▾	100	101	102	103	104	105	Grand Total
18		Advil	434	469	499	207	301	226	2136
19		Aleve	229	169	274	106	125	93	996
20		Anacin	105	64	93	29	11	63	365
21		Bayer	213	223	312	65	111	95	1019
22		Bufferin	32	32	46	8	26	12	156
23		Excedrin	211	235	444	132	188	115	1325
24		Motrin	120	128	183	76	98	60	665
25		Tylenol	737	543	705	270	222	293	2770
26		Grand Total	2081	1863	2556	893	1082	957	9432
27									

The admissions process operates on a rolling basis, with a series of five decision periods, or rounds. In developing a strategy for round-by-round selections, it is helpful to know whether there are systematic differences among the rounds. To probe this topic, we return to the Applicants database and set up a pivot table. At the Layout step, we place ROUND in the ROW box and Average GMAT in the DATA box. Figure 7.20 displays the result. Evidently, there is a trend toward lower GMAT scores during the course of the overall admission period.

ANALYZING SAMPLE DATA

As explained earlier, our context for data analysis is determining parameters for our models. For example, we might want to determine the price parameter in the Advertising Budget model. If we have data on past prices—say, quarterly data for ten years—we can expect to use this information to help determine the price parameter for next year. But next year's price could be different from any of the prices we have seen over the past ten years. We think of the past data as a sample from some population of prices, just as next year's price is another sample, perhaps from the same or a related population.

We call the set of all possible values for a parameter the **population.** If we were to obtain data for the entire population, then we could build a comprehensive numerical picture of the parameter we are using in our model. Numerical features of populations are described by probability distributions, and, in modeling applications, we are often interested in three measures related to the probability distribution:

- the mean of the distribution
- the variance of the distribution
- a tail probability, or proportion, in the distribution

It is seldom the case, however, that we find ourselves with data covering an entire population. For one thing, the population may have infinite size, making it impossible to obtain all the data. But even with manageable populations, it may be prohibitively time-consuming or expensive to collect population data. Instead, we find ourselves working with information from a portion of the entire population; this portion is called the **sample.** In this situation, **statistics** are summary measures about the values in the sample, and the goal is to construct statistics that are representative of the overall population.

When we were analyzing the Analgesics database, we assumed implicitly that our data were complete. In other words, the database contains data on *all* sales for the given stores and time periods. By contrast, the Executives database does not cover all executives; it is a sample of 100 records drawn from a larger population.

FIGURE 7.20
Pivot Table Showing
Average GMAT Scores
by Round

Applicants.xls

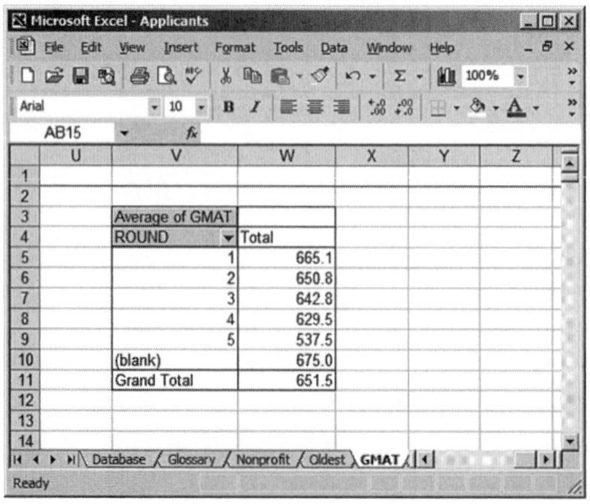

ROUND	Total
1	665.1
2	650.8
3	642.8
4	629.5
5	537.5
(blank)	675.0
Grand Total	651.5

TERMS USED IN SAMPLING

Population: the set of all possible values of a parameter

Sample: a subset of the population

Statistic: a summary measure of sample values

The analysis of sample data provides a basis for estimating each of the three measures that help to describe a population (mean, variance, and tail probability). Ideally, the sample data points are drawn from the population of interest. As a practical matter, this may not be possible, but we might have a situation where the population from which samples are drawn is considered to be equivalent to the population of interest. For example, if we are interested in modeling customer demand for *next* month, we may use data on demand in the *previous* twelve months. At some level, observations from six months ago cannot be considered samples from the population of future demand levels, but there may be enough stability in the demand process that we can consider future populations to be essentially equivalent to six-month-old populations. This is an area where judgment is a crucial element in model building.

Samples can be generated in different ways, and the sampling process can determine whether the data are valuable or not. The most common forms of sampling are convenience sampling and random sampling. As its name implies, **convenience sampling** refers to a situation where we have easy access to information about a particular subset of the population. However, a convenience sample may not be representative. Suppose an insurance company wants a sample of customers in order to estimate family incomes, and it happens that one of its staff members is about to process the forms for all of this month's new customers. Can we use the income data from this group of customers as a sample? It is certainly convenient, because the processing will be taking place in any event. But new customers tend to be younger than the set of all customers, and their incomes tend to be lower. Thus, if we use the convenience sample to estimate income, we will be working with a sample that is not representative.

By contrast, **random sampling** refers to a situation where all values in the population have an equal chance of appearing in the sample. We assume random sampling in our examples unless we specify otherwise, because it is the simplest form of representative sampling. As an example, suppose we wish to take a random sample of 100 applicants from our Applicants database (Applicants.xls). One quick way to do so is to enter random numbers into the cells of column U, by entering the random number function RAND() in the range U2:U2917. Then, using Paste Special to preserve the numbers generated, copy and paste the random values into column V. Next, sort the database by the values in column V. The first 100 applicants make up the desired random sample.

Classical methods in statistics deal with situations involving a random sample of observations. The data points in the sample are drawn from a population that can be described by a probability distribution, but the parameters of that distribution are unknown. Sampling and the analysis of sample information produce statistical data regarding the sample. Statistical data can be used in two ways—**descriptive** and **inferential.** Descriptive statistics summarize information in the sample. They have a limited purpose: they simply give a numerical picture of the observations. Inferential statistics have a different orientation. They use the information in the sample to make inferences about the population and thereby become the basis for estimating model parameters. However, we have to recognize that this type of estimation is subject to two important kinds of errors. First, there is **systematic error,** which occurs if the sample is not representative of the population. We can avoid systematic error by taking some time to design the sampling process and making sure that no unwanted patterns or biases occur in the sample. Second, there is **sampling error** (sometimes called statistical error), which occurs because the sample is merely a subset of the entire population. Because the subset is hardly ever a perfect representation of the population, sampling error is inevitable. The effects of sampling error can be mitigated (e.g., by taking large samples), but they cannot be avoided entirely.

Sampling error is influenced by two factors—the size of the sample and the amount of variation in the population. Obviously, we can't do much about the latter; it is the nature of the population that we want to learn about, and we have to work with the extent of variation in it, whatever it may be. For example, there may be great variation in executive compensation, or there may be limited variation in applicants' GMAT scores. Whatever the case, we have to accept the level of variation in the population when we are devising our samples. On the other hand, we can do something about the size of the sample. The larger the sample, the more it resembles the entire population, so the less chance there is for sampling error to occur. Moreover, when we're working on a computer and can obtain data in electronic form, it is only slightly more difficult to manage a large sample than a small one. Thus, a large sample can mitigate the effect of sampling error, even if we cannot overcome it completely.

Recall from our earlier remarks that it is a good idea to do some sensitivity analysis before collecting data. One of the outcomes of sensitivity analysis is insight into how precisely we need to know certain parameters. From that information, we can determine how large a sample we really need. The convenience of collecting data aside, we may often find that we need only a small sample to achieve the precision we desire.

ESTIMATING PARAMETERS

As introduced in Chapter 2, parameters are numerical inputs, or uncontrollable variables, in a model. Parameters can be natural constants, such as the speed of sound or the density of water. These are numerical values that we would want to look up in a reference book. Parameters can also be quantitative phenomena in our environment, such as overhead rates, lead times, or process yields. These are numerical values that we might want to estimate from empirical data. When we are building a deterministic model, where we assume that all elements in the model are known with certainty, we want to use the most accurate values possible for our parameters. For such models, we are most likely to be interested in a single value to represent each parameter. When we are building a probabilistic model, where some parameters are described by probability distributions, we want to estimate the means and variances of those distributions. The information on which estimates are based may come from a database or from a specialized study organized explicitly for the purpose of obtaining estimates. In either case, we can use standard statistical techniques to provide the estimates we seek.

Point Estimates

We estimate parameters in two ways, with **point estimates** and with **interval estimates.** The point estimate approach produces a single number that becomes our "best guess" for the value of the parameter. We then use this estimate in our model as the parameter's value. The interval estimate approach produces a range of values in which we are fairly sure that the parameter lies, in addition to a single-value point estimate. A range of values for a parameter allows us to perform sensitivity analysis in a systematic fashion, and it provides input for tornado charts or sensitivity tables, as described in Chapter 6. Point estimates are summary statistics, and we deal first with those.

Following standard practice, we assume that the given data represent a random sample of n observations. The ith observation in the sample has the value x_i, and n is the sample size. Three summary statistics for the sample are the sample average, the sample variance, and the sample standard deviation.

The **sample average** is calculated as:

$$\bar{x} = \frac{1}{n} \sum_{i=1}^{n} x_i \tag{1}$$

The **sample variance** is calculated as:

$$s^2 = \sum_{i=1}^{n} \frac{(x_i - \bar{x})^2}{n-1} \tag{2}$$

and its square root is the **sample standard deviation:**

$$s = \sqrt{\frac{\sum_{i=1}^{n} (x_i - \bar{x})^2}{n-1}} \tag{3}$$

The sample average is the point estimate of the population mean. For example, in a production model, we might want to represent the time required for a product's final assembly. We might collect data on the ten most recent assemblies in order to estimate the final assembly time. If we take the sample average of these ten observations, using (1), that calculation gives us a point estimate of the assembly time to use in our model. The sample average is an estimate of the mean assembly time in the population.

The sample variance is the point estimate of the population variance. Consider an investment model in which we need to estimate the variance in week-to-week changes in a particular stock index. By creating a historical sample of the index and tracking its weekly changes, we can compute the sample variance as a point estimate, using (2), for the purposes of our model. The sample variance is an estimate of the variance of weekly values of the stock index in the population.

For purposes of illustration, we use our sample in the Executives database to estimate an average salary. If we select Tools→Data Analysis, we will see a window listing a collection of Excel-based statistical analyses. (If the Data Analysis tool does not appear on the Tools menu, load it by selecting Tools→Add-Ins. Then, check the box for Analysis ToolPak.) If we select Descriptive Statistics, we will see another window for this specific tool. We select D2:D101 as the input range (since column D contains salaries) and choose the button that places output in a separate worksheet. Then, Excel produces a standard table of descriptive statistics based on our sample, as shown in Figure 7.21. Some of the entries in this table involve advanced material beyond our present coverage, but a few of the items are worth noting. The sample average is listed as the Mean, with a value of 679.138. This result indicates that the average salary in our sample was slightly more than $679,000. The sample variance and the sample standard deviation are also shown as 118,307 and 343.9585, respectively. (These calculations can also be made separately, using Excel's AVERAGE, VAR, and STDEV functions.) We use these results later on.

In some cases, we might be interested in **categorical,** or qualitative, information rather than numerical information. Examples might include good (versus defective) output items, in-the-money (versus worthless) stock options, or profitable (versus unprofitable) product introductions. We have two approaches for dealing with this kind of information. First, we can define the value x_i to be 1 or 0, according to whether the ith

FIGURE 7.21
Descriptive Statistics
Summarized for
Executive Salaries

Executives.xls

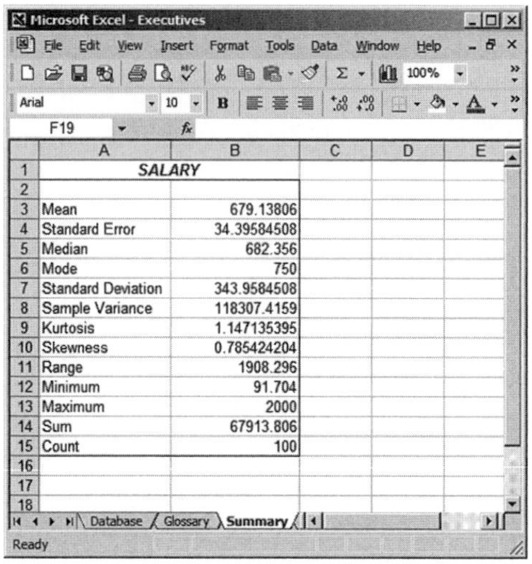

	A	B	C	D	E
1		**SALARY**			
2					
3	Mean	679.13806			
4	Standard Error	34.39584508			
5	Median	682.356			
6	Mode	750			
7	Standard Deviation	343.9584508			
8	Sample Variance	118307.4159			
9	Kurtosis	1.147135395			
10	Skewness	0.785424204			
11	Range	1908.296			
12	Minimum	91.704			
13	Maximum	2000			
14	Sum	67913.806			
15	Count	100			
16					
17					
18					

observation in the sample is, say, good or defective. Having created a quantitative measure out of the categorical information, we can use the three formulas above. A second approach is to use the proportion p observed in the sample as the summary statistic. Since this approach is sometimes the most convenient, we treat the **sample proportion** as a fourth summary statistic of interest. We usually use p to denote the observed proportion in a sample. For example, we may be interested in the number of executives in our sample who received a bonus as part of their compensation. We can construct a small pivot table, based on column E in the Executives database, to verify that 81 of the 100 executives received bonuses that were larger than zero. Therefore, $p = 0.81$ is our sample proportion for positive bonuses. In the spirit of inferential statistics, the calculated proportion is an estimate of the proportion in the population.

Interval Estimates

An interval estimate is expressed as the point estimate "plus or minus" some amount. In the case of our executive salaries, an interval estimate for the mean might be

$$679.138 \pm 58.525$$

In other words, the interval consists of a range on either side of the point estimate. The width of the range depends on how confident we wish to be at capturing the true value of the parameter. (Recall that, because of sampling error, the sample may not be perfectly representative of the population.) A wide range gives us considerable confidence that we've captured the true mean value, while a narrow range gives us less confidence.

We sometimes state an interval estimate in the form of a probability:

$$P(L <= \mu <= U) = 1 - \alpha$$

In this form, L and U represent the lower and upper limits of the interval, and $1 - \alpha$ (usually a large percentage) represents the **confidence level.** The symbol μ represents the true value of the parameter. The confidence level gives the long run probability that the interval contains the true value of the parameter we're estimating. In other words, if we were to repeat the sampling process many times, about $1 - \alpha$ percent of our confidence intervals would contain the true value. However, given any one estimate, the true value is either within the confidence interval or not, with probability 1 or 0. In the case of our salary estimate, the interval estimate could be stated as:

$$P(679 - 58 <= \text{true mean salary} <= 679 + 58) = 1 - \alpha$$

where we discuss below how to determine the value of α.

In order to appreciate the reasoning that lies behind interval estimates, we return briefly to sampling theory. (See Appendix A for background information on sampling theory.) Suppose, for the moment, that we are working with a population that is described by a normal probability model with mean μ and standard deviation σ. Imagine that we take repeated samples of n items from that population and calculate the sample average each time. How will this collection of sample averages be distributed? The answer is that the sample averages also follow a normal distribution, with a mean of μ and a variance of σ^2/n. As a specific illustration, suppose we start with a normal population with a mean of 100 and standard deviation of 10. In our experiment, we take samples of size 100 and calculate the sample average for each one. Figure 7.22A shows the sample averages in a histogram. Note that the histogram resembles the shape of a normal distribution and that, although most of the *population* lies between 70 and 130, the *sample averages* cluster in a much narrower range, from about 97 to 103. Sample averages show far less variability than the population they are drawn from because high outcomes tend to be balanced by low ones.

We use the term **standard error** to refer to the standard deviation of some function being used to provide an estimate. Here, the sample average (or sample mean) provides our estimate. Its standard deviation is called the **standard error of the mean,** defined as the square root of the variance of the sample average, or:

$$\sigma_{\bar{x}} = \sigma / \sqrt{n}$$

(We assume here that σ is known; later, we discuss how to proceed when it, too, must be estimated.)

As usual with a normal distribution, the z-score measures the number of standard deviations (in this case, standard deviations of the sample average) away from the mean. Here, the z-score corresponding to any particular sample average is the following:

$$z = \frac{\bar{x} - \mu}{\sigma_{\bar{x}}} = \frac{\bar{x} - \mu}{\sigma / \sqrt{n}} \qquad (4)$$

The z-score tells us how many standard errors we are from the mean. We know that 90 percent of the sample averages will have z-scores between -1.64 and $+1.64$. In other words, they differ from μ by at most 1.64 standard errors. Stated another way, the chances

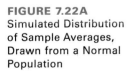

FIGURE 7.22A
Simulated Distribution of Sample Averages, Drawn from a Normal Population

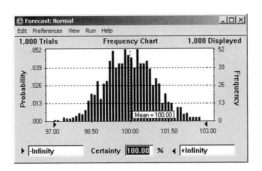

are 90 percent that the sample average will fall no more than 1.64 standard errors from the true mean. In our example, the standard error is 1.0 ($\sigma / \sqrt{n} = 10 / \sqrt{100} = 1.0$), so we expect 90 percent of the sample averages to fall between 98.36 and 101.64, which is approximately the case in Figure 7.22A.

Now imagine that we run the same experiment (calculating a sample average for a sample of size n), but without knowing the probability model that describes the original population. Even if the population does not follow a normal distribution, the sample averages will still follow a normal distribution with mean μ and variance σ^2/n, as long as n is sufficiently large. A value of $n > 30$ is considered large enough for the normal distribution to hold, but n can be a good deal smaller if the original population resembles the normal. (A value as small as $n = 6$ is large enough if the population is symmetric with a single peak.) Thus, for large samples, we can conclude that the chances are 90 percent that the sample average will fall no more than 1.64 standard errors from the true mean. The figure of 90 percent is the confidence level, and it helps determine the size of the relevant interval.

To continue our illustrative experiment, we take samples of size 100 from a uniform distribution with a range from 80 to 120. Again, we calculate sample averages and construct their histogram, as shown in Figure 7.22B. As expected, the form of the histogram resembles the normal distribution. In addition, the standard error in this case turns out to be about 1.15, so that we expect 90 percent of the sample averages to fall between 98.1 and 101.9, which is approximately the case in Figure 7.22B.

To calculate a range for an interval estimate, then, we begin by expressing the confidence level as a percentage. A typical confidence level would be 90 percent, but other levels commonly used are 95 percent and 99 percent. Using (4), we can obtain the upper and lower limits of a 90 percent confidence interval for the mean:

$$\bar{x} \pm z(\sigma / \sqrt{n}) \tag{5}$$

The z-value in this formula corresponds to a tail probability of 0.05 in a normal distribution. (Including 90 percent of the area under a standard normal distribution in a particular interval is equivalent to 5 percent of the area in each tail.) The well known numerical value corresponding to a 90 percent confidence interval is $z = 1.64$, which can be verified using the Excel formula NORMSINV(0.95).

We mentioned earlier that the formula (5) for the interval estimate assumes that the standard deviation σ in the underlying population is known. But this will rarely be the case. When the standard deviation is not known, its value also must be estimated from the sample data. To do so, we replace σ by its point estimate, the sample standard deviation s, and then we can use (5), provided that our sample is larger than about $n = 30$. (When n is less than 30, other approaches are needed, which are beyond the level of this book.) In the case of our sample of executive salaries, we have $s = 343.9585$. The form of a 90 percent confidence interval for the mean becomes

FIGURE 7.22B
Simulated Distribution of Sample Averages, Drawn from a Uniform Population

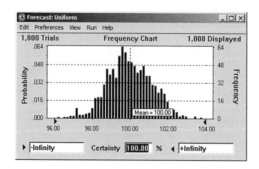

EXCEL TIP: CALCULATING Z-VALUES

Note that Excel's standard normal inverse function computes a z-value from a value of the cumulative distribution function (see Appendix A). Since the confidence interval of 90 percent corresponds to 5 percent in each of two tails, the cumulative distribution function corresponds to 0.95 in this case. The Excel formula returns a value of approximately 1.645. Some common z-values are summarized in the table below:

confidence level	90%	95%	99%
z-value	1.645	1.960	2.576

$$\bar{x} \pm z(s/\sqrt{n}) \tag{6}$$

Thus, our interval estimate for the population mean becomes

$$679.138 \pm 1.64(34.396) = 679.138 \pm 56.409$$

The 90 percent confidence interval for the true mean extends from \$622,729 to \$735,547. (In Excel's Descriptive Statistics tool, there is an option to calculate the half width of the confidence interval and include it in the summary table. When Excel makes this calculation, it does not use the normal approximation mentioned earlier for sample sizes above 30, but instead uses a more precise formula. In the case of our example, the half width is reported as 57.111, as compared to the approximate value of 56.409.)

Thinking back to our discussion of tornado charts in Chapter 6, an interval estimate calculated from (6) could provide a useful guideline for the high and low values of the parameter. If one of the parameters in our model is an executive's salary, then we can use \$679,138 as a point estimate; and when we perform sensitivity analysis, we can use upper and lower limits of \$622,729 and \$735,547 to generate a tornado chart.

Interval Estimates for a Proportion

The confidence interval for a proportion takes a form very similar to that of the confidence interval for the mean. When we estimate the sample proportion p, the interval estimate takes the form

$$p \pm z\sqrt{\frac{p(1-p)}{n}} \tag{7}$$

Usually, a sample size of at least 50 is needed for this formula to be reliable.

As an example, recall that 81 percent of our sample of executives received bonuses. The 90 percent confidence interval for this estimate becomes $0.81 \pm 1.64(0.0392)$, or 0.81 ± 0.06. The limits of the confidence interval are therefore 75 percent and 87 percent. The true proportion, of course, either lies in this interval or not. But if we were to take many samples, we would capture the true proportion with (7) about 90 percent of the time.

Sample-Size Determination

Formulas for interval estimates—such as (5), (6), and (7)—express the range of the interval as a function of the sample size n. To this point, we have started with a sample of size n and proceeded to calculate an interval estimate. However, if we know what precision we want, we can use this same relationship to calculate the minimum necessary sample size.

For example, suppose we wish to estimate the mean of a sample to within a range of $\pm R$. We can manipulate (5) algebraically to obtain

$$n = (z\sigma / R)^2 \qquad (8)$$

This formula applies to the conditions associated with (5): sampling from a normal distribution with a known variance. When the standard deviation is unknown, we simply substitute its estimate. But where do we find an estimate if we haven't yet taken the sample? The solution is to take a fairly small sample (say, 10 or 20) to get an initial estimate s of the standard deviation, then use (8), with s in place of σ, to determine more precisely how large the sample size should be.

For example, if we take our entire sample of 100 executives, we estimate the standard deviation of salaries to be 343.958. If we wish to estimate the mean salary to within $25,000 with 90 percent confidence, then the necessary sample size, from (8), must be

$$n = [(1.64)(343.958)/25]^2 = 509$$

Therefore, in order to produce an estimate with the desired precision, we need a sample more than five times as large as what we have. This assumes, of course, that our original estimate of the standard deviation is accurate.

The same reasoning applies to the case of estimating a proportion. Since the formula in (7) involves the sample size, we can solve for the minimum necessary sample size in terms of the proportion p. The algebra leads us to the following sample-size formula:

$$n = z^2 p(1 - p) / R^2 \qquad (9)$$

If we have only a rough idea of the unknown proportion p, we can use that value in the formula, but if we have absolutely no idea at all about p, we can still proceed. The term $p(1 - p)$ is maximized when $p = 0.5$. So a conservative value would be obtained by substituting this value into (9) to obtain

$$n = (z/2)^2 / R^2 \qquad (10)$$

If we wish to estimate the proportion of executives who receive bonuses to within 0.02, at 90 percent confidence, then (9) tells us that we would need a sample size of 1,035, based on our estimate of the proportion p as 0.81. The more conservative formula in (10) prescribes a sample size of 1,681, using $p = 0.5$.

Capacity Planning in the BPI Example

We return to the example of Bundy Pharmaceuticals to illustrate how confidence intervals can be used in sensitivity analysis. Earlier, we created a tornado chart that ordered the parameters according to their influence on the NPV, based on 10 percent changes in all input values. Using a common percentage for all parameters can be misleading, however, because we can usually estimate some parameters with considerable precision, while others are very uncertain. A case in point is initial demand. It is a fact that last year's sales were 1.01 million. To vary this parameter by 10 percent above and below this level makes no sense. On the other hand, the growth rate in demand is not known, although some historical information is available. Can we use this information to improve our analysis?

Looking back at the data, we have ten years of demand history and therefore nine observations of annual growth. Although this is a fairly small sample, it is at least plausible to assume that year-to-year growth follows a normal distribution. For our sample of nine observations, we first compute the mean and standard deviation from the data. Then, we form a 90 percent confidence interval using (6), as summarized in Figure 7.23. Several

FIGURE 7.23
Confidence Interval
Calculations

Bundy.xls

	A	B	C	D	E	F	G
1	Demand Data						
2	Growth Rate Estimation						
3							
4	Year	Demand	Growth	Estimates			
5	1	487,000		Average			
6	2	560,000	73,000	58,111			
7	3	601,000	41,000				
8	4	689,000	88,000	St. Deviation			
9	5	788,000	99,000	25,896			
10	6	854,000	66,000				
11	7	902,000	48,000	Conf. Interval		Interval	
12	8	957,000	55,000	72,310		90%	
13	9	991,000	34,000	43,913		z-value	
14	10	1,010,000	19,000			1.645	
15							

conclusions can be drawn from this data. First, our assumption that demand will grow by 50,000 per year may be somewhat low: the average in our sample is just over 58,000. The corresponding 90 percent confidence interval ranges from 43,913 to 72,310, corresponding to a range of ±49 percent around the point estimate.

If we believe that these observations are relevant to future growth, we might replace our base-case value with our estimated mean of 58,111. When we do so, we find that the optimal plant capacity is about $1.30 million, slightly above our base-case value, with an NPV of about $2.090 million.

As for the confidence intervals, our earlier tornado-chart analysis suggested that annual demand growth had relatively little impact. In the chart, we varied its value from 45,000 to 55,000 and observed that NPV varied over a range of about $1.25 million. If we use the lower and upper limits of the confidence interval, we find that the NPV varies over a range of $1.78 million. From this perspective, the tornado chart may have led us to underestimate the sensitivity of NPV to the growth rate in demand.

Confidence intervals can be useful, when appropriate data are available, in refining a sensitivity analysis. The standard tornado chart allows each parameter to be varied by the same percentage amount, using the Constant Percentage option. While this is handy for a quick analysis, it may be misleading when parameters can vary significantly more or less than the given percentage. A better guideline would be to vary each parameter by a percentage equal to the size of its 90 percent confidence interval, using the Variable Percentage option. In our case, we found that a 90 percent confidence interval for the annual growth in demand was considerably wider than the standard ±10 percent, leading the tornado chart to underestimate the impact of this parameter in the base-case model.

However, our ultimate interest is in the best choice of plant capacity, and this involves an optimization step (represented by a sensitivity table) that cannot be contemplated by a tornado chart. Over the range of the 90 percent confidence interval, from 43,913 to 72,310, we find that the optimal NPV varies from $1.829 million to $2.601 million, or about $0.77 million (as compared to a range of about $1.08 million in the tornado chart). In this case, we may have overestimated the sensitivity of the *optimal* NPV when we varied the growth rate by the standard 10 percent in constructing the chart. Furthermore, the optimal capacity ranges from 1.26 million to 1.37 million, or a difference of only about 0.11 million. The main point here is that the tornado chart is most appropriate to a model in which decisions have already been determined; it is not necessarily very helpful when the model contains decisions yet to be optimized.

ESTIMATING RELATIONSHIPS

In the previous section, we dealt with point estimates and interval estimates for individual parameters of our models. Parameters represent the simplest type of quantitative assumption, in the sense that each parameter takes on a single value in the model. Unless otherwise specified, the various parameters are assumed to be completely independent—that is, we can estimate one parameter separately from the way we estimate any other parameter. However, in some cases, we want to recognize some form of dependence between two variables. Indeed, a relationship between two variables may be an important part of a model. For example, a planning model for a firm's best selling product may have variables for advertising and sales volume. We may suspect that these two quantities are related, and we may want to devote part of the overall model to the specific relationship between volume and advertising. The numerical values in this relationship will become parameters in our model. In another example, the monthly sales at a drugstore might well depend on its business hours, shelf space, national advertising, and number of nearby competitors. In this kind of example, the monthly sales figure is dependent on several variables, all of which could be treated as uncontrollable in the overall model. In cases like these, the economics of the situation suggest a relationship between variables, but in other cases, we may want to simply explore the data to see whether there is evidence that a relationship even exists.

The first and most important step in exploratory data analysis is simply to *plot the data.* Excel provides us with the option of building an X-Y chart, also called a **scatter plot,** to investigate the relationship between two variables. When we look at data in this manner, we can get a hint as to whether there is a positive or negative association, how strong that association is, and whether it seems to be linear or not. We can then back up our visual impressions with some basic statistical analyses to refine our understanding of the dependency.

The first statistical step involves the correlation between two variables. Suppose we have a sample consisting of n pairs of observations for the variables x and y. Using the definitions of the previous section, we can compute the average and the standard deviation for x and for y. Then, the **correlation** is defined as

$$ r = \frac{1}{(n-1)} \sum_{i=1}^{n} \left(\frac{(x_i - \bar{x})}{s_x} \right) \left(\frac{(y_i - \bar{y})}{s_y} \right) $$

Here, we use s_x to represent the standard deviation of the variable x and similarly for s_y. The quantity r measures the strength of a linear association between the two variables x and y. In other words, it is a measure of the degree to which the relationship between x and y follows a straight line.

The r-statistic has a number of convenient features. The value of r will always lie in the range between -1 and 1. A value of $r > 0$ indicates a positive association between the two variables. In other words, when one variable is above its mean, the other tends to be above its mean as well. A value of $r < 0$ indicates a negative relationship; that is, when one variable is above its mean, the other tends to be below its mean. When r is close to 1 (or -1), the association is a strong one, but when r is close to 0, the association is weak. Also, because the calculation of r is based on z-values, it is independent of the units of measurement. In other words, we may scale the variables x and y before we make the calculation, but we still get the same value for r.

If we find that r is close to zero, the data do not show a strong linear association between the two variables. We may look for a different kind of data set, or we may retreat from the assumption that a relationship exists between the two variables. If we find that r

is large (and there is no formal cutoff for "large"), we know that there is a strong linear relationship between the variables, and we can proceed to investigate what straight line best describes that relationship.

The calculation of the correlation r can be obtained from the Excel function CORREL. As an example, suppose we take the ten-year history of annual demand at BPI. Even a casual look at the figures will suggest a relationship, but the scatter plot (see Figure 7.24) underscores the possibility. The calculation of the correlation r can be obtained from the Excel function CORREL(A8:A17,B8:B17), which yields a value of $r = 0.988$, as shown in the figure. This value tells us that demand has risen over time, in a near linear fashion. We may ultimately decide that a nonlinear relationship makes more economic sense, but the scatter plot and the calculation of r provide strong evidence that a simple linear trend model is justifiable, at least over the range of the given observations.

For a different example, suppose that, in the Executives database, we are curious about the relation between executive salaries and company sales. We calculate the correlation as $r = 0.473$. This positive value tells us that salaries tend to be high in firms whose sales are high (and vice versa). When we look at a scatter plot of the data (Figure 7.25), we may be able to detect a bit of a pattern, but there is a great deal of scatter. In other words, the relation is a positive one, but there is not a strong indication of a linear relationship between sales and salary. (Note that Figure 7.25 omits a small number of points representing very high salaries.)

The kind of dependency we address here is a *probabilistic* dependency, not a *deterministic* one. An example should illustrate the difference. Suppose our firm orders circuit boards from a supplier. If we place an order for x boards this month, then, according to the price schedule, we will pay $\$y$. If we place another order next month for x boards, then we will again pay $\$y$. The price schedule represents a deterministic dependency: for every quantity we order, there is a corresponding price; and if we order the same quantity twice, we will pay the same amount each time. Suppose also that we place x advertisements for our product in a trade journal this month and obtain orders for $\$y$ of our product. Then, next month, we again place x advertisements for our product in the same trade journal. Should we expect to obtain orders for $\$y$ again next month? Probably not—next month will be different. At a minimum, some unknown factors will be at work influencing the relationship

FIGURE 7.24
Scatter Plot for BPI
Demand History

Bundy.xls

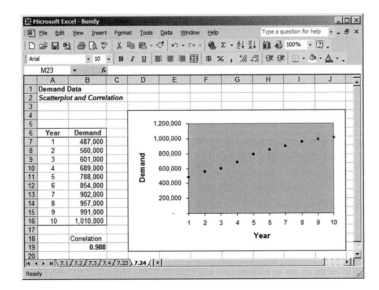

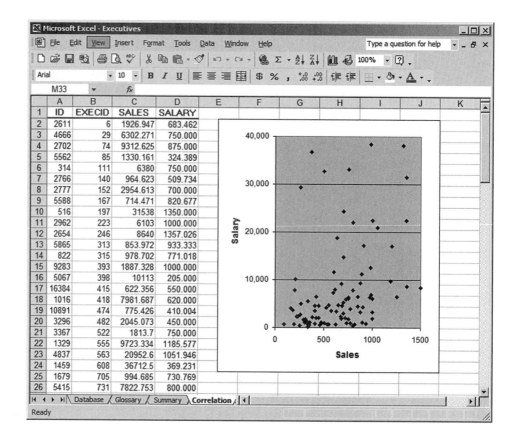

between advertising and sales revenue. Such factors are probabilistic: we will not be able to predict sales revenue with complete precision, because the revenue relationship is a probabilistic one (subject to the influence of unknown factors), whereas the price schedule is a deterministic one. A probabilistic dependency always leaves some influences unexplained.

Our spreadsheet models may be either deterministic or probabilistic. In a deterministic model, we assume that all numerical values are known with certainty. In the case of an individual parameter, we might estimate its value with an average value calculated from some data set; and in a deterministic model, we would represent that parameter as if it were perfectly known. The same is true of dependencies in a deterministic model. We would represent a dependency as if it were deterministic, even though we might estimate the numerical values in the relationship by treating it as a probabilistic dependency.

In the same sense that we can incorporate parameters into a model without first collecting data, provided we later do some sensitivity analysis, we can also incorporate dependency into a model by assuming a particular relationship between two or more parameters. Similarly, just as we sometimes find ourselves collecting data to estimate parameters, we are sometimes in the position of collecting data to estimate relationships. When we base our estimates on empirical data, we refer to dependent relationships as **regression** relationships, in the sense that we can build and test regression models in order to support the dependencies we hypothesize. In this approach, we identify one variable as the **dependent variable,** which means that it can be predicted from the values of other variables. In other words, the variable can be explained—at least in part, and in a quantitative fashion—by the other variables. Those other variables are called **independent variables.** The concept is that we may need to collect information about the independent variables, but, having done so, we should then be able to *predict* the dependent variable.

We classify regression models as **linear** or **nonlinear,** depending on their structural form, and **simple** or **multiple,** depending on whether there is one independent variable or more than one. In the case of simple regression, where there is one independent variable, the ability to plot graphs of observed relationships is very helpful. Figure 7.26 shows three types of graphs we might encounter when we construct a scatter plot. In the first figure, there appears to be a systematic relationship between y and x, and a linear (or straight line) dependence would be plausible. In the second figure, there again appears to be a systematic relationship, but this time it appears to be nonlinear. (The term **curvilinear** is sometimes used.) Finally, in the third figure, it is difficult to discern any relationship at all. Discriminating among these three cases is an important step, and the scatter plot provides us with an early indication of what shape the model could take.

Simple Linear Regression

The simple linear regression equation takes the form

$$y = a + bx + e \tag{11}$$

where y is the dependent variable, x is the independent variable, and the constants a and b represent the intercept and slope, respectively, of the regression line. The term e represents an "error" term. In other words, we may think of the relationship between x and y as if it follows the straight line formed by the function $y = a + bx$, subject to some unexplained "noise" captured in the error term. The noise component may simply represent the limitations of our knowledge about the true relationship. Alternatively, we can think of the dependent variable as following a probability model, with y as its mean value, for any given value of x. The error term then represents the random deviation of the dependent variable from its mean value, y. We will write the error term explicitly when introducing a new type of model, but we'll omit it when discussing examples.

The regression problem is to find the line that most closely matches the observed relationship between x and y. Although the concept of "most closely" could be implemented in alternative ways, the most common approach is to minimize the sum of squared differences between the observed values and the model values. (Approaches to the problem of finding the closest match fall into the general category of optimization methods that we cover in more detail in Chapter 8.)

Why is minimizing the sum of squared differences such a popular approach? At first, we might think that it would be a good idea to minimize just the sum of differences between the observed values and the model values. However, it is possible to show that the sum of differences is always zero when y is set equal to the mean y-value. Since this value obviously ignores the relationship between y and x, it would not be satisfactory; we therefore need some other measure of how closely a line fits the data. The sum of squared differences is almost as simple as the sum of differences, and it has the virtue of "penalizing" large differences more than small differences, so it is a natural candidate. (The sum

FIGURE 7.26
Three Types of
Scatter Plots

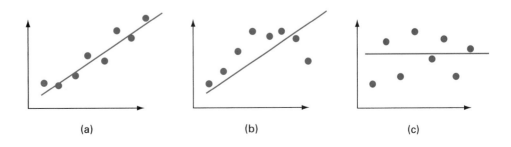

(a)   (b)   (c)

of squared differences has some technical virtues as well, but they involve statistical concepts that go beyond our coverage here.)

Specifically, let's suppose that our sample contains n observations of x-y pairs. Let x_i represent the ith observation of the independent variable, and let y_i represent the corresponding observation of the dependent variable. The model predicts that when the independent variable takes on the value x_i, then the dependent variable should be $y = a + bx_i$. The difference between the observed value and the model's prediction is called the **residual,** which can be written as

$$e_i = y_i - y = y_i - (a + bx_i) \tag{12}$$

and the sum of squared differences (between observation and model) becomes

$$SS = \sum_{i=1}^{n} e_i^2 = \sum_{i=1}^{n}(y_i - a - bx_i)^2$$

The regression problem reduces to choosing a and b so that we minimize SS. One of the assumptions in the analysis is that the residuals follow a normal distribution with a mean of zero.

Regression theory gives us formulas that solve the simple regression problem, as shown below:

$$b = \frac{n\sum_{i=1}^{n} x_i y_i - \sum_{i=1}^{n} x_i \sum_{i=1}^{n} y_i}{n\sum_{i=1}^{n} x_i^2 - (\sum_{i=1}^{n} x_i)^2} \text{ and } a = \bar{y} - b\bar{x} \tag{13}$$

However, it is not necessary to solve these equations, as Excel can perform these calculations once we have recorded the observed data in a spreadsheet.

As an example, we return to the Executives database and examine the relation between executive salaries and company sales. Our equation takes the form $y = a + bx + e$, where y represents salary (in thousands) and x represents sales (in millions). For our sample of 100 executives, the formulas in (13) yield the estimates $a = 583$ and $b = 0.00897$. These results suggest that an increase of $1 million in sales is associated with an increase of about $8,970 in salary.

Having found the values of the constants a and b that give the best fit of the model to the observed data, we might still wonder, how *good* a fit is the best fit? Given that we are working with a linear model, the three graphs in Figure 7.27 suggest the spectrum of outcomes. In Figure 7.27a, the regression is perfect: every observation falls right on the regression line, and the residual values are all zero. Another way to interpret this outcome is that *all* of the variation in y-values is completely accounted for (or "explained") by their dependence on x-values (and therefore on the variation in x-values). In Figure 7.27b, the regression is imperfect, so the residuals are nonzero but small. Nevertheless, *much* of the variation in y-values can be explained by variation in x. That is, changes in x account for most of the variation in y, although there is some "unexplained" variation. Finally, in Figure 7.27c, there is little or no dependency between y and x. In this case, the variation in the residuals is roughly the same as the variation in the y-values; *none* of the variation in y-values can be explained by variation in x.

In order to quantify the outcomes and to provide a measure of how well the regression equation fits the data, we introduce the **coefficient of determination,** known as R^2, to measure the closeness of fit. Values of R^2 must lie between zero and one, and the closer R^2 is to one, the better the fit. (Its square root is the correlation, r.) A useful interpretation

FIGURE 7.27
Three Types of
Regression Results

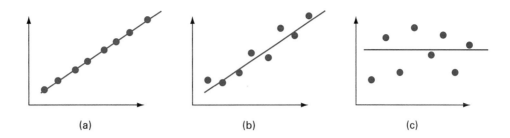

(a)   (b)   (c)

is that R^2 is relatively large when the model explains much of the variation in observed y-values. When R^2 is equal to one, the regression equation is perfect—it explains all of the observed variation. (This would be the case for Figure 7.27a.) When R^2 is zero, the regression equation explains none of the observed variation. (This would be approximately the case for Figure 7.27c.) Thus, R^2 measures how much of the variation in y-values is explained by the relation in the model.

In our example involving executive salaries and company sales, $R^2 = 0.223$. In other words, about 22 percent of the variation in salaries can be explained by variation in company sales. The rest of the variation is due either to "noise" or to systematic factors—other than sales—that we have not included in the regression equation.

Excel's Data Analysis tool contains a Regression option that automates the calculations we have just discussed. To use the tool, we select Regression on the Data Analysis menu. The Regression window, shown in Figure 7.28, asks for a range for the y-values and for the x-values. If we use the original Executives database, we can specify the y-range as D1:D101 and the x-range as N1:N101, checking the Labels box to reflect the fact that these ranges include field names. For this illustration, we need not check other boxes, although the Line Fit Plot provides a convenient graphical look at the results. The figure illustrates the output option of using a new worksheet (named Regression) as a home for the regression report. Excel then produces the regression tables shown in Figure 7.29, which have been slightly modified for display purposes.

Much of the information in the regression tables is quite detailed and beyond the scope of our coverage. We focus on four measures of how well the regression model is supported by the data: R^2, the F-statistic, the p-statistics, and confidence intervals. The first two of these measures apply to the regression model as a whole; the last two apply to individual regression coefficients.

As we have seen, the R^2 value provides an overall, quantitative measure of how close the regression model fits the data. The higher the R^2, the more the regression model explains, or accounts for, the variation in the dependent variable. There is, however, no magic level for R^2 that distinguishes a good model from a bad model. All we can really say is that if we have two competing models, the one with the higher R^2 fits the data more closely. But there are situations in which our business judgment would suggest that we work with a model with a lower R^2 than a competing model.

The **F-statistic** provides a different measure of the overall quality of the regression. It answers this question: How likely is it that we would get the R^2 we observe (or higher) if, in fact, all the true regression coefficients were zero? In other words, if our model really had no explanatory power at all, how likely is it that, sampling at random, we would encounter the explained variation we observed? If sufficient thought has gone into a model before turning to regression, so that the analyst has cogent reasons for believing the form of the model is realistic and the initial parameter values are plausible, it is very unlikely that the F-statistic will suggest that the R^2 we observe could have come about when all the true coefficients are zero. In effect, this result would imply that the data do not support

FIGURE 7.28
The Regression Window in the Data Analysis Tool

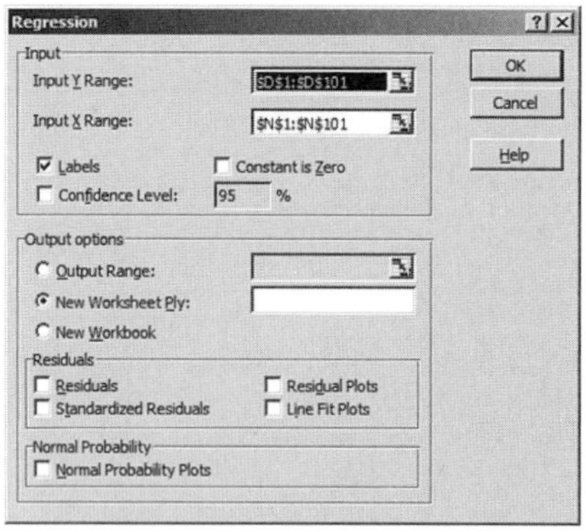

Regression ? ×

Input
Input Y Range: `$D$1:$D$101`
Input X Range: `$N$1:$N$101`

☑ Labels   ☐ Constant is Zero
☐ Confidence Level: 95 %

Output options
○ Output Range:
● New Worksheet Ply:
○ New Workbook

Residuals
☐ Residuals   ☐ Residual Plots
☐ Standardized Residuals   ☐ Line Fit Plots

Normal Probability
☐ Normal Probability Plots

OK | Cancel | Help

FIGURE 7.29
Regression Results for the Executives Example

Executives.xls

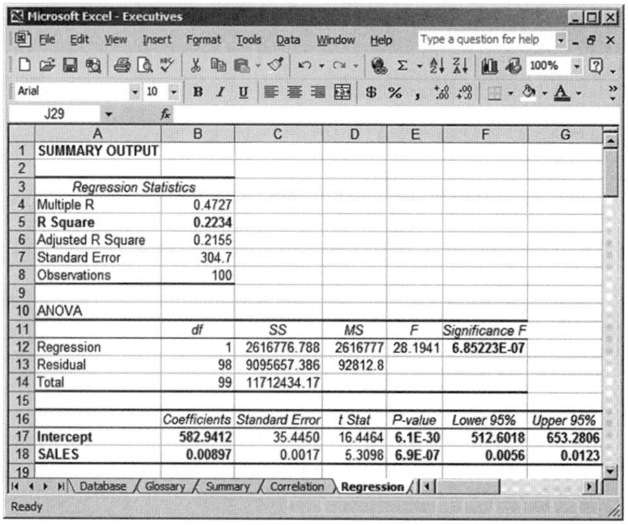

Microsoft Excel - Executives

File Edit View Insert Format Tools Data Window Help   Type a question for help

	A	B	C	D	E	F	G
1	SUMMARY OUTPUT						
2							
3	Regression Statistics						
4	Multiple R	0.4727					
5	R Square	0.2234					
6	Adjusted R Square	0.2155					
7	Standard Error	304.7					
8	Observations	100					
9							
10	ANOVA						
11		df	SS	MS	F	Significance F	
12	Regression	1	2616776.788	2616777	28.1941	6.85223E-07	
13	Residual	98	9095657.386	92812.8			
14	Total	99	11712434.17				
15							
16		Coefficients	Standard Error	t Stat	P-value	Lower 95%	Upper 95%
17	Intercept	582.9412	35.4450	16.4464	6.1E-30	512.6018	653.2806
18	SALES	0.00897	0.0017	5.3098	6.9E-07	0.0056	0.0123
19							

Database / Glossary / Summary / Correlation \ Regression /

any aspect of the model. If the *F*-statistic suggests that it is *unlikely* that the observed R^2 could occur when all the true regression coefficients are zero, this should not be taken as a positive sign that the model is somehow proven, since we had strong reasons before performing the regression to believe that the overall form of the model was realistic. On the other hand, if the *F*-statistic suggests that it is *likely* that the R^2 we observe could occur when all the true coefficients are zero, the most sensible conclusion is that the data are not appropriate for refining the parameter estimates in our model, and we should look for more appropriate data or rely on our judgment for our parameter estimates.

We turn our attention now from evaluating the regression model as a whole to evaluating each regression coefficient individually, using *p*-statistics and confidence intervals. The **p-statistic** is somewhat akin to the *F*-statistic. It answers this question: How likely is it that we would get an estimate of the regression coefficient at least this large (either positive or negative) if, in fact, the true value of the regression coefficient were zero? In other words, if there really was no influence of this particular independent variable on the dependent variable, how likely is it that we would encounter the estimated coefficient we observed? Again, this is not usually a particularly strong test of the model. Imagine, for example, that we are attempting to determine the impact of a growing patient population on the sales of a drug. We have hypothesized, based on expert experience in the industry, that an additional 100 patients will increase annual sales by 800 to 1,200 doses. We would expect, then, that the regression coefficient would be around 10, but could be as low as 8 or as high as 12. After collecting data and running a regression (perhaps getting an estimated coefficient of 9.5), we would probably not be surprised to find that it is very unlikely that the estimated coefficient would have arisen by chance when the true coefficient was zero. After all, we know that an increase in the patient population has *some* positive effect on sales. What we are really interested in is whether the coefficient is 8 or 12 or somewhere in between, and we hope that the regression procedure will shed light on this question. The most useful way to determine the range of uncertainty in a regression coefficient is to form a confidence interval. (A check box is provided in the Excel Regression window for confidence intervals for the regression coefficients. Excel automatically provides a report on the 95 percent confidence intervals, so the user needs to check this box only when a different confidence interval is desired.) A confidence interval for the coefficient in our example will tell us whether the actual parameter is likely to lie between 9.0 and 10.0, for example, or between 8.0 and 11.0. This information, along with the point estimate of the coefficient itself and our judgment, will help us to select a final parameter value for this coefficient in our model.

Returning to the regression results in Figure 7.29, we first observe that R^2, displayed in cell B5, is 0.223. In cell F12, under the heading *Significance F,* we find the probability of observing this R^2 or higher when all the true regression coefficients are zero. The reported value is 6.852×10^{-7} (or 0.0000006852), which means that this probability is negligible.

In rows 17 and 18, we find results for each of the regression coefficients, the constant or intercept, and Sales. In cells B17 and B18, we find point estimates for the values of the coefficients—$a = 583$ for the constant term and $b = 0.00897$ for the coefficient of Sales. The *p*-values in cells E17 and E18 are both essentially zero, suggesting that these estimated coefficients would be unlikely to occur randomly if the true coefficients were zero. In cells F17 and G17, we are given the 95 percent confidence interval on the intercept: 512.6 to 653.3. Finally, in cells F18 and G18, we have the 95 percent confidence interval on the coefficient on Sales: 0.0056 to 0.0123. Thus, while our point estimate for the coefficient on Sales is about 0.009, these data suggest that it could range between 0.006 and 0.012, approximately.

To provide another example, we return to the Applicants database and the analysis of GMAT levels in different admission rounds. For this separate analysis, we construct the pivot table of Figure 7.30 in a new worksheet and proceed. For the Regression tool, we specify the *y*-range as B5:B9 and the *x*-range as A5:A9 (see Figure 7.30). The regression table reveals the following results:

- The value of R^2 is about 0.745, which suggests that the model fits the data rather well.

- The probability under *Significance F* is about 6 percent, which suggests that it is unlikely that this R^2 value could have arisen when all the true coefficients were zero.

- The estimated coefficients are $a = 708$ and $b = -27.7$, indicating that the average GMAT scores drop by almost 28 points each round in the admission process. The *p*-value for the intercept is very small, which suggests that this estimate would be unlikely if the true value of the coefficient were zero. However, the *p*-value for Round is 6 percent, which suggests that we cannot be so sure that this estimate could not have arisen by chance when the true coefficient was zero. The 95 percent confidence interval for Round is extremely wide, from −57 to +2. This suggests that our point estimate, from which we concluded that GMAT scores drop by almost 28 points each round, is rather imprecisely estimated. (Notice that the confidence interval for this coefficient does extend past zero, which is consistent with the low but nonzero *p*-value.)

FIGURE 7.30
Regression Results for
the Applicants Example

Applicants.xls

	A	B	C	D	E	F	G	H	I	J
1										
2										
3	Average of GMAT			SUMMARY OUTPUT						
4	ROUND	Total								
5	1	665.1		*Regression Statistics*						
6	2	650.8		Multiple R	0.8631					
7	3	642.8		R Square	0.7449					
8	4	629.5		Adjusted R Square	0.6598					
9	5	537.5		Standard Error	29.5452					
10	(blank)	675.0		Observations	5					
11	Grand Total	651.5								
12				ANOVA						
13					*df*	*SS*	*MS*	*F*	*Significance F*	
14				Regression	1	7646.3	7646.3	8.7595	0.0596	
15				Residual	3	2618.8	872.9			
16				Total	4	10265.1				
17										
18					*Coefficients*	*Standard Error*	*t Stat*	*P-value*	*Lower 95%*	*Upper 95%*
19				Intercept	708.0815	30.9873	22.8507	0.0002	609.466	806.697
20				X Variable 1	-27.6520	9.3430	-2.9596	0.0596	-57.386	2.082
21										

Simple Regression in the BPI Example

In our base-case model for Bundy Pharmaceuticals, we used a very simple idea to project demand. We calculated the rough average annual growth in demand over the past ten years, and we used that figure to project forward from the previous year. Thus, our initial conclusions were based on demand growing from about 1.05 million to 1.50 million units over the life of the plant. This initial model was only loosely derived from past experience. But since we have historical data on past sales, it is natural to ask whether we could use regression methods to create demand models that exploit the available historical data more fully. Whether these models will materially change the *conclusions* of the base case is an open question. We test three such models here, using time, lagged demand, and the number of patients with arthritis as independent variables.

First, we look at time as the independent variable. Perhaps the simplest interpretation of the available data is that demand increases over time at a constant rate. In fact, this is the reasoning behind our base-case model, although, for the purposes of that model, we made a quick calculation of the growth rate without using statistical methods. Later, we used a scatter plot, along with the calculation of correlation, to support the original reasoning. Here, we assume that there is a linear model describing the relation between demand and time (with time indexed from 1 to 10). The Data Analysis tool, applied to the ten years of historical data, produces the following regression equation:

REGRESSION STATISTICS

Four measures are used to judge the statistical qualities of a regression:

R^2: Measures the percent of variation in the independent variable accounted for by the regression model.

F-statistic (Significance F): Measures the probability of observing the given R^2 (or higher) when all the true regression coefficients are zero.

p-statistic: Measures the probability of observing the given estimate of the regression coefficient (or a larger value, positive or negative) when the true coefficient is zero.

Confidence interval: Gives a range within which the true regression coefficient lies with given probability.

$$Demand = 443{,}600 + 61{,}873 \times Time$$

The fit of this regression is very good: the R^2 is high (0.98); the probability corresponding to the F-value (*Significance F*) is essentially zero, and the p-values for both the slope and intercept are essentially zero as well. The 95 percent confidence interval for the slope coefficient is 53,964 to 69,782. Recall that in our base model, we assumed sales growth of 50,000 each year, so the regression results suggest a point estimate closer to 60,000, although our original estimate is not far outside the confidence interval for this parameter.

When we introduce annual growth of 61,873 into the base-case spreadsheet, demand grows to 1.63 million units ten years out, compared to the base-case value of 1.51 million units. After creating a sensitivity table for NPV as a function of capacity, we find that the best capacity choice for this model is 1.3 million units, with an estimated NPV of $2.201 million. This contrasts to our base-case conclusion that capacity of 1.25 million would give an optimal NPV of $1.811 million.

It is worth asking how wrong we would be if this current model were actually to represent reality, and we were to choose instead a capacity of 1.25 million units, as suggested by our base-case analysis. The NPV at 1.25 million units is about $2.138 million. The difference between this value and the optimum of $2.201 million is about 3 percent—not a particularly large error, given the complications of forecasting future values of the other parameters.

It is also instructive to test the sensitivity of these conclusions to the regression parameters, the slope parameter in particular. Suppose we vary the slope parameter from 50,000 to 70,000, which is roughly the range of the 95 percent confidence interval from the regression. Repeated visits to a sensitivity table show that the optimal capacity varies from 1.25 million to 1.35 million units over this range. As in the base case, we conclude that optimal capacity is only moderately sensitive to the annual growth in demand.

A second regression approach takes lagged demand as the independent variable. While it is plausible that demand grows as a function of time alone, it is more likely that demand is influenced directly by economic and business forces. One way to incorporate these influences is to use last year's demand to forecast this year's demand, on the assumption that this year's activity will be influenced by much the same underlying factors as last year's.

The Data Analysis tool produces the following regression model:

$$Demand = 124{,}247 + 0.913 \times LastYearDemand$$

This regression also fits quite well, with high R^2 (0.99); the probability corresponding to the F-value (*Significance F*) is essentially zero, and the p-values for both the slope and intercept are essentially zero as well. The 95 percent confidence interval for the slope coefficient is 0.81 to 1.01. This model, however, suggests that demand will grow only to 1.24 million in year 10, far lower than in our base-case model. Why is this? The answer lies in the estimated regression equation, which suggests that demand in any given year is a constant plus 91 percent of the previous year's demand. According to this equation, demand would actually *decline* over time were it not for the influence of the constant term. Not surprisingly, under these assumptions, the optimal value of capacity is lower, around 1.15 million, and the best NPV we can expect is only $1.219 million.

A better model for demand based on lagged values would force the regression constant to be zero. (This is a check-box option offered in the Regression window shown, for example, in Figure 7.28.) This model would take the form *Demand* = $a \times$ *LastYearDemand*, so we would expect the parameter a to exceed 1.0. The Data Analysis tool produces the following regression model:

$$Demand = 1.069 \times LastYearDemand$$

This regression fits well, with an R^2 of 0.96 and the other indicators in line. The slope coefficient indicates that annual growth will occur at a rate just under 7 percent (its 95 percent confidence interval is from 1.033 to 1.10, suggesting that annual growth could range from 3 percent to 10 percent). Under this model, demand reaches 1.97 million units by year 10, and the optimal plant capacity is 1.40 million units (with an NPV of $2.708 million), higher than the base case, but more in line with the results using the first regression model with time as the independent variable.

How sensitive is our decision to the slope coefficient? Suppose we vary the annual growth rate from 1 percent to 15 percent. (Recall that the estimated value is 6.9 percent.) Optimal capacity varies from 1.05 million to more than 3 million units in this range. How should we interpret these results? The answer to this question depends on how much we know about the growth rate in demand over the next ten years. If we actually believe that any growth rate between 1 percent and 15 percent is equally likely, we can say only that the optimal capacity choice is indeterminate over a wide range. However, suppose we believe that growth will lie in a range around 7 percent—perhaps between 3 percent and 10 percent, as suggested by the confidence interval. Then, we can conclude that the optimal plant capacity lies between 1.14 million and 1.80 million units.

A third regression approach takes the number of arthritis patients as the independent variable. The two previous models fit the given data well, from a purely statistical point of view. However, neither relates demand directly to any of the underlying economic forces. Such a model, while it may involve more effort to build, may also provide insights unachievable with the previous models.

Sales of an antiarthritis drug obviously have a direct connection to the number of people suffering from this condition. Drawing on some work done by an industry association, BPI has gathered data covering the past ten years on the number of patients diagnosed with arthritis (see Figure 7.31). Two plausible models suggest themselves: either demand is proportional to the number of patients (and the regression line goes through the origin), or it is linear in the number of patients. The first approach does lead to a plausible model (*Demand = 0.050 × Patients*), with R^2 of 0.84 and the other statistical measures in line. However, this model may overestimate the growth in demand if some doctors experiment with a new drug and prescribe it frequently to the first patients they see, but prescribe it less often to subsequent patients. The alternative approach, using a nonzero intercept, produces the following regression equation:

$$Demand = 190{,}543 + 0.0387 \times Patients$$

This regression has a higher R^2 (0.93) than the previous model. It suggests that if the number of patients were to rise by 100,000, demand would rise by 3,870. However, the 95 percent confidence interval on the critical slope parameter is 0.030 to 0.047, so the actual increase in demand could be as low as 3,000 or as high as 4,700. In a detailed analysis, we would want to test the sensitivity of our results to values in this range.

FIGURE 7.31
Data on Arthritis Patients

Bundy.xls

Year	Demand	Patients
1	487,000	9,123,000
2	560,000	10,189,000
3	601,000	11,570,000
4	689,000	12,584,000
5	788,000	13,965,000
6	854,000	15,191,000
7	902,000	17,321,000
8	957,000	19,247,000
9	991,000	21,096,000
10	1,010,000	23,095,000

Before we can use this regression model to forecast demand, we need to develop a forecast for the independent variable, the number of arthritis patients. We assume the number of patients will grow at a constant rate (5 percent) over the ten-year horizon. With this assumption, demand will grow to 1.65 million units by year 10. The optimal capacity for this case is 1.35 million, with an estimated NPV of $2.696 million. Again, this conclusion is in line with earlier results from regressions based on time and based on lagged sales. However, this conclusion depends both on our forecast of the number of arthritis patients *and* on our estimated relationship between patients and demand. Therefore, errors in forecasting the growth in arthritis patients will lead to errors in selecting the optimal plant capacity.

To test the sensitivity of the optimal capacity to the assumed growth in the number of patients, we determined the optimal capacity for growth rates between 0 percent and 10 percent by incorporating the patient-based regression equation into our model and then building a sensitivity table to compare different capacity choices. If there is no future growth in the patient population, the optimal capacity is 1.10 million. With 5 percent growth, we should build a plant for 1.35 million; at 10 percent, the optimal capacity is 1.80 million. Any uncertainty we have about the growth of the patient population adds to the uncertainty in determining the optimal plant capacity. This is a major drawback of regression models based on independent variables that themselves require forecasting.

Simple Nonlinear Regression

In many cases, a straight line relationship will not be the most plausible description of a dependency between two variables. Consider the dependency of sales volume on advertising, or any relationship involving diminishing returns. When we compare linear and nonlinear equations (see, for instance, the graphs in Figures 7.26a and 7.26b), the nonlinear version may well be better.

How should we attack the nonlinear case in regression? Since the formulas for the linear case are so convenient, the approach most widely used is to transform the model back into a linear one. For example, suppose we are trying to estimate the parameters (*a* and *b*) of a power function

$$y = ax^b \tag{14}$$

Following the approach introduced for simple linear regression, we could calculate predicted values from this equation and compare them to the observed values, minimizing the sum of squared differences between the observations and the predictions. There are no simple formulas available for this case, analogous to those in (*13*). Moreover, it is difficult to locate software that automates the calculations, as Excel does for linear regression. (We can, however, create our own custom analysis for this purpose, using optimization techniques, and we discuss this application in Chapter 8.)

Alternatively, we can transform the equation in (*14*) by taking the logarithm of both sides:

$$\log y = \log a + b \times \log x$$

Note that this transformation creates a linear equation: $\log a$ is the constant term, and the constant *b* now plays the role of a slope, not an exponent. With this transformation, we can use all of the results for simple linear regression, including the Data Analysis tool in Excel. However, this also means that we have to think in terms of a graph that plots $\log y$ versus $\log x$, rather than *y* versus *x*. Because most of us find it difficult to think in "logarithm space," this version of the model is probably not as intuitive or transparent as the original. So we give up some intuition for the convenience of using the transformed model.

We should not expect to get identical answers from the two approaches. An example will illustrate this point. A chain of drugstores has pharmacies in different types of locations, such as shopping malls, grocery stores, and independent storefronts. Stores in different types of locations are open for different hours, and the company can therefore study a natural experiment to see how revenue varies with store hours. For a sample of ten stores, the following data show the number of hours the store is open each week and the average revenue.

Store	1	2	3	4	5	6	7	8	9	10
Hours	40	44	48	48	60	70	72	90	100	168
Revenue	5,958	6,662	6,004	6,011	7,250	8,632	6,964	11,097	9,107	11,498

If we work with the data directly, with the form of (*14*), we need a specialized analysis to find the best fit. It is possible to show (using methods that we introduce in Chapter 8) that the best fit is given by the equation

$$Revenue = 1{,}022 \times Hours^{0.482}$$

The choice of $a = 1{,}022$ and $b = 0.482$ leads to a sum of squared differences equal to approximately 7.55 million.

By contrast, if we work with the transformed equation, we can use Excel's Regression tool to analyze the relation between the logarithm of *Revenue* and the logarithm of *Hours*. The best fit turns out to be

$$\log(Revenue) = 2.954 + 0.510 \times \log(Hours)$$

When this equation is transformed back into the original dimensions, it becomes

$$Revenue = 899.2 \times Hours^{0.510}$$

Obviously, the two equations are not very different; however, the sum of squared differences for the transformed equation is equal to about 7.68 million, or nearly 2 percent higher than the best fit. This example illustrates the trade-off in a choice of a modeling strategy. If we use the direct equation, we need to develop a specialized analysis, but we can find the best fit. On the other hand, if we use the transformed equation, we can take advantage of Excel's built-in regression analysis, but we will likely not find the best fit.

The power function in (*14*) is just one example of the model structures that could be useful in describing the dependence of one variable on another. As we discussed in Chapter 3, it is helpful to be familiar with a few families of functions. In the regression context, these functions would be the curves we might sketch to fit data points on a scatter plot. In Chapter 8, we present a general method for fitting nonlinear curves to data.

Multiple Linear Regression

A simple regression equation may not always be sufficient for our purposes. The use of a single independent variable may lead to acceptable results in statistical terms, but to be useful, the relationship may need additional variables. In these cases, an appropriate predictive equation contains multiple independent variables. When there are m such variables, the linear regression model takes the form

$$y = a_0 + a_1 x_1 + a_2 x_2 + \ldots + a_m x_m + e \tag{15}$$

Here, we're using subscripts differently than in the discussion of simple regression. In (*15*), the subscripts are used to index the different independent variables, from 1 to m. However, the main regression concepts resemble those for the case of simple regression.

As before, we work with n observations, where each observation consists of one value for the dependent variable and one value for each of the m independent variables. We compare the observations with the prediction of the equation and find the sum of squared differences. Then, we find the values of the coefficients, a_0 through a_m, that minimize this sum. These coefficients provide the best fit.

Excel's Regression tool provides an extensive analysis of the regression equation. Its first table lists a number of statistics, including three measures of fit. As in the case of simple regression, we can use R^2 as a basic measure of fit. In the case of multiple regression, R^2 is called the **coefficient of multiple determination,** and its square root, R, is called the **multiple R,** or the **multiple correlation coefficient.** Excel reports both values. The table also reports an **adjusted R^2.** The reason for introducing another measure is that adding independent variables to the regression equation will never decrease the value of R^2, and will usually increase it, even if there is no reason why the added variable should help predict the dependent variable. A suitable adjustment accounts for the effect of the number of variables in the equation and will cause the adjusted R^2 to decrease unless there is a compensating reduction in the differences between observed and predicted values. One informal guideline for how many independent variables to include in a regression equation is to find the largest value of the adjusted R^2. However, we strongly recommend including variables that can be justified on practical or theoretical grounds, even if the adjusted R^2 is not at its largest possible value.

The regression report also lists a value for the F-statistic (labeled *Significance F*), which has the same interpretation as in a simple regression: it measures the probability of getting the observed R^2 or higher if, in fact, all the true regression coefficients were zero. This is a measure of the overall fit of the regression model to the data, but it is not a particularly stringent test. We would expect this probability to be low in any well-considered model for which relevant data were being used.

The estimated coefficients of the regression equation, which we denoted as a_0 through a_m, can be found under the *Coefficients* heading in the Excel regression output. Corresponding to each coefficient, the table provides a *p*-value, which measures the probability that we would get an estimate at least this large if the true regression coefficient were zero. While the *p*-value does provide a quick check on each coefficient, the respective confidence intervals generally provide more useful information.

As a brief example, we return to the Executives database. This time, we explore a multiple regression model for the relation between executive salaries and various measures of firm performance. In particular, for independent variables, we select Sales, Profits, Assets, and ROA, because one or more of these financial measures would seem to be logical explanatory variables. Thus, our regression equation takes the following form:

$$Salary = a_0 + a_1 \times Sales + a_2 \times Profit + a_3 \times Assets + a_4 \times ROA$$

To invoke Excel's tool for multiple regression, we must have the independent variables in contiguous cells on the spreadsheet, so that we can specify a single range for the *x*-variables. In this case, that range is N1:Q101, with labels included. The output table is shown in Figure 7.32. We observe the following:

- The multiple regression model achieves $R^2 = 0.275$. If we are comparing the multivariable model to the simple regression model we examined earlier, a relevant comparison involves the Adjusted R^2, which has gone up slightly, from 0.215 to 0.244.

- The F-value of 3.277×10^{-6} shows that it would be extremely unlikely to observe this value of the R^2 if all the true regression coefficients were zero.

- Although the increased value of R^2 is achieved with four independent variables, two of them (*Assets* and *ROA*) have high *p*-values (0.63 and 0.20, respectively), which suggests that these estimates would not be unlikely even when the true coefficients are zero. As we would expect, the confidence intervals for these coefficients range on either side of zero. As for the coefficient on Sales, the point estimate is 0.0172, with a 95 percent confidence interval from 0.0098 to 0.0246. The coefficient on Pretax has a point estimate of –0.0513, with a 95 percent confidence interval from –0.1030 to 0.0004. Notice that this confidence interval extends over zero, and the *p*-value of 5.16 percent suggests that there is a nonnegligible chance of observing the estimate we have when the true coefficient is zero.

Our attempts to develop a model for executive salaries have not gone very far at this point. Although the level of company sales appears to be a key explanatory factor in our analysis, we must also recognize that we are limited by the data. In particular, if we had a larger data set, with data from successive years, we might be able to fashion a more convincing model by relating salaries to *changes* in profits or returns. Here again, judgment about the nature of salaries in practice might be more beneficial than a series of regression runs in helping us formulate a good predictive model.

Multiple Regression in the BPI Example

Could we improve the capacity decision by adding explanatory factors to the demand model—in other words, by performing a multiple regression? We have already discussed data on the number of patients with arthritis; additional data are available on the average price of the drug and on the level of sales effort (measured in terms of the size of the sales force dedicated to this product). Let's see if we can improve our decision with this information.

First, we should think through the implications of a multiple regression model in this context. The regression equation would take the form

$$Demand = a_0 + a_1 \times Patients + a_2 \times Price + a_3 \times Effort$$

We expect that two factors, *Patients* and *Effort*, would have positive effects on Demand, so a_1 and a_3 should be positive numbers. Similarly, we expect *Price* to have a negative effect, so a_2 would be negative. However, since most patients don't pay for drugs directly, or don't pay the full price, it is possible that this effect is weak.

This model is based on the following strong assumptions:

- *Demand* would be a_0 even if *Patients, Price,* and *Effort* were all zero.

- If any one of the independent variables—for example, *Price*—were to increase by *x*, *Demand* would increase by $a_2 \times x$, regardless of the level of *Price*. Thus, an increase in *Price* from \$10 to \$11 will have the same effect as an increase from \$100 to \$101.

- The effects of two or more independent variables are independent. Thus, an increase of \$1 in *Price* has the same impact on *Demand* whether *Effort* is high or low.

In a first attempt, we include all three independent variables. Our results (see Figure 7.33) show an adjusted R^2 of 0.98, which is higher than we achieved with the simple regression (0.93) using patients only. (The *F*-value is once again essentially zero.) The regression equation takes the following form:

$$Demand = 1,397,473 + 0.0258 \times Patients - 79,351 \times Price - 3,383 \times Effort$$

FIGURE 7.32
Multiple Regression
Results for Executive
Salaries

Executives.xls

	A	B	C	D	E	F	G
1	SUMMARY OUTPUT						
2							
3	*Regression Statistics*						
4	Multiple R	0.5244					
5	R Square	0.2750					
6	**Adjusted R Square**	**0.2444**					
7	Standard Error	299.0					
8	Observations	100					
9							
10	ANOVA						
11		df	SS	MS	F	Significance F	
12	Regression	4	3220345	805086.3	9.0064	3.27673E-06	
13	Residual	95	8492089	89390.4			
14	Total	99	11712434				
15							
16		Coefficients	tandard Err	t Stat	P-value	Lower 95%	Upper 95%
17	Intercept	541.3234	44.3163	12.2150	3.46E-21	453.3445	629.3023
18	SALES	0.0172	0.0037	4.6128	1.24E-05	0.0098	0.0246
19	PRETAX	-0.0513	0.0260	-1.9714	0.0516	-0.1030	0.0004
20	ASSETS	-0.0002	0.0005	-0.4788	0.6332	-0.0012	0.0007
21	ROA	6.9400	5.4625	1.2705	0.2070	-3.9043	17.7844
22							

However, a high p-value (11 percent) suggests that the estimated coefficient on Effort could arise even when the true coefficient is zero. (The 95 percent confidence interval is –7,803 to 1,036.) Worse than that, the estimated coefficient on Effort is *negative*. Unless our sales force is utterly inept, this is not a very reasonable result. If we include it in the model, it will lead us to conclude that less sales effort is better than more, when more appropriate conclusions might be that the data on effort are somehow biased or that we should fix a broken sales process.

With these results in hand, we estimate another equation in which we use only Patients and Price as independent variables. This equation takes the following form:

$$Demand = 1{,}100{,}233 + 0.0169 \times Patients - 76{,}745 \times Price$$

The adjusted R^2 is 0.99, and now all three regression coefficients have low p-values. Moreover, the coefficients on *Patients* and *Price* have the sign we would expect. However, there is still substantial uncertainty as to the true value of the coefficients, as indicated by their confidence intervals. For example, the coefficient on *Price*, which may be crucial to determining future pricing policy, is estimated at –76,745 but could lie between –117,269 and –36,220. In other words, increasing price by $1 could lower demand by anywhere from 36 to 117 thousand units.

If we accept this equation as the best regression model possible using these data, what implications does it have for the capacity decision? First, notice that to use this equation, we have to make projections of the independent variables, *Patients* and *Price*, just as we did before when we used only *Patients* as the independent variable. To keep this manageable, we assume that *Patients* will grow at 10 percent and that *Price* will not grow at all over the next ten years. Under these assumptions, the optimal capacity is about 1.28 million units, with an associated NPV of $1.963 million.

But does this multiple regression really make our decision better? Even if our regression model is highly accurate, how accurate are our forecasts of *Patients* and *Price*? If those forecasts are inaccurate, and actual demand differs from our forecasts, then our decision on capacity may be off as well. We can test this by varying our growth rate assumptions for *Patients* and *Price* and then testing the sensitivity of optimal capacity. For example, if the

FIGURE 7.33
Multiple Regression
Results for BPI Demand

Bundy.xls

	A	B	C	D	E	F	G
13	SUMMARY OUTPUT						
14							
15	*Regression Statistics*						
16	**Multiple R**	0.994373061					
17	R Square	0.988777784					
18	**Adjusted R Square**	0.983166675					
19	Standard Error	24601.59061					
20	Observations	10					
21							
22	ANOVA						
23		*df*	*SS*	*MS*	*F*	*Significance F*	
24	Regression	3	3.19961E+11	1.067E+11	176.21791	3.07857E-06	
25	Residual	6	3631429562	605238260			
26	Total	9	3.23593E+11				
27							
28		*Coefficients*	*Standard Error*	*t Stat*	*P-value*	*Lower 95%*	*Upper 95%*
29	Intercept	1397473.03	237341.4827	5.8880269	0.001065	816718.9217	1978227.1448
30	Patients	0.025820	0.006541285	3.9471715	0.007562	0.009814	0.041826
31	Price	-79350.92	14770.29026	-5.372333	0.001708	-115492.5467	-43209.2973
32	Effort	-3383.08	1806.158	-1.873078	0.110207	-7802.5882	1036.4371
33							

growth in *Patients* is 0 percent, capacity should be 1.04 million; if the growth is 20 percent, capacity should be 1.81 million. Now setting the growth rate for *Patients* back to 10 percent, we find that if Price grows by 10 percent, capacity should be set at 1.00 million units; if Price declines at 10 percent, capacity should be 1.46 million. Clearly, forecasting the growth rates in Patients and Price is particularly critical to making a good decision.

These results suggest that inaccuracy in our forecasts of independent variables could have a major impact on our decision. Thus, we should not be too confident in the value of this model to improve our decision making unless we think we can make a fairly accurate forecast of the growth in *Price*. The lesson is this: always remember that multiple regression models require forecasts of the independent variables. If these forecasts themselves cannot be made with precision, the regression equation may not provide a better decision than a simpler approach that does not require forecasting.

Regression Assumptions

We have introduced the regression equation as a means for estimating relationships between two or more parameters in our model. We have not attempted to develop the full coverage of regression as a statistical topic; rather, we have drawn on statistical results where they suit our purposes in modeling. Nevertheless, we should point out that the validity of statistical inferences from regression analysis rests on several important assumptions. These are as follows:

- Errors in the regression model follow a normal distribution.
- Errors in the regression model are mutually independent.
- Errors in the regression model have the same variance.
- Linearity is assumed to hold (for single and multiple linear regression).

The first of these assumptions relates to our basic probabilistic model. The dependent variable is viewed as having a mean value on the regression line, and the observation is viewed as being equal to the mean value plus an error term. The error terms are assumed to follow a normal distribution. This might be a plausible assumption whenever differences between observed and model values can be thought of as the combined effect of several unobservable and independent factors, such as would be the case for the relationship between sales and advertising. One way to use the data to help confirm this assumption is to examine the residual values. For the case of simple regression, the residuals are given by the formula in (*12*), but in this and other cases, residuals can be plotted automatically by Excel. Either by scanning the residuals, or by displaying them in a histogram, there should be an indication that they follow a normal distribution.

The second assumption states that there are no systematic dependencies among different observations. This would be the case, for example, if we hypothesized a linear relationship when there was actually a cycle in operation. In this situation, some observations would fall above the regression equation, and others below it, in a discernible, systematic pattern. Such dependencies can often be detected by looking for systematic patterns in the graph of residuals.

The third assumption states that the normal distribution for errors does not become more narrow, or more spread out, as we proceed through the data. Qualitatively, this means that the size of the errors should be roughly the same early in the sample as late in the sample. Again, we would find evidence to the contrary by scanning the residuals to see whether small and large values are distributed randomly throughout the sample.

Finally, the fourth assumption may be based on our knowledge of the underlying economics in a model, or from a well intended attempt at a reasonable first cut. If linearity is a poor assumption, the evidence is likely to show up in the pattern of residuals. For example, if the plot of residuals shows values that are first negative, then positive for a while, and then finally negative again, there is good reason to believe that a nonlinear relationship exists in the data.

FORECASTING WITH TIME-SERIES MODELS

Regression represents a general modeling approach to predicting the value of one variable based on knowledge of other variables. In particular, if we know the values of the independent variables, we may be in a good position to predict the value of the dependent variable. However, when we want to forecast the routine behavior of an input variable, regression may be of limited usefulness. While it does afford us an opportunity to "explain" one variable's behavior in terms of several other variables, it still leaves us with the task of finding or predicting those values. In short, regression replaces the problem of forecasting y (the dependent variable) with the problem of forecasting x (the independent variable). For some kinds of forecasting, we can make reasonable predictions of a variable's future value merely by basing our calculations on its own history, while avoiding the necessity of predicting independent variables.

The basic problem in short-term forecasting is to estimate the value of an important parameter, such as next week's demand for a product. Two features of short-term forecasting are important. First, we make use of historical data. In other words, we have some recent data on hand, and we assume that the near-term future will resemble the past. That makes it sensible to project historical observations into the future. Second, we seek a routine calculation that may be applied to a large number of cases and that may be automated, without relying on any qualitative intelligence about the underlying phenomena. Some people use the term **forecasting** to imply the use of a routine method, preferring the term **prediction** to suggest the use of subjective judgment in addition to calculations. In that sense, we are dealing here with forecasting techniques.

At the outset, we hypothesize a model for systematic behavior in the time series of interest. The major components of such a model are usually the following:

- an average level
- a trend
- a seasonal or cyclic fluctuation

Figure 7.34 shows these three basic categories in graphical form. Thus, we start by adopting one of these models as a representation of the process we're forecasting. Later, we will see how we might choose one of the models based on how well the forecasts match our observations.

By adopting one of the models in Figure 7.34, we are assuming that future observations will be samples drawn from a probability distribution whose mean value follows the model. The simplest case is the model for a stable mean demand (Figure 7.34a), without trend or seasonality. In that case, our model becomes:

$$x_t = \mu + e \qquad (16)$$

where x_t represents the observed value for time period t, and μ represents the mean value. The term e represents randomness. In other words, the actual observations can be thought of as a systematic but unknown mean value (μ), modified by a random or "noise" term (e). The random term captures all of the uncertainty, and the purpose is to forecast the non-random term as precisely as possible. In order to produce that forecast, we can draw on the previous observations, x_t, x_{t-1}, x_{t-2}, and so on.

The Moving-Average Model

If we were perfectly confident in our assumption about the model in (16), then we could use our entire history of observations to construct a forecast. In fact, the more of our past data we used, the more precise our forecast would tend to be. However, we may suspect that there has been, or will be, some systematic change in the mean of the process (that is, a change in μ). If such a change had occurred without our knowing about it, then some of the data used in the construction of the forecast would be outdated. To guard against this possibility, we can limit ourselves to only the most recent observations in order to construct a forecast. In particular, the n-period **moving average** builds a forecast by averaging the observations in the most recent n periods:

$$F_t = (x_t + x_{t-1} + \ldots + x_{t-n+1}) / n \qquad (17)$$

where F_t denotes the forecast, and x_t represents the observation from period t.

The formula in (17) simply takes the average of the n most recent observations. One period from now, there will be a new observation to include in the average, while the oldest observation will be dropped. Thus, in the event that a systematic change occurs in the underlying process, the oldest data point, which reflects how the process looked prior to the change, will be purged from the forecast calculation.

As an example, the distributor for Aleve is tracking weekly volumes, for inventory control purposes, using the data in the Analgesics database for service to all of the stores. The volumes over the past ten weeks are shown in the table below. We renumber the weeks for convenience.

FIGURE 7.34
Graphs for the Level, Trend, and Seasonal Forecasting Models

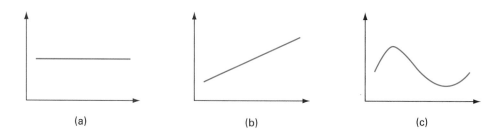

(a)   (b)   (c)

Week	1	2	3	4	5	6	7	8	9	10
Sales	6,486	4,502	4,308	3,728	3,782	3,782	5,102	5,238	5,594	4,766

Now the distributor's task is to develop a forecast for week 11 (and beyond) from this history. In the worksheet of Figure 7.35, we find the observations in column B and the forecast calculations in column C. The first forecast we can calculate, using a four-week moving average, occurs after the fourth observation, so we see entries in the Forecast column starting in week 4. Cell C8 contains the formula AVERAGE(B5:B8), and this formula has been copied to the cells below it. The last calculation in column C contains the moving average after the observation in week 10, a value of 5,175.

How good are the forecasts produced by this moving-average calculation? There is no standard measure of performance for forecast accuracy, but several measures are used frequently. We suggest three measures:

- MSE: the Mean Squared Error between forecast and actual
- MAD: the Mean Absolute Deviation between forecast and actual
- MAPE: the Mean Absolute Percent Error between forecast and actual

The MSE is a traditional squared-error calculation that echoes results in statistics. The MAD looks only at error sizes, without squaring them, and the MAPE looks at relative error sizes. For now, we simply record these measures, calculated from the pairs of forecasts and observed data points that correspond to weeks 5 through 10. These are shown in the spreadsheet in cells I4, I5, and I6.

How many periods' worth of observations should we include in the moving average? There is no definitive answer to this question, but there is a trade-off to consider. Suppose the mean of the underlying process remains stable. If we include very few data points, then the moving average will exhibit more variability than if we include a larger number of data points. In that sense, we get more *stability* from including more points. (In our example, the three measures of forecast accuracy are all a little better for a six-week moving average than for the four-week moving average.) On the other hand, suppose there is an unanticipated change in the mean of the underlying process. If we include very few data points, our moving average will tend to track the changed process more closely than if we include a larger number of data points. In that case, we get more *responsiveness* from including fewer points. An idealized example will help demonstrate this fact. Suppose a demand process is perfectly stable at a level of 200, but at week 10, the process jumps to 400 and stays there. If we use a four-week moving average, the forecast will move gradually from 200 to 400, and after week 13, the forecast will be 400. If instead we use a six-week moving average, the forecast will move more gradually. After week 13, the forecast will be 333; it won't

EXCEL TIP: MOVING-AVERAGE CALCULATIONS

Moving averages are simple enough to calculate on a spreadsheet, and we don't really need specialized software or commands to do the work. However, Excel's Data Analysis tool does contain an option for calculating moving averages. Excel assumes that the data appear in a single column, and the program provides an option of recognizing a title for this column, if it is included in the data range. Other options include a graphical display of the actual and forecast data and a calculation of the standard error after each forecast. (This is equivalent to the square root of the MSE; however, Excel pairs the forecast F_t and the observation x_t. In the calculations of Figure 7.35, we adopted a more standard convention in which the forecast F_t is compared with the next observation, x_{t+1}.)

FIGURE 7.35
Moving Average
Forecasts for
the Example

Forecasting.xls

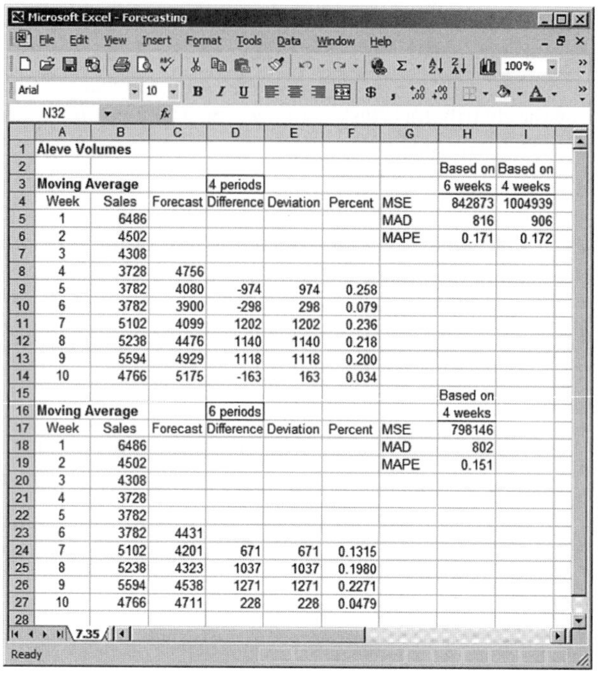

Microsoft Excel - Forecasting

	A	B	C	D	E	F	G	H	I
1	Aleve Volumes								
2								Based on	Based on
3	Moving Average			4 periods				6 weeks	4 weeks
4	Week	Sales	Forecast	Difference	Deviation	Percent	MSE	842873	1004939
5	1	6486					MAD	816	906
6	2	4502					MAPE	0.171	0.172
7	3	4308							
8	4	3728	4756						
9	5	3782	4080	-974	974	0.258			
10	6	3782	3900	-298	298	0.079			
11	7	5102	4099	1202	1202	0.236			
12	8	5238	4476	1140	1140	0.218			
13	9	5594	4929	1118	1118	0.200			
14	10	4766	5175	-163	163	0.034			
15								Based on	
16	Moving Average			6 periods				4 weeks	
17	Week	Sales	Forecast	Difference	Deviation	Percent	MSE	798146	
18	1	6486					MAD	802	
19	2	4502					MAPE	0.151	
20	3	4308							
21	4	3728							
22	5	3782							
23	6	3782	4431						
24	7	5102	4201	671	671	0.1315			
25	8	5238	4323	1037	1037	0.1980			
26	9	5594	4538	1271	1271	0.2271			
27	10	4766	4711	228	228	0.0479			
28									

reach 400 until after week 15. The MSE will be lower for the four-week moving average than for the six-week moving average. Thus, the answer to the question of how many periods to include depends on what we think might be happening to the underlying process. If it is stable, we prefer to include a larger number of data points in the average; but if it is apt to change, we prefer to include a smaller number. The trade-off involves stability and responsiveness, and our choice depends on the risk that the underlying process will change.

The Simple Exponential Smoothing Model

The essence of a time-series forecast is that we use historical observations—x_t, x_{t-1}, x_{t-2}, and so on—we apply some weights to these observations, and then we compute a weighted average in order to project future mean values. In the case of a four-period moving average, the weights are 0.25 on each of the last four observations and zero on all of the previous observations. But if the philosophy is to weight recent observations more and older ones less, then why not allow the weights to decline gradually as we go back in time? This is the approach taken in **exponential smoothing** forecasts.

Specifically, for the stable demand model of (*16*), we make the following calculation:

$$F_t = \alpha x_t + (1 - \alpha)F_{t-1} \tag{18}$$

where the *smoothing constant* α is some number between zero and one. We can think of (*18*) as describing the weighted average of two numbers: the latest observation (x_t) and our previous best guess (F_{t-1}). Similarly, one period previously, we would have made the calculation

$$F_{t-1} = \alpha x_{t-1} + (1 - \alpha)F_{t-2}$$

Substituting this equation into (*18*) yields

$$F_t = \alpha x_t + \alpha(1 - \alpha)x_{t-1} + (1 - \alpha)^2 F_{t-2}$$

Continuing to substitute in this way, we can eventually express (*18*) as follows:

$$F_t = \alpha x_t + \alpha(1 - \alpha)x_{t-1} + \alpha(1 - \alpha)^2 x_{t-2} + \alpha(1 - \alpha)^3 x_{t-3} + \ldots \qquad (19)$$

In this form, we can see that the forecast is a weighting of all observations, but with the largest weight on the most recent observation, the second largest weight on the second most recent observation, and so on. (Since $\alpha < 1$, the term $\alpha(1 - \alpha)^t$ declines with t.) Thus, the exponential smoothing formula is not as drastic as the moving average formula, in that it doesn't discard old data after n periods. Instead, the exponential smoothing calculation simply gives less weight to observations as they become older. In fact, the exponential decay exhibited by the weights in (*18*) is the basis for the name of the forecasting technique.

As written in (*18*), the new forecast is a weighted average of the most recent observation and the last forecast. An algebraic restatement of the relationship is the following:

$$F_t = F_{t-1} + \alpha(x_t - F_{t-1}) \qquad (20)$$

In other words, our new forecast (F_t) is equal to our old one (F_{t-1}), modified by an amount proportional to the difference, or error, between our latest observation and our previous forecast. Thus, we are willing to adjust our old forecast in the direction of that difference, and, in some sense, the value of α describes the strength of that adjustment. A larger value of α gives more weight to the adjustment. However, since there is likely to be some randomness in the difference between x_t and F_{t-1}, we do not want to make the value of α too large.

The formula illustrated in (*19*) strikes something of a balance between stability (by including all observations) and responsiveness (by weighting recent observations most heavily). However, even this balance can be influenced by the choice of the smoothing constant. When α is large (close to 1), the forecasts are responsive but tend to be volatile; when α is small (close to 0), the opposite is true. Most analysts opt for a conservative choice; that is, a relatively small value of α.

We can get an additional perspective by examining the coefficients in the expression (*19*). Figure 7.36 shows the weight applied to observation x_{t-k} (the observation that is $k - 1$ periods old) for two values of the smoothing constant α, $\alpha = 0.2$ and $\alpha = 0.6$. The use of the larger value, $\alpha = 0.6$, leads to 99 percent of the weight being placed on the most recent five observations, whereas the use of the smaller value, $\alpha = 0.2$, leads to only 67 percent of the weight being placed on the same observations. The graph also shows that the weights for $\alpha = 0.2$ are almost identical from period to period, while for $\alpha = 0.6$, the weights decline rapidly for earlier periods.

For the Aleve example, we illustrate forecasts obtained from exponential smoothing in Figure 7.37 for two cases, $\alpha = 0.6$ and $\alpha = 0.2$. We initialize the calculations by setting $F_1 = x_1$, as is customary. Both values of the smoothing constant lead to similar forecasts after week 10, and the forecasts are a little less variable than those produced by the moving averages. In Figure 7.38, we compare the forecasts for different values of the smoothing constant. The set of graphs shows that the use of a relatively large value of α allows the forecast to track the observations fairly closely, while a small value of α keeps the forecast much more insulated from fluctuations in the observed values.

EXCEL TIP: IMPLEMENTING EXPONENTIAL SMOOTHING

Excel's Data Analysis tool contains an option for calculating forecasts using exponential smoothing. The Exponential Smoothing module resembles the Moving Average module, but instead of asking for the number of periods, it asks for the **damping factor,** which is the complement of the smoothing factor, or $(1 - \alpha)$. Again, there is an option for chart output and an option for a calculation of the standard error.

FIGURE 7.36
Comparison of Weights
in Exponential
Smoothing

Forecasting.xls

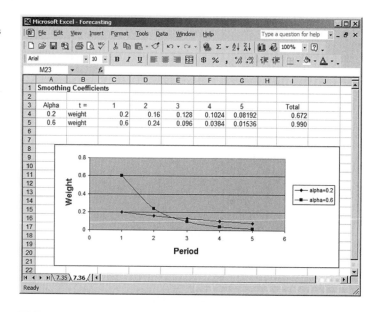

FIGURE 7.37
Exponential Smoothing
Forecasts for the
Aleve Example

Forecasting.xls

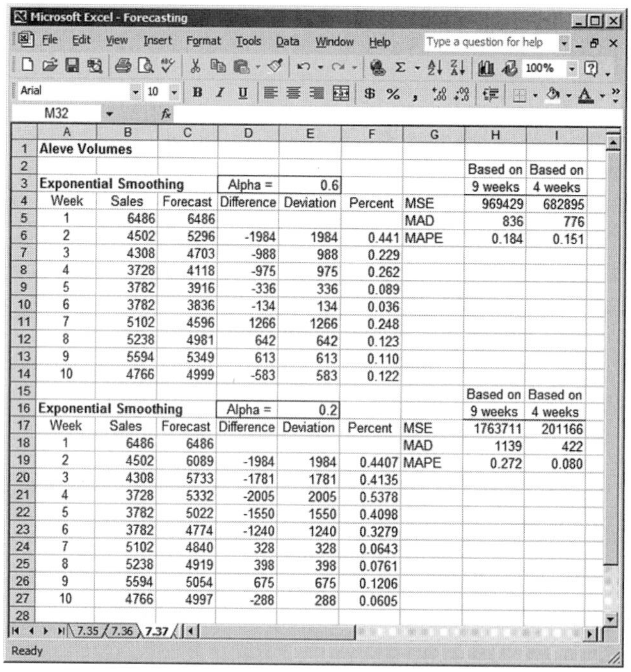

The Exponential Smoothing Model with Trend

In the previous discussions, our introduction to moving-average and exponential smoothing methods for forecasting was based on the stable demand model, $x_t = \mu + e$. Another of the choices available to us is the model with a linear trend in systematic demand:

$$x_t = \mu + \beta t + e$$

where β is the slope of the mean value line, usually called the **trend,** and t is time. When a trend is present, there are two tasks—to forecast the mean and to forecast the trend. Loosely speaking, we ask, where is the process now, and how fast is it changing? A pair of smoothing formulas does the work:

FIGURE 7.38

Comparison of Forecasts for Different Values of the Smoothing Constant

Forecasting.xls

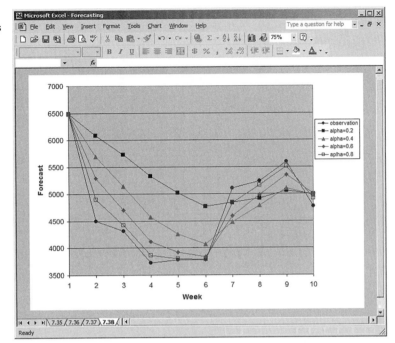

$$F_t = \alpha x_t + (1 - \alpha)(F_{t-1} + T_{t-1}) \qquad (21)$$

and

$$T_t = \beta (F_t - F_{t-1}) + (1 - \beta)T_{t-1} \qquad (22)$$

Equation 21 is a close analogue of (*18*), where we weight the most recent observation and our previous best guess as to where the mean value should lie in period *t*. Equation 22 is similar, except that instead of observing the trend directly, we use the difference in the two most recent forecasts as a proxy, and then we weight that along with our previous best guess about the value of the trend.

As an example, we return to Aleve volumes, assuming that a trend is present. We initialize F_t by setting it equal to the first observation at $t = 1$, and we initialize T_t at zero. In the spreadsheet of Figure 7.39, we show the calculated values of F_t and T_t, along with the forecast, which is calculated as $F_t + T_t$ for the period to follow. In this example, we can see that the observations induce a negative trend estimate in the early periods, as volumes decline. Then, after week 7, the trend estimate turns positive as volumes start to grow. The trend model can be a little more responsive than the stable mean model. As a result, the forecasts tend to be more accurate, as long as the underlying data are not too volatile.

In the trend model, and especially where we initialize the trend forecast at zero, it makes sense to use a relatively large smoothing factor in the trend equation (*22*), whereas a smaller factor is still reasonable for the main equation (*21*).

Exponential Smoothing in the BPI Example

In our final variation on this example, we use time-series methods to estimate demand. Since the historical data clearly show a trend, we use the exponential smoothing procedure with trend (equations 21 and 22). The results suggest that demand will grow to 1.57 million over the next ten years (see Figure 7.40). The optimal capacity under these assumptions is around 1.30 million units, with a projected NPV of $2.018 million. This conclusion is in line with those we made using simple linear regression models based on

FIGURE 7.39
Exponential Smoothing
Forecasts, with Trend,
for the Example

Forecasting.xls

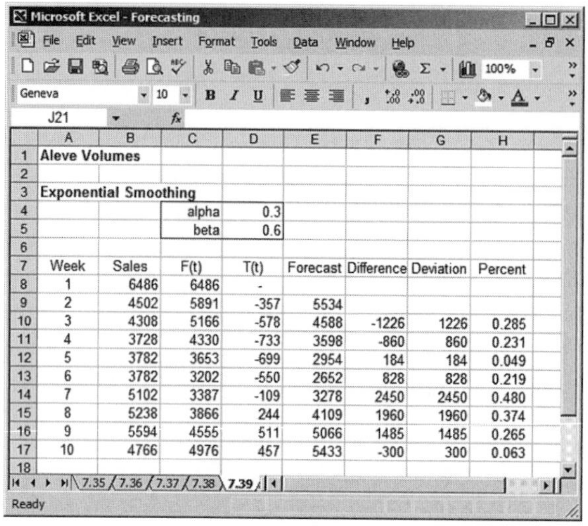

Microsoft Excel - Forecasting

Week	Sales	F(t)	T(t)	Forecast	Difference	Deviation	Percent
1	6486	6486	-				
2	4502	5891	-357	5534			
3	4308	5166	-578	4588	-1226	1226	0.285
4	3728	4330	-733	3598	-860	860	0.231
5	3782	3653	-699	2954	184	184	0.049
6	3782	3202	-550	2652	828	828	0.219
7	5102	3387	-109	3278	2450	2450	0.480
8	5238	3866	244	4109	1960	1960	0.374
9	5594	4555	511	5066	1485	1485	0.265
10	4766	4976	457	5433	-300	300	0.063

Aleve Volumes — Exponential Smoothing — alpha 0.3, beta 0.6

FIGURE 7.40
Results for Exponential
Smoothing in the BPI
Example

Bundy.xls

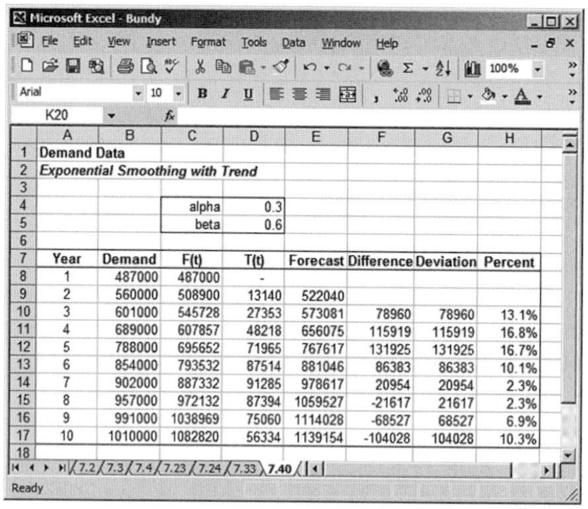

Microsoft Excel - Bundy

Year	Demand	F(t)	T(t)	Forecast	Difference	Deviation	Percent
1	487000	487000	-				
2	560000	508900	13140	522040			
3	601000	545728	27353	573081	78960	78960	13.1%
4	689000	607857	48218	656075	115919	115919	16.8%
5	788000	695652	71965	767617	131925	131925	16.7%
6	854000	793532	87514	881046	86383	86383	10.1%
7	902000	887332	91285	978617	20954	20954	2.3%
8	957000	972132	87394	1059527	-21617	21617	2.3%
9	991000	1038969	75060	1114028	-68527	68527	6.9%
10	1010000	1082820	56334	1139154	-104028	104028	10.3%

Demand Data — Exponential Smoothing with Trend — alpha 0.3, beta 0.6

time or lagged sales. Like those earlier models, this one does not require us to forecast an independent variable, which can be a distinct advantage.

The Exponential Smoothing Model with Trend and Seasonality

We can take the exponential smoothing model further, to include a seasonal or cyclical factor, as anticipated by Figure 7.34. Actually, graphs b and c of that figure are combined in the extended model. The form of the model is

$$x_t = (\mu + \beta t)S_t + e$$

where the seasonal factor is multiplicative and denoted by S_t. If we let p represent the number of periods in a cycle (i.e., the number of different seasonal factors), then there will be p distinct values of S_t to estimate. This means that the forecast calculated after the observation for period t will be calculated as $(F_t + T_t)S_{t-p+1}$ for the period to follow.

This time, there are three smoothing formulas and three smoothing constants (α, β, and γ). The formulas are as follows:

$$F_t = \alpha x_t / S_{t-p} + (1 - \alpha)(F_{t-1} + T_{t-1}) \tag{23}$$

$$T_t = \beta(F_t - F_{t-1}) + (1 - \beta)T_{t-1} \tag{24}$$

$$S_t = \gamma x_t / F_t + (1 - \gamma) S_{t-p} \tag{25}$$

We demonstrate this approach in Figure 7.41, again using data on Aleve. We start with a history of four quarterly observations of demand. Based on the first cycle of observations, the components of the forecast are initialized as follows:

$$S_t = x_t/(x_1 + x_2 + x_3 + x_4), \text{ for } t = 1 \text{ to } 4.$$

$$F_t = (x_1 + x_2 + x_3 + x_4) / 4, \text{ for } t = 4.$$

$$T_t = 0 \text{ for } t = 4.$$

Then, formulas (23)–(25) are used to compute new values of S_t, F_t, and T_t each time a new observation is made. Once entered into a spreadsheet, the set of formulas in (23)–(25) provides a general and powerful way to create forecasts with exponential smoothing. In particular, if there is no trend, then we can set all T-values equal to zero. If there is no seasonality, then we can set all S-values equal to one. Alternatively, we can allow the formulas to calculate these values, and, if there is not too much volatility in the observations, we expect to see calculations of T_t near zero and calculations of S_t near one.

SUMMARY

Our premise in this chapter is that modeling is the central task; data collection and analysis support the modeling task where appropriate. Nevertheless, when early sensitivity testing indicates that certain parameters must be estimated precisely, we turn to data analysis for locating relevant information, estimating parameters and relations among parameters, and constructing routine forecasts.

The process of finding facts in data is aided by a facility with Excel and in particular with its database capabilities. As more data sets become available through public sources

FIGURE 7.41
Exponential Smoothing
Forecasts, with Trend
and Seasonality

Forecasting.xls

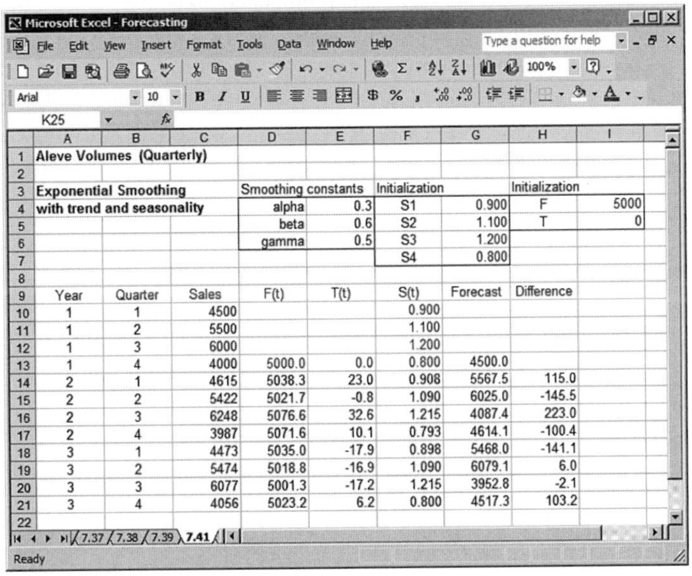

	A	B	C	D	E	F	G	H	I
1	Aleve Volumes (Quarterly)								
2									
3	Exponential Smoothing			Smoothing constants		Initialization		Initialization	
4	with trend and seasonality			alpha	0.3	S1	0.900	F	5000
5				beta	0.6	S2	1.100	T	0
6				gamma	0.5	S3	1.200		
7						S4	0.800		
8									
9	Year	Quarter	Sales	F(t)	T(t)	S(t)	Forecast	Difference	
10	1	1	4500			0.900			
11	1	2	5500			1.100			
12	1	3	6000			1.200			
13	1	4	4000	5000.0	0.0	0.800	4500.0		
14	2	1	4615	5038.3	23.0	0.908	5567.5	115.0	
15	2	2	5422	5021.7	-0.8	1.090	6025.0	-145.5	
16	2	3	6248	5076.6	32.6	1.215	4087.4	223.0	
17	2	4	3987	5071.6	10.1	0.793	4614.1	-100.4	
18	3	1	4473	5035.0	-17.9	0.898	5468.0	-141.1	
19	3	2	5474	5018.8	-16.9	1.090	6079.1	6.0	
20	3	3	6077	5001.3	-17.2	1.215	3952.8	-2.1	
21	3	4	4056	5023.2	6.2	0.800	4517.3	103.2	
22									

or on the Internet, it will become more valuable to be able to probe data sets quickly and intelligently. Excel provides an array of commands for searching, sorting, filtering, and tabulating data. These kinds of skills should be available to support spreadsheet modeling.

The basic numerical task involving data is to estimate model parameters. For this purpose, Excel provides statistically-oriented tools that make the process convenient. The Data Analysis tool for calculating descriptive statistics enables rapid construction of point estimates and interval estimates from raw data. The accompanying tool for implementing linear regression enables rapid building of simple models to show how certain variables can predict the values of other variables. However, the tool has technical limitations, in that it addresses only linear models, as well as practical limitations, as our example suggested.

Finally, routine forecasting is easy to adapt to the spreadsheet, as a means of tracking and predicting future values of key parameters. Although there is a Data Analysis tool for calculating moving-average and exponentially-smoothed forecasts, the tool does not accommodate the most powerful version of exponential smoothing, which includes trend and seasonal components. Fortunately, the formulas for these calculations are straightforward and lend themselves easily to spreadsheet use. Even without an add-in to perform the work, analysts can adapt exponential smoothing techniques to spreadsheets without extensive preparation.

Some review comments are also in order about our extended example, Bundy Pharmaceuticals. We began with a simple prototype and incorporated several alternative statistical analyses. Some of these analyses enriched our understanding. For example, the use of interval estimates (confidence intervals) allowed us to perform a more intelligent sensitivity analysis than naive use of a tornado chart would permit. However, other analyses, though mathematically powerful, may have had the opposite effect. For example, a somewhat forced multiple regression approach simply converted the challenge of predicting demand to the challenge of predicting patients, price, and sales effort. Our original message remains: model structure, not the analysis of data, has the largest effect on results. It is the structure of the model, and in particular the cost structure, that dictates an optimal capacity around 1.3 million units. Different forecasts of demand modify that conclusion in only minor ways. Figure 7.42 summarizes the various cases we examined for BPI, and we can see that our first prototype was not changed drastically by any of the statistical embellishments. Its assumption about annual growth in demand was perhaps conservative, and the most convincing statistically-based enhancements would lead us to a capacity choice of 1.30 million. On the other hand, an argument could be made that, linear projections notwithstanding, demand is beginning to level off, and a choice of 1.25 million makes a lot of sense.

Data analysis represents one of the three technical areas that supplement the art of modeling. In the next two chapters, we elaborate on the other areas of expertise.

SUGGESTED READINGS

The popularity of spreadsheets, both in education and in industry, has influenced the writing of textbooks in several areas, including statistics. The list below contains textbooks on basic statistics, mostly with a classical treatment of the subject, except that they rely on a spreadsheet perspective.

Albright, S. Christian, Wayne L. Winston, and Christopher Zappe. 1999. *Data Analysis and Decision Making with Microsoft Excel.* Pacific Grove, CA: Duxbury.

Evans, James R. and David L. Olson. 2000. *Statistics, Data Analysis, and Decision Modeling.* Upper Saddle River, NJ: Prentice–Hall.

Levine, David M., Mark L. Berenson, and David Stephan. 1999. *Statistics for Managers using Microsoft Excel.* Upper Saddle River, NJ: Prentice–Hall.

Pelosi, Marilyn K. and Theresa M. Sandifer. 2002. *Doing Statistics for Business with Excel,* 2d ed. 2002. New York: John Wiley.

FIGURE 7.42	Case	Optimal Capacity	Optimal NPV
Summary of the Various BPI Analyses	Base Case	1.25	$1.811
	Point estimate	1.30	$2.090
	Time regression	1.30	$2.201
	Lagged demand	1.15	$1.303
	Proportional regression	1.40	$2.708
	Patients regression	1.35	$2.816
Bundy.xls	Patients & Price	1.15	$1.566
	Smoothing	1.30	$2.018

EXERCISES

Database analysis

Examine the appropriate database and answer the questions posed.

1. The database Dish.xls contains a transaction history describing more than 4,000 purchases of detergent at a number of stores in a grocery chain over a period of several weeks. Compile the following pivot tables from this database:

   Questions

   a. A tabulation of sales by brand. In this analysis, "sales" refers to the number of sales units.

   b. A tabulation of sales broken down by brand and by week.

   c. A tabulation of sales broken down by brand, by week, and by store.

   d. A tabulation of sales broken down by brand and by size of container. From this breakdown, find the sales volume for each brand. In this analysis, "sales" refers to the number of ounces purchased.

2. The database Tissue.xls contains a transaction history describing more than 3,700 purchases of bathroom tissues at a number of stores in a grocery chain over a period of several weeks. Compile the following pivot tables from this database:

   Questions

   a. A tabulation of sales by brand. In this analysis, "sales" refers to the number of sales units.

   b. A tabulation of sales broken down by brand and by week.

   c. A tabulation of sales broken down by brand, by week, and by store.

   d. A tabulation of sales broken down by brand and by size of container. From this breakdown, find the sales volume for each brand. In this analysis, "sales" refers to the number of rolls purchased. Assume that all sizes refer to the number of rolls.

3. The database Applicants.xls contains a description of an MBA applicant pool for an unspecified year in the 1990s. For each of the following requirements, create a separate worksheet and extract the data from the original database.

   Questions

   a. Among enrolling students, what is the average GMAT score? What is the average in the applicant pool as a whole?

   b. How many in the applicant pool represented Financial Services in terms of job background? What was their average age? What was their average work experience (months)? What was their average GMAT score?

   c. How many in the applicant pool represented Consulting in terms of job background? What was their average age? What was their average work experience (months)? What was their average GMAT score?

   d. What proportion of the applicant pool had two or more degrees?

Estimation

4. Your company is changing its name, and you've been asked to study the impact of a name change announcement on the subsequent return generated by the firm's stock. In a sample of 400 companies that have made such announcements, you discover that over the twenty-eight-day period after a name change announcement, the average company experiences a 17 percent increase in price, with a standard deviation of 8 percent.

Questions

a. What is a 90 percent confidence interval for the mean stock price change for companies announcing a name change?

b. The range from 16 percent to 18 percent would constitute what (percentage) confidence interval for the mean change?

c. Do the data suggest that there is at least a 75 percent chance that a company's stock price will go up after a name change announcement?

5. Five years ago, an automobile manufacturer started offering an extended warranty to buyers of its sport-utility vehicle. The extended warranty covered defects occurring after the initial three-year warranty expired. Of the 10,000 people who bought the sport-utility vehicle in the first year of the program, 15 percent purchased the extended warranty.

   In the Warranty Department, you have recently received data on a random sample of 200 of the cars sold in the first year that the extended warranty was available. For this sample, the average extended-warranty expenditure per car for the one-year period after the initial warranty elapsed was $350 with a standard deviation of $100.

Questions

a. What is a 95 percent confidence interval for the mean one-year extended-warranty expenditure per automobile?

b. At its introduction, the extended warranty was priced at $225 per year per automobile. Compute a 95 percent confidence interval for the one-year profitability of the extended warranty.

c. How large a sample would the Warranty Department require if it wanted its 95 percent confidence interval for the mean warranty expenditure to be no more than ±$5?

6. The Luxor Computer Company plans to introduce a pyramid-shaped desktop computer. The company is interested in the proportion of prospective customers who find the unusual shape a positive selling point. In a random sample of 350 potential customers, 203 of the respondents indicated that the shape was a positive selling point.

Questions

a. What is an estimate of the proportion of prospective customers who find the unusual shape a positive selling point?

b. What is a 90 percent confidence interval for the proportion of prospective customers who find the unusual shape a positive selling point?

c. How many prospective customers would have to be queried for Luxor to be 90 percent certain that its estimated proportion was within 5 percent of the true value?

7. The number of staff personnel needed to handle patients at a medical center is determined by the mean time that patients must wait before being attended to by a physician. For a random sample of 100 previously recorded emergencies, the sample mean waiting time was seventy-two minutes, with a standard deviation of twenty-eight minutes.

Questions

a. What is a 50 percent confidence interval for the actual mean waiting time?

b. What is a 99 percent confidence interval for the actual mean waiting time?

8. Oxbridge University is contemplating a policy under which they would pay employees to not bring their vehicles to campus. Instead of paying an annual fee for on-campus parking, employees would receive a rebate from the university, provided that they found alternative means of getting back and forth to work. Since this idea is unusual, the university wants to

estimate the proportion of its employees who would sign up. When the option was offered to a random sample of forty employees, five signed up.

Questions

a. What is the estimated proportion that will sign up? What is the estimated standard deviation of the proportion that will sign up?

b. What is a 95 percent confidence interval for the proportion that will sign up?

c. How large a sample size is required in order to obtain a 95 percent confidence interval of ±0.05?

9. An engineer working on the auto assembly line is preparing to estimate the mean time required to install a dashboard. Assuming that the standard deviation of assembly time is ten seconds, determine the sample size under the following conditions:

Questions

a. The desired confidence level of being in error by no more than one second (in either direction) is 0.99.

b. The desired confidence level is 0.95 for a tolerable error of one second.

c. A confidence level of 0.99 is desired with a tolerable error of two seconds. How does the sample size you obtain compare with your answer to (a)?

d. Repeat (σ), assuming that s = 20 seconds. By how much does the sample-size change?

Regression

10. A food products company believes that storing frozen foods at low temperatures for several weeks might cause a noticeable weight loss in the product. Some data were collected to test this belief, as summarized in the table below:

Weeks stored	26	32	35	27	25	31	30	36
Weight loss (%)	1.05	1.35	1.32	1.12	1.01	1.24	1.28	1.41

Questions

a. Explore the possibility of a linear relation between percentage weight loss and weeks in storage. Does there seem to be a strong linear relationship, based on the calculation of the correlation?

b. Build a linear model to represent the relation between storage time and weight loss. What weight loss would the model predict for this product, if it were stored at low temperatures for twenty-eight weeks? For fifty-two weeks?

c. As an alternative way of building the model, suppose we measure excess storage time as weeks beyond twenty-four along with weight loss in percentage above 1 percent. Find the coefficients of the linear model corresponding to this alternative specification of the variables. How do they compare to the coefficients in (b)? Explain.

11. A toy company has been marketing souvenir toys in conjunction with various professional sports teams in a number of cities. Over the past few years, this experience has provided some data on the effect of advertising on sales, because the advertising expenditures have tended to be different in each case. Although the lengths of advertising campaigns vary, the vast majority of the sales occur within the first three months, which is the time period covered in the data. A summary is shown in the table.

Advertising ($M)	18	12	5	4	24	26	15	12	16	10	15	12
Revenues ($M)	105	72	40	44	135	122	88	77	105	67	98	54

Questions

a. Explore the possibility of a linear relation between advertising expenditures and three-month sales revenue. Does there seem to be a strong linear relationship, based on the calculation of the correlation?

b. Build a linear model to represent the relation between advertising and revenue. What revenues would the model predict for expenditures of $2 million?

c. As an alternative way of building the model, suppose that instead of measuring gross revenues (as reported in the table), we measure revenues net of advertising expenditures. Build a new linear model for this specification. How do the coefficients in the model compare with those in the model in (b)? Which model would be preferred?

12. A marketing manager for a computer manufacturer was interested in whether consumers could evaluate the price of laptops and desktops with different features. An experiment was devised in which a set of consumers were randomly shown one computer from an inventory and were asked to guess its price. Four computers were used in the study, with list prices of $1,800, $2,400, $3,600, and $4,000. The table below summarizes the findings. Each column represents a different computer, with its price in the first row. The rest of the column contains the various guesses by randomly selected customers. (Each guess came from a different customer.)

1,800	2,500	3,000	4,500
1,400	2,500	3,600	3,600
2,300	2,600	3,300	5,500
2,200	2,400	3,600	4,900
3,000	2,700	3,600	5,600
1,000	2,500	3,700	4,600
1,500	2,600		4,300
1,400	1,800		6,100
	2,400		

Questions

a. Explore the possibility of a linear relation between a customer's guesses and actual prices. Does there seem to be a strong linear relationship, based on the calculation of the correlation?

b. Build a linear model to represent a customer's price guess for a given computer price. What guess would the model predict for a computer that has a list price of $3,600?

c. Build a linear model with an intercept of zero to represent a customer's price guess for a given computer price. What guess would the model predict for a computer that has a list price of $3,600?

d. What advantages or disadvantages does the model in (b) have?

13. The Energy Conservation Committee at National Electronics Company is trying to understand energy use at their plant. As a first step, the committee wants to build a model that will predict monthly energy use as a function of production volumes, daily outside temperature, and number of workdays. The table below summarizes the data they have been able to collect for the previous year.

Month	Energy Use	Temperature	Days	Production
1	450	42	24	121
2	442	56	21	116
3	499	62	24	132
4	484	68	25	109
5	479	78	25	115
6	507	85	26	119
7	515	89	25	118
8	501	81	24	116
9	513	73	24	132
10	480	67	25	127
11	492	58	24	122
12	466	50	23	117

Questions

a. What is the regression equation that provides the prediction the committee was seeking?

b. What level of energy use would the model predict for a month in which there was an average temperature of forty-four, monthly production of 120, and twenty-five days of work at the plant?

Forecasting

14. The database Population.xls contains data from the U.S. Census showing the population of each state for the ten years from 1990 to 1999.

Questions

a. Calculate a forecast for the population of each state for 2000 using five-year moving averages.

b. Calculate a forecast for the population of each state for 2000 using exponential smoothing with $\alpha = 0.2$.

c. Calculate a forecast for the population of each state for 2000 using exponential smoothing with $\alpha = 0.4$.

15. The database Population.xls contains data from the U.S. Census showing the population of each state for the ten years from 1990 to 1999.

Questions

a. Calculate forecasts for years 1995–1999 using exponential smoothing with different smoothing constants from $\alpha = 0.1$ to $\alpha = 0.6$ in steps of 0.1. Which value achieves the smallest value of MSE?

b. For the same range tested in (a), which value achieves the smallest value of MAD?

16. The operations manager at a manufacturing facility is about to begin an energy-efficiency initiative. As this program begins, it will be helpful to have benchmark data on energy use, in order to determine whether the initiative is having an effect. The facilities department has provided data on the monthly energy use (in kilowatt hours) over the past three years, as shown in the table below:

Year 1	Usage	Year 2	Usage	Year 3	Usage
Jan	31,040	Jan	24,540	Jan	32,410
Feb	28,720	Feb	26,560	Feb	21,380
Mar	20,540	Mar	22,060	Mar	20,370
Apr	22,260	Apr	16,220	Apr	18,300
May	11,550	May	12,920	May	10,020
Jun	13,100	Jun	9,740	Jun	11,420
Jul	14,790	Jul	10,160	Jul	10,020
Aug	12,360	Aug	12,740	Aug	11,800
Sep	12,890	Sep	9,240	Sep	13,120
Oct	9,790	Oct	11,220	Oct	10,410
Nov	14,840	Nov	13,780	Nov	13,510
Dec	14,610	Dec	19,040	Dec	17,340

Questions

a. Use the exponential smoothing model (with trend and seasonality) to estimate the monthly usage for the coming twelve months. Use smoothing parameters of $\alpha = 0.3$, $\beta = 0.4$, and $\gamma = 0.5$.

b. For the forecasting problem in (a), which value of α achieves the minimum value of MSE, holding the other smoothing parameters constant?

17. The town of Hillside has a surface reservoir that supplies water to the homes in the town's central residential district. A committee of residents is concerned about the system's capacity and wants to project future use. The town's water department has promised to develop its best forecast of water use in the next two years. The department has collected quarterly data on water use (in millions of gallons) over the past decade, as shown in the table below:

Year	Q1	Q2	Q3	Q4
1	55	34	39	65
2	59	54	46	46
3	41	38	33	65
4	37	36	35	51
5	34	21	23	60
6	39	27	23	47
7	42	25	21	55
8	23	22	25	40
9	28	26	21	53
10	30	25	21	54

Questions

a. Use the exponential smoothing model (with trend and seasonality) to estimate the quarterly water use for the coming eight quarters. Use smoothing parameters of $\alpha = 0.3$, $\beta = 0.4$, and $\gamma = 0.5$.

b. For the forecasting problem in (a), which value of α achieves the minimum value of MSE, holding the other smoothing parameters constant?

CHAPTER 8

OPTIMIZATION

INTRODUCTION

Optimization is the process of finding the best set of decisions for a particular measure of performance. For example, in the Advertising Budget example of Chapter 5, we measure performance in terms of annual profit, and we would like to determine how to set advertising expenditures in the four quarters in order to achieve the *maximum* profit.

In Chapter 6, we introduced a framework for spreadsheet analysis in which optimization represents one of the higher order levels of analysis, generally coming after a base case has been established, some what-if questions have been explored, and perhaps some back-solving calculations have been made. In this chapter, we'll assume that the steps in that framework have already been explored. However, the framework does not necessarily apply to every spreadsheet model. There are spreadsheets that do not lend themselves to optimization. In some models, for example, the purpose is simply to forecast future outcomes or to explore past relationships. But managers and analysts generally use models in order to improve future operations. We refer to the levers they use to bring about improved performance as **decision variables.** If there are decision variables in a model, it is natural to ask what are the *best* values of those variables? This chapter explores in some detail how to answer this question by building and analyzing optimization models.

Optimization refers both to the goal of finding the best values of the decision variables and to a set of procedures, also known as **algorithms,** that accomplish this goal and are implemented by software. In the case of Excel, the optimization software is known as **Solver.** A version of Solver is built into every copy of Excel. In this book, we use **Premium Solver for Education,** which is a more advanced version than the standard Solver in Excel. Premium Solver for Education is included on the disk that comes with this book and should be installed before reading this chapter.

These days, the word "solver" is often a generic reference to optimization software, whether or not it is implemented in a spreadsheet. However, optimization tools have been available on computers for several decades, predating the widespread use of spreadsheets and even personal computers. Before spreadsheets, optimization was available through stand-alone software, but was often accessible only by technical experts. Managers and business analysts had to rely on those experts to build and interpret optimization models. The process of "building" such models typically referred to the construction of algebraic statements that defined the optimization problem mathematically. Now, however, the spreadsheet permits end users to develop their own models without relying explicitly on the algebra of model building. Moreover, the same end users can then call on Solver to find optimal solutions for the models they build themselves.

Because there are an infinite variety of possible spreadsheet models, finding the optimal values of decision variables in any one of those models can sometimes present quite a challenge. Although the Excel Solver is a very powerful and highly sophisticated piece of software, it is still possible to formulate otherwise acceptable spreadsheet models for which Solver cannot find the optimal solution. To use Solver effectively, end users must have some understanding of how to formulate spreadsheet models that exploit the power of Solver while avoiding its pitfalls. This chapter is designed to provide that understanding.

One way to avoid some of the pitfalls is to follow the principles of spreadsheet design covered in Chapter 5. For instance, it remains desirable in this context to modularize the spreadsheet, to isolate parameters, and to separate decision variables from calculations and intermediate calculations from final results. In this chapter, we also advocate some specific guidelines for optimization models. These guidelines help us to debug our own models, and when we're finished debugging and testing, the guidelines help us communicate the results of our models to others. Solver actually permits users considerable flexibility in designing models, but if we were to use all of that flexibility, we might confuse the people we want to communicate with, as well as ourselves. For that reason, it is good practice to impose some discipline on the building of optimization models.

We begin the chapter by demonstrating the optimization approach in the Advertising Budget example. We next provide general principles for building models for Solver. Then, we give an overview of the algorithms in the Solver software, so the user can form a mental image of what Solver is actually doing and can learn how to avoid misusing it. Optimization problems are categorized in various ways, with the categories corresponding roughly to the algorithm used to solve them. In subsequent sections of the chapter, we discuss three categories: nonlinear, linear, and integer optimization problems. In each case, we provide several examples, give advice on how to formulate models effectively, show how to solve problems, and illustrate how to interpret the results.

AN ILLUSTRATION OF OPTIMIZATION

Recall that in the Advertising Budget example of Chapters 5 and 6, the goal is to plan the spending of advertising dollars over the coming year. Planning is done on a quarterly basis, so we must choose advertising expenditures for each of the four quarters. Whatever plan we devise, we will evaluate it in terms of annual profits. Also, we have an annual advertising budget of $40,000 that we should not exceed.

Optimizing Q1

We first consider a limited optimization question: What is the best choice of advertising expenditures in the first quarter (Q1)? For the moment, we ignore the existence of the budget, and we assume that the expenditures in the three other quarters remain at $10,000. We could approach this problem by using the Data Sensitivity tool. In Figure 8.1, we show a table of Q1 expenditures and the corresponding annual profits, along with a graph of the relationship. The graph reveals that expenditures beyond the base-case level of $10,000 increase annual profits; but eventually, such expenditures become counterproductive, and annual profits drop. The graph and the table both show that the maximum profit level is achieved for expenditures of about $17,000. With two or three systematic refinements of this table, we could easily determine the optimal expenditures to a higher level of precision. However, we would not be able to extend the sensitivity table to more than two variables, which is our goal given that we have four decision variables.

To illustrate the optimization approach to this problem, we access Solver on the Tools menu. Assuming we have installed the Premium Solver for Education, we could toggle back and forth between this version and the standard version of Solver. The Premium version is always preferred. To invoke it, we click on the Premium button in the Solver Parameters window. This step will alter the window layout and substitute a Standard button for the Premium button, as shown in Figure 8.2. In the Solver Parameters window, there are three basic selections for the model: a **target cell,** or "set" cell; a set of **changing cells;** and a set of

FIGURE 8.1
Annual Profits as a
Function of Advertising
Expenditures in Q1

Adbudget8.xls

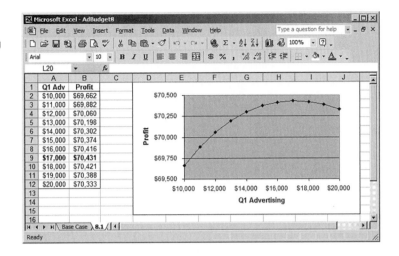

constraints. The syntax in the window asks Solver to set the target cell equal to a maximum by altering the changing cells, subject to constraints. In our problem, there are no constraints; we are simply interested in maximizing profit (our target cell) by altering Q1 expenditures (our single changing cell). In the Solver Parameters window, we enter the references to the target cell (C21) and the changing cell (D18). Then, we select the Standard GRG Nonlinear algorithm from the pull-down menu. (If this menu is not visible in the Solver Parameters window, it is likely that the standard version of Solver is running. Click on the Premium button to toggle to the Premium version.) Figure 8.2 shows the Solver Parameters window at this stage.

When we click on the Solve button, Solver searches for the optimal expenditure level and places it in the changing cell. If no technical problems are encountered, Solver displays a window stating, "Solver found a solution. All constraints and optimality conditions are satisfied." Here, we can simply choose OK. In this case, the optimal expenditure in Q1 is $17,093, and the corresponding revenue is $70,431. This is essentially the same result we found using the Data Sensitivity tool in Figure 8.1, with somewhat more precision.

Optimization Over All Four Quarters

If we optimized the advertising expenditures in each of the other quarters individually, as we did with Q1, we would find a different optimal level of expenditures for each quarter. The table below summarizes the results of those four one-at-a-time optimization runs.

	Quarter			
	1	2	3	4
Expenditures	17,093	27,016	12,876	32,721
Profits	70,431	73,171	69,806	75,284

FIGURE 8.2
The Solver Parameters
Window

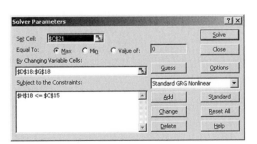

We get the same results if we optimize all four quarters simultaneously, by entering their cell addresses (D18:G18) as changing cells. Unfortunately, this result is infeasible, because it calls for total expenditures of more than $40,000 ($89,706, in fact). Although this solution is infeasible, it is useful to explore our model in this way. For one thing, this solution immediately suggests that we may want to lobby for a larger budget. It also reveals interesting structure in the solution, in that the expenditure profile reflects the seasonal factors, with the highest and lowest values coming in the last two quarters.

Having provided a glimpse of Solver's capability by optimizing our decisions without constraints, we look next at Solver's real power, the optimization of decision variables simultaneously, with constraints. We return to the Advertising Budget example and suppose that we want to operate within the original $40,000 budget. How should we allocate expenditures across the four quarters?

Incorporating the Budget Constraint

To investigate this question, we return to the base-case model and select Solver from the Tools menu. Solver presents its three basic selections: a target cell, a set of changing cells, and a set of constraints. Again, the syntax asks Solver to set the target cell equal to a maximum by altering designated changing cells subject to specified constraints. In our model, the target cell remains C21, and there are four changing cells, corresponding to the range D18:G18. We next click on the Add button, so that we can enter constraint information. This brings up the Add Constraint window, allowing us to designate the restriction that the sum of the advertising expenditures (H18) must be less than or equal to the size of the budget (C15), as shown in Figure 8.3. One of our design guidelines for Solver models calls for referencing a *formula* in the left-hand window and referencing a *number* in the right-hand window when specifying constraints. In this case, cell H18 contains a formula, and cell C15 contains a number. By relying on cell references rather than entering numbers directly, we assure that the key parameters are visible on the spreadsheet itself, rather than in the less accessible windows of the Solver interface. Finally, we click on OK and return to the Solver Parameters window, where we select the Standard GRG Nonlinear algorithm from the pull-down menu.

At this point, the model has been specified well enough to solve, but it is always a good habit to examine the Options window before proceeding. There are some options (check boxes) in this window that we might want to consider, as displayed in Figure 8.4. In this example, the decision variables must be nonnegative, so we check the Assume Non-Negative box. We also check the box for bypassing Solver reports, which we generally do not use. The option to show iteration results might occasionally be used to help in debugging, but it is normally unchecked. Usually, we leave the Automatic Scaling option box unchecked as well, although there are some exceptions, as we discuss later.

Although the optimization of a model such as the Advertising Budget model can be done quickly and smoothly, we don't advocate a rapid click of the Solve button to obtain a solution. Rather, we like to see users pause before running Solver, in order to think about what the outcomes might be. In the case at hand, should we expect the advertising budget to be allocated equally across the quarters? If so, why should this occur? If not, should we expect one of the allocations to be zero? Why or why not? These kinds of questions are informal hypotheses that can be very valuable to an analyst. They provide an opportunity for us to test our intuition with respect to the model. Only two things can happen, and they

FIGURE 8.3
The Add Constraint
Window

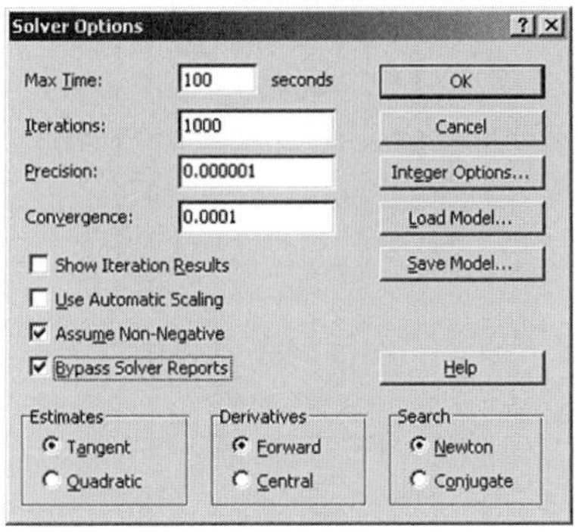

FIGURE 8.4
The Solver Options
Window

are both good. Either our intuition will be confirmed, in which case our confidence in the model will increase; or else our intuition will be contradicted, in which case we can learn something unexpected about the situation that might help us in the future.

In this example, we have already explored the differences among the quarters, so we should expect the allocations to be unequal across quarters, reflecting differences in the seasonal factors. Our limited examination of the relationship between Q1 expenditures and profit (Figure 8.1) suggested that profits were enhanced even by small expenditures, at least in Q1. We might expect the same phenomenon to occur in other quarters, making it desirable to use nonzero advertising expenditures.

By entering the addresses of the target cell and the changing cells and by specifying a constraint, we have prepared the model for optimization. When we click on the Solve button, Solver searches for the optimal expenditures and displays the results in our spreadsheet. The Solver Results window allows us to either keep the optimal solution and write over the original contents, or restore the values that were in the spreadsheet before Solver ran. In this case, we keep the solution and note that the optimal profit is $71,447, as shown in Figure 8.5. As we can see in the figure, the optimal allocation contains different expenditures in each quarter, and in every quarter the expenditure exceeds $5,000. The highest expenditures occur in Q4 and Q2, as we would expect, given their high seasonal factors. Finally, we note that the entire $40,000 advertising budget is used.

BUILDING MODELS FOR SOLVER

As we mentioned earlier, most of our general guidelines about effective spreadsheet design apply to the specific case of building models for use with Solver. In addition, Solver requires specific information about our optimization problem, so we must be able to identify a target cell, a set of changing cells, and the constraints (if any). The process of identifying these elements is called **formulating** an optimization problem.

Formulation

Every optimization model is made up of **decision variables,** an **objective function,** and a set of **constraints.** Before setting up a spreadsheet for optimization, it is a good idea to identify these elements, at least in words if not in symbols.

To guide us toward decision variables, we ask ourselves, "What must be decided?" Decision variables must be under the control of the decision maker. (Other quantitative inputs, not under the decision maker's control, are treated as parameters.) From the start, we should be explicit about the units in which we measure each decision variable. Common examples of decision variables would include quantities to buy, quantities to deploy, quantities to produce, or quantities to deliver (or combinations of the above list). Whatever the

FIGURE 8.5
Optimal Expenditures in
the Advertising Budget
Example

Adbudget8.xls

	A	B	C	D	E	F	G	H
1	Advertising Budget Model							
2	SGP/KRB							
3	1/1/2000							
4								
5	PARAMETERS							
6				Q1	Q2	Q3	Q4	
7		Price	$40.00					
8		Cost	$25.00					
9		Seasonal		0.9	1.1	0.8	1.2	
10		OHD rate	0.15					
11		Sales Parameters						
12			35					
13			3000					
14		Sales Expense		8000	8000	9000	9000	
15		Ad Budget	$40,000					
16								
17	DECISIONS							Total
18		Ad Expenditures		$7,273	$12,346	$5,117	$15,263	$40,000
19								
20	OUTPUTS							
21		Profit	$71,447		Base case	$69,662		
22								
23	CALCULATIONS							
24		Quarter		Q1	Q2	Q3	Q4	Total
25		Seasonal		0.9	1.1	0.8	1.2	
26								
27		Units Sold		3193	4769	2523	5676	16161
28		Revenue		127709	190776	100906	227039	646430
29		Cost of Goods		79818	119235	63066	141899	404019
30		Gross Margin		47891	71541	37840	85140	242411

decision variables are, once we know their numerical values, we should have a resolution of the problem. In Solver models, the changing cells contain the values of decision variables.

To guide us toward an objective function, we ask ourselves, "What measure will we use to compare alternative sets of decision variables?" Imagine that two consultants have come to us with their recommendations on what action to take (i.e., what decision variables to use), and we must choose which action we prefer. For this purpose, we need a yardstick—some measuring function that will tell us which action is better. That function will be an expression involving the decision variables, and it will normally be obvious whether we wish to maximize or minimize. Maximization criteria usually focus on such measures as profit, revenue, return, or efficiency. Minimization criteria usually focus on cost, time, distance, size, or investment. Only one measure can play the role of the objective function. In Solver models, the target cell contains the value of the objective function.

To guide us toward constraints, we ask ourselves, "What restrictions limit our choice of decision variables?" We are typically not free to choose any set of decisions we like; there are some limitations intrinsic to the decision problem that have to be respected. For example, we may look for capacities that provide upper limits on certain activities or commitments that place thresholds on other activities. Sometimes, we may specify equations to assure consistency among a set of variables.

Constraints thus appear in three varieties in optimization models. Each constraint involves a relationship between a "left-hand side" and a "right-hand side." By convention, the right-hand side (RHS) is usually a number (i.e., a parameter), and the left-hand side (LHS) is a function. We refer to the RHS as the constraint constant, the RHS constant, or simply the RHS. The three varieties of constraints are:

LHS <= RHS   (less than, or LT, constraint)
LHS >= RHS   (greater than, or GT, constraint)
LHS = RHS   (equality, or EQ, constraint)

We use LT constraints to represent capacities or ceilings. For example, we might require that labor hours scheduled must be less than or equal to labor hours available. In that case, hours scheduled would make up the LHS, and hours available would be the RHS of an LT constraint. We use GT constraints to represent commitments or thresholds. For example, we might require that components purchased must be at least as large as the minimum quantity in the purchasing contract. In that case, components purchased would make up the LHS, and the contractual minimum would be the RHS of a GT constraint. Finally, we use EQ constraints to represent material-balance constraints or simply to define related variables consistently. For example, we might include a material-balance constraint that end-of-month inventory must equal start-of-month inventory plus production minus demand. In symbols, this relationship translates into the following algebraic expression:

Ending Inventory = Starting Inventory + Production – Demand

In such a case, demand levels usually play the role of given parameters, and the other quantities are usually variables. For that reason, start-of-month inventory plus production minus end-of-month inventory would become the LHS, and demand would be the RHS of an EQ constraint. Algebraically, this means rewriting the above expression as:

Starting Inventory + Production – Ending Inventory = Demand

Layout

We prefer a disciplined approach to building optimization models, and we advocate conformance to a relatively standardized model template. Standardization helps us in several ways. First, it enhances our ability to communicate with others. A standardized structure provides a common language for describing optimization problems and reinforces our understanding about how these models are shaped. This is especially true when spreadsheet models are being shown to someone knowledgeable about optimization. Second, it improves our ability to diagnose errors while we are building the model. A standardized structure has certain recognizable features that make it easier to spot modeling errors or simple typographical errors than in an unstructured approach. Third, it permits us to "scale up" the model more easily. That is, we often want to expand a model by adding variables or constraints, allowing us to move from a prototype to a practical size, or from a "toy" version to an "industrial strength" version.

SOLVER TIP: RANGES IN THE SOLVER WINDOW

We could reference the changing cells one at a time, separated by commas. We prefer, however, to arrange the spreadsheet so that all the decision variables are in adjacent cells, since this allows us to make a single reference to their range. Since most optimization problems have several decision variables, it saves time if we place all of them in adjacent cells. This design also makes the Solver Parameters window easier to interpret if someone else is trying to follow our work, or if we are reviewing it after not having seen it for a long time.

In a similar way, it helps to reference a set of constraints as a range, rather than referencing one constraint at a time. There is one added complication with constraints: the Add Constraint window allows us to specify LT, GT, or EQ. We cannot mix two of those types in the same constraint window. Therefore, the best we can do is to cluster similar constraints together (for example, placing all the LT constraints together)—with their left-hand side values in adjacent cells and their right-hand side values in another set of adjacent cells. This organization allows us to use ranges in the Add Constraint window as well as in the Parameters window.

Here are the main elements of our structured approach:

■ Organize the spreadsheet in modules. We suggest separate portions of the worksheet for decision variables, objective function, and constraints, but sometimes other forms of organization are more appropriate. For data-intensive models, it is also a good idea to devote a separate module to the input data.

■ Place all decision variables in a single row (or column) of the spreadsheet if possible. (It is sometimes advantageous to use a rectangular range for decision variables.) It also helps to use color or border highlighting for the decision variable cells. Later, we discuss circumstances where we might want to choose an alternative layout.

■ Place the objective function in a single cell (also highlighted), using a SUM or a SUMPRODUCT formula if possible.

■ Arrange constraints to facilitate the comparison of left-hand and right-hand sides, and use a SUMPRODUCT formula to express the left-hand side when it's convenient. For the most part, "left" and "right" can be respected in the layout, although other formats occasionally make sense. Sometimes, it is also helpful to calculate the difference between the left and right-hand sides for each constraint, or at least to indicate whether the constraint has been met exactly.

As indicated, there are reasonable exceptions to these guidelines. However, the standard structure is a useful starting point for the several reasons we have enumerated.

Results

Just as there are three modules in our spreadsheet, there are three kinds of information to examine in the optimization results. First, there are the optimal values of the decision variables. They tell us the best course of action. Second, there is the optimal value of the objective function, which tells us the best level of performance we can achieve. Third,

---

SOLVER TIP: SCALING THE MODEL

Rescaling the parameters of a model—so that they appear in thousands (or even millions)—has the virtue that it saves us the work of entering lots of zeros. As a consequence, we may avoid some data-entry errors, and the spreadsheet looks a little less crowded than it would with many large numbers on it. However, there is an important practical reason for scaling as well. The way that the computer carries out its arithmetic sometimes makes scaling desirable. As a guideline, the values of the objective function and the constraints should not differ from each other, or from the values of the decision variables, by more than a factor of 1,000, or at most 10,000. A model that tracks cash flows in the millions while also computing percentage returns as decimal fractions violates this rule.

Sometimes, scaling problems are difficult to avoid when we're trying to keep the model easy to understand. In these cases, we can ask Solver to perform some internal scaling of the model if we check the option box for Use Automatic Scaling. This might also be a good option to check in a linear program, if Solver gives an error message that the linearity conditions are not met or, in a nonlinear model, if Solver reports convergence but not that the optimality conditions are satisfied. As helpful as the Automatic Scaling option is, however, it is always preferable for the model builder to do the scaling.

Finally, if we need to display our model results in units that are more natural for our audience, we can create a separate presentation worksheet. On this sheet, the numbers can be displayed in any desired format without impacting the optimization process.

there are the constraint outcomes. In particular, an LT constraint or a GT constraint in which the left-hand side equals the right-hand side is called a tight, or **binding,** constraint. Prior to solving the model, each constraint is a *potential* limitation on the set of decisions, but optimization generally leads to an outcome where only some of the constraints are *actually* binding. These are the true economic limitations in the model: they are the constraints that actually prevent us from achieving even better levels of performance.

We can think of the solution to an optimization problem as providing what we might call **tactical** information and **strategic** information. By tactical information, we mean that the optimal solution prescribes the best possible set of decisions under the conditions given. Thus, if the model represents an actual situation, its optimal decisions represent a plan to be implemented. By strategic information, we mean that the optimal solution tells us what factors could lead us to even better levels of performance. In particular, the model identifies the binding constraints as the economic factors that restrict the value of the objective function. If we are not faced with the need to implement a course of action immediately, we can think about altering one or more of the constraints in a way that could improve the situation. Thus, if the model represents a situation with given parametric conditions, we can examine the possibility of changing the "givens" in order to raise the level of performance.

MODEL CLASSIFICATION AND SOLVER ALGORITHMS

Optimization models come in only a few basic types or categories. It is important to recognize the category into which a model falls, because the algorithm used to optimize the model must match its type. The fundamental distinction among models arises from linearity.

Every relationship in a model is either **linear** or **nonlinear.** In a linear relationship, each variable is multiplied by a constant, such as the straight line

$$y = ax + b$$

or the plane

$$z = ax + by$$

where x, y, and z represent variables.

Any relationship that is *not* of this form is nonlinear; for example, the power function

$$y = ax^b$$

when $b \neq 1$.

Optimization problems are classified as linear if the objective function and all the constraints are linear functions of the decision variables. If any one of these components is not linear, the problem is classified as a nonlinear optimization problem. We also refer to linear optimization as **linear programming** and to nonlinear optimization as **nonlinear programming.**

It is important to know whether an optimization model is linear, because Solver offers a different solution technique for linear models than for nonlinear models. This technique is more powerful and delivers more insight than its nonlinear counterpart. Although this is largely a technical reason for favoring linear models, there is a practical reason, too. Many real-world relationships are linear, especially the ones that managers and analysts tend to be interested in. Moreover, even those relationships that are not truly linear might well be close to linear, at least as a first cut, or in the region where realistic decisions are likely to lie. Thus, a linear model often represents an appropriate base case for beginning the analysis. We should therefore try to harness the capability of the linear solver whenever possible. To do so, we must adhere to the requirements of linearity in building the model.

As the default choice, the Solver Parameters window always shows the selection of the nonlinear solver (Standard GRG Nonlinear) when we first enter information describing our model. The nonlinear solver can be used for linear problems or for nonlinear problems, although it is not the best algorithm to use for linear problems. The main alternative is the linear solver (Standard Simplex LP), which is specialized for linear cases. We now compare these two procedures.

Hill Climbing: The Nonlinear Solver

The algorithm used by Solver for nonlinear optimization is called the **GRG algorithm** (short for Generalized Reduced Gradient), which is often likened to hill climbing in the fog. Because of the fog, we can't tell where the peak is located relative to our starting point, so we can use only the conditions close around us to choose a direction. One practical approach, or heuristic, would be to follow the steepest path we can see. After we proceed a few steps in that direction, we look again for the steepest path available from our new location, and we proceed in that direction. Again, after a few steps, we reach the limit of what we were able to see in the fog, and we reassess which direction seems to be the steepest, modifying our path as we go. Eventually, we will come to a point from which no path leads up. As far as we can tell, this must be the top, so we will stop.

The GRG algorithm uses a very similar procedure to locate a maximum for a complicated function. It starts at the point represented by the values of the decision variables in the changing cells, tests different directions in which it could modify those variables, and selects the direction that goes up most steeply; that is, in which the objective function increases the most. After taking a step in that direction, the procedure tests different directions from its new location and again selects the steepest path. Eventually, the procedure comes to a point where no step in any direction goes up. At that point, the procedure stops. (In a minimization problem, we could think of the procedure as descending into a crater, looking for the lowest point.)

The GRG algorithm has some additional intelligence built into its procedure. For example, it is capable of adjusting the size of its steps—first taking large steps while steep paths are available, but then taking smaller steps as the path levels out. The algorithm can also cope with constraints. However, hill climbing in the fog has one serious limitation. When we stop the search, fog obscures our long range view, so we can't see whether another location some distance away is higher than where we stopped. In other words, the fog may prevent us from seeing a higher peak than the one we found. In an analogous fashion, the GRG algorithm may stop at a solution that we call a **local optimum.** This point is better than any other point close by, but there could well be an even better solution some distance away, unseen by the search procedure. Although we wish to find the highest peak, or **global optimum,** the GRG procedure will not guarantee that we always find it with one run, except in special circumstances.

A graphical interpretation should underscore this point. Figure 8.6 shows a graph of a hypothetical objective function, where the single decision variable is plotted along the horizontal axis. The maximum value of the function lies at point D. However, if we begin our hill-climbing procedure at points A, E, or G, we will stop at points B or F, which are local optima. On the other hand, if we start at point C, our hill-climbing procedure will take us to the global optimum at point D, as desired.

As our graph shows, the final solution produced by the GRG algorithm may depend on where it started. This would be true in problems where there are several local optima distinct from the global optimum. In such cases, there can never be a guarantee that a single run of Solver has found the optimal solution, so it makes sense to rerun Solver several

FIGURE 8.6
Graph of a Hypothetical
Function for which the
Maximum Is Sought

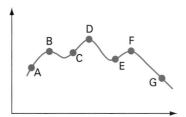

times, trying a different starting point each time. The **starting point** is the set of values of the decision variables in the spreadsheet when Solver begins its search. If Solver finds the same solution from many different starting points, that should increase our confidence that we have found the global optimum. On the other hand, there is no recipe for how many starting points to try or where they should be located. As the graph suggests, the set of starting points that lead to the global optimum can be a small one.

In many practical cases, the objective function has only one local optimum, which is also a global optimum. A figure corresponding to Figure 8.6 for this type of function would exhibit only one peak. Such functions are sometimes referred to as shaped like an "inverted bowl." (In minimization problems, the analogy would be a "bowl-shaped" function.) For these kinds of functions, the GRG algorithm in Solver is perfectly **reliable** when the model contains either no constraints or a set of linear constraints, which we discuss below. We use the term "reliable" to mean that the algorithm finds the global optimum.

The Linear Solver

The term "linear" in linear programs refers to a feature of the objective function and the constraints. A linear function exhibits three properties:

- additivity
- proportionality
- divisibility

By **additive,** we mean that the contribution from one decision gets added to (or sometimes subtracted from) the contributions of other decisions. In an additive function, we can separate the contributions that come from each decision. By **proportional,** we mean that the contribution from any given decision grows in proportion to the value of the corresponding decision variable. When a decision variable doubles, then its contribution to the objective also doubles. By **divisible,** we mean that a fractional decision variable is meaningful.

As an example, suppose that we compute profit from the function

Profit = (*Unit Revenue*) × (*Quantity Sold*) – (*Unit Cost*) × (*Quantity Purchased*)

where *Unit Revenue* and *Unit Cost* are parameters known to be 100 and 60, while *Quantity Sold* and *Quantity Purchased* are decisions, which we'll denote by x and y, respectively. In symbols, we can simply write:

$$Profit = 100x - 60y$$

where x and y are decision variables. Note that Profit separates into two additive terms, which we can call total revenue and total cost. The total revenue term ($100x$) is proportional to the decision variable Quantity Sold. Likewise, the total cost term ($60y$) is proportional to the decision variable Quantity Purchased. Fractional values for the decisions could well make sense. Suppose, for example, that the product is fuel and that the unit of measurement is gallons. Then certainly a fractional value such as $x = 72.4$ is plausible. Even if we think of discrete items, such as televisions, the unit of measurement could be dozens, in which case a fractional value such as $x = 15.5$ would be meaningful. In summary, our Profit function exhibits all three of the properties of a linear function.

We turn now to an algebraic perspective. When we have several decision variables, we may give them letter names, such as x, y, and z; or we may number them and denote them by x_1, x_2, x_3, and so on. When there are n decision variables, we can write a linear objective function as follows:

$$z = c_1 x_1 + c_2 x_2 + \ldots + c_n x_n$$

where z represents the value of the objective function, and the c's are a set of given parameters called **objective function coefficients.** Note that the x's appear in separate terms (i.e., they are additive), they appear with exponents of 1 (i.e., their contributions to the objective function are proportional), and they are not restricted to integers (i.e., they are divisible). In a spreadsheet, we recognize the structure of z as a calculation that could be made by the SUMPRODUCT function (i.e., SUMPRODUCT($\{c_1, c_2, \ldots c_n\}, \{x_1, x_2, \ldots x_n\}$). Thus, for spreadsheet purposes, we can recognize a linear function if it consists of a sum of pairwise products—where one of the pairs in each product is a parameter, and the other is a decision variable.

Suppose, for example, that we had three items with unit prices of 2, 3, and 4, with sales volumes of u, v, and w, respectively. Then total revenue would come to $2u + 3v + 4w$, which could be computed from the formula SUMPRODUCT $(\{2,3,4\}, \{u,v,w\})$. When the volumes are $u = 30$, $v = 33$, and $w = 36$, the total revenue function takes on the value 303.

For a constraint to be linear, its left-hand side must be a linear function. In other words, the left-hand side can be represented by a SUMPRODUCT function made up of a sum of pairwise products, where one element of each product is a parameter, and the other is a decision variable. In most cases, we will actually use the SUMPRODUCT formula, although, in some special cases, we can get by with the SUM formula.

The solution procedure for linear models is referred to as the **simplex algorithm,** or the linear solver. The simplex algorithm employs a strategy that shares some of the features of hill climbing, but it is able to exploit some special properties of linearity to find an optimal solution efficiently. For instance, if we can imagine a diamond that represents the set of feasible decision variables, then the simplex algorithm can be viewed as a procedure for moving along the edges of the diamond's surface until an optimal point is encountered. The simplex algorithm does not require a starting point in the spreadsheet; or, to put it another way, it determines its own starting solution. That means that Solver ignores the information in the changing cells when solving a linear model. Once the solution procedure finds a **feasible solution,** it proceeds from there to an optimal solution. A feasible solution is one that satisfies all the constraints, but may not be optimal. An optimal solution must satisfy all constraints and is therefore feasible. Moreover, the simplex method *guarantees* that it will find a global optimum (if there is one), and in that sense the simplex method is completely reliable. We cannot say the same for the GRG algorithm, except under special conditions.

In mathematical terms, linear models are a special case of nonlinear models, and, in principle, the GRG algorithm could be used as a solution procedure. However, the simplex algorithm is especially suited to linear models, and it avoids some numerical problems that sometimes affect the performance of the GRG algorithm. The simplex algorithm is the preferred choice for any linear programming problem.

Integer Optimization

The divisibility property of linear models means that a solution may contain fractional values for decision variables. Such an outcome may also occur in the solution of nonlinear models. Fractional decision variables are appropriate in many, perhaps most, applications. When they are not, we must restrict Solver to integer solutions.

Solver offers the possibility of designating some of the decision variables as integer valued. Adding an integer requirement to a model that is otherwise a nonlinear programming problem or a linear programming problem will give rise to an **integer nonlinear programming problem,** or to an **integer linear programming problem.** In the case of integer linear programs, Solver employs an algorithm that checks all possible assignments of integer values to variables, although some of the assignments may not have to be examined explicitly. This procedure may require the solution of a large number of linear programs, but since Solver can do this very reliably with the simplex algorithm, it will eventually locate a global optimum. In the case of integer nonlinear programs, however, certain problems can arise, although Solver will always attempt to find a solution. Since it builds on the GRG algorithm, which cannot distinguish local optima from global optima, Solver is somewhat handicapped in its solution procedure for these problems. In practice, Solver is seldom used to find solutions to integer nonlinear programs.

NONLINEAR PROGRAMMING

Because nonlinear functions include a wide variety of possible relationships, there are many different kinds of problems that lend themselves to solution by nonlinear programming. The Advertising Budget example was such a problem, where the nonlinearity arose in the function relating sales and advertising. Thus, we found ourselves confronting a nonlinear objective function and (in the case of the advertising budget) a linear constraint. In this section, we illustrate the formulation and solution of nonlinear programs related to some other common problem structures. Each involves the maximization or minimization of a nonlinear objective function.

Revenue Maximization

A common business problem involves maximizing revenue in the presence of a demand curve. A demand curve is simply a function that relates demand volume to price. But because revenue is the product of price and volume, and volume is itself a function of price, revenue will generally be a nonlinear function of price. We illustrate with the Coastal Telephone Company example.

EXAMPLE

Coastal Telephone Company

Coastal Telephone Company (CTC) is a regional supplier of long-distance telephone services. CTC is trying to determine the optimal pricing structure for its daytime and evening long-distance calling rates. The daytime price applies from 8:00 A.M. to 6:00 P.M., and the evening price applies the rest of the time. With the help of a consultant, the company has estimated the average demand for phone lines (per minute) as follows:

$$Daytime\ Lines\ Demanded = 600 - 5{,}000 \times Day\ Price + 300 \times Evening\ Price$$
$$Evening\ Lines\ Demanded = 400 + 600 \times Day\ Price - 2{,}500 \times Evening\ Price$$

CTC wants to find prices that will maximize its revenue.

To determine the decision variables in this problem, we ask, "What must be decided?" Here, the answer is obviously the pair of prices, which we write as DP for the daytime price and EP for the evening price. To determine the objective function, we ask, "What measure will we use?" As stated, CTC is interested in maximizing its total revenue. Total revenue consists of a daytime component and an evening component. The daytime component per minute is $DD \times DP$, where DD represents daytime demand. Similarly, the evening component per minute is $ED \times EP$, where ED represents evening demand. Noting that there are 600 minutes in the daytime period and 840 minutes in the evening period, we can write our objective function as shown below, together with the demand curve constraints:

$$\text{Maximize } Revenue = 600DD \times DP + 840ED \times EP$$

subject to

$$DD = 600 - 5{,}000DP + 300EP$$
$$ED = 400 + 600DP - 2{,}500EP$$

Note that since DD is a function of both DP and EP, the objective function is nonlinear because it involves products of decision variables (i.e., $DP \times DP$ and $DP \times EP$). Moreover, DD is not, strictly speaking, a decision variable. Rather, we view it as a derived variable, or an intermediate variable, in the sense that its value is determined once we know the values of the decision variables.

In the spreadsheet shown in Figure 8.7, we devote column B to daytime variables and column C to evening variables. First, we place the daytime and evening prices in row 4. Since we do not know the optimal prices when we are building the spreadsheet, we can place initial guesses (such as 0.10) in these cells. The demand parameters appear in the next module, with demands calculated in row 10, and from these values, the revenues are calculated in row 13. These last two figures are summed to obtain total revenue in cell B14. We invoke Solver and specify:

Target cell: B14 (maximize)
Changing cells: B4:C4

No constraints need to be specified, since the demand curves are embedded in the revenue calculation.

FIGURE 8.7
Spreadsheet Model for
Coastal Telephone
Company

NLP.xls

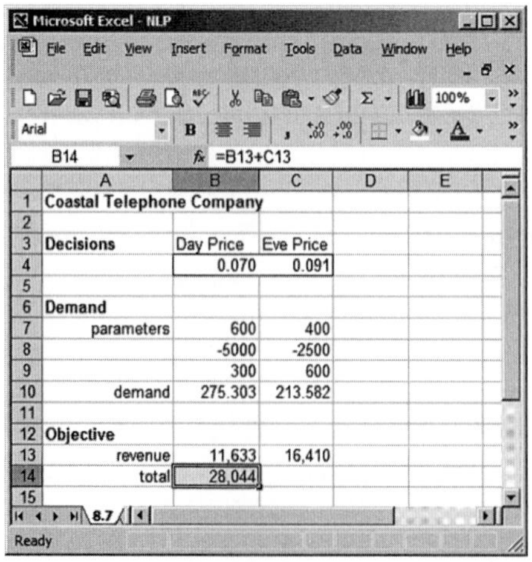

	A	B	C	D	E
1	Coastal Telephone Company				
2					
3	Decisions	Day Price	Eve Price		
4		0.070	0.091		
5					
6	Demand				
7	parameters	600	400		
8		-5000	-2500		
9		300	600		
10	demand	275.303	213.582		
11					
12	Objective				
13	revenue	11,633	16,410		
14	total	28,044			
15					

When we click on the Solve button, Solver searches for an optimal solution. The optimal prices turn out to be roughly $DP = 0.070$ and $EP = 0.091$, with maximum revenue of $28,044 per day. (When the objective is a quadratic function, as it is here, and there are no constraints, the GRG algorithm reliably finds the global optimum. This could be confirmed by running Solver from a variety of initial starting values for the decision variables.)

Curve Fitting

As a second example of optimization without constraints, we describe a general approach to regression, or, more accurately, the process of fitting a function to observed data points. In particular, we return to an example we first encountered in Chapter 7, where we want to predict pharmacy revenue as a function of the number of hours the store is open in a week. The given data consist of ten observations of store hours and revenue. These are shown in cells B5:C14 in the spreadsheet of Figure 8.8.

The scatter plot in Figure 8.8 suggests a nonlinear relationship, so we will work with a simple nonlinear function. Recalling our list of functions in Chapter 3, we first hypothesize that the relationship takes the form of the power curve

$$Revenue = a \times (Hours)^b$$

As we know from our coverage of regression in Chapter 7, the decision variables are the parameters a and b, and the objective function is the sum of squared differences between the model and the data. In the spreadsheet of Figure 8.9, we reserve cells D1 and D2 for the parameters a and b, respectively, and we enter the formula for Revenue into cells D5:D14. As tentative values, we set $a = 1,000$ and $b = 0.5$, though we know those arbitrary choices can certainly be improved. We now have the observed values and the model values for Revenue next to each other in columns C and D. In column E, we calculate the difference between model and observation and, in column F, the square of each difference. The sum of these squared differences appears in cell F2 and represents the objective function. We invoke Solver and specify:

Target cell: F2 (minimize)
Changing cells: D1:D2

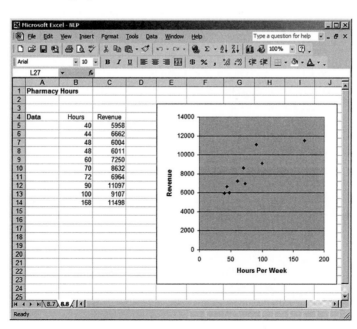

FIGURE 8.9
Optimal Curve Fitting for
the Pharmacy Revenue
Example

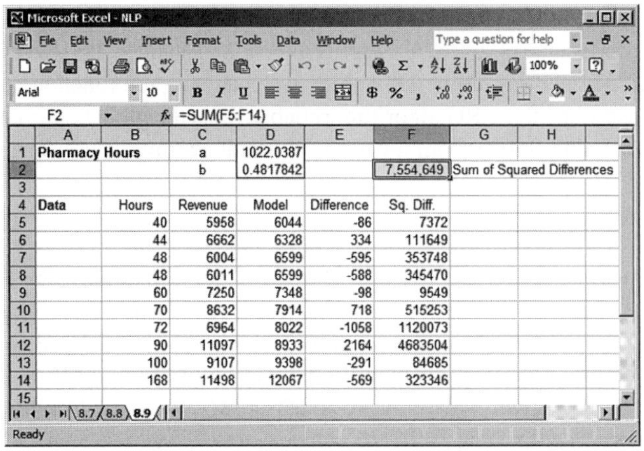

NLP.xls

	A	B	C	D	E	F	G	H
1	Pharmacy Hours		a	1022.0387				
2			b	0.4817842		7,554,649	Sum of Squared Differences	
3								
4	Data	Hours	Revenue	Model	Difference	Sq. Diff.		
5		40	5958	6044	-86	7372		
6		44	6662	6328	334	111649		
7		48	6004	6599	-595	353748		
8		48	6011	6599	-588	345470		
9		60	7250	7348	-98	9549		
10		70	8632	7914	718	515253		
11		72	6964	8022	-1058	1120073		
12		90	11097	8933	2164	4683504		
13		100	9107	9398	-291	84685		
14		168	11498	12067	-569	323346		
15								

F2 = =SUM(F5:F14)

No constraints are necessary, and we need not even require nonnegativity of the decision variables. When we click on the Solve button, Solver searches for the optimal values
of the model parameters. In this case, the values turn out to be $a = 1,022$ and $b = 0.482$,
with a minimum sum of squares approximately equal to 7.55 million, as shown in Figure
8.9. (When the objective is in the form of a sum of squared differences, the objective function is a quadratic, and the GRG algorithm reliably finds the global optimum. This could
be confirmed by running Solver from a variety of initial starting values for the decision
variables.) As we pointed out in Chapter 7, standard regression software will not be able
to achieve a sum of squares as small as this value.

The model that we have built is quite flexible because of its modular structure. For
example, we could easily modify the spreadsheet to fit an alternative model of the form

$$Revenue = a + b \times LOG(Hours)$$

This modification requires that we enter the model function into cell D5 and then
copy it throughout the column below. Thus, column D is a module corresponding to the
form of the model we wish to fit. (In Chapter 7, we summarized the results of using a variation of the logarithmic model.)

A second module corresponds to the measure of fit. Although minimizing the sum of
squared differences would be the typical objective function for regression analysis, other
measures of fit are sometimes desirable. For example, we could minimize the sum of
absolute differences. For this criterion, we calculate the absolute difference between
model and observation in column F, as shown in Figure 8.10. The sum in cell F2 does not
have to change. When we run Solver, we do not have to modify the information in the
Solver Parameters window, because the modifications have all been made on the spreadsheet. The target cell and changing cells remain the same. Thus, column F is a module corresponding to the *criterion* for the model we wish to fit. Together, the modules for form
and criterion give us a flexible tool for fitting a model to data, a tool that provides flexibility unavailable in the standard regression package.

SOLVER TIP: TARGET CELL OPTIONS IN SOLVER

Solver provides us with the opportunity to maximize a target cell, or to minimize a target cell,
simply by choosing a button in the Solver Parameters window. A third option allows us to
specify a target value and find for our variables a set of values that achieves the target value.
This target capability is similar to that of the Goal Seek tool, except that Solver can handle
many variables at once. However, it is the maximization and minimization modes for which
Solver is primarily used.

FIGURE 8.10
Optimal Curve Fitting for
the Absolute Value
Criterion

NLP.xls

	A	B	C	D	E	F	G	H	I
1	Pharmacy Hours		a	1107.908					
2			b	0.456619		5719	Sum of Absolute Differences		
3									
4	Data	Hours	Revenue	Model	Difference	Abs. Diff.			
5		40	5958	5971	-13	13			
6		44	6662	6236	426	426			
7		48	6004	6489	-485	485			
8		48	6011	6489	-478	478			
9		60	7250	7185	65	65			
10		70	8632	7709	923	923			
11		72	6964	7809	-845	845			
12		90	11097	8647	2450	2450			
13		100	9107	9073	34	34			
14		168	11498	11498	0	0			
15									

F2 ▼ f_x =SUM(F5:F14)

Starting with the *a* and *b* values of Figure 8.10, Solver produces a solution with an objective function of 5,719. However, in the Solver Results window, we read the message, "Solver has converged to the current solution. All constraints are satisfied." This message indicates that Solver may not have reached even a local optimum. In fact, Solver's stopping criterion is related to the Convergence parameter on the Options menu, for which the default is usually 0.0001. This means that Solver will stop when the last few solutions in its hill-climbing procedure have been unable to improve the objective function by more than 0.01 percent. In response to this stopping message, we should simply rerun Solver, starting from the latest solution. In this instance, Solver achieves an improved value of the objective function of 5,717, and the message in the Solver Results window now reads, "Solver found a solution. All constraints and optimality conditions are satisfied." This is the message we're looking for, as it indicates that a local optimum has been found.

Unlike the minimization of the sum of squares, this nonlinear program has several local optima. If we had started the search at a different pair of values for *a* and *b*, Solver could have produced a different solution. The table below summarizes some alternative results:

Starting Values		Final Values		
a	*b*	*a*	*b*	Objective
1,022	0.482	1,108	0.457	5,717
500	0.500	1,142	0.451	5,712
500	0.000	1,136	0.452	5,713
1,000	1.000	1,003	0.479	5,911
1,000	0.000	1,129	0.453	5,714
2,000	2.000	1,663	0.369	7,323

This example illustrates one of the potential problems with the nonlinear solver: its solution may depend on the starting point. As a result, we normally want to try out a variety of starting points, to give us the best chance to find the global optimum.

Economic Order Quantities

A basic inventory problem requires the trade-off of ordering costs and carrying costs. We are given a product's annual demand, D, and we need to determine the order quantity, Q. By placing orders so that replenishment occurs just as stock is depleted, we assure that the

SOLVER TIP: SOLUTIONS FROM THE GRG ALGORITHM

When the GRG algorithm concludes with the message, "Solver has converged to the current solution. All constraints are satisfied," the algorithm should be rerun from the point at which it finished. This message may reappear, in which case Solver should be rerun once more. Eventually, the algorithm should conclude with the message, "Solver found a solution. All constraints and optimality conditions are satisfied," which signifies that it has found a local optimum. (If the first message persists, it may be helpful either to check the box for Automatic Scaling or to increase the Convergence parameter by a factor of 10, for example, from 0.0001 to 0.001.) To help determine whether the local optimum is also a global optimum, Solver should be restarted at a different set of decision variables and rerun. If several widely differing starting solutions lead to the same local optimum, that is some evidence that the local optimum is likely to be a global optimum, but there is no way in general to know for sure.

Although there are conditions under which we can guarantee that the GRG algorithm is reliable—that is, it finds a global optimum—the theoretical details are beyond the scope of our treatment. It is always a good idea to try starting with different sets of decision variables, to see whether Solver will always converge to the same local optimum. If we encounter two different local optima in this process, we know that we had better test a variety of starting points if we hope to find the global optimum.

inventory level fluctuates between a low of zero and a high of Q. The average inventory is therefore $Q/2$. Meanwhile, the number of orders placed per year is D/Q. The total annual costs are the sum of ordering costs and carrying costs, or:

(Cost per order) $\times$ (Orders per year) + (Carrying charge) $\times$ (Average inventory)

Suppose that a fixed ordering cost of K is incurred with each order, independent of the order size. Suppose also that items held in inventory incur an annual carrying cost of h. This cost is often expressed as a percentage of the product's unit cost, in the form $h = ic$, where i denotes the carrying cost percentage, and c denotes an item's cost. Then, the total annual cost (TAC) is the sum of these two components:

$$TAC = KD/Q + hQ/2 \qquad (1)$$

The next example illustrates the determination of an optimal ordering policy.

EXAMPLE

Woodstock Appliance Company

The Woodstock Appliance Company carries four products. The spreadsheet in Figure 8.11 shows the annual demands for each of these products, along with the purchase cost, order cost, and holding cost. It also shows how much space each product occupies. Woodstock stores inventory in its warehouse, which contains 12,000 square feet that can be devoted to the four products. The problem is then to find the lowest annual total cost consistent with respecting the limit on storage space.

What must be decided? We want to determine the four order quantities, and these serve as decision variables in our model. How do we measure performance? We evaluate a set of order quantities by calculating the total annual cost across all four products. For product j, the total annual cost is given by a function TAC_j, which follows (1). The sum of the four functions TAC_j serves as the objective function. What constraints apply? The only important constraint is the ceiling on storage space. In words, we require that the storage space consumed must be less than or equal to the space available. (Note that each product consumes a certain amount of space, as given in row 10 in the spreadsheet.) In addition,

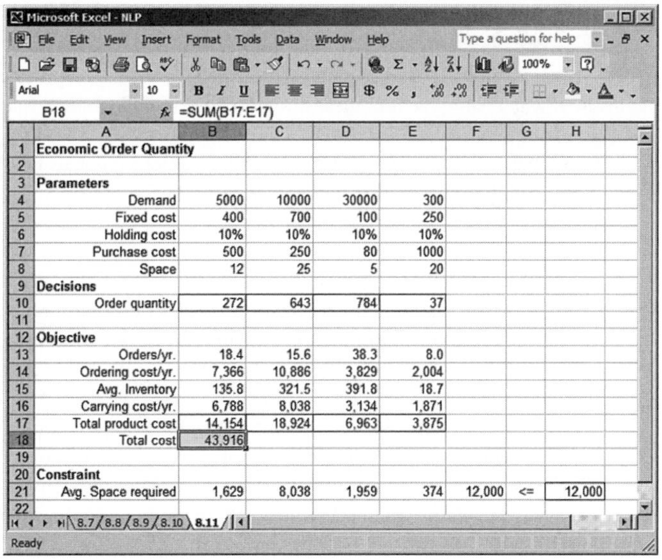

FIGURE 8.11
Spreadsheet Model for
the Woodstock Appliance
Company

NLP.xls

	A	B	C	D	E	F	G	H
1	Economic Order Quantity							
2								
3	Parameters							
4	Demand	5000	10000	30000	300			
5	Fixed cost	400	700	100	250			
6	Holding cost	10%	10%	10%	10%			
7	Purchase cost	500	250	80	1000			
8	Space	12	25	5	20			
9	Decisions							
10	Order quantity	272	643	784	37			
11								
12	Objective							
13	Orders/yr.	18.4	15.6	38.3	8.0			
14	Ordering cost/yr.	7,366	10,886	3,829	2,004			
15	Avg. Inventory	135.8	321.5	391.8	18.7			
16	Carrying cost/yr.	6,788	8,038	3,134	1,871			
17	Total product cost	14,154	18,924	6,963	3,875			
18	Total cost	43,916						
19								
20	Constraint							
21	Avg. Space required	1,629	8,038	1,959	374	12,000	<=	12,000
22								

we might want to add the constraints $Q_j >= 1$, just to be explicit that order quantities of less than 1 are not feasible. An algebraic formulation of our problem becomes:

$$\text{Minimize } TAC = TAC_1 + TAC_2 + TAC_3 + TAC_4$$
$$\text{Subject to: } 12Q_1 + 25Q_2 + 5Q_3 + 20Q_4 <= 12,000$$
$$Q_1 >= 1$$
$$Q_2 >= 1$$
$$Q_3 >= 1$$
$$Q_4 >= 1$$

In Figure 8.11, the individual product costs are calculated in cells B17:E17. Cell B18 then sums the four individual product costs in order to determine the cost for the product line. The space required for each product is calculated in cells B21:E21, and the total space used is calculated in cell F21.

We invoke Solver and specify:

Target cell: B18 (minimize)
Changing cells: B10:E10
Constraints: F21 <= H21
B10:D10 >= 1

When we click on the Solve button, we obtain a solution with a minimum annual cost of $43,916. Once again, we test this solution by choosing different initial values of the decision variables as starting points. The results indicate that the solution is likely to be a global optimum.

Sensitivity Analysis for Nonlinear Programs

Sensitivity analysis involves relating our conclusions to our initial assumptions. In a typical spreadsheet model, we might ask what-if questions regarding the choice of decision variables, looking for effects on the performance measure. Eventually, instead of asking how a particular change in the decision variables would affect the performance measure, we might search for those values of the decision variables that will have the *best possible*

SOLVER TIP: AVOID DISCONTINUOUS FUNCTIONS

There are a number of functions that experienced Excel programmers use that should be avoided when using the nonlinear Solver. These include logical functions (such as IF or AND), mathematical functions (such as ROUND or CEILING), lookup and reference functions (such as CHOOSE or VLOOKUP), and statistical functions (such as RANK or COUNT). In general, any function that *changes discontinuously* is to be avoided. For example, the IF function

$$IF(X <= 0,0,1)$$

jumps abruptly from 0 to 1 when the variable X reaches 0.

The problem these functions create for the hill-climbing algorithm in Solver is that they can turn a smooth hill into one with abrupt cliffs. Since the hill-climbing procedure cannot "see" beyond its immediate surroundings, when it comes to a cliff, it simply stops. Thus, the Solver may stop at suboptimal solutions when used on models that include these functions.

Premium Solver for Education contains a third optimization algorithm, the Evolutionary Solver, which is suited to nonlinear optimization problems that have discontinuities, such as would be the case if the model were to use such functions as IF, VLOOKUP, or ROUND. However, the principles behind this algorithm are beyond the scope of our coverage.

effect on performance. As we saw in Chapter 6, the use of the Data Sensitivity tool allows us to conduct such a search, but only for one or two decision variables at a time. An optimization procedure performs this kind of search in a sophisticated manner and can handle large numbers of decision variables and constraints. Thus, we can think of optimization as an ambitious form of what-if analysis with respect to decision variables.

Now consider another kind of sensitivity analysis—this time with respect to parameters rather than decision variables. In a simple spreadsheet model, we might change a parameter and, with the decision variables held fixed, record the effect on the objective function. Again, the Data Sensitivity tool automates this kind of analysis for one or two parameters at a time. For example, in the Advertising Budget problem, we might fix advertising at $10,000 each quarter and ask how changes in the price affect profit. But how can we determine the effect of varying a parameter on the *optimal* value of the objective function? In the Advertising Budget example, we might find ourselves in the situation where we do not know next year's price at the present time, but we will know it before we have to implement our advertising plan. In this case, we would like to vary the price and determine the optimal advertising plan and optimal profit for each possible price. For this purpose, we would need to run Solver for each value of the price that we wish to study. Fortunately, there is an analogous tool to Data Sensitivity, called **Solver Sensitivity,** which automates this procedure. It is also a module in the Sensitivity Toolkit add-in. Before using Solver Sensitivity, we must run Solver on the active worksheet. Then, after optimizing the base-case model, we can select Solver Sensitivity from the Sensitivity Toolkit menu.

We illustrate the use of Solver Sensitivity by revisiting the Advertising Budget example of Figure 8.5. In our first sensitivity analysis, we vary the unit price, which is $40.00 in the base case. The first step is to optimize the base-case model. Then, when we select Sensitivity Toolkit→Solver Sensitivity, the first panel in Figure 8.12 appears. Solver Sensitivity automatically identifies the objective function in cell C21. For Other Cell(s), we specify the decision variables (in this case, the range D18:G18), although, in general, we could track any set of cells on the worksheet. Finally, we select One-Way Table and click on Next. On the next input screen (see Figure 8.12), we select C7, which contains the price, as Cell to Vary. Using the Begin–End–Increment mode of data entry, we enter a First Value (or minimum) of 30.00, a Last Value (or maximum) of 40.00, and an Increment of 0.50. (Dollar signs should be omitted.) The second panel of Figure 8.12 shows the Solver Sensitivity input windows after this information has been entered, just before clicking Finish.

The Solver Sensitivity add-in now runs Solver 21 times, once for each value of price between $30.00 and $40.00. It then produces a new worksheet, containing the information shown after some reformatting in Figure 8.13. Column A contains the values we specified for Price: $30.00 to $40.00 in steps of $0.50. In column B, we find the corresponding optimal profit values, each produced by a Solver run. In column C, Solver Sensitivity calculates the rate of change in the optimal values, from one price to the next. Finally, the last four columns (D–G) show the values of the "Other Cells" we designated, with column headings showing the cell addresses for each of those outputs.

In the table, we can see in one place how the optimal solution (that is, the objective function value and the optimal values of the decision variables) varies with the unit price. At relatively low prices (at or below $32.00), the margins are so small that it is best not to spend anything on advertising. As the unit price increases, it first becomes desirable to spend advertising money in Q4; then in Q2 as well; then in Q1 as well; and, at $34.50, it becomes desirable to spend advertising money in all four quarters. When the price rises to $37.00, the advertising budget is completely spent, and the allocation of the $40,000 budget remains the same as price rises even further. Thus, we can see that the base-case result (that the budget should be completely spent) is dependent, in part, on the fact that the unit price is sufficiently high. This is not an insight we could obtain without doing this kind of sensitivity analysis.

A sensitivity analysis can also show the effects on the optimal solution of altering the budget. This is a common type of sensitivity analysis, in which we explore the consequences of altering a constraint that was binding in the base case. Figure 8.14, created with Solver Sensitivity, shows how optimal profit changes when the budget is increased from $30,000 to $100,000 in steps of $5,000. These inputs are shown in column A, with the corresponding optimal profit given in column B. In column C, we see a calculation of the rate at which profit changes, per unit change in the budget. For example, the first nonblank entry indicates that, between $30,000 and $35,000, each additional $1.00 of advertising budget adds 51.2 cents to profit.

A graphical perspective on these results is shown in Figure 8.15. The top chart plots the optimal profit as a function of the budget. In this graph, we can see that optimal profits expand as the budget increases. However, there are **diminishing marginal returns,** reflecting the fact that the profit function gets flatter as the budget increases. Eventually,

FIGURE 8.12
The Solver Sensitivity
Windows

FIGURE 8.13
Sensitivity of the
Advertising Budget
Solution to the Price

Adbudget8.xls

	A	B	C	D	E	F	G
1	Price	Objective	Change	$D$18	$E$18	$F$18	$G$18
2	$30.00	-$30,166		$0	$0	$0	$0
3	$30.50	-$26,907	$6,517.89	$0	$0	$0	$0
4	$31.00	-$23,648	$6,517.89	$0	$0	$0	$0
5	$31.50	-$20,389	$6,517.89	$0	$0	$0	$0
6	$32.00	-$17,130	$6,517.89	$0	$0	$0	$0
7	$32.50	-$13,871	$6,518.16	$0	$0	$0	$39
8	$33.00	-$10,511	$6,720.85	$0	$447	$0	$1,101
9	$33.50	-$6,875	$7,271.23	$0	$1,475	$0	$2,325
10	$34.00	-$2,902	$7,946.11	$773	$2,636	$0	$3,708
11	$34.50	$1,487	$8,778.44	$1,640	$3,932	$666	$5,249
12	$35.00	$6,330	$9,685.58	$2,597	$5,361	$1,422	$6,950
13	$35.50	$11,626	$10,592.76	$3,643	$6,924	$2,249	$8,810
14	$36.00	$17,376	$11,499.96	$4,779	$8,621	$3,147	$10,830
15	$36.50	$23,580	$12,407.14	$6,005	$10,452	$4,115	$13,009
16	$37.00	$30,237	$13,313.80	$7,273	$12,346	$5,117	$15,263
17	$37.50	$37,105	$13,736.64	$7,273	$12,346	$5,117	$15,263
18	$38.00	$43,974	$13,736.64	$7,273	$12,346	$5,117	$15,263
19	$38.50	$50,842	$13,736.64	$7,273	$12,346	$5,117	$15,263
20	$39.00	$57,710	$13,736.65	$7,273	$12,346	$5,117	$15,263
21	$39.50	$64,578	$13,736.65	$7,273	$12,346	$5,117	$15,263
22	$40.00	$71,447	$13,736.65	$7,273	$12,346	$5,117	$15,263
23							

profit actually levels out, because the advertising budget is more than we can effectively use. The bottom chart plots the rate of change in profit as a function of the budget. Here, we observe diminishing returns in the form of a declining rate of change. The rate of change in profit reaches zero when the budget exceeds a useful level, around $90,000.

We have added four columns in Figure 8.14 (columns H:K) that translate the quarterly expenditures into percentages of the overall budget. As we can see, the percentage split changes very slightly over this range. For a budget of $30,000, the optimal expenditure in Q4 is about 39 percent of the year's budget, and for a budget of $90,000, this figure drops to about 36 percent.

Perhaps the most important feature of these results is a qualitative one. *When we relax a binding constraint, the objective function cannot get worse.* In fact, it usually gets better, as illustrated in Figure 8.14. This is an intuitive but important result, and we will encounter it in both linear and nonlinear optimization models.

FIGURE 8.14
Sensitivity of the
Advertising Budget
Solution to Budget Size

Adbudget8.xls

	A	B	C	D	E	F	G	H	I	J	K
1	Budget	Objective	Change	$D$18	$E$18	$F$18	$G$18	Q1	Q2	Q3	Q4
2	$30,000	$66,715.5		$5,298	$9,395	$3,556	$11,751	17.7%	31.3%	11.9%	39.2%
3	$35,000	$69,277.5	0.512	$6,285	$10,871	$4,337	$13,507	18.0%	31.1%	12.4%	38.6%
4	$40,000	$71,446.8	0.434	$7,273	$12,346	$5,117	$15,263	18.2%	30.9%	12.8%	38.2%
5	$45,000	$73,279.0	0.366	$8,261	$13,822	$5,898	$17,020	18.4%	30.7%	13.1%	37.8%
6	$50,000	$74,817.5	0.308	$9,249	$15,298	$6,678	$18,776	18.5%	30.6%	13.4%	37.6%
7	$55,000	$76,097.3	0.256	$10,237	$16,773	$7,459	$20,532	18.6%	30.5%	13.6%	37.3%
8	$60,000	$77,146.8	0.210	$11,224	$18,249	$8,239	$22,288	18.7%	30.4%	13.7%	37.1%
9	$65,000	$77,989.6	0.169	$12,212	$19,724	$9,020	$24,044	18.8%	30.3%	13.9%	37.0%
10	$70,000	$78,645.7	0.131	$13,200	$21,200	$9,800	$25,800	18.9%	30.3%	14.0%	36.9%
11	$75,000	$79,131.8	0.097	$14,188	$22,676	$10,580	$27,556	18.9%	30.2%	14.1%	36.7%
12	$80,000	$79,462.3	0.066	$15,176	$24,151	$11,361	$29,312	19.0%	30.2%	14.2%	36.6%
13	$85,000	$79,649.9	0.038	$16,163	$25,627	$12,141	$31,068	19.0%	30.1%	14.3%	36.6%
14	$90,000	$79,705.6	0.011	$17,093	$27,016	$12,876	$32,721	19.0%	30.0%	14.3%	36.4%
15	$95,000	$79,705.6	0.000	$17,093	$27,016	$12,876	$32,721	18.0%	28.4%	13.6%	34.4%
16	$100,000	$79,705.6	0.000	$17,093	$27,016	$12,876	$32,721	17.1%	27.0%	12.9%	32.7%
17											

FIGURE 8.15
Graphical Display of the
Sensitivity Analyses

Adbudget8.xls

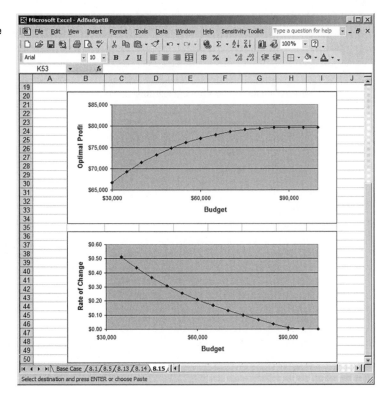

LINEAR PROGRAMMING

We now turn to the topic of linear optimization—or linear programming, as it is more typically called. These are models with a linear objective function and linear constraints. A large variety of linear programming applications have been developed in the fifty years or so that computers have been available for this kind of decision support. Linear programming models have proved to be valuable tools for understanding business decisions.

Linear programming models come in many sizes and shapes, but there are only a few standard types. It is helpful, therefore, to think in terms of a few basic structures when learning how to build and how to interpret linear programming models. In what follows, we present four different types. Most linear programming models are, in fact, combinations of these four types, but understanding the building blocks will help clarify the key modeling concepts. In our framework, the four types are *allocation* models, *covering* models, *blending* models, and *network* models.

Allocation Models

The allocation model calls for maximizing an objective (usually profit) subject to LT constraints on capacity. Consider the Veerman Furniture Company as an example.

EXAMPLE

Veerman Furniture Company

Veerman Furniture Company makes three kinds of office furniture: chairs, desks, and tables. Each product requires some labor in the parts fabrication department, the assembly department, and the shipping department. The furniture is sold through a regional distributor, who

SOLVER TIP: DATA SENSITIVITY OR SOLVER SENSITIVITY?

It is easy to confuse when to use the Data Sensitivity tool and when to use the Solver Sensitivity tool. Both tools are used to explore the results of varying an input parameter, but they answer different types of questions.

Solver Sensitivity answers questions about how the *optimal solution* changes with a change in a parameter. In this case, Solver Sensitivity varies an input parameter and reruns Solver to determine the optimal values of the decision variables for that parameter. The output can trace the implications for a result cell (or several result cells). However, it is not appropriate to use Solver Sensitivity unless the decision maker actually has the opportunity to optimize decisions in response to a parameter change.

The Data Sensitivity tool answers questions about how specific outputs change with a change in one or two parameters. In this case, Data Sensitivity varies an input parameter and traces the implications on a result cell (or several result cells). If there are decision variables in the model, they are held constant when the input parameter changes. There is no opportunity to reoptimize their values when the input changes.

The Data Sensitivity tool can also be used to answer questions about how specific outputs change with a change in one or two decision variables. This usage amounts to a simple search for optimal decision variables. It is a form of what-if analysis that explores the change in outputs when an input is varied, where the input just happens to be a decision variable. For this purpose, Solver itself would be a more powerful tool. However, Data Sensitivity may be appropriate if we are interested in the nonoptimal values of the decision variables as well as the optimal values.

has estimated the maximum potential sales for each product in the coming quarter. Finally, the accounting department has provided some data showing the profit contributions on each product. The decision problem is to determine the product mix—that is, to maximize Veerman's profit for the quarter by choosing production quantities for the chairs, desks, and tables. The data shown below summarize the parameters of the problem:

| Department | Hours per Unit | | | Hours |
	Chairs	Desks	Tables	Available
Fabrication	4	6	2	1,850
Assembly	3	5	7	2,400
Shipping	3	2	4	1,500
Demand Potential	360	300	100	
Profit	$15	$24	$18	

Once again, to determine the decision variables, we ask, "What must be decided?" The answer is the product mix, so we define decision variables as the number of chairs, desks, and tables produced. For the purposes of notation, we use C, D, and T to represent the number of chairs, the number of desks, and the number of tables in the product mix, respectively.

Next we ask, "What measure will we use to compare alternative sets of decision variables?" To choose between two different product mixes, we would calculate the total profit contribution for each one and choose the higher profit. To calculate profit, we add the profit from chairs, the profit from desks, and the profit from tables. Thus, an algebraic expression for total profit is:

$$Profit = 15C + 24D + 18T$$

To identify the model's constraints, we ask, "What restrictions limit our choice of decision variables?" In this scenario, there are two kinds of limitations: one due to production capacity and the other due to demand potential. In words, a production capacity constraint states that the number of hours *consumed* in the fabrication department must be less than or equal to the number of hours *available.* In symbols, we write:

Fabrication hours consumed $= 4C + 6D + 2T <= 1{,}850$ (Fabrication hours available)

Similar constraints hold for the assembly and shipping departments:

Assembly hours consumed $= 3C + 5D + 7T <= 2{,}400$ (Assembly hours available)
Shipping hours consumed $= 3C + 2D + 4T <= 1{,}500$ (Shipping hours available)

For the demand potential constraint, a word statement is that the number of chairs *produced* must be less than or equal to the estimated demand *potential* for chairs. In symbols, we write:

Chairs produced $= C <= 360$ (Chair demand potential)

Similar constraints hold for desks and tables:

Desks produced $= D <= 300$ (Desk demand potential)
Tables produced $= T <= 100$ (Table demand potential)

We now have six constraints that describe the restrictions limiting our choice of decision variables C, D, and T. The entire model, stated in algebraic terms, reads as follows:

Maximize $z =$ $15C \quad + 24D \quad + 18T$
subject to

$4C$	$+ 6D$	$+ 2T$	$<=$	$1{,}850$
$3C$	$+ 5D$	$+ 7T$	$<=$	$2{,}400$
$3C$	$+ 2D$	$+ 4T$	$<=$	$1{,}500$
C			$<=$	360
	D		$<=$	300
		T	$<=$	100

This algebraic statement reflects a widely used format for linear programs. Variables appear in columns, constraints appear as rows, and the objective function appears as a special row at the top of the model. We will adopt this layout as a standard for spreadsheet display.

A spreadsheet model for this allocation problem appears in Figure 8.16. Notice the three modules in the spreadsheet, including a highlighted row for the decision variables, a highlighted single cell for the objective function value, and a set of constraint relationships. The cells containing the symbol <= have no function in the operation of the spreadsheet; they are intended as a visual aid to the user, helping to convey a sense of the information in the constraints. We place them between the left-hand side value of the constraint (a formula) and the right-hand side value (a parameter). To the right of each constraint parameter, we construct a cell that displays the status of the constraint. The constraint is binding if it is satisfied as an equality; otherwise, it is nonbinding. (Although this status indicator is a desirable feature of linear programming models for most beginners, we will often omit it, so that we can focus on the information in the constraints themselves.)

Figure 8.17 shows the formulas in this model. Note here that the model consists of only two kinds of cells: those containing a number (either a parameter or a decision variable) and those containing a SUMPRODUCT formula.

The set of values for the decision variables in Figure 8.16 was an arbitrary one. We could try different sets of three values in order to see whether we could come up with a good product mix by trial and error. Such an attempt might also be a useful debugging

FIGURE 8.16
Spreadsheet Model for the Allocation Problem

LP.xls

	A	B	C	D	E	F	G	H
1	Allocation: Furniture Production							
2								
3	Decision Variables							
4		C	D	T				
5	Product mix	100	200	50				
6								
7	Objective Function				Total			
8	Profit	15	24	18	7200			
9								
10								
11	Constraints				LHS		RHS	
12	Fabrication	4	6	2	1700	<=	1850	Not Binding
13	Assembly	3	5	7	1650	<=	2400	Not Binding
14	Distribution	3	2	4	900	<=	1500	Not Binding
15	Chair market	1	0	0	100	<=	360	Not Binding
16	Desk market	0	1	0	200	<=	300	Not Binding
17	Table market	0	0	1	50	<=	100	Not Binding
18								

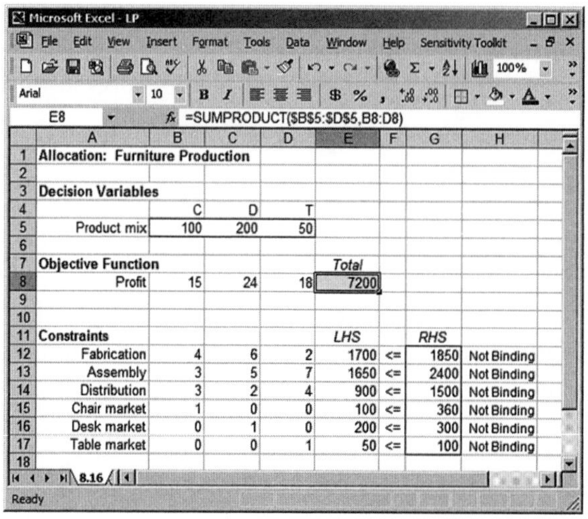

FIGURE 8.17
Formulas in the Model for the Allocation Problem

LP.xls

	A	B	C	D	E	F	G	H
1	Allocation: Furniture							
2								
3	Decision Variables							
4		C	D	T				
5	Product mix	100	200	50				
6								
7	Objective Function				Total			
8	Profit	15	24	18	=SUMPRODUCT($B$5:$D$5,B8:D8)			
9								
10								
11	Constraints				LHS		RHS	
12	Fabrication	4	6	2	=SUMPRODUCT($B$5:$D$5,B12:D12)	<=	1850	=IF(E12=G12,"Binding","Not Binding")
13	Assembly	3	5	7	=SUMPRODUCT($B$5:$D$5,B13:D13)	<=	2400	=IF(E13=G13,"Binding","Not Binding")
14	Distribution	3	2	4	=SUMPRODUCT($B$5:$D$5,B14:D14)	<=	1500	=IF(E14=G14,"Binding","Not Binding")
15	Chair market	1	0	0	=SUMPRODUCT($B$5:$D$5,B15:D15)	<=	360	=IF(E15=G15,"Binding","Not Binding")
16	Desk market	0	1	0	=SUMPRODUCT($B$5:$D$5,B16:D16)	<=	300	=IF(E16=G16,"Binding","Not Binding")
17	Table market	0	0	1	=SUMPRODUCT($B$5:$D$5,B17:D17)	<=	100	=IF(E17=G17,"Binding","Not Binding")
18								

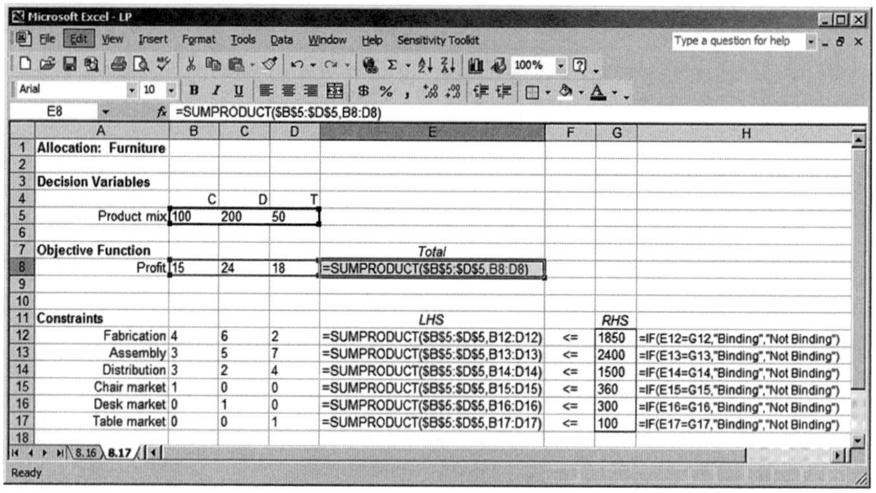

step, to provide some assurance that the model is correct. For example, suppose we start by fixing the number of desks and tables at zero and varying the number of chairs. For fabrication capacity, chairs consume 4 hours each, and there are 1,850 hours available, so we could put 1,850/4 = 462.5 chairs into the mix (that is, into cell B5), and the result would be feasible for the first constraint. However, we can see immediately—by comparing LHS and RHS values—that this solution violates the ceiling on chair demand. So we can reduce the number of chairs to 360, which will give us a feasible product mix and a profit of $5,400. (Recall that a feasible solution satisfies all constraints.) Keeping the number of chairs fixed, we can now add desks to the product mix (by entering a number into cell C5). Using trial and error (or Goal Seek), we can determine that it is possible to raise the number of desks to 68, achieving a profit of $7,032. However, this choice consumes all of the remaining fabrication capacity, leaving no room for tables in the product mix. Similar kinds of explorations, with other values of the decision variables, can help us confirm that the model is working properly and give us a feel for the profit that might be achievable. Although we will not discuss this step as we build other models in this chapter, we wouldn't skip it unless we were dealing with a familiar type of problem.

Once we are satisfied that the model is valid, we proceed to the optimization procedure. We invoke Solver and specify:

Target cell: E8 (maximize)
Changing cells: B5:D5
Constraints: E12:E17 <= G12:G17

Note that in this last step, we reference parameters that have been entered in the spreadsheet. We usually do *not* enter the right-hand side constants in the constraint window, even though Solver permits us to do so.

We select the linear solver (Standard Simplex LP) from the pull-down menu in the Solver Parameters window. Next, we proceed to the Options menu and check the box for Assume Non-Negative.

Before running Solver, we should create some hypotheses about the solution. For example, do we expect that the optimal solution will call for all three products? Will it consume all of the available hours? At the very least, we should recognize that desks have the highest profit margin, and thus we might expect to make the maximum number of them (300). As we mentioned earlier, this is an excellent opportunity to test our intuition.

As we see in Figure 8.18, the optimal solution calls for no chairs, 275 desks, and 100 tables. Evidently, the profit margin on chairs is not sufficiently attractive for us to want to devote scarce resources to their production. (We discuss the nature of the solution in more detail in the following section.) The maximum profit contribution is $8,400, and the two binding constraints are fabrication hours and the demand ceiling for tables. (We also have unused time in assembly and shipping and unmet demand in chairs and desks.) These results—decision variables, objective function, and binding constraints—are the three key pieces of information provided in the solution.

Recall the distinction made earlier between tactical and strategic information in the solution to an optimization problem. If we are faced with implementing a production plan for the next quarter at Veerman Furniture, we would pursue the tactical solution, producing no chairs, 275 desks, and 100 tables. (We might first want to make sure that our marketing department approves the idea of bringing a limited range of products to the market in order to maximize short term profits. This is one of the places where the simplifications in a model must be assessed against the realities of the actual situation.) On the other hand, if there is time to adjust the resources available at Veerman Furniture, we should

FIGURE 8.18
Optimal Solution for the Allocation Problem

LP.xls

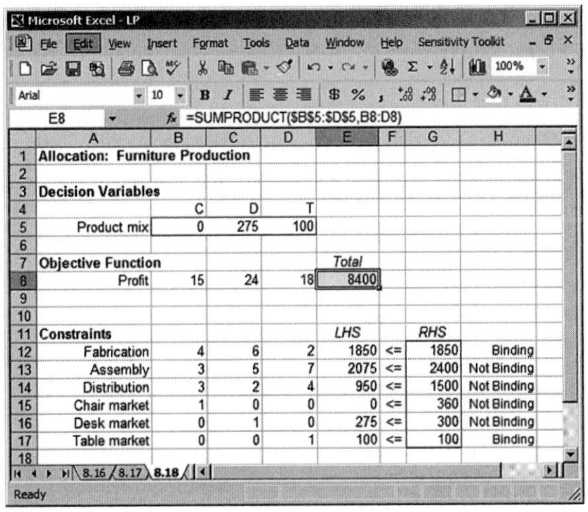

	A	B	C	D	E	F	G	H
1	Allocation: Furniture Production							
2								
3	Decision Variables							
4		C	D	T				
5	Product mix	0	275	100				
6								
7	Objective Function				Total			
8	Profit	15	24	18	8400			
9								
10								
11	Constraints				LHS		RHS	
12	Fabrication	4	6	2	1850	<=	1850	Binding
13	Assembly	3	5	7	2075	<=	2400	Not Binding
14	Distribution	3	2	4	950	<=	1500	Not Binding
15	Chair market	1	0	0	0	<=	360	Not Binding
16	Desk market	0	1	0	275	<=	300	Not Binding
17	Table market	0	0	1	100	<=	100	Binding
18								

explore the possibility of acquiring more fabrication capacity or expanding the demand potential for tables, as these are the binding constraints. In addition, if there is time to adjust marketing policies, we might also want to look into the possibility of raising the price on chairs.

Covering Models

The covering model calls for minimizing an objective (usually cost) subject to GT constraints on required coverage. Consider Dahlby Outfitters as an example.

EXAMPLE

Dahlby Outfitters

Dahlby Outfitters wishes to introduce packaged trail mix as a new product. The ingredients for the trail mix are seeds, raisins, flakes, and two kinds of nuts. Each ingredient contains certain amounts of vitamins, minerals, protein, and calories. The marketing department has specified that the product be designed so that a certain minimum nutritional profile is met. The decision problem is to determine the optimal product composition—that is, to minimize the product cost by choosing the amount for each of the ingredients in the mix. The data shown below summarize the parameters of the problem:

| Component | Grams per Pound | | | | | Nutritional |
	Seeds	Raisins	Flakes	Pecans	Walnuts	Requirement
Vitamins	10	20	10	30	20	20
Minerals	5	7	4	9	2	10
Protein	1	4	10	2	1	15
Calories	500	450	160	300	500	600
Cost/pound	$4	$5	$3	$7	$6	

What must be decided? Here, the answer is the amount of each ingredient to put into a package of trail mix. For the purposes of notation, we use S, R, F, P, and W to represent the number of pounds of each ingredient in a package.

What measure will we use to compare sets of decision variables? This should be the total cost of a package, and our goal is the lowest possible total cost. To calculate the total cost of a particular composition, we add the cost of each ingredient in the package:

$$Cost = 4S + 5R + 3F + 7P + 6W$$

What restrictions limit our choice of decision variables? In this scenario, the main limitation is the requirement to meet the specified nutritional profile. Each dimension of this profile gives rise to a separate constraint. An example of such a constraint would state, in words, that the number of grams of vitamins *provided* in the package must be greater than or equal to the number of grams *required* by the specified profile. In symbols, we write:

$$\text{Vitamin content} = 10S + 20R + 10F + 30P + 20W >= 20 \quad \text{(Vitamin floor)}$$

Similar constraints must hold for the remainder of the profile:

$$\text{Mineral content} = 5S + 7R + 4F + 9P + 2W >= 10 \quad \text{(Mineral floor)}$$
$$\text{Protein content} = 1S + 4R + 10F + 2P + 1W >= 15 \quad \text{(Protein floor)}$$
$$\text{Calorie content} = 500S + 450R + 160F + 300P + 500W >= 600 \quad \text{(Calorie floor)}$$

In this basic scenario, no other constraints occur, although we could imagine that there might also be limited quantities of the ingredients available (expressed as LT constraints), or a weight requirement for the package (expressed as an EQ constraint).

A spreadsheet model for the basic scenario appears in Figure 8.19. Again, we see three modules: a highlighted row for decision variables, a highlighted single cell for the objective function value, and a set of constraint relationships. If we were to display the formulas for this model, we would again see that the model is made up of only numbers and cells containing the SUMPRODUCT formula.

Once we are satisfied that the model is valid, we proceed to the optimization procedure. We invoke Solver and specify:

> Target cell: G8 (minimize)
> Changing cells: B5:F5
> Constraints: G12:G15 >= I12:I15

We select the linear solver and, in the Options menu, check the box for Assume Non-Negative. After contemplating some hypotheses about the problem (for example, will the solution require all five ingredients?), we run Solver and obtain a solution. The optimal solution, shown in Figure 8.19, calls for 1.32 pounds of flakes, 0.33 pound of raisins, and 0.48 pound of seeds, with no nuts at all. Evidently, nuts are prohibitively expensive, given the nature of the required nutritional profile and the other ingredients available. The optimal mix achieves all of the nutritional requirements at a minimum cost of $7.54. The three binding constraints in this solution are the requirements for minerals, protein, and calories.

Of course, we might decide that a trail mix without nuts is not an appealing product. If we wish, we can amend the model in order to force nuts into the optimal mix. One way to do so is to specify a minimum amount of nuts. In Figure 8.20, we show an amended model that requires at least 0.15 pound of *each* ingredient. The value of 0.15 is placed in row 6, just below the corresponding decision variable. In the Solver Parameters window, we add the constraint that the range B5:F5 must be greater than or equal to the range B6:F6. A requirement that a particular decision variable must be greater than or equal to a given value is called a **lower bound** constraint. Analogously, a requirement that a particular decision variable must be less than or equal to a given value would be called an **upper bound** constraint.

After including the lower bound constraints, a new run of Solver produces the optimal solution shown in Figure 8.20. Note that the lower bounds create an optimal solution that contains all five of the ingredients, as expected. We might have anticipated that nuts would appear at their lower limit, because before we added the lower bound constraints,

FIGURE 8.19
Optimal Solution for the
Covering Problem

LP.xls

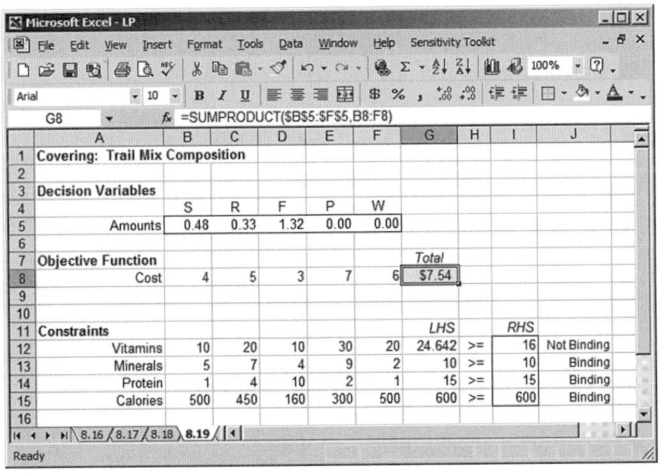

	A	B	C	D	E	F	G	H	I	J
1	Covering: Trail Mix Composition									
2										
3	Decision Variables									
4		S	R	F	P	W				
5	Amounts	0.48	0.33	1.32	0.00	0.00				
6										
7	Objective Function						Total			
8	Cost	4	5	3	7	6	$7.54			
9										
10										
11	Constraints						LHS		RHS	
12	Vitamins	10	20	10	30	20	24.642	>=	16	Not Binding
13	Minerals	5	7	4	9	2	10	>=	10	Binding
14	Protein	1	4	10	2	1	15	>=	15	Binding
15	Calories	500	450	160	300	500	600	>=	600	Binding
16										

FIGURE 8.20
Amended Model for the
Covering Problem, with
Lower Bounds

LP.xls

	A	B	C	D	E	F	G	H	I	J
1	Covering: Trail Mix Composition									
2										
3	Decision Variables									
4		S	R	F	P	W				
5	Amounts	0.39	0.15	1.36	0.15	0.15				
6	Floor levels	0.15	0.15	0.15	0.15	0.15				
7	Objective Function						Total			
8	Cost	4	5	3	7	6	$8.33			
9										
10										
11	Constraints						LHS		RHS	
12	Vitamins	10	20	10	30	20	27.97	>=	16	Not Binding
13	Minerals	5	7	4	9	2	10.0791	>=	10	Not Binding
14	Protein	1	4	10	2	1	15	>=	15	Binding
15	Calories	500	450	160	300	500	600	>=	600	Binding
16										

the optimization process kept nuts completely out of the mix. The cost is also higher in the amended model than in the original, at $8.33. This fact reflects an intuitive principle that complements the one we stated earlier: *When we add constraints to a model, the objective function cannot improve.* In most cases, as in this example, the objective function will get worse when we add a constraint.

Blending Models

The blending model involves mixing materials with different individual properties and describing the properties of the blend with weighted averages. Consider the Diaz Coffee Company as an example.

EXAMPLE

The Diaz Coffee Company

The Diaz Coffee Company blends three types of coffee beans (Brazilian, Colombian, and Peruvian) into ground coffee to be sold at retail. Suppose that each kind of bean has a distinctive aroma and strength, and the company has a chief taster who can rate these features on a scale of 1 to 100. The features of the beans are tabulated below.

Bean	Aroma Rating	Strength Rating	Cost/lb
Brazilian	75	15	$0.50
Colombian	60	20	$0.60
Peruvian	85	18	$0.70

The company would like to create a blend that has an aroma rating of at least 78 and a strength rating of at least 16. Its supplies of the various beans are limited, however. The available quantities are 1,500 pounds of Brazilian, 1,200 pounds of Colombian, and 2,000 pounds of Peruvian beans, all delivered under a previously arranged purchase agreement. Diaz wants to make 4,000 pounds of the blend at the lowest possible cost.

Suppose, for example, that we blend Brazilian and Peruvian beans in equal quantities of 25 pounds each. Then we should expect the blend to have an aroma rating of 80, just halfway between the two pure ratings of 75 and 85. Mathematically, we take the weighted average of the two ratings:

$$Aroma\ rating = \frac{25(75)+25(85)}{25+25} = \frac{4000}{50} = 80$$

Now suppose that we blend the beans in amounts B, C, and P. The blend will have an aroma rating calculated by a weighted average of the three ratings, as follows:

$$Aroma\ rating = \frac{B(75)+C(60)+P(85)}{B+C+P}$$

To impose a constraint that requires an aroma rating of at least 78, we write:

$$\frac{B(75)+C(60)+P(85)}{B+C+P} >= 78$$

This GT constraint has a parameter on the right-hand side and all the decision variables on the left-hand side, as is usually the case. Although this is a valid constraint, it is not in *linear* form, because the quantities B, C, and P appear in both the numerator and denominator of the fraction. If we were to include this form of the constraint in Solver, we would be forced to use the nonlinear solver to get a solution. However, we can convert the nonlinear inequality to a linear one with a bit of algebra and thereby continue to use the linear solver. First, multiply both sides of the inequality by $(B + C + P)$, yielding:

$$75B + 60C + 85P >= 78(B + C + P)$$

Next, collect terms on the left-hand side, so that we get:

$$-3B - 18C + 7P >= 0$$

This form conveys the same requirement as the original fractional constraint, and we recognize it immediately as a linear constraint. The coefficients on the left-hand side turn out to be just the *differences* between the individual aroma ratings (75, 60, 85) and the requirement of 78, with the signs indicating whether the individual rating is above or below the target. In a similar fashion, a requirement that the strength of the blend must be at least 16 leads to the constraint

$$-1B + 4C + 2P >= 0$$

Thus, blending requirements are stated initially as fractions, and, in that form, they lead to nonlinear constraints. We are interested in converting these to linear constraints because with a linear model, we can harness the full power of Solver. As discussed earlier, this means that we can find a global optimum reliably.

Now, with an idea of how to incorporate the blending requirements, we return to our scenario. What must be decided? The decision variables are the quantities to purchase, which we can continue to represent as B, C, and P. What measure will we use? Evidently, it is the total purchase cost of meeting our 4,000-pound requirement. What restrictions must we meet? In addition to the blending constraints, we will need a constraint that generates a 4,000-pound blend, along with three constraints that limit the supplies of the different beans. Figure 8.21 shows the spreadsheet for our model, which contains a GT constraint and three LT constraints, in addition to the blending constraints. The three decision variables have been set arbitrarily to 1,000. In a sense, the model has two key blending constraints, and it also has what we might think of as covering and allocation constraints. Each of the constraints takes the same form: a SUMPRODUCT formula on the left-hand side and a parameter on the right-hand side. Note that this model contains both LT and GT constraints, and it is helpful, when filling in the Solver Parameters window, to keep like constraints together.

FIGURE 8.21
Spreadsheet Model for
the Blending Problem

LP.xls

	A	B	C	D	E	F	G	H
1	Blending: Coffee beans							
2								
3	Decision Variables							
4		B	C	P				
5	Inputs	1000	1000	1000				
6								
7	Objective Function				Total			
8	Cost	0.50	0.60	0.70	$1,800			
9								
10								
11	Constraints				LHS		RHS	
12	Blend aroma	-3	-18	7	-14000	>=	0	Not Binding
13	Blend strength	-1	4	2	5000	>=	0	Not Binding
14	Output	1	1	1	3000	>=	4000	Not Binding
15	B-supply	1	0	0	1000	<=	1500	Not Binding
16	C-supply	0	1	0	1000	<=	1200	Not Binding
17	P-supply	0	0	1	1000	<=	2000	Not Binding
18	Actual aroma	75	60	85	73.3		78	
19	Actual strength	15	20	18	17.7		16	
20								

Cell E8: =SUMPRODUCT($B$5:$D$5,B8:D8)

Notice that the Output constraint requires that we produce *at least* 4,000 pounds, not exactly 4,000 pounds. Thus, as formulated here, there is some flexibility in the Output constraint. Although Diaz wishes to produce 4,000 pounds, our model allows the production of a larger quantity if this will reduce costs. (Our intuition probably tells us that we should be able to minimize costs with a 4,000-pound blend, but we would accept a solution that lowered cost while producing more than 4,000 pounds because we could simply throw away the excess and remain better off.) In many situations, it is a good idea to use the weaker form of a constraint, giving the model some additional flexibility and avoiding EQ constraints. In other words, *we build the model with some latitude in satisfying the constraints of the decision problem, whenever possible.* The solution will either confirm our intuition (as this one does) or else teach us a lesson about the limitations of our intuition.

We now invoke Solver and specify:

> Target cell: E8 (minimize)
> Changing cells: B5:D5
> Constraints: E12:E14 >= G12:G14
>   E15:E17 <= G15:G17

We select the linear solver and check the box for Assume Non-Negative. We obtain the optimal blend of 1,500 pounds of Brazilian, 520 pounds of Colombian, and 1,980 pounds of Peruvian beans, for a total cost of $2,448 (see Figure 8.22). Of the two blending constraints, only the first (aroma) constraint is binding; the optimal blend actually has better-than-required strength. The output constraint is also binding (consistent with our intuitive expectation), as is the limit on Brazilian supply.

In Figure 8.22, which displays the optimal solution, the last two rows of the spreadsheet are not part of our Solver model. Instead, they provide a more conventional calculation of the blended properties, and we add them simply for convenience in interpretation of the results. Thus, where the first constraint of the model is binding (left-hand side and right-hand side both equal to zero), the aroma calculation in the next-to-last row shows that the weighted average exactly equals the requirement of 78. Where the second constraint shows that the strength requirement is not binding, the comparison of left-hand side (4,540) with right-hand side (zero) gives us little obvious indication of the meaning of the

FIGURE 8.22
Optimal Solution for the
Blending Problem

LP.xls

	A	B	C	D	E	F	G	H
1	Blending: Coffee beans							
2								
3	Decision Variables							
4		B	C	P				
5	Inputs	1500	520	1980				
6								
7	Objective Function				Total			
8	Cost	0.50	0.60	0.70	$2,448			
9								
10								
11	Constraints				LHS		RHS	
12	Blend aroma	-3	-18	7	0	>=	0	Binding
13	Blend strength	-1	4	2	4540	>=	0	Not Binding
14	Output	1	1	1	4000	>=	4000	Binding
15	B-supply	1	0	0	1500	<=	1500	Binding
16	C-supply	0	1	0	520	<=	1200	Not Binding
17	P-supply	0	0	1	1980	<=	2000	Not Binding
18	Actual aroma	75	60	85	78.0		78	
19	Actual strength	15	20	18	17.1		16	
20								

difference between the LHS and RHS in the constraint. However, the last row of the spreadsheet shows that the optimal blend's strength is 17.1 (see cell E19), as compared to the requirement of 16.

Network Models

The network model describes patterns of flow in a connected system, where the flow might involve material, people, or funds. Consider Bonner Electronics as an example.

EXAMPLE

Bonner Electronics

Bonner Electronics is planning next week's shipments from its three manufacturing plants to its four distribution warehouses and is seeking a minimum-cost shipping schedule. Each plant has a potential capacity, expressed in cartons of product, and each warehouse has a week's requirement that must be met. There are twelve possible shipment routes, and for each route, the unit shipping cost is known. This is an instance of the classical **transportation problem,** which is described by a set of capacities, demands, and unit costs of transportation. The transportation problem is a common one in distribution logistics, and the corresponding transportation model is often useful as a building block in models of complicated supply chains. The table below provides the given information for this example:

Plant	Warehouse				Capacity
	Atlanta	Boston	Chicago	Denver	
Minneapolis	$0.60	$0.56	$0.22	$0.40	10,000
Pittsburgh	0.36	0.30	0.28	0.58	15,000
Tucson	0.65	0.68	0.55	0.42	15,000
Requirement	8,000	10,000	12,000	9,000	

A flow diagram, showing the possible routes, is depicted in Figure 8.23. In the diagram, the letters on the left designate the manufacturing plants, which supply the product. The letters on the right stand for the warehouses, where the demands occur. In this case, all supply-demand pairs represent feasible choices for the shipment plan.

M
P
T
A
B
C
D

FIGURE 8.23
Flow Diagram for the Transportation Problem

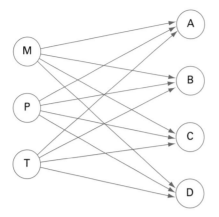

Network terminology refers to flow along **arcs,** or arrows, in the diagram. Each arc connects two **nodes,** or circles, and the direction of the corresponding arrow indicates the direction of flow in the network. Each flow incurs a cost: the unit cost of flow from any plant to any warehouse is given in the table that describes the parameters of the problem. The flows along each of the twelve possible routes constitute the decision variables in the model. Although the diagram does not contain labels for the arcs, it would be natural to use the notation *MA* for the quantity shipped on the route from Minneapolis to Atlanta, *MB* for the quantity shipped on the route from Minneapolis to Boston, and so on. In network problems, each arc in our diagram represents a decision.

Figure 8.24 displays the spreadsheet model. Notice the distinctive From/To structure in the table describing the problem's data. This structure lends itself readily to a row-and-column format, which is the essence of spreadsheet layout. Here, we adopt the convention that flow moves conceptually *from* rows in the spreadsheet *to* columns—for example, from M to A. Because of this From/To structure, it is helpful to depart from the standard linear programming layout and adopt a special format for this type of model. In particular, we can construct a spreadsheet model in rows and columns to mirror the table of parameters given above. In the Parameters module of the spreadsheet, we see all of the given information, displayed in an array, or rectangular range. In the Decisions module, the decision variables (shaded for highlighting) appear in an array of the same size. At the

FIGURE 8.24
Spreadsheet Model for the Transportation Problem

LP.xls

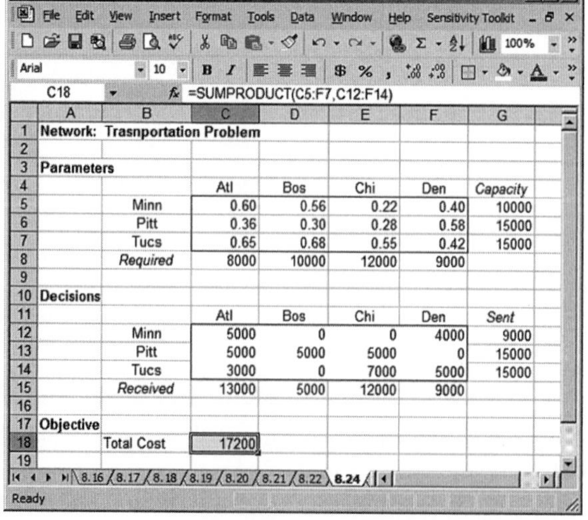

Microsoft Excel - LP
C18 =SUMPRODUCT(C5:F7,C12:F14)

	A	B	C	D	E	F	G
1	Network: Trasnportation Problem						
2							
3	Parameters						
4			Atl	Bos	Chi	Den	*Capacity*
5		Minn	0.60	0.56	0.22	0.40	10000
6		Pitt	0.36	0.30	0.28	0.58	15000
7		Tucs	0.65	0.68	0.55	0.42	15000
8		*Required*	8000	10000	12000	9000	
9							
10	Decisions						
11			Atl	Bos	Chi	Den	*Sent*
12		Minn	5000	0	0	4000	9000
13		Pitt	5000	5000	5000	0	15000
14		Tucs	3000	0	7000	5000	15000
15		*Received*	13000	5000	12000	9000	
16							
17	Objective						
18		Total Cost	17200				
19							

right of each row is the "Sent" quantity, which is simply the sum of the flows along the row. Below each column of the array is the "Received" quantity, which is the sum down the column. The objective function, which is expressed as a SUMPRODUCT in cell C18, is the total transportation cost for the system.

The transportation model has two kinds of constraints: LT capacity constraints and GT demand constraints, at least as long as demand does not exceed capacity. For the Minneapolis plant, we can express the capacity constraint as follows, using MA to represent the quantity shipped from Minneapolis to Atlanta, as suggested earlier:

$$MA + MB + MC + MD <= 10,000$$

In words, the total amount shipped out of Minneapolis must be less than or equal to the Minneapolis capacity. For Pittsburgh and Tucson, we have similar constraints:

$$PA + PB + PC + PD <= 15,000$$
$$TA + TB + TC + TD <= 15,000$$

Note that the left-hand side of these constraints simply adds the outbound shipment quantities from a given location. For that reason, we don't really need to use the SUMPRODUCT formula; we can get by with the simpler SUM formula.

For the Atlanta warehouse, the demand constraint reads:

$$MA + PA + TA >= 8,000$$

In words, the amount received at Atlanta must be greater than or equal to the Atlanta demand. Similarly, for the other three warehouses, the demand constraints become:

$$MB + PB + TB >= 10,000$$
$$MC + PC + TC >= 12,000$$
$$MD + PD + TD >= 9,000$$

Again, the left-hand sides of these constraints can easily be expressed using the SUM formula.

We now invoke Solver and specify:

Target cell: C18 (minimize)
Changing cells: C12:F14
Constraints: G12:G14 <= G5:G7 (Sent <= Capacity)
                   C15:F15 >= C8:F8 (Received >= Required)

We select the linear solver and check the box for Assume Non-Negative. We obtain the solution shown in Figure 8.25, which achieves the minimum cost of $13,830. All requirement constraints in this solution are binding, even though we permitted the model to send more than the requirement to each warehouse. This result makes intuitive sense, because shipping more than is required to any warehouse would merely incur excess cost. Once we understand why there is no incentive to exceed demand, we can anticipate that there will be some excess capacity in the solution. This follows from the fact that total capacity comes to 40,000 cartons, while total demand comes to only 39,000. In particular, capacity constraints are binding at Pittsburgh and Minneapolis, but an excess of 1,000 cartons remains at Tucson.

Building Network Models with Balance Equations

The transportation model is a special kind of network. As we can readily see in the diagram of Figure 8.23, the locations can be separated into a set of supply nodes and a set of demand nodes. This partitioning allows us to use a From/To structure and display decision

FIGURE 8.25
Optimal Solution for the
Transportation Problem

LP.xls

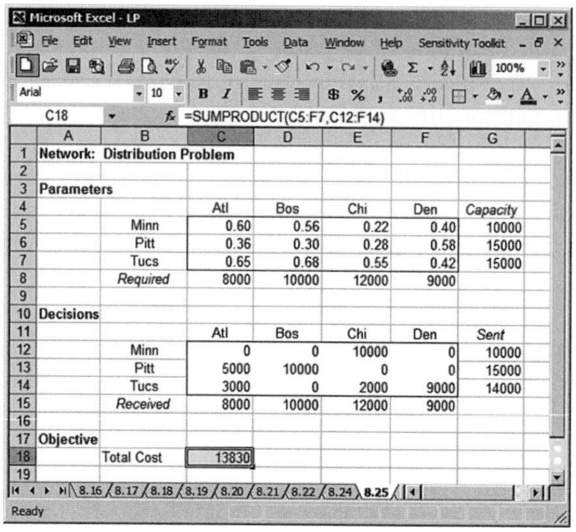

		Atl	Bos	Chi	Den	Capacity
Parameters						
	Minn	0.60	0.56	0.22	0.40	10000
	Pitt	0.36	0.30	0.28	0.58	15000
	Tucs	0.65	0.68	0.55	0.42	15000
	Required	8000	10000	12000	9000	
Decisions		Atl	Bos	Chi	Den	*Sent*
	Minn	0	0	10000	0	10000
	Pitt	5000	10000	0	0	15000
	Tucs	3000	0	2000	9000	14000
	Received	8000	10000	12000	9000	
Objective						
	Total Cost	13830				

variables in an array. However, some network structures do not lend themselves as easily to an array layout for decision variables. For these networks, it is desirable to use the standard linear programming format, with decision variables in a single row and a SUMPRODUCT function in each of the constraints. In what follows, we provide a glimpse of how to approach network models in such a manner.

The distinguishing features of this approach are a **flow diagram** and the use of **material-balance equations.** Flow diagrams were introduced in Chapter 4, primarily as visual aids in modeling. As discussed in Chapter 4, each node in the network corresponds to a material-balance equation—the requirement that total outflow must equal total inflow. This requirement means that there are no "leaks" in the network, nor is there a place for storage. Moreover, if total supply capacity exceeds total demand, we can always add a dummy demand, just for capturing unused supply. That way, all of the supply capacity would get shipped somewhere. Similarly, if demand exceeds supply, then we could add a node to capture unmet demand.

We can translate a network problem into a linear program by using a simple procedure. We first build a flow diagram for the flows in the problem. We then build the model by following these simple steps:

- Define a variable for each arc.
- Include the input flows for supply and the output flows for demand.
- Construct the balance equation for each node.

In addition, a sign convention for right-hand side constants can provide improved clarity. Under this convention, we write a balance equation with a positive right-hand side when there is flow *into* the network and with a negative right-hand side when there is flow *out of* the network. To illustrate how to build linear programming models from network diagrams, we recall an example from Chapter 4.

EXAMPLE

Planning for Tuition Expenses

Two parents want to provide for their daughter's college expenses with some of the $80,000 they have recently inherited. They hope to set aside part of the money and establish an account that would cover the needs of their daughter's college education, which begins four years from now, with a one-time investment. Their estimate is that first-year college expenses will come to $24,000 and will increase $2,000 per year during each of the remaining three years of college. The following investment instruments are available:

Investment	Available	Matures	Return at Maturity
A	Every year	in 1 year	5%
B	In years 1, 3, 5, 7	in 2 years	11%
C	In years 1, 4	in 3 years	16%
D	In year 1	in 7 years	44%

Investment and funds-flow problems of this sort lend themselves to network modeling. In this type of problem, nodes represent points in time at which funds flows occur. We can imagine tracking a bank account, with funds flowing in and out, depending on our decisions. In this problem, there needs to be a node for Now (the start of year 1) and for the start of years 2 through 8. (Note that the end of year 3 and the start of year 4 are, in effect, the same point in time.) To construct a typical node, we list the potential inflows and outflows that can occur:

Inflows

Initial investment

Appreciation of investment A from one year ago

Appreciation of investment B from two years ago

Appreciation of investment C from three years ago

Appreciation of investment D from seven years ago

Outflows

Expense payment for the coming year

Investment A for the coming year

Investment B for the coming two years

Investment C for the coming three years

Investment D for the coming seven years

Not all of these inflows and outflows apply at every point in time, but if we sketch the eight nodes and the flows that do apply, we come up with a diagram such as the one shown as Figure 8.26. In this diagram, $A1$ represents the amount allocated to investment A at the start of year 1, $A2$ represents the amount allocated to investment A at the start of year 2, and so on. The initial fund in the account is shown as $INIT$, and the expense payments are shown as $E5$ through $E8$. The diagram shows the end-of-year nodes as independent elements, which is all we really need; however, Figure 8.27 shows a tidier diagram in which the nodes are connected in a single flow network; this is equivalent to Figure 4.19. (In Chapter 4, we took an additional step, splitting each arc into two arcs, for the purpose of tracking the details of funds flow. Here, however, the linear programming model will perform much of that function, so we can work directly with the diagram in Figure 8.27 or the one in Figure 8.26.)

Note that there is no variable $B7$ in the model. A two-year investment starting in year 7 would extend beyond the eight-year horizon, so this option is omitted. However, the variable $A8$ does appear in the model. We can think of $A8$ as representing the final value in the account. Perhaps it is intuitive that, if we are trying to minimize the initial investment, there is no reason to have money in the account in the end. Still, to verify this intuition, we include $A8$ in the model, anticipating that we will find $A8 = 0$ in the optimal solution.

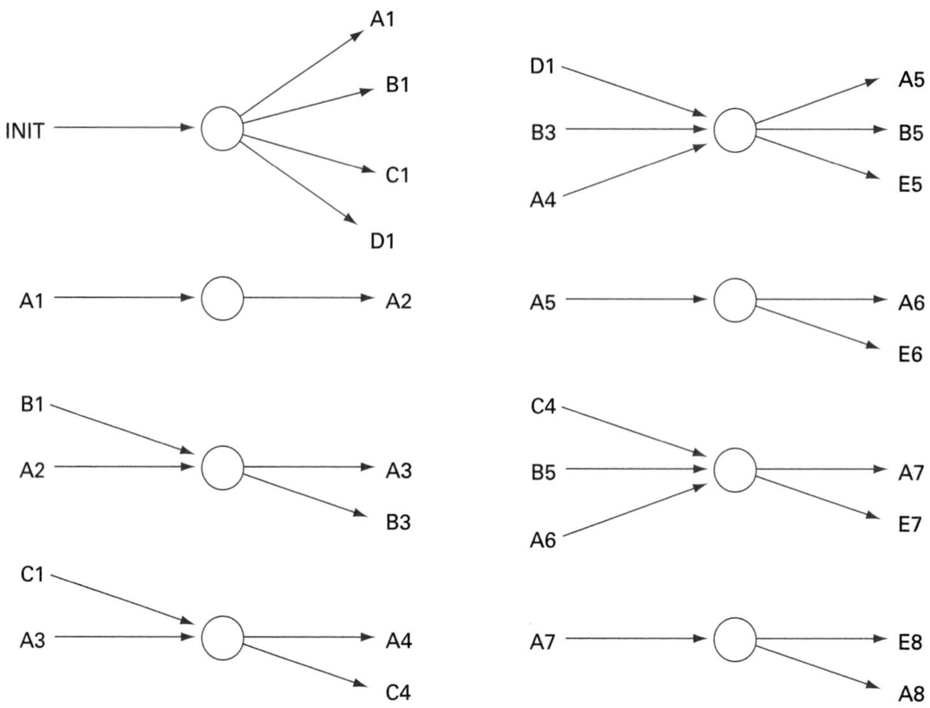

FIGURE 8.26
Diagram for the Network Problem, with Separate Nodes

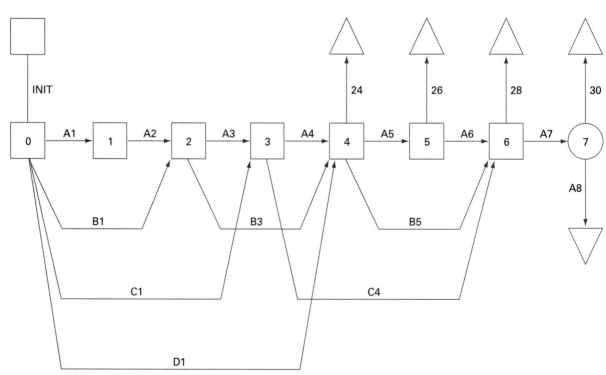

FIGURE 8.27
Alternative Network Diagram, with Connected Nodes

The next step is to convert the diagram into a linear programming model. For this purpose, the flows on the diagram become decision variables. Then, each node gives rise to a balance equation, as listed below.

Start of year 1: $A1 + B1 + C1 + D1 - INIT = 0$
Start of year 2: $A2 - 1.05A1 = 0$
Start of year 3: $A3 + B3 - 1.05A2 - 1.11B1 = 0$
Start of year 4: $A4 + C4 - 1.05A3 - 1.16C1 = 0$
Start of year 5: $A5 + B5 + 24{,}000 - 1.05A4 - 1.11B3 = 0$
Start of year 6: $A6 + 26{,}000 - 1.05A5 = 0$
Start of year 7: $A7 + 28{,}000 - 1.05A6 - 1.11B5 - 1.16C4 = 0$
Start of year 8: $A8 + 30{,}000 - 1.05A7 - 1.44D1 = 0$

These EQ constraints are shown as part of the spreadsheet model in Figure 8.28. Notice the systematic pattern formed by the coefficients in the columns of the constraint equations. Each column has two nonzero coefficients, a positive coefficient (of one), corresponding to the time the investment is made, and a negative coefficient (reflecting the appreciation rate), corresponding to the time the investment matures. The only exceptions are $INIT$ and $A8$, which essentially represent flows into and out of the network. In other funds-flow models, the column coefficients portray the investment-and-return profile for each of the variables (on a per-unit basis). The right-hand side constants, following our sign convention, show the profile of planned flows into and out of the system over the various time periods. In this case, the constants in the last four constraints are negative, reflecting required outflows from the investment account in the last four years of the plan.

The objective function in this example is simply the initial size of the investment account, which is the variable $INIT$. Thus, we can depart from the usual format and designate the objective function in cell B7 simply by referencing cell B5.

We now invoke Solver and specify:

Target cell: B7 (minimize)
Changing cells: B5:P5
Constraints: Q11:Q18 = S11:S18

When we minimize $INIT$, Solver provides the optimal solution shown in Figure 8.28, calling for an initial investment of about \$80,883.

FIGURE 8.28
Spreadsheet Model for
the Network Problem

LP.xls

	A	B	C	D	E	F	G	H	I	J	K	L	M	N	O	P	Q	R	S
1	Network: Tuition Problem																		
2																			
3	Decisions																		
4		INIT	A1	A2	A3	A4	A5	A6	A7	A8	B1	B3	B5	C1	C4	D1			
5		80.883	0.00	0.00	0.00	0.00	24.76	0.00	0.00	0.00	60.05	66.66	25.23	0.00	0.00	20.83			
6	Objective																		
7		80.883																	
8																			
9	Constraints																		
10	Year																		
11	0	-1	1	0	0	0	0	0	0	0	1	0	0	1	0	1	1.07E-14	=	0
12	1	0	-1.05	1	0	0	0	0	0	0	0	0	0	0	0	0	0	=	0
13	2	0	0	-1.05	1	0	0	0	0	0	-1.11	1	0	0	0	0	1.42E-14	=	0
14	3	0	0	0	-1.05	1	0	0	0	0	0	0	0	-1.16	1	0	0	=	0
15	4	0	0	0	0	-1.05	1	0	0	0	0	-1.11	1	0	0	0	-24	=	-24
16	5	0	0	0	0	0	-1.05	1	0	0	0	0	0	0	0	0	-26	=	-26
17	6	0	0	0	0	0	0	-1.05	1	0	0	0	-1.11	0	-1.16	0	-28	=	-28
18	7	0	0	0	0	0	0	0	-1.05	1	0	0	0	0	0	-1.44	-30	=	-30
19																			

The nature of the optimal solution may not be easy to anticipate. First, note that the return of 16 percent on investment C exceeds the return of 5 percent annually, even when we allow for compounding. Thus, we might have expected to see some use of investment C, rather than investment A, in the optimal solution. However, the equivalent annual rate of return is highest on investment B and next highest on investment D, which is still better than investment C. Thus, we should expect to see the use of B and D in the solution, and we do. The use of investment A is dictated by timing. Since it is the only investment maturing at the end of year 5, it becomes the vehicle to meet the $26,000 requirement at the end of year 5. Prior to that, the solution uses $B3$ (funded in turn by $B1$) to cover the first year of expenses and to fund $A5$. Then, $B5$ covers the third year of expenses, funded by $B3$. Meanwhile, $D1$ covers the fourth year of expenses. As anticipated, the account is empty at the end of the planning horizon.

Note that the optimal value of the objective function in our spreadsheet model appears as 80.883, because we have scaled our model in thousands of dollars. The scaling was accomplished by entering the tuition expenses in thousands of dollars on the right-hand side of the last four constraints. In a model such as this one, scaling is obviously convenient. It allows us to avoid entering a lot of zeros when we type in the model, and it makes the model easier to debug.

Sensitivity Analysis for Linear Programs

As we stressed in Chapter 6, sensitivity analysis is a vital part of all spreadsheet modeling. In optimization modeling, some of the most valuable insights come not from the optimal solution itself, but from a sensitivity analysis around the optimal solution. As we will see, the special structure of linear programs gives rise to certain characteristic results. We again use the Solver Sensitivity option in the Sensitivity Toolkit.

We implement Solver Sensitivity with the Veerman Furniture model to illustrate some of the features of sensitivity analysis in linear programs. Recall that the model allows us to find the profit-maximizing product mix among chairs, desks, and tables. The optimal product mix (see Figure 8.18) is made up of desks and tables, with no chairs. Two constraints are binding: fabrication hours and the tables market. The optimal total profit contribution in the base case is $8,400.

Suppose that we are using the Veerman Furniture model as a planning tool and that we wish to explore a change in the price of chairs. We might not yet know what the exact price will be, pending more information about the competition, but we want to explore the impact of a price change, which translates into a change in the profit contribution of chairs. For the time being, let's assume that if we vary the price, there will be no effect on the demand potential for chairs. We invoke Solver Sensitivity with the following entries:

Objective Function: E8
Other Cell(s): B5:D5
Cell to Vary: B8
First Value: 12
Last Value: 24
Increment: 1

The Solver Sensitivity results appear on a new worksheet (see Figure 8.29). They show how the optimal product mix and the optimal profit both change as the profit contribution on chairs increases. For the range of profit contributions we chose ($12 to $24), we see two distinct profiles. For values up to $16, the base-case solution prevails, but above $16, the optimal mix changes, as follows:

FIGURE 8.29
Sensitivity of the
Optimal Allocation to
Profit on Chairs

LP.xls

	A	B	C	D	E	F	G
1	Unit Profit	Objective	Change	C	D	T	
2	$12	$8,400		0	275	100	
3	$13	$8,400	$0	0	275	100	
4	$14	$8,400	$0	0	275	100	
5	$15	$8,400	$0	0	275	100	
6	$16	$8,400	$0	0	275	100	
7	$17	$8,730	$330	330	55	100	
8	$18	$9,060	$330	330	55	100	
9	$19	$9,390	$330	330	55	100	
10	$20	$9,720	$330	330	55	100	
11	$21	$10,050	$330	360	40	85	
12	$22	$10,410	$360	360	40	85	
13	$23	$10,770	$360	360	40	85	
14	$24	$11,130	$360	360	40	85	
15							

- Chairs stay at zero until the unit profit contribution on chairs reaches $16; then chairs enter the optimal mix at a quantity of 330.

- When the unit contribution reaches $21, the number of chairs in the optimal mix increases to 360.

- Desks and tables are not affected until the unit contribution on chairs reaches $16; then the optimal number of desks drops from 275 to 55. When the unit profit on chairs reaches $21, the optimal number of desks drops again, to 40.

- Tables stay level at 100 until the unit contribution on chairs reaches $21; then the optimal number of tables drops to 85.

- The optimal total profit remains unchanged until the unit contribution on chairs reaches $16; thereafter, it increases.

From this information, we can conclude that the optimal solution is insensitive to changes in the unit profit contribution of chairs, up to $16. Beyond that point, however, the profit contribution on chairs becomes sufficiently attractive that we want to have all three products in the mix. In effect, chairs substitute for desks (though not at a ratio of 1:1) when the profit contribution exceeds $16. Subsequently, when the profit contribution exceeds $21, chairs substitute for both desks and tables and are limited only by their demand potential. Thus, if we decide to alter the price for chairs, we can anticipate the impact on our product mix from the information in the sensitivity table.

In all linear programs, there is a distinct pattern to the changes in the optimal solution when we vary a coefficient of a decision variable in the objective function. In some interval around the base-case value, there is no change at all in the optimal decisions, but the objective function value will change if the decision variable is positive. Outside of this interval, a different set of values for the decision variables is optimal. As we saw in this example, the change from one set of values to the other will not be gradual. Instead, it will often be dramatic, as illustrated by the optimal number of chairs changing from 0 to 330 when the profit contribution increases from $16 to $17.

We noticed in the optimal solution that two constraints are binding: fabrication hours and the demand for tables. If fabrication time is limiting our ability to increase profits, perhaps we should acquire more of it. How much should we pay for additional time? Notice that this is a sensitivity question that involves one of the right-hand side constants rather than an objective function coefficient. To obtain an answer, we can invoke Solver Sensitivity again. In this case, our entries are the following:

Objective Function: E8
Other Cell(s): B5:D5
Cell to Vary: G12
First Value: 1,500
Last Value: 2,400
Increment: 100

The Solver Sensitivity tool adds another new worksheet, as shown in Figure 8.30. The table shows how the optimal product mix and the optimal profit both change as the number of fabrication hours increases. Its columns correspond to the same outputs as in the first table, and its rows correspond to the values we designated for the input. Thus, we see the following changes in the optimal product mix:

- Chairs stay at zero until the number of fabrication hours reaches 2,000; then chairs enter the optimal mix and continue to increase thereafter.

- Desks increase until the number of fabrication hours reaches 2,000; then desks stay level at 300.

- Tables stay level at 100 until the number of fabrication hours reaches 2,200; then tables drop.

- The optimal total profit increases as the number of fabrication hours increases, but not at a constant rate.

From this information, we can conclude that as we increase fabrication capacity, we should alter the product mix—first by increasing the number of desks, then by adding chairs to the mix, and then by swapping chairs for tables.

To determine how much we should be willing to pay for additional time, we examine the marginal value of additional fabrication hours. The **marginal value** is defined as the improvement in the objective function from a unit increase in the number available (i.e., an increase of 1 in the right-hand side of the fabrication constraint). We could calculate this marginal value by changing the number of fabrication hours to 1,851, re-solving the problem, and noting the improvement in the objective function. (It increases to $8,404, an improvement of $4.)

Marginal values are calculated automatically by Solver Sensitivity and are displayed in the third column of the table, where we see that the marginal value of fabrication hours is $4.00 in the region of the base case. As the number of fabrication hours increases, the marginal value stays level for a while, then drops to $3.75, stays level at this value for a

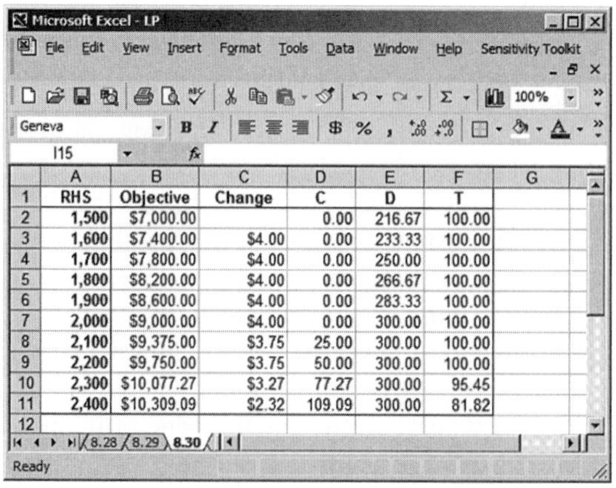

FIGURE 8.30
Sensitivity of the
Optimal Allocation to
Fabrication Hours
Available

LP.xls

	A	B	C	D	E	F	G
1	RHS	Objective	Change	C	D	T	
2	1,500	$7,000.00		0.00	216.67	100.00	
3	1,600	$7,400.00	$4.00	0.00	233.33	100.00	
4	1,700	$7,800.00	$4.00	0.00	250.00	100.00	
5	1,800	$8,200.00	$4.00	0.00	266.67	100.00	
6	1,900	$8,600.00	$4.00	0.00	283.33	100.00	
7	2,000	$9,000.00	$4.00	0.00	300.00	100.00	
8	2,100	$9,375.00	$3.75	25.00	300.00	100.00	
9	2,200	$9,750.00	$3.75	50.00	300.00	100.00	
10	2,300	$10,077.27	$3.27	77.27	300.00	95.45	
11	2,400	$10,309.09	$2.32	109.09	300.00	81.82	
12							

while, then later drops to about $2.32. This pattern is another instance of diminishing marginal returns: if someone were to offer us more and more of a scarce resource, its value would eventually decline. In this case, the scarce resource (or binding constraint) is fabrication capacity. Limited fabrication hours prevent us from achieving higher total profits; that is what makes fabrication hours economically scarce.

Starting with the base case, we should be willing to pay up to $4.00 for each additional fabrication hour because profit increases by this amount. This marginal value is also called the **shadow price.** In economic terms, the shadow price is the break-even price at which it would be attractive to acquire more of a scarce resource. In other words, imagine that someone were to offer us additional fabrication hours (for example, if we could lease fabrication equipment). We can improve total profit by acquiring those additional hours, as long as their price is less than $4.00.

We observe in this example that the marginal value of the scarce resource remains constant in a neighborhood around the base-case value. In particular, the $4.00 shadow price holds for additional fabrication hours until we reach 2,000; then it drops to $3.75. In the interval from 1,850 hours to 2,000 hours, the incremental hours allow more desks to be manufactured. In fact, we can see from the table that each additional 100 hours leads to an increment of 16.67 desks in the product mix. This increment, in turn, accounts for an increase of $400.00 in total profit, since desks contribute $24.00 each.

Above 2,000 fabrication hours, the pattern is a little different. With additional hours available, there are more chairs in the optimal product mix, and the optimal profit grows by $375.00 for each additional 100 hours. Thus, the shadow price is $3.75, and this value persists until around 2,200 hours. Actually, the shadow price changes at 2,266.67 hours, but our table is too coarse for us to see the precise change point. (We could see it more readily if we were to repeat the analysis with a step size of 1 hour.) Above 2,266.67 fabrication hours, the total profit increases at an even smaller rate ($2.32). In this interval, we see that chairs are added to the product mix, and tables are removed from it. Chairs consume more fabrication time than do tables. Therefore, with a relatively small amount of fabrication capacity (1,850 hours), we are better off not making chairs. As fabrication capacity increases (to, say, 2,300 hours), we are willing to swap chairs for tables, in light of other capacities available, in pursuit of optimal profits.

In linear programs, there is typically a distinct pattern in sensitivity tables when we vary the availability of a scarce resource. The marginal value of capacity remains constant over some interval of increase or decrease. (This contrasts with the marginal value in nonlinear models, such as Figure 8.15, where we saw marginal values that changed continuously as we altered the availability of a scarce resource.) Within this interval, some of the decision variables change linearly with the change in capacity, while other decision variables stay the same. If someone were to give us more and more of a scarce resource, its value would drop and eventually fall to zero. In the case of our product mix problem, we could confirm that the value of additional hours drops to zero at a capacity level of 3,000.

The Solver Sensitivity tool has the limitation that we must specify in advance the grid over which we change the input parameter. If we choose too coarse a grid, we may not identify the precise point at which the solution changes. In this case, we can always refine the search and run the analysis again. An alternative is to use Solver's own Sensitivity Report, which provides information on the local sensitivity to both objective function coefficients and right-hand sides. The chapter appendix provides some details on the information in the Sensitivity Report.

We have illustrated the sensitivity of linear programs to two fundamental types of parameters: an objective function coefficient and a constraint constant. These cases are particularly interesting because each produces a characteristic pattern in the optimal solution.

SOLVER TIP: SOLVER SENSITIVITY AND SHADOW PRICES

Solver Sensitivity is a general purpose tool for sensitivity analysis of optimization models. It is used to determine the sensitivity of the optimal solution to *any* input parameter. It automatically calculates the change in the objective function per unit change in the input parameter, which we call the *marginal change* in the objective.

Solver Sensitivity can, of course, be used to assess the impact on the optimal solution of changes in the constraint constants, which typically represent resources. In this case, the marginal change in the objective can be interpreted as the marginal value of the resource. The marginal value of a resource is the change in the objective per unit change in the resource, or the maximum we would be willing to pay to acquire additional resource.

In the special case of linear optimization problems, the marginal value of a resource is given the special name **shadow price.** Shadow prices are special because they are constant for some range of changes in the RHS. This feature is central to our interpretation of the economic patterns in the solutions to linear optimization models. In nonlinear models, the marginal values of resources are typically not constant.

However, we should not lose sight of the fact that with the Solver Sensitivity tool, we can analyze the sensitivity of the optimal solution to *any* parameter in the model.

Patterns in Linear Programming Solutions

In linear programming models, one form of insight comes from seeing a qualitative pattern in the solution. Stated another way, the optimal solution tells a "story" about a pattern of economic priorities, and it's the recognition of these priorities that provides useful insight. When we know the pattern, we can explain the solution more convincingly than when we simply read Solver results. When we know the pattern, we can also anticipate some of the answers to "what if" questions without having to modify the spreadsheet. In short, the pattern provides a level of understanding that enhances decision making. Therefore, after we optimize a linear programming model, we should always try to discern the qualitative pattern in the optimal solution.

Spotting a pattern involves observations about both variables and constraints. In the optimal solution, we pay special attention to which constraints are binding and which are not, as well as to which decision variables are positive and which are zero. Grasping the pattern of binding constraints and positive decision variables often allows us to reconstruct the solution in a step-by-step fashion. To the untrained observer, we seem to be solving the problem methodically, from scratch; in fact, we are only providing a retrospective interpretation of the solution, and we need to know that solution before we can devise the interpretation. Nevertheless, we are not merely reflecting information in the computer output. Rather, we are describing a set of economic imperatives at the heart of the model. When we can see those imperatives, and communicate them, then we have gained some insight. In the examples that follow, we show how to uncover these patterns, and we provide a test to determine whether we have been successful in recognizing a pattern.

In the example of Bonner Electronics discussed earlier (see Figure 8.25), there are three sources (Minneapolis, Pittsburgh, and Tucson) and four destinations (Atlanta, Boston, Chicago, and Denver). As the spreadsheet model indicates, the optimal total cost is $13,830.

The first thing to notice is that we need to use only six of the twelve available routes in order to minimize costs. In other words, six decision variables are positive, and six are zero. As the Solver solution reveals, the *best* routes to use are *MC, PA, PB, TA, TC,* and *TD.* The other routes can, in effect, be ignored.

The solution also tells us that all of the demand constraints are binding. (This makes intuitive sense, because unit costs are positive on all routes, so there is no incentive to ship more than demand to any destination, even though the GT constraints permit it.) A consequence of exactly meeting all demands is that at least one of the supply capacities will be underutilized, since there is a total of 39,000 units demanded compared to a total capacity of 40,000. In general, there is no way to anticipate how many sources will be fully utilized and how many will be underutilized, so one useful part of the optimal pattern is the identification of *critical* sources—that is, those that are fully utilized. The critical sources correspond to binding capacity constraints in the model. In the example, Tucson is underutilized, and the other capacities are binding. The decision variables associated with Tucson are not determined by the capacity at Tucson; instead, they are determined by other constraints in the model.

Thus, the elements of the pattern are as follows:

- All demand constraints are binding.

- Capacity constraints are binding at Minneapolis and Pittsburgh.

- Six routes are used (*MC, PA, PB, TA, TC,* and *TD*); the others play no role in the optimal solution.

So far, we have relied on Solver's solution to tell us which constraints were binding and which routes were worth using. In describing the pattern at this level, we need no numbers. However, the next step is to convert this description of the pattern into a scheme for computing the numerical values in the optimal solution.

In the optimal solution, some demands are met entirely from a unique source. For example, demand at Boston is all met from Pittsburgh, and demand at Denver is all met from Tucson. In some sense, these are high priority allocations, and we can think of them as if they were made *first*. There is also a symmetrical feature: supply from Minneapolis all goes to Chicago. Allocating capacity to a unique destination also marks a high priority allocation.

Once we assign the high priority allocations, we can ignore the supply at Minnesota and the demands at Boston and Denver, and we can turn to the problem that remains. Thus, we proceed to a second priority level, where we are left with a reduced problem containing two sources and two destinations. Now the list of best routes tells us that the remaining supply at Pittsburgh must go to Atlanta, since *PA* is a high priority allocation in the reduced problem. Similarly, the remaining demand at Chicago is entirely met from Tucson.

Having made the second priority assignments, we can ignore the supply at Pittsburgh and the demand at Chicago. We are left with a net demand at Atlanta and unallocated supply at Tucson. Thus, the last step, at the third priority level, is to meet the remaining demand with a shipment along route *TA*.

To review the steps in priority order, we have the following:

- Identify a high priority demand—one that is met from a unique source—and allocate the entire demand to this route. Remove this destination from consideration.

- Identify a high priority capacity—one that supplies a single destination—and allocate the remaining supply to this route. Remove this source from consideration.

- Repeat the previous two steps using remaining demands and remaining supplies each time, until all shipments are accounted for.

Using this set of steps, we ship as much as possible on routes *PB, TD,* and *MC*. Then, we proceed to the reduced problem at the second priority level and ship as much as possible on routes *PA* and *TC*. Finally, we proceed to the reduced problem at the third priority level and ship as much as possible on route *TA*. At each allocation, "as much as possible" is dictated by the minimum of capacity and demand. Looking back, note that this description characterizes the optimal solution without explicitly using a number. By describing the optimal solution without using the parameters in the problem, we have portrayed a qualitative pattern in the solution and translated it into a list of economic priorities. At first, the pattern was just a collection of positive decision variables and binding constraints. But a closer look enabled us to convert that pattern into a prioritized list of allocations that establish the values of the decision variables one at a time.

This retrospective description of the solution has two important features: it is **complete** (that is, it specifies the entire shipment schedule), and it is **unambiguous** (that is, it leads to just one schedule). Anyone who constructs a solution using these steps will reach the same result. The following table lays out the numerical steps in priority order:

Route	PB	TD	MC	PA	TC	TA
Priority	1	1	1	2	2	3
Shipment	10,000	9,000	10,000	5,000	2,000	3,000

The significance of this pattern is that it holds not just for the specific problem that we solved, but also for similar problems that have some of the parameters slightly altered. For example, suppose that demand at Boston were raised to 10,500. We could verify that the same pattern applies. The revised details of implementing the same pattern are shown below:

Route	PB	TD	MC	PA	TC	TA
Priority	1	1	1	2	2	3
Shipment	10,500	9,000	10,000	4,500	2,000	3,500
Change in Shipments	500	0	0	−500	0	500
Cost change	150			−180		325

Following the pattern, additional demand at Boston is met from Pittsburgh, which forces a reduction in the shipment from Pittsburgh to Atlanta, which in turn requires Tucson to make up the shortfall at Atlanta. Summing the cost changes in the last row, we find that an increase of 500 in Boston demand leads to an increase in total cost of $295. In effect, we have derived the shadow price on the constraint for Boston demand, since the per-unit change in total cost would be $295/500 = $0.59. Of course, we could confirm this result by rerunning the model with the additional demand at Boston.

More generally, we can alter the original problem in several ways at once. Suppose demands at Atlanta, Boston, and Chicago are *each* raised by 100 simultaneously. What will the optimal plan look like? In qualitative terms, we already know. The qualitative pattern of economic priorities allows us to write down the optimal solution to the revised problem without reinvoking Solver, but rather, by using the priority list and adjusting the shipment quantities for the modifications in demands:

Route	PB	TD	MC	PA	TC	TA
Original Shipment	10,000	9,000	10,000	5,000	2,000	3,000
Revised	10,100	9,000	10,000	4,900	2,100	3,200
Change in Shipment	100	0	0	−100	100	200
Cost change	30			−36	55	130

Tracing the cost implications, we find that the 100-unit increases in the three demands will combine to increase the optimal total cost by $179. On a per-unit basis, this is an increase of $1.79, which corresponds to the sum of the shadow prices on the first three demand constraints.

While it can be extremely helpful to identify the pattern in the solution to a linear program, we should not assume that the pattern holds for anything other than small changes in the parameters. We can always check whether the pattern changes by rerunning Solver with the new input parameters.

EXAMPLE

A Product Portfolio Decision

The product portfolio problem asks which products a firm should be making. If there are contracts that obligate the firm to enter certain markets, then the question is which products to make in quantities beyond the required minimum. Consider Grocery Distributors (GD), a company that distributes fifteen different vegetables to grocery stores. GD's vegetables come in standard cardboard cartons that each take up 1.25 cubic feet in the warehouse. The company replenishes its supply of frozen foods at the start of each week and rarely has any inventory remaining at week's end. An entire week's supply of frozen vegetables arrives each Monday morning at the warehouse, which can hold up to 18,000 cubic feet of product. In addition, GD's supplier extends a line of credit amounting to $30,000. That is, GD is permitted to purchase up to $30,000 worth of product each Monday.

GD can predict sales for each of the fifteen products for the coming week. This forecast is expressed in terms of a minimum and a maximum level of sales. The minimum quantity is based on a contractual agreement that GD has made with a few retail grocery chains; the maximum quantity represents an estimate of the sales potential in the upcoming week. The unit cost and unit selling price for each product are known. The given data are tabulated in Figure 8.31.

GD solves the linear programming model shown in Figure 8.31. In this model, the constraints are shown in columns rather than in rows, as would be the case in a standard

FIGURE 8.31
Spreadsheet Model for
the Product Portfolio
Problem

LP.xls

Vegetable	Cost	Given Price	Data Min	Max	Objective (Profit)	Decisions (Cartons)	Constraints Credit	Space	Ratio
Whipped potatoes	2.15	2.27	300	1500	0.12	300	2.15	1.25	1.056
Creamed corn	2.20	2.48	400	2000	0.28	2000	2.20	1.25	1.127
Black-eyed peas	2.40	2.70	250	900	0.30	900	2.40	1.25	1.125
Artichokes	4.80	5.20	0	150	0.40	0	4.80	1.25	1.083
Carrots	2.60	2.92	300	1200	0.32	1200	2.60	1.25	1.123
Succotash	2.30	2.48	200	800	0.18	200	2.30	1.25	1.078
Okra	2.35	2.20	150	600	-0.15	150	2.35	1.25	0.936
Cauliflower	2.85	3.13	100	300	0.28	100	2.85	1.25	1.098
Green peas	2.25	2.48	750	3500	0.23	750	2.25	1.25	1.102
Spinach	2.10	2.27	400	2000	0.17	400	2.10	1.25	1.081
Lima beans	2.80	3.13	500	3300	0.33	2150	2.80	1.25	1.118
Brussels sprouts	3.00	3.18	100	500	0.18	100	3.00	1.25	1.060
Green beans	2.60	2.92	500	3200	0.32	3200	2.60	1.25	1.123
Squash	2.50	2.70	100	500	0.20	100	2.50	1.25	1.080
Broccoli	2.90	3.13	400	2500	0.23	400	2.90	1.25	1.079
Obj. Fn.					3395.50	LHS	30000	14938	
							<=	<=	
						RHS	30000	18000	

F20   fx =SUMPRODUCT(F5:F19,$G$5:$G$19)

layout. The model's objective is maximizing profit for the coming week. Sales for each product are constrained by a minimum quantity and a maximum quantity. In addition, aggregate constraints on warehouse space and purchase expenditures make up the model.

Our Solver parameters are as follows:

> Target cell: F20 (maximize)
> Changing cells: G5:G19
> Constraints: G5:G19 >= D5:D19
>   G5:G19 <= E5:E19
>   H20 <= H22
>   G20 <= G22

The solution shows that all of the decision variables are positive except for artichokes, and the minimum cost is $3,395.50.

Examining the variables in the solution in more detail, we notice that all but one of the purchase quantities match either the maximum or the minimum, with lima beans as the only exception. Any product that has a nonzero minimum must appear in the solution at a positive amount, but some products are purchased at even higher levels. These can be considered high priority products. Products purchased at their minimum levels can be considered low priority products.

Examining the constraints in the solution, we see that the credit limit is binding, but the space constraint is not. In effect, the credit limit serves as a bottleneck on purchases, but we can ignore the space constraint. A description of the pattern could take the following form:

- Set the volume of each high priority product equal to its maximum level.
- Set the volume of each low priority product equal to its minimum level.
- Use the entire credit limit.

In other words, we are actually solving a simpler problem than originally given: produce the highest possible value from the fifteen products under a tight credit limit. To solve this problem, we can use a common sense rule: pursue the products in the order of highest to lowest *profit-to-cost ratio*. The only proviso is that we must meet the given minimum quantities. Therefore, we can convert the pattern into a calculation scheme for the decision variables, as follows:

- Purchase each product at its minimum sales level.
- Rank the products from highest to lowest ratio of profit to cost.
- For the highest ranking product, raise the purchase quantity toward its maximum sales level. Two things can happen: either we increase the purchase quantity until the maximum is attained (in which case we go to the next highest priority product), or else we use up the credit limit (in which case we are done).

The ranking mechanism prioritizes the products. Using these priorities, we essentially separate the products into three groups: a set of high priority products, produced at their maximum levels; a set of low priority products, produced at their minimum levels; and a *single* medium priority product, produced at a level in between its minimum and maximum. (This product is the one we are adding to the purchase plan when we use up the credit limit.) This procedure is complete and unambiguous, and this pattern describes the optimal solution without explicitly using any numbers. At first, the solution was just a collection of positive decision variables and binding constraints. But we were able to convert the solution into a prioritized list of allocations that establish the values of the decision variables one at a time.

Actually, Solver's solution merely distinguishes the three priority classes; it does not reveal the profit-to-cost ratio rule explicitly. That insight might come from reviewing the makeup of the priority classes, or from some intuition about how single-constraint problems are optimized. (The profit-to-cost ratios are shown for confirmation in column J of Figure 8.31.) But this brings up an important point. Usually, Solver will not reveal the economic reason for why a variable should have high priority. It is not always necessary (or even possible) to know *why* an allocation receives high priority. However, when available, the insights that come from these patterns can be extremely valuable.

Again, we can alter the base-case model slightly and follow the consequences for the optimal purchase plan. For example, if we raise the credit limit, the only change in the solution will be the purchase of additional cartons of the medium priority product. Thus, the marginal value of raising the credit limit is equivalent to the incremental profit per dollar of purchase cost for the medium priority product, or $0.1179. We could confirm this result by rerunning Solver with one additional dollar of credit.

Suppose instead that we were to increase the amount of a low priority product in the purchase plan. Then, following the optimal pattern, we would have to purchase less of the medium priority product. Consider the purchase of more squash than the 100-carton minimum. Each additional carton of squash will cost $2.50, substituting for about 0.892 cartons of lima beans in the credit constraint. The net effect on profit is as follows:

- Add a carton of squash (increase profit by $0.20).
- Remove 0.892 carton of lima beans (decrease profit by $0.2946).
- Therefore, net cost = $0.0946.

Thus, each carton of squash we force into the purchase plan, above the minimum sales level of 100, will reduce profits by 9.46 cents. If we were to rerun the model requiring 101 cartons of squash, we would confirm that profit declined by this same amount.

Comparing the analysis of GD's problem with the transportation problem considered earlier, we see that the optimal pattern, when translated into a computational scheme, is complete and unambiguous in both cases. We can use the pattern to determine the shadow price on a binding constraint or to derive marginal costs of introducing nonoptimal decisions. A specific feature of GD's model is the focus on one particular bottleneck constraint. This feature helps us understand the role of a binding constraint when we interpret a pattern; however, in many problems, there will be more than one binding constraint.

EXAMPLE

Production Planning

The production planning problem has several formulations. In one version, a company has contracted to meet a certain demand schedule and faces constraints on production capacity. The problem is to find a least-cost production plan. In our example, a company produces two products (A and B) using two types of machines (X and Y) over a planning period of three months. The products can be produced on either machine, and the following table describes the machine hours required to make a single unit of each product:

	Product A	Product B
Hrs. on Machine X	2.0	1.5
Hrs. on Machine Y	2.5	2.0

Machine capacities on X and Y are given for each of the three months. In addition, the quantities to be delivered each month, according to the contract, are also given.

Month	X-Capacity	Y-Capacity	A-Demand	B-Demand
1	140	250	50	30
2	60	80	100	60
3	150	100	50	50

The relevant costs are labor on each machine ($30.00/hour) and inventory held ($10.00/unit/month, for either product).

Figure 8.32 provides a linear programming model for this problem, with the optimal solution shown. The variables in this model are of two kinds. One kind is the number of units of each product scheduled for production, broken down by machine and by month—for example, *AX*1. The other kind is the inventory of each product held from one month to the next—for example, *AI*1. The inventory variables allow us to express demand constraints using the basic accounting definition of inventory: final inventory must be equal to starting inventory plus production minus shipments. One such equation applies to each product in each month.

Our Solver parameters are as follows:

Target cell: R13 (minimize)
Changing cells: B10:Q10
Constraints: R15:R20 <= T15:T20
R21:R26 = T21:T26

A look at the optimal solution in Figure 8.32 leads us to the following description of the pattern:

- All product shipment constraints are binding (because they were cast as equations in the model).

FIGURE 8.32 Spreadsheet Model for the Production-Planning Problem

LP.xls

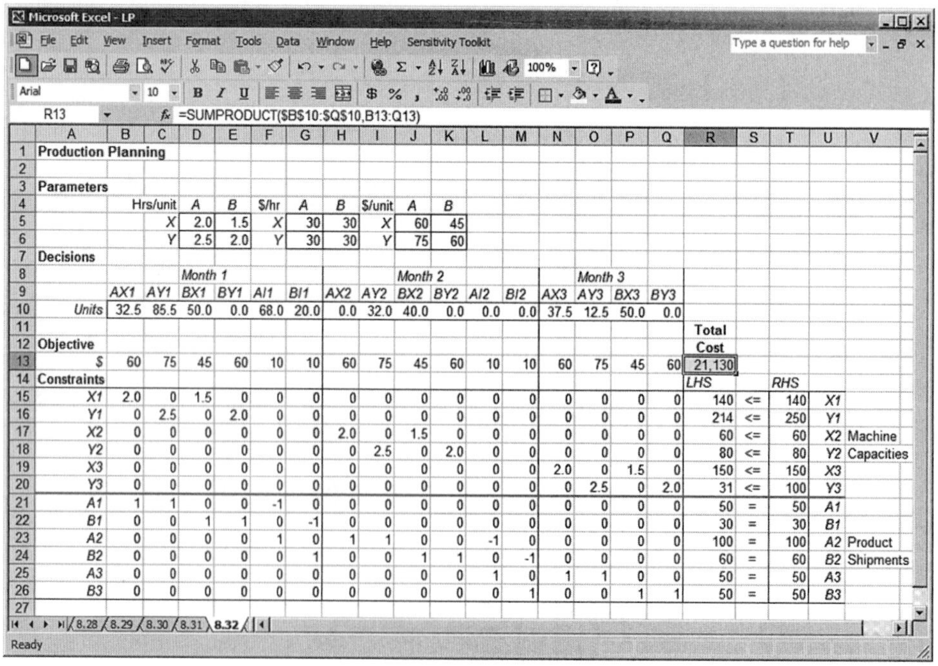

	A	B	C	D	E	F	G	H	I	J	K	L	M	N	O	P	Q	R	S	T	U	V
1	Production Planning																					
2																						
3	Parameters																					
4			Hrs/unit	A	B	$/hr	A	B	$/unit	A	B											
5			X	2.0	1.5	X	30	30	X	60	45											
6			Y	2.5	2.0	Y	30	30	Y	75	60											
7	Decisions																					
8				Month 1						Month 2					Month 3							
9		AX1	AY1	BX1	BY1	AI1	BI1	AX2	AY2	BX2	BY2	AI2	BI2	AX3	AY3	BX3	BY3					
10	Units	32.5	85.5	50.0	0.0	68.0	20.0	0.0	32.0	40.0	0.0	0.0	0.0	37.5	12.5	50.0	0.0					
11																		Total				
12	Objective																	Cost				
13	$	60	75	45	60	10	10	60	75	45	60	10	10	60	75	45	60	21,130				
14	Constraints																	LHS		RHS		
15	X1	2.0	0	1.5	0	0	0	0	0	0	0	0	0	0	0	0	0	140	<=	140	X1	
16	Y1	0	2.5	0	2.0	0	0	0	0	0	0	0	0	0	0	0	0	214	<=	250	Y1	
17	X2	0	0	0	0	0	0	2.0	0	1.5	0	0	0	0	0	0	0	60	<=	60	X2	Machine
18	Y2	0	0	0	0	0	0	0	2.5	0	2.0	0	0	0	0	0	0	80	<=	80	Y2	Capacities
19	X3	0	0	0	0	0	0	0	0	0	0	0	0	2.0	0	1.5	0	150	<=	150	X3	
20	Y3	0	0	0	0	0	0	0	0	0	0	0	0	0	2.5	0	2.0	31	<=	100	Y3	
21	A1	1	1	0	0	-1	0	0	0	0	0	0	0	0	0	0	0	50	=	50	A1	
22	B1	0	0	1	1	0	-1	0	0	0	0	0	0	0	0	0	0	30	=	30	B1	
23	A2	0	0	0	0	1	0	1	1	0	0	-1	0	0	0	0	0	100	=	100	A2	Product
24	B2	0	0	0	0	0	1	0	0	1	1	0	-1	0	0	0	0	60	=	60	B2	Shipments
25	A3	0	0	0	0	0	0	0	0	0	0	1	0	1	1	0	0	50	=	50	A3	
26	B3	0	0	0	0	0	0	0	0	0	0	0	1	0	0	1	1	50	=	50	B3	
27																						

- Capacity constraints on machine X capacity are binding in each period, but machine Y capacity is binding only in month 2.
- In the optimal production plan, the following variables are positive:

  *AX*1, *AX*3
  *AY*1, *AY*3
  *BX*1, *BX*2, *BX*3

- The positive inventory variables are *AI*1 and *BI*1.

To convert this pattern into a scheme for calculating the values of the decision variables, we again start by noticing which variables are positive and which are zero. If we focus on product-month combinations, we may not see a distinct pattern, although it becomes clear that the optimal schedule calls for overproduction in the first month, creating inventory that gets consumed in the second month. In the third month, production matches demand exactly. When we focus on product-machine combinations, on the other hand, a detailed pattern begins to take shape. We see that product B is never produced on machine Y, whereas product A is produced on both X and Y. Since machine X capacity is binding in each month, it is evidently important to produce B on X and to avoid producing B on Y. In fact, we see that it is also preferable to produce B on X in an earlier period, and to hold it in inventory, as compared to producing B on Y in the period when demand occurs. This observation suggests that the solution can be constructed by the following procedure:

- First, assign X capacity in each month to make the number of units of B demanded in the current period.
- If X capacity is inadequate to meet current demand, then assign X capacity in the previous month and hold the items in inventory.
- If X capacity is more than adequate for B, then assign X capacity to make the number of units of A demanded in the current period.
- If X capacity is fully consumed, then assign Y capacity to make the remaining number of units of A demanded in the current period.
- If Y capacity is inadequate to meet current demand, then assign Y capacity in the previous month and hold the items in inventory.

Clearly, machine X has a cost advantage over machine Y in making both products, because its hourly cost is the same, and it takes less time to produce either product. It is this relative cost advantage that leads to the pattern in the optimal solution. Here again, we have interpreted the optimal solution without explicitly using a number; yet we have provided a complete and unambiguous description of the solution. This description can be viewed as a system of priorities that determines the variables one at a time, in sequence.

Again, we can test our characterization of the optimal pattern by deriving the shadow prices. For example, suppose that the capacity of X were increased by one hour in month 1. Given the optimal pattern, we should want to transfer some production of A at the margin from machine Y to machine X. The extra hour of X would accommodate ½ unit of A. This would reduce production of A by ¾ of an hour on Y. In cost terms, the extra hour of X incurs a cost of $30.00, while ¾ of an hour on Y will be saved, at a benefit of $37.50. The net benefit is $7.50, which is the shadow price on the capacity constraint for machine X in month 1. We could, of course, confirm this result by rerunning Solver with one more hour of capacity on X.

As another example of altering the problem slightly, suppose that we increase by one unit the quantity of product A to be delivered in month 1. The marginal cost of meeting this shipment is just the cost of producing one more unit of product A on Y. This amount is $75.00, which turns out to be the shadow price for the corresponding constraint. Suppose instead that we increase by one unit the quantity of product A to be delivered in month 2. In this case, the marginal cost is $85.00, since the marginal unit must be produced in month 1 (at a cost of $75.00) and held in inventory one month (at a cost of $10.00), because no capacity remains in month 2 under the optimal plan. Suppose now that we increase by one unit the quantity of product B to be delivered in month 2. According to the pattern, we prefer to make this unit on machine X, but X is fully committed to product B during month 2. Following the pattern, we will want to make product B on X during month 1 and hold it in inventory; but to do so, we will have to transfer some production of A from machine X to machine Y. To find the marginal cost of this entire adjustment, we have to follow the economic implications of each element of the marginal change:

- Make one unit of B on X (time = 1.5 hrs.; cost = $45.00).
- Hold one unit of B one month (cost = $10.00).
- Remove 1.5 hrs. of A production from X (cost saved = $45.00; ¾ unit).
- Add ¾ unit of A production to Y (time = 15/8 hrs.; cost = $56.25).
- Therefore, net cost = $45.00 + $10.00 − $45.00 + $56.25 = $66.25.

Once again, knowing the qualitative pattern in the optimal solution allows us to anticipate how that solution will change when the problem is modified. Moreover, we can calculate shadow prices by quantifying the implications of the pattern for changes in the constraint constants.

General Comments on Patterns

The foregoing examples illustrate the process of extracting insight from the pattern in a linear programming solution. The first step, of course, is to understand the situation leading to the model. This allows us to examine the optimal decision variables and look for positive quantities. We can ignore the zero-valued variables when developing the pattern. We can also examine the constraints and determine whether they are binding; then we can ignore the nonbinding constraints. By focusing just on positive variables and on binding constraints, we next try to "construct" the optimal solution from the given parameters, with the determination of one variable at a time. This construction can often be interpreted as a list of priorities, and those priorities reveal the economic forces at work.

The pattern that emerges from the economic priorities is essentially a qualitative one, in that we can describe it without using specific numbers. However, once we supply the parameters of the constraints, the pattern leads us to the optimal quantitative solution. In a sense, it is almost as if Solver first spots the optimal pattern and then says, "Give me the numerical information in your problem." For any specification of the numbers (within certain limits), Solver could then compute the optimal solution by simply following the sequential steps in the pattern. In reality, of course, Solver cannot know the pattern until the solution is determined, because the solution is a critical ingredient in the pattern.

Two diagnostic questions help determine whether we have been successful at extracting a pattern. First, is the pattern complete and unambiguous? That is, the pattern must lead us to a full solution of the problem, not just to a partial solution; and if there are different ways of implementing it, the pattern should lead to the same solution. Second, where do the shadow prices come from? In each case, the shadow price comes from slightly altering one constraint constant in the original problem. We should be able to trace the incremental changes in the variables, through the various steps in the pattern, and ultimately derive the shadow price for the corresponding constraint. We can, of course, determine marginal values for changing several parameters simultaneously in much the same way.

Patterns have certain limits, as suggested above. If we think of testing our specification of a pattern by deriving shadow prices, we have to recognize that a shadow price has a limited range over which it holds. (Recall in Figure 8.30 that the shadow price on fabrication time was $4.00 up to 2,000 hours and then dropped to $3.75.) Beyond this range, a different pattern prevails. As we change a right-hand side constant, there will eventually be a change in the shadow price. The same is true of the pattern: beyond the range in which the shadow price holds, the pattern may change. In the production-planning example, however, the pattern was described in a fairly general way, so that it holds even when the shadow price changes. In that example, we were able to articulate a pattern at a high enough level that the "story" continues to hold even for substantial changes in the given data.

Unfortunately, it is not always the case that the pattern can be reduced to a list of assignments, in priority order. Occasionally it happens that, once we identify the positive variables and the binding constraints in the optimal solution, we might be able to say no more than that the pattern comes from solving a system of equations determined by the binding constraints and the positive variables. Nevertheless, in most cases, as the foregoing examples indicate, we can learn much more about the underlying economics from looking for patterns in the optimal solution.

Integer Programming

We mentioned earlier that an integer programming model contains a requirement that some or all of the decision variables must be integers. As we also mentioned, integer versions of nonlinear programs are particularly challenging, so we will concentrate here on integer linear programs.

Before we discuss how to handle the integer requirement with Solver, we return briefly to the subject of fractional values for decision variables. Recall that one of the three conditions of linear programs is divisibility—that is, fractional values make sense for decision variables. Consider the product mix for chairs, desks, and tables discussed in the Veerman Furniture model. As it turned out, the optimal solution contains no chairs, 275 desks, and 100 tables, so that the decisions are all integers. Suppose instead that the problem had been posed with only 1,800 fabrication hours available, rather than the 1,850 of the base case. Then the optimal product mix would have been 266.67 desks and 100 tables. Is the fractional number of desks meaningful?

On the surface, it may seem to make no sense to talk about two-thirds of a desk in the product mix. Certainly, if we were interested in the tactical implications of the solution, it would not make sense for us to prescribe the production of two-thirds of a desk to help meet demand. However, there are two interpretations of the fraction that do make sense. For one, we should be willing to round off or truncate fractional values. That is, we might interpret the optimal solution as 266 desks and 100 tables. Although this truncated solution does not use every last hour of capacity, the unused time is about a tenth of a percent of fabrication capacity. The impact on the objective function is equally small. The underlying uncertainty in our knowledge of all the parameters in the model is likely to be much larger than a tenth of 1 percent. Thus, *any* solution to the model is somewhat approximate. Therefore, rounding is often an acceptable solution to fractional decision variables.

A second interpretation is also possible. We might want to think of the model as representing a planning model that specifies conditions in a typical week. In that context, when we encounter a figure such as 266.67 in the optimal mix, we could interpret it as prescribing 267 desks for the first two weeks and then 266 desks in the third. That is, we might interpret the solution as the long run average of a repeated activity, where, again, fractions could easily make sense. Thus, rounded-off values and planning averages provide us with two reasons why we might tolerate fractional answers to linear programming problems when they seem impractical in literal terms. Still, there are some cases where only integers will suffice (for example, when projects must be funded in full or not at all, or when producing a small quantity of large things such as airplanes). In those cases, we must be able to specify that the decision variables be integers.

The use of Solver for integer programming models, once they are formulated, is relatively straightforward. The requirement that a variable must be an integer is treated like an additional constraint in Solver. Notice that, along with the constraint choices of <=, >=, and =, the Solver constraint window also permits **int** and **bin**. The *int* constraint forces a variable to be *int*eger valued, while the *bin* constraint forces a variable to be either zero or one (i.e., *bin*ary valued).

Once the model has been built and particular variables have been designated as integer or binary, the next step is to select Integer Options from the menu in the Solver Options window. The key option is the Tolerance parameter, for which the default value is normally set at 5 percent. At this setting, Solver is guaranteed only to find a solution that is no worse than 5 percent away from the optimal solution. Clearly, we want to find the very best solution, and this calls for setting the Tolerance parameter equal to 0 percent. However, the tighter Tolerance level may require the solution procedure to take much more time. Therefore, we usually keep the level at 5 percent while we are debugging the model, and we leave it at that level if we find ourselves working on a large problem. If we find that Solver will locate a solution at the 5 percent Tolerance level in a reasonable amount of time, we can experiment by lowering the Tolerance toward the 0 percent level.

To illustrate how to use Solver for integer programming, consider the following example:

EXAMPLE: AIRPORT SERVICES, INC.

Airport Services operates seven days a week and requires a specified minimum number of employees to be at work each day, in order to provide the necessary level of customer service. Under union regulations, employees at the company must all work full-time schedules, which means five consecutive workdays and two days off per week. The minimum daily need for workers is described in the following table. The company wishes to minimize the number of employees hired to provide the necessary service.

Day	Su	M	Tu	W	Th	F	Sa
Requirement	16	11	17	13	15	19	14

For this problem, there are seven possible work shifts. Each shift starts a five-day work period on a particular day. For example, the number of employees starting work on Sunday is denoted SU. The constraints state that the number of employees assigned to work a given day must be at least as large as the daily requirement. For example, the number working on Wednesday ($SA + SU + MO + TU + WE$) must be greater than or equal to 13. Figure 8.33 shows the complete spreadsheet model: it takes the form of a standard covering model. Our Solver parameters are as follows:

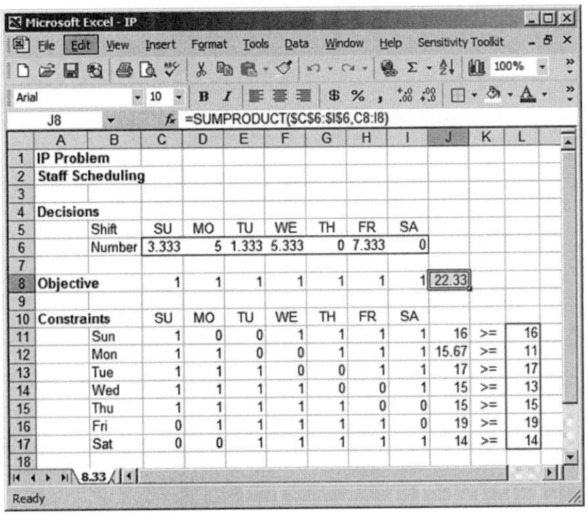

FIGURE 8.33
Spreadsheet Model for
the Staffing Problem

IP.xls

	A	B	C	D	E	F	G	H	I	J	K	L
1	IP Problem											
2	Staff Scheduling											
3												
4	Decisions											
5		Shift	SU	MO	TU	WE	TH	FR	SA			
6		Number	3.333	5	1.333	5.333	0	7.333	0			
7												
8	Objective		1	1	1	1	1	1	1	22.33		
9												
10	Constraints		SU	MO	TU	WE	TH	FR	SA			
11		Sun	1	0	0	1	1	1	1	16	>=	16
12		Mon	1	1	0	0	1	1	1	15.67	>=	11
13		Tue	1	1	1	0	0	1	1	17	>=	17
14		Wed	1	1	1	1	0	0	1	15	>=	13
15		Thu	1	1	1	1	1	0	0	15	>=	15
16		Fri	0	1	1	1	1	1	0	19	>=	19
17		Sat	0	0	1	1	1	1	1	14	>=	14
18												

Target cell: J8 (minimize)
Changing cells: C6:I6
Constraints: J11:J17 >= L11:L17

When we treat this model as a linear programming problem, Solver produces a solution containing some fractions and a total workforce size of 22.33. To produce an integer solution, we add constraints that require all of the decision variables to be integers. Then, we reset the Tolerance parameter to be 0 percent (as this is not a large problem) and ask for a solution. Solver produces a workforce with a size of 23. Aside from having faith in Solver, we know this must be an optimal solution because even if we ignored the integer requirements, we could never do better than 22.33. In this case, since the size of the workforce is simply the sum of the integer decision variables, and since that sum must be larger than 22, we know from the linear programming solution that a workforce of size 23 is the best that can be achieved.

As this example suggests, many integer programming models are simply linear programs with certain variables constrained to be integers. To solve these models using Solver requires only one or two additional steps beyond those required to solve linear programs. It might appear, therefore, that integer programming is just a minor technical extension of linear programming. However, binary variables allow us to model a number of frequently occurring situations that cannot be modeled using standard linear programming techniques. In this section, we discuss the elements of that class of models.

All-or-Nothing Variables

A binary variable, which takes on the values zero or one, can be used to represent a "go/no-go" decision. We usually think in terms of discrete projects, where the decision to undertake the project is represented by the value 1, and the decision to reject the project is represented by the value 0. A classical example is the capital budgeting model.

EXAMPLE

Capital Budgeting

Division A of a large corporation has been allocated $40 million for capital projects this year. Managers in Division A have examined various possibilities and have proposed five projects for the capital budgeting committee to consider. The projects cover a variety of activities, such as introducing a new product, purchasing real estate, and so on, but there is just one of each type. Each project has an estimated net present value (NPV), and each requires a capital expenditure, which must come out of the budget for capital projects. The following table summarizes the possibilities, with all figures in millions of dollars:

Project	P1	P2	P3	P4	P5
NPV	2.0	3.6	3.2	1.6	2.8
Expenditure	12	24	20	8	16

The committee would like to maximize the total NPV from projects selected, subject to expenditures of no more than $40 million.

This problem can be posed as an allocation model with one constraint, as shown in Figure 8.34. (A feasible but suboptimal set of choices is displayed in the model.)

If we were to optimize the model as if it were a simple linear program, the NPV would be $8.0 million, but the solution would be to select project P4 *five times*. This is because P4 has the lowest cost per dollar of NPV. However, these are one-of-a-kind projects; none can be implemented more than once.

If we were to optimize the model as a linear program with each of the variables constrained to be no more than 1, the NPV would be $7.04 million, and the optimal mix of projects would be P1, P4, P5, and 20 percent of P3. However, no fractional projects are possible. We must treat the projects as indivisible: the decision on each one is to either accept it or reject it entirely. Therefore, we must use binary variables, as all-or-nothing variables, for this purpose.

When we add the constraint that each variable is binary, we obtain the maximum NPV of $6.8 million, by accepting projects P1, P3, and P4 (see Figure 8.35).

FIGURE 8.34
Spreadsheet Model for the Capital Budgeting Problem

IP.xls

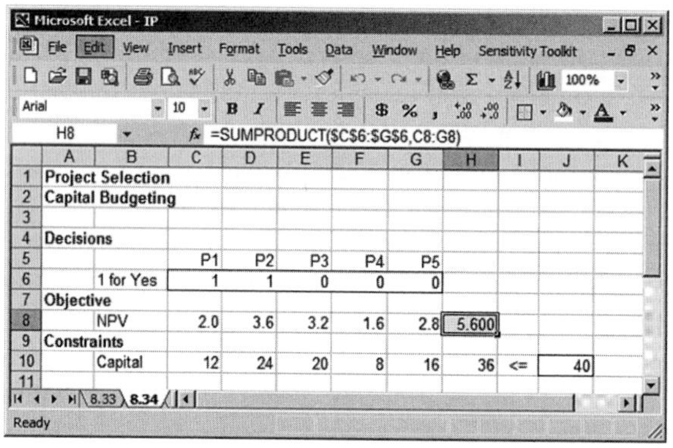

FIGURE 8.35
Optimal Solution for the Capital Budgeting Problem

IP.xls

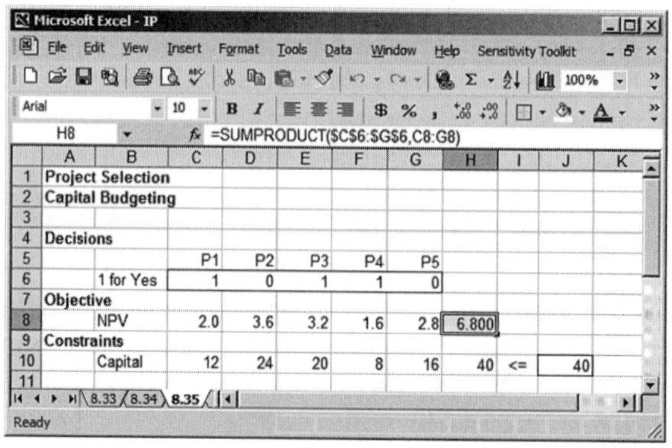

Logical Relationships

We often encounter additional conditions affecting the selection of projects in problems like the previous one. For example, suppose that projects P2 and P5 are international projects, while the others are domestic. Suppose also that the committee wishes to select at least one of its projects from the international arena. We can then add a covering constraint to the base case:

$$P2 + P5 >= 1$$

This constraint will ensure that P2 or P5, or both, will be selected, thus satisfying the requirement of one international selection. Of course, the addition of a new constraint may make the objective function worse. In this case, the optimal NPV drops to $6.4 million, by accepting only projects P2 and P5 (see Figure 8.36).

This additional constraint illustrates the fact that we can use binary variables to represent structural or policy relationships of the form

- Select *at least m* of the possible projects.
- Select *at most n* of the possible projects.

Other relationships that we normally think of as "logical" relationships can also be expressed with binary variables. Suppose that projects P2 and P5 are **mutually exclusive** (for example, they could require some of the same staff resources). Then we could interpret this feature as a special case of the condition for selecting at most *n*, and write:

$$P2 + P5 <= 1$$

In addition, we sometimes encounter **contingency** relationships. Suppose that project P5 requires that P3 be selected. In other words, P5 is contingent on P3. To analyze logical requirements of this sort, consider all of the selection combinations. The brief table below shows that three of the four combinations are consistent with the contingency condition:

P3	P5	Consistent?
0	0	Yes
1	0	Yes
0	1	No
1	1	Yes

We can accommodate the three consistent combinations and exclude the inconsistent combination by adding the following constraint:

$$P3 - P5 >= 0$$

FIGURE 8.36
Optimal Solution for
Capital Budgeting with
a Logical Constraint

IP.xls

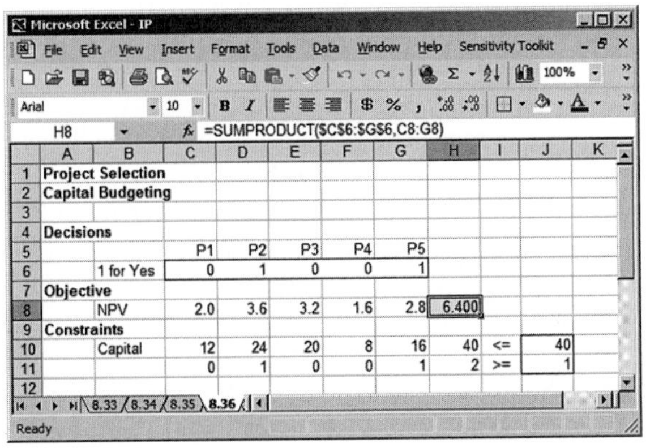

	Microsoft Excel - IP										
	File	Edit	View	Insert	Format	Tools	Data	Window	Help	Sensitivity Toolkit	

H8   =SUMPRODUCT($C$6:$G$6,C8:G8)

	A	B	C	D	E	F	G	H	I	J	K
1	Project Selection										
2	Capital Budgeting										
3											
4	Decisions										
5			P1	P2	P3	P4	P5				
6		1 for Yes	0	1	0	0	1				
7	Objective										
8		NPV	2.0	3.6	3.2	1.6	2.8	6.400			
9	Constraints										
10		Capital	12	24	20	8	16	40	<=		40
11			0	1	0	0	1	2	>=		1
12											

8.33 / 8.34 / 8.35 / 8.36

Ready

SOLVER TIP: LOGICAL FUNCTIONS

In setting up integer programming models, an experienced Excel programmer might be tempted to use the logical functions in Excel (IF, AND, OR, etc.) to express certain relationships among decision variables. For example, a direct means of assuring the selection of either project P1 or project P5 would be:

IF(OR(P1,P5) = 1, 1, 0) = 1

This equation holds when either one of the project variables P1 and P5 is selected. We could ensure selection of P1 or P5 by adding this EQ constraint to the model.

While this approach is logically sound, the IF function is nonlinear. Thus, we would not be able to use the linear solver on a model that contained this constraint. Even worse, the presence of the IF function tends to make the nonlinear solver stop its search at a local optimum (as discussed earlier). For these reasons, we formulate logical relationships using binary variables.

Thus, we can represent all-or-nothing decisions, and we can add provisions for related logical constraints, all within the framework of linear programming with binary variables.

Fixed Costs

One of the assumptions in linear models is strict proportionality: the cost contributed by an activity is proportional to its activity level. However, we commonly encounter situations in which activity costs are composed of fixed costs and variable costs, with only the variable costs being proportional to activity level. With an integer programming model, we can also integrate the fixed component of cost.

Imagine that we have already built a linear programming model, but one variable (x) has a fixed cost that we want to represent in the objective function. To incorporate this fixed cost into the model, we separate the fixed and variable components of cost. In algebraic terms, we write cost as

$$Fy + cx$$

where F represents the fixed cost, and c represents the linear variable cost. The variables x and y are decision variables, where x is a normal (continuous) variable, and y is a binary variable. Constraints in the linear program involve only the variable portion—that is, they involve only the variable x, not the variable y. In this situation, we also want to make sure that the variables x and y work together consistently. In particular, we want to have $y = 1$ (so that we incur the fixed cost) when $x > 0$, and we want to have $y = 0$ (so that we avoid the fixed cost) when $x = 0$. To achieve consistent linking of the two variables, we add the following **linking constraint:**

$$x <= My$$

where the number M represents an upper bound on the variable x. In other words, M is at least as large as any value we can feasibly select for x.

Why does the linking constraint work? As seen by Solver, this is just another condition of feasibility to be satisfied. When $y = 0$, the right-hand side becomes zero, and Solver interprets the constraint as $x <= 0$. Since we also require $x >= 0$, these two constraints together force x to be zero, so that there will be no fixed cost. Thus, when $y = 0$, it will be consistent to avoid the fixed cost. On the other hand, when $y = 1$, the right-hand side will be so large that Solver does not need to restrict x at all, permitting its value to be positive while we incur the fixed cost. Thus, when $y = 1$, it will be consistent to incur the fixed cost. Of course, since we are optimizing, Solver will never produce a solution with the combination of $y = 1$ and $x = 0$, because it would always be preferable to set $y = 0$.

The following example illustrates the use of linking constraints:

EXAMPLE

Mayhugh Manufacturing Company

Mayhugh Manufacturing, a medium size job shop, has been producing and selling three product families. Each product family requires production hours in each of three departments. In addition, each product family requires its own sales force, which must be supported no matter how large or small the sales volume happens to be. The parameters describing the situation are summarized in the following table:

	Product Family		
	F1	F2	F3
Profit per unit	$1.20	$1.80	$2.20

	Hours Required per Thousand Units			Hours Available
Department A	3	4	8	2,000
Department B	3	5	6	2,000
Department C	2	3	9	2,000
Sales cost ($000)	60	200	100	
Demand (000)	300	200	50	

At the heart of this situation lies a product mix problem. The linear programming representation of the product mix problem (with no fixed costs) is shown in Figure 8.37. By defining the x-values in thousands, we have scaled the model so that the objective function is actually in thousands of dollars. The optimal product mix calls for producing all three families, with F1 and F3 at their demand ceilings and F2 at 160,000. This product mix creates $758,000 in variable profits. If we subtract the total fixed costs of $360,000, we are left with a net profit of $398,000.

FIGURE 8.37
Spreadsheet Model for the Product Mix Problem, Without Fixed Costs

IP.xls

	A	B	C	D	E	F	G	H	I
1	Product Mix (Kernel)								
2	Linear Programming Analysis								
3	Decisions								
4			F1	F2	F3				
5			300	160	50	K-units			
6									
7	Objective								
8		Variable profit	1.20	1.80	2.20	758			
9	Constraints								
10		X	3	4	8	1940	<=	2000	
11		Y	3	5	6	2000	<=	2000	
12		Z	2	3	9	1530	<=	2000	
13			1			300	<=	300	
14				1		160	<=	200	
15					1	50	<=	50	
16									
17		Fixed costs	60	200	100	360			
18									
19		Net Profit				398			
20									

The linear programming solution might represent the situation in a firm that has introduced and supported various new products over the years and that now finds itself carrying out activities in three product markets. The linear programming framework suggests how to allocate capacity, provided that all three product families are active. However, there is no basis for determining whether any one of the families should be dropped, because fixed cost considerations are not part of the linear programming analysis.

To formulate the full problem as an integer programming model, we make two changes. First, we write the objective function with variable profit and fixed cost terms:

$$\textit{Net Profit} = 1.20x_1 - 60y_1 + 1.80x_2 - 200y_2 + 2.20x_3 - 100y_3$$

where x_j represents the volume for family j, in thousands. Here, y_j is a binary variable that must take either the value 1 when x_j is positive (and the fixed cost is incurred) or the value 0 when x_j is zero (and the fixed cost is avoided). Next, we add three linking constraints to assure consistency between the x-y pairs:

$$x_1 - My_1 \leq 0$$
$$x_2 - My_2 \leq 0$$
$$x_3 - My_3 \leq 0$$

Now we need to identify a large number to play the role of M. Essentially, we need a number large enough so that it will not limit the choice of these variables in any of the other (demand and supply) constraints. For example, a value of 300 (thousand) would work, since that represents the largest demand ceiling, and none of the volumes could ever be larger.

Thus, when $y_2 = 1$, the constraint on product family F2 becomes $x_2 \leq 300$; and when $y_2 = 0$, the constraint becomes $x_2 \leq 0$. Similar interpretations apply to families F1 and F3. These are valid linking constraints, but we can streamline the model slightly. Instead of retaining separate constraints to represent the demand ceilings and the linking relationship, we can let the linking constraint do "double duty" if we choose a different value of M for each family and set it equal to the demand ceiling. For example, the value of M selected for the F2 constraint could be 200 instead of 300. Then, when $y_2 = 1$, the constraint on product family F2 becomes $x_2 \leq 200$, which also serves as a demand-ceiling constraint. When $y_2 = 0$, the constraint becomes $x_2 \leq 0$, and the choice of M does not matter. The streamlined model becomes:

$$\text{Maximize } 1.20x_1 - 60y_1 + 1.80x_2 - 200y_2 + 2.20x_3 - 100y_3$$

subject to:

$$
\begin{array}{rcl}
3x_1 + 4x_2 + 8x_3 & \leq & 2{,}000 \\
3x_1 + 5x_2 + 6x_3 & \leq & 2{,}000 \\
2x_1 + 3x_2 + 9x_3 & \leq & 2{,}000 \\
x_1 - 300y_1 & \leq & 0 \\
x_2 - 200y_2 & \leq & 0 \\
x_3 - 50y_3 & \leq & 0
\end{array}
$$

Our spreadsheet model uses just three columns (one for each product family), where the corresponding pairs of x and y variables appear in the same column. In this spreadsheet, the linking constraints for each x-y pair appear in the corresponding column, as shown in Figure 8.38. For example, the formula in cell C16 is C5 – C6*C15, and this value is constrained to be negative or zero. We invoke Solver and specify:

Target cell: F9 (maximize)
Changing cells: C5:E6
Constraints: F11:F13 <= H11:H13
          C16:E16 <= 0

The optimal solution achieves a net profit of $460,000. In order to attain this level of profits, the company must eliminate production of product family F3 and produce families F1 and F2 up to their respective ceilings. In other words, the integer programming model detects that family F3 does not pay its way, and the company would be better off not producing and selling that family at all.

Threshold Levels

Sometimes, we encounter situations where, in order to do business, we are required to participate at a specified minimum level. For example, in manufacturing, a setup is sufficiently disruptive that the line would be set up to assemble a batch of motors only if we're making a dozen of them, not merely one or two. As another example, in purchasing, we might be able to qualify for a discounted price if we buy in quantity. These examples illustrate a **threshold level requirement:** a decision variable is either at least as large as a specified minimum, or else it is zero.

The existence of a threshold level does not directly affect the objective function of a model, and it can be represented in the constraints with the help of binary variables. Suppose we have a variable x that is subject to a threshold requirement. Let m denote the minimum feasible value of x if it is nonzero. Then we can capture this structure in an integer programming model by including the following pair of constraints:

$$x - my >= 0$$
$$x - My <= 0$$

where, as before, M is a large number that is greater than or equal to any value x could feasibly take. To see how these two requirements work, consider the two possibilities for the binary variable. When $y = 1$, the constraints reduce to $m <= x <= M$, so that x is forced to be at or above the threshold level. When $y = 0$, the constraints reduce to $x = 0$. Thus, the pair x and y will behave consistently.

For example, in the Mayhugh example, we might want to require that product family 1 have a production threshold of at least 100 units. Since the model already includes the fixed cost constraint $x - 300y <= 0$, we need only to add the threshold constraint $x - 100y >= 0$, and the search will be restricted to production values between 100 and 300, or zero.

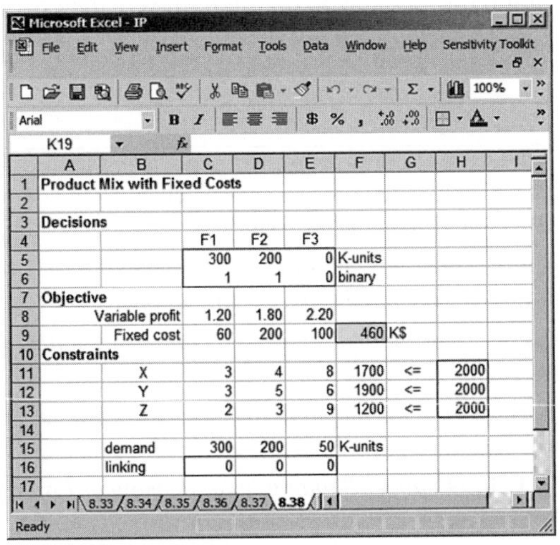

FIGURE 8.38
Alternative Layout for
the Product Mix Problem,
with Fixed Costs

IP.xls

	A	B	C	D	E	F	G	H	I
1	Product Mix with Fixed Costs								
2									
3	Decisions								
4			F1	F2	F3				
5			300	200	0	K-units			
6			1	1	0	binary			
7	Objective								
8		Variable profit	1.20	1.80	2.20				
9		Fixed cost	60	200	100	460	K$		
10	Constraints								
11		X	3	4	8	1700	<=	2000	
12		Y	3	5	6	1900	<=	2000	
13		Z	2	3	9	1200	<=	2000	
14									
15		demand	300	200	50	K-units			
16		linking	0	0	0				
17									

SUMMARY

We introduced optimization in Chapter 6 as one phase in a general analytic procedure for spreadsheet models. Optimization answers the question, "What's the best we can do?" or, "What values of the decision variables lead to the best possible value of the objective?" In a sense, optimization is simply a sophisticated tool for performing what-if analysis.

In Excel, optimization is carried out using Solver. Solver is actually a collection of optimization procedures—one for linear programs, another for (linear) integer programs, and yet another for nonlinear programs. (There is an additional procedure, the Evolutionary Solver, which is suited to nonlinear optimization problems that have discontinuities. However, the principles behind this algorithm are beyond the scope of our coverage.)

To develop facility with Solver, it helps to practice formulating, solving, and interpreting optimization problems. Formulation and layout for optimization require some additional considerations that tend not to arise in simpler kinds of modeling, and we mentioned a number of principles that bear repeating. These are guidelines for the model builder and, in our experience, the craft skills exhibited by experts:

- Follow a standard form whenever possible.
- Enter cell references in the Solver windows; keep numerical values in cells.
- Use a linear model in preference to a nonlinear model.
- Use the weak form of a constraint and give the model maximum flexibility.
- Explore some feasible (and infeasible) possibilities as a way of debugging the model.
- Test intuition and suggest hypotheses before running Solver.
- Identify the patterns of economic priorities that appear in the solution.

Along with the technical information that we have covered, these guidelines provide help in learning how to implement optimization analyses in spreadsheet models.

While optimization is a powerful technique, we should not assume that a solution that is optimal for a model is also optimal for the real world. Since every model is a simplification, any optimal solution from a model must be interpreted before it can be applied in the real world. Often, the realities of the real world will force changes in the optimal solution as determined by the model. One powerful method for making this translation is to look for the pattern, or the economic priorities, in the optimal solution. These economic priorities are often more valuable to decision makers than the precise solution to a particular instance of the model.

SUGGESTED READINGS

Some advanced perspectives on optimization techniques, along with some guidance in constructing optimization models, can be found in the following books:

Fourer, Robert, David F. Gay, and Brian W. Kernighan. 1993. *AMPL: A Modeling Language for Mathematical Programming.* South San Francisco, CA: Scientific Press.

Rardin, Ronald L. 1998. *Optimization in Operations Research.* Upper Saddle River, NJ: Prentice–Hall.

Schrage, Linus. 1997. *Optimization Modeling with LINDO,* 5th ed. Pacific Grove, CA: Duxbury Press.

Williams, H. P. 1999. *Model Building in Mathematical Programming,* 3rd ed. Chichester: John Wiley.

EXERCISES

1. *Cost Modeling.* General Widget Corporation has collected data on the daily output and daily production cost of widgets produced at its factory. (Data for the study are shown in the table below.) The company believes that daily output (DO) and daily production cost (PC) ought to be linearly related. Thus, for some numbers a and b:

   $PC = a + b*DO$

	Output	Production Cost
Day 1	5,045	2,542
Day 2	6,127	2,812
Day 3	6,360	2,776
Day 4	6,645	3,164
Day 5	7,220	4,102
Day 6	9,537	4,734
Day 7	9,895	4,238
Day 8	10,175	4,524
Day 9	10,334	4,869
Day 10	10,855	4,421

   Questions

   a. Build a least squares model to estimate the parameters a and b in the linear relationship. In other words, minimize the sum of squared differences between the model's predicted values and the observations. Find the best values of the parameters a and b for this criterion and give the minimum value of the objective function. (Verify your results by using Excel's Regression tool.)

   b. Suppose instead that a better criterion is thought to be minimizing the sum of absolute deviations between the model's predicted values and the observations. Find the best values of the parameters a and b for this criterion and give the minimum value of the objective function.

   c. Suppose instead that a better model than the linear model is thought to be the power function

   $$PC = a(DO)^b$$

   Using the sum of absolute deviations (as in the previous part), find the values of a and b that provide the best fit and give the minimum value of the objective function.

2. *Profit Maximization with Demand Curves.* Campbell Motors is an auto dealership that specializes in the sales of station wagons and light trucks. Due to its reputation for quality and service, Campbell has a strong position in the regional market, but demand remains somewhat sensitive to price. While evaluating the new models, Campbell's marketing consultant has come up with the following demand curves in which prices are expressed in thousands of dollars:

   $$\text{Truck Demand} = 500 - 18 \text{ (Truck Price)}$$

   $$\text{Wagon Demand} = 400 - 11 \text{ (Wagon Price)}$$

   The dealership's unit costs are \$20,000 for trucks and \$25,000 for wagons. Each truck requires three hours of prep labor, and each wagon requires two hours of prep labor. The current staff can supply 250 hours of labor.

   Question

   Determine prices at which Campbell Motors can maximize the profit it generates from sales of trucks and wagons. (Allow fractional demands.)

3. *Allocation.* A regional beer distributor has \$100,000 to spend on advertising in four markets, where each market responds differently to advertising. Based on observations of the market's response to several advertising initiatives, the distributor has estimated the sales response by fitting a power curve $R = ax^b$, where R represents sales revenue, and x represents advertising dollars, both measured in thousands. The estimated curves are shown in the table below:

Market	Sales Revenue
Domestic	$100x^{0.4}$
Premium	$80x^{0.5}$
Light	$120x^{0.3}$
Microbrew	$60x^{0.6}$

Question

Determine how the advertising dollars can be allocated to the four markets so that the sales revenue for the distributor is maximized.

4. *Selecting an Advertising Budget.* A well-known charity is interested in conducting a television campaign to solicit contributions. The campaign will be conducted in two metropolitan areas. Past experience indicates that, in each city, the total contributions are a function of the amount of money expended for TV advertisements. Specifically, the charity has estimated response functions that indicate the percentage of the population making a donation as a function of the dollars spent on TV advertising. The form of this function is $y = 1 - \text{EXP}(-\alpha x)$, where x represents the advertising expenditure (in thousands of dollars), y represents the fraction donating, and α is a parameter that differs from city to city. The charity has earmarked a fund of $400,000 for advertising between the two cities and wants to determine the best allocation of these funds.

	City 1	City 2
Response parameter	$\alpha = 0.006$	$\alpha = 0.004$
Population	750,000	600,000
Average donation per donor	$2.00	$1.50

Questions

a. Suppose the charity decides to maximize total donations, given its budget limit on advertising. How should advertising funds be spent, and what amount will be raised in donations as a result?

b. Is the budget binding in the solution of (a)? If so, how much additional budget would the charity like to obtain? If not, how much of the budget should actually be spent?

5. *Planning Automobile Production.* The Auto Company of America (ACA) produces four types of cars: subcompact, compact, intermediate, and luxury. ACA also produces trucks and vans. Vendor capacities limit total production capacity to, at most, 1.2 million vehicles per year. Subcompacts and compacts are built together in a facility with a total annual capacity of 620,000 cars. Intermediate and luxury cars are produced in another facility with capacity of 400,000; and the truck/van facility has a capacity of 275,000. ACA's marketing strategy requires that subcompacts and compacts must constitute at least half of the product mix for the four car types. The Corporate Average Fuel Economy (CAFE) standards in the Energy Policy and Conservation Act require an average fleet fuel economy of at least 27 mpg.

Profit margins, market potential, and fuel efficiencies are summarized below:

Type	Profit Margin ($/vehicle)	Market Potential (sales in '000)	Fuel Economy (mpg)
Subcompact	150	600	40
Compact	225	400	34
Intermediate	250	300	15
Luxury	500	225	12
Truck	400	325	20
Van	200	100	25

Questions

a. What is the optimal profit for ACA?

b. What is the pattern in the optimal allocation?

c. How much would annual profit drop if the fuel economy requirement were raised to 28 mpg?

6. *Distributing Coal.* The Calcio Coal Company produces coal at three mines and ships it to four customers. The cost per ton of producing coal, the ash and sulfur content of the coal, and the production capacity (in tons) for each mine are given in Table A. The number of tons of coal demanded by each customer is given in Table B. The cost (in dollars) of shipping a ton of coal from a mine to each customer is given in Table C. The total amount of coal shipped to each customer must contain, at most, 5 percent ash and, at most, 3.75 percent sulfur. Calcio wishes to minimize the cost of meeting customer demands.

Table A

	Production Cost	Capacity (tons)	Ash Content	Sulfur Content
Mine 1	$50	120	8%	5%
Mine 2	$55	100	6%	4%
Mine 3	$62	140	4%	3%

Table B

	Customer 1	Customer 2	Customer 3	Customer 4
Demand (tons)	80	70	60	40

Table C
Cost of Shipping 1 Ton

	Customer 1	Customer 2	Customer 3	Customer 4
Mine 1	4	6	8	12
Mine 2	9	6	7	11
Mine 3	8	12	3	5

Questions

a. Suppose that Calcio were to ignore the ash- and sulfur-content requirements. What would be the minimum cost?

b. Now suppose the ash- and sulfur-content requirements must be met. How much of an increase do these requirements add to the company's total cost?

7. *Make or Buy.* A sudden increase in the demand for smoke detectors has left Acme Alarms with insufficient capacity to meet demand. The company has seen monthly demand from its retailers for its electronic and battery-operated detectors rise to 20,000 and 10,000, respectively. Acme's production process involves three departments: fabrication, assembly, and shipping. The relevant quantitative data on production and prices are summarized below:

Department	Monthly Hours Available	Hours/Unit (Electronic)	Hours/Unit (Battery)
Fabrication	2,000	0.15	0.10
Assembly	4,200	0.20	0.20
Shipping	2,500	0.10	0.15
Variable cost/unit		$18.80	$16.00
Retail price		$29.50	$28.00

The company also has the option to obtain additional units from a subcontractor, who has offered to supply up to 20,000 units per month in any combination of electric and battery-operated models, at a charge of $21.50 per unit. For this price, the subcontractor will test and ship its models directly to the retailers without using Acme's production process.

Questions

a. What are the maximum profit and the corresponding make/buy levels? (This is a planning model; fractional decisions are acceptable.)

b. Describe the qualitative pattern in the solution.

c. Use the pattern in (b) to trace the effects of increasing the fabrication capacity by 10 percent. How will the optimal make/buy mix change? How will the optimal profit change?

d. For how much of a change in fabrication capacity will the pattern persist?

8. *Leasing Warehouse Space.* Cox Cable Company needs to lease warehouse storage space for five months at the start of the year. Cox knows how much space will be required in each month, and the company can purchase a variety of lease contracts to meet these needs. For example, Cox can purchase one-month leases in each month from January to May. The company can also purchase two-month leases in January through April, three-month leases in January through March, four-month leases in January and February, or a five-month lease in January. In total, there are fifteen possible leases the company could use. Cox must decide which leases to purchase and how many square feet to purchase on each lease.

Since the space requirements differ month to month, it may be economical to lease only the amount needed each month on a month-by-month basis. On the other hand, the monthly cost for leasing space for additional months is much less than for the first month, so it may be desirable to lease the maximum amount needed for the entire five months. Another option is the intermediate approach of changing the total amount of space leased (by adding a new lease and/or having an old lease expire) at least once, but not every month. Two or more leases for different terms can begin at the same time.

The space requirements (in square feet) and the leasing costs (in dollars per thousand square feet) are given in the two tables below:

Month	Space Requirements	Lease Length	Lease Cost
January	15,000	1 month	$280
February	10,000	2	450
March	20,000	3	600
April	5,000	4	730
May	25,000	5	820

The task is to find a leasing schedule that provides the necessary amounts of space at the minimum cost.

Questions

a. Determine the optimal leasing schedule. What is the optimal total cost and the corresponding schedule?

b. Describe the qualitative pattern in the solution.

c. Use the pattern in (b) to trace the effects of increasing the space required for January. How will the leasing schedule change? How will the total cost change?

d. For how much of a change in January's requirement will the pattern persist?

9. *Oil Blending.* An oil company produces three brands of oils: Regular, Multigrade, and Supreme. Each brand of oil is composed of one or more of four crude stocks, each having a different viscosity index. The relevant data concerning the crude stocks are:

Crude Stock	Viscosity Index	Cost ($/barrel)	Supply per Day (barrels)
1	20	7.10	1,000
2	40	8.50	1,100
3	30	7.70	1,200
4	55	9.00	1,100

Each brand of oil must meet a minimum standard for viscosity index, and each brand thus sells at a different price. The relevant data concerning the three brands of oil are:

Brand	Minimum Viscosity Index	Selling Price ($/barrel)	Daily Demand (barrels)
Regular	25	8.50	2,000
Multigrade	35	9.00	1,500
Supreme	50	10.00	750

Questions

Determine an optimal production plan for a single day, assuming that all oil produced during this day can be either sold or stored at negligible cost. This exercise is subject to alternative interpretations. Investigate the following:

a. The daily demands represent potential sales. In other words, the model should contain demand ceilings (upper limits). What is the optimal profit?

b. The daily demands are to be met precisely. In other words, the model should contain demand constraints in the form of equalities. What is the optimal profit?

c. The daily demands represent minimum sales commitments, but all output can be sold. In other words, the model should permit production to exceed daily demand. What is the optimal profit?

10. *Coffee Blending and Sales.* Hill-O-Beans Coffee Company blends four component beans into three final blends of coffee: one is sold to luxury hotels, another to restaurants, and the third to supermarkets for store label brands. The company has four reliable bean supplies: Robusta, Javan Arabica, Liberica, and Brazilian Arabica. The table below summarizes the very precise recipes for the final coffee blends, the cost and availability information for the four components, and the wholesale price per pound of the final blends. The percentages indicate the fraction of each component to be used in each blend.

Component	Hotel	Restaurant	Market	Cost per Pound	Max Weekly Availability (lbs)
Robusta	20%	35%	10%	$0.60	40,000
Javan Arabica	40%	15%	35%	$0.80	25,000
Liberica	15%	20%	40%	$0.55	20,000
Brazilian Arabica	25%	30%	15%	$0.70	45,000
Wholesale Price					
Per Pound	$1.25	$1.50	$1.40		

The processor's plant can handle no more than 100,000 pounds per week, and Hill-O-Beans would like to operate at capacity. There is no problem in selling the final blends, although the marketing department requires minimum production levels of 10,000, 25,000, and 30,000 pounds, respectively, for the hotel, restaurant, and market blends.

Questions

a. In order to maximize weekly profit, how many pounds of each component should be purchased?

b. What is the economic value of an additional pound's worth of plant capacity?

c. How much (per pound) should Hill-O-Beans be willing to pay for additional pounds of Liberica in order to raise total profit?

d. Construct a graph to show how the optimal profit varies with the minimum weekly production level of the hotel blend.

e. Construct a graph to show how the optimal profit varies with the unit cost of Robusta beans.

11. *Distributing a Product.* The Lannon Lock Company manufactures a commercial security lock at plants in Atlanta, Louisville, Detroit, and Phoenix. The unit cost of production at each plant is $35.50, $37.50, $37.25, and $36.25, respectively; the annual capacities are 18,000, 15,000, 25,000, and 20,000, respectively. The locks are sold through wholesale distributors in seven locations around the country. The unit shipping cost for each plant-distributor combination is shown in the following table, along with the demand forecast from each distributor for the coming year:

	Tacoma	San Diego	Dallas	Denver	St. Louis	Tampa	Baltimore
Atlanta	2.50	2.75	1.75	2.00	2.10	1.80	1.65
Louisville	1.85	1.90	1.50	1.60	1.00	1.90	1.85
Detroit	2.30	2.25	1.85	1.25	1.50	2.25	2.00
Phoenix	1.90	0.90	1.60	1.75	2.00	2.50	2.65
Demand	5,500	11,500	10,500	9,600	15,400	12,500	6,600

Questions

a. Determine the least costly way of shipping locks from plants to distributors.

b. Suppose that the unit cost at each plant were $10 higher than the original figure. What change in the optimal distribution plan would result? What general conclusions can you draw for transportation models with nonidentical plant related costs?

12. *Planning Investments.* Your uncle has $90,000 that he wishes to invest now in order to use the accumulation for purchasing a retirement annuity in five years. After consulting with his financial adviser, he has been offered four types of fixed income investments, labeled as investments A, B, C, and D.

Investments A and B are available at the beginning of each of the next five years (call them years 1 to 5). Each dollar invested in A at the beginning of a year returns $1.20 (a profit of $0.20) two years later, in time for immediate reinvestment. Each dollar invested in B at the beginning of a year returns $1.36 three years later.

Investments C and D will each be available at one time in the future. Each dollar invested in C at the beginning of year 2 returns $1.66 at the end of year 5. Each dollar invested in D at the beginning of year 5 returns $1.12 at the end of year 5.

Your uncle is obligated to make a balloon payment on an existing loan, in the amount of $24,000, at the end of year 3. He wants to make that payment out of his investment account.

Questions

a. Devise for your uncle an investment plan that maximizes the amount of money that can be accumulated at the end of five years. How much money will be available for the annuity in five years?

b. Describe the pattern in the optimal plan.

13. *Gulfport Oil Case.* Review the network diagram generated for this case in conjunction with the corresponding exercise in Chapter 4.

Questions

a. Find the optimal flows (i.e., optimal decisions) for this problem.

b. What is the optimal total cost?

14. *Coastal Refining Case.* Review the network diagram generated for this case in conjunction with the corresponding exercise in Chapter 4.

Questions

a. Find the optimal flows (i.e., optimal decisions) for this problem.

b. What is the optimal total cost?

15. *Quincy Chocolate Case.* Review the network diagram generated for this case in conjunction with the corresponding exercises in Chapter 4.

Questions

a. Find the optimal flows (i.e., optimal decisions) for this problem.

b. What is the optimal total cost?

16. *Workforce Management Case.* Review the network diagram generated for this case in conjunction with the corresponding exercises in Chapter 4.

Questions

a. Find the optimal flows (i.e., optimal decisions) for this problem.

b. What is the optimal total cost?

17. *Cargo Loading.* You are in charge of loading cargo ships for International Cargo Company (ICC) at a major East Coast port. You have been asked to prepare a loading plan for an ICC freighter bound for Africa. An agricultural commodities dealer would like to transport the following products aboard this ship:

Commodity	Tons Available	Volume per Ton (cu. ft.)	Profit per Ton ($)
1	4,000	40	70
2	3,000	25	50
3	2,000	60	60
4	1,000	50	80

You can elect to load any or all of the available commodities. However, the ship has three cargo holds with the following capacity restrictions:

Cargo Hold	Weight Capacity (tons)	Volume Capacity (cu. ft.)
Forward	3,000	100,000
Center	5,000	150,000
Rear	2,000	120,000

More than one type of commodity can be placed in the same cargo hold. However, because of balance considerations, the weight in the forward cargo hold must be within 10 percent of the weight in the rear cargo hold, and the center cargo hold must be between 40 percent and 60 percent of the total weight on board.

Questions

a. Determine a profit-maximizing loading plan for the commodities. What is the maximum profit and the loading plan that achieves it?

b. Suppose each one of the cargo holds could be expanded. Which holds and which forms of expansion (weight or volume) would allow ICC to increase its profits on this trip, and what is the marginal value of each form of expansion?

18. *Optimizing Product Mix.* California Products Company has the capability of producing and selling three products. Each product has an annual demand potential (at current pricing and promotion levels), a variable contribution, and an annual fixed cost. The fixed cost can be avoided if the product is not produced at all. This information is summarized below:

Product	Demand	Contribution	Fixed Cost
I	290,000	$1.20	$60,000
J	200,000	1.80	200,000
K	50,000	2.30	55,000

Each product requires work on three machines. The standard productivities and capacities are given below:

Hours per 1,000 Units

Machine	Product I	Product J	Product K	Hours Available
A	3.205	3.846	7.692	1,900
B	2.747	4.808	6.410	1,900
C	1.923	3.205	9.615	1,900

Questions

a. Determine which products should be produced, and how much of each should be produced, in order to maximize profit contribution from these operations.

b. Suppose the demand potential for product K were doubled. What would be the maximum profit contribution?

19. *Vendor Allocation with Price Breaks.* Universal Technologies, Inc. has identified two qualified vendors with the capability to supply certain of its electronic components. For the coming year, Universal has estimated its volume requirements for these components and has obtained price break schedules from each vendor. (These are summarized as "all-units" price discounts in the table below.) Universal's engineers have also estimated each vendor's maximum capacity for producing these components, on the basis of available information about equipment in use and labor policies in effect. Finally, because of its limited history with vendor A, Universal has adopted a policy that permits no more than 60 percent of its total unit purchases on these components to come from vendor A. Find the minimum cost purchase plan for Universal.

		Vendor A		Vendor B	
Product	Requirement	Unit Price	Volume Required	Unit Price	Volume Required
1	500	$225	0–250	$224	0–300
		$220	250–500	$214	300–500
2	1,000	$124	0–600	$120	0–1,000
		$115	600–1,000	(no discount)	
3	2,500	$ 60	0–1000	$ 54	0–1,500
		$ 56*	1,000–2,000	$ 52	1,500–2,500
		$ 51	2,000–2,500		
Total Capacity (Units)		2,800		2,400	

*For example, if 1,400 units are purchased from vendor A, they cost $56 each, for a total of $78,400.

20. *Vendor Allocation with an Incremental Quantity Discount.* In the previous problem, suppose that vendor A provides a new price discount schedule for component 3. This one is an "incremental" discount, as opposed to an "all-units" discount, as follows:

> Unit price = $60 on all units up to 1,000
> Unit price = $56 on the next 1,000 units
> Unit price = $51 on the next 500 units

Question

What is the impact on the optimal purchase plan and its cost?

21. *Plant Location.* The Spencer Shoe Company manufactures a line of inexpensive shoes in one plant in Pontiac and distributes to five main distribution centers (Milwaukee, Dayton, Cincinnati, Buffalo, and Atlanta) from which the shoes are shipped to retail shoe stores. Distribution costs include freight, handling, and warehousing costs. To meet increased demand, the company has decided to build at least one new plant with a capacity of 40,000 pairs per

week. Surveys have narrowed the choice to three locations: Cincinnati, Dayton, and Atlanta. As expected, production costs would be low in the Atlanta plant, but distribution costs are relatively high compared to the other two locations. Other data are as follows:

Distribution Costs per Pair

To Distribution Centers	From Pontiac	Cincinnati	Dayton	Atlanta	Demand (pairs/wk)
Milwaukee	$0.42	$0.46	$0.44	$0.48	10,000
Dayton	0.36	0.37	0.30	0.45	15,000
Cincinnati	0.41	0.30	0.37	0.43	16,000
Buffalo	0.39	0.42	0.38	0.46	19,000
Atlanta	0.50	0.43	0.45	0.27	12,000
Capacity (pairs/wk.)	27,000	40,000	40,000	40,000	
Production cost/pair	$2.70	$2.64	$2.69	$2.62	
Fixed cost /wk.	$7,000	$4,000	$6,000	$7,000	

Questions

a. Determine for Spencer Shoe the plant locations that will minimize total costs, including production, distribution, and fixed costs. Which locations are optimal, assuming that the Pontiac plant has no resale value and must remain open?

b. Determine the optimal locations, assuming that the Pontiac plant could be closed at zero net cost.

APPENDIX 8.1. THE SOLVER SENSITIVITY REPORT

The Solver Sensitivity tool duplicates for optimization models the functionality of the Data Sensitivity tool for basic spreadsheet models. That parallelism makes Solver Sensitivity the vehicle of choice for most of the sensitivity analyses we might want to perform with optimization models. However, it is sometimes useful to draw on Excel's own sensitivity tool. The Sensitivity Report is one of three reports offered after a Solver run, once the optimal solution has been found. The other two reports are completely superfluous if a model has been constructed effectively, but the Sensitivity Report sometimes provides additional insight or efficiency.

To provide access to the Sensitivity Report, we must uncheck the box for Bypass Solver Reports in the Solver Options menu. After the optimal solution has been produced, we highlight Sensitivity in the Reports list on the Solver Results window. The Sensitivity Report for linear programs has two sections. The top section (titled Adjustable Cells) deals with the objective function and, in particular, with the coefficients in the objective function corresponding to each of the decision variables. The bottom section (titled Constraints) deals with the values of the constants on the right-hand sides. Figure 8A.1 shows the Sensitivity Report for the Veerman Furniture (allocation) example.

In the top section, the report provides the values of the decision variables in the optimal solution (under Final Value) and the values of the coefficients in the objective function (under Objective Coefficient). The Allowable Increase and Allowable Decrease show how much we could change any one of the objective function coefficients without altering the optimal product mix—that is, without altering any of the decision variables. For example, the objective function coefficient for desks is $24 in the base case. This figure could rise to $54.00 or drop to $22.50 without having an impact on the optimal product mix. (Of course, the optimal profit would change, because the number of desks remains fixed.) A similar range is provided for the other two variables, with 1E+30 symbolizing infinity in the

FIGURE 8A.1
Sensitivity Report for the
Allocation Example

LP.xls

Microsoft Excel 10.0 Sensitivity Report
Worksheet: [LP.xls]8.18

Adjustable Cells

Cell	Name	Final Value	Reduced Cost	Objective Coefficient	Allowable Increase	Allowable Decrease
$B$5	Product mix C	0	-1	15	1	1E+30
$C$5	Product mix D	275	0	24	30	1.5
$D$5	Product mix T	100	0	18	1E+30	10

Constraints

Cell	Name	Final Value	Shadow Price	Constraint R.H. Side	Allowable Increase	Allowable Decrease
$E$12	Fabrication LHS	1850	4	1850	150	1650
$E$13	Assembly LHS	2075	0	2400	1E+30	325
$E$14	Distribution LHS	950	0	1500	1E+30	550
$E$15	Chair market LHS	0	0	360	1E+30	360
$E$16	Desk market LHS	275	0	300	1E+30	25
$E$17	Table market LHS	100	10	100	60.9375	75

report's output. Finally, there is a column labeled Reduced Cost. Entries in this column are zero for variables that are not at their bound (in this case, the bound is zero). For chairs, the reduced cost of –1 reflects the fact that the objective function coefficient of $15 would have to improve by more than $1 before there would be an incentive to use chairs in the optimal mix. However, this same information is available in the Allowable Increase column for chairs. In most cases, the Reduced Cost information in the report is redundant.

In the bottom section, the report provides the values of the constraint left-hand sides (under Final Value) and the right-hand side constraint constants (under Constraint R.H. Side), along with the shadow price for each constraint. The Allowable Increase and Allowable Decrease show how much we could change any one of the constraint constants without altering any of the shadow prices. For example, the number of Fabrication hours (1,850 in the base case) could change from 200 to 2,000 without affecting the shadow price of $4.00.

The ranging analysis for right-hand side constraint constants is omitted for constraints that involve a simple lower bound or upper bound. That is, if the form of the constraint is Variable <= Ceiling or else Variable >= Floor, then the sensitivity analysis will not appear. On the other hand, if the same information is incorporated into the model using the standard SUMPRODUCT constraint form, as in the case of the product mix model, then the Sensitivity Report will treat the constraint in its usual fashion and include it in the Constraints table. As an example, consider the modified version of the Dahlby Outfitters (covering) example, with a floor of 0.15 for each of the decision variables. Although there are four original constraints and five additional constraints limiting the decision variables to values no less than 0.15, the Sensitivity Report shows information for only the four original constraints (see Figure 8A.2).

Compared to the Solver Sensitivity output, the Sensitivity Report is more precise but less flexible. The Sensitivity Report is more precise than Solver Sensitivity with respect to the question of where the decision variables change or where a shadow price changes. Recall in our allocation example that we could not tell precisely when the shadow price drops from $3.75 to $2.32. Only by searching on a smaller grid could we detect where the change takes place, and even that would require some careful interpolation in the table to obtain the exact value. By contrast, if we were to solve a base-case model in which there were 2,200 Fabrication hours, and if we asked for the Sensitivity Report, we would be able to see from the Allowable Increase on Fabrication hours that the shadow price holds up to 2,666.67 hours.

FIGURE 8A.2
Sensitivity Report for the
Covering Example

LP.xls

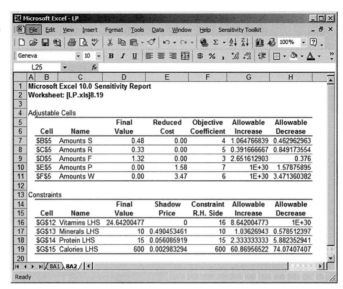

The Sensitivity Report is less flexible than Solver Sensitivity output with respect to the user's ability to tailor the analysis. The Sensitivity Report cannot "see" beyond the Allowable Increase or the Allowable Decrease. However, a coarse grid search using Solver Sensitivity can show changes beyond these ranges. In addition, Solver Sensitivity can track the effect of varying a parameter on any cells in the spreadsheet. The Sensitivity Report, by contrast, does not tell us explicitly how the objective function changes when we vary one of the objective function coefficients, nor does it tell us how the decision variables change when we vary one of the constraint constants. Solver Sensitivity can even track the effect of varying a parameter that is not, strictly speaking, within the model itself. For example, suppose there were several constraint constants that represented capacities, and that these capacities could all be increased by a common percentage. Solver Sensitivity could be set up to track the decision variables and the objective function as functions of this percentage.

In addition, Solver Sensitivity can perform two-way analyses, in the same spirit as the two-way analysis in the Data Table tool. When we also consider the user's ability to tailor the analysis, something that is lacking in the Sensitivity Report, we conclude that the Solver Sensitivity is the more valuable way of doing sensitivity analysis, in spite of the loss in precision.

CHAPTER 9

SIMULATION

INTRODUCTION

Change and uncertainty are ubiquitous features of the business world. The effective business analyst and model builder, whose work always involves planning for an uncertain future, must therefore have tools for dealing with these aspects of business life. **Simulation,** the topic of this chapter, is an essential tool for modeling situations involving uncertainty.

In previous chapters, we generally assumed that the parameters and relationships in our models were known with certainty. We did not entirely ignore uncertainty, but we dealt with it as a secondary feature of the situation, perhaps using what-if analysis or scenario analysis to explore how our model results would change if our assumptions changed. There are situations, however, in which uncertainty is a central, unavoidable feature of the problem, so that if we ignore it, our analysis is sure to be flawed. In this chapter, we provide methods to help recognize and address situations in which uncertainty is a key factor.

The Advertising Budget example provides a good illustration of the role uncertainty can play in spreadsheet modeling. When we introduced this problem in Chapter 5, we took it for granted that the price would be $40 and the cost $25, yet future prices and costs are seldom what we expect. Nevertheless, the first step in most modeling efforts involves building a prototype that ignores the uncertainties in the situation, at least temporarily. Sometimes, the parameter values chosen at this stage of the analysis represent the most likely values, or perhaps average values. In a first model, the uncertainty is often not even recognized. Using the given parameters for price and cost, we determined that profits of $71,447 were attainable with the optimal advertising expenditures. But if price and cost were uncertain and could take on values different from those we had assumed, we would want to know how much the resulting profit could vary. In particular, we might be interested in the average profit for a range of possible prices and costs. In addition, we might wish to determine how likely it is that we will lose money through an unfortunate combination of low price and high cost. These are typical of the questions that can be answered using simulation.

The automobile-leasing decision described in Chapter 4 provides another instance of a situation in which uncertainty is a central factor. The challenge for a leasing company is to choose the price at which a customer can purchase the car at the end of the lease. This price is called the contract residual value. If it is set too high, a large proportion of lease customers will return their vehicles at the end of the lease. Leasing companies typically take losses when they must sell large numbers of returned vehicles on the used market. On the other hand, if the residual value is set too low, the monthly payments for the lease will not be competitive. If the leasing company could know the value of used cars three years out, it would have little trouble in setting contract residual values to avoid losses. It is only because these future values are uncertain that the decision makers must consider the implications of forecast error. It would be shortsighted to assume that the best policy is to set contract residual values equal to the forecast of used car prices. But setting the contract residual value above or below the forecast of the used car price is a decision that can be reached systematically only through an analysis that recognizes uncertainty.

We describe how to analyze uncertainty in spreadsheet models using a technique known as **Monte Carlo simulation.** To do this, we use the Excel add-in **Crystal Ball.** (This software is provided on the CD that accompanies this book.) In a nutshell, simulation can describe not only what the **outcomes** of a given decision could be, but also the **probabilities** with which these outcomes will occur. In fact, the result of a simulation is the entire probability distribution of outcomes. In a sense, simulation is an advanced form of sensitivity analysis in which we attach a probability to each possible outcome. We are often concerned primarily with the average outcome, which is one way of summarizing the distribution of all possible outcomes. For example, we might wish to determine average profit in the Advertising Budget example or the auto-leasing case. In addition, we often wish to determine the probability of certain critical events occurring, such as the probability of negative profits in the Advertising Budget example, or the probability of residual losses in the auto-leasing case. Both kinds of analyses can be carried out using simulation.

We assume that the reader is familiar with the basic concepts of probability, since these are essential to analyzing situations involving uncertainty. The relevant concepts are reviewed in Appendix A, which covers probability distributions (discrete and continuous), cumulative distribution functions, expected values, tail probabilities, variability, and sampling theory.

Decision trees provide a simple means for analyzing decisions with uncertainty and risk. We discussed in Chapter 4 how to construct decision trees and how to determine the expected outcome and the probability distribution of outcomes given a choice of actions. Simulation provides a more general approach to similar problems. Simulation is the tool of choice when there are a large number of uncertainties, especially when these are represented by continuous distributions. Simulation is also a practical method when the underlying model is complex, as we illustrate later. However, it is important to realize that, just as with decision trees, the result of a simulation is a **probability distribution** of the outcome or outcomes of interest. Analyzing these distributions and extracting managerial insights is an important part of the art of simulation.

We begin this chapter with a demonstration of the steps involved in a simulation analysis, using the Advertising Budget example we have used throughout the book. We follow this with several additional applications, to show how simulation is used in other contexts. We then systematically treat each of the steps in a simulation study: selecting uncertain parameters, choosing probability distributions, ensuring appropriate precision in the outcomes, and interpreting outcome distributions. Finally, we address the topic of optimization in simulation: how to determine the optimal values of decision variables when simulation must be used to measure the value of the objective. We also provide two appendixes that describe details of using Crystal Ball. Appendix 9.1 covers Crystal Ball settings for running simulations, while Appendix 9.2 describes advanced features of Crystal Ball.

THE SIMULATION-MODELING PROCESS

In this section, we first illustrate the process of carrying out a simulation analysis using the Advertising Budget example. Then, we recapitulate the process more formally to provide a structured approach for simulation modeling. (If you have not already done so, install Crystal Ball at this time from the CD that accompanies this book. Note that Crystal Ball adds three options to the Excel menu bar: Cell, Run, and CBTools.)

In Chapter 8, we established that the optimal profit in the Advertising Budget example using the base-case inputs was $71,447. Of course, this result assumes that the input parameters are accurate forecasts of next year's values. In reality, next year's market price is subject to considerable uncertainty. The **expected value** of the price may be $40, but it could turn out to be as low as $30 or as high as $50. Given this uncertainty, what is our

expected profit? And what are the **risks** of implementing the advertising allocation we previously found to be optimal? In particular, what are the chances that we could actually lose money next year? We next explore how simulation can answer these two common questions: What are the expected results, and What are the corresponding risks?

We begin with a version of our spreadsheet in which the quarterly advertising decision variables are already set to their optimal levels, as shown in Figure 9.1. Our first task is to replace the price parameter in cell C7 with a probability distribution. We place the cursor on C7 and select Cell→Define Assumption. (An input that is described by a probability distribution is called an **Assumption cell** in Crystal Ball.) The Distribution Gallery window appears, displaying a number of probability distributions. To reflect our assumption that any value between $30 and $50 is equally likely, we choose a uniform distribution. (In a later section, we discuss how to choose an appropriate probability distribution.) We click on Uniform Distribution and enter 30 for the minimum and 50 for the maximum. After we select Enter, the distribution changes shape to reflect the parameters that we entered. Finally, we select OK to return to the spreadsheet. Cell C7 changes color to indicate that it has become an Assumption cell; that is, it is now determined by a probability distribution.

The next step in setting up a simulation is to choose the output cell. Total profit is the best measure of the results of our advertising plan, so we select cell C21 as the output cell. (An outcome we wish to describe is called a **Forecast cell** in Crystal Ball.) We place the cursor on C21 and select Cell→Define Forecast. The Forecast Name should be Profit, and we can, as an option, specify Dollars for the Units. Cell C21 changes color to indicate that it has become a Forecast cell. (We can modify the appearance of Assumption cells and Forecast cells by selecting Cell→Cell Preferences and specifying details in the window that appears.)

We can now trace the impact of price uncertainty on profit by selecting Run→Single Step. In response, Crystal Ball does three things:

FIGURE 9.1
Spreadsheet for the Advertising Budget Example

Adbudget9.xls

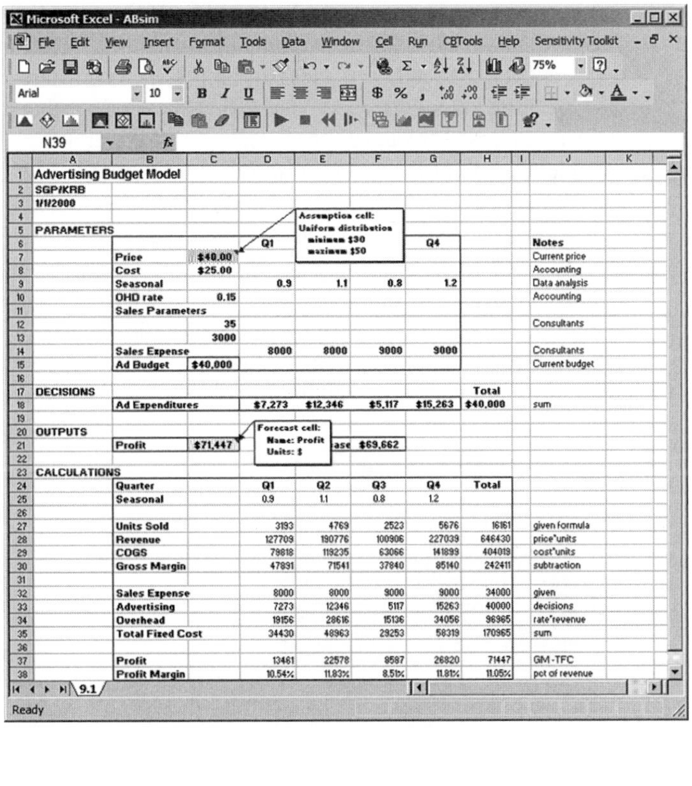

- It draws a random sample from the distribution we have chosen for price.
- It enters that number in cell C7.
- It calculates the resulting profit in cell C21.

When we repeat this procedure five or ten times, we get a rough impression of the range of possible outcomes, given our assumptions about uncertainty. We probably observe at least one case in which profit is negative, which suggests that this outcome is not entirely unlikely.

It is possible to repeat this sampling procedure hundreds or even thousands of times, record the results, and build up a complete picture of the probability distribution for profit. Fortunately, there is an easier way. We can select Run→Run Preferences and specify 1,000 for Maximum Number of Trials; this tells Crystal Ball to repeat the sampling procedure 1,000 times. To construct the resulting histogram of profits, we select Run→Run; a Forecast window opens in which Crystal Ball gradually plots the 1,000 outcomes in the form of a histogram for profit. The results are shown in Figure 9.2. (Note: It may be necessary to select Run→Reset before the Run→Run option is available. This action clears the temporary file that Crystal Ball uses for storing results.)

Two modifications to the look of the Forecast window are often desirable. One is to ensure that all the outcomes of a simulation are displayed. The data in the upper right-hand corner of Figure 9.2 ("989 Displayed") shows that only 989 of the 1,000 outcomes are actually displayed. To obtain a complete display, we select Preferences→Display Range from the menu in the Forecast window. In the Display Range Preferences window, we click the button for Using Fixed Endpoints, where the endpoints are –Infinity and +Infinity. This assures that all simulated outcomes are shown in the histogram. The second modification involves checking the box for Round Axis Values. This usually makes the histogram easier to interpret visually.

This histogram represents a probability distribution for the profit that would occur next year if price were uncertain and the budget of $40,000 were allocated optimally, as in Chapter 8. This distribution allows us to determine, among other things, that the average profit is about $71,459, and the probability of a loss is about 24 percent. Here's how to uncover these facts. In the Forecast window, we select View→Statistics and see that the Mean is $71,459. (To display the mean on the frequency chart itself, select Preferences→Chart→Mean Line.) This is the simple average of the 1,000 profit outcomes generated by our simulation, each one of which is equally likely. To find the probability of a loss, we return to the distribution by selecting View→Frequency Chart. We enter 0 in the data box in the lower right-hand corner to the right of the dark triangle and then press Enter. The outcomes to the right of 0 change color from blue to red, and the Certainty window reads 24.10 percent, as shown in the updated histogram of Figure 9.3. This means that the probability of making a profit is about 76 percent, and the probability of a loss is about 24 percent. (Note that results may differ slightly in different runs because of the variability in random samples.)

FIGURE 9.2
Histogram of Profits for the Advertising Budget Example

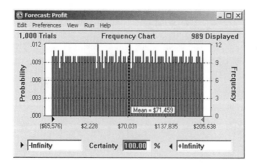

FIGURE 9.3
Negative Profit
Outcomes in the
Advertising Budget
Example

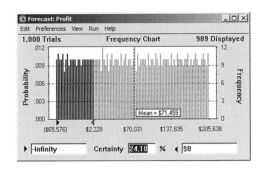

When Not to Simulate

This example illustrates an important point about simulation: sometimes it is *not necessary* to carry out a simulation in order to understand the effects of uncertainty. Recall that the optimal profit in the Advertising Budget example was $71,447 when we assumed that the product would be sold at $40. When we replaced this deterministic assumption with a uniform distribution for price, we found that the estimated mean profit, $71,459, was within about 0.02 percent of the base-case value of $71,447. In other words, replacing an input with a distribution can leave the expected result essentially unchanged. We can also calculate (using Goal Seek) that the break-even price is $34.80; at this price, profit is zero. If we examine the uniform distribution for price, we see that the probability is 24 percent that price lies below its break-even value, so we could have anticipated that the probability of a loss with this distribution is 24 percent. In this example, the simulation was not necessary for us to determine either the mean profit or the probability that profit would be negative. There is a general principle at work here, which is worth a brief elaboration.

The impact that uncertainty in an input parameter (such as price) has on the output (such as profit) depends on the form of the relationship between the two. If that relationship is *linear,* then the expected value of the output is related by the same linear relationship to the expected value of the input. Thus, if we replace an input by a distribution without changing the expected value, then the expected value of the output does not change, and simulation is not needed. An analogous relationship holds for tail probabilities when the relationship between input and output is linear.

As a simple example, consider a firm's profit as affected by uncertainty about sales revenue. We might think of profit as described by the equation

$$Profit = Margin \times Revenue - Fixed\ cost$$

where *Margin* is stated as a proportion. For example:

$$Profit = 0.4 \times Revenue - 100$$

This equation takes the linear form $Z = aX + b$, with Z in the role of *Profit* and X in the role of *Revenue*. Clearly, *Profit* becomes uncertain when we treat *Revenue* as uncertain. We might want to estimate the expected value of *Profit,* or perhaps the probability that *Profit* is positive. Since the relationship is linear, it follows that

$$Expected\ Profit = Margin \times (Expected\ Revenue) - Fixed\ cost$$

Also:

$$P(Profit > 0) = P(Margin \times Revenue - Fixed\ cost > 0)$$
$$= P(Revenue > Fixed\ cost/Margin)$$

In the Advertising Budget case, the uniform distribution for price translates directly into a comparable distribution for profit. The reason is the linear relation between profit and price. In fact, if we express the model in algebraic terms, we have the following equation for profit:

$$Profit = Sales \times (1 - Overhead\ Rate) \times Price - Unit\ Cost \times Sales - Fixed\ Cost$$

Now, if *Price* is the only input that we treat as uncertain, this expression is linear, so that we can write:

$$Expected\ Profit = Sales \times (1 - Overhead\ Rate) \times (Expected\ Price) - Unit\ Cost \times Sales - Fixed\ Cost$$

$$Expected\ Profit = 16{,}160 \times (1 - 0.15) \times 40 - 478{,}019$$

$$Expected\ Profit = 71{,}447$$

Similarly, with respect to the probability of breaking even:

$$P(Profit > 0) = P(13{,}737 \times Price - 478{,}019 > 0) = P(Price > 34.8) = 0.24$$

Of course, inputs and outputs are not always related in a linear fashion. To illustrate, we examine the impact of uncertainty on another parameter in this model. Cell C13 contains the parameter from the sales-response function that determines the base level of sales when advertising is zero. In the original analysis, this parameter took on the value 3,000. To illustrate the effect of uncertainty in this parameter, we replace this single value with a uniform distribution having the same mean value but a minimum of –5,000 and a maximum of 11,000. (To make the comparison clearer, we also assume for the moment that price is $40 for sure.) When we run a simulation under these assumptions, we see that uncertainty *reduces* mean profit, from $71,447 in the no-uncertainty case to $68,438 under uncertainty (see Figure 9.4). We also see that the shape of the profit distribution is no longer uniform. In fact, values toward the upper end of the range are more likely than lower ones. (To emphasize this result visually, we have altered the number of groups in the histogram using Preferences→Chart→Groups, where we selected 25.) Since the relationship here is not linear, the expected profit is not linear in the expected value of the input parameter.

To summarize these two cases: uncertainty in price gives us no new information about the expected profit or about the probability of breaking even, while uncertainty in the sales parameter shifts the mean profit and changes the shape of the profit distribution. Why are these two cases different? The explanation lies in the relationship between the outcome variable and the uncertain parameters. In the case of price, we saw that profit is linear in price. Equivalently, a graph of profit versus price is a straight line, as in Figure 9.5. The relationship between the profit and the sales parameter, on the other hand, is not linear. Recall that, in this model, sales are related to the square root of the product of advertising and the sales parameter. When we construct a graph of profit versus the sales parameter, we get a gradually diminishing increase in profit, as shown in Figure 9.6. These examples

FIGURE 9.4
Second Histogram for the Advertising Budget Example

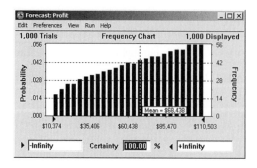

FIGURE 9.5
Profit as a Function
of Price

Adbudget9.xls

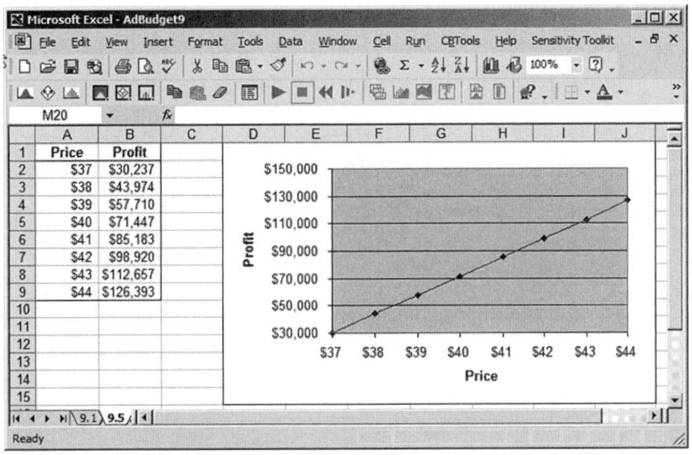

FIGURE 9.6
Profit as a Function
of the Second Sales
Parameter

Adbudget9.xls

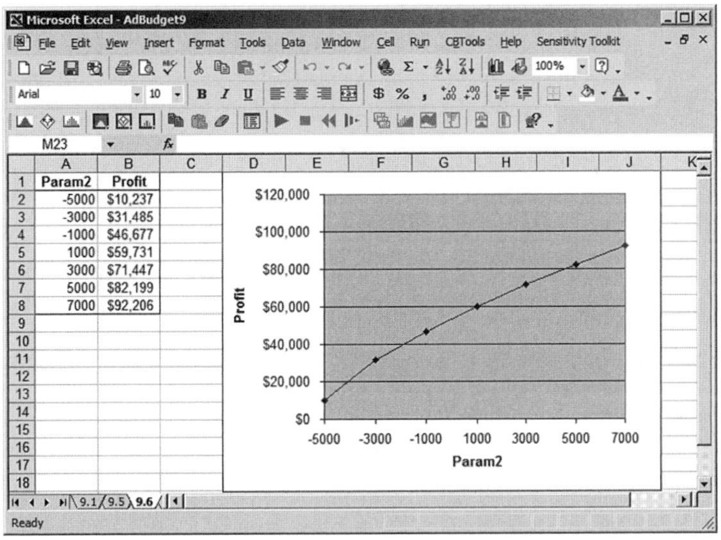

illustrate the point that we can detect whether the relationship between an input and an output is linear either by creating an algebraic model that is equivalent to the spreadsheet or by drawing a graph (perhaps using the Data Sensitivity tool). The graphical procedure is not fail-safe, as the graph can appear linear when it is not, or the range chosen can be too limited to reveal nonlinearity. Nonetheless, it is often an effective approach.

There are other cases in which it is possible to determine the expected value of the output without using simulation. Occasionally we may go to the trouble of conducting a simulation only to discover that the effort could have been avoided. However, in complex models with many uncertain parameters, it is often difficult to determine whether simulation can be avoided. Moreover, we often do not know in advance exactly which outputs we want to analyze. Thus, unless our model is particularly simple and we suspect that linearity holds, simulation is our general-purpose tool for analyzing uncertain situations.

Summary of the Simulation Process

The Advertising Budget example provides a rudimentary understanding of simulation and how to implement Crystal Ball. Now, we recapitulate the procedure to reinforce the main concepts.

1. Selecting Uncertain Parameters

The first step in any simulation (after building a deterministic spreadsheet) is to select parameters to treat as uncertain. Each of these parameters requires its own probability distribution. Since it takes time and effort to find a suitable distribution, some economy is called for in selecting uncertain parameters. As we saw in Chapter 6, changes in some parameters generate only modest changes in the outcome. These parameters probably do not warrant treatment as uncertain. Therefore, we recommend performing an initial sensitivity analysis to select those parameters that have the most influence on the results. A tornado chart is a natural tool in this selection process. Among the most influential inputs, some may be decision variables: these should *never* be considered uncertain, because they are under our control. Only the most influential and uncertain parameters should be replaced with probability distributions. In a later section, we describe in more detail how to select uncertain parameters.

2. Selecting Probability Distributions

Once we have decided that a particular input parameter should be treated as uncertain, we need to develop a probability distribution for it. In most cases, this step involves a mixture of data analysis and judgment. A small set of probability distributions is commonly used in business analysis. We describe these in a later section and indicate when each is suitable.

3. Selecting Output(s)

Every simulation produces a probability distribution for one or more outputs. Generally the output cell represents the single most important aspect of the model. But in simulation, we are not confined to considering only one output variable. In fact, one of the powerful aspects of simulation is that any cell in the spreadsheet can be considered an output cell. We might, for example, be interested not only in the profit we generate, but also in the NPV, the ratio of cost to revenues, and so on. Any variable we can represent in a single cell can be treated as an output. We illustrate this in the Netscape example below.

4. Running a Simulation

Executing a simulation consists of sampling from the input distributions and storing the results of the outputs. This involves a number of choices, only a few of which we mention here. The key choice is how many samples to draw—selecting the number of **Trials,** in Crystal Ball language. Whether we are interested in the mean profit or the probability of a loss, the more samples we take, the more precise our estimates become. We elaborate later on how to select an appropriate level of precision and how to choose other Crystal Ball settings.

5. Analyzing Outputs

The result of running a simulation is a histogram, which we interpret as a probability distribution, for each of the output cells. How we analyze this distribution depends on the problem. Often, we are concerned simply with the expected value, or mean outcome, which in Crystal Ball is listed as part of the statistical summary in the Forecast window and which can be displayed on the histogram. Many other useful aspects of the distribution are summarized under View→Statistics, such as the minimum and maximum outcomes. Probabilities for any event of interest can be found in various ways, which we discuss subsequently.

SIMULATION EXAMPLES

In this section, we discuss some additional examples in order to provide a broader understanding of the simulation approach. Each example illustrates the application of simulation to a new type of problem as well as several new features of Crystal Ball. Although we report detailed numerical results, it is important to keep in mind that results may differ slightly in repeated runs because of the variability in random samples.

EXAMPLE

Valuing Netscape

The initial public offering (IPO) of Netscape Communications Corporation on August 9, 1995, is thought to have signaled the beginning of the Internet boom. The underwriters of the IPO planned to offer five million shares at $28 per share, thereby raising $140 million. Up to that point, about $27 million had been invested in Netscape, and the company had yet to show a profit. At $28 per share, Netscape's market value would be more than $1 billion, despite a book value of just $16 million.[1]

The IPO underwriters calculated the value of the firm by adding the present value of the free cash flows through 2005 to the present value of the firm after 2005. This latter value, known as the **terminal value,** was calculated under the assumption that the free cash flows after 2005 would grow forever at a constant rate.

The underwriters' valuation was based on an annual revenue growth rate of 65 percent. Also, the terminal value growth rate was set at 4 percent, and the tax rate was assumed to be 34 percent. Some of the other assumptions included:

Cost of sales	10.4% of revenues
R&D	34.6% of revenues
Depreciation	5.5% of revenues
Operating expenses	80% of revenues in 1995 decreasing to 20% by 2005
Capital expenses	45% of revenues in 1995 decreasing to 10% by 2005

With these assumptions, a discounted cash-flow model for Netscape gave a valuation of $28 per share, supporting the underwriters' plans.

Our deterministic model for this problem is shown in Figure 9.7. As usual, we have isolated the parameters in one location and have grouped the calculations separately. The model includes actual values for 1995 in column B and builds the forecasts for the years 1996–2005 using recursive formulas along with growth rates and ratios given in the Assumptions section. For example, we calculate 1996 revenues in cell C19 by taking 1995 revenues and augmenting them by the revenue growth rate in cell B4. By using a relative address for the previous year's revenues and by using an absolute address for the growth rate, we can copy this formula across the row for the years 1997–2005.

The free cash flows shown in row 31 are negative until 1999, but turn positive in 2000 and grow dramatically thereafter. The terminal value of the firm, which is an estimate of its value after 2005, is calculated in cell B32. Here, we take the 2005 cash flows and project them forward one year using the terminal value growth rate, then we divide by the difference between the cost of equity and the terminal value growth rate. This calculation gives the present value in 2005 of an endless stream of cash flows growing at the terminal value growth rate.

One interesting feature of this model is that we can measure four or five different aspects of the value of Netscape (see cells N4:O8). The single most important measure of the value of the firm is the total present value (cell O4), which adds the present value of free cash flows from 1996–2005 to the present value of the terminal value. Another interesting measure is the ratio of the terminal value to the total present value (cell O5), which

---

[1] This example is based on work of Professor Anant Sundarum.

FIGURE 9.7 Deterministic Spreadsheet for Netscape Valuation

Netscape.xls

	A	B	C	D	E	F	G	H	I	J	K	L	N	O
1	**Netscape Valuation Model - Deterministic Version**													
2														
3	**Assumptions**		**1996**	**1997**	**1998**	**1999**	**2000**	**2001**	**2002**	**2003**	**2004**	**2005**	**Performance**	
4	Revenue growth rate	65%											**Total NPV**	1,057,167
5	Terminal value growth rate	4.00%											**Ratio TV/Tot.**	0.77
6	Cost of sales (% revenues)	10.40%											**Year FCF >0**	2002
7	R&D (% revenues)	36.80%											**Max loss**	(172,278)
8	Tax rate	34.00%											**Price/Share**	27.82
9	Other operating expenses		0.80	0.65	0.55	0.45	0.35	0.25	0.20	0.20	0.20	0.20		
10	Capital expenditure		0.45	0.40	0.30	0.20	0.10	0.10	0.10	0.10	0.10	0.10		
11	Depreciation (% revenues)	5.50%												
12	ΔNWC	0.00%												
13	Beta	1.50												
14	Riskless rate	6.71%												
15	Market risk premium	7.50%												
16	Cost of equity (CAPM)	17.96%												
17	**Model**													
18		**1995 actual**	**Forecast**										Shares	
19	Revenues	33250	54863	90523	149363	246449	406641	670958	1107081	1826683	3014027	4973145	outstanding	33000
20	Cost of goods sold	3472	5706	9414	15534	25631	42291	69780	115136	189975	313459	517207	to be issued	5000
21	R&D expenses	12230	20189	33313	54966	90693	149644	246913	407406	672219	1109162	1830117	total	38000
22	Depreciation	1836	3017	4979	8215	13555	22365	36903	60889	100468	165771	273523		
23	Other operating expenses	26898	43890	58840	82150	110902	142324	167739	221416	365337	602805	994629		
24	Profit before taxes	(11186)	(17940)	(16023)	(11501)	5668	50017	149624	302233	498684	822829	1357668		
25	Taxes	(3803)	(6100)	(5448)	(3910)	1927	17006	50872	102759	169553	279762	461607		
26	Net income	(7383)	(11840)	(10575)	(7591)	3741	33011	98752	199474	329132	543067	896061		
27														
28	Capital expenditure	15236	24688	36209	44809	49290	40664	67096	110708	182668	301403	497314		
29	ΔNWC	0	0	0	0	0	0	0	0	0	0	0		
30														
31	Free cash flow	(20783)	(33511)	(41805)	(44185)	(31994)	14712	68558	149655	246931	407436	672270		
32	Terminal value (2005)	5008313												
33	PV Free cash flow	243196												
34	PV Terminal value	813971												
35	Total PV	**1057167**												
36														
37														
38														
39	**Cumulative FCF**	(20,783)	(54,294)	(96,099)	(140,284)	(172,278)	(157,566)	(89,007)	60,648	307,579	715,015	1,387,285		
40														
41	**Test for positive FCF**	0	0	0	0	0	0	0	60648	307579	715015	1387285		
42		0	0	0	0	0	0	0	60648	0	0	0		
43		0	0	0	0	0	0	0	2002	0	0	0		

reflects how much of the overall value comes after 2005. A third measure is the year in which cash flows first turn positive (cell O6), which is 2002 in the base case. Another measure that relates to financing is the maximum loss (cell O7), or the cumulative free cash flow during the initial years before the cash flow turns positive. Since this is the amount that must be financed, it can suggest whether the current IPO will raise sufficient funds. Finally, we calculate the price per share (cell O8), by apportioning the total present value of the firm to the 38,000 shares that will be outstanding after the IPO.

Our deterministic model gives us some interesting insights. The total present value of Netscape comes to more than $1 billion under this set of assumptions, thereby justifying the IPO share price. Netscape's cumulative free cash flows are expected to turn positive by 2002, but the maximum loss is more than $170 million, indicating that the proceeds from the IPO may not be sufficient to cover the investment Netscape needs to fuel its growth. Finally, the terminal value of more than $800 million makes up more than three-quarters of the total value of $1 billion. This suggests that the valuation is heavily dependent on assumptions that affect the terminal value.

Before we turn to the uncertainty analysis, we should undertake some sensitivity testing with the deterministic model. Since we know that the terminal value makes up about 77 percent of the total present value, it is natural to ask how sensitive the terminal value is to its driving variables: the terminal value growth rate and the market risk premium. The two-way Data Sensitivity table shown in Figure 9.8 illustrates how small changes in either the terminal value growth rate or the market risk premium have significant effects on the terminal value of Netscape and hence on the total valuation. With the market risk premium at 7.5 percent, the terminal value ranges from about $650 million to $1.5 billion for terminal value growth rates between 1 percent and 10 percent. Similarly, when we vary the market risk premium from 5 percent to 10 percent with the terminal value growth rate at 4 percent, the terminal value ranges from $1.6 billion to $450 million.

FIGURE 9.8
Data Sensitivity
for Netscape

Netscape.xls

			Microsoft Excel - Netscape												

	A	B	C	D	E	F	G	H	I	J	K	L	M	N
1	Sensitivity of Terminal Value (TV)													
2														
3							Terminal value growth rate							
4		813971.2	0%	1%	2%	3%	4%	5%	6%	7%	8%	9%	10%	
5		5.0%	1096993	1191836	1302215	1432286	1587836	1777165	2012615	2313378	2711005	3261271	4072946	
6		5.5%	969611	1049458	1141627	1249209	1376423	1529182	1716039	1949844	2250835	2652830	3216920	
7		6.0%	859582	927198	1004677	1094348	1199334	1323925	1474179	1658935	1891616	2193652	2601479	
8		6.5%	764133	821695	887219	962479	1049818	1152401	1274598	1422629	1605655	1837751	2141702	
9	Market	7.0%	681007	730248	785965	849523	922705	1007030	1100037	1228260	1374347	1556021	1788091	
10	Risk	7.5%	608352	650664	698278	752258	813971	Base Case: 7.5% and 4% 58		1066680	1184747	1329167	1509874	
11	Premium	8.0%	544640	581147	622024	668104	720450		62	931129	1027584	1143906	1286938	
12		8.5%	488600	520218	555459	594981	639617	690426	748784	816510	896056	990811	1105599	
13		9.0%	439168	466650	497150	531194	569439	612713	662077	718916	785064	863014	956233	
14		9.5%	395451	419416	445909	475351	508266	545306	587298	635305	690721	755404	831890	
15		10.0%	356693	377656	400745	426303	454747	486595	522498	563282	610016	664103	727429	
16														
17														
18														

Since we have a large number of input parameters in this model, it is also useful to create a tornado chart to evaluate which parameters most affect the valuation. Recall that a tornado chart is a deterministic sensitivity analysis in which we vary each parameter independently. The tornado chart in Figure 9.9 is based on the assumption that each parameter in the range from B4 to B15 varies up and down by the same percentage (10 percent) of its base-case value. The results suggest that the valuation is most dependent on four parameters: revenue growth rate, R&D as a percentage of revenues, beta, and the market risk premium. Since the value of beta can be estimated with reasonable accuracy from the performance of comparable companies, our uncertainty analysis focuses on the other three parameters.

Having built a deterministic model and having carried out various sensitivity analyses, we are now ready to undertake a risk analysis using simulation. We have identified three parameters that have a particularly strong impact on the valuation: the revenue growth rate, the R&D percentage, and the market risk premium. After considerable discussion about the uncertainties governing each of these parameters, the following probability distributions were adopted:

Revenue growth rate	Normal, with a mean of 65 percent and a standard deviation of 5 percent
R&D as a percentage of revenues	Triangular, with a minimum of 32 percent, most likely value of 37 percent, and a maximum of 42 percent
Market risk premium	Uniform, with a minimum of 5 percent and a maximum of 10 percent

The questions before us now are: How does the uncertainty in these parameters affect the valuation of Netscape, and was the IPO valuation justified in light of these uncertainties?

Our second model for this problem, shown in Figure 9.10, includes the appropriate probability distributions for the revenue growth rate, R&D as a percentage of revenues, and the market risk premium. In the spreadsheet, these three cells are defined as Assumptions and appear with color shading. All five of the result cells discussed above are defined as Forecast cells, and they also appear with color shading. We can use the Single Step feature in Crystal Ball to get a rough idea of the range of valuations that result from these uncertain inputs. We then run 1,000 trials to generate histograms for each of

FIGURE 9.9
Tornado Chart for Netscape

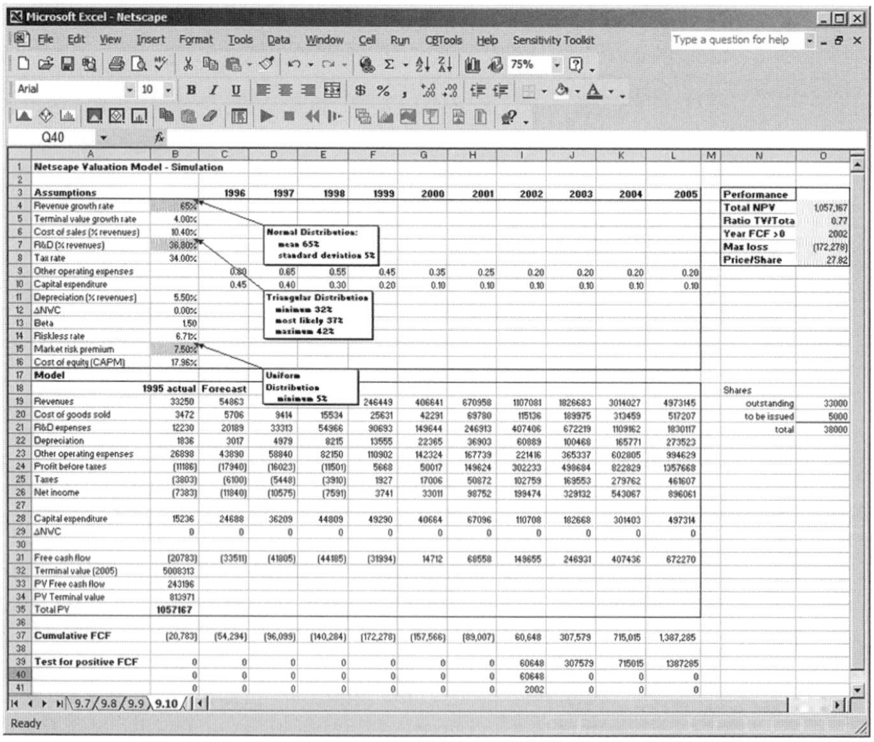

Netscape.xls

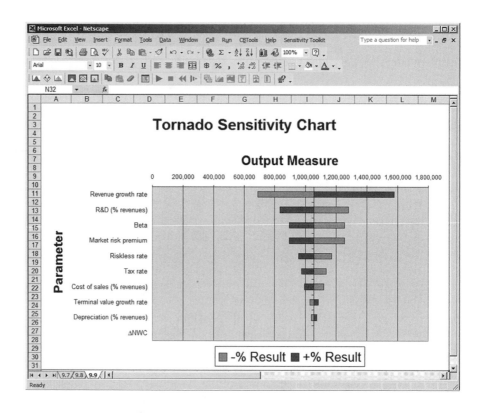

FIGURE 9.10
Simulation Spreadsheet for Netscape

Netscape.xls

	A	B	C	D	E	F	G	H	I	J	K	L
1	**Netscape Valuation Model - Simulation**											
2												
3	**Assumptions**		**1996**	**1997**	**1998**	**1999**	**2000**	**2001**	**2002**	**2003**	**2004**	**2005**
4	Revenue growth rate	65%										
5	Terminal value growth rate	4.00%										
6	Cost of sales (% revenues)	10.40%										
7	R&D (% revenues)	36.80%										
8	Tax rate	34.00%										
9	Other operating expenses		0.80	0.65	0.55	0.45	0.35	0.25	0.20	0.20	0.20	0.20
10	Capital expenditure		0.45	0.40	0.30	0.20	0.10	0.10	0.10	0.10	0.10	0.10
11	Depreciation (% revenues)	5.50%										
12	ΔNWC	0.00%										
13	Beta	1.50										
14	Riskless rate	6.71%										
15	Market risk premium	7.50%										
16	Cost of equity (CAPM)	17.96%										
17	**Model**											
18		**1995 actual**	**Forecast**									
19	Revenues	33250	54863			246449	406641	670958	1107081	1826683	3014027	4973145
20	Cost of goods sold	3472	5706	9414	15534	25631	42291	69780	115136	189975	313459	517207
21	R&D expenses	12230	20189	33313	54966	90693	149644	246913	407406	672219	1109162	1830117
22	Depreciation	1836	3017	4979	8215	13555	22365	36903	60889	100468	165771	273523
23	Other operating expenses	26898	43890	58840	82150	110902	142324	167739	221416	365337	602805	994629
24	Profit before taxes	(11186)	(17940)	(16023)	(11501)	5668	50017	149624	302233	498684	822829	1357668
25	Taxes	(3803)	(6100)	(5448)	(3910)	1927	17006	50872	102759	169553	279762	461607
26	Net income	(7383)	(11840)	(10575)	(7591)	3741	33011	98752	199474	329132	543067	896061
27												
28	Capital expenditure	15236	24688	36209	44809	49290	40664	67096	110708	182668	301403	497314
29	ΔNWC	0	0	0	0	0	0	0	0	0	0	0
30												
31	Free cash flow	(20783)	(33511)	(41805)	(44185)	(31994)	14712	68558	149655	246931	407436	672270
32	Terminal value (2005)	5008313										
33	PV Free cash flow	243196										
34	PV Terminal value	813971										
35	Total PV	**1057167**										
36												
37	**Cumulative FCF**	(20,783)	(54,294)	(96,099)	(140,284)	(172,278)	(157,566)	(89,007)	60,648	307,579	715,015	1,387,285
38												
39	**Test for positive FCF**	0	0	0	0	0	0	0	60648	307579	715015	1387285
40		0	0	0	0	0	0	0	60648	0	0	0
41		0	0	0	0	0	0	0	2002	0	0	0

	N	O
3	**Performance**	
4	**Total NPV**	1,057,167
5	**Ratio TV/Tota**	0.77
6	**Year FCF >0**	2002
7	**Max loss**	(172,278)
8	**Price/Share**	27.82
18	Shares	
19	outstanding	33000
20	to be issued	5000
21	total	38000

the five outcome measures described above (see Figures 9.11–9.15). Analysis of these histograms sheds light on the nature of the uncertainties facing the Netscape IPO.

■ Figure 9.11 shows that, while the mean valuation remains around $1 billion, the present value can be as low as $219 million or as high as $4.0 billion. There is a 10 percent chance that the value will be less than about half a billion, a far cry from the deterministic valuation of $1 billion. Thus, simulation analysis allows us to quantify the extreme uncertainty in the overall value for this IPO.

■ Figure 9.12 shows that the terminal value is consistently 70 percent or more of the total valuation. As in the deterministic case, the great majority of the total value of this firm appears to come after ten years' time.

■ Figure 9.13 shows that the maximum cumulative loss averages $173 million, but can be as large as $220 million. More significantly, if the current IPO raises $140 million, there is less than a 1 percent chance that this amount will be sufficient to fund the entire future development of the company.

■ Figure 9.14 shows that cumulative free cash flows turn positive in either 2002 or 2003. There is relatively little variation in the turning point.

■ Figure 9.15 shows that the stock price ranges from a low of about $6 to a high of $106, with a mean value of about $31. Although the stock price is closely related to the total value of the firm, this outcome measure may be more valuable to a potential investor. This result shows that stock purchased at $28 today may actually be worth as little as $6; nevertheless, it has a 10 percent chance of being worth more than $50.

The foregoing simulation analysis has allowed us to quantify the uncertainty in the future value of Netscape along a number of different dimensions. It suggests that we

FIGURE 9.11
Distribution of Total Value for Netscape

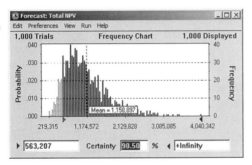

FIGURE 9.12
Distribution of Ratio of Terminal Value to Total Value for Netscape

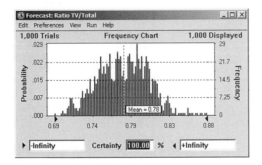

FIGURE 9.13
Distribution of Maximum
Cumulative Loss for
Netscape

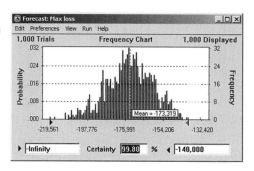

FIGURE 9.14
Distribution of the Year
that Cash Flows Turn
Positive for Netscape

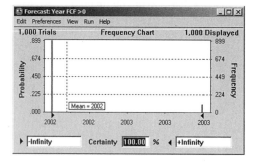

FIGURE 9.15
Distribution of Stock
Price for Netscape

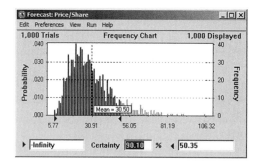

should be somewhat skeptical that the company's future value really supports a share price of $28. Questions remain, however. We might ask, for example, how our simulation estimates would vary if one of the underlying parameters were to change. We pointed out above that the terminal value growth rate strongly influences the terminal value of the firm, which in this case accounts for most of the overall value. Thus, it is natural to ask how sensitive the expected NPV is to the terminal value growth rate.

To answer this and similar sensitivity questions with a simulation model, we need to run Crystal Ball once for each value of the parameter we wish to test. Our Sensitivity Toolkit includes an option to do this called **CB Sensitivity.** CB Sensitivity runs Crystal Ball over a range of input parameters and records the mean (or other statistics) for as many Forecast cells as we define. This is analogous to running Solver in a loop, using Solver Sensitivity, to evaluate the sensitivity of the optimal solution to an underlying parameter.

CRYSTAL BALL TIP: CB SENSITIVITY

CB Sensitivity is a tool that allows us to run an entire set of Crystal Ball simulations while varying one or two input parameters. The CB Sensitivity input window (for one input parameter) is shown in Figure 9.16A. The first panel lists all the Forecast cells defined in the model. The user can choose to capture results from one or more Forecast cells in a given run. The second panel lists various statistics that can be recorded for each Forecast, including the mean, MSE, minimum, and maximum. Finally, the user must specify which input cell to vary and over what range, from Initial Value to Final Value and with what Increment.

As an illustration, we run CB Sensitivity on the Netscape model, varying the terminal value growth rate from 1 percent to 10 percent in increments of 1 percent (see Figure 9.16B). The resulting values for the mean NPV are shown in graphical form in Figure 9.17. We see that as the terminal value growth rate varies from 1 percent to 10 percent, the expected NPV varies from just under $1 billion to $2 billion. The CB Sensitivity tool also allows us to capture the minimum and maximum values of a Forecast cell. Figure 9.17 shows that the minimum value varies little over this range, from about $0.2 billion to $0.3 billion. However, the maximum value increases from $3 billion to more than $7 billion, indicating that the likelihood of extremely high valuations increases rapidly with the terminal value growth rate.

The Netscape valuation illustrates an approach to valuing a company that is used throughout the finance industry. One weakness of this approach is that a single growth rate is used for revenues over a period as long as ten years, with no detailed modeling to explain the sources for this growth. Another weakness is that the terminal value often dominates the overall value of the firm, and, as we have seen, the terminal value is highly sensitive to the assumptions on which it is based. Without simulation, no insights into the effects of uncertainty would be possible, and the evaluation could easily be optimistic.

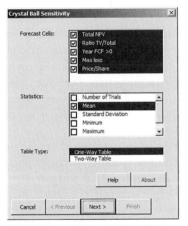

FIGURE 9.16A CB Sensitivity Input Window

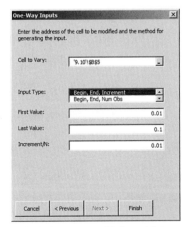

FIGURE 9.16B CB Sensitivity Input Window

FIGURE 9.17
NPV as a Function
of Terminal Value
Growth Rate

Netscape.xls

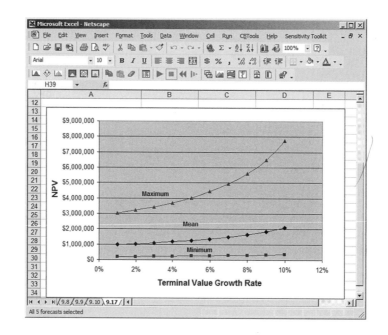

Simulation reveals the range of uncertainty in the valuation itself, as well as in other important aspects of the firm's future, such as the adequacy of funding.

EXAMPLE

Pricing a European Call Option

An **option** is the right to buy or sell an asset, without the corresponding obligation. For example, we might negotiate an option to purchase a sports franchise at any time in the coming year for a set price. If the team does well and its value increases, we might decide to exercise the option and make the purchase, but if the team does poorly, there is no obligation to buy.

Financial options, which include the right to buy or sell stocks, have become central to modern finance and investment. Financial options have value primarily because they allow the holder to hedge against changes in the value of the underlying stock. Billions of dollars' worth of options are traded each year. Every buyer or seller of an option has a stake in determining a fair price for the option. The theory behind option pricing is based on rather advanced mathematics, but the principles involved can be readily understood. In this example, we develop the basic concepts behind pricing options, and we use simulation to make those concepts concrete.

A **European call option** on a stock gives the owner the right to purchase the stock at a specified price on a given date. The specified purchase price is called the **strike price,** and the given date is called the **expiration date.** Imagine that we had a call option with a strike price of $100.00 and an expiration date six months away. If the stock price on the expiration date turns out to be $105.00, we could make a profit of $5.00 by exercising the option to purchase the stock for $100.00 and then selling it for $105.00. If the stock price on the expiration date turns out to be $90.00, we would lose $10.00 if we exercised the option to buy at $100.00, so we would not exercise the option. This example shows that the higher the actual price is *above* the strike price, the higher the profit. But no matter how far the actual price is *below* the strike price, the owner loses nothing except the cost of acquiring the option.

A particular stock is currently selling at $35.00. A call option is available on this stock with an expiration date six months from today and a strike price of $40.00. What would be a fair market price for this option?

As the example shows, the value of an option depends on the actual price of the underlying stock at the expiration date. Stock prices, of course, are not easily predicted, so it is natural to develop a probability distribution for the stock price at the expiration date. We first illustrate the concepts behind option pricing by using a simple but unrealistic distribution. Then, we develop a more realistic model for the evolution of stock prices over time, and we use it to determine option prices.

For the moment, assume there is a 50 percent chance that the stock price at expiration will be $45.00 and a 50 percent chance the stock price will be $35.00. If the price is $45.00, we can exercise the option and gain a profit of $5.00. If it is $35.00, we will not exercise, and we will lose nothing. The value of the option at the expiration date is called its **intrinsic value.** The intrinsic value is $5.00 when the price is $45.00; it is $0.00 when the price is $35.00.

Since we are considering buying the option today, we have to adjust for the time difference between now and the expiration date. The present value of the possible $5.00 gain is $4.83, assuming a 7 percent annual discount rate [= 5 / (1 + 0.07 / 2)]. The present value of the $0.00 gain if the price falls is obviously $0.00. The *expected value* of the option would be $2.41 (= 0.5 × 4.83 + 0.5 × 0). Financial theory and practice both confirm that this expected value is a suitable market price for the option.

Now let's return to the question of what is a realistic probability distribution for stock prices. Studies of the actual behavior of stock prices over time indicate that stocks are subject to small random changes every day, with a small upward trend. In other words, while daily prices vary, stocks show an average gain in price over longer periods. The evidence also suggests that stock prices at any date in the future tend to follow an asymmetrical distribution, with a maximum value farther above the mean than the minimum is below it. Figure 9.18 shows a lognormal distribution, which is generally accepted as fitting actual stock prices quite well.

A realistic model that reproduces these aspects of actual stock prices takes the form

$$P_t = P_0 e^N$$

where P_t is the price at some future time t, P_0 is the price today, and the exponential term e^N gives the required growth factor. N is itself a sample from a normal distribution with a mean of μ and a standard deviation of σ. The specific values for these parameters depend on the length of time between the current date and the future time t. These parameters are usually derived from the stock's average annual return and the standard deviation of the

FIGURE 9.18
Lognormal Distribution

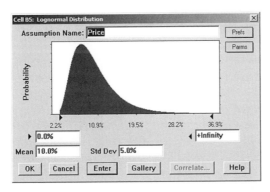

annual return. Note that stock returns are measured as the logarithm of the ratio of prices—that is, $\ln(P_t / P_0)$. We need to convert these annual parameters to daily equivalents, in order to build a model that shows how stock prices move over shorter time periods. Since there are about 250 trading days in a year, we divide the annual price growth rate by 250 to get a daily mean, and we divide the annual standard deviation by the square root of 250 to get a daily standard deviation. For a stock with an average annual price growth of 12 percent and an annual standard deviation of 30 percent, the equivalent daily parameters are 4.8 percent (= 12 / 250) for the mean and 1.9 percent (= 30 / 250^0.5) for the standard deviation, respectively.

Our model for projecting stock prices is shown in Figure 9.19. We begin the simulation with the known stock price at time zero, $35.00, in cell C4. This value becomes the initial value at the start of day 1 (cells E16 and C17). In cell D17, we take the exponential function of a sample from the appropriate normal distribution, as in the formula above. The Excel formula here is:

=EXP(CB.NORMAL($C$11,$C$12))

The Crystal Ball function in this formula, CB.NORMAL(mean, standard deviation), samples from the normal distribution. This value becomes the argument for the Excel function EXP(). Crystal Ball functions for probability distributions are a useful alternative to the Distribution Gallery for specifying Assumption cells. The available functions can be displayed using Insert→Function and looking under the heading Crystal Ball.

Returning to the spreadsheet, in cell E17, we calculate the ending price for day 1 by multiplying the initial price (cell C17) by the growth factor (cell D17). This ending price becomes the initial price for day 2 (cell C18), and the process is repeated with another independent sample from the normal distribution in cell D18 and with a new ending price in cell E18. Since all the formulas in cells C18:E18 involve Excel and Crystal Ball functions, we can complete the model for 125 days (six months) simply by using the Copy and Paste commands in Excel. We do not need to use the Copy Data and Paste Data commands

FIGURE 9.19
Options Pricing
Spreadsheet

Options.xls

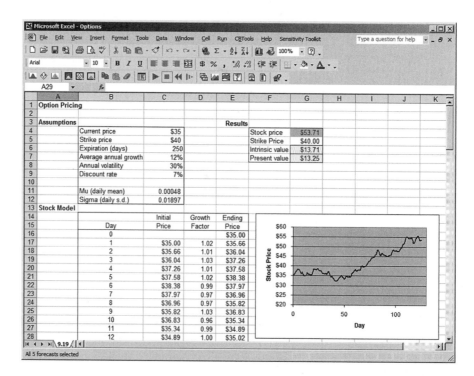

in Crystal Ball, because the probability distributions are entered as functions, not Assumption cells. This is generally a more efficient procedure when the model involves a large number of Assumption cells.

One projected price path over the six-month period is shown in the graph on the spreadsheet. By using Run→Single Step and observing the graph, we can get a visual sense of the price paths this model generates. Figure 9.20 shows five of these price paths. The upward tendency in prices is evident in this graph, as well as the large degree of variability in the price.

We can determine the distribution of prices at the end of the 125-day period by designating the final price as a Forecast cell. Figure 9.21 shows the distribution of prices in a simulation of 1,000 trials. The mean price is $38.23, which is consistent with the 12 percent annual growth we have assumed. The distribution also has the asymmetrical shape that actual stock prices show, with a minimum value of about $18.00, or roughly half the mean, and a maximum about $78.00, more than twice the mean.

Now that we have a realistic model for the evolution of stock prices over time, we can return to the question of pricing the option. In the spreadsheet of Figure 9.19, we calculate the present value of the option for every randomly generated stock price. In cell G4, we reproduce the stock price at the end of six months. The strike price is in cell G5. In cell G6, we calculate the intrinsic value of the option, using the formula MAX(0,G4 – G5). Finally, in cell G7, we discount this future value to the present at the given discount rate. When we use Crystal Ball to generate 1,000 trials, we obtain 1,000 values for the stock price as well as 1,000 corresponding values for the present value of the intrinsic value of the call option. The average of these 1,000 values becomes our estimate of the fair market value for this option.

Figure 9.22 shows the distribution of option prices. Here, we observe that 72 percent of the time, the option has no value. In these cases, the price of the stock has not risen above

FIGURE 9.20
Five Stock Price Paths

Options.xls

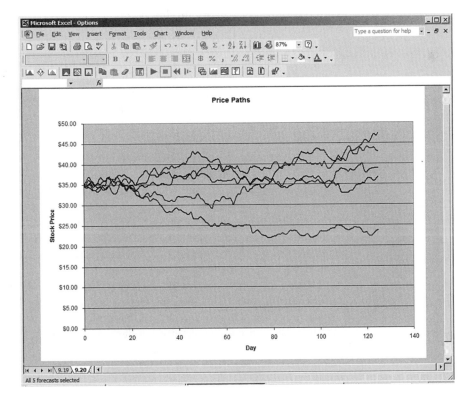

FIGURE 9.21
Distribution of Stock
Price after Six Months

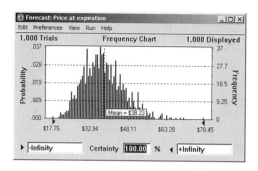

FIGURE 9.22
Distribution of Option
Prices

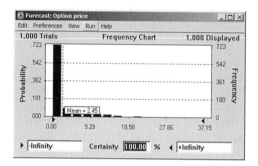

the strike price ($40.00) at the end of six months, so the option is not exercised. In the other 28 percent of the cases, the stock price is above the strike price, and the option does have value. In the extreme case, the price rises to about $77.00, giving an intrinsic value of about $37.00. On average, in our sample of 1,000, the discounted value is $2.45, which is an estimate of the fair market value for this option.[2] Note the extreme asymmetry of the distribution of option prices. As we mentioned, options are used to hedge risk. In our example, however, roughly 70 percent of the time, the option has no value. But when the stock price rises sharply, an owner of this option can make significant profits. At the extreme, for an investment of about $2.00, the owner can make a profit of more than $30.00 in just six months' time. No wonder many investors are tempted to invest in options!

We can get some additional insight into the forces behind the value of options by considering the impact of variability in the stock price. We have assumed that the underlying stock has an annual standard deviation of 30 percent. Would the option be worth more or less if the stock price were more or less volatile? To answer this question in the abstract, recall our two-price model for price uncertainty, where prices could go up to $45.00 or down to $35.00 with equal probabilities. We found that the option under these assumptions had a value of $2.41. But what if the stock price were more variable and could be $50.00 or $30.00 with equal probabilities? When the price is low, we still make nothing, but when the price is high, we make $10.00 instead of $5.00. In this case, the option is worth more than in the original case: its value is $9.66 (= 10 / 1.035). It follows that increasing the standard deviation of a stock increases the value of an option, because the gains increase while the losses never go below zero.

Figure 9.23 shows the results of varying the standard deviation in our option price model from 10 percent to 90 percent. Once again, we use the CB Sensitivity tool to carry out this set of simulations. We can see that option prices are worth very little when the underlying stock has little volatility, but they can be worth a great deal when the stock is

---

[2] This is actually an approximation to the true option value. According to current finance theory, in order to find the true market value of this option, we would need to simulate the stock growing at the risk-free rate.

FIGURE 9.23
Sensitivity of Option
Price to Standard
Deviation of Stock Price

Options.xls

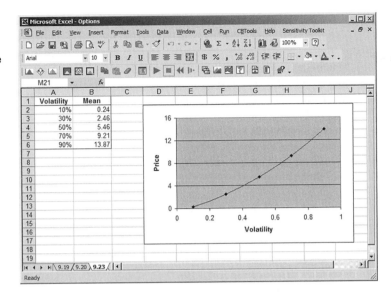

highly volatile. Of course, the exact value is also influenced by the strike price and the time to expiration.

We mentioned previously that our option prices were estimates, based on a simulation of 1,000 stock prices six months out. How accurate are these estimates? One simple way to answer this question is to take repeated samples of 1,000 prices and compare estimates of the mean values. The table below shows the results of ten simulations, each with 1,000 trials:

Run	Option Price
1	$2.34
2	$2.37
3	$2.19
4	$2.56
5	$2.22
6	$2.05
7	$2.18
8	$2.28
9	$2.38
10	$2.30

Our original estimate of $2.45 is certainly in the right ballpark, but these estimates range from a low of $2.05 to a high of $2.56. We would have to take a much larger sample than 1,000 trials if we needed to determine the option price to within $0.05 or $0.10. (Later, we discuss more formal methods of achieving acceptable levels of precision with simulation estimates.)

EXAMPLE

Cash Budgeting at Butson Stores

Butson Stores faces a problem in maintaining sufficient cash balances for operations over the first six months of the year. Each month, they must pay certain fixed costs and taxes, as well as materials costs that run about 80 percent of the current month's sales. Monthly cash receipts consist of revenues from the previous month's sales, as well as 0.5 percent interest on short-term cash balances. The company enters the six-month period with a cash balance of $250,000 and wishes to maintain at least that balance each month in order to cover cash needs. December sales of $1.54 million have just been recorded.

If Butson finishes a month with less than $250,000 in cash, the company can take out a one-month loan at 1 percent interest. The principal and interest are repaid in the following month. Butson's marketing department has made estimates for the mean and standard deviation of sales in each of the next six months. Given the uncertainty in sales, Butson would like to know how large their maximum monthly loan is likely to be, and how likely they are to exceed their current credit limit of $750,000. Finally, the company would like to know how much they will have to pay in interest costs for loans.

Our spreadsheet model for this problem is shown in Figure 9.24, where all dollar amounts are shown in thousands. We first forecast sales for each month from January through June. Assuming a normal distribution for sales, we use the Distribution Gallery to enter a normal distribution with the mean and standard deviation given in cells E6 and E7. (Using the Gallery, we can enter cell references for the parameters as long as we enter an equal sign before the cell address—for example,=E6 for Mean and =E7 for Std Dev. If we use relative references here, we can copy the formula along the row, accessing the monthly means and standard deviations from rows 6 and 7 of the worksheet.) Having entered the distribution for cell E18, we can use Crystal Ball to copy this distribution for the remaining months. To do this, we first highlight cell E18 and choose Cell→Select Data. Then, we highlight the range F18:J18 and choose Cell→Paste Data. The cells change color to show they have all become Assumption cells. We can then use Cell→Define Assumption to confirm that each of these cells has the correct normal distribution. (Be warned that using Excel Copy and Paste here would *not* copy the Assumption cell—only the *value* in cell E18.)

FIGURE 9.24
Spreadsheet for
Butson Stores

Butson.xls

	A	B	C	D	E	F	G	H	I	J	K
1	Butson Stores										
2											
3	Assumptions					December sales figure is assumed known.					
4											
5		Monthly sales			Dec	Jan	Feb	Mar	Apr	May	Jun
6		Mean			1540	1800	1500	1900	2600	2400	1900
7		Standard deviation				80	80	100	125	120	90
8		Fixed Costs and taxes				250	250	400	250	250	350
9		Cost of Goods Sold %	80%								
10		Monthly interest rates									
11		Interest cost of loan	1.0%								
12		Interest return on cash	0.5%								
13		Initial cash in Jan ($000)	250								
14		Min cash balance ($000)	250								
15											
16	Simulation model										
17					Dec	Jan	Feb	Mar	Apr	May	Jun
18		Actual sales ($000)			1540	1896	1506	1823	2719	2449	1873
19		Cash and receipts									
20		Beginning cash balance				250	250	465	250	250	250
21		Interest on cash balance				1.3	1.3	2.3	1.3	1.3	1.3
22		Receipts				1540	1896	1506	1823	2719	2449
23		Costs									
24		Fixed costs and taxes				250	250	400	250	250	350
25		Cost of Goods Sold				1517	1205	1459	2175	1959	1498
26		Loan payback (principal)					225	0	136	738	234
27		Loan payback (interest)					2	0	1	7	2
28		Cash balance before loan				25	465	114	-488	16	616
29		Loan amount				225	0	136	738	234	0
30		Final cash balance				250	465	250	250	250	616
31	Results										
32		Maximum loan	738								
33		Loan interest	13								

We can best explain the logic behind this model by concentrating on the month of February, cells F18 to F30. Cash inflows in February come from three sources: the cash balance available from the previous month, interest earned on that balance, and sales receipts. In cell F20, we set the initial cash balance for February equal to the final balance for January. In cell F21, we calculate interest on this balance, and in cell F22, we record sales receipts (equal to the previous month's sales).

The cash available at the end of each month must cover the cash outflows: fixed costs and taxes, cost of sales, and repayment of the previous month's loan (if any), with interest. Fixed costs and taxes are given (cell F24), cost of goods sold is 80 percent of the current month's sales (cell F25), and the loan principal and interest (cells F26 and F27) are calculated based on the loan taken in January (cell E29).

In cell F28, we subtract the uses for cash from the sources of cash, to determine net cash on hand. If this is less than $250,000, we must take out a loan to make up the difference. This amount is calculated in cell F29 using the function MAX(Minimum cash balance − F28, 0). Finally, in cell F30, we determine the actual end-of-month cash balance, which is either $250,000, when we have taken a loan, or higher, when the cash on hand exceeds $250,000 without a loan.

Two Forecast cells are needed. In cell C32, we track the maximum loan taken out between January and June. We then measure the total amount of interest paid on short term loans in cell C33, which is the sum of entries in the range F27:J27. (We ignore any loans taken out in December.) These two measures summarize performance. The results of a simulation of 1,000 trials are shown in Figures 9.25 and 9.26.

- Figure 9.25 shows that the maximum loan over the six months averages $648,000. The credit limit is sufficient with a probability of 83.4 percent. Finally, the actual maximum loan can range from a low of $314,000 to a high of $1,004,000.

- Figure 9.26 shows the distribution of interest costs. On average, Butson can expect to pay $12,000 in interest, but this amount could range from a low of $8,000 to a high of $16,000.

FIGURE 9.25 Distribution of Maximum Loan

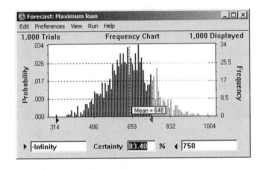

FIGURE 9.26 Distribution of Interest Costs

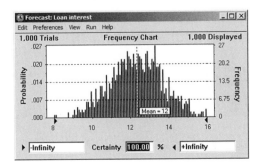

One of the assumptions behind these results is particularly questionable. We have assumed to this point that sales are statistically independent each month. Thus, if for some reason, sales are high in January, that gives us no reason to think that sales in February will be high or low. In many situations, this assumption is not realistic. January sales probably reveal something about how sales will progress for the entire year. Sales could be high because the product line is attractive, incomes are high, and competitors are weak. If so, and these underlying factors continue to hold in the coming months, then we can expect sales to be high in February and beyond. In order to model these kinds of interactions between different random inputs, it is necessary to understand how to deal with correlation.

Two random variables are **correlated** if the outcomes on each variable tend to move together. Positive correlation implies that high values of one outcome are associated with high values of the other, and low with low. Negative correlation implies that high values are associated with low, and low with high. In this case, we assume that sales in successive months are positively correlated with a correlation of 0.9.

Crystal Ball supports several different methods of creating correlated distributions. We illustrate only one of them here. (Other methods are described in Appendix 9.2.) To correlate sales in January with those in December:

1. Highlight cell F18.
2. Choose Cell→Define Assumption.
3. Click on the Correlate . . . button.
4. Click and hold Select Assumption.
5. Choose Jan.
6. Enter 0.9 for Correlation Coefficient.
7. Press Enter.

At this point, Crystal Ball draws a scatter plot of the two random inputs to suggest the strength of the correlation. Experimenting with inputs of –0.9, –0.5, 0, +0.5, and +0.9 gives us a sense of the meaning of correlation. By repeating this procedure, we can correlate each of the samples for February through June with the previous month's sales.

How much does correlation in monthly sales change our earlier conclusions? Figure 9.27 shows the distribution of the maximum loan for this model. We see that the mean value changes very little. The probability that the credit limit is sufficient rises to 94.5 percent. Finally, the range of outcomes—from a minimum of $435,000 to a maximum of $863,000—is narrowed somewhat from the uncorrelated case. Thus, in the Butson example, correlated sales lead to less risk than do uncorrelated sales.

EXAMPLE

Forecasting Sales of a New Product

Kardjian Brothers has invented a fundamentally new way to control the photolithography process used in manufacturing computer chips. Before they sell or license this

FIGURE 9.27
Distribution of Maximum Loan with Correlated Demand Samples

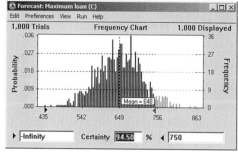

technological breakthrough, they would like to have some idea of how rapidly it might gain market share.

We base our model on three assumptions:

- There is a fixed population of potential users, all of whom will eventually adopt.
- Adoptions from *innovators* are proportional to the current number of potential adopters.
- Adoptions from *imitators* are proportional to the product of the current number of adopters and the remaining potential adopters.

While there are many interpretations of this general model, it is common to attribute the innovation effect to marketing efforts such as advertising, which convert some percentage of potential adopters every time period. The imitation effect is thought to operate through word of mouth, in which every contact between an adopter and a potential adopter results in a new adoption with some probability.

Some algebraic manipulation of these assumptions leads to the following model:

$$n(t) = pN_0 + (q - p) \times N(t) - (q/N_0) \times N(t)^2$$

where

$n(t)$ = customers adopting at time t
N_0 = total number of potential adopters
$N(t)$ = cumulative adopters at time t
p = propensity to innovate (percentage of potentials per time period)
q = propensity to imitate (percentage of potentials times adopters per time period)

Kardjian Brothers must find suitable values for the critical parameters, p and q, if they are to use this model in their planning. Fortunately, the process and the market they face have some features in common with earlier new process introductions from which values of the parameters can be estimated. Still, some uncertainty remains over the appropriate input values.

Forecasting sales of a new product or technology is a common but daunting challenge. Sales of some new products start high and taper off; others increase rapidly and steadily after introduction until the market is saturated; still others grow fast initially but reach a peak and decline. The model we employ in this example, known in marketing as the **Bass diffusion model,** is flexible enough to accommodate almost any realistic pattern of sales over time. It is particularly applicable for forecasting the long term sales (or penetration generally) of a new technology or durable good for which no close alternatives exist.

Our initial model is shown in Figure 9.28. We assume an initial population of 1,000 and parameter values of 0.03 for p and 0.38 for q. (These are the average values found over dozens of new products and technologies ranging from toasters to CT scanners). The number of new adopters in period t is calculated in column B using the equation for $n(t)$ and the total number of adopters from the previous time period. The cumulative number of adopters is calculated in column C by adding the number of new adopters in period t to the previous total.

The two charts in Figure 9.28 show that, for these parameter values, the rate of new adoptions rises to a peak of about 110 in year 8 and then falls off to zero as the population of potential adopters drops toward zero. The cumulative number of adopters increases slowly at first, then accelerates, and finally slows as it nears 1,000. Experimentation with the parameters of this model can suggest which parameter values give qualitatively different patterns of behavior.

FIGURE 9.28
Deterministic Bass Model

Diffusion.xls

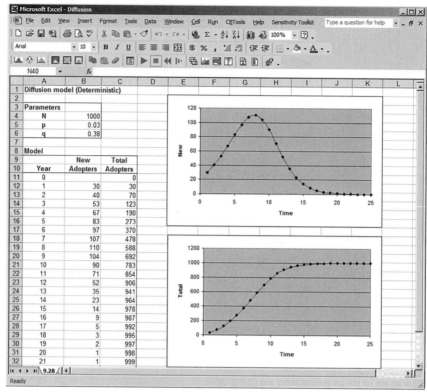

While we have empirical estimates of the parameters p and q for dozens of products and technologies introduced in the past, it is impossible to precisely determine these parameters for any particular product. We could select all similar technologies and products, and we could then average their parameter values. However, we would still face uncertainty in the input parameters and thus in the time path for adoptions. One measure of particular interest is the time to achieve a target market share—say, 50 percent.

It is straightforward to adapt our earlier deterministic model to accept probability distributions for the parameters p and q. In Figure 9.29, we display a version of this model in which we have used uniform distributions for the parameters (p lies between 0 and 0.5; q lies between 0.28 and 0.48). In column D of the model, we insert an IF statement that tests whether the total number of adopters in column C remains less than the target market share, returning 1 if so and 0 otherwise. In cell E4, we sum the entries in this column and add 1, thus obtaining the year in which the target share is achieved. This cell becomes our Forecast cell.

The results of running 1,000 trials with random parameters p and q are shown in Figure 9.30. Although a 100 percent market share is always achieved with this model, the speed with which it is achieved varies widely depending on the strength of the innovation and imitation effects. On average, it takes less than 3.5 years to achieve 50 percent penetration. However, it can take as few as 2 and as many as 20 years to do so. There is a 90 percent chance of achieving this level of penetration in 6 years or less; similarly, there is a 3 percent chance it will take 10 years or more.

Now that we have illustrated the uses of Monte Carlo simulation with several examples, we return to describe in more detail the essential steps in any simulation analysis:

- selecting uncertain parameters
- selecting probability distributions

FIGURE 9.29
Bass Model with Uncertain Parameters

Diffusion.xls

	A	B	C	D	E
1	Diffusion model (Probabilistic)				
2					
3	Parameters			Target	Years to Target
4	N	1000		50%	8
5	p	0.03			
6	q	0.38			
7					
8	Model				
9		New	Total	Less than	
10	Year	Adopters	Adopters	Target	
11	0		0		
12	1	30	30	1	
13	2	40	70	1	
14	3	53	123	1	
15	4	67	190	1	
16	5	83	273	1	
17	6	97	370	1	
18	7	107	478	1	
19	8	110	588	0	
20	9	104	692	0	
21	10	90	783	0	
22	11	71	854	0	
23	12	52	906	0	
24	13	35	941	0	
25	14	23	964	0	
26	15	14	978	0	
27	16	9	987	0	
28	17	5	992	0	
29	18	3	995	0	
30	19	2	997	0	
31	20	1	998	0	

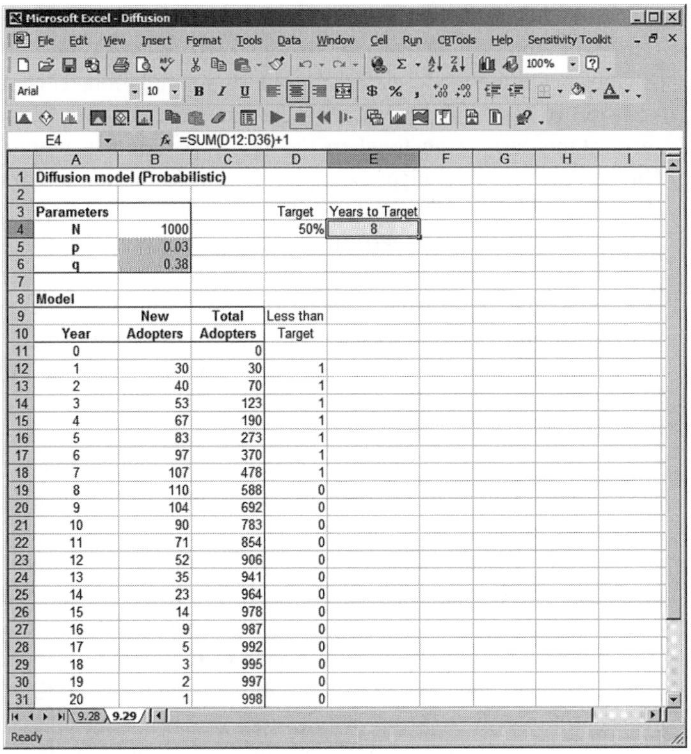

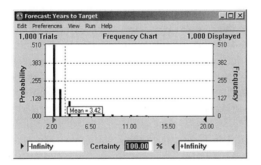

FIGURE 9.30
Distribution of Year in which 50 Percent Penetration is Reached

- ensuring appropriate precision in the outcomes
- interpreting outcomes

SELECTING UNCERTAIN PARAMETERS

With few exceptions, there is some degree of uncertainty surrounding the true value of *every* parameter in a model. Nevertheless, it would be a mistake to treat every parameter as uncertain in a simulation analysis. As we know from our discussion of sensitivity analysis in Chapter 5, variations in many parameters have little effect on the outcomes. Therefore, it is likely that randomness in these parameters will generate negligible randomness in the outcomes. Since it takes time and effort to develop an appropriate probability distribution for a parameter, this time and effort can be better used elsewhere if that parameter has little impact on the outcome.

Selecting which parameters to treat as uncertain is more an art than a science. However, some guidelines are useful. First, it is essential to carry out a deterministic analysis with the model *before* considering simulation. This involves establishing a base-case set of inputs and calculating the base-case outputs. Some thought should be given, even at this early stage, to where the base-case inputs lie within their ranges of uncertainty. In the Advertising Budget example, if we assume that the price next year is $40, do we have in mind the average price or the minimum price?

The next step is to perform sensitivity analysis, not only to test the model and learn about the range of possible outcomes, but also to get a sense of whether simulation is needed. In the Advertising Budget example, we might test prices as low as $30 and as high as $50. If profit does not vary significantly within this range, it is a good indication that uncertainty in price is not a central concern. (We can think of this range of variation as a crude first attempt at defining a probability distribution for the parameter. In this context, we should test values at or near the extremes rather than values near the mean.)

A tornado chart is a useful way to determine which of an entire set of parameters have a significant impact on the outcome. In Chapter 6, we illustrated the use of tornado charts in the Advertising Budget example. We first varied each of thirteen parameters within 10 percent of its base-case value, using the Constant Percentage option in the Tornado Chart tool. The results, summarized in Figure 6.8, suggest that four parameters have a significant impact on profits. For the remaining nine parameters, the impact was negligible. At this point, we could conclude that none of these nine parameters needs to be modeled as random, unless its true range of variability is much larger than ±10 percent. Hereafter, we concentrate on the top four parameters.

We also pointed out in Chapter 6 that using a single uncertainty range for all the parameters could lead to false conclusions. A 10 percent range may be realistic for one parameter, while 20 percent is realistic for another, and 5 percent for a third. The critical factor is the size of the forecast error for each parameter. If these ranges are significantly different, we should assign different percentages to different inputs using the Variable Percentage option in the Tornado Chart tool. In the Advertising Budget model, consider the four parameters that appear to have the biggest impact on profits: price, cost, overhead rate, and the first sales parameter. Based on our knowledge of the situation, suppose we knew that price could vary by 5 percent around its base-case value and that cost could vary 15 percent. Similarly, suppose we knew that the sales parameter and overhead rate could both vary by 10 percent. Using these facts as the basis for a tornado-chart run, we generate the results shown in Figure 9.31. With these more carefully chosen ranges of variation, we conclude that cost has the biggest impact on profits, followed by price, sales parameter, and overhead rate.

To this point in our sensitivity analysis, we have not associated probabilities with any of the variations we have considered. We have assigned ranges to each input, but we have not addressed the likelihood that the parameter will take on specific values within this range. Of course, if we ultimately decide to perform a simulation, we have to assign a specific probability distribution to each uncertain input. Creating these distributions can be time consuming. Therefore, it is useful to have the option to perform a deterministic sensitivity analysis, but with parameter variations that carry probabilistic interpretations. This is the purpose of the Percentiles option within the Tornado Chart tool.

The idea behind this method is to use the 10th and 90th percentiles of the distribution for each uncertain parameter as the endpoints of a deterministic sensitivity analysis. The 10th percentile is the number *below* which the outcome falls with probability 10 percent; the 90th percentile is the number *above* which it falls with probability 10 percent. One virtue of using this approach is that these values are not restricted to being symmetrical about the base-case value. For example, when we specified a 5 percent range for price

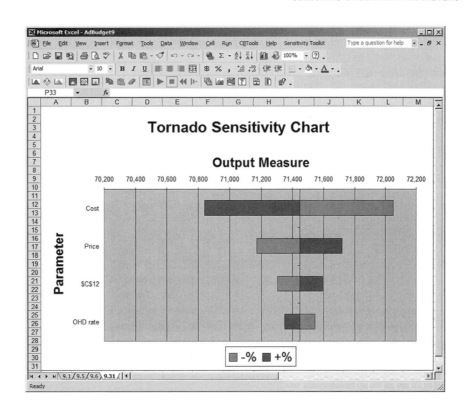

(around the $40 base-case value), we allowed it to vary from $38 to $42. This might represent a rough estimate of one standard deviation about the base-case value. But the 10th percentile value could be $33, and the 90th percentile $52, if we believe that extremely high values are more likely than extremely low ones.

Figure 9.32 illustrates the results of this approach using the Advertising Budget model. We assume the following values for the critical four parameters:

Parameter	10th Percentile	Base Case	90th Percentile
Price	33	40	52
Cost	19	25	31
Sales Parameter	30	35	40
Overhead Percentage	0.12	0.15	0.19

Price and cost continue to appear to be the most sensitive inputs, but this analysis provides additional insights over the earlier approaches. Figure 9.32 suggests that the uncertainty in cost can lead to a profit as low as –$26,000 and as high as $170,000. But the uncertainty in price leads to a highly asymmetrical range, from –$25,000 to $236,000. The upside potential caused by the likelihood of an extremely high price is an important factor that can be uncovered only by using this method of analysis.

To summarize, uncertain parameters should be selected only after a thorough sensitivity analysis. The purpose of this sensitivity testing should be to discover which parameters have a significant impact on the results, and what the likely range of uncertainty is for each parameter. The process begins with simple what-if testing of high and low values. The Data Sensitivity tool can also be used to test a range of inputs and to determine whether the model is linear in the given parameter. The Tornado Chart tool can then be used to test the impact of entire sets of parameters. The easiest approach, although not the most revealing, is to vary each parameter by the same percentage (the Constant Percentage

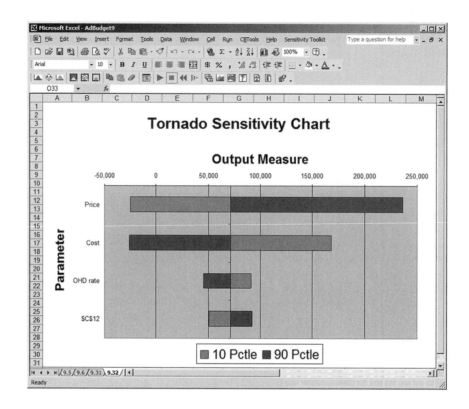

option). More information is required to assign a separate range of variation to each parameter (the Variable Percentage option), but the results are more meaningful. Finally, we can assess the extreme values of the distribution of each parameter (with the Percentiles option), to show how carefully selected extreme (and possibly asymmetrical) inputs affect the outputs. While none of these methods requires us to develop a complete probability distribution, the Variable Percentage and Percentiles options do require us to think carefully about uncertainty.

SELECTING APPROPRIATE PROBABILITY DISTRIBUTIONS

Once we have selected a set of uncertain parameters, the next step is to choose probability distributions for each one. But which type of distribution should we choose: discrete, uniform, normal, triangular, or perhaps something else? And once we have chosen a type of distribution, how do we choose its specific parameters (such as the mean and standard deviation for the normal distribution)? While Crystal Ball provides a menu of seventeen types of distributions, most business analysts use only a small handful of these.

Empirical Data and Judgmental Data

In considering how to choose probability distributions, it is important to distinguish between **empirical data** and **judgmental data.** Empirical data consists of numerical observations from experience, such as monthly sales for the past four years or daily stock returns over the previous year. It is often assumed, especially in textbooks, that empirical data are available and are directly relevant to the problem at hand. That is often not the case in problems encountered by the business analyst. Where, for example, could we hope to get relevant empirical data on the sales of an entirely new kind of product or service, such as the sales of an Internet company a year or two after its founding?

There is, however, another source of highly relevant data for the business analyst—one that is often overlooked or devalued. This is judgmental data, such as estimates made by experts in the field or by the decision makers most closely involved in the analysis. While the marketing department may not have empirical data on new product sales, its senior members probably have many years of experience in marketing new products. This experience is legitimate knowledge, and when a group of experts such as these are carefully queried for their judgment on a particular question, that judgment should be taken seriously. With a little prior training, we can learn to ask decision makers for probability estimates such as the mean, the minimum, or the 10th and 90th percentiles needed for tornado-chart analysis. As we discuss below, some probability distributions are especially suited for fitting to judgmental data, because their parameters correspond to probability questions that business experts find relatively easy to answer.

In Chapter 3, we noted that expert modelers focus more on the structure of the model, and less on collection of empirical data, while novices do the reverse. Novice modelers tend to be naive about empirical data, while experts know that most data contain hidden biases and errors. By the same token, experts are typically far more aware of the benefits of using judgmental data, and more willing to use it, than are novices. Judgmental data can often be gathered very quickly, sometimes just with a few phone calls. Within the prototyping process, judgmental data can be useful early on to test and debug an initial model. If sensitivity testing suggests that more accurate information is needed about a particular parameter, then the time and effort to acquire empirical data may be justified.

The traditional answer to the question of which distribution to choose is to select the distribution that provides the best fit to the data, where the reference is usually to empirical data. However, at least four aspects of this advice can be misleading:

- In most cases, unless we are doing scientific research, no empirical data at all will be available. (Judgmental data, on the other hand, are usually available.)

- Even if empirical data are available, the information may be biased or otherwise ill-suited for the purposes at hand.

- Even if relevant empirical data are available, it requires judgment to determine whether the distribution that provides the best fit to the given empirical data is appropriate in the model.

- In many cases, the results of interest depend on the mean and variance of an uncertain parameter, but not on the specific form of the probability distribution.

For all these reasons, we believe that empirical data alone are seldom sufficient. Even when empirical data are available, it takes careful judgment to decide whether some or all of that data should be used. Often, we also have some judgmental data at hand, if only the opinions of the decision makers, and these data should be combined with the empirical data when choosing a probability distribution. Effectively using data requires good judgment, not merely good statistical technique.

Four Essential Distributions

While Crystal Ball provides seventeen types of probability distributions, many of these are specialized and rarely used. In business analysis, four families of distributions are used most heavily: the discrete, uniform, triangular, and normal.

The discrete distribution is used in situations where an uncertain parameter can take on one of only a few possible values. For example, a competitor can either enter the market next year or not. This uncertain event can be described by a discrete distribution having the outcome 1 (for entry) and 0 (for no entry), with suitable probabilities. For another example, we might model market share with states of High with probability 0.25, Medium with probability 0.50, or Low with probability 0.25. If we used the number 2 for High, 1 for Medium, and 0 for Low, the states would be numerically valued. These numerical values can be entered into Crystal Ball using the Custom distribution.

Three continuous distributions provide a good deal of flexibility in capturing the kind of variability encountered in decision problems. The uniform distribution describes an outcome that is equally likely to fall anywhere between a minimum and a maximum value. It is particularly appropriate when we can make a reasonable guess about the smallest and largest possible outcomes, but have no reason to suspect that any values in between are more likely than others. The triangular distribution describes an outcome that has a minimum and maximum value, but is most likely to occur at an intermediate point. The triangular distribution is more flexible than the uniform because it can have a peak anywhere in its range. It is well suited to situations where we can identify a most likely outcome as well as the smallest and largest possible outcomes. Finally, the normal distribution describes an outcome that is most likely to be in the middle of the distribution, with progressively smaller likelihoods as we move away from its most likely value. This distribution, which is familiar to many analysts, can describe a symmetrical uncertain quantity using only two parameters (the mean and the standard deviation).

The uniform distribution is often the first distribution we use when prototyping a model. We choose the uniform distribution because it is so easy to specify, requiring only a minimum and maximum value. Figure 9.33 shows a uniform distribution whose outcomes lie between 50 and 150. The mean for a uniform distribution is midway between the minimum and maximum values (100 in this case). The critical property that defines the uniform distribution is that every outcome between the minimum and the maximum is equally likely. Often, this is a reasonable assumption, especially when first testing the effects of uncertainty in a model and when no empirical data or other kinds of information are available to suggest different likelihoods.

The triangular distribution is a more flexible family of continuous distributions. These distributions are specified by three parameters: the minimum, maximum, and most likely values. Figure 9.34 shows a triangular distribution from 50 to 150, with a most likely value of 125. Triangular distributions are particularly useful for representing judgmental estimates. Very few managers can specify offhand a probability distribution for an uncertain quantity, but most can give reasonable estimates for the minimum, maximum, and most likely values.

The normal distribution is a symmetrical distribution, usually specified by its mean and standard deviation. The normal distribution shown in Figure 9.35 has a mean of 100

FIGURE 9.33
A Uniform Distribution

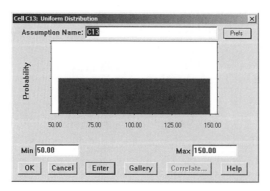

FIGURE 9.34
A Triangular Distribution

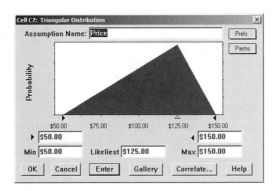

FIGURE 9.35
A Normal Distribution

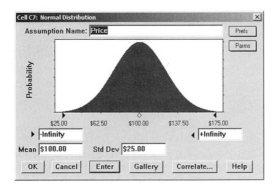

and a standard deviation of 25. The normal is often appropriate for representing uncertain quantities that are influenced by a large number of independent factors, such as the heights of a group of people or the physical measurements of a manufactured product. But the normal is often overused, perhaps because it is prominent in statistics, where it plays a central role. The normal should not be used unless there is reason to believe the distribution is symmetrical. It also has the sometimes problematic property that negative outcomes are possible, especially if the standard deviation is large relative to the mean. Thus, the normal would not be a suitable probability model for demand or price, unless the standard deviation were small relative to the mean (say, 25 percent of the mean or less).

While the normal distribution is usually defined in terms of its mean and standard deviation, Crystal Ball provides the option to use alternative input parameters. (This option is also available for many other continuous distributions.) For example, when we click on the Parms button in the upper right of the Normal Distribution window, Crystal Ball offers these options: 10th and 90th percentile, 5th and 95th percentile, mean and 90th percentile, mean and 95th percentile, or Custom. (With the Custom option, we can define the distribution using any two percentile values.) This option is particularly convenient if we have already determined the 10th and 90th percentiles for a tornado-chart analysis. Then, if a normal distribution seems indicated, it is not necessary to determine the mean and standard deviation, since the 10th and 90th percentiles can be entered directly. Crystal Ball calculates the corresponding mean and standard deviation when given the 10th and 90th percentiles. To invoke this capability, we click Parms again and click Mean–StDev to see these values.

Fitting Distributions to Data

While it is important to understand the limitations of empirical data, it is also important to know how to utilize empirical data when they are available. Assume we have

CRYSTAL BALL TIP: ENTERING DISTRIBUTIONS

Crystal Ball provides two distinct ways to enter probability distributions: through the Distribution Gallery (Cell→Define Assumption) or through Crystal Ball functions (such as CB.NORMAL). Each has its advantages and disadvantages.

The Distribution Gallery is a convenient method for entering distributions, especially for new users of Crystal Ball. It has the advantage that it displays all of the available distributions in a visual format. Once we select a particular family of distributions, such as the uniform or triangular, we can enter different sets of parameter values and see how they change the shape of the distribution. For most distribution types, we can either enter parameter values directly, or through relative or absolute cell references.

The Distribution Gallery has several disadvantages as well. First, it does not provide the standard documentation we expect in Excel: highlight a cell defined as a distribution, and the cell contents are simply a number. We have to use other methods, such as color coding, to remind us there is a distribution behind the cell. We also cannot take cells defined this way and copy and paste them using the normal Excel commands, but must use the Copy Data and Paste Data options within Crystal Ball. This is a common source of errors. Finally, a distribution entered this way cannot be embedded into an Excel function.

The alternative to using the Distribution Gallery is to use Crystal Ball functions for distributions, such as CB.NORMAL or CB.TRIANGULAR. Crystal Ball provides a function for every distribution available in the Distribution Gallery. These functions act just like any other Excel functions, so they can be embedded in other functions, are self-documenting, and can take inputs from other cells. They can also be copied using the standard Excel Copy and Paste functions. Most users of Crystal Ball eventually gravitate toward using these functions instead of using the Distribution Gallery.

There are also some drawbacks to using the Crystal Ball functions for distributions. One is that the user must learn the required inputs and their order. Another is that the shape of the distribution is not visible. Finally, Crystal Ball does not recognize a distribution function as an Assumption cell. Because there are certain specialized tasks in Crystal Ball itself that require the use of Assumption cells, it is still sometimes necessary to use the Distribution Gallery.

relevant data on a given parameter, and we wish to choose a probability distribution. For example, Figure 9.36 gives 50 observations on sales of a particular product. The essential first step is to create a histogram of the data and calculate the mean and standard deviation, as shown in the figure. We see that the mean is a little over 100, and the standard deviation is about 24. The histogram suggests that values close to the mean are more likely than values at the extremes, but the histogram does not strongly suggest any one type of distribution. If we were to select a normal distribution, we would probably choose a mean of 100 and a standard deviation somewhat higher than that observed in the data, say 30 or 35. If we were to select a triangular distribution, we might pick a minimum of 40 (somewhat below the lowest value observed), a maximum of 170 (somewhat higher than observed), and a most likely value of 110 or 120. When choosing a distribution based on empirical data, it is generally advisable to widen the range because actual results tend to underestimate the extremes. By contrast, the sample average is usually an accurate estimate of the population mean, and there is no built-in bias, even with a small sample.

Crystal Ball provides several more formal methods for fitting a distribution to a set of empirical data. One alternative, which is useful for fitting one distribution at a time, is to use the Fit option in the Distribution Gallery. If we need to fit a number of distributions, the Batch Fit tool (on the CBTools menu) is the preferred approach. More details about how to use these tools can be found in Appendix 9.2.

FIGURE 9.36
Using Data to Choose
a Distribution

Data.xls

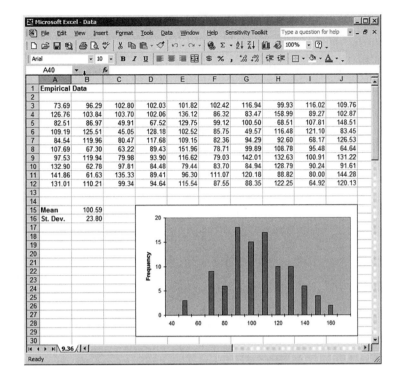

Summarizing this section, we recommend tackling the problem of choosing probability distributions with a liberal amount of judgment supported by judicious use of data analysis. In our experience, it is often the mere recognition of variability in the critical parameters that gives rise to the vital business insights, not the specific form of the probability distributions chosen to represent that variability. For example, it would be a rare case in which the essential decisions were sensitive to the choice of a triangular over a normal distribution. This can happen, but it is unusual unless there are major benefits or costs corresponding to outcomes in the tails of the probability distribution. Thus, time spent trying to identify the best probability distribution for a parameter is probably not time well spent.

ENSURING APPROPRIATE PRECISION IN OUTPUTS

Every time we run a simulation, we are performing an experiment. The purpose of this experiment is to estimate some quantity, such as the expected value of profit or the probability of a loss. With any simulation result, there is some difference, or error, between our estimate and the true value we are after. Thus, our estimate of the mean profit and the true value of the mean profit differ by some amount of **simulation error.** As with any good experiment, a well planned simulation study requires effort to measure this error. More specifically, we must ensure that whatever conclusions we draw from the simulation study are not seriously compromised by simulation error.

Simulation error is not the only source of error in our modeling efforts. It may not even be the most important source of error. All models are abstractions of the real situation they mimic, and for that reason, they differ in their behavior from the real thing. We can use the term **model error** to refer to this divergence between the behavior of the model and the behavior of the real thing. The essence of modeling is to abstract the essential features of the problem and then to interpret the model results in order to gain useful insights about the behavior of the real system. In most practical situations, model error is a much larger problem than simulation error. Nonetheless, simulation error itself can cause problems in interpreting model results, and for that reason, it should be measured and controlled.

Illustrations of Simulation Error

We begin with the simplest possible illustration, one in which we know the answer in advance. We can simulate one roll of a fair die by entering a discrete distribution in Crystal Ball, with the outcomes 1 through 6 all having probability 1/6 (We use the Custom Distribution, entering the outcomes under Value and the probability 0.1667 under Prob.) We know that the probability of getting, say, a four on one roll is 0.1667; how well does simulation work at finding this result?

Each time we take a sample from this distribution, we get one outcome of rolling the die. When we run *one* sample (or "trial" in Crystal Ball language), we may get the value three. Based on this information alone, we would have to conclude the probability of getting a four is zero. The difference between the true value of 0.1667 and the estimated value of zero is very large: 0.1667. This is the error in our simulation at this point. When we run a second trial, we may get a one. Still, the probability of a four is 0 (= 0/2), and still the error is high. When we run ten samples, we may get these results:

Trial	Result
1	3
2	1
3	5
4	4
5	3
6	2
7	5
8	5
9	4
10	3

In these ten trials, we find that four appears twice, so our estimate of the probability of getting a four is now 0.20 (= 2/10). The simulation error is now 0.0333 (= 0.2 − 0.1667), which is much smaller than it was with one or two trials. If we run 100 trials, we get sixteen fours. Our estimate now is 0.16 with an error of 0.0067. Finally, if we run 1,000 trials, we get 161 fours, and our estimate of the probability of a four is 0.161 with an error of 0.0057.

This example illustrates several important points. To begin with, small samples can lead to large errors. However, even a sample of 1,000 trials is insufficient to determine the answer perfectly. We do, however, seem to get closer and closer to the right answer as the number of trials increases. We exploit this fact in developing methods for estimating simulation outcomes with acceptable precision.

Let's take a closer look at simulation error in a realistic application before we suggest strategies for dealing with it. Refer again to the Advertising Budget example. We know that profit is $71,447 when the price is $40 for certain. We also know that mean profit remains $71,447 even when price is uniformly distributed between $30 and $50, due to the linear relationship between price and profit. Now let's see how the number of trials of a simulation affects our estimate of the mean profit.

For dramatic effect, we start with one trial: choosing Single Step from the Run menu creates a single sample from the distribution for price, and displays a single sample for profit. In our run, we found that price is $42.05 and profit is $99,617. (In other trials, we would get different results.) Since we have only one sample for profit, it becomes our best estimate for the mean, but the simulation error is huge: $99,617 – $71,447 = $28,170 (or 39 percent above the true mean). Of course, no one would seriously suggest taking only a single sample in a simulation. How much closer to the true value would we get if we took, say, ten samples and averaged them? The table below shows typical results:

Trial	Result
1	$99,617
2	–2,246
3	84,813
4	189,680
5	–206
6	10,663
7	66,730
8	185,044
9	83,019
10	201,057

The average of these ten trials is $78,579, with a simulation error of $7,132 (10 percent). This is still a significant error, but we see that the larger sample has brought us considerably closer to the true mean of $71,447. Would 100 samples be good enough? When we run 100 trials, we get an average of $73,911, or an error of only $2,464 (3 percent). Now we're getting close. With 1,000 trials, we get an average of $71,444, which is indistinguishable from the true mean profit.

What have we learned? Clearly, a sample of one or even ten is not nearly enough in this situation. But a sample of size 1,000 is probably close enough for even the most demanding client. In fact, 1,000 trials may be overkill for practical purposes. As we should expect, the precision of any simulation estimate increases as the run length increases.

Precision versus Accuracy

It is important to develop some terminology before we address simulation error from a technical point of view. We assume there is a probability distribution for the outcome of interest—profit in our example—although we do not know what this distribution is. Our interest is in particular aspects of this distribution, such as its expected value or the probability of a particular range of profit outcomes. Because of the complexity of our model, we cannot determine these quantities exactly, but must resort to simulation. Using simulation, we create a set of sample outcomes for profit from which we can estimate features of the probability distribution for profit. If our goal is to determine the expected value of profit, we compute the average of all the simulation outcomes. For clarity, we refer to this average as the **sample average,** to distinguish it from the true mean profit. The sample average is an estimate of the true mean. (The sample average of the ten trials for the Advertising Budget example was $78,579.) Likewise, if we wish to determine the probability of a loss in our simulation, we compute the percentage of outcomes in which a loss occurs. This percentage is the **sample proportion,** an estimate of the true probability of a loss. Whether we are interested in a mean value or a tail probability, our simulation produces an estimate of the true quantity. Our goal here is to understand and control the error in this estimate.

It is important to distinguish here between precision and accuracy. A single sample gives us a perfectly accurate estimate of the true mean profit, as long as there is no bias in the process. Technically, we are saying that the expected outcome of a single sample is the true mean. In this sense, a sample average from a large sample is no more *accurate* than from a sample of size one. But an estimate based on the larger sample is more *precise* than an estimate based on a sample of one. This is so because the variance of the sample average declines with the sample size. In other words, a second sample of size one will most likely be very different from the first, whereas another sample of size 1,000 will most likely not be very different from the first, at least for the purposes of estimating the true mean. Repeated samples are more like each other (that is, they show less variance) as the sample size increases, and they are therefore more precise.

An Experimental Method

The simplest approach to determining the precision of a simulation estimate is to experiment with multiple independent runs. To do this, we first make sure the Use Same Sequence of Random Numbers box is *not* checked in the Sampling window under Run Preferences. This option ensures that different random numbers are used each time we run a simulation. Now we pick an initial sample size—say, 100. We perform five to ten simulations using this run length and compare the estimates of the outcome measure. Are they close to each other or far apart? If they are too far apart for our purposes, we have not achieved sufficient precision in our estimates, and so we cannot rely on any single run at the current run length. We therefore increase the run length, possibly to 500 or 1,000. We make another five or ten runs at this new run length and again compare the results. When the set of results has a sufficiently small range, we have a sufficient sample size.

We can illustrate this procedure with the Advertising Budget model. We set the run length to 100 trials and carry out five runs. The five successive estimates of profit are given in the table below:

Trial	Result
1	$64,766
2	70,017
3	69,759
4	64,441
5	71,046

If we didn't know that the true mean profit was $71,447, so that we had only these five observations to work with, we might conclude that there was too much variability in these results to rely on them. If we increase the run length to 500 trials and run five runs, we get the following results:

Trial	Result
1	$71,453
2	71,452
3	71,450
4	71,438
5	71,455

Whereas the range from lowest to highest was $6,280 with 100 trials, with 500 trials, it is only $17, quite possibly enough precision for our purposes. Just to be sure, we can perform five runs at 1,000 trials. Here, the results range from $71,442 to $71,449, a difference of only $7. The range of results on independent runs gets narrower as the number of trials increases.

Using the MSE

An important measure of precision in a simulation estimate is the mean standard error (MSE). We referred to the same concept as the standard error of the mean in Chapter 7 when we described how to construct interval estimates. In a simulation experiment, we are essentially estimating the mean value of a population, and an interval estimate describes the precision associated with our estimate. In Chapter 7, we also explained that each interval estimate corresponds to a particular confidence level. For example:

- A 68 percent confidence interval for the true mean extends to one MSE on either side of the sample average.

- A 90 percent confidence interval for the true mean extends to 1.645 MSEs on either side of the sample average.

- A 95 percent confidence interval for the true mean extends to 1.960 MSEs on either side of the sample average.

- A 99 percent confidence interval for the true mean extends to 2.576 MSEs on either side of the sample average.

In the Advertising Budget simulation model, for example, a run length of 1,000 trials generates an MSE of 2,510. This is reported in the Statistics view on the Forecast window, as shown in Figure 9.37. (Results may vary slightly due to simulation error when this experiment is repeated.) Thus, a 68 percent confidence interval for the mean is 71,447 ± 2,510. This range of outcomes, from 68,934 to 73,954, represents the uncertainty in our estimate of the mean, with a confidence level of 68 percent.

If we want a confidence level higher than 68 percent, we have to widen the range. For example, a 95 percent confidence level corresponds to 71,447 ± 1.96(2,510). This range of outcomes, from 66,524 to 76,364, represents the uncertainty in our estimate of the mean with a confidence level of 95 percent.

With a smaller sample size, we would expect the possible errors, and therefore the MSE, to be larger. For an experiment consisting of 100 trials, the sample average is $62,162, and the MSE is 9,155, or about 15 percent. Thus, we would expect the true mean to lie within the range from 53,007 to 71,317 about 68 percent of the time. Notice that in

FIGURE 9.37
Statistics View

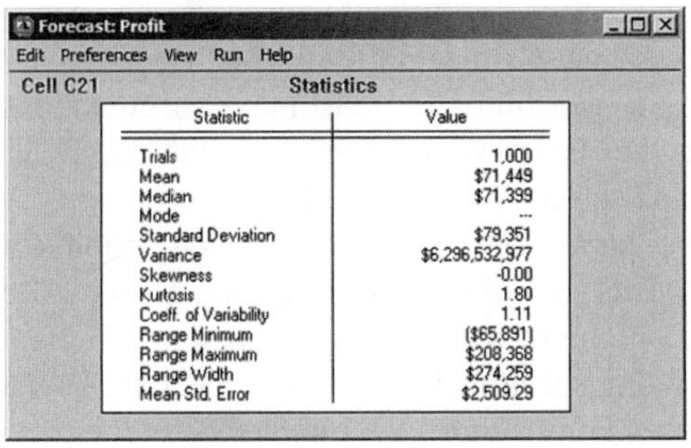

Statistic	Value
Trials	1,000
Mean	$71,449
Median	$71,399
Mode	---
Standard Deviation	$79,351
Variance	$6,296,532,977
Skewness	-0.00
Kurtosis	1.80
Coeff. of Variability	1.11
Range Minimum	($65,891)
Range Maximum	$208,368
Range Width	$274,259
Mean Std. Error	$2,509.29

this case, a range of one MSE on either side of the sample average does *not* include the true mean (71,447). This should be sobering, if not startling. There is, after all, no *guarantee* that a range of even 1.96 MSEs around the sample mean contains the true mean. All we can say is that the probability of this outcome is 95 percent.

In Chapter 7, we pointed out that the standard error of the mean declines with the square root of the sample size. More formally, a confidence interval for the mean has the form

$$\bar{x} \pm z(s/\sqrt{n}) \qquad (1)$$

where $\bar{x}$ is the sample mean and s is the standard error of the mean. In the simulation context, we use confidence intervals of the form

$$\text{sample average} \pm z \text{ (MSE)}$$

Since the MSE also declines with the square root of the sample size, as we increase the sample size, we increase the precision of our estimates, but not in a linear fashion. In fact, if we want to cut the MSE in half, we have to *quadruple* the sample size, due to the square root relationship. More samples are always better, but successive samples of a given size contribute less and less additional precision.

One way to use the MSE is to determine the acceptable error before running a simulation. In the Advertising Budget model, we might be willing to accept an MSE that is roughly 5 percent of the mean, or about 3,600. Suppose we run 100 trials and find that the MSE is about 15 percent of the mean. We could then increase the sample size, on a trial-and-error basis, until the MSE is sufficiently small. Or, drawing on the square root relationship in the formula, we could increase the sample size by a factor of about 9. Note that this approach always requires us to run at least a small simulation experiment, in order to estimate the MSE.

Alternatively, we can specify the size of a required confidence interval at the start. From (*1*), the length of the confidence interval is $zs/n^{0.5}$ in either direction. Therefore, if we specify a confidence interval of length R in either direction, we require a sample size of

$$n = (zs/R)^2 \qquad (2)$$

where we would use $z = 1$ for a 68 percent confidence interval, $z = 1.645$ for a 90 percent confidence interval, and so on. For example, suppose we want a 90 percent confidence interval to be ±1,500, or about 2 percent of the mean. Our simulation run of 1,000 trials produced a standard deviation of $s = 79,375$. Therefore, from the formula, we need a sample size of about $n = 7,577$ trials.

Using Precision Control

Crystal Ball provides another approach to the problem of controlling simulation error, known as Precision Control. With this feature, we can specify, in advance, the required precision in any outcome. Crystal Ball will then run trials until the desired precision is reached. To set up this capability, we must make specifications in two places.

First, consider the Forecast cell for which the required precision is specified. We highlight the cell and select Cell→Define Forecast from the Crystal Ball menu. Then, we click on the More>> button. We select the Precision option to access a section of the window headed by a check box for Select Precision Using. After making sure this box is checked, we click on one of the buttons for Absolute Units or Relative Percentage and enter the corresponding specification. We also check the box for Mean (or for one of the alternative measures). For example, we might specify the precision using Absolute Units of 100. This parameter sets the half-width of the desired confidence interval.

The second set of arrangements must be made under Run→Run Pre
Trials option. We check the box for Precision Control and enter the per
desired confidence interval. For example, if we select a confidence interv..
then Crystal Ball runs until the half-width of a 95 percent confidence interval is 100. At
this time, we should also make sure that the number of trials is a large number, since
Crystal Ball stops the simulation when the number of trials is reached or the precision is
reached, whichever comes first.

When we run a simulation under Precision Control, Crystal Ball periodically calculates the confidence interval for the Forecast cell we have specified, and it stops the simulation when the required precision is reached. In other words, Precision Control allows
us to set the maximum acceptable width of a confidence interval around the result.

Controlling Precision in Tail Probabilities

The MSE can also be used when we are estimating a probability related to the outcome.
We know that we can estimate a probability from a single simulation run by calculating
the percentage of trials in which the event occurred. But, just as with the sample average,
this estimate of the probability differs from the true probability by some unknown amount.
To determine the precision in such an estimate, we add a cell to the spreadsheet that shows
the value 1 when the event occurs and a 0 otherwise. For example, the statement IF(Profit
> 0,1,0) returns the value 1 when profit is positive and the value 0 otherwise. We define
the new cell as a Forecast cell. Since this cell takes on only the values 1 and 0, the Forecast
window reports under the Mean the percentage of times a 1 appeared. The MSE then represents the standard error of the estimate of this proportion.

Here is an illustration. We created a simple model with one Assumption cell containing a normal distribution with a mean of 100 and a standard deviation of 25. Then, we
added an IF statement to determine whether each sample was above or below 100. We
know, because the normal distribution is symmetrical, that precisely 50 percent of such
samples in the long run should be above 100. Let's experiment to see how close we get to
this known value for different sample sizes. The results are shown in the table below:

Trials	Sample Mean	MSE
10	0.30	0.15
100	0.47	0.05
1000	0.50	0.02

With ten trials, three exceed 100, so our estimate of the probability is 0.3. The MSE
is understandably high, at 0.15, or one-half the sample mean. At 100 trials, our estimate
is much closer to the true value of 0.5, and the MSE has dropped to 0.05, or 11 percent of
the sample mean. With 1,000 trials, the sample mean is right on target, and the MSE has
fallen to around 4 percent of the sample mean.

Precision versus Run Time

We have yet to raise an important issue in this discussion of run lengths, and that is the
trade-off between the *precision* of the results and the *time* it takes to get them. We know
that time is valuable for practical modelers, and time spent doing simulation runs may
come at the expense of time spent formulating the model, testing, collecting data, or performing some other aspect of the modeling process. Thus, an effective modeler does not
waste time on long simulation runs unless the additional precision has more value than the
next best use of that time.

On a 400 MHz computer, it takes about five seconds to run 1,000 trials for the Advertising Budget model, or less than a minute to run 10,000 trials. This suggests that we can easily afford the time for the precision we get at 1,000 trials, and we might even think about increasing the run length if more precision is valuable. But this is a very simple simulation model, so the trade-off between time and precision favors precision. However, it is not difficult to construct a spreadsheet model for which 1,000 trials would take hours. In such a case, it is worthwhile to investigate more carefully how much precision is really needed and to choose a run length that provides sufficient precision without taking too much time.

Simulation Error in a Decision Context

We offer one final word on the subject of simulation error. Sometimes, because they have lost sight of the broader context, analysts devote excessive effort to ensuring that individual simulation runs are highly precise. Rarely is the ultimate goal of a simulation study to estimate a single number. The broader goal is to provide help in making a decision. The ultimate test of our efforts is whether we have made a good *decision*, not whether our simulation results are highly precise. True, simulation error can lead to bad decisions, but it is only one source of such errors. As we have pointed out, the modeling process itself introduces errors by the very nature of the abstraction process; the model is not the real world. So the model we use to represent the world itself contains errors, and increasing the simulation run length cannot in any way reduce those errors. In addition, extreme precision may not be necessary if our goal is to make the best decision. (We return to this issue later, when we discuss optimization in simulation.)

For example, imagine we are estimating the NPV of a single project in which the choices are simply to accept or reject. Our decision criterion is to accept the project if the NPV is positive and otherwise to reject. Our simulation model, using a run length of 100, shows an NPV of $12.7 million with an MSE of $3.5 million. Now this is not a very precise estimate of the NPV, since a 95 percent confidence interval is from $5.7 million to $19.7 million. But the chances are slim that the NPV is negative, so the decision to accept is pretty clear. In this case, a run length of 100 trials seems fully justified. On the other hand, if we were choosing between two projects, this level of precision might not be sufficient. If the competing project were to show an estimated NPV of 13.9 million, with an MSE of 4.1, we could not be confident that the second project was actually better than the first. In this case, a longer run length would be needed to correctly identify the better of these two projects.

INTERPRETING SIMULATION OUTCOMES

When we run a simulation with, say, 1,000 trials, the raw result is simply a file of 1,000 values for each outcome, or Forecast cell. Fortunately, we rarely have to work with the raw data directly. Instead, we use Crystal Ball to display and summarize the results for us. Most often that summary takes the form of a histogram, or frequency chart, but there are other ways of summarizing output data. We first discuss how to use the Forecast chart and then the Statistics and Percentile views.

In the Advertising Budget example, our outcome cell is Profit, and the Forecast window is shown in Figure 9.2. Normally the Forecast window displays the histogram in the form of a probability distribution, but options are available (under View) to display it as a cumulative or reverse cumulative distribution. We can modify the appearance of this chart

CRYSTAL BALL TIP: SETTING RUN LENGTH

Experimental method

Use independent random seeds.

Select a short run length.

Perform a small number of independent samples and compare results.

If the range of results is too wide, increase the run length and repeat the process from the start.

MSE method

Use independent random seeds.

Choose an acceptable MSE. (Remember: a 95 percent confidence interval is about twice the MSE on either side of the mean.)

Run a simulation with a short run length and determine the MSE.

If the MSE is too large, increase the run length.

Precision Control method

Set the half-width of the confidence interval (in relative or absolute terms) when defining the Forecast cell.

Set the confidence level under Run Preferences.

Crystal Ball then runs until the confidence level is reached.

in various ways by selecting Preferences→Format, Chart, or Display Range. The Format option allows us to change the way the numerical data are displayed on the chart. The Chart option allows us to add the mean value to the chart. It also allows us to change the size of the bins that define the histogram. Finally, the Display Range option allows us to choose the range over which the data are displayed. We recommend using the Display Fixed Endpoints option from –Infinity to +Infinity, since this ensures that all of the simulation results are included in the chart. (The number of trials actually run and the number displayed are shown on the Frequency chart; if these differ, the chart can be misleading.)

Figure 9.3 also illustrates the use of the certainty sliders, the small black triangles at the extreme right and left of the histogram. These triangles can be moved to select a range of outcomes. Crystal Ball displays the percentage of trials that lie in the highlighted range in the Certainty window at the bottom of the chart. This is one way to determine a tail probability. As an alternative, we can enter numbers directly in the boxes at the bottom of the window; when we press Enter, Crystal Ball uses these limits to calculate the Certainty value.

While it can be very convenient to use the Forecast window to determine tail probabilities, this method can sometimes be quite inaccurate. Crystal Ball does not calculate the probabilities from the underlying simulation data, but rather, from the histogram itself. Since the histogram is only a summary of the underlying data, the required estimate can be poor. A better alternative is to define a Forecast cell in the model that takes on the value 1 when the event in question occurs (such as NPV > 0) and 0 otherwise. When the Forecast window for this cell is displayed, it shows the probability without any error due to summarizing the data.

More detailed information on the outcome distribution can be found by choosing View→Statistics in the Forecast window (see Figure 9.37). This table shows the number of trials, the mean outcome, and a host of other summary measures. The most useful of these are the minimum, maximum, and the mean standard error. The minimum and maximum are simply the extreme values encountered during the simulation run. They correspond to the best and worst cases, which are often of special interest. The mean standard error, discussed above, is a useful tool in determining the precision of the outcome estimates.

In most cases, we refer to the Forecast window to find the results of a simulation. Sometimes, especially when we must run a simulation many times, it is more convenient to record the results directly on the spreadsheet. Crystal Ball provides a special function for this purpose: CB.GETFORESTATFN. This function records any of the statistics from the Statistics view. Its inputs are the cell address of the Forecast cell and the number of the statistic. The statistics are numbered from 1 to 13, in the same order they appear in the Statistics view, starting with the number of trials. Thus, number 1 is the number of trials, number 2 is the mean, and number 13 is the MSE. To record the mean value for forecast cell E11, we would use the function CB. GETFORESTATFN (E11,2). (Note that this function returns the result #Value until a simulation has been run, at which point it takes on the numerical value.)

The third view of the outcomes provided by Crystal Ball is the Percentiles view (see Figure 9.38.) This table reports the percentiles of the outcome distribution. The default is to show every 10th percentile. For other percentiles, we can use the Crystal Ball function CB.GETFOREPERCENTFN, which returns the given percentile value of a Forecast cell. For example CB.GETFOREPERCENTFN(E11,25) returns the 25th percentile of the Forecast cell E11.

In some circumstances, it is useful to work directly with the simulation data itself and not with the various Crystal Ball Forecast windows. The option Run→Extract Data allows the user to create a spreadsheet containing the raw results for each Forecast cell. This is particularly useful if custom graphs are desired. A related option is Run→Create Report, which allows the user to create a spreadsheet with both the input assumptions and the outputs. This is a useful means of documenting multiple runs of the same model.

While most of this discussion has been devoted to the details of finding specific summary measures for simulation results, there is more to the art of interpreting simulations. First, we must take care in defining outcome variables. Unless we capture the essential aspects of the model, our interpretations will be handicapped. Having done this, we must then ensure that our estimates are sufficiently precise to support meaningful interpretation. Finally, we come to the results themselves. In most simulations, we are interested in both the expected outcome and the variability in outcomes. These two aspects of the situation are captured in the mean value, in the variance (or standard deviation), and in tail probabilities. Often, the value of simulation comes from providing insight into the trade-off between the expected outcome and the associated risks. This trade-off is illustrated well in the Netscape IPO example discussed earlier, where a deterministic analysis supported a high value for the company, while the simulation analysis revealed some extreme risks associated with the IPO.

FIGURE 9.38
Percentiles View

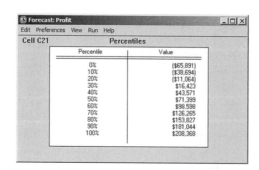

OPTIMIZATION IN SIMULATION

As we have seen, simulation is simply a method for estimating the distribution of an outcome variable for any specified set of decisions and other input variables. By itself, it offers no assistance in identifying an *optimal* (or even good) set of decisions. Ideally, we would like to marry the power of optimization to identify the best decision variables with the power of simulation to estimate outcome distributions. Unfortunately, the optimization approaches we covered in Chapter 8 are all based on the premise that the objective function can be measured deterministically. But when the objective function is a random variable, or even an expected value of a random variable, there is no simple way to employ Solver in finding the optimal decision variables. However, there are a number of other approaches to optimization using simulation. For illustration, we draw on the following example.

EXAMPLE

Hastings Sportswear

In November, Jeff Hastings of the fashion skiwear manufacturer Hastings Sportswear, Inc., faces the task of committing to specific production quantities for each skiwear item the company will offer in the coming year's line. Commitments are needed immediately, in order to reserve space in production facilities located throughout Asia. Actual demand for these products will not become known for at least six months. In fact, demand for the current year's line is only beginning to become available.

In an initial experiment, Jeff has asked six of his most knowledgeable people to make forecasts of demand for the various models of parkas. Forecasts for one product are given in the table below, along with the average and standard deviation of the forecasts. Experience suggests that the actual standard deviation in demand is roughly twice that of the standard deviation in the forecasts.

Forecaster 1	900	units
Forecaster 2	1,000	
Forecaster 3	900	
Forecaster 4	1,300	
Forecaster 5	800	
Forecaster 6	1,200	
Average	1,017	
Standard deviation	194	

Production costs for a typical parka run about 75 percent of the wholesale price, which in this case is $110. Unsold parkas can be sold at salvage for around 8 percent of the wholesale price.

What quantity should Jeff order for this model of parka?

Our first model for this situation is shown in Figure 9.39. This model has one decision variable, the number of parkas ordered. We have arbitrarily set it equal to the mean demand of 1,017 (cell C13). We have also assumed a normal distribution for demand, with a mean of 1,017 units and a standard deviation of 388, or twice the standard deviation of the six forecasts. Random samples from this distribution are created in cell C16 using the Crystal Ball function CB.NORMAL(C8,C10*C9). Since a normal distribution with a standard deviation nearly 40 percent of the mean can produce negative results, we truncate the normal sample with the maximum function to ensure that demand is nonnegative. The rest of the model is as follows:

- Cell C17 calculates regular sales by taking the minimum of demand and the number ordered.

FIGURE 9.39
Hastings Sportswear
Spreadsheet

Hastings1.xls

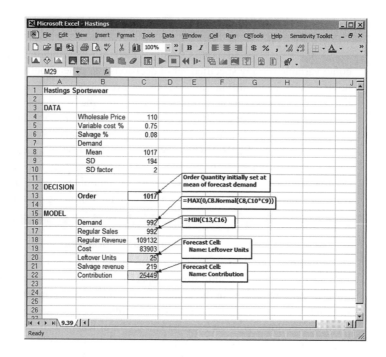

- Cell C18 is normal revenue, the number of units sold times the wholesale price.
- Cell C19 computes the costs, applied not to units sold but to units ordered.
- Cell C20 calculates the number of units left unsold.
- Cell C21 calculates the salvage revenue on unsold units.
- Cell C22 calculates profit contribution, the sum of normal revenue and salvage revenue, less costs.

Two outcomes of this analysis are of interest: one is profit contribution; the other is leftover units. Accordingly, we have designated two Forecast cells: contribution in cell C22 and leftover units in C20. Hastings Sportswear would like to determine an order quantity that leads to a large profit contribution, but without running the risk of having too many parkas left unsold. Since we cannot optimize two objective functions, we take contribution as our objective to be maximized, but we impose an informal constraint on the number of leftover units.

When we run a simulation of this model using a sample size of 1,000, we get the results shown in Figures 9.40 and 9.41. Figure 9.40 suggests that our average contribution from this product is $11,602 if we order 1,017 units. Contribution cannot exceed $27,968,

FIGURE 9.40
Distribution of Profit
Contribution for
Hastings Sportswear

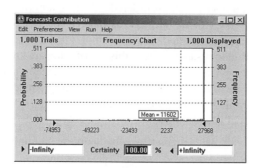

FIGURE 9.41
Distribution of Leftover
Units for Hastings
Sportswear

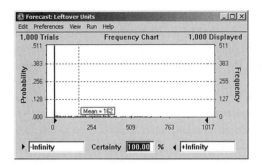

but it can fall as low as –$74,953. Evidently, there is considerable financial risk associated with this decision, in addition to the risk of having leftover units. The upper limit on the contribution ($27,968) is determined by the order quantity. Since we cannot sell more than we order, revenues cannot exceed the value of the wholesale price times the order quantity. Whenever demand exceeds the order quantity, we sell exactly what we ordered, and the contribution is $27,968. According to Figure 9.40, this occurs about 50 percent of the time. One of the interesting aspects of this case is how the normal distribution for demand is transformed by the lost-sales structure into the highly skewed distribution of profit contribution shown in Figure 9.40.

Figure 9.41 shows the distribution of leftover units associated with ordering 1,017 parkas. On average, we can expect to have 162 units left over, but this amount could range from zero to 1,017. In about half the cases simulated, demand exceeds supply, and so no units are left over. But there is a small chance that demand will be zero and that the entire stock will be left over.

We remarked earlier that simulation should be used only in situations where uncertainty is an essential feature of the problem. This is one of those situations. If there were no uncertainty in demand, and we knew demand would be 1,017, we would simply order 1,017 and be guaranteed to make $27,968 with no units left over. With uncertainty, however, our expected profit is only $11,602. Without uncertainty, the decision is obvious, and the results are entirely predictable. But this analysis misses the essential challenge of the problem—that when demand is uncertain, we must strike a balance between two kinds of risks. In one direction, there is the risk of ordering too many and having costly leftovers; in the other, there is the risk of ordering too few and having unmet demand. Simulation analysis reveals the risks associated with ordering mean demand, but to this point, it does not suggest an optimal order quantity.

Grid Search

Our goal in this problem is not merely to estimate the contribution we would receive for a particular order quantity, but to determine the *best* order quantity. The term "best" involves a large expected contribution, but it might also involve ensuring that the risk of a low contribution is not too great and that the number of parkas left over is acceptable. At this stage of our analysis, we have determined only that we would make $11,602 on average if we were to order 1,017 parkas. We also observed that we would have an average surplus of 162 parkas. These results might suggest that we consider ordering fewer than 1,017 parkas, since having so many units left over seems to be a waste of resources.

It is straightforward to change the number of parkas ordered (cell C13) and rerun the simulation to determine a new expected contribution. The results are as follows: when we order 900, we make $14,223 on average, which is better than when we order 1,017. The average number of unsold parkas declines, as we would expect, to 97. If we reduce the order quantity still further, to 800, average contribution rises to $14,767, and the average unsold stock drops to 64. If we order 700, we make $14,480 with an average of 40 unsold; at 600, we make $13,496 with an average of 25 unsold. It appears that ordering fewer parkas than the mean demand can increase contribution while also decreasing the leftover stock.

It is worthwhile to pause and think through the implications of these results. Parkas cost Hastings Sportswear $82.50 (= 0.75 × 110) and sell for $110. Ordering one parka less than demand results in one lost sale. The forgone profit is $27.50 (= 110 − 82.5). But ordering one too many results in $82.50 of excess production cost, of which only 8 percent, or $8.80, is recouped in salvage revenue. The surplus cost is $73.80 (= 82.5 − 8.8). Thus, there is a basic asymmetry in the costs of ordering one too many ($73.80) or one too few ($27.50). The economics favor ordering too few, because the incremental cost of this error is only one-third the incremental cost of ordering too many.

This conclusion is, of course, true only within the model world. One of the implications of ordering less than demand is that it may lead to unsatisfied customers, people who wanted our product but found it out of stock. This result can have serious consequences in the long run for our company, if unsatisfied customers tend to drift away to competitors. Such costs are not captured in our model. If they were, we would probably recommend a higher order level.

The procedure we have illustrated here is a form of **grid search.** In a grid search, we select a series of values we wish to test for a decision variable, and we run the simulation at each of these values. Our grid in this case consists of the order levels 600, 700, 800, and 900. We show the results of an expanded grid search in the table below:

Parkas Ordered	Expected Contribution	Expected Leftovers
600	$13,496	25
650	14,070	32
700	14,480	40
750	14,726	51
800	14,764	64
850	14,617	79
900	14,223	97
950	13,609	117
1,000	12,766	139
1,050	11,639	165
1,100	10,195	193
1,150	8,468	224
1,200	6,525	257

These results suggest that contribution is highest in the vicinity of 800 units, with an average of about 64 units unsold. (For more precision in our estimate of the best order quantity, we could refine the grid search by using a step size smaller than the 50 used in this table.)

Replicating the Model

When our model is particularly simple, there is another, more efficient approach to grid search. The trick is to replicate the model for each value of the decision variable we wish to test. This is illustrated in Figure 9.42, in which we have taken the one column model from Figure 9.39 and essentially copied it thirteen times, for order levels between 600 and 1,200. These alternatives for the order level appear in cells D13:P13. For each different

FIGURE 9.42
Hastings Sportswear
Spreadsheet with
Replications

Hastings2.xls

	A	B	C	D	E	F	G	H	I	J	K	L	M	N	O	P
1	Hastings Sportswear (with Replications)															
2																
3	DATA															
4		Wholesale Price	110													
5		Variable cost %	0.75													
6		Salvage %	0.08													
7		Demand														
8		Mean	1017													
9		SD	194													
10		SD factor	2													
11																
12	DECISION															
13		Order	1017	600	650	700	750	800	850	900	950	1000	1050	1100	1150	1200
14																
15	MODEL															
16		Demand	1147	1147	1147	1147	1147	1147	1147	1147	1147	1147	1147	1147	1147	1147
17		Regular Sales	1017	600	650	700	750	800	850	900	950	1000	1050	1100	1147	1147
18		Regular Revenue	111870	66000	71500	77000	82500	88000	93500	99000	104500	110000	115500	121000	126212	126212
19		Cost	83903	49500	53625	57750	61875	66000	70125	74250	78375	82500	86625	90750	94875	99000
20		Leftover Units	0	0	0	0	0	0	0	0	0	0	0	0	3	53
21		Salvage revenue	0	0	0	0	0	0	0	0	0	0	0	0	23	463
22		Contribution	27968	16500	17875	19250	20625	22000	23375	24750	26125	27500	28875	30250	31360	27675
23						CB.GetForeStatFN(D20,2)										
24																
25		Mean leftovers		25	32	40	51	64	79	97	117	139	164	192	222	254
26		Mean contribution		13,984	14,652	15,153	15,428	15,508	15,362	14,968	14,327	13,417	12,258	10,831	9,157	7,264
27						CB.GetForeStatFN(D22,2)										
28																

order level, there may be different outcomes in the cells below. However, the parameters in the range C4:C10 are used in the calculations for each alternative.

Several aspects of this model are noteworthy. One is that we have simulated demand only once, in cell C16, and then used this random value for all the other values of the decision variable. In other words, the cells to the right of C16 all reference the contents of C16. The alternative would be to sample from a different distribution for each decision variable. However, in that design, there would be two possible sources of variability in the profit contribution—the randomness in demand and the choice of an order quantity. Sampling once not only cuts down on simulation run time, it also removes one of these sources of variability. In the design of Figure 9.42, the only source of difference between one profit outcome and another is the choice of an order quantity.

Since we are interested both in contribution and in the number of leftover units as the order level changes, we must create Forecast cells for each of these results for each order quantity. First, we remove the Forecast status of cell C20. We select this cell and then choose Cell→Clear Data, clicking OK to confirm our intention. Next, we define cells D22:P22 as Forecast cells. Although it's a little tedious, it helps to give each of these cells a descriptive name. Since we are searching among order levels, we might name the cells according to the corresponding order level, Contribution at 600 for cell D22, Contribution at 650 for E22, and so on. We repeat this procedure for the leftover units in cells D20:P20, using appropriate names. This gives us a total of twenty-six forecasts. Then, when we run the simulation, twenty-six Forecast windows open on the screen. (If the windows seem distracting, we can send them to the background by clicking on the spreadsheet itself. Alternatively, when the simulation completes, we can choose Run→Forecast Windows and can then click the button for Close All Forecasts. To turn off the display of Forecast windows during a simulation, choose Run Preferences→Speed→Suppress Forecast Windows.)

One convenient way to record the results on the spreadsheet itself is to use the Crystal Ball function CB.GETFORESTATFN, which we described briefly in an earlier section. In the

Results section of Figure 9.42, we have used this function to record the mean values for both the leftover units (in row 25) and the contribution (in row 26) for each order level. For example, the formula for cell D25 is CB.GETFORESTATFN(D20,2). Once the simulation has been completed, this cell displays the mean value of the forecast for leftover units in cell D20.

In Figure 9.43, we show graphs of these results as the order level varies from 600 to 1,200. The graph for mean contribution shows that the maximum occurs at an order level of about 750 or 800. It also suggests that any order level between about 700 and 850 may be acceptable, since mean contribution is within 1 percent of the optimum in this range. Over this same range, the mean number of leftover units varies from 40 to 80. If we wish to take risk into account, we can choose an order level anywhere in this range and be sure we are not giving up too much in contribution. Moreover, we can select an order level at the lower end to save about 40 leftover units, on average, at a cost of only 1 percent of contribution.

Crystal Ball provides a specialized chart called a **trend chart,** which can be used to depict the sensitivity of Forecast cells to decision variables or other inputs. After the simulation run is finished, we select Run→Open Trend Chart. Under Choose Forecasts, we select the thirteen outputs for contribution. Under Chart Preferences, we select Vertical for the Forecast Axis and Zero Based for the Value Axis. Then, we check the box for 0 percent Certainty Band, leaving the other boxes unchecked. The result, shown in Figure 9.44, shows the median level of contribution for each of the thirteen order levels from 600 to 1,200 units. Recall that the median of a distribution divides the outcomes in half. Referring back to Figure 9.40, we can see that the median lies above the mean in this case because the outcomes are skewed to the left. Figure 9.44 shows that if we wanted to optimize the median contribution (rather than the mean), we would choose an order level around 1,000 units, close to mean demand.

Figure 9.45 displays another trend chart for the same data. This version gives an indication of the range of outcomes, or the risks, associated with these alternatives. To produce

FIGURE 9.43
Expected Contributions and Expected Leftovers for Hastings Sportswear

Hastings2.xls

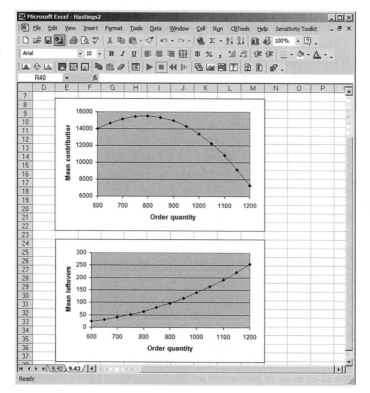

FIGURE 9.44
Trend Chart for Median
Contribution

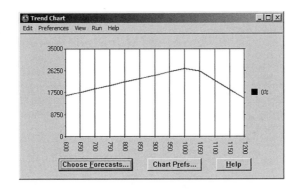

FIGURE 9.45
Trend Chart for Median
Contribution with
Uncertainty Bands

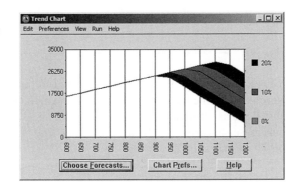

this display, we check the boxes for 0 percent, 10 percent, and 20 percent Certainty Bands. In the chart, the thin black line represents the median (for example, $13,878 at an order level of 1,200). The interior bands show outcomes that represent levels at percentiles of 45 percent and 55 percent. For an order level of 1,200, the 10 percent band extends from about $8,750 to about $19,640. The next pair of bands corresponds to percentiles of 40 percent and 60 percent The chart shows that the risk, or range of outcomes, increases as the order quantity increases above 950 units. Again, if we wish to reduce risk, we might want to order fewer than 1,000 parkas, although we lower the median contribution by doing so.

The Crystal Ball trend chart is a convenient way to display the sensitivity of an output variable to any input that ranges over multiple values. It is a natural way to perform optimization in simple simulation models with a single decision variable, provided that the median outcome is a reasonable objective. It also provides a convenient device for displaying the trade-off between the median outcome and the risks of extreme outcomes.

Using CB Sensitivity

The CB Sensitivity tool, which we discussed earlier in the context of sensitivity analysis, can also be used for optimization. It is particularly useful for models that are too complex for the replication approach, or when we want to vary two inputs (either decision variables or other parameters). We illustrate using the original Hastings Sportswear model of Figure 9.39. When we call up CB Sensitivity, we find the two Forecast cells are already identified. We choose to record not only the mean values, but also the minimum and maximum values for each. To find the optimal value for the order level, we vary it from 600 to 1,200 in steps of 50. The results are shown in Figure 9.46. As we have already determined, the optimal order level for maximizing mean profit is around 800. However, the *range* of outcomes from minimum to maximum increases as we increase the order quantity, so it might

FIGURE 9.46
CB Sensitivity Table
for Order Level

Hastings1.xls

	A	B	C	D	E	F	G
1	Order	Contribution: Mean	Contribution: Min	Contribution: Max	Leftover Units: Mean	Leftover Units: Min	Leftover Units: Max
2	600	14171	-44220	16500	23	0	600
3	650	14799	-47905	17875	30	0	650
4	700	15234	-51590	19250	40	0	700
5	750	15488	-55275	20625	51	0	750
6	800	15533	-58960	22000	64	0	800
7	850	15332	-62645	23375	79	0	850
8	900	14887	-66330	24750	97	0	900
9	950	14155	-70015	26125	118	0	950
10	1000	13200	-73700	27500	141	0	1000
11	1050	11964	-77385	28875	167	0	1050
12	1100	10464	-81070	30250	196	0	1100
13	1150	8687	-84755	31625	227	0	1150
14	1200	6638	-88440	33000	260	0	1200

be advantageous to order fewer than 800 if we wanted to limit the downside risk. Also shown in Figure 9.46 are the mean, minimum, and maximum values for leftovers. Here, we can see that the maximum number of units left over is always the order quantity, so this measure increases linearly with the order quantity. The mean number left over, however, increases at an increasing rate.

In this model, the only true decision variable is the number of parkas ordered, cell C13. We would like to optimize this variable, but we might also like to know how sensitive the results are to the cost of parkas. Using the CB Sensitivity tool, we can run a simulation and record the expected contribution for each combination of input values for order quantity and unit cost. We let the order level range from 600 to 1,200 in increments of 100, and we let the cost range from 0.70 to 0.90 in increments of 0.05.

For these settings, CB Sensitivity runs Crystal Ball thirty-five times (seven values for the order level times five values for costs) and builds the table shown in Figure 9.47. For a fixed order level, we can see how sensitive the mean contribution is to the cost by reading across the rows. For a given cost, we can determine how sensitive the mean contribution is to the order level by reading down the columns. The optimal expected contribution for each value of the cost parameter is highlighted in bold. One interesting message emerging from this table is that the optimal number of parkas drops from around 800 to around 600 as costs increase from 70 percent to 90 percent.

FIGURE 9.47
CB Sensitivity Table for
Order Level and Price

Hastings1.xls

	A	B	C	D	E	F	G	H
1	Contribution: Mean							
2		Variable cost %						
3	Order	0.70	0.75	0.80	0.85	0.90		
4	600	17417	14117	10817	7517	4217		
5	700	19047	15197	11347	7497	3647		
6	800	19818	15418	11018	6618	2218		
7	900	19791	14841	9891	4941	-9		
8	1000	18726	13226	7726	2226	-3274		
9	1100	16481	10431	4381	-1669	-7719		
10	1200	13169	6569	-31	-6631	-13231		

Complex Optimization Problems: Using Optquest

The Hastings Sportswear example represents a simple optimization problem in the sense that it has only one decision variable. In general, grid search is a practical approach to optimization when we have one or two decision variables. The CB Sensitivity tool automates a grid search, but it, too, is limited to one or two variables. When the problem involves three or more decision variables, and possibly constraints as well, these approaches have limited usefulness. In such cases, we turn to a sophisticated Crystal Ball tool called **Optquest,** which optimizes the choice of decision variables when the objective function is based on simulation outcomes.

Optimizing decision variables based on simulation outcomes can be an extremely challenging task. We saw in Chapter 8 that optimizing deterministic models requires some attention to model structure so that the optimization algorithm matches the problem at hand. Simulation models make the problem one level more complex, because we cannot measure the objective function precisely. Instead, we can only estimate it within the limits of precision achieved by our simulation. This "fuzziness" in the objective function rules out the possibility of directly adapting the deterministic optimization algorithms (hill climbing or the linear solver) to problems involving randomness. Optquest takes a novel approach to this problem, which we describe in general terms later.

The concepts needed to use Optquest should be familiar from our study of deterministic optimization in Chapter 8. Optquest attempts to maximize or minimize an **objective function,** by changing the values of **decision variables,** possibly subject to one or more **constraints.** Optquest also introduces a new concept, that of a **requirement,** which is a restriction on the distribution of forecast values, such as the mean or 10th percentile.

The objective function in Optquest can be any summary measure of a Forecast cell. Typically, we would maximize or minimize the mean value of the forecast. However, there are circumstances in which we might wish to minimize the variance, minimize the probability of a loss, or maximize the 5th percentile of the distribution of forecast values.

Decision variables are specified directly in Crystal Ball by highlighting a cell and choosing Define→Decision Variable. Each decision variable can be assigned lower and upper limits (the tighter these limits, the better Optquest works). Also, decision values can be made discrete or continuous. With the discrete option, we can specify the number of evenly spaced discrete alternatives between a minimum and maximum value. In the case of continuous decision variables, fractional values are allowed.

As we saw in Chapter 8, constraints or relationships among decision variables are a common feature of optimization problems. Optquest allows the user to specify *linear* constraints among the decision variables. For example, in a portfolio problem, the total amount invested must add up to the amount available. Optquest does not consider candidate solutions that violate any of the constraints.

Sometimes, we wish to impose a constraint on the distribution of a Forecast cell. For example, we might wish to maximize the mean return from a portfolio, but also impose a ceiling on the standard deviation of the return (a measure of risk). The objective here is to maximize mean return. The constraint, or requirement in Crystal Ball language, is that the standard deviation must not exceed a given upper limit. In this case, the objective function and the requirement apply to different measures of the distribution of the same forecast. In other cases, the objective function and the requirement could apply to different forecasts. Requirements are different from constraints because they cannot be imposed before a simulation is run, only afterward.

CRYSTAL BALL TIP: OPTQUEST CONCEPTS

Key features of Optquest include:

Objective: Forecast cell to be maximized or minimized. Optquest allows the user to optimize any one of various summary measures of the objective—for example, mean, standard deviation, or 10th percentile.

Decision variable: Spreadsheet parameters Optquest uses to optimize the objective. These must be defined as Decision cells in Crystal Ball.

Constraint: Optquest allows any number of linear constraints among the decision variables. Solutions that violate these constraints are not considered feasible and are not reported.

Requirement: A constraint on a summary measure of a Forecast. For example, one could require that the standard deviation not exceed a set limit. Requirements can be evaluated only after a simulation run; thus, Optquest may report a solution that violates a requirement, but Optquest labels the solution infeasible.

The algorithms used by Optquest are complex and beyond the scope of this book, so we only sketch them here.[3] Since the problems Optquest is designed to tackle involve uncertainty, it cannot use the same approach as Solver takes for deterministic problems. Optquest takes a **heuristic** approach to optimization, by which we mean that it searches intelligently for better and better solutions, but Optquest cannot guarantee that it finds the global optimum. As a consequence, we must take extra care to ensure that the results Optquest gives us are sensible.

Optquest uses three distinct heuristics in its search for optimal solutions: scatter search, tabu search, and neural networks. Scatter search generates an initial population of candidate solutions and uses simulation to estimate the objective for each one. It then creates another generation of solutions by taking combinations of the previous solutions. At each generation, the best solutions are saved and the worst discarded. In this fashion, the general quality (by which we mean the value of the objective function) of the population of solutions improves over time. Tabu search is superimposed on the scatter search to control and direct the generation of solutions. Tabu search uses computer memory in various ways to ensure that the search does not reinvestigate solutions that have already been evaluated (such solutions are "tabu") and to ensure that the population remains sufficiently diverse over time. Finally, neural networks can be used (at the option of the user) to quickly screen out candidate solutions that are likely to result in poor values of the objective. A neural network is a predictive model that, in this case, predicts the objective function value for a candidate solution based on all the past solutions that have been evaluated. Using these heuristics, Optquest can evaluate hundreds or thousands of candidates, depending on the time it is given and the complexity of the model, and it often finds optimal or near optimal solutions to quite complex problems. By using several examples, we illustrate how Optquest works.

Veerman Furniture Company (Revisited)

In Chapter 8, we discussed the allocation problem facing Veerman Furniture, which was to choose how much to produce of three products (chairs, desks, and tables) to maximize profits, without using more production time than is available in three departments (fabrication, assembly, and shipping) and without exceeding demand. We solved this problem as a deterministic linear program, and we found that maximum profits of $8,400 were achieved by making 275 desks, 100 tables, and no chairs (see Figure 8.18).

While this solution is unambiguously optimal for the problem as we stated it, it may not be directly applicable in the real world. For one thing, demands are usually forecasts,

---

[3] A more complete description can be found at the Web site www.decisioneering.com/optquest/methodology.html.

and those forecasts are somewhat uncertain. If the actual demands turn out to be higher or lower than forecasts, the optimal solution to the deterministic problem may no longer be optimal, or even feasible. For example, in the optimal solution, we make 100 tables, which meets the demand exactly. If actual demand is 110, we might wish we had made more tables. On the other hand, if demand is 90, we will have 10 tables in surplus and would clearly have done better to reallocate our resources. For simplicity, we assume that solutions in which demand is less than production for at least one product are considered infeasible. That is, Veerman Furniture wants to avoid a surplus.

Our first step in introducing uncertainty into this model is to analyze the performance of the optimal deterministic solution when demand is uncertain. We assume that demand for each product is normally distributed, with a mean equal to our point forecast and a standard deviation equal to 10 percent of the mean. Likewise, we assume that the profit contributions from each product are normally distributed, with a mean given by our point forecasts and a standard deviation equal to 10 percent of the mean. We modify the original spreadsheet by using the CB.NORMAL function for the profit contributions in cells B8:D8 and demands in cells G15:G17 (see Figure 9.48). We also determine whether the solution is feasible by adding a formula in cell H19 that takes on the value 1 when demands for all the products exceed production (i.e., there is no surplus) and the value 0 otherwise. The Forecast cells are Total Profit in E8 (our original objective function) and Feasibility in cell H19.

When we run a simulation using the optimal deterministic solution, we find that the mean profit is \$8,365, essentially unchanged from the deterministic solution. However, that solution results in surplus production, and is thereby infeasible, 62 percent of the time. (We obtain this estimate as the mean value of the Feasibility Forecast cell.) Note that since the demand constraint on tables was binding in the original model, half the time the simulated demand falls below the mean and makes the solution infeasible. The constraint on desk demand was not binding, but the excess demand was small enough that, an additional 12 percent of the time in the simulation, this constraint is violated when table demand is not.

A solution that is infeasible 62 percent of the time is unlikely to be attractive to management. But we cannot simply impose a constraint that our solution must be feasible, because we do not know demand in advance. The best we can do is find a set of decisions that offers high average profit and is highly likely to be feasible. This is a task for Optquest.

FIGURE 9.48
Veerman Furniture
Spreadsheet for
Optquest

Veerman.xls

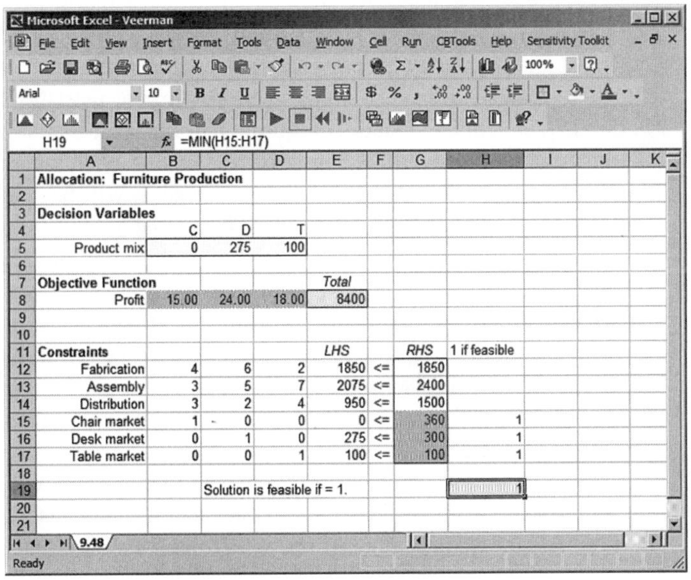

	A	B	C	D	E	F	G	H	I	J	K
1	Allocation: Furniture Production										
2											
3	Decision Variables										
4			C	D	T						
5		Product mix	0	275	100						
6											
7	Objective Function				Total						
8		Profit	15.00	24.00	18.00	8400					
9											
10											
11	Constraints					LHS		RHS	1 if feasible		
12		Fabrication	4	6	2	1850	<=	1850			
13		Assembly	3	5	7	2075	<=	2400			
14		Distribution	3	2	4	950	<=	1500			
15		Chair market	1	0	0	0	<=	360	1		
16		Desk market	0	1	0	275	<=	300	1		
17		Table market	0	0	1	100	<=	100	1		
18											
19				Solution is feasible if = 1.				1			
20											
21											

To set up the spreadsheet for Optquest, we must define decision variables, constraints, the objective function, and requirements. Uncertain parameters (Assumption cells), outputs (Forecast cells), and decision variables (Decision cells) are all defined before opening the Optquest program; the remaining inputs are defined within Optquest itself.

We define the decision variables in cells B5:D5 one at a time, using the Crystal Ball command Cell→Define Decision. This is also an opportunity to assign names to the variables, for clarity in the steps that follow. Initially, we specify that each decision variable is discrete, with a step size of 10 units, a lower bound of zero, and an upper bound equal to mean demand. Since our goal is to limit the percentage of time the solution is infeasible, we can anticipate that the optimal values of the decision variables lie below mean demand.

Finally, it is necessary to determine a suitable run length before opening Optquest, since it uses whatever simulation run length has been specified in Run Preferences. Again, recall that results may differ slightly in different runs because of the variability in random samples. Recall also that we can control such differences by selecting the simulation run length. A preliminary simulation run with 1,000 trials yields an MSE for profit of 21, or about 0.2 percent (= 21/8,400). Another run with 100 trials yields an MSE of 74, or about 1 percent. Since 1 percent accuracy is probably sufficient for our purposes, and the shorter run length allows Optquest to examine more alternative solutions, we specify a run length of 100 trials. It is also important to set the random number seed (in Crystal Ball, check Use Same Sequence of Random Numbers under Run Preferences→Sampling) so that the same random outcomes are used on every Optquest run. This reduces the variance between runs and makes the search for an optimum more efficient.

We open Optquest by choosing CBTools→Optquest. Within Optquest, we choose File→New, and Optquest prepares the spreadsheet for optimization. (It is a good idea to have only one spreadsheet open in Crystal Ball when running Optquest.) Optquest brings up four windows in turn: Decision Variable Selection, Constraints, Forecast Selection, and Options. We can edit the default information in these windows, or click OK to accept them as given. We can also return to any of these windows by making a selection from the Optquest Tools menu or its Window menu.

The Decision Variables window in this case simply confirms the definitions of the variables specified earlier in Crystal Ball. In the Constraints window, we enter the three production constraints (Fabrication, Assembly, and Distribution). The easiest way to do this is to click on Sum all Variables and edit the text as necessary. When all three constraints have been entered, we click OK. The next window is Forecast Selection. Here, we see two rows, one for each Forecast cell (Total Profit and Feasibility). Total Profit is our objective, so we specify Select→Maximize Objective and then Forecast Statistic→Mean. Our requirement is that the solution be feasible at least 90 percent of the time, so for Feasibility, we choose Select→Requirement, Forecast Statistic→Mean, and in the Lower Bound column, we enter 0.9. This ensures that cell H19, which takes on the value 1 when the solution is feasible and the value 0 otherwise, will be 1 on at least 90 percent of the trials. In other words, the solution will be feasible at least 90 percent of the time.

These three windows can be resized so that they are displayed simultaneously, as shown in Figure 9.49. The last window is Options. For example, run-time options are shown on a drop-down list under the Time tab. However, the user can override the options given. (Five minutes represents the shortest run time on the drop-down list of times, but shorter run times are useful during debugging and preliminary testing, while longer run times ensure higher quality solutions.) We enter three minutes as a run time and click on OK. Then, we select Run→Start.

When Optquest begins a run, it opens a Status and Solutions window. This window shows the values of the decision variables and the Forecast cells for the current run, the best run so far, and a number of previous runs. Two other useful windows can be opened

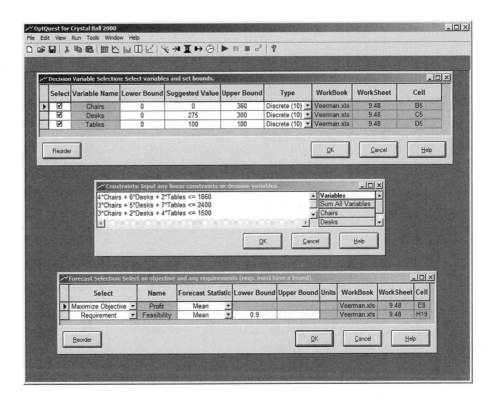

from the Optquest menu: the Performance Graph and the Current Decision Variables bar graph. The Performance Graph shows the value of the objective for the best alternative found so far during the search. This graph generally increases (for maximization) or decreases (for minimization) as the search progresses. In most cases, it changes quickly early in the run, as improvements are being found frequently, and then it changes more slowly as better solutions become harder to find. It is a good idea to watch this graph during an Optquest run, as it gives a good overall indication of how the search is progressing. The Current Decision Variables window, which shows the values of the decision variables being tested on the current run, may also be helpful by providing a visual sense of which combinations of decision variables have generated improved solutions.

The results of this first run are shown in Figure 9.50. The best solution found was to produce 50 chairs, 250 desks, and 80 tables. This solution has an estimated profit of $8,190 and is feasible 93.2 percent of the time. The Performance Graph shows that the best alternative was found rather early in the search and could not be improved with further testing. We can learn more about the search by choosing Run→Solution Analysis from the Optquest menu, selecting the top 5 percent of the runs, and then selecting Analyze. The results are shown in Figure 9.51. Among the top 5 percent of the cases tested, the average value of profit was $7,913, and the average values of the decision variables were 108 for chairs, 210 for desks, and 70 for tables. It appears that the optimal solution involves production of all three products, with a higher number of desks and chairs and fewer tables. However, we also notice in Figure 9.51 that in the top five solutions, the optimal values of the decision variables are not very consistent. The number of chairs, for example, varies from 50 to 140. This suggests that a more refined search might be valuable. One way to improve the search would be to allow the decision variables to vary by one unit rather than ten. This can be done by selecting Tools→Decision Variables, changing the necessary parameters, and clicking OK.

FIGURE 9.50
Optquest Results for
Step Size 10

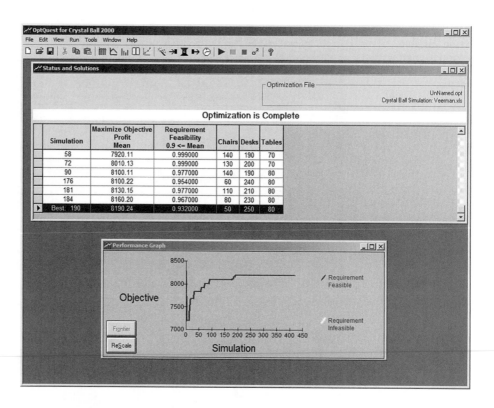

FIGURE 9.51
Optquest Solution
Analysis

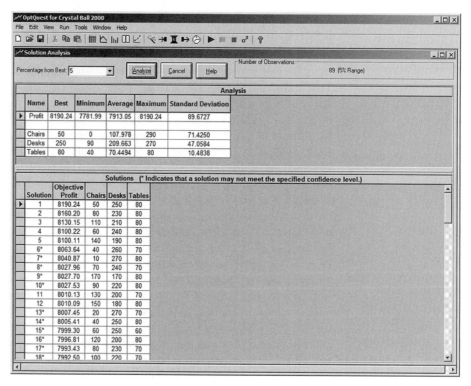

Another three-minute run of Optquest gives the results shown in Figure 9.52. With Optquest searching over a finer grid, we would expect the solution to improve, and it does. The best solution found in this run shows a profit of $8,196, feasible 90.5 percent of the time, producing 54 chairs, 244 desks, and 85 tables. The Solution Analysis shows that the top 5 percent of the cases tested had an average profit of $8,009. More importantly, the top ten cases showed much more stability in the values of the decision variables. For chairs, the solution values varied from 52 to 70, a much smaller range than in the previous run. We might expect the percentage of time the solution is feasible to decline as profit increases. The fact that both runs produced solutions somewhat above our 90 percent requirement suggests that it may still be possible to locate a better mean profit by allowing feasibility to drop closer to 90 percent. (A longer run would confirm this hypothesis.) Remember, however, that both the objective function and the requirement are measured with some degree of imprecision, so we should not expect the requirement to be met exactly.

The solution found above is probably good enough for practical purposes. But it is a good idea to test this solution by redefining the decision variables again, this time as continuous. The optimal solution shows no improvement in a short run, but with longer runs, we have encountered a profit of $8,380, feasible 90 percent of the time, producing 54.8 chairs, 243.6 desks, and 84.3 tables. The Solution Analysis shows a limited range of variation in the values of the decision variables. The number of chairs produced ranges from 54.5 to 95.6, desks from 216.1 to 243.9, and tables from 84.1 to 85.9. The continuous runs of Optquest confirm what we found earlier using a discrete search. We can construct a solution in which production exceeds demand for any product only about 10 percent of the time by producing around 50 chairs, 240 desks, and 85 tables. The profit from this plan

FIGURE 9.52
Optquest Results for
Step Size 1

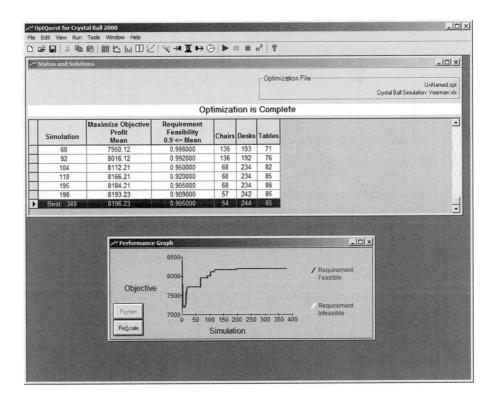

is not quite as high as in the deterministic formulation of the problem, but it is not radically lower. Finally, there is some degree of freedom in our choice of production levels, at least for chairs and desks, since these can vary somewhat from the optimal levels without significantly impacting profit.

This set of decision variables is quite different from the deterministic solution—not only quantitatively, but qualitatively as well. In the deterministic formulation of the problem, we produce no chairs at all, and the binding constraints are fabrication capacity and tables demand. In the current version of the problem, we find it advantageous to produce some of all three products, although we continue to produce more desks than either chairs or tables. From a deterministic point of view, *none* of the constraints is binding under this solution. We actually have unused production resources in all three departments. While this makes no sense from the point of view of linear programming, it does make sense when we take into account the desire to maintain a high probability of feasibility in demand, given uncertainty.

We conclude this example with some rules of thumb for using Optquest effectively. First, experiment with different values of the decision variables *before* running Optquest, to make sure that the objective function is not flat. If widely different values of the decision variables give essentially the same values of the objective, the problem may not be well specified, and the results from Optquest will be misleading. Second, set the simulation run length as short as possible, since that allows Optquest to try the maximum number of solutions in a given amount of time. Use the MSE for each of the Forecast cells in the model to determine an acceptable level of simulation error. (If the error is too high, Optquest could settle on a solution that appears optimal only because simulation error leads to a good value of the objective.) Third, start with discrete decision variables and a coarse grid, then refine the grid in later runs. Specify continuous variables only if needed. The coarser the grid, the fewer alternatives Optquest can search through. (Of course, if the grid is too coarse, as it was in our initial run in this example, the results may not be sufficient.) Consult the Performance Graph to suggest whether the run length is long enough or whether a longer run is likely to produce an improvement. Fourth, use Solution Analysis to examine the top 5 percent or 10 percent, or perhaps the top ten alternative solutions. Look for fairly consistent values of the decision variables among these alternatives, as a sign of robustness in the optimal solution. Also, look for suboptimal solutions that are close to optimal and preferred for reasons outside the model.

Portfolio Optimization

A standard problem in finance is to find the best way to allocate a pool of money to a set of investments. Each investment vehicle has its own characteristics for return and risk. Some, such as government bonds, have low returns and low variability. Others, such as technology stocks, may have high returns but high variability. The objective is to formulate

---

CRYSTAL BALL TIP: OPTQUEST RULES OF THUMB

Before running Optquest, experiment with various values of the decision variables to determine that the objective function is shaped like a hill and not flat.

Set the run length to the smallest possible value consistent with an acceptable simulation error.

Start with discrete decision variables and a coarse grid and gradually refine the search.

Use Solution Analysis to determine whether the top solutions are consistent, suggesting that a true optimal solution has been identified.

an investment portfolio that has an attractive average return with low risk. In general, these goals conflict: high mean return is usually associated with high risk.

Investing in Four Stocks

A particular investor has $100,000 to invest. She is considering investing her money in four stocks: Microsoft, GM, GE, and AT&T. The table below gives the average returns on these investments as well as the standard deviation of returns. (For simplicity in this example, we assume that returns among these assets are uncorrelated.) We want to determine how much to invest in each fund to maximize the average return, while keeping risk at an acceptable level. Since risk can be measured in different ways, it is important to explore the sensitivity of the solution to the risk measure used.

Investment	Annual Return	Standard Deviation
MSFT	40%	28%
AT&T	16%	22%
GM	20%	24%
GE	30%	18%

Our initial spreadsheet for this problem is shown in Figure 9.53. We have entered the returns data in cells C5:F6 and, for future use, have calculated the variances in cells C7:F7. The four decision variables in cells C11:F11 represent the proportion of the portfolio allocated to each investment. The total invested is calculated in cell G11 by adding the four decision variables. The decision variables are squared for future use in cells C12:F12. Cell E14 contains the target standard deviation we want our portfolio not to exceed. Finally, the mean portfolio return and the standard deviation of the return are calculated in cells C18 and E18, respectively. The mean return of the portfolio is the weighted average of the mean returns of the individual stocks, with the weights being the proportions invested. Similarly, the variance of the portfolio return is the weighted average of the variances of the individual stocks, with the weights being the squared proportions. The standard deviation of the portfolio return is simply the square root of its variance.

FIGURE 9.53
Spreadsheet for the Portfolio Application Problem

Portfolio.xls

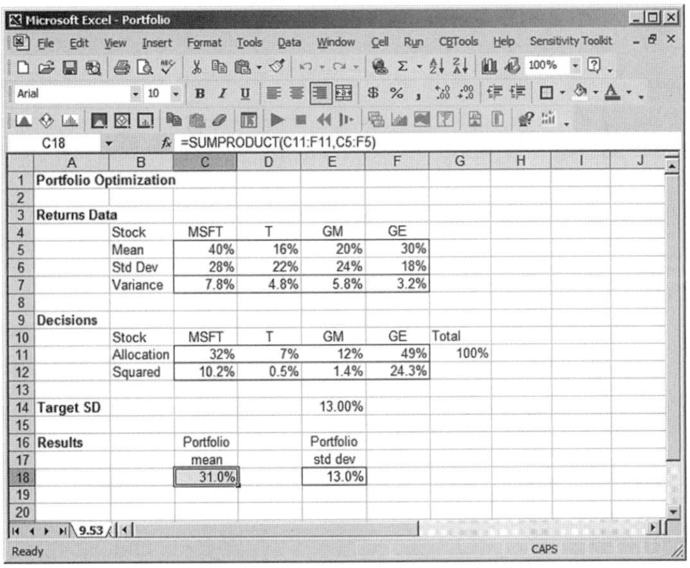

	A	B	C	D	E	F	G	H	I	J
1	Portfolio Optimization									
2										
3	Returns Data									
4		Stock	MSFT	T	GM	GE				
5		Mean	40%	16%	20%	30%				
6		Std Dev	28%	22%	24%	18%				
7		Variance	7.8%	4.8%	5.8%	3.2%				
8										
9	Decisions									
10		Stock	MSFT	T	GM	GE	Total			
11		Allocation	32%	7%	12%	49%	100%			
12		Squared	10.2%	0.5%	1.4%	24.3%				
13										
14	Target SD				13.00%					
15										
16	Results		Portfolio		Portfolio					
17			mean		std dev					
18			31.0%		13.0%					
19										
20										

C18 =SUMPRODUCT(C11:F11,C5:F5)

The investor's major objective is to make the portfolio mean return as high as possible. This could be achieved by investing the entire portfolio in Microsoft, since it has the highest mean return of the four stocks. However, the portfolio would then have a very high risk, as measured by the standard deviation of 28 percent for Microsoft. One way to control the risk would be to maximize the mean return subject to a constraint on the portfolio standard deviation. This can be accomplished using Solver. The objective is the portfolio mean return in cell C18. The decision variables are the portfolio weights in cells C11:F11. There are two constraints: one is that the weights must sum to one; the other is that the portfolio standard deviation in cell E18 must be less than or equal to the target given in cell E14 (in this case, 13 percent). The objective function is linear in the decision variables, as is the first constraint. However, the second constraint is nonlinear since it involves the squared values of the decision variables. Thus, the entire problem is nonlinear, and we can use the nonlinear Solver option to find an optimal solution.

The solution is shown in Figure 9.53. The mean return for the optimal portfolio is 31 percent, with the standard deviation at its ceiling of 13 percent. The optimal portfolio weights are 32 percent in Microsoft, 7 percent in AT&T, 12 percent in GM, and 49 percent in GE. This portfolio achieves the highest possible mean return while limiting risk (as measured by the standard deviation) to an acceptable level.

We can gain additional insight into this problem by varying the investor's tolerance for risk, as expressed by the limit on the standard deviation of the portfolio return. Figure 9.54 shows the results of running Solver Sensitivity on this model for values of the standard deviation target from 12 percent to 30 percent (no feasible portfolios have lower levels of risk). Several interesting observations can be made based on these results. First, as we increase the allowable risk, the portfolio mean increases, but at a decreasing rate. In fact, above a standard deviation of 28 percent, no improvement is possible, since the entire portfolio is invested in Microsoft. When the allowable risk is low, the optimal plan involves investing in all four stocks—most heavily in Microsoft and GE. As the allowable risk increases, the optimal plan invests more in Microsoft and less in both AT&T and GM. The share invested in GE first increases, reaching a maximum of 55 percent, and then decreases to zero.

FIGURE 9.54
Sensitivity of the Optimal Solution to Risk Tolerance

Portfolio.xls

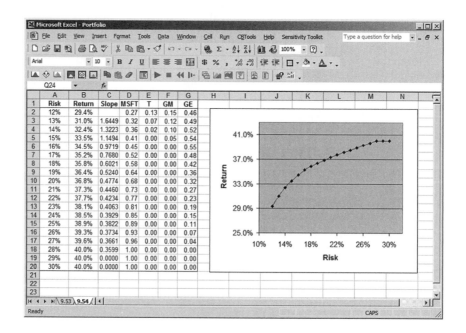

The analysis we have carried out to this point is technically deterministic, although we have calculated the mean and standard deviation of the portfolio. This approach gives us some important information about the distribution of returns for any allocation, but it does not give us the entire distribution of returns. To generate this distribution, and to prepare for using Optquest, we modify our model to simulate actual returns from each stock and to determine the resulting distribution of portfolio returns. Figure 9.55 shows the modified model. In cells C8:F8, we have entered lognormal distributions for each stock, using the given means and standard deviations. Then, in cell C21, we have calculated the resulting portfolio return, the weighted average of the stock returns with the proportions in cells C12:F12 as weights. (Cell D21 is a duplicate of cell C21, for later use.)

A simulation of 1,000 trials gives the distribution of returns shown in Figure 9.56. The mean return is 30.9 percent, with a standard deviation of 12.9 percent. These results confirm the earlier deterministic analysis. However, the frequency distribution shows that the portfolio return is itself skewed to the right—with a maximum return above 90 percent and a minimum of about 7 percent. More indicative of the distribution, perhaps, are the 10th and 90th percentiles: 17 percent and 48 percent, respectively.

We illustrate two different uses of Optquest in this problem. First, we duplicate the problem we analyzed with Solver: maximize the mean return while ensuring that the standard deviation does not exceed a limit. Then, we change our measure of risk to the 10th percentile of the return distribution. Solver cannot handle this formulation, since no formula exists for the 10th percentile of the distribution, but it is a straightforward application of Optquest.

The model shown in Figure 9.55 is almost ready for using Optquest. The four proportions invested are the decision variables, defined in Crystal Ball as continuous variables between zero and one. The Forecast cell is the total return in cell C21. The random inputs are the returns on the stocks, defined using the Crystal Ball function CB.LOGNORMAL(mean,standard deviation). We choose a run length of 1,000 trials, with an MSE of 0.4 percent on a mean return of 30 percent. The only additional input is needed because of a peculiar feature—one might even call it a bug—of Optquest. Optquest does not operate correctly unless one or more of the random inputs are defined using the Distribution

FIGURE 9.55
Simulation Model for the Portfolio Problem

Portfolio.xls

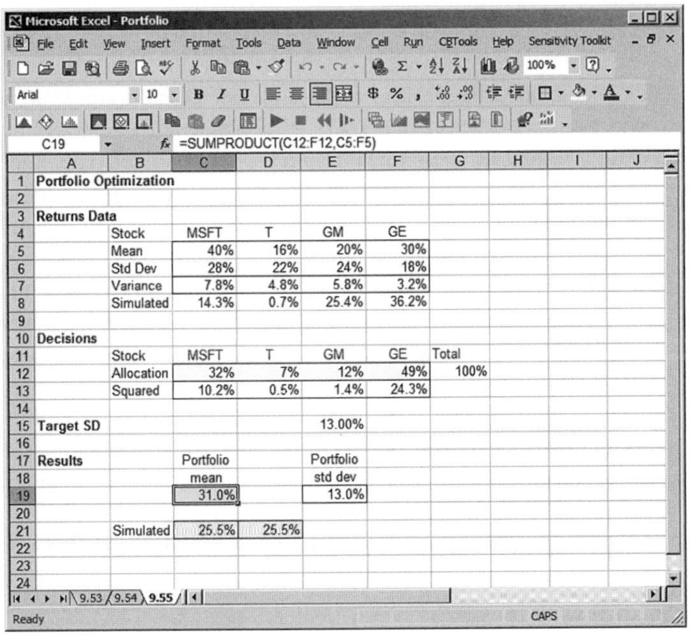

	A	B	C	D	E	F	G
1	Portfolio Optimization						
2							
3	Returns Data						
4		Stock	MSFT	T	GM	GE	
5		Mean	40%	16%	20%	30%	
6		Std Dev	28%	22%	24%	18%	
7		Variance	7.8%	4.8%	5.8%	3.2%	
8		Simulated	14.3%	0.7%	25.4%	36.2%	
9							
10	Decisions						
11		Stock	MSFT	T	GM	GE	Total
12		Allocation	32%	7%	12%	49%	100%
13		Squared	10.2%	0.5%	1.4%	24.3%	
14							
15	Target SD				13.00%		
16							
17	Results		Portfolio		Portfolio		
18			mean		std dev		
19			31.0%		13.0%		
20							
21		Simulated	25.5%	25.5%			
22							
23							
24							

FIGURE 9.56

Simulation Results for the Portfolio Problem

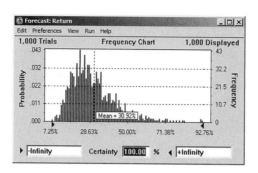

Gallery. We have four random inputs in cells C8:F8, but all use Crystal Ball functions, not the Distribution Gallery. To get around this peculiarity, we add a random input in cell K21 (out of view), defined as a uniform distribution using the Distribution Gallery. This cell has no influence on the results; it simply tricks Optquest into running correctly. [If none of the random inputs is entered using the Distribution Gallery, Optquest attempts to find an optimal solution without taking any random samples. One way to detect the error is to observe that each run takes only a second or two. Alternatively, we can check the Options window to see if the Deterministic (no assumptions) option is checked. In either case, the work-around is to enter into the spreadsheet at least one random variable using the Distribution Gallery.]

When we open Optquest, it recognizes the four decision variables as continuous between zero and one. We set the initial allocation at 25 percent in each stock in order to test Optquest's ability to find the known optimal solution from an arbitrary starting point. In general, we would choose starting values for the decision variables as close to the optimum as we could. There is one constraint to add: that the four proportions add to 1.0. The Forecast window in Optquest devotes one row to the return. We can use this to define the objective as maximizing mean return. To impose the requirement that the standard deviation not exceed 13 percent, we must first duplicate the Forecast cell (Edit→Duplicate), then specify that Return2 (the name given to the duplicate value in cell D21) is a requirement with an upper bound on the standard deviation of 0.13. Finally, we set the time limit to five minutes and run Optquest. The results are shown in Figure 9.57.

The optimal portfolio has a mean return of 30.0 percent with a standard deviation of 12.7 percent. The proportions to invest in each stock are as follows: 37 percent in Microsoft, 12 percent in AT&T, 19 percent in GM, and 32 percent in GE. This solution closely resembles the one we found by using Solver. The objective function value is a little lower, and the constraint on the standard deviation is not quite binding, but the stock proportions are close. If we isolate the top twenty solutions using Solution Analysis (see Figure 9.58), we can see there are many solutions that give a mean return of 29 percent or higher. Among these solutions, most invest about 36 percent in Microsoft and 20 percent in GM; the remainder can be split between AT&T and GE in various proportions.

The standard deviation of the return distribution is just one of many ways to measure risk. One shortcoming of the standard deviation is that it penalizes deviations above the mean as much as those below, whereas, when it comes to returns on a portfolio, deviations above the mean are actually good, not bad. A better approach to limiting risk is to limit the downside outcomes. This can be operationalized, for example, by placing a limit on the 10th percentile of the distribution. In Optquest, this requires only that we change the requirement from an upper bound on the standard deviation to a lower bound on the 10th percentile.

FIGURE 9.57
Optquest Results for the
Portfolio Problem

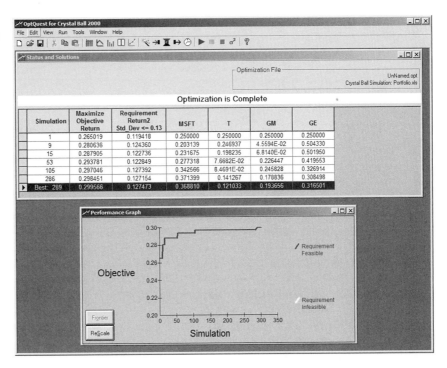

FIGURE 9.58
Solution Analysis for the
Portfolio Problem

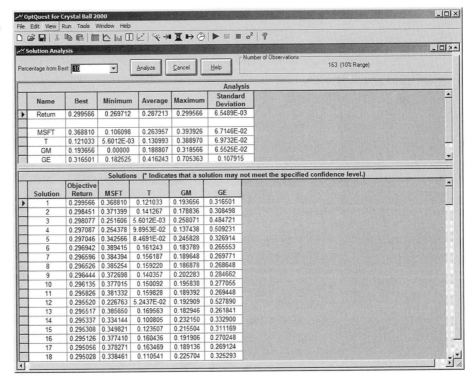

Figure 9.59 shows the results of an Optquest run in which we have maximized the mean return while requiring the 10th percentile to exceed 17 percent. The resulting solution has a mean return of 35.1 percent, with a 10th percentile of 17.7 percent. The proportions invested are about 58 percent in Microsoft, 3 percent in AT&T, 0 percent in GM, and 39 percent in GE. This is a very different investment strategy than resulted from the earlier problem formulation in which we imposed a ceiling on the standard deviation of returns. Much higher allocations are invested in Microsoft, with lower allocations in all other stocks. The result is a higher mean, 35 percent versus 31 percent in the case of the standard deviation constraint. Of course, the standard deviation is also higher. Figure 9.60 shows the distribution of returns for this solution. This distribution should be contrasted with the corresponding distribution for the standard deviation-constrained solution in Figure 9.56. Both are skewed to the right, but the maximum outcome in this case is much higher. The estimated mean is 35 percent versus 31 percent, and the standard deviation is 17 percent versus 13 percent. When we control risk by controlling the 10th percentile, the result is a distribution that is more skewed to the right, so high outcomes are significantly more likely. Since the mean also increases, this solution arguably dominates the earlier one. However, the quantitative measurement of risk is itself an individual choice.

This example illustrates a number of approaches to using Optquest. It is always helpful to solve a deterministic version of the problem first, if possible. When we can do so, we produce a baseline against which to measure the performance of Optquest. Compare the Optquest solution to the deterministic solution; if they are significantly different, then explore why they are different. Next, vary the objective function and requirements to explore how the solution changes. When performing risk analysis, recognize that risk can be measured in different ways and that the method must be tailored to the problem at hand. Often, as in this case, the solution changes as the measure of risk changes. Optquest is well designed to support this type of model exploration.

FIGURE 9.59
Solution to the Portfolio
Problem with 10th
Percentile Requirement

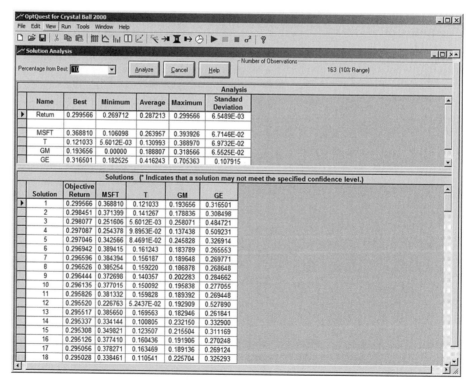

FIGURE 9.60
Distribution of Portfolio
Returns with 10th
Percentile Requirement

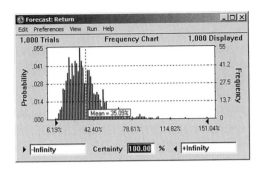

Embedded Optimization: Using Solver within Crystal Ball

In a typical application of simulation, decisions must be made *before* the outcomes of the uncertainties become known. In the Advertising Budget example, next year's price and cost are uncertain at budgeting time, when we must make a commitment to our advertising plan for the entire coming year. But it can happen that some of our decisions can be made *after* the uncertainties have been resolved. For example, we might know next year's price either exactly, or with much less uncertainty than at present, by the time we begin the third quarter of the year. In that case, we could choose our advertising expenditures for the third and fourth quarters after we know the price for those quarters.

When decisions can be made after uncertainties are resolved, we are worse off to ignore the fact. If we do ignore the option to act later with more complete knowledge, we must make our plans taking all the uncertainties into account. On the other hand, if we can make our decision after we know the outcome of an uncertain event or parameter, we can match our decision exactly to that outcome and eliminate the risks. In the Hastings Sportswear example, if we must make our production decision before we know demand, we have to balance the risks of producing too many or too few. However, if we already know demand when we come to decide on production, we simply produce to demand and thereby avoid both leftovers and stockouts. Once we know demand, risk is removed.

A somewhat more complex example involves a decision to purchase several types of production machinery, each of which has some flexibility to produce different products. Today, we face the decision of how much machine capacity of each type to purchase. Future demand for each product is uncertain. In future years, we will know demand fairly accurately each month, and we can assign machines to products so as to minimize costs. This choice of optimal production plan, however, is constrained in the future by the capacity choices we make today. To model this problem realistically, we first need to model the uncertainty in demand. Then, we need to formulate the optimization problem of allocating production capacity to minimize costs, given demand. Finally, we evaluate total costs over a range of choices for the initial capacities, taking into account the uncertainty in demand and the fact that the production plan will be optimized for each demand level.

We call problems of this type, where some decisions are made after uncertainty has been resolved, **embedded-decision problems.** Their main characteristics are the following:

- At the first stage, there is a need to make a set of long-term decisions in the face of uncertainty.

- Subsequently the uncertainty is resolved, and conditions become known.

- At the second stage, there is a need to make short-term decisions, given the outcomes of uncertain conditions and the constraints persisting from the long-term decisions.

We cannot use Crystal Ball in the usual manner to model these problems, because Crystal Ball alone has no facility to choose the optimal decisions on each simulation trial. To do this, we need to call on Solver to carry out the optimization at the appropriate point within each Crystal Ball trial. We first describe the process of linking Solver and Crystal Ball in this way, and then we provide an example to illustrate the process.

Optimization within a Crystal Ball simulation requires the use of a macro to invoke Solver. A **macro** is simply a stored series of Excel commands that can be executed automatically, without user intervention. Excel has the capability of recording the commands entered by a user at the keyboard, so the simplest way to create a macro is to set up the macro recorder and click through the sequence of commands.

The first step is to build a deterministic spreadsheet, treating both decision variables and random inputs as fixed numbers. Next, we reserve a separate part of the spreadsheet for generating the random inputs. (The separation is necessary because we do not want the random inputs to change within a Solver run.) Then, we invoke Solver and define the objective function, decision variables, and constraints in our short-term model. We must actually run Solver once for the overall process to work properly. Finally, we create the random inputs in their reserved location (using CB functions or the Distribution Gallery), copy their values into the reserved cells in the model, and execute Solver. At this point, we are ready to record the macro.

The details of recording the macro are outlined in the box below:

Three steps remain. One is to edit the macro, since this macro as recorded does not work exactly as intended. The second step is to coordinate the macro with Crystal Ball. The last step is to search for good long-term decisions using Optquest. We illustrate this process using an example.

Capacity Planning[4]

A producer of industrial chemicals has three manufacturing facilities from which it ships its products to five regions of the country. The chemical company must decide how much capacity to create at each manufacturing site to produce a new product. Because shipping costs are substantial, the profit margin on each unit sold depends on the distance it must

---

CRYSTAL BALL MACRO: EMBEDDING SOLVER

1. Start the macro recorder: Tools→Macros→Record New Macro.
2. Give the macro a name, and save it in This Workbook.
3. Press Enter, and the Stop Recording Macro button appears on the spreadsheet.
4. Highlight the random inputs.
5. Choose Edit→Copy.
6. Highlight the range where the random inputs are needed.
7. Choose Edit→Paste Special.
8. Select Paste→Values. Click on OK.
9. Choose Tools→Solver→Solve.
10. When Solver finishes, click on OK.
11. Select the objective function cell.
12. Click on the Stop Recording icon in the Macro Recording window.

---

[4] Wayne Winston. 1999. *Decision Making Under Uncertainty with RISKOptimizer*. Newfield, NY: Palisade Corporation.

be shipped. That is, the unit profit depends on the location of manufacture and the region where the sale takes place. Since industrial chemicals are sold mostly on annual contracts, demand for a given year is quite predictable. Thus, we can choose the optimal production and distribution plan once we know demand. However, at the time the capacity decision must be made, demand is uncertain.

This is an embedded-decision problem because we can choose the amounts to produce and the shipment schedule (short-term decisions) *after* we know demand, but we have to choose capacity (long-term decisions) *before* we know demand. We simulate demand using Crystal Ball, and we then optimize the shipments given demand by embedding a macro to run Solver within Crystal Ball. We then call on Optquest to search for the optimal capacities, knowing that we can obtain optimal shipments for each random demand.

Our spreadsheet model is shown in Figure 9.61. The unit profit margins are given in cells C4:G6. The short-term decision variables are the shipment quantities in cells C9:G11. The total amount sold in each region appears in row 12, while demands appear in row 13. The fixed cost per unit of capacity is shown in I4, and the capacities appear in cells I9:I11. Profit is calculated in cell B15 by subtracting annual fixed costs on total capacity from the total margin on units sold. We set up Solver to maximize short-term profit by choosing the shipment quantities. There are two constraints: the amount sold in each region cannot exceed demand, and the amount produced at each site cannot exceed capacity, which is treated as given.

To prepare this model for the embedded-optimization process, we first create random demands. The means and standard deviations are given in rows 18 and 19, and the actual demands are sampled in the Assumption cells of row 17 using a normal distribution. (The objective function in cell B15 should be designated as a Forecast cell.) The macro copies these random demands into row 13 before running Solver. To create the macro to run Solver, we follow the steps outlined above, naming the macro Capacity, designating Ctrl-A as the keystroke shortcut, and saving it in the current workbook.

Two corrections are required to the macro as recorded. Choose Tools→Macro→ Macros. With Capacity highlighted, choose Edit. First, make sure Solver is linked to the macro by checking Solver.xla under Tools→References. Second, change SolverSOLVE to SolverSOLVE (True) where it appears in the macro itself. (This command turns off the Solver completion message so that the Crystal Ball run is not interrupted when Solver finishes execution.) At this stage, it is a good idea to save the workbook.

FIGURE 9.61
Spreadsheet Model for
Capacity-Planning
Example

Plant.xls

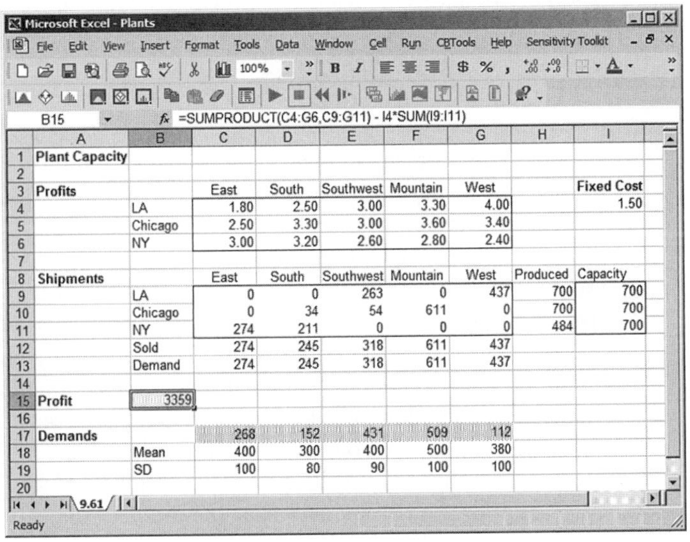

	A	B	C	D	E	F	G	H	I
B15				fx =SUMPRODUCT(C4:G6,C9:G11) - I4*SUM(I9:I11)					
1	Plant Capacity								
2									
3	Profits		East	South	Southwest	Mountain	West		Fixed Cost
4		LA	1.80	2.50	3.00	3.30	4.00		1.50
5		Chicago	2.50	3.30	3.00	3.60	3.40		
6		NY	3.00	3.20	2.60	2.80	2.40		
7									
8	Shipments		East	South	Southwest	Mountain	West	Produced	Capacity
9		LA	0	0	263	0	437	700	700
10		Chicago	0	34	54	611	0	700	700
11		NY	274	211	0	0	0	484	700
12		Sold	274	245	318	611	437		
13		Demand	274	245	318	611	437		
14									
15	Profit	3359							
16									
17	Demands		268	152	431	509	112		
18		Mean	400	300	400	500	380		
19		SD	100	80	90	100	100		
20									

We can test the macro before proceeding. By choosing Run→Single Step, we sample a new set of demands. Then, we run the macro by hitting the designated keys (Ctrl-A in our example). The macro should copy the random samples to the demand cells and reoptimize the shipment schedule. If this does not occur as expected, the macro should be reentered.

Now we return to Crystal Ball and choose Run→Run Preferences and set the run length to 100 trials. Under Sampling, we check Use Same Sequence of Random Numbers and enter a seed value. Under Macros, we enter the name of the macro in the space under After Recalculations. Specifically, the name of the macro here consists of the spreadsheet name followed by the macro name, in the following format:

‘Plants.xls’!Capacity

At this stage, we can again save the file and check our progress by choosing Run→Single Step. This command should sample a new set of demands *and* reoptimize the shipments, without our intervention. We can also run a simulation of any particular long-term policy, as represented by the contents of cells I9:I11.

Finally, we proceed to the long term decision problem, where we rely on Optquest to find a good policy. First, we define the capacities as discrete decision variables, each with a range from 300 to 900.

For the purposes of illustration, we use a run length of 100 trials. This run length achieves an MSE of roughly 1 percent, although the actual figure depends somewhat on the capacity choices. As we discussed earlier, the choice of a run length should be determined by the level of precision we wish to maintain in our estimates of the objective function. A single run of 100 trials for this model may take half a minute, even on a very fast computer. Clearly, we cannot expect Optquest to find a high quality solution in just a few minutes. This is the kind of application where we should expect to run our computer for a matter of hours, even overnight, to get respectable results. To give an idea of the quality of solutions as the Optquest run time increases, we ran this model for ten, thirty, and 720 minutes (twelve hours). The results are summarized in the table below:

Minutes	Simulations	Profit	Optimal Capacities (LA/CHI/NY)
10	30	3,454	591/749/595
30	104	3,459	603/761/584
720	1,445	3,470	612/900/469

The Performance Graph for the twelve-hour run suggests that very good solutions were found during the early portion of the run, but the best solution was encountered late in the run. In addition, Solution Analysis confirms that most of the top twenty candidate solutions are very similar to the best solution. This evidence for stability suggests that we are at least very close to the optimal solution.

As a basis for comparison, we can set up a deterministic version of this model that includes the long-term decision variables as well as the short-term decision variables. Taking demands at their mean values, we can optimize this model using Solver. The maximum profit is $3,740, with total capacities of 780 in Los Angeles, 800 in Chicago, and 400 in New York City. (Note that this is not an embedded-optimization problem, because we have suppressed randomness entirely and have substituted mean values.) Interestingly, the total capacity in this solution is almost identical to the total capacity in the Optquest solution, although the distribution across the three locations is different. The fact that the maximum profit is higher than the best value found by Optquest reflects the fact that there is no uncertainty in the deterministic model. Thus, the plant capacities, however they are chosen, can always be fully utilized. Uncertainty about demand in the embedded-optimization problem makes this virtually impossible to achieve.

Finally, Figure 9.62 shows the distribution of profits in the best solution found by Optquest. The wide range of potential profits is remarkable. Even when we can optimize our production decisions after demand is known, profits can vary from about $2,000 to about $5,000. This gives a far more realistic picture of the true uncertainties facing this company than does the deterministic solution.

SUMMARY

We introduced simulation in Chapter 6 as one phase in a general analytic procedure for spreadsheet models. Simulation answers the question, "What are the risks?"—showing us how uncertainty in the inputs influences the outputs of our analysis. Like optimization, simulation can be seen as a sophisticated form of sensitivity analysis.

In Excel, simulation can be carried out conveniently using Crystal Ball. Crystal Ball provides all the probability models needed to express the uncertainties in our assumptions, and it automates the repetitive process of sampling from these distributions. Finally, it provides extensive methods for displaying and analyzing the results.

Simulation is a powerful tool when used effectively, but it should never be used *before* sensitivity analysis is carried out on a deterministic version of the model. What-if analysis, involving use of the Data Sensitivity tool or perhaps the Tornado Chart tool, uncovers those input parameters that have the biggest impact on the outcomes. These should be the focus of any uncertainty analysis. We have designed the Tornado Chart tool to support a sequence of analyses that can lead to simulation and that can help focus the analysis on the critical parameters.

Every simulation analysis involves four major activities:

- selecting uncertain parameters
- selecting probability distributions
- ensuring appropriate precision in the outcomes
- interpreting outcome distributions

The parameters that are treated as uncertain in a simulation analysis should be those that are subject to substantial uncertainty and have a significant impact on the outcome. Selecting uncertain parameters is a natural outgrowth of sensitivity analysis. While many probability models are available, only a small number are used routinely by business analysts. We have described these models (the uniform, triangular, normal, and discrete distributions), and we have indicated the most suitable applications for each. Ensuring that our simulation results are sufficiently precise is primarily a matter of choosing a suitable run length. However, we have stressed the importance of determining how much precision is really needed in a given analysis before making this decision. Finally, simulations produce probability distributions

FIGURE 9.62
Profit Distribution for the
Optquest Solution

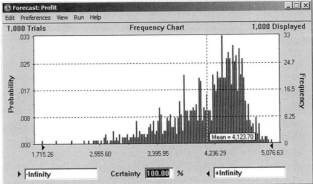

as outcomes, which are by their nature complex. We have emphasized the importance of summarizing and simplifying these results, in order to make them useful to managers.

Simulation is primarily a way to describe the range of uncertainty in the results of a model. It does not automatically provide insight into the question of which values of the decision variables lead to the best possible value of the objective. Thus, optimizing within a simulation analysis is not routine. The tools of deterministic optimization covered in Chapter 8—Solver with its various algorithms—do not directly apply because, in a simulation model, the objective can only be estimated. However, there are a number of approaches to optimization within simulation, ranging from simple grid search to Optquest. We provided a range of examples and guidelines for using these tools.

While simulation is more sophisticated than simple spreadsheet modeling, it is one of the most widely used of the advanced management science tools. It is relatively easy for business analysts to learn, and it provides a means for expressing and understanding the uncertainty that is so prevalent in business. It does require some familiarity with probability, the language of uncertainty, but many analysts have this familiarity, and most can acquire what they need. Often, the bigger challenge with simulation is translating the results into a form that managers can understand and act upon.

SUGGESTED READINGS

Evans, James R. and David L. Olson. 2002. *Introduction to Simulation and Risk Analysis,* 2d ed. Upper Saddle River, NJ: Prentice Hall.

This is the only full length text devoted to simulation using Crystal Ball. The coverage of Crystal Ball is somewhat less detailed than in this chapter, but there are many more examples and applications. Discrete event simulation using *ProModel* is also covered.

Seila, Andrew F., Vlatko Ceric, and Pandu Tadikamalla. 2003. *Applied Simulation Modeling.* Belmont, CA: Brooks/Cole.

This book covers simulation from the business and engineering points of view. It uses @*Risk* and the discrete event simulation language *Arena*. @Risk is Crystal Ball's main competitor in the marketplace. It is not difficult to learn how to use @Risk after working with Crystal Ball for a while. In addition, @Risk is paired with RISKOptimizer, roughly the equivalent of the Optquest package. The following books are also based on @Risk, although it would not be difficult to read the material and translate the exercises and examples into Crystal Ball.

Winston, Wayne. 1999. *Financial Models using Simulation and Optimization.* Newfield, NY: Palisade.

Winston, Wayne. 2001. *Simulation Modeling with @Risk.* Pacific Grove, CA: Duxbury.

Winston, Wayne. 1999. *Decision Making under Uncertainty with RISKOptimizer.* Newfield, NY: Palisade.

Financial Models contains sixty-three examples of simulation applications, most with a financial flavor. *Simulation Modeling* is more like a textbook, with some introductory chapters on simulation in general. The body of this book consists of a large number of worked examples from planning, marketing, finance, and operations. *Decision Making* contains thirty-four worked examples for optimization in simulation.

EXERCISES

1. *NPV Analysis.* You have been asked to evaluate the following investment opportunity. A small firm is available for purchase at an initial cost of $150,000, to be paid to the current owner in equal installments over the next five years. The firm has been generating annual revenues of $100,000. Operating costs are 65 percent of revenues. For tax purposes, the firm's earnings would appear on your personal income tax return, and the applicable tax rate would be about 36 percent. Your investment would be deductible when calculating taxes. Under these assumptions, the NPV (at a discount rate of 10 percent) for this project is $12,131.

In light of the fact that most of your information about this firm comes from the current owner, you are concerned that some of your assumptions may be inaccurate. After some research, you have determined the following about the key inputs to this problem:

- Actual revenues each year could be as low as $60,000 or as high as $125,000. The most likely amount is $100,000. Revenues in successive years are independent.

- Operating costs each year could be as low as 55 percent of revenues or as high as 75 percent, with any values in between being equally likely. Costs in successive years are independent.

- The tax rate in any year will be 36 percent with probability 0.4 and 40 percent with probability 0.6, depending on factors outside your control and independent from year to year.

In the case of negative taxable income, you will have other income, so the tax effects represented in the model will still hold.

Questions

a. What probability distributions are appropriate for the three uncertain quantities in this analysis?

b. Estimate the mean NPV under the assumptions given above.

c. Estimate the probability that the NPV will be negative.

d. Estimate the probability that the cash flow will be positive in all five years.

2. *Production Planning with Returns.* A computer manufacturer sells its laptop model through a Web-based distributor, who buys at a unit cost of $200 and sells at a unit price (revenue) of $500. The product life cycle is so short that the distributor is given only one opportunity to order stock before the technology becomes obsolete and a new model becomes available. At the beginning of the cycle, the distributor orders a stock level in the face of uncertain retail demand. Based on similar experiences in the past, the distributor believes that a reasonable demand model is a uniform distribution with a minimum of 1,000 and a maximum of 8,000 laptops. The items originally stocked are ultimately sold, returned, or scrapped. Customers place orders on the Web, and the distributor tries to satisfy their orders from stock. If there is a stockout, demands are lost.

The computer manufacturer offers the distributor a returns policy of the following form: it will pay $100 for each returned unit at the end of the product life cycle, but only up to a maximum of 20 percent of the original number of units ordered. Excess stock that cannot be returned to the manufacturer is picked up as scrap material by an electronics recycling center, with no cost or revenue involved. The decision facing the distributor is to choose the optimal stock level.

Questions

a. Suppose there were no ceiling on the return of excess laptops. How many laptops should the distributor stock in order to maximize its expected profit? (Answer to within ± 200.)

b. With the returns ceiling in place, how many laptops should the distributor stock? (Answer to within ± 200.)

c. In (b), what would be the maximum expected profit for the distributor?

d. What would be the corresponding expected profit for the manufacturer if the manufacturing cost is $125 per laptop, and the distributor uses the policy in (b)?

3. *Value of a Customer.* As the manager of credit card services at Bank of Hanover (BOH), you're aware that the average profitability of a credit card customer grows with the number of years they have used the credit card. Two probabilistic factors affect actual profitability. The mean profitability function is given in the table below, which has been gathered from data on BOH customers. The actual profit in a given year follows a normal distribution, with a standard deviation equal to 25 percent of the mean profit.

In addition, there is a probability less than one that a customer will continue to use the card during year t. This probability is sometimes called the *retention rate*. For instance, an 80 percent retention rate means that, during any year, there is a 20 percent chance the customer will cancel their credit card. Assume that if a customer cancels during year t, then the cancellation occurs at the end of the year, and BOH still gets profits from year t. The current retention rate has been estimated at 80 percent.

BOH uses a discount rate of 10 percent for calculating net present values.

Year	Mean Profit
1	40
2	66
3	72
4	79
5	87
6	92
7	96
8	99
9	103
10	106
11	111
12	116
13	120
14	124
15	130
16	137
17	142
18	148
19	155
20	161

Questions

a. When the retention rate is 80 percent, what is the average NPV from a customer?

b. When the retention rate is 80 percent, what is the probability that the NPV for a given customer will exceed $100?

c. Determine the average NPV from a customer when the retention rate is 85 percent, 90 percent, and 95 percent. Sketch a graph that describes how the average NPV varies with the retention rate, and interpret the sketch.

4. *Production Scheduling.* A simple model is sometimes used in order to illustrate the production-scheduling maxim, "balance flow, not capacity." Consider a factory that consists of three workstations where each customer order must proceed through the workstations in sequence. Next, suppose that a fair amount of industrial engineering work has gone into designing the operations and that the workloads are balanced. This means that, on average, each order requires equal amounts of work at each of the three stations. Assume that the average operation time is sixty minutes.

Now suppose that six orders are to be scheduled tomorrow. Using average times, we would expect that completion times would look like the following:

Order	1	2	3	4	5	6
Complete Station 1	60	120	180	240	300	360
Complete Station 2	120	180	240	300	360	420
Complete Station 3	180	240	300	360	420	480

and we would expect that the schedule length would be 480 minutes.

Suppose that actual operation times follow a triangular distribution with a minimum of thirty minutes and a maximum of ninety minutes.

Questions

a. What is your estimate for the mean schedule length?

b. What is your estimate for the probability that the schedule length will exceed 480 minutes?

c. Change the range of the distribution from sixty to forty and to twenty, and then repeat (a) . What are your revised estimates for the mean schedule length? What do you conclude from these observations?

5. *Reliability.* Your company is responsible for the design of a commercial satellite that will make a 100-week flight, sending back valuable information via a battery-powered transmitter. The lifetime of a battery is known to follow an exponential distribution with a mean of twenty-five weeks. (Equivalently, this means a failure rate of 0.04 per week, which is the "rate" parameter for the exponential distribution.) The design calls for backup batteries, in order to assure that the transmitter will function for a longer period. Whenever a battery fails, it is immediately replaced as a power source by a backup, if one is available. The design problem is to determine how many batteries (including the original) are required to be 99 percent sure that the transmitter will function for the entire flight.

Questions

a. What is the minimum number of batteries required to provide the 99 percent assurance?

b. In the design of (a), what is the probability that all batteries will be used?

c. In the design of (a), what is the mean number of batteries used?

6. *Competitive Bidding.* Two partners have decided to sell the manufacturing business they have been running. They have lined up five prospective buyers and have hired a consultant to help them with the bidding and the sale. The consultant, an expert in assessments of this sort, has told the partners that the business is worth $10 million.

The consultant has obtained indications that the prospective buyers would be willing to participate in a sealed-bid auction to determine who will buy the business and at what price. Under the rules of the auction, the sale price would be the highest bid.

Due to their limited information about the business, the bidders may overestimate or underestimate what the business is actually worth. After listening to some of their preliminary thoughts, the consultant concludes that limited information will lead each of them to value the business at a minimum of $8 million and a maximum of $15 million. Their most likely value is $10 million. (We interpret this to mean that a suitable model for an individual value will be a triangular distribution.) The bidders, however, have an instinct about the Winner's Curse, and they each plan to bid only 75 percent of their estimated value for the business. (The Winner's Curse is a phenomenon in competitive bidding where the winner is generally the one that most overestimated the value of the prize.)

Questions

a. What is the expected price that the partners will receive for their business?

b. What is the probability that the partners will receive more than $10 million for the business?

c. Suppose the consultant asks for a fee in order to identify five more bidders to participate in the auction. How large a fee should the partners be willing to pay for this service?

7. *Airline Revenue Management.* Alpha Airlines has ordered a new fleet of DC-717s. At this stage of the contract, Alpha's operations manager must specify the seating configuration on the aircraft that will be used on the Boston-Atlanta-Chicago-Boston circuit. Alpha flies this route once each day.

The configuration decision involves specifying how many rows will be allocated for first class and how many for tourist class. If the aircraft were configured entirely of tourist rows (containing six seats each), there would be forty rows. First-class seats are wider and afford more legroom, so that, in order to make room for one first-class row (containing four seats), two tourist rows must be removed. Thus, conversion from tourist to first-class seating involves the loss of some seats, but the conversion may be appealing because the revenues are higher for first-class passengers than for tourist passengers (see Exhibit 1).

A perfect match between the configuration and the demand for seats is seldom possible. Historical data suggest a probability distribution of demand for seats on each leg (as detailed in Exhibit 2). There is another distribution for the fraction of demand that corresponds to first-class seats (Exhibit 3), which seems to apply on all legs, although the fraction that occurs in one market on any day is independent of the fraction in the other markets. Finally, there is some chance that all seats in either seating category will be booked on a given leg when demand for that category occurs. Under present management policies, such demand is simply lost to competitors.

Exhibit 1. Revenue per Seat

	First-class	Tourist
Boston-Atlanta	$400	$175
Atlanta-Chicago	$400	$150
Chicago-Boston	$450	$200

Exhibit 2. Distribution of Total Demand for Seats

	Min.	Most Likely	Max.
Boston-Atlanta	160	180	220
Atlanta-Chicago	140	200	240
Chicago-Boston	150	200	225

Exhibit 3. Distribution of Fraction First Class

Fraction	5%	12%	15%
Probability	0.2	0.5	0.3

The fixed cost of operating the full circuit is $100,000 per day. Alpha Airlines is seeking a profit-maximizing configuration.

Questions

a. What is the expected profit per day for a configuration of three first-class rows and thirty-four tourist rows? For convenience, you may allow fractional values of demand in your model.

b. With the suggested configuration, what proportion of the days will Alpha at least break even on the Atlanta-Chicago-Boston-Atlanta circuit?

c. For the demand that Alpha faces, what is the maximum expected profit, and what is the seat configuration that achieves it?

8. *Inventory Planning.* Rowers North, Inc. (RNI) would like to develop an inventory policy that will minimize the total cost associated with the company's inventory of rowing machines, while ensuring that few customers are unable to purchase a machine the day they walk in the store.

The type of inventory policy they prefer involves a fixed reorder point and order quantity. The *reorder point* is the level of inventory at which an order is placed to the supplier. The *order quantity* is the amount ordered each time. These are decision variables, but once chosen, they will not be changed.

Inventory planning at RNI is complicated by several factors. One is uncertainty in demand. Weekly demand can range from zero to five machines. Data covering the past year is given in Exhibit 1. A further complication is that the time it takes for an order to arrive from the manufacturer is variable. This lead time has been as long as four weeks. Exhibit 2 gives the actual lead times for the twenty most recent orders. (Once an order has been placed, the lead time is determined by the supplier and communicated to RNI.)

Some of the relevant cost data are known. For example, it costs $1 per week to hold a rowing machine in inventory, and it costs $50 to place an order (regardless of its size).

One of the central issues for RNI is the cost of being out of stock. Since there are a number of competing retailers in the area, it is common for a customer who doesn't find the preferred machine in stock to leave and look for it elsewhere. Some customers may be loyal enough to wait until the product is back in stock, but even those customers may be displeased by the service they receive. The VP of marketing has suggested that the cost of an unsatisfied customer is simply the forgone margin on the lost sale (roughly $50 per machine). Others in the company argue that the cost is less, perhaps much less.

Note that if RNI places an order in every week in which final inventory falls below the reorder point, it may find itself with multiple, redundant orders arriving in subsequent weeks. To control this, firms typically track their *order backlog* (i.e., the quantity of units ordered but not yet received). They then take the backlog into account when deciding whether to order in a given week.

Build a simulation model with which you can help RNI determine an effective inventory policy.

Question

Use your model to determine the optimal reorder point and order quantity.

Exhibit 1

Week	Demand	Week	Demand	Week	Demand
1	3	21	4	41	1
2	0	22	1	42	0
3	1	23	1	43	1
4	1	24	2	44	0
5	0	25	0	45	1
6	1	26	1	46	4
7	5	27	1	47	1
8	1	28	0	48	1
9	1	29	1	49	1
10	1	30	5	50	1
11	1	31	0	51	0
12	0	32	1	52	2
13	1	33	1		
14	2	34	1		
15	2	35	1		
16	4	36	3		
17	2	37	1		
18	1	38	5		
19	3	39	0		
20	1	40	1		

Exhibit 2

Order	Lead Time (wks.)	Order	Lead Time (wks.)
1	3	11	4
2	1	12	2
3	2	13	3
4	3	14	3
5	1	15	2
6	4	16	3
7	3	17	3
8	3	18	3
9	2	19	3
10	1	20	2

9. *Equilibrium in Competitive Bidding.* A sealed-bid auction is going to be held in the near future for Medex Pharmaceuticals. You represent one of two companies expected to enter bids. The basic data available to your firm consist of an estimate of the value of Medex and some information on the uncertainty surrounding that value. Your task is to prepare a quantitative bidding strategy for this auction. The attached letter from your boss explains his thinking about the problem and offers some suggestions for your approach.

Here are some guidelines for your analysis:

- Your boss has provided an estimate, based on his past experience, of the range of errors that are likely to be made in valuing companies such as Medex. Errors up to 50 percent above and below the true value are possible. If we assume that the true value is $100 million, we could represent the range of possible estimates by a uniform probability distribution with a minimum value of $50 million and a maximum value of $150 million. Other probability models would also be plausible.

- We know that our competitor, National, is similar to our company in all important ways. Thus, we may assume that their probability distribution for the value of Medex is the same as ours.

- Bidding theory suggests that we should bid less than our estimated value in a common-value auction such as this. Formulate your strategy in terms of a *bid level,* which is the percentage of our estimated value we will bid.

- We clearly cannot know for certain what bid level National will choose. But we can determine what our bid level should be for any given bid level they might choose.

- While your boss has specified the problem rather precisely, you should explore the sensitivity of your results to your assumptions, including the range of uncertainty, the form of the probability distribution, and the number of bidders.

MEMO

TO: Susan Morganstern

FROM: Vaughn Newman

RE: Bidding for Medex

As promised, I am following up our conversation of a few days ago with more information. You mentioned that your staff group might be able to help us prepare our bid for Medex Pharmaceuticals. Here are some of the details you asked about.

First of all, I don't want you to get the impression that our primary objective is simply to win the bid. We'd like to own Medex, of course, but only if the net effect is to increase our shareholder value. One of my big concerns is that we might win the bid but overestimate the value of Medex. That would not be a success.

Second, I'm confident that my Valuation Committee is doing its best to determine how much Medex is worth, but, as you said, we have to recognize the uncertainty we're dealing with. Medex might be worth a lot more or a lot less than our estimate—it really depends on how their R&D division does and on what happens to the market for the new drug they just got approved. I looked back at some of our previous work, and it looks like we've been high or low in our assessment by as much as 50 percent. That's a lot of uncertainty, but it just seems to be the nature of the situations we've been in.

Third, I am pretty sure that the only other bidder for Medex will be National, in which case we'll have only one rival to worry about. Somehow, this ought to make things simpler than if there were several bidders out there.

Finally, as a corporation, National resembles us closely, and whichever one of us gets Medex should be able to extract the same value from the assets. National's access to information is about the same as ours, so their level of uncertainty should be the same. In addition, National has had some experience in this sort of bidding, and they're not naive about bidding strategy. Judging from their track record, they'll want to avoid overbidding, too. In essence, I guess I'm saying that they are likely to analyze the deal pretty much the way we are.

Any insight you could give us on how we should approach the bidding would be appreciated. The sealed bid is due at Morgan Stanley next Friday.

10. *Pricing Exotic Options.* A given stock currently is priced at $100. Historically, its annual return has been 12 percent with a standard deviation of 15 percent. Build a spreadsheet simulation model for the stock price, using the lognormal pricing model described in the text. Build the model to simulate the stock price over 126 days, or six months. The risk-free rate of return is 3 percent.

Questions

a. A particular European call option gives the owner the right to purchase this stock after six months at a strike price of $105. What is the price of the option? Note: remember to discount the value at six months to the present using continuous compounding. You can assume the relevant discount rate is 6 percent, so the discount factor for half a year is $EXP(-0.5 \times 0.06)$.

b. Create a graph of the option price as a function of the strike price, for strike prices from $100 to $110 in increments of $1.

c. A particular *European put option* gives the owner the right to sell this stock after six months at a strike price of $95. What is the price of the put?

d. A *lookback call option* on this stock has an exercise price given by the minimum price observed during its six-month term. What is the price of the lookback?

e. An *Asian option* on this stock has a strike price set by the average value of the stock during its term. What is the price of the Asian option?

f. A *knockout call option* on this stock terminates if the stock price reaches or exceeds $125 (that is, the option cannot be exercised). Otherwise, it has the same structure as the normal call. What is the price of the knockout?

11. *Capacity Planning.* Lang Drug needs to determine the proper capacity level for a new drug, Niagara. Our goal is to maximize the expected NPV earned from the drug during years 0–15, assuming a discount rate of 10 percent per year. It costs $10 to build enough capacity to produce one unit of drug per year. All construction cost is incurred during year 0. It costs $1 per year to maintain a unit of annual production capacity. In year 1, we know demand will be for 160,000 units of Niagara. We believe that the mean annual percentage growth of demand for Niagara is equally likely to assume any value between 10 percent and 20 percent. The actual growth rate of demand during any year is normally distributed with the given mean and a standard deviation of 6 percent. During year 1, each unit of Niagara sells for $8. The price of Niagara will almost surely grow at 5

percent per year. Unit variable cost is known to be 40 percent of sales price. The depreciation rate is 10 percent and the tax rate is 35 percent.

Suppose that Lang Drug has the additional opportunity to review demand during year 5 and, if desired, build additional capacity. How will this change Lang Drug's strategy? Now Lang Drug may not need to build as much capacity during year 1, because they can wait and see whether demand will be high. If demand is high, they can ramp up capacity during year 5 for future years; if not, they can stick with their year 1 capacity. To model this situation, we assume that after observing year 5 demand, Lang Drug proceeds as follows: If the ratio of year 5 demand to capacity exceeds some cutoff point C, then Lang Drug will add capacity. If capacity is added, then Lang Drug will add enough capacity to bring total capacity to a multiple M of year 5 demand. We assume it costs $12 to build one unit of capacity at the end of year 5. Thus, Lang Drug's capacity strategy is defined by three decisions:

- initial capacity (year 1)
- the cutoff value C, which determines whether capacity is added after year 5 (assume that capacity arrives in time for year 6)
- the multiple M that defines how much capacity is added

Questions

a. Assuming Lang *cannot* build additional capacity in year 5, what capacity level will maximize expected discounted profit? Assume that all building costs are incurred during year 0 and that all cash flows occur at the beginning of the year.

b. With the additional opportunity to review demand and add capacity in year 5, what values would you recommend for the initial capacity, for C, and for M? How much does the option to expand increase the NPV?

12. *Valuing a Real Option.* You have been hired to estimate the value of the startup company Garcia, Ltd. Garcia has one product, which is expected to sell in the first year for $100. The price will grow in subsequent years by an amount given by a normal distribution with a mean of 5 percent and a standard deviation of 3 percent. Initial sales will be 5,000 units, expected to grow at 5 percent. The unit cost will initially be $75, and this will grow at a rate given by a normal distribution with a mean of 10 percent and a standard deviation of 3 percent. The valuation will be based on a time horizon of ten years. The discount rate is 10 percent.

Garcia wants to investigate an option to decide in year 6 whether to continue in business or go out of business. (This is what is known as a *real option*, as opposed to the *financial options* discussed in the text.) Specifically, they intend to execute the option to go out of business at the end of year 6 if the year 6 contribution is less than some cutoff value. If they opt to go out of business, they will receive zero contribution in years 7–10.

Questions

a. Build a model to estimate the NPV of the business *without* the option to go out of business.

b. What is the *optimal* cutoff value? That is, what cutoff value should Garcia use in year 6 so as to maximize the expected NPV of the company from the start?

c. The value of this option is the *difference* between the expected NPV *with* the option and expected NPV *without* the option. What is the value of this option?

APPENDIX 9.1. CHOOSING CRYSTAL BALL SETTINGS

Crystal Ball provides a number of choices under Run→Run Preferences for tailoring the simulation. Many of these options are useful only to advanced users, but all users must understand a few of them. In this appendix, we describe the most important options and provide guidelines for making wise choices. This section is organized in the same order as the options are listed in the Run Preferences window.

Trials

Earlier, we discussed the question of how to choose a suitable run length. In the Run Preferences→Trials window, this parameter is entered next to Maximum Number of Trials. Below that are two check boxes. If we check Stop on Calculation Errors, the simulation stops and issues a warning when Excel encounters an error, such as trying to divide by zero. It is a good idea to keep this box checked since it can help reveal bugs in the model. If we check Enable Precision Control, the simulation stops either when the maximum number of trials is reached or when the output measure has been estimated with sufficient precision, whichever comes first. The Confidence Level parameter entered into this window sets the target level of precision in the forecast cell at which Crystal Ball stops the run.

Sampling

This panel gives the user several options for controlling the process of generating random inputs. To fix the random number sequence and use the same values on each simulation run, check Use Same Sequence of Random Numbers. The Initial Seed Value specifies the starting point for the sampling process within Crystal Ball. A unique set of random numbers will be drawn for any positive integer specified in this window. If this option is checked, Crystal Ball chooses the same samples from the input distributions on each run, and the outputs are thus identical. If this option is not checked, Crystal Ball chooses different samples from the input distributions on each run, and the outcomes are different as well. In general, we should use the same sequence of random numbers when we are comparing alternatives, but different sequences when we are determining run length.

As an example, consider the Hastings Sportswear case (discussed in the chapter), where we are interested in maximizing the mean profit. If we choose an order quantity of 1,000 and run the simulation with a sample size of 100, we might get a sample mean profit of $10,461. We know that if we were to rerun the simulation, we would likely get a different estimate, but we are interested mainly in spending our time finding a good order quantity. So we change the order quantity to 900 and run the simulation again. This time, we might get a sample mean profit of $14,850. The figure is higher by $4,389, but is this difference due to the fact that the order quantity of 900 is truly better? The difference could simply be a coincidence, reflecting a favorable set of input values sampled in the second run or unfavorable values sampled in the first run. These same questions continue to plague us as we look for an order quantity that improves on 900.

Without more investigation, we cannot know the answer to these questions unless we can replicate the samples taken on each run. By fixing the process of sampling input values (that is, by checking the box for Use Same Sequence of Random Numbers), we know that any differences must be due to the decision variable and not to the results of our sampling method.

Now imagine that we first check the box for setting the random number seed and specify some arbitrary value for the seed, such as 1,234. Then, a production level of 1,000 yields an estimated mean profit of $10,195, and a production level of 900 yields $12,067. Using this procedure, we can be confident that the improvement from the lower order quantity is due to the change in the decision, rather than a chance outcome due to a favorable or unfavorable set of samples on one of the runs.

As this example shows, setting the random number seed can be a very useful option when we are using simulation to *compare* decisions. Anytime we are making comparisons, we prefer to remove randomness in the sampling processes as a source of difference and to focus only on differences due to the decisions. Even with the random number seed set, we must still be sure that the run length is sufficient to detect the magnitude of differences we encounter.

The next option in this panel is Sampling Method: Monte Carlo or Latin Hypercube. As a general rule, we recommend using Latin Hypercube sampling, which is a form of stratified sampling, over Monte Carlo sampling because it achieves the same precision with fewer trials. It does, however, require more computer memory, so problems may arise if computer memory is limited.

The final option here is Sample Size for Correlation and Latin Hypercube. The technical issues here can be complex. Our advice is to set this parameter to an even fraction of the run length. For example, when the run length is 1,000 trials, set this parameter to 500.

Speed

Two options here are useful for speeding up simulation runs. If we check Minimize While Running→Microsoft Excel, Crystal Ball minimizes the Excel window while it is running a simulation. This speeds up the process by eliminating the need to refresh the spreadsheet after each sample. Likewise, we can check Suppress Forecast Windows, and Crystal Ball does not redraw each of the forecast windows as the sampling proceeds.

Macros

On some occasions, it is desirable to run an Excel macro during a Crystal Ball simulation. This window allows the user to enter the name of a macro and to specify the point during the Crystal Ball run when the macro will be executed. We can use this option, as we explained in the chapter, to run Solver within Crystal Ball.

Options

There are two sets of options presented here. The first, Update Forecast Windows and Check Precision Every . . . Trials, sets the frequency with which Forecast windows are redrawn during a simulation run. If speed is an issue, this number can be made as large as the simulation run length itself. The second set of options allows us to turn on or off the Sensitivity Analysis feature and any correlated Assumption cells.

Turbo

These options are for advanced users only.

APPENDIX 9.2. ADDITIONAL FEATURES OF CRYSTAL BALL

As with Excel itself, Crystal Ball has more features than a typical user will employ in a lifetime of modeling. A few of the more commonly used features are described briefly here.

Editing in Crystal Ball

It is sometimes easy to confuse operations in Excel with similar ones in Crystal Ball. This is especially so with copying distributions entered using the Distribution Gallery. In this case, the confusion is between the Copy→Paste operation in Excel and the Copy Data→Paste Data operation in Crystal Ball.

If we have entered a distribution into cell B2 using the Distribution Gallery and we want to copy that distribution to cells B3:B10, we must use Crystal Ball, not Excel. Excel would copy only the *number* in cell B2, not the *distribution*. To copy the distribution, we need to highlight B2 and choose Cell→Copy Data. Then, highlight B3:B10 and choose Cell→Paste Data. We should then see the same distribution that was in cell B2 copied to the cells in B3:B10. When we recalculate the spreadsheet, we get independent samples from this distribution in cells B2:B10.

It is sometimes necessary to find all the Assumption cells in a spreadsheet. This can be accomplished by choosing Cell→Select All Assumptions. Crystal Ball highlights all the Assumption cells—that is, those cells that contain distributions entered through the Distribution Gallery. (Unfortunately, this does not work to highlight distributions entered using Crystal Ball functions.) Similar options exist on the Cell menu for locating Forecast and Decision cells.

Occasionally one can run into a bug in Crystal Ball that has its origins in an Assumption or Forecast cell that has been misplaced during revision of the spreadsheet. The solution is to first locate those cells using Cell→Select All. . . . . Then, if necessary, one can delete unneeded Assumptions or Forecasts using Cell→Clear Data.

Crystal Ball Functions

In our examples, we have often used the Distribution Gallery to input probability distributions. This feature is one of our favorite aspects of Crystal Ball, not only because it is easy to use, but also because it reinforces the idea that the choice of a probability distribution for an uncertain parameter is just another modeling choice requiring judgment. However, the Distribution Gallery has several drawbacks. One is that the distribution is not visible as a formula in the spreadsheet. Another is that we cannot embed these distributions in formulas. Finally, copying distributions entered this way is somewhat clumsy. Fortunately, Crystal Ball provides an alternative method.

Crystal Ball provides seventeen special functions for taking samples from probability distributions. For example, if we enter the formula

CB.NORMAL(100,25)

in a cell, Crystal Ball interprets that formula just as if we had entered a normal distribution with mean of 100 and standard distribution of 25 from the Distribution Gallery. This formula returns a random sample from this distribution each time the spreadsheet is recalculated. Since Excel interprets this function as a standard Excel function, we can copy and paste it just as we would any other function (using Excel, not Crystal Ball), and we can embed it in a more complex formula, for example:

IF((D20>=$B$7), CB.NORMAL(100,25),0).

The formulas for the other major types of distributions take a similar form, for example:

CB.UNIFORM(minimum,maximum)
CB.TRIANGULAR(minimum,most likely,maximum)
CB.CUSTOM(I1:J4)

In the last example, we enter a discrete distribution using the CB.CUSTOM function and specify the cell range where the outcomes and probabilities are located. More details on these functions and their arguments are available by choosing Insert Function and finding the Crystal Ball category.

Crystal Ball provides a number of other functions besides probability distributions. Most of these are specialized and beyond the level of this book. One particularly useful function records any of the statistics from the Statistics view of the Forecast window in the spreadsheet. This is particularly useful when a model has a large number of Forecast cells. For example, if we enter the formula

CB.GETFORESTATFN(E11,2)

in a cell, Crystal Ball records the mean value of the forecast cell in E11 after a simulation is run. (Note that this function returns the result #VALUE until a simulation has been run, at which point it takes on the numerical value.)

The first input in this function is the cell address of the Forecast cell; the second is the number of the statistic. The statistics are numbered from 1 to 13, in the same order they appear in the Statistics window, starting with the number of trials. Thus, number 1 is the number of trials, number 2 is the mean, number 10 is the minimum, number 11 is the maximum, and number 13 the MSE.

Filtering Output Values

Occasionally we want a Forecast report involving only certain selected values from a Forecast cell. Here's an example: we are studying the inventory situation at a warehouse. Each week, we are either able to meet all orders for a given item, or we are short some number of items. Using a simple IF statement, we can determine the percentage of weeks in which we are unable to fill all orders. But we also want to know the expected number of units we fall short of demand in those weeks in which we are not able to meet all demand. In a simulation of 1,000 weeks, we might completely meet demand 80 percent of the time. If we examine a Forecast window for the cell representing unmet demand, it takes on the value zero 80 percent of the time and a positive value the remaining 20 percent of the time. The reported expected value combines these two types of outcomes and reports the overall number of units short, rather than the units short in just those weeks in which we are short, which is what we want to know.

A Crystal Ball option comes in handy here. When we define a Forecast cell, we normally enter just its name and appropriate units. But if we select More>>, we are given additional options. Under the Filter option, we can filter out of the Forecast window values that fall inside or outside defined ranges. In the example above, we would filter out all zero values for unmet demand. This window also provides the option to apply the filter on one forecast to other forecasts. So we could also use this approach to calculate the mean profit for those weeks in which unmet demand was positive.

Overlay Chart

We have seen that Crystal Ball produces a Forecast window for every Forecast cell in a model. Because each of these windows contains so much information, it is often difficult to compare results across several forecasts. The Overlay Chart can help here by displaying two or more distributions superimposed in the same graph.

In the Butson Stores example, recall that we built a model for both the base case and a correlated case. Suppose we place each case on a separate worksheet and designate the maximum loan as a forecast on each sheet. Then, when we run Crystal Ball, we obtain two Forecast windows, one for each case. When the run completes, we select Run→Open Overlay Chart. If we select the Choose Forecasts button, we can select the particular forecasts we wish to include in the overlay chart. (This would be cell C32 for each worksheet, in the model of Figure 9.24.) Then, we click OK and select the Chart Prefs button. As an illustration, suppose we choose a line chart (with parameters 2 and 0, respectively for line and dots), a frequency distribution, and groups of size 50. The resulting chart is shown as

Figure 9A.1. As the chart shows, the distribution for the correlated case, denoted by (C), has a smaller variance and approximately the same mean, as the distribution for the uncorrelated case.

Sensitivity Chart

Throughout this book, we have emphasized the importance of sensitivity analysis. In Chapter 6, we discussed using Data Sensitivity to determine the relationship between a single parameter or decision variable and the outcome. We also introduced the concept of a tornado chart, which provides a ranking of parameters in terms of the impact they have on the outcome. Recall that in a tornado chart, we assume each parameter takes on its high and low values one at a time, with all other parameters fixed. While a tornado chart can help determine which variables have the strongest impact on the outcome, it cannot take into account the probability distribution behind a parameter, nor can it vary all parameters simultaneously.

Crystal Ball's Sensitivity Chart feature does precisely this: it takes into account both the uncertainty in a parameter and the mathematical relationship between that parameter and the outcome. In a nutshell, this feature determines the extent to which each Assumption cell is correlated with the Forecast cell. If large values of one Assumption tend to occur in the same trial as large values of the Forecast (regardless of the values of other Assumptions) and vice versa, then the sensitivity of the Forecast to this Assumption is high.

To illustrate this feature, we use the Advertising Budget example. We use three Assumption cells for this illustration: price has a uniform distribution between 30 and 50; cost has a uniform distribution between 20 and 30; and overhead percentage has a triangular distribution with a minimum of 10 percent, a maximum of 20 percent, and a most likely value of 15 percent. After the simulation run, we can select Run→Open Sensitivity Chart. The result is shown in Figure 9A.2.

This chart shows that price is most strongly correlated with profit: the higher the price, the higher the profit. Cost is next most strongly correlated, and the relationship is negative, as we would expect. The overhead percentage ranks third in terms of impact.

Fitting Distributions to Data

Chapter 9 contains a discussion of how to select a particular probability distribution for an uncertain parameter. We advocate considerable judgment in this process, since data are usually not available or are biased. However, there are formal methods for determining which family of distributions (for example, normal or triangular) fits a given set of data most closely. Crystal Ball provides the Batch Fit tool to help carry out this process.

FIGURE 9A.1
Overlay Chart for
Maximum Loan at
Butson Stores

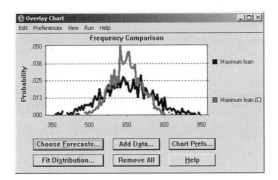

FIGURE 9A.2
Sensitivity Chart for the
Advertising Budget
Example

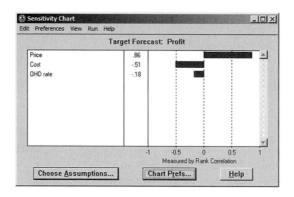

(Warning: the Batch Fit tool should be used only after determining that the data are appropriate for the parameter in question and have been adjusted for any biases.)

To implement the Batch Fit tool, we place data in a row or a column (as in Figure 9A.3) and select Batch Fit from the CBTools menu. Choose Fit from this window, and Crystal Ball fits a continuous distribution to data provided in the spreadsheet. (By fit, we mean that Crystal Ball chooses parameters for each type of distribution that make it correspond as closely as possible to the given data.) In the first stage, we have the option to fit some or all of the continuous distributions on the standard list provided. Suppose we select all of the distribution options. In the second stage (which we reach by clicking Next), we specify the range in which the data can be found. In this example, there are a hundred data points, in the range A2:A101, with a histogram summary appearing in the same worksheet. At the second stage, the Batch Fit tool offers three different tests of "goodness of fit:" the Chi-squared, Kolmogorov-Smirnov (K-S), and Anderson-Darling (A-D) tests. (More information on these tests is available in the Crystal Ball user manual.) We select the Chi-squared to get started. Then, at the third stage, we choose a location for the analysis, checking the boxes Format output and Show table of goodness-of-fit statistics.

The result, for the example data set, is shown in Figure 9A.4, in columns C and D. The values of the Chi-squared statistic are shown in D27:D37 for the eleven distributions tested. The best results are shown in D23:D25. For the Chi-squared test, a larger p-value is desirable, and a Weibull distribution is selected as providing the best fit among the distributions tested. (A p-value above 0.5 is an indication of a close fit; in this example, the value turns out to be about 0.61.) In columns F and G, we show the parallel results for the

FIGURE 9A.3
Empirical Data Set

Data.xls

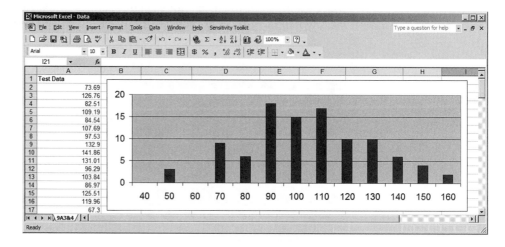

FIGURE 9A.4
Results from the Batch
Fit Tool

Data.xls

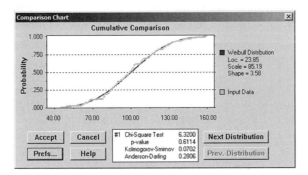

	C	D	E	F	G	H	I	J
20	Results							
21								
22	Data Series:	1		Data Series:	1		Data Series:	1
23	Chi-squared p-value:	0.61143481		Kolmogorov-Smirnov:	0.05079848		Anderson-Darling:	0.236812
24	Distribution:	0		Distribution:	0		Distribution:	0
25	Best fit:	Weibull		Best fit:	Gamma		Best fit:	Gamma
26								
27	Normal	0.337688407		Normal	0.065703486		Normal	0.256289
28	Triangular	0.43347013		Triangular	0.084252107		Triangular	0.757118
29	Lognormal	0.031637333		Lognormal	0.065299173		Lognormal	0.606338
30	Uniform	7.84527E-06		Uniform	0.169469757		Uniform	5.730367
31	Exponential	0		Exponential	0.424771259		Exponential	26.65662
32	Weibull	0.61143481		Weibull	0.070157596		Weibull	0.280578
33	Beta	0.457258423		Beta	0.064408993		Beta	0.242462
34	Gamma	0.020634647		Gamma	0.05079848		Gamma	0.236812
35	Logistic	0.098919846		Logistic	0.054897099		Logistic	0.323238
36	Pareto	0		Pareto	0.385236576		Pareto	21.08754
37	Extreme Value	0.114040422		Extreme Value	0.079415928		Extreme Value	1.00427
38								

K-S test, and in columns I and J, we show the result for the A-D test. Interestingly, for these two tests, the Gamma distribution provides the closest fit.

One final comment on this example is in order. We created the data in this example by simulating 100 independent trials from a *normal* distribution with a mean of 100 and a standard deviation of 25. The best fitting distributions had mean values of 100.6, but the normal was not the closest fit or even the second closest fit. This example shows that the estimated mean and standard deviation can be quite close to the true values, yet the shape of the distribution may not appear to be normal. The lesson is that if there is this much difference between a data sample and the distribution that generated it, we should be very skeptical that actual empirical data accurately reveal the *shape* of the underlying probability distribution. Judgment in this matter, as always, is unavoidable.

An alternative to the process described above is to fit a distribution to data using the Distribution Gallery. Suppose we wish to input one Assumption cell using the Distribution Gallery. We select Fit from among the buttons at the bottom of the Distribution Gallery. This selection implements a variant of the Batch Fit tool. If we specify the same 100 data points (Figure 9A.3) as input data, then we obtain the same information in a slightly different format. Here, the candidate distributions are presented graphically, one at a time, in order of goodness of fit. The first distribution displayed for the Chi-squared test is the Weibull distribution, as shown in Figure 9A.5. Here, we have reformatted the display to show the cumulative distribution functions for both the empirical data and the Weibull distribution. The

FIGURE 9A.5
Comparison of the
Weibull Distribution and
the Empirical Data

buttons for Next Distribution and Prev Distribution allow us to examine this comparison for any of the fitted distributions, and the button for Accept allows us to ultimately select one of the candidates to serve as the distribution in our Assumption cell.

Creating Reports

Consistent documentation of simulation results is difficult because each run contains so much data. Crystal Ball provides a Report option that creates a separate spreadsheet in which we can store all the necessary information from a simulation. After running a simulation, we simply select Run→Create Report, and a window appears that permits us to save selected results. This can include the values of decision variables, the distributions of Assumption cells, and all aspects of Forecast cells. We can also select Overlay Charts, Trend Charts, or Sensitivity Charts. This is a useful feature when we begin to use a simulation model in production mode and need to save the essential features of our results in a single place.

Extracting Data

Occasionally the data-analysis and graphing capabilities of Crystal Ball may not be adequate for our purposes. In these cases, it is helpful to create a file of the raw output data. This can be accomplished using Run→Extract Data. This command creates a new spreadsheet containing the results of the simulation in one of six different forms. These six choices are provided in the Type of Data section of the Extract Data window. The statistics form follows the standard Excel statistical summary (also used in the Statistics View, for forecasts in Crystal Ball). The worksheet obtained from the Extract Data command can also tabulate the information on which the Overlay Chart is based.

Tornado Charts

Crystal Ball provides a tool (under CBTools) for generating tornado charts and spider charts. We do not recommend using this tool for tornado charts, since the Tornado Chart add-in provided with this book provides many of the same capabilities and more. The Crystal Ball tool performs only a Common Percentage tornado chart. As we explain in Chapter 6, this is a quick first step in sensitivity analysis, but we would usually recommend supplementing it with the Variable Percentage option or the Percentiles option, neither of which is available in Crystal Ball.

A spider chart is a line chart that plots the values of the objective for two values above and two values below the base-case value of each input. It is similar to a tornado chart, in that the sensitivity to multiple inputs can be tested at one pass. It is different in that it tests two values on each side of the base case so any nonlinearities in the response can be uncovered. Spider charts can be useful, and we do recommend using this tool for them.

Correlated Sampling

Crystal Ball provides several methods for creating correlations between various probability distributions. In the Butson Stores example in this chapter, we illustrated the method of entering correlations directly into the Distribution Gallery. Although we did not illustrate it, this method also allows for calculating the required correlation from data in the spreadsheet. This method is straightforward, but can become tedious if many correlated distributions are needed.

The Correlation Matrix option (under CBTools) provides a more powerful method for entering correlations among Assumptions. With this tool, we can select some or all of the Assumption cells in a model, as needed. It then creates a matrix into which we can enter the correlation parameters directly. When Crystal Ball comes to taking samples from the Assumption cells during a simulation, it uses this matrix of correlations to relate the random samples as required.

Bootstrapping

Sometimes, we use unusual or complex output statistics, such as the minimum, maximum, or the ratio of the mean to the standard deviation. To determine how accurate our estimates of these statistics are, we need to know their *sampling distributions*. Recall that the sampling distribution of the mean is normal with a standard deviation (MSE) equal to the standard deviation of the output divided by the square root of the sample size. We can use the MSE to determine a suitable sample size for the mean because we know its sampling distribution is normal. However, the sampling distributions for unusual statistics are not necessarily normal. The bootstrap is a statistical tool for determining these sampling distributions. It works by taking repeated samples from the model and constructing the sampling distribution empirically. Crystal Ball provides the Bootstrap tool (under CBTools) for bootstrap estimation. Refer to the user manual for more details.

MODELING CASES

RETIREMENT PLANNING

Bob Davidson is a forty-six-year-old tenured professor of marketing at a small New England business school. He has a daughter (Sue, age six) and a wife (Margaret, age forty). Margaret is a potter, a vocation from which she earns no appreciable income. Before she was married, and for the first few years of her marriage to Bob (she was married once previously), Margaret worked at a variety of jobs, mostly involving software programming and customer support.

Bob's grandfather died at age forty-two; Bob's father died in 1980 at the age of fifty-eight. Both died from cancer, although unrelated instances of that disease. Bob's health has been excellent; he is an active runner and skier. There are no inherited diseases in the family with the exception of glaucoma. Bob's most recent serum cholesterol count was 190.

Bob's income from the school where he works consists of a nine-month salary (currently $95,000), on which the school pays an additional 10 percent into a retirement fund. He also regularly receives support for his research, which consists of an additional ⅔ of his regular salary, although the college does not pay retirement benefits on that portion of his income. (Research support is additional income; it is not intended to cover the costs of research.) Over the twelve years he has been at the college, Bob's salary has increased by 4 percent to 15 percent per year, although faculty salaries are subject to severe compression, so he expects not to receive such generous increases in the future. In addition to his salary, Bob typically earns $10,000 to $20,000 per year from consulting, executive education, and other activities.

In addition to the 10 percent regular contribution the school makes to his retirement savings, Bob also contributes a substantial amount. He is currently setting aside $7,500 per year (before taxes). The maximum tax-deferred amount he can contribute is currently $10,000; this limit rises with inflation. If Bob were to increase his retirement contributions above the limit, he would have to invest after-tax dollars. All of Bob's retirement savings are invested with TIAA-CREF (Teachers Insurance and Annuity Association–College Retirement Equities Fund; home page: www.tiaa-cref.org), which provides various retirement, investment, and insurance services to university professors and researchers. Bob has contributed to Social Security for many years as required by law, but in light of the problems with the Social Security Trust Fund, he is uncertain as to the level of benefits that he will actually receive upon retirement (the Social Security Administration's Web site is www.ssa.gov).

Bob's TIAA-CREF holdings currently amount to $137,000. These are invested in the TIAA long term bond fund (20 percent) and the Global Equity Fund (80 percent). The Global Equity Fund is invested roughly 40 percent in U.S. equities and 60 percent in non-U.S. equities. New contributions are also allocated in these same proportions.

In addition to his retirement assets, Bob's net worth consists of his home (purchase price $140,000 in 1987; Bob's current equity is $40,000), $50,000 in a rainy-day fund (invested in a short term money-market mutual fund with Fidelity Investments), and

$24,000 in a Fidelity Growth and Income Fund account for his daughter's college tuition. He has a term life insurance policy with a value of $580,000; this policy has no asset value, but pays its face value (plus inflation) as long as Bob continues to pay the premiums. He has no outstanding debts in addition to his mortgage, other than monthly credit card charges.

Should Bob die while insured, the proceeds on his life insurance are tax-free to his wife. Similarly, if he dies before retirement, his retirement assets go to his wife tax-free. Either one of them can convert retirement assets into annuities without any immediate taxation; the monthly income from the annuities is then taxed as ordinary income.

Bob's mother is seventy-two and in good health. She is retired and living in a co-op apartment in Manhattan. Her net worth is on the order of $300,000. His mother-in-law, who is seventy, lives with her second husband. Her husband is eighty-seven and has sufficient assets to pay for nursing home care, if needed, for his likely remaining lifetime. Upon her husband's death, Bob's mother-in-law will receive ownership of their house in Newton, Massachusetts, as well as one-third of her husband's estate (the remaining two-thirds will go to his two children). Her net worth at that point is expected to be in the $300,000 to 400,000 range.

Bob's goals are to work until he is sixty or sixty-five. He would like to save enough to pay for his daughter's college expenses, but not for her expenses beyond that point. He and his wife would like to travel, and they do so now as much as his job and their family responsibilities permit. Upon retirement, he would like to be able to travel extensively, although he expects to live quite modestly otherwise. He does not foresee moving from the small town where he now lives.

Bob has a number of questions about how he should plan for his retirement. Will the amount he is accumulating at his current rate of savings be adequate? How much *should* he be setting aside each year? How much will he have to live on when he retires? How long after retirement will he be able to live comfortably? What are the risks he faces, and how should his retirement planning take these risks into account?

DRAFT TV COMMERCIALS*

Your client directs TV advertising for a large corporation that currently relies on a single outside advertising agency. For years, ads have been created using the same plan: the agency creates a draft commercial and, after getting your client's approval, completes production and arranges for it to be aired.

Your client's budget is divided between creating and airing commercials. Typically about 5 percent of the budget is devoted to creating commercials, and 95 percent is devoted to airing them. Lately, your client has become dissatisfied with the quality of the ads being created. Along with most advertising people, he believes that the ultimate profitability of an advertising campaign is much more strongly influenced by the content of the advertisement than by the level of expenditure on airing or the media utilized (assuming reasonable levels of expenditure). Thus, he is considering increasing the percentage of his budget devoted to the first, "creative" part of the process.

One way to do this is to commission multiple ad agencies to each independently develop a draft commercial. Your client would then select for completion and airing the one that he determines would be most effective in promoting sales. Of course, since his budget is essentially fixed, the more money your client spends on creating draft commercials, the less he has to spend on airing commercials. Note that he will have to pay up front for all of the draft commercials before he has a chance to evaluate them.

* Source: Tom Willemain. This case was supported by National Science Foundation Grant SES 9012094.

The standard technique for evaluating a draft commercial involves showing it to a trial audience and later asking what they remembered about it (this is known as "next-day recall"). Ads with higher next-day recall are generally those with higher effectiveness in the marketplace, but the correlation is far from perfect. A standard method for assessing the effectiveness of a commercial *after* it has been aired is to survey those who watched the show and to estimate "retained impressions." Retained impressions are the number of viewers who can recall the essential features of the ad. Ads with higher retained impressions are usually more effective in generating sales, but again, the correlation is not perfect. Both the effectiveness of a commercial (the number of retained impressions it creates) and the exposure it receives (the number of times it is aired) will influence sales.

How would you advise your client on the budget split between creating and airing a commercial?

ICEBERGS FOR KUWAIT*

The cost of desalinating seawater using conventional technology in the Persian Gulf is high (around £0.1 per cubic meter), and the process requires extensive amounts of oil. Sometime ago, scientists suggested that it could well prove both practically feasible and less expensive to tow icebergs from the Antarctic, a distance of about 9,600 kilometers. Although some of the ice would undoubtedly melt in transit, it was thought that a significant proportion of the iceberg would remain intact upon arrival in the Gulf. Bear in mind that since water expands upon freezing, 1 cubic meter of ice produces only 0.85 cubic meter of water.

A study was carried out to evaluate the practical problems associated with such a proposal and to quantify the factors that were likely to influence the economics of such a venture. One factor was the difference in rental costs and capacities of towing vessels (summarized in Table 1). Note that each vessel has a maximum iceberg it can tow (measured in cubic meters). It was found that the melting rate of the iceberg depends on both the towing speed and the distance from the South Pole (see Table 2). The data in this table represent the rate at which a hypothetical spherical iceberg shrinks *in radius* over a day at the given distance from the Pole and at the given towing speed. Finally, fuel cost was found to depend on the towing speed and the (current) size of the iceberg (see Table 3).

Determine whether it is economically feasible to produce water from icebergs in the Persian Gulf, and if it is, determine the best means to do so.

Table 1
Towing Vessel Data

Ship size	Small	Medium	Large
Daily rental (£)	400	600	800
Maximum load (m³)	500,000	1,000,000	10,000,000

Table 2
Melting Rates (meter/day)

	Distance from Pole (km)			
	1,000	2,000	3,000	$\geq 4,000$
Speed				
1 km/hr.	0.06	0.12	0.18	0.24
3 km/hr.	0.08	0.16	0.24	0.32
5 km/hr.	0.10	0.20	0.30	0.40

---

* Source: M. Cross and A.O. Moscardini, 1985. *Learning the Art of Mathematical Modeling.* Chichester, UK: Ellis Horwood, Ltd.

Table 3
Fuel Costs (£/km)

| | Current Volume (m^3) | | |
	100,000	1,000,000	10,000,000
Speed			
1 km/hr.	8.4	10.5	12.6
3 km/hr.	10.8	13.5	16.2
5 km/hr.	13.2	16.5	19.8

THE RACQUETBALL RACKET*

It is early in 1999, and a friend of yours has invented a new manufacturing process for producing racquetballs. The resulting high quality ball has more bounce, but slightly less durability, than the currently popular high quality ball, which is manufactured by Woodrow, Ltd. The better the player, the more they tend to prefer a lively ball. The primary advantage to the new ball is that it can be manufactured much more inexpensively than the existing ball. Current estimates are that full variable costs for the new ball are $0.52 per ball, as compared to $0.95 for the existing ball. (Variable costs include all costs of production, marketing, and distribution that vary with output. Variable costs exclude the costs of plant and equipment, overhead, etc.)

Because the new process is unlike well-known production processes, the only reasonable alternative is to build a manufacturing plant specifically for producing these balls. Your friend has calculated that this would require $4 million to $6 million of initial capital. He figures that if he can make a good case to the bank, he can borrow the capital at about a 10 percent interest rate and start producing racquetballs in a year.

Your friend has offered to make you a partner in the business and has asked you in return to perform a market analysis for him. He has already hired a well-known market research firm, Market Analysis, Ltd., to do some data gathering and preliminary market analysis. The key elements of their final report are given in the attachments.

Your problem is to determine how the new balls should be priced, what the resultant market shares will be and whether the manufacturing plant is a good investment. Your friend is especially concerned about the risks involved and would like some measures of how solid the investment appears to be. He would like you to make a formal presentation of your analysis.

RACQUETBALL MARKET ANALYSIS

Market Analysis, Ltd.

January 20, 2000

1. The market for this type of high quality ball is currently dominated by a single major competitor, Woodrow, Ltd. Woodrow specializes in manufacturing balls for all types of sports. They have been the only seller of high quality racquetballs since the late 1970s. Their current price to retail outlets is $1.25 per ball (the retail markup is typically 100 percent, so these balls retail around $2.50 each, or $5.00 for the typical pack of two).

2. Historical data on the number of people playing the sport, the average retail price of balls, and the (estimated) total sales of balls are given in the following table:

* Source: Dick Smallwood and Peter Morris.

Year	Number of Players (thousands)	Retail Price (per ball)	Balls Sold (millions)
1985	600	$1.75	5.932
1986	635	$1.75	6.229
1987	655	$1.80	6.506
1988	700	$1.90	6.820
1989	730	$1.90	7.161
1990	762	$1.90	7.895
1991	812	$2.00	7.895
1992	831	$2.20	8.224
1993	877	$2.45	8.584
1994	931	$2.45	9.026
1995	967	$2.60	9.491
1996	1,020	$2.55	9.996
1997	1,077	$2.50	10.465
1998	1,139	$2.50	10.981

3. According to industry trade association projections, the total number of players will grow about 10 percent a year for the next ten years and then stabilize at a relatively constant level.

4. In order to assess relative preferences in the marketplace, a concept test was performed. In this test, 200 customers were asked to use both balls over a three-month period and then to specify which ball they would buy at various prices. Many customers indicated they would pay a premium for the Woodrow ball, based on their satisfaction with it and its better durability. Nevertheless, about 11 percent of the customers interviewed indicated a preference for the new bouncier ball at equal prices. The actual observed distribution of price premiums is tabulated below:

Price Ratio*	Percentage Who Would Buy New Ball
0.5	0
1.0	11
1.5	41
2.0	76
2.5	95
3.0	100

* Price of Woodrow ball/Price of new ball.

THE XYZ COMPANY[†]

The XYZ Company makes widgets and sells to a market that is just about to expand after a period of stability. As the year starts, the widgets are manufactured at a cost of $0.75 and sold at a market price of $1.00. In addition, the firm has 1,000 widgets in finished goods inventory and a cash account of $875 at the beginning of January. During January, sales amount to 1,000 units, which is where they have been in the recent past.

Profitability looks good in January. The 1,000 units of sales provide profits for the month of $250. This amount goes right into the cash account, increasing it to $1,125.

[†] Source: Clyde Stickney

In February, the sales level rises to 1,500 units. For the next several months, it looks as though demand will rise by 500 each month, providing a very promising profit outlook.

The XYZ Company keeps an inventory of finished goods on hand. This practice allows it to meet customer demand promptly, without having to worry about delays in the factory. The specific policy is always to hold inventory equal to the previous month's sales level. Thus, the 1,000 units on hand at the start of January are just the right amount to support January demand. When demand rises in February, there is a need to produce for stock as well as for meeting demand, because the policy requires that inventory must rise to 1,500 by March. February production is therefore 2,000 units, to provide enough widgets to both meet demand in February and raise inventory to 1,500 by the end of the month.

1. Build a spreadsheet model to trace the performance of the XYZ Company on a monthly basis, as demand continues to increase at the rate of 500 units per month. Assume that all revenues are collected in the same month in which sales are made, all costs are paid in the same month in which production occurs, and profits are equal to the difference between revenues and costs. The cost of producing items for inventory is included in the calculation of monthly profit. Trace profits, inventory, and cash position on a monthly basis through the month of June. This model will give us an initial perspective on the financial health of the XYZ Company. Does the company seem to be successful?

In reality, the XYZ Company behaves like many other firms: it pays its bills promptly, but it collects cash from its customers a little less promptly. In fact, XYZ Company takes a full month to collect the revenues generated by sales. This means that the firm has receivables every month, which are collected during the following month.

XYZ Company actually starts the year with receivables of $1,000, in addition to inventory worth $750 and a cash account worth $875. (Therefore, its total assets come to $2,625 at the start of the year.) A month later, receivables remain at $1,000, inventory value remains at $750, and cash increases to $1,125 (reflecting receivables of $1,000 collected, less production expenses of $750).

When February sales climb to 1,500 units, XYZ Company produces 2,000 widgets. Of this amount, 1,500 units are produced to meet demand and 500 units are produced to augment inventory. This means that a production bill of $1,500 is paid in February. During February, the January receivables of $1,000 are collected, and at the end of February, there are receivables of $1,500, reflecting sales made on account during the month.

For accounting purposes, XYZ Company calculates its net income by recognizing sales (even though it has not yet collected the corresponding revenues) and by recognizing the cost of producing the items sold. The cost of producing items for inventory does not enter into its calculation of net income. In January, net income is therefore calculated as $250, representing the difference between the revenue from January sales of $1,000 and the cost of producing those 1,000 units, or $750.

2. Build a second spreadsheet model to trace the performance of the XYZ Company, again with demand increasing at the rate of 500 units per month. Assume that all revenues are collected in the month following the month in which sales occur, but that all costs are paid in the same month in which they occur. Trace net income, receivables, inventory, and cash on a monthly basis through the month of June. This will give us another perspective on the financial health of the XYZ Company. What financial difficulty does the model portray?

GULFPORT OIL COMPANY

Gulfport Oil Company markets three products—regular gasoline, premium gasoline, and distillate. In order to make these products, Gulfport imports three types of crude oil under purchase contracts that stipulate the maximum weekly supply and the cost per barrel, as tabulated below:

Crude Oil	Cost per Barrel	Maximum Availability
Crude 1	$22.50	10,000 bbl.
Crude 2	24.00	17,000
Crude 3	24.75	15,000

Gulfport uses three basic refinery units—a distillation column (DC), a catalytic cracking (CC) unit, and an ultraformer (UF). When crude oil is processed in the DC, four intermediate products, or *cuts,* are produced. The relative yields of the four cuts depend on the type of crude oil processed, as shown below:

	Crude 1	Crude 2	Crude 3
Gas oil	0.49	0.51	0.48
Ultraformer feed	0.20	0.17	0.19
Gasoline	0.15	0.22	0.17
Distillate	0.16	0.10	0.16

The various cuts can be processed further, or else they can be blended and sold directly. For example, gas oil can be blended directly into distillate (a generic product) or used as feedstock for the CC unit. When processed, the CC feedstock results in a 55 percent cut of medium octane gasoline and a 45 percent cut of distillate. The UF feedstock is a valuable cut that is used only for further processing, ultimately yielding a high octane gasoline. The gasoline cut is ready to be used as low octane gasoline without further processing, while the remaining cut is additional distillate.

At present, the DC has a capacity of 40,000 barrels of crude oil per week, while the weekly capacities at the CC unit and the UF are 25,000 and 20,000, respectively. The operating costs per barrel are $0.55, $0.50, and $0.65 for the DC, the CC unit, and the UF, respectively. These figures are all based on barrels of input.

Gulfport has long-term contracts to provide 10,000 barrels, 4,000 barrels, and 12,000 barrels per week of regular gasoline, premium gasoline, and distillate, respectively, to a few large customers. These long term contracts bring in revenues of $1 million per week. On the spot market, Gulfport can also sell extra regular, premium, and distillate production for $38, $45, and $32 per barrel, respectively.

Each of the final products has a quality requirement imposed by the market. The minimum octane numbers for regular and premium gasoline are 87 and 91, respectively. These two products are blended only from the three gasoline inputs. Distillate requires a maximum contamination number of 56 when sold, and it is blended from a combination of the distillate produced by the DC and the distillate produced by the CC unit. The quality of the cuts from the refinery units is described below:

Source	Octane Number	Contamination Number
Gas oil	—	50
Distillation column	85	54
Catalytic cracker	90	64
Ultraformer	92	—

In effect, there is flexibility in choosing crude-oil quantities, the amount of gas oil processed by the catalytic cracking unit, and the composition of the gasoline products. A plan is needed to coordinate these choices with the selection of output quantities to sell on the spot market.

COASTAL REFINING COMPANY

Coastal Refining Company operates a refinery with a distillation capacity of 12,000 barrels per day. As a new member of Coastal's management team, you have been given the task of developing a production schedule for the refinery—that is, determining how much of what to produce and how.

In simplified form, the refinery process starts with distillation, which feeds crude oil into a *pipestill,* as it is commonly called. Here, the crude is heated, and as the temperature rises, different products are given off in vapor form. These products can be collected separately and sold as produced, or blended and sold, or else processed further in a *catalytic cracker.* In the cracker, less profitable products such as heating oil can be converted to more profitable products such as naphtha. Finally, the various products of the pipestill and the cracker are blended and sold on the marketplace.

To streamline the analysis, the lighter distillation products have been grouped under the single category of *naphtha.* Similarly, the lighter streams from the catalytic cracker have been grouped under the single category of *catalytic naphtha.* Based on present operation, a satisfactory gasoline blend can be obtained by combining the straight-run naphtha (directly from the pipestill) and catalytic naphtha in the ratio of, at most, five parts straight run to four parts catalytic.

Two crude oil sources are available to the refinery, in quantities up to 10,000 barrels per day for each source of crude. The yields from distillation and the delivered cost of the inputs are as follows:

	Crude 1	Crude 2
Naphtha	0.20	0.15
Diesel Fuel	0.25	0.20
Gas Oil	0.40	0.30
Heating Oil	0.10	0.20
Pitch	0.05	0.10
Cost/barrel	$34	$32

The yields for each of the crude oil sources add to less than one because there is always some residue from the process, averaging 10 percent.

Heating oil can be used as feedstock to the catalytic cracker, or, alternatively, it can be treated and sold in the form produced by the pipestill. Gas oil can also be fed to the cracker, or, with some blending, it can be sold as equipment fuel. The blending process requires that at least one part diesel fuel must be mixed with four parts gas oil.

In the catalytic cracking process, the feedstock is recycled through the cracker until fully converted. For example, each barrel of gas oil originally fed into the catalytic cracker uses an average of 4.0 barrels of capacity when fully cycled. The products of this process will be catalytic naphtha, catalytic heating oil, and pitch. When heating oil is used as feedstock, the possibilities are a bit more complicated. In normal mode, each barrel of heating oil originally fed into the catalytic cracker uses an average of 2.5 barrels of capacity when fully cycled; but there is also a "high-severity" mode of operation, which uses an average of 2.0 barrels of capacity. The capacity of the catalytic cracker is 15,000 barrels of throughput per day, and its yields are as follows:

	Heating Oil Normal	Heating Oil High-Severity	Gas Oil
Catalytic Naphtha	30%	35%	50%
Catalytic Heating Oil	70%	80%	50%
Pitch	10%	5%	15%

The sums exceed 100 percent because the cracking process reduces the density of the output.

Current prices (in dollars per barrel) for the major final products are as follows: gasoline $42, diesel fuel $38, catalytic heating oil $36, straight-run heating oil $35, equipment fuel $32, and pitch $25. The marketing department has indicated that the company could probably not sell more than 4,000 barrels per day each of diesel fuel and catalytic heating oil, but it could sell as much of the other products as the refinery is able to produce.

A recent internal study has reported that the direct processing cost per barrel of crude oil going into the pipestills is $1.20 and that the direct cost for the catalytic cracker is $1.50 per barrel of input, with a 15 percent premium for the high-severity mode of operation.

QUINCY CHOCOLATE COMPANY

Quincy Chocolate Company purchases cocoa beans to manufacture candy bars and powder mixes for consumer use, as well as a variety of ingredients for industrial use. Its factory is specifically responsible for the production of milk chocolate, chocolate powder, cocoa butter, and cocoa liquor. Milk chocolate is sold by the Manufacturing Division directly to wholesalers. Chocolate powder, obtained as a by-product, is sent to the Marketing Division for further refinement and packaging. Cocoa butter and cocoa liquor are intermediate products that are used in the production of milk chocolate and sold as by-products to the Marketing Division.

The processing of raw cocoa beans consists of a number of stages, starting with cleaning and roasting, followed by grinding, then pressing, and finally, mixing of intermediate products with sugar and milk powder to obtain milk chocolate.

The cleaning-and-roasting stage begins with a filtering machine that removes foreign matter and unusable fragments normally found in cocoa bags. The machine then washes the beans and screens them by size, in preparation for uniform roasting. At the factory, the filtering machine, which averages about 220 hours of productive time per month, can process 25,000 pounds of beans per hour. This is a "pre-yield" figure. Due to impurities in the input, a pound of purchased Brazil beans yields only 0.96 pound after filtering, while a pound of purchased African beans yields only 0.92 pound. The purified flows emerging from the filtering machine proceed to the roasting ovens and from there to grinding. The roasting ovens provide 300 hours of capacity per month and can accommodate 10,000 pounds of Brazil beans per hour. African beans take about 10 percent more time in roasting than Brazil beans.

In the grinding stage, cocoa beans are first blended to maintain quality standards. After blending, the mixture is milled between pairs of grindstones. Milling generates heat, which liquifies the fat content of the beans. The grinding process continues until it forms a dark brown liquor mass. The effective monthly grinding capacity is about 240 hours, and the equipment can process about 15,000 pounds per hour of either type of bean. The yield from grinding is 82 percent by weight.

After the grinding process, the liquor moves in one of two paths. One direction is to the cocoa press, which separates liquor into its two basic constituents: butter and powder (which are obtained from the press in equal amounts). The press stage compresses pods of liquor, squeezing out predetermined amounts of cocoa butter and leaving behind a hard cake of cocoa solids. This cake is cooled after being discharged, crushed between rollers, and then pulverized to yield chocolate powder. The monthly pressing capacity is about 250 hours, and the production rate is 8,000 pounds per hour.

The second direction is to the mixer, which produces milk chocolate by combining liquor and cocoa butter, while adding sugar and milk powder to increase palatability. Cocoa butter, which is squeezed out of the liquor by the press, gets mixed with liquor that comes from grinding, along with prescribed amounts of sugar and powdered milk, to obtain the milk chocolate. Specifically, half of the mix must be sugar, and another 10 percent must be milk powder. The remaining 40 percent is a combination of cocoa butter and liquor, with the ratio of cocoa butter to liquor falling between 0.8 and 1.2. After sufficient mixing and conditioning to enhance shelf life, the milk chocolate gets molded and packaged. The capacity in mixing, molding, and packaging far exceeds any conceivable level of milk chocolate production.

The price quoted for delivery of raw Brazil beans is $1.87 per pound, and the price quoted for raw African beans is $1.66 per pound. These two price quotations reflect, among other things, a difference in quality between the two types of beans. Corporate Procurement is responsible for assessing the quality of the raw product. They use a numerical scale with a range from 1 to 4. Recently the Brazil beans have been averaging 3 points per pound, while African beans have been averaging 2 points per pound. The minimal quality requirement on raw cocoa beans used in milk chocolate is 2.7 points.

Corporate Procurement has also set a transfer price of $2.10 per pound on liquor for sales to the Marketing Division, a price of $2.25 for chocolate powder, and a price of $2.40 for cocoa butter. A production plan is needed that will guarantee the Manufacturing Division output of 2 million pounds of milk chocolate, sufficient to meet its existing delivery contracts for the month.

WORKFORCE MANAGEMENT

A software company is anticipating an increase in demand for its products. However, management is concerned about the adequacy of their programmers to meet the increased demand, given the history of workforce turnover (an average of 5 percent of the programmers leave the company at the end of each month). Rather than hiring new workers, management is contemplating enrolling some or all of their programmers in a monthlong intensive training program. After the successful completion of the training program, a programmer would receive an increase in salary and would sign a contract not to leave the company for at least six months. Trained programmers would therefore be immune from normal turnover.

Management believes that successful completion of the program would increase a programmer's productivity by 20 percent, and management will implement a no-layoff policy to encourage participation. However, only 90 percent of the programmers are estimated to be able to complete the training program successfully. Those who enroll in training but do not complete the program successfully will return to the workforce at their pretraining skill level. (For simplicity, assume that they are not candidates for turnover during their training month and that they can enroll in the training program again later.)

The monthly demand for untrained programmers for the next six months is shown in the table below. Note that if there are trained programmers available, their higher productivity allows management to satisfy demand with fewer programmers. For example, the demand in January can be satisfied with 100 untrained programmers, or with 82 untrained and 15 trained programmers (since $100 = 82 + 1.20 \times 15$).

Number of Untrained Programmers Required

Month	Jan.	Feb.	Mar.	Apr.	May	June
Programmers	100	100	115	125	140	150

A programmer cannot be engaged in production and participate in the training program during the same month. At the beginning of January, there are 145 (untrained) programmers on the workforce. Monthly payroll costs to the company are $3,000 per untrained programmer (engaged in either production or the training program) and $3,300 per trained programmer. A workforce plan for the six-month period will specify hiring and training volumes, while assuring that the demand for programmers can be met.

FLEXIBLE INSURANCE COVERAGE

A company health plan offers four alternatives for coverage, from a low-cost plan with a high deductible to a high-cost plan with a low deductible. The details of coverage are given in the table below. The human resources department would like to develop a spreadsheet that can be used to help any employee—whether single or married, small family or large, low medical expenses or high—to compare these plan alternatives.

Plan Options and Costs

	Deductible*	Coinsurance†	Annual Premium‡		
			1-Person	2-Person	Family
Option 1	$1,500/$2,500	none	$1,825	$3,651	$4,929
Option 2	500/1,000	20%	2,016	4,032	5,444
Option 3	250/500	20%	2,245	4,491	6,063
Option 4	100/200	10%	2,577	5,154	6,959

* The deductible amount is paid by the employee. The first figure applies to an individual; the second applies to two-person or family coverage. In the case of Option 1, for example, this means that the insurance coverage takes effect once an individual has paid for $1,500 worth of expenses. (This limit holds for any individual under two-person or family coverage, as well as for an individual with one-person coverage.) In the case of two-person or family coverage, the insurance also takes effect once the household has incurred $2,500 worth of expenses.

† The coinsurance is the percentage of expenses that must be paid by the employee when the insurance coverage takes effect. In the case of Option 2, for example, this means that the insurance covers 80 percent of all expenses after the deductible amount has been reached.

‡ The annual premium is the cost to the employee of the insurance.

THE TWO-PART TARIFF*

For many types of services, customers can be segmented into classes on the basis of their willingness to pay for the service as a whole as well as for incremental use. For example, some customers may be willing to pay a high monthly *access fee* for cell phone access, but only a small *usage fee* for each call. For others, it may be the reverse. For the firm providing the service, the problem is to set prices for each type of customer.

Management is responsible for selecting an access fee and a usage fee for each segment. The objective is to maximize profit, which is the sum of each segment's revenue minus variable cost. Revenue per customer equals the access fee plus the customer's demand (e.g., calls per month) multiplied by the usage fee. For simplicity, we assume that there is a representative customer for each segment and that the number of customers in each segment is fixed.

In each segment, the value placed on services is represented by a demand function. This function tells us how much demand there will be at any given price. In other words, at any price, the function gives the customer's willingness to buy, which is measured as a demand volume.

Several constraints must be taken into account in this problem. One is that the consumer surplus for each segment must be positive. Otherwise, demand from that segment will be zero. Likewise, the consumer surplus for the customers in segment 1 must be greater when using the access fee and usage rate for segment 1 than when using the access fee and usage rate for segment 2. Otherwise, segment 1 customers would switch to segment 2. A symmetrical condition holds for segment 2.

Suppose that linear demand curves apply. Let $D1$ represent demand (in thousands) from segment 1 when the usage fee is $U1$. Also let the access fee for segment 1 be denoted $A1$. Segment 2 is represented using $D2$, $U2$, and $A2$, respectively. Assume that there are 1,000 customers in each segment and that variable costs are $1 per call.

Demand for calls from segment 1 is elastic, with the demand curve

$$D1 = 11 - 3.67 \times U1$$

Segment 2 has different characteristics, with a demand curve

$$D2 = 2 - 0.5 \times U2$$

Consumer surplus for segment 1 can be calculated using the following formula:

$$CS1 = 0.5 \times (3 - U1) \times D1 - A1$$

For segment 2:

$$CS2 = 0.5 \times (4 - U2) \times D2 - A2$$

The task is to find a viable pricing scheme for each segment.

PRODUCER RESPONSIBILITY AT BMW

Late in the summer of 1989, the government of Germany was seriously considering an innovative policy affecting the treatment of scrapped vehicles. This policy would make auto manufacturers responsible for recycling and disposal of their vehicles at the end of their useful lives. Sometimes referred to as a "Producer Responsibility" policy, this regulation would obligate the manufacturers of automobiles to take back vehicles that were ready to be scrapped.

*Source: Praveen Kopalle and Sam Wylie

The auto take-back proposal was actually the first of several initiatives that would also affect the end-of-life (EOL) treatment of such other products as household appliances and consumer electronics. But in 1989, no other industry had faced anything like this new policy. Managers at BMW and other German automakers struggled to understand the implications for their own companies. Perhaps the first exercise was to gauge the magnitude of the economic effect. Stated another way, management wanted to know what the cost of the new policy was likely to be if BMW continued to do business as usual.

Background

A loose network of dismantlers and shredders managed most of the recycling and disposal of German vehicles, accounting for about 95 percent of EOL volume, or roughly 2.1 million vehicles per year. Dismantling was a labor intensive process that removed auto parts, fluids, and materials that could be resold. The hulk that remained was sold to a shredder. Shredding was a capital intensive business that separated the remaining materials into distinct streams. Ferrous metals were sold to steel producers, nonferrous metals were sold to specialized metal companies, and the remaining material was typically sent to landfills or incinerators. The material headed for disposal was known as Automobile Shredder Residue (ASR) and consisted of plastic, rubber, foam, glass, and dirt. ASR was virtually impossible to separate into portions with any economic value, so shredders paid for its removal and disposal. As of 1989, the annual volume of ASR came to about 400,000 tons. On average, an automobile stayed in service for about ten years.

Although dismantlers and shredders were unaffiliated private businesses in 1989, it was conceivable that, under the new government policy, they would be taken over by the auto companies. Even if they remained independently owned businesses, the costs of dismantling and shredding would ultimately be borne by the auto companies, since the policy made them legally responsible for the waste.

Economics of Disposal

The costs in this system had been increasing and in fact were about to increase more quickly due to two major trends—one involving disposal costs and the other involving material composition. On the material side, automobiles were being designed each year with less metal and more plastics. In the 1960s, a typical car was made up of more than 80 percent metal, but the new models of 1990 were only about 75 percent metal. This meant that more of the vehicle was destined to end up as ASR. Averaged across the market, autos weighed an average of about 1,000 kilograms each. See Table 1 for some representative figures.

TABLE 1   Material Trends in Automobile Composition

Material	1965	1985	1995 (est.)
Iron and Steel	76.0%	68.0%	63.0%
Lead, Copper, and Zinc	4.0%	4.0%	3.0%
Aluminum	2.0%	4.5%	6.5%
Plastics	2.0%	9.0%	13.0%
Fabric, Rubber, and Glass	16.0%	14.5%	14.5%

BMW 1989 Models	Weight (kg)	Plastics Content
3 series	1,150	11.3%
5 series	1,400	10.9%
7 series	1,650	10.3%

On the disposal side, a much more significant trend was in progress. As in most of Europe, landfill options were disappearing in Germany. In 1989, about half of the waste stream found its way to landfills, with 35 percent going to waste-to-energy incinerators, and the remaining 15 percent going to recycling of some kind. But the number of landfills was declining, and it looked like this trend would continue, so that by 1999, landfill and incineration would handle approximately equal shares. The effects of supply and demand were visible in the costs of disposal at landfills. Table 2 summarizes recent and projected costs.

TABLE 2   Recent and Projected (*) Landfill Costs

Year	Cost (DM/ton)
1987	30
1988	40
1989	60
1990	120
1991*	200
1993*	500 ±100
1995*	1,200 ±600

Many landfills were of older designs, and public concern about their environmental risks had grown. Recent environmental regulations were beginning to restrict the materials that could be taken to landfills, and there was a good chance that ASR would be prohibited. Specially designed hazardous waste landfills were an alternative, but they tended to be three or four times as costly as the typical solid waste landfill.

Meanwhile, the number of incinerators had grown from a handful in the early 1960s to nearly fifty by 1989, with prospects for another twenty-five or more in the coming decade. However, incinerators were expensive to build, and awareness of their environmental impacts was growing. In particular, the incineration of plastics had come under special scrutiny. The net effect was that incineration was about twice as costly as landfill disposal in 1989, and it was uncertain how the relative cost of incineration would evolve in the years to come.

Trends in the Market

Prior to the 1980s, BMW cars were known for their reliability and quality. Only during the 1980s did BMW acquire a reputation for performance and begin to compete in the high-end market. As a result, the company's domestic market share had risen from about 5.6 percent at the start of the decade to 6.7 percent in 1989. Some details of financial and market performance for BMW are summarized in Tables 3 and 4.

TABLE 3   Selected Company-Wide Financial Data for BMW

	1989	1988	1987	1986	1985
Net Sales (DM millions)	20,960	19,880	17,660	15,000	14,240
Sales (Vehicles)	511,000	486,600	459,500	446,100	445,233
Production (Vehicles)	511,500	484,100	461,300	446,400	445,200
Net Income (DM millions)	386.0	375.0	375.0	337.5	300.0

TABLE 4 Selected Market Data for BMW Automobiles

	1989 Sales	1989 Share	1988 Sales	1988 Share
Germany	191,000	6.7%	180,200	6.4%
Europe (rest)	163,200	1.7%	153,100	1.9%
N. America	69,200	6.4%	78,800	6.8%
Other	57,300	1.1%	47,700	1.1%

In 1989, BMW seemed poised to benefit from its successes over the previous several years, having consolidated its position in the marketplace. Long range forecasts predicted that the economy would grow by about 2 percent in the coming decade, with inflation at no more than 4 percent. However, the proposed take-back policy raised questions about whether the company's profitability could endure. Assuming that, in the new regulatory regime, automakers bear the cost of disposal, the task is to estimate how much of the firm's cost will be devoted to EOL vehicles ten years into the future.

VERSIONING AT SNOEY SOFTWARE

Snoey Software Company is developing a new piece of software that can be tailored to various market segments. At this stage, the developers envision three versions of the software: an Educational version, a Large-Scale version, and a High-Speed version. Each is built around the same basic design, but a number of data handling and input/output procedures are different in the different versions. By creating these versions, Snoey hopes to extract more value from the marketplace than it could obtain with just one version.

Currently, the developers are close to completing the Educational version, but they have done little more than outline the other two versions. The estimated R&D expenditures required to finish those tasks are $100,000 for the Large-Scale version and $150,000 for the High-Speed version. The actual variable costs are estimated to be $10 for the Educational version, $20 for the Large-Scale version, and $36 for the High-Speed version.

The marketing director at Snoey Software has identified five market segments that would respond differently to the new software. These segments are: (1) university students, (2) academic and government laboratories, (3) consultants, (4) small companies, and (5) large companies. The potential sales in each of these markets, together with the cost of advertising in each market, are listed below:

Segment	Market Size	Marketing Costs
Students	400,000	$350,000
Laboratories	1,200	75,000
Consultants	12,000	150,000
Small companies	24,000	200,000
Large companies	6,000	100,000

In a series of surveys and focus groups, the marketing staff has tested the interest of each market segment in the three different versions of the software. The results of the tests have been summarized in a table of values that represent the prices each segment would be willing to pay for each of the versions. This information is shown below:

Segment	Educational	Large-Scale	High-Speed
Students	$ 25	$ 40	$ 75
Laboratories	125	300	1,000
Consultants	100	500	750
Small companies	75	250	500
Large companies	150	1,000	2,500

In order to develop a price structure for the software, the marketing director uses the following logic. For each segment and for each version, the potential customer will calculate the difference between the price and the value. The highest difference will dictate what the customer will purchase. On that basis, it will be possible to estimate the sales volumes of each version in each segment and compute the resulting profits.

You have been hired to build a model that will compute the sales of each version in each market segment and then calculate the resulting profit for Snoey Software. Given the approach they have taken thus far, the company is committed to the Educational version, but it could halt development activities on either or both of the other versions. Which versions should be brought to market?

PRODUCTION AND FINANCIAL PLANNING AT DAMON APPLIANCES

Damon Appliances is a manufacturer of consumer products with a marked seasonality in its sales. The company engages in a careful process of annual planning, so that its yearly cycle can be accommodated. Particular attention is paid to managing the size of the labor force and controlling the investment in working capital, as these are major factors in coping with seasonal demand. This type of planning requires good communication between the vice president of manufacturing (VPM) and the chief financial officer (CFO).

At the start of the year, the VPM uses a forecast of monthly sales to come up with a proposed production plan. This plan describes, on a monthly basis, the planned regular time and overtime levels of production, the expected inventory levels, and any expansions or contractions of the workforce. Traditionally, the company builds some inventory during its low sales months and then draws down that inventory during its high sales months late in the year. The sales forecasts for the coming year are shown below:

Jan.	Feb.	Mar.	Apr.	May	June	July	Aug.	Sept.	Oct.	Nov.	Dec.
48	56	64	56	56	56	56	648	736	856	912	448

Figures in this table are predicted sales revenues, in thousands, for each month. For planning purposes, the output is treated as if there were a single "average" product, which sells for $800. Of that figure, $240 represents the direct material cost, and $150 represents the direct labor cost. The remainder consists of indirect cost, overhead, and contribution margin.

Although December is a month in which sales are high, it also marks the end of the sales peak. Consequently, Damon's policy at the end of the year has always been to scale down workforce levels and inventories to what they had been at the start of the year, even though this might mean some layoffs in the holiday season. Fortunately, seasonal employment is tolerated in the local labor market.

An initial production plan worked out by the VPM is shown below:

Jan.	Feb.	Mar.	Apr.	May	June	July	Aug.	Sept.	Oct.	Nov.	Dec.
32	32	32	32	32	32	32	32	75	75	75	68
256	256	256	256	256	256	256	256	600	900	900	544

The first row of this table gives the workforce size, and the second row gives the production quantity each month. Specifically, this means that there will be a workforce expansion of forty-three late in August (when the training costs will be incurred). There will also be a contraction at the end of November and another at the end of December, bringing the workforce back to thirty-two. The layoff expenses will be incurred in

November and December. Meanwhile, the peak regular-time capacity will grow to 600 units in September through November, and, in addition, there will be overtime production of 300 units in October and November. The year's production will approximately match the year's projected sales.

Given the VPM's production and material plans, the CFO examines the financial implications. The main purpose at this stage is to forecast cash needs and determine whether credit arrangements with the bank need to be revised. A first cut at this evaluation is made as follows. The CFO builds a pro forma income statement containing sales revenue, cost of goods sold, and fixed overhead. (For this purpose, cost of goods sold is taken as $420 per unit, and fixed overhead is taken as $12,000 each month.) This information allows the CFO to compute gross profit each month. Taxes are due on profits earned and are paid quarterly. The tax rate is assumed to be 40 percent.

Next, the CFO builds a statement of projected cash flows each month. With few exceptions, Damon's accounts are paid off within thirty days, and the same discipline is followed by its customers. Thus, the cash-flow projection takes payables as the current month's material purchases and receivables as the current month's sales. From the VPM's production plan, it is possible to include salaries ($1,200 per employee per month), expansion costs ($2,000 per unit increase in workforce size), contraction costs ($1,500 per unit decrease), overtime premiums (one-third of regular time rates), and inventory handling costs ($2/month for each item kept in stock). In addition, 75 percent of fixed overhead cost corresponds to capital expenditures. By replacing machines and equipment on a gradual basis, Damon keeps its balance sheet entry for plant and equipment at a stable level. The tax payments identified in the pro forma income statement are also included. Finally, the CFO plans to pay off the current loan outstanding as soon as possible, since the annual interest rate is 8 percent.

The purpose of the cash-flow projections is to estimate monthly cash positions. The typical buildup of inventory would result in a negative cash position if the firm were to rely solely on cash flows. By tracing how negative this position would otherwise become later in the year, the CFO gets an idea of how large a bank loan will be necessary.

The CFO might report that credit restrictions make the proposed production plan unattainable, and the VPM would then try alternatives. This exchange of information would then continue until a satisfactory plan emerges. In any event, the analysis is not intended to produce precise accounting reports. The participants recognize, for example, that the calculations are based on an estimated value for the unit cost of goods sold. Moreover, since the purpose of the exercise is to determine how large a loan is needed, interest expenses are left out of the analysis at this stage. Nevertheless, the process would be easier if there were a spreadsheet model available to support the analysis. As a starting point, it could display the balance sheet at the end of the previous year, reproduced below:

Assets		Liabilities	
Cash	300,000	Accounts Payable	132,000
Accounts Receivable	384,000	Loan Outstanding	372,000
Inventory	124,000	Accrued Taxes	0
Plant & Equipment	744,000	Stockholders' Equity	400,000
		Retained Earnings	648,000
Total Assets	1,552,000	Total Liabilities	1,552,000

As an internal consultant, you have been asked to build a spreadsheet that contains the VPM's production plan, the corresponding income statement, and the resulting cash-flow statement, under the assumptions given. Specifically, you've been asked to determine the size of the maximum cash deficit Damon Appliances faces during the coming year.

To test your work, you will want to repeat the previous analysis for the alternative production plan described below. The first row gives workforce levels, and the second row gives production output.

Jan.	Feb.	Mar.	Apr.	May	June	July	Aug.	Sept.	Oct.	Nov.	Dec.
40	40	40	40	40	40	56	56	56	56	56	40
320	320	320	320	320	508	523	548	548	548	395	320

For the two plans, compare the profitability for each, along with the maximum cash deficit.

APPENDIX **A**

BASIC PROBABILITY CONCEPTS

INTRODUCTION

Probability is the *language* of risk and uncertainty. Since risk and uncertainty are essential elements of business life, a basic understanding of this language is essential for the business analyst. In this appendix, we present some of the elements of probability as they are used in business modeling. We begin by describing probability distributions for uncertain parameters; then we discuss expected values, variances, and tail probabilities, describing why they are generally appropriate measures for decision making. Finally, we describe the elements of sampling theory, in order to provide the background for the text's coverage of data analysis and simulation.

The orientation in this appendix is not toward a broad introduction to probability theory. Instead, we focus particularly on the knowledge that an analyst might want to draw on during a model-building project.

PROBABILITY DISTRIBUTIONS

For any parameter in a model, we should give some thought to how precisely we know its value. Very few parameters are really known for certain, especially in models that predict the future. In various chapters of the book, we discuss ways to take this uncertainty into account. The simplest approach is sensitivity analysis, in which we vary one or more parameters to determine how sensitive the model results are to changes in the parameter values. For example, we might determine that if sales are high next year (50 percent above this year's level), our profits will be $5 million, while if sales are low (25 percent below this year's level), our profits will be only $1 million. With just this kind of information—an optimistic alternative and a pessimistic alternative—we have the beginnings of a probability model for the parameter in question. In Chapter 9, we forge an important link between sensitivity analysis and uncertainty. However, to appreciate this link, we need some basic concepts related to probability distributions.

A **probability distribution** is simply a description of an uncertain event or parameter. A simple and familiar probability distribution is based on tossing two coins and counting the number of heads. The distribution can be described in a table as follows:

Number of Heads	0	1	2
Probability	0.25	0.50	0.25

The same distribution can be described in a chart, as shown in Figure A.1. Both the table and the chart depict the **outcomes** of the coin toss and the **probabilities** of each outcome. Any probability distribution must describe these two aspects of an uncertain event.

A **random variable** is a numerically-valued outcome of an uncertain event. In the case of tossing two coins, we could have described the outcomes qualitatively (with the list HH, HT, TH, and TT), and we could still associate probabilities with those outcomes.

FIGURE A.1
Probability Distribution
for Coin Toss

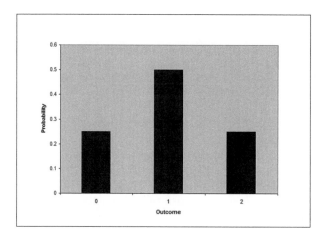

However, when we describe the outcome as the number of heads, we are using a numerical value to describe the outcome. In this sense, we can look at a numerical parameter in our models as if it were a random variable. Our three-outcome table is thus the probability distribution for the random variable "number of heads."

When we can conveniently list the possible outcomes of a random variable or identify them with integers, as in the coin-tossing example, we refer to the random variable, and the probability distribution, as **discrete.** We can describe a discrete probability distribution (or, more simply, a discrete distribution) with a table like the one in our example: a list of outcomes together with a list of corresponding probabilities. Since the outcomes are mutually exclusive and exhaustive, the probabilities must sum to 1.

Conceptually, we use a discrete distribution when we are describing a quantity that involves measurement by counting, such as the number of heads or the number of customers or the number of defects. A discrete distribution might not be suitable, however, if we were measuring a time interval or the length of an object. When we deal in intervals, especially where fractions of any size are possible, we refer to the random variable, and its probability distribution, as **continuous.** In such a case, we describe a continuous probability distribution (or, more simply, a continuous distribution) not with a table but rather, with a function—one that we might depict in a graph. The function gives the relative likelihood of various outcomes, and, conceptually, there could be an infinite number of outcomes. For example, how long will it take to drive to the airport? The graph of the function labeled $f(x)$ in Figure A.2 shows a continuous distribution for the length of the airport trip. In the graph, x-values for which the function is high are more likely to occur than x-values for which the function is low. In addition, the probability that the length of the trip will lie between two values a and b corresponds to the area under the curve between $x = a$ and $x = b$, as shown in the figure. Since probabilities correspond to areas, the area under the entire function must be equal to 1.

What if we were dealing with an event that has a vast number of discrete outcomes? Suppose we want to model the number of light bulbs that will be sold in our hardware chain next month. Although we could use a discrete distribution and enumerate the individual possibilities for sales quantity, the list of outcomes could be unmanageably long. It would be more convenient to use a continuous approach, ignoring the fact that fractions are not possible (because we cannot sell a fraction of a light bulb). Thus, the graph resembling Figure A.2 could represent a continuous distribution used as a model for light bulb sales.

Alternatively, we might describe the outcomes with ranges of values. We might classify next year's sales into three outcome ranges: sales below 50,000, sales between 50,000 and 100,000, and sales between 100,000 and 150,000. One way to simplify the ranges is to substitute their midpoints as a single outcome representing the entire range. Thus, the

FIGURE A.2
Probability Distribution
for Time to Airport

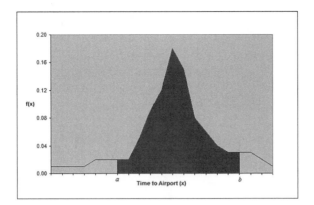

first outcome would be sales of 25,000; the second outcome, sales of 75,000; and the third outcome, sales of 125,000. Figure A.3 shows a distribution for these events in which the probability of sales in either the middle or high range is twice that of sales in the low range. This is a discrete distribution with three distinct outcomes and three corresponding probabilities. For some purposes, this model would be a sufficient representation of the possibilities for next year's sales, even though it involves a good deal of simplification.

These two examples show that phenomena in the real world are not intrinsically discrete or continuous. Rather, we can choose to use discrete or continuous models to represent those phenomena. The choice sometimes comes down to what is convenient for modeling purposes and what is plausible for the user.

A frequency distribution, or **histogram,** is a commonly encountered chart that shows how members of a population are distributed according to some criterion. Figure A.4 shows how grades are distributed in a certain class of 100 students. Note that the bars depict the number of students whose grades fall in the given ranges (for example, from 85 to 89).

To construct a histogram in Excel, we can use the Histogram function in the Data Analysis tools. We select Tools→Data Analysis and then select Histogram from the window of options presented. The Histogram tool draws on two types of information: one is an array of raw data; the other is the set of "bins" defining the columns of the histogram. For example, suppose that we have the scores for the 100 students entered in cells B20:K29 and that we list the upper limit for each of the bins in column A of the first worksheet. (The entries in column B are simply used as labels for the x-axis of the chart.) Then, we can invoke the Histogram function in order to produce the result in Figure A.4, where we have edited the chart's format.

FIGURE A.3
Probability Distribution
for Sales

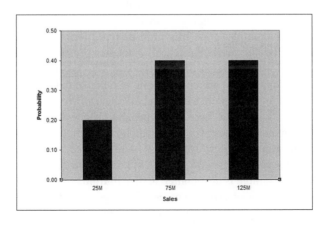

FIGURE A.4
A Histogram for
Student Grades

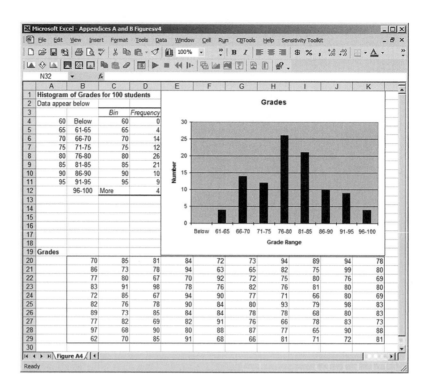

This histogram can also be interpreted as a probability distribution. For example, the chances are $21/100 = 0.21$ that a randomly selected student's grade will fall in the range 81–85. Similarly, by adding up the heights of the relevant bars, we can determine that the chances are 52 percent that a randomly selected student's grade will fall between 66 and 80.

EXAMPLES OF DISCRETE DISTRIBUTIONS

Although we can specify any discrete distribution by constructing a table of outcomes and probabilities, as we did for the coin-tossing example, there are some specific distributions that correspond to particular real-world phenomena. For example, the **Poisson distribution** describes a random variable that counts the occurrences of random events. In particular, suppose we wish to know the number of times our computer system will break down next week. The possible outcomes are the numbers 0, 1, 2, . . . , and so on. If we know that breakdowns occur at an average rate of 2 per day, then the number that occurs next week (seven days) can be modeled as following a Poisson distribution with a mean of 14. We need only one parameter—the mean value—to specify a Poisson distribution.

Another example is the **binomial distribution,** which describes a random variable that counts the number of successful outcomes in a series of n independent experiments (trials), each with a success probability of p. The possible outcomes are the numbers 0, 1, 2, . . . , n. Suppose we are counting the number of defective chips in a production batch of $n = 100$. (As is often the case in quality control, we can represent a defective as a "success.") If we know that there is a 5 percent chance than an individual chip is defective, then the number of defectives in the batch can be modeled as following a binomial distribution with parameters $n = 100$ and $p = 0.05$. We need two parameters—the number of trials and the success rate—to specify a binomial distribution.

A third example is the **geometric distribution,** which describes a random variable that counts the number of experiments needed to generate the first success, in a series of independent experiments like the one we described above, each with a success probability of p.

The possible outcomes are the numbers 1, 2, 3, . . . , and so on, without an upper limit. Suppose we are counting the number of days until our computer system will break down. (Here, a "success" is a breakdown.) If we know that there is an 80 percent chance that there will be a breakdown on a given day, then the number of days until a breakdown occurs can be modeled as following a geometric distribution with parameter $p = 0.8$.

EXAMPLES OF CONTINUOUS DISTRIBUTIONS

Three continuous probability distributions are particularly useful in modeling uncertainty in business situations: the uniform, triangular, and normal distributions. There are many more types of distributions, but these three provide us with a good deal of flexibility in capturing the kind of variability we usually encounter in decision problems. The **uniform distribution** describes an outcome that is equally likely to fall anywhere between a prescribed minimum and a prescribed maximum. It is particularly appropriate when we can make a reasonable guess about the smallest and largest possible outcomes but have no reason to suspect that any values in between are more likely than others. The **triangular distribution** describes an outcome that has a minimum and maximum value but is most likely to occur at an intermediate point. The triangular distribution is more flexible than the uniform because it can have a peak anywhere in its range. It is well suited to situations where we can identify a most likely outcome as well as the smallest and largest possible outcomes. Finally, the **normal distribution** describes an outcome that is most likely to be in the middle of the distribution, with progressively smaller likelihoods as we move away from its most likely value. This distribution, which is familiar to many analysts, can describe a symmetrical uncertain quantity using only two parameters (the mean and standard deviation).

The uniform distribution is often the first distribution we use when prototyping a model, because it is so easy to specify, requiring only a minimum and maximum value. Figure A.5 shows a uniform distribution whose outcomes lie between 50 and 150. The mean for a uniform distribution is midway between the minimum and maximum values (100 in this case). The critical property that defines the uniform distribution is that every outcome between the minimum and the maximum is equally likely. Often, this is a reasonable assumption, especially when first testing the effects of uncertainty in a model and when no data or other information are available to suggest different likelihoods.

A somewhat more flexible family of continuous distributions is the triangular. These distributions are specified by three parameters: the minimum, maximum, and most likely values. Figure A.6 shows a triangular distribution from 50 to 150 with a most likely value of 125. Note that the mean of this distribution is not 100 but somewhat higher, because values above 100 are more likely than those below it. The mean of a triangular distribution is always one-third the sum of the minimum, maximum and most likely values (108.3 in this case.) Triangular distributions are particularly useful for representing subjective uncertainty. Very few managers can specify offhand a probability distribution for an uncertain quantity, but most can give reasonable estimates for the minimum, maximum, and most likely values.

The normal distribution is a symmetrical distribution specified by its mean and standard deviation. The normal distribution shown in Figure A.7 has a mean of 100 and a standard

FIGURE A.5
A Uniform Distribution

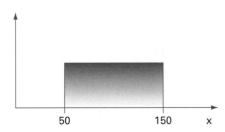

50   150   x

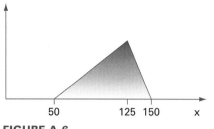

FIGURE A.6
A Triangular Distribution

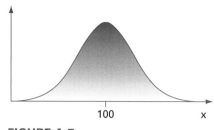

FIGURE A.7
A Normal Distribution

deviation of 25. The normal is often appropriate for representing uncertain quantities that are influenced by a large number of independent factors, such as the heights of a group of people or the physical measurements of a manufactured product. But the normal is probably overused, perhaps because it is prominent in statistics, where it plays a central role. The normal should not be used unless there is reason to believe the distribution is symmetrical. It also has the sometimes problematic property that negative outcomes are possible, especially if the standard deviation is large relative to the mean. Thus, the normal would not be an appropriate probability model for demand or price, unless the standard deviation were small relative to the mean (say, 25 percent of the mean or less).

EXPECTED VALUES

We use probability distributions in two ways in spreadsheet modeling: first to describe uncertain parameters as inputs and then to describe the resulting outcomes. While distributions are important, they are also quite complex. In particular, many decision makers cannot easily understand the implications of a probability distribution for their situation. Therefore, it is important to be able to capture the essential features of a distribution in a single number. Usually, that number is the expected value. Most often the symbol μ is used to represent the expected value of a distribution.

An **expected value** is simply an average, but an average of a somewhat special kind. Recall that Figure A.4 depicts the grades of 100 students in a class. One way to summarize this chart is with the average grade, which we calculate simply by adding all 100 grades and dividing by 100. But this procedure does not work as well in calculating the average sales in Figure A.3. Here, the outcomes (sales of 25M, 75M, or 125M) do not occur with equal probabilities—the outcome of 25M is half as likely as the other outcomes. Any estimate of the average outcome should take the probabilities into account. The expected value does so by multiplying each outcome by its probability. Thus, the expected value of sales in this distribution is

$$0.2 \times 25M + 0.4 \times 75M + 0.4 \times 125M = 85M$$

If S represents the random variable sales in this example, then we write its expected value as $E[S] = 85M$. Note that, as this example illustrates, the expected value is not necessarily one of the actual outcomes of the distribution.

Another way to think about an expected value is as a probability-weighted average. Indeed, someone who has studied mechanics would recognize the expected value as the center of gravity of a one-dimensional object (the random variable), where outcomes play the role of distances, and probabilities play the role of weights.

To clarify terminology, we use the terms expected value and mean interchangeably in this book. However, we reserve the word **average** to refer to the simple (unweighted) average. Thus, we might refer to the expected value of the exam scores in Figure A.4 as an average, but the expected value of sales in Figure A.3 would be called a mean.

When distributions contain a discrete set of outcomes, it is straightforward to calculate the expected value: we simply multiply each outcome by its probability and add the products. (The calculation can easily be carried out using the SUMPRODUCT function in Excel.) Even if the number of outcomes is infinite, as in the Poisson distribution, there may be a formula that allows us to calculate the required summation. Alternatively, we might be willing to leave out very unlikely outcomes and make an approximate calculation of the expected value. However, in the case of continuous distributions, there is always an infinite number of outcomes, and the procedure for calculating the expected value is more complex. When any distribution is symmetrical, however, the expected value lies at the center of the distribution. Thus, the mean for both the uniform and normal distributions is the center of the distribution. As we pointed out earlier, there also happens to be a simple formula for the expected value of the triangular distribution.

One of the important properties of the expected value is **linearity.** Essentially this means that if an outcome is related in a linear fashion to an uncertain parameter, then the expected value of the outcome is also related in the same linear fashion to the expected value of the parameter. An example will make this clearer. Consider the following simple model for profit:

$$Profit = Margin \times Sales - Fixed\ Cost$$

In this model, we assume that Margin and Fixed Cost are known with certainty. Sales, on the other hand, is uncertain. Consequently, Profit is uncertain. But because the relationship is linear, if we want to find the expected value of Profit, we need to know only the expected value of Sales, that is:

$$E[Profit] = Margin \times E[Sales] - Fixed\ Cost$$

This property of linearity becomes important when we consider the implications of uncertainty in a parameter for the outcomes of a model. We noted earlier that most parameters are uncertain, although we may choose to ignore the fact. Often, the uncertainty present in the situation is not sufficient to justify a full uncertainty analysis. This discussion of linearity points out one such situation: if our model is linear (that is, if the output is related in a linear fashion to uncertain inputs), and if we want to determine the expected value of the *output,* then we can simply use the expected values of the *parameters* as our inputs and not use probability distributions in our evaluation. The flip side of this conclusion is that if either of these requirements is not met, then we will need to take a probabilistic view when analyzing the model.

Why is the expected value of the output a reasonable summary measure of all the possible outcomes? There are several reasons, but the most important is that the expected value is actually the long-run average outcome if the uncertain situation represented by the model is repeated many times. For example, consider a simple game in which we flip a fair coin and receive $10 for Heads and pay $5 for Tails. Let *W* represent our winnings when we play the game. The expected winnings can be calculated as a probability-weighted average:

$$E[W] = 0.5 \times 10 - 0.5 \times 5 = 2.5$$

This is not a bad deal, of course: our *expected* winnings are $2.50 each time we play. If we were to play 1,000 times, we would probably make very close to $2,500, since, in such a large number of repetitions, we would win close to 50 percent of the time. So if we could play this game many times, it would be reasonable to use the expected value of the outcome as a measure of its long-run value. In effect, we can ignore the uncertainty on a single repetition of this game because we are planning to play many times. The general notion here is that a manager facing a series of decisions influenced by uncertainty will maximize profits in the long run by maximizing expected profit on each individual decision.

But what if the outcomes were not in dollars but in *millions* of dollars? The expected outcome is still attractive, at $2.5 million, but we might not be able to ignore the uncertainty we face on each repetition. For example, if we had resources of less than $5 million available, then a loss on the first coin flip would leave us incapable of continuing, and thus incapable of reaching the long run, where our winnings would be great. In this case, the expected value is *not* a sufficient measure of the outcome, even if we can play many times, because it does not recognize the possibility that we could go bankrupt at the first coin flip. Thus, we have to qualify the principle of maximizing long-run profits by acknowledging that the manager can reach the long run only if the firm survives. The risk of an extreme outcome, especially if it jeopardizes the manager's ability to persist, should therefore be considered explicitly.

Throughout this book, we advocate a two-phased approach to summarizing the distribution of outcomes. The first phase is almost always to consider the expected value of the outcome. Even in situations where this is not completely sufficient, it is a necessary first step. But as our simple example shows, sometimes the risks associated with a course of action are so high that the expected outcome is not the only measure to consider. We should then be looking at the probability of extreme outcomes as well.

CUMULATIVE DISTRIBUTION FUNCTIONS

The cumulative distribution function (or **cdf**) gives, for any specified value, the probability that the random variable will be *less than or equal to* that value. For example, suppose we are using a Poisson distribution with a mean of 2 to model the number of breakdowns in a day. The distribution is shown in the following table:

Outcome	0	1	2	3	4	5	6	7	8
Probability	0.135	0.271	0.271	0.180	0.090	0.036	0.012	0.003	0.001

The cdf at a particular value, y, gives the probability that the random variable will be less than or equal to y. Thus, the cdf at 1 is equal to 0.406, the sum of the probabilities for outcomes 0 and 1. The cdf at 2 is equal to 0.677, the sum of the probabilities for outcomes 0, 1, and 2. Simple addition allows us to construct a table of cumulative distribution values, as shown below:

Outcome	0	1	2	3	4	5	6	7	8
Probability	0.135	0.271	0.271	0.180	0.090	0.036	0.012	0.003	0.001
Cumulative	0.135	0.406	0.677	0.857	0.947	0.983	0.995	0.999	1.000

The cdf is usually written as the function $F(y)$, and, mathematically speaking, it is defined for all possible values of y. For instance, in the Poisson example, it follows from the table that $F(4.3) = 0.947$. A graph of this particular cdf is shown in Figure A.8.

FIGURE A.8
A Cumulative Distribution Function for the Poisson Distribution

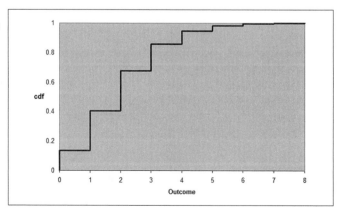

In the case of continuous random variables, there is also a cumulative distribution function. It is again defined by the function $F(y)$, representing the probability that the random variable is less than or equal to y. However, in some cases (such as the normal distribution), this function cannot be expressed algebraically. Therefore, it is common to describe a cdf graphically. In Figures A.9 through A.11, we show pairs of graphs for the uniform, triangular, and normal distributions. The first graph of the pair is the probability distribution, and the second graph is the cdf. Mathematically, the cdf $F(y)$ gives the area under the probability distribution graph to the left of y.

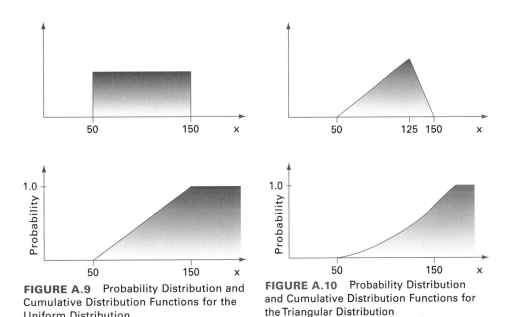

FIGURE A.9 Probability Distribution and Cumulative Distribution Functions for the Uniform Distribution

FIGURE A.10 Probability Distribution and Cumulative Distribution Functions for the Triangular Distribution

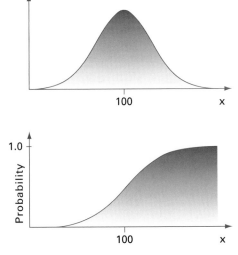

FIGURE A.11
Probability Distribution and Cumulative Distribution Functions for the Normal Distribution

TAIL PROBABILITIES

While the expected value is a useful summary of the long run average value of an uncertain situation, we are sometimes interested in a particular set of outcomes, especially extreme outcomes. An example would be the outcomes that lead to bankruptcy in our coin-flip example discussed earlier. Another example might be related to our probability distribution of breakdowns, discussed earlier in conjunction with the Poisson distribution. Suppose our system can tolerate only as many as two breakdowns in a day without exhausting our repair capabilities. What is the probability that our repair capabilities will be sufficient on a given day?

Another way to ask this question is: what is the probability that there will be at most two breakdowns in a day, or what is the probability that the number of breakdowns will be less than or equal to 2? The answer is the sum of probabilities on the left-hand side of the Poisson table (see above), or, in terms of the cdf, we want $F(2)$. Referring to our table of Poisson cdf values, we can see that this value is 0.677.

Probabilities relating to a set of outcomes at one side of the distribution are called **tail probabilities**. In some cases, we might be interested in the side of the distribution containing the larger values. For example, in our breakdown example, the risk is that our repair capabilities will be outstripped. The probability of this event is the probability of an outcome larger than 2, which we may write as the complement of the cdf: $1 - F(2) =$ 0.323. The probability represented by a cdf value is a tail probability, or, more precisely, a **left-hand** tail probability, since it involves probabilities of outcomes to the "left" of a given value in the table or distribution. The probability represented by the complement of a cdf value is a **right-hand** tail probability. Such tail probabilities are often helpful in assessing risk.

In this context, *risk* is measured as the probability of some undesirable event, such as running out of funds or losing money on an investment. The probability of such events is often easy to describe as a tail probability. Thus, tail probabilities give us a means of quantifying the extent of particular risks.

VARIABILITY

Another sense of the term risk relates to the unpredictability of an outcome. In terms of a probability distribution, this means considering the variance. In particular, for a quantity X that is subject to a probability distribution, we define the **variance** as follows:

$$\sigma^2 = E[(X - \mu)^2]$$

In words, the variance is the expected value of the squared deviation from the mean. In the case of our Poisson distribution, we can illustrate the calculation of the variance as follows. Recall that the mean is known to be $\mu = 2$.

Outcome (X)	0	1	2	3	4	5	6	7	8
Probability	0.135	0.271	0.271	0.180	0.090	0.036	0.012	0.003	0.001
$(X - \mu)$	−2	−1	0	1	2	3	4	5	6
$(X - \mu)^2$	4	1	0	1	4	9	16	25	36

Taking the SUMPRODUCT of the last row and the probabilities, we obtain a value for the variance of $\sigma^2 = 1.99$. Actually, this calculation is only approximate, because we were using Poisson outcomes up to 8. In fact, there are small probabilities of outcomes larger than 8. If we were to use four decimal places and extend the list of outcomes to 9, we would find that the variance is essentially 2.00.

In the case of continuous probability distributions, the calculation of a variance is complicated, as in the case of calculating the mean itself, although there are some cases where relatively simple formulas exist. A normal distribution is usually specified by supplying the mean (μ) and the variance (σ^2), so there is rarely a need to compute the variance if the normal distribution has already been specified.

The variance is an important feature of a probability distribution because it measures dispersion—that is, the extent of the unpredictability in the outcome. In some settings, the extent of unpredictability is a reasonable measure of risk, and therefore the variance is sometimes used to assess the level of risk. The variance and tail probabilities are two types of features associated with probability distributions, but they have special importance in business modeling because of their use as measures of risk.

SAMPLING THEORY

One important application of basic probability concepts helps lay the groundwork for statistical analysis. In this application, we take a set of n independent numerical observations (or samples) from an unknown population, and then we compute the average of the observations. We are interested in the nature of this computed average.

We refer to the value of the jth observation as X_j, and we treat it as a random variable, with unknown mean μ and unknown variance σ^2. When we compute the average of the sample observations, we use the standard formula shown below, giving rise to another random variable:

$$M = \Sigma_j \, X_j/n$$

When we compute the variance in the sample observations, we use another standard formula, as follows:

$$S = \Sigma_j \, (X_j - M)^2/(n - 1)$$

Next, we wish to know the probability distribution of the random variable M. It turns out that the distribution is approximately normal if n is reasonably large, due to the formal result known as the Central Limit Theorem. Since this result allows us to deal with a normal distribution, we need a mean and variance in order to specify the distribution completely, and for this purpose, we use the observed values of M and S. In particular, the linearity property of expected values leads to the following result:

$$E[M] = \mu$$

This result means that when we treat the sample average as a random variable, its mean value is μ, identical to the mean of the unknown distribution for X_j.

A companion result states that the variance of the random variable M is equal to σ^2/n. This means that when we treat the sample average as a random variable, its variance is equal to the variance of the unknown distribution for X_j, divided by the sample size. It follows that in a large sample, the variance of M is small. Figure A.12 reinforces these results by showing the distribution of the sample average when sampling from a uniform distribution with a minimum of 50 and a maximum of 100 for three sample sizes: 10, 50, and 100. The charts show that the variability in the sample average declines as the sample size increases.

FIGURE A.12
Distribution of the
Sample Mean

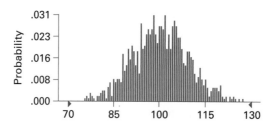

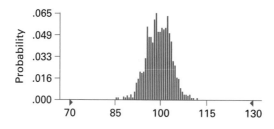

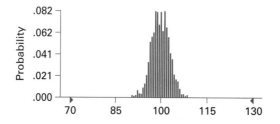

EXCEL TOOLS FOR MODELING

INTRODUCTION

While Excel is a powerful and highly flexible software tool, it contains many specialized and rarely used features. Most analysts will not need to master a majority of the tools in Excel, but they would be well served to gain total command of a few essential ones. In this appendix, we describe the basic Excel skills we think are prerequisites for learning to model with Excel. We also summarize a number of Excel features that every business analyst should know. In the main text, we cover advanced features that are especially useful in modeling, such as Data Sensitivity or Solver.

This appendix is not intended to serve as a beginner's tutorial on Excel. Those who are new to Excel and who need a tutorial should work through one of the excellent training guides listed below or take an on-line course from one of the vendors listed. Those who have a working knowledge of Excel will find in this appendix some reminders about familiar tools and perhaps pointers to some new ones as well.

Excel Training Guides:

- Gips, James C. 1997. *Mastering Excel.* New York: John Wiley.

  This book covers the fundamentals of Excel as well as some advanced features, such as financial functions and data analysis. The first eight chapters are essential. Chapters 10, 11, 12, and 14 would also be useful.

- Reding, Elizabeth and Lynne Wermers. 2001, *Microsoft Excel 2002—Illustrated Introductory.* Cambridge, MA: Course Technology.

  This is an elementary workbook. Chapters A through E are essential. The remaining chapters are quite advanced and can be omitted by the beginner.

- Reding, Elizabeth and Lynne Wermers. 2001. *Microsoft Excel 2002—Illustrated Complete.* Cambridge, MA: Course Technology.

  This book contains the previous one. Its additional chapters make it a handy reference manual.

- Taylor, A.J. Hamish. 2002. *Excel Essentials: Using Microsoft Excel for Data Analysis and Decision Making.* Pacific Grove, CA: Duxbury Press.

  This is a CD that focuses on Excel skills useful in analyzing business problems. It consists of nine modules, starting with Excel menus and moving through more advanced topics, including Solver, graphing, regression, and pivot table.

Excel On-line Programs:

- ElementK (www.elementk.com) offers a variety of on-line courses in Excel. Excel 2002: Level 1 covers the basics, while Excel 2002: Level 2 covers charts and simple data analysis.
- The e-Learning Center (www.e-learningcenter.com) offers a basic course in Excel (Office 2002: Excel Introduction) and a series of somewhat more advanced modules in the Excel 2002 MOUS Series.

EXCEL PREREQUISITES

What are the basic spreadsheet skills required of an analyst who would like to learn to *model* in Excel? The most basic skill, and one that doesn't show up in the books, is the ability to *learn by trial and error*. Few successful users of software learn from manuals or help facilities. Most have learned to scan the menus and search in a partly random, partly intelligent fashion for the tool they need and to experiment freely, knowing that (almost) nothing they do cannot be undone. In fact, the Undo command is one of the most important features in Excel!

Getting down to Excel, the first necessary skill is to be able to *navigate* around a spreadsheet and between spreadsheets in a workbook. This includes moving the cursor, scrolling, using the Home and End keys, and so on. Even the novice modeler needs to *enter text* and *enter data* and to choose the *format* of these entries. It is handy to be able to change the font and pitch size, to use bold and italics, and to color a cell or its contents. The ability to *edit* cells is important. Other necessary skills include *inserting* and *deleting* rows or columns and entire worksheets; *cutting, copying,* and *pasting; printing;* and *drawing charts* (using the *Chart Wizard*).

Skillful use of *formulas* and *functions* separates the novice spreadsheet user from the advanced user. To create formulas effectively, users must understand both *relative cell addressing* and *absolute cell addressing*. Excel has innumerable built-in functions that can drastically simplify calculations. Some of the most useful are SUM, IF, MAX, MIN, AVERAGE, and NPV. The *Function Wizard* (Insert→Function) not only lists all the available functions by category, but also specifies the syntax of each function, explaining what inputs each requires and in what order.

Beyond these basic tools, Excel contains literally hundreds of specialized tools. Few modelers use more than a dozen of these routinely, and even fewer can remember all of them between uses. It is *not* necessary to master all of these specialized tools in order to succeed at modeling.

WINDOW FEATURES

Each Excel file is called a *workbook*. A workbook consists of a number of individual spreadsheets.

The basic spreadsheet layout consists of a grid of rows and columns of cells (see Figure B.1). The rows are labeled with numbers (1 to 65,536), and the columns are labeled with letters (A to IV). The address of a cell corresponds to its column and row label—for example, C3 or AB567.

Excel displays a portion of this grid surrounded by other information. Some of the important features of the Excel window are described below and noted in Figure B.1:

FIGURE B.1
Features of the
Excel Window

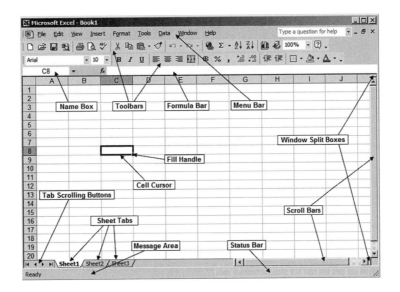

Menu bar: A row of words (File, Edit, etc.) corresponding to basic command categories appears at the top of the window. Click on any word, and a pull-down menu of detailed commands appears. For example, the Save command appears in the File menu. We refer to this command as File→Save. Other examples include Insert→Worksheet or Tools→Solver.

Toolbars: Various sets of icons that provide shortcuts to commands appear below the Menu bar. For example, there are icons for Save, Copy, Paste Function, and Font Color. Normally, the Standard toolbar and the Formatting toolbar are displayed. Toolbars can be added to or deleted from this area with the command View→Toolbars. The contents of the toolbars can be edited with the command Tools→Customize. Add-ins, such as Crystal Ball, often add their own specialized toolbar when loaded.

Message area: When Excel performs lengthy calculations, a message will appear in this area giving information on the progress of the procedure. For example, during a Crystal Ball simulation, the message will show how many trials have been performed to this point.

Status bar: Messages appear in this area that point out any special state the spreadsheet may be in. For example, if Manual Calculation is in use and the current spreadsheet has not been recalculated, the message "Calculate" will appear.

Scroll bars: These bars allow the user to change the portion of the spreadsheet displayed on the screen.

Sheet tabs: These tabs allow the user to select which worksheet is displayed. The selection allows the user to move from sheet to sheet within a workbook.

Tab-scrolling buttons: These small triangles allow the display of different tabs, in workbooks where not all of the tabs are visible at once.

Name box: This box displays the cell address where the cursor is located, as well as the names of any named ranges. (We elaborate on named ranges later on.)

> **Formula bar:** This box displays the contents of the cell where the cursor is located, whether a number, formula, or text. This is usually the area in which the user enters information into a cell.
>
> **Mouse cursor:** The location of the mouse is shown with an open cross symbol.
>
> **Cell cursor:** When a cell has been selected, it is outlined with a dark border.
>
> **Fill handle:** At the lower right-hand corner of the cell border is a cross that can be selected for copying the contents of the cell to adjacent cells. When this cross is selected, the mouse cursor changes to a darkened cross.

OPTIONS CONFIGURATION

Many users are not aware that they can control the look and behavior of their spreadsheets by setting certain parameters. Select Tools→Options, and a window with eight tabs appears. Most of the choices provided on these tabs can safely be left at their default values. We recommend the following choices:

> **View tab:** Check the boxes for these options: Formula bar, Status bar, Windows in task bar, Page breaks, Gridlines, Row & column headers, Zero values, Vertical scroll bar, Horizontal scroll bar, and Sheet tabs.
>
> **General tab:** Under Recently used file list, there is an opportunity to select how many recently used Excel files are displayed on the File menu. Another entry selects the number of Sheets in new workbooks. It can also be helpful to select a Standard font throughout the workbook.
>
> **Edit tab:** Check the boxes for these options: Edit directly in cell, Allow cell drag and drop, and Alert before overwriting cells.
>
> **Calculation tab:** In most uses, it is preferable to have the spreadsheet calculate all formula cells each time a change is made to any cell. This updating occurs if Automatic Calculation is selected. On occasion, it is useful to turn this feature off. To do so, check Manual Calculation. When this option is chosen, the spreadsheet can be recalculated at any time by pressing F9. However, it will not recalculate when a cell is changed. The message "Calculate" will appear in the Message area when a cell has been changed but the spreadsheet has not been recalculated.

When a spreadsheet contains simultaneous relationships, calculations cannot be made in the usual manner. This situation typically generates an error message warning of a *circular reference*. The error message is useful because circular references usually occur when there is a mistake in the logic; however, there are circumstances where a circular reference is sensible. In these cases, it is necessary to use a number of iterations to calculate the desired values. The Iteration check box on the Calculation tab allows the user to implement an iterative approach.

MANIPULATING WINDOWS AND SHEETS

There are several ways to make it easier to view a spreadsheet. The Tools→Zoom command can be used to increase or decrease the number of cells displayed. Increasing the Zoom setting, which decreases the number of cells displayed, makes each displayed cell larger and easier to read. For example, when Zoom is set to 100 percent, a typical configuration, such as the one in Figure B.1, might show 22 rows and 11 columns, or a total of 242 cells. Set Zoom to 75 percent, and 450 cells are displayed: 30 rows by 15 columns. Set Zoom to 150 percent, and 98 cells are displayed: 14 rows by 7 columns.

The Window command makes it possible to simultaneously display more than one spreadsheet on the screen. These sheets may be from the same workbook or from different workbooks. This command can be particularly useful when we are building formulas in a second sheet using cells located in the first. Select Window→New Window to add a spreadsheet window; then select Window→Arrange to display multiple windows side-by-side or in some other fashion.

Excel provides an option to display two sets of rows or columns in the same spreadsheet. If, for example, we wish to enter formulas in row 100 that reference cells in rows 1–10, we can select the Window Split box that lies just above the row scroll bar on the right side of the spreadsheet. If we click and drag this box down ten rows, Excel will open a second pane of rows with its own scroll bar, splitting the window horizontally. We can then display row 100 in the lower pane while displaying rows 1–10 in the upper pane. The window can also be split vertically, using a Window Split box that lies just to the right of the column scroll bar. The window can even be split both horizontally and vertically.

SELECTING CELLS

There are many ways to select some or all of the cells in a spreadsheet. Here are the essentials:

Selecting all cells: Click on the box immediately to the left of column A and above row 1.

Selecting a column or a row: Click on a single row label or column label (for example, A or 1). To select several adjacent columns or rows, click on the first label and drag the cursor to the last.

Selecting rectangular ranges: Any rectangular range of cells can be selected by selecting any one of its four corner cells and dragging the cursor across to the diagonal corner. The same effect can be achieved by selecting a corner, dragging across the row to the opposite corner and then to the diagonal corner, or vice versa.

Selecting noncontiguous ranges: To select two distinct rectangles of cells, select the first range, hold down the Control key, and select the second range.

EDITING CELLS

There are several ways to edit the information in cells. Here are the most useful alternatives:

Formula bar: The simplest way is to click on the Formula bar. A vertical cursor will appear in the Formula bar, and formulas can be entered or modified using all the normal Windows typing options. If the selected cell is not empty, its contents will appear in the Formula bar. Clicking on the text there will make the editing cursor appear.

Double-click: A handy alternative approach is to double-click on a cell, or, equivalently, to press the F2 key. This allows editing in the cell itself. If the selected cell is not empty, any cells referred to in the formula will be highlighted in color, a useful debugging device. We can then enter modifications by placing the cursor and typing directly into the cell or by moving the vertical cursor to the formula bar and typing there. Alternatively, we can alter any cell reference in a formula by dragging the highlighted outline to another location. This option provides a visual device for editing, which is convenient when the formula is based on distinctive reference patterns.

Equals tool: Yet another handy device is to click on the Equals tool (the icon immediately to the left of the Formula bar) during formula editing. This will open a window in which the formula will be explained briefly and evaluated, thus providing helpful feedback on whether the formula being entered is giving the expected results. In addition, a list of most recently used functions is available from the pull-down menu at the triangle to the left of the Equals tool.

Function Wizard: An alternative for editing a formula is the Function Wizard (the f_x icon on the Standard toolbar). If we click on this wizard when the cursor is on a cell that does not contain a function, it will bring up the Paste Function window, which lists all available functions. If a specific function is then selected, it will be entered into the formula, and its own window will appear, which facilitates entering the inputs properly. If we click on this wizard when the cursor is on a cell that already contains a function, it will bring up the corresponding function window, allowing the definition of the function to be verified or the arguments of the function to be revised.

Absolute and relative cell references: These are useful primarily to make copying of complex formulas easy and reliable. Rather than typing in the appropriate dollar signs, it can be easier to enter all addresses in relative form (without dollar signs), highlight one or more addresses, and then press F4 repeatedly until the desired combination of absolute and relative addresses appears.

ENTERING TEXT AND DATA

To copy a formula from one cell to adjacent cells, first enter the formula, and then either use the Fill handle and drag the formula to adjacent cells, or else use Edit→Fill→Right (or Edit→Fill→Down).

We often need to enter a series of numbers or dates. Examples include the numbers of successive customers (1, 2, 3, 4, . . .) or successive quarters in a year (Q1, Q2, Q3, . . .). Excel provides alternative ways to enter these series quickly. The Edit→Fill→Series command will enter various kinds of series. The same effect can be accomplished by entering the first two cell entries, highlighting them, and copying to the rest of the range using the Fill handle. Excel can usually guess the pattern correctly. For example, enter 1 and 2 in one column. Highlight the two cells. Copy down to the next eight cells using the Fill handle, and the remainder of the series (3, 4, 5, 6, 7, 8, 9, 10) will appear. To enter the numbers between 10 and 50 in steps of 5, enter 10 and 15 in adjacent cells and fill down until 50 is reached.

FORMATTING

We can change individual column widths and row heights by moving the vertical or horizontal lines between the column and row labels. Widths or heights of multiple columns or rows can be set using the Format→Row (or Column) command.

Any range of cells can be formatted by selecting the range and then selecting Format→Cells. This opens a window with the following six tabs:

Number: Choose a type of formatting—for example, Currency or Date—and specify parameters such as the number of decimal places displayed.

Alignment: Align text horizontally and vertically, and choose Wrap Text to fit long text labels into cells.

Font: Specify font, size, color, and superscript or subscript for the cell contents.

Border: Set various borders around a range of cells.

Patterns: Set a background pattern or a color shade for the cell (not its contents).

Protection: Lock or hide cells for safety.

Many of these options are also available on the Formatting toolbar. The most frequently used tools are Increase Decimal and Decrease Decimal, which change the number of decimals displayed in selected cells by one decimal place each time they are clicked.

NAMING CELLS

Individual cells and ranges of cells can be given names, and these names can be used in formulas to make them more readable. This approach to model building is highly recommended in corporate settings for models that are used by many people over many years. However, for the solo modeler, it is an open question whether the additional complexity of range names justifies their use.

The simplest way to define a range name for a single cell is to place the cursor on that cell and note that the address of the cell appears in the Name box above column A. Click in the Name box and enter the name of the cell there.

To define several range names it is more convenient to access the Define Name window by selecting Insert→Name→Define. This window makes it possible to enter range names and their cell addresses (in the Refers to: box). Names can be entered for single cells, consecutive cells in a row, consecutive cells in a column, or rectangular ranges. Enter a name for the range, and it will appear in the Name box, where clicking on it will highlight the named range in the spreadsheet. Likewise, selecting the named range will highlight its name in the Name box. Press F3 and all the named ranges will appear in the Paste Name box.

WIZARDS

Two of the many wizards in Excel are particularly useful for modelers: the Function Wizard and the Chart Wizard. The Function Wizard (the f_x icon on the Standard toolbar) brings up a list of all functions in Excel, including those in add-ins such as Crystal Ball or Solver. Select one of the functions, and a window opens that displays the syntax of the function (which inputs need to be entered and in what order), as well as the results of the formula when sufficient inputs are entered.

The Chart Wizard is the standard means of creating graphs. First select the data to be charted, and then select Chart Wizard from the Standard toolbar. The Chart Wizard contains four steps in which a chart is designed. Each step contains tabs to visit, and each tab contains design options to select. Progress along the four-step design path is controlled by the Next and Back options available at each step, until the Finish is reached. To use the same four-step path in editing an existing chart, select the chart and click on the Chart Wizard icon. This will open the window from the first step of chart design. At each step, the open window will display the design choices that were made in the construction of the existing chart, for possible revision.

INDEX